SOL PLAATJE

South African Nationalist, 1876–1932

PERSPECTIVES ON SOUTHERN AFRICA

SOL PLAATJE

South African Nationalist, 1876–1932

BRIAN WILLAN

UNIVERSITY OF CALIFORNIA PRESS
BERKELEY and LOS ANGELES

University of California Press
Berkeley and Los Angeles

© Brian Willan 1984
First published 1984 by University of California Press,
Berkeley and Los Angeles

Library of Congress Cataloging in Publication Data

Willan, Brian
Sol Plaatje, South African nationalist, 1876–1932.
Bibliography: p.
Includes index.
1. Plaatje, Sol. T. (Solomon Tshekisho), 1876–1932.
2. South Africa—Race relations. 3. South Africa—
Politics and government—1836–1909. 4. South Africa—
Politics and government—1909–1948. 5. Journalists—
South Africa—Biography. 6. Blacks—South Africa—
Biography. 7. Nationalists—South Africa—Biography.
I. Title.
DT779.8.P54W54 1984   968.2′04′0924 [B]   84–2471
cloth ISBN 0–520–05274–9
paper ISBN 0–520–05334–6

Typeset and printed in Great Britain

CONTENTS

PREFACE

This book tells the story of the life of Solomon Tshekisho Plaatje. Plaatje was an African of Barolong ancestry, who was born in the Orange Free State in 1876, and died in Johannesburg in 1932. One of the most talented South Africans of his generation, Plaatje was in the forefront of the public affairs of the African people for the greater part of his adult life, one of their best-known political leaders and spokesmen, and a prolific writer and journalist. He led a life of almost ceaseless endeavour and commitment, sustained by a vision of a South Africa free from all forms of discrimination on grounds of race or colour. A pioneer in the little-known history of the African press, Plaatje was one of the founders of the South African Native National Congress (later the African National Congress) in 1912, became its first General Secretary, and twice travelled overseas to represent the interests of his people. He wrote a political book, *Native Life in South Africa*, which stands to this day as one of the most powerful polemics – and there have been many – to have been written on South Africa; he was well known as a political journalist, both as editor of his own newspaper and later in life as a contributor to many others. And he made an outstanding contribution in the field of literature – both in his native tongue, Setswana, and in writing a historical novel, *Mhudi*, the first novel in English to have been written by a black South African, and one of the earliest African novels from any part of the continent.

Simply to outline some of Plaatje's accomplishments in this way is to suggest an immense versatility and range of achievement. No wonder then that the journalist Vere Stent, a lifelong friend of Plaatje's since they first met during the siege of Mafeking, should have called him 'one of the greatest of the sons of South Africa'; or that another journalist, G. A. Simpson, editor of the *Diamond Fields Advertiser*, the daily paper from Plaatje's home town of Kimberley, should have acknowledged, when unveiling a memorial tombstone to him in 1935, three years after Plaatje's death, that 'no mere words of mine can adequately pay tribute to his memory – the memory of one who was an outstanding figure in the life of the people of South Africa'.

Fifty years on it is remarkable how little is generally known of Plaatje's life and career. The vast majority of South Africans, it would be true to say, have never even heard of his name. Such a state of affairs stems not so much from the lack of recognition accorded to Plaatje during his own lifetime – the comments of Vere Stent and G. A. Simpson suggest otherwise – but rather from South Africa's capacity to obscure and distort its own past, to neglect the lives of those whose ideals and aspirations have been in conflict with official orthodoxies, past and present. The South African historical memory, to put it another way, has been highly selective in its recall.

I hope this book may contribute to challenging the dominance of this form of historical memory; and in showing that it is possible to write a book such as this, I hope I may encourage others to undertake biographical research into the lives of other men and women of Plaatje's background and generation. The longer this is left, it need scarcely be added, the less there will be to recover.

Writing this book has presented a variety of difficulties and challenges. Foremost amongst them has been Plaatje's own extraordinary range of talents, particularly in the field of languages – he spoke eight different languages, European and African, and wrote regularly in half of these. I make no claims to such linguistic competence myself. Where appropriate, I have relied upon others for assistance in translation, and have taken comfort in the knowledge that were Plaatje to await a biographer with a range of linguistic skills which matched his own, it is doubtful if an account of his life would ever be written. I hope that others more qualified than myself to assess Plaatje's contribution in the field of Tswana literature, in particular, will be encouraged by my findings to investigate this subject further.

ACKNOWLEDGEMENTS

During the course of researching and writing this book I have incurred innumerable debts of gratitude. I am indebted, first and foremost, to the family and relatives of the man who forms the subject of this book: to Mrs Mary Plaatje, Solomon Plaatje's only surviving daughter-in-law; Mr Johannes Plaatje, a grand-nephew; the late Mrs Martha Bokako, a niece, who was gifted with a remarkable memory and an encyclopaedic knowledge of the Plaatje family history; and four members of the Molema family – Mr Morara Molema, Mrs Lucretia Molema, Mr Victor Molema and Mr Batho Molema. All have given generously of their time and knowledge, and extended a welcome to me which made the research for this book an unforgettable experience. It could not have been written without their assistance, and I hope it provides some recompense for my intrusions into their lives, some vindication of the faith they so readily placed in me. For that, above all, I shall always remain grateful.

Those who knew Plaatje as friend or colleague have been equally generous in sharing their memories with me – in particular the late Mr Michael van Reenen, who for some fifteen years lived opposite Plaatje's home in Angel Street, Kimberley; Mr Simon Lekhela, now living in London, once a fellow student of Plaatje's youngest son, Halley; the late Mrs Maud Zibi, whose memories extended as far back as the siege of Mafeking in 1899–1900; and Miss E. M. Westphal, for her vivid recollections of her mother and father, Ernst and Elizabeth Westphal.

I have used a great number of libraries and archives in Britain, southern Africa, and the United States. Without exception their librarians and archivists have been unfailingly helpful. Of those in southern Africa I should like to thank particularly Mrs Muriel Macey, of the Kimberley Public Library; Dr M. H. Buys, De Beers archivist, Kimberley; Mrs P. E. Stevens, University of Cape Town Library; Mrs Anna Cunningham and Marcelle Jacobson, University of the Witwatersrand Archives (Historical and Literary Papers); Mike Berning and Sandy Fold, Cory Library, Rhodes University, Grahamstown; Audrey Renew, Mafeking Museum; Miss M. F. Cartwright, South African Library, Cape Town; Annica van Gylswyk, University of South Africa, Pretoria; and the staff of the South African Archives Depots in Cape Town, Bloemfontein, Pietermaritzburg and Pretoria. In the UK, I am indebted to the staff of the four libraries I have used most frequently: the Institute of Commonwealth Studies, the Royal Commonwealth Society, the School of Oriental and African Studies, and the British Library Newspaper Library.

Many other people have assisted by passing on references and other helpful information, commented upon what I have written, provided hospitality during the course of my research, helped with translations, or taken time off their own work to seek out material for me. I would particularly like to thank the following: Mr D. J. M. Abdey, Dr Randall K. Burkett, Lord Brockway, Dr Heinz Blauert, Dr William Beinart, Dr Tony Clayton, Dr John Comaroff, Mr A. A. Crovo, Professor D. C. Cole, Rev. J. Dire, Mrs R. Davidowitz, Dr Peter Delius, Dr Robert Edgar, Professor Adelaide Cromwell Gulliver, Dr Albert Grundlingh, Ian and Catherine Glenn, Professor Stephen Gray, Mr Jeffrey Green, Mr Connie Guettler, Bessie Head, Professor Robert Hill, Mr Baruch Hirson, Rev. Derek Jones, Professor Kenneth King, Dr Hilda Kuper, Peter and Jackie Kallaway, Tim and Margy Keegan, Professor E. P. Lekhela, Mrs Frieda Matthews, Mrs Connie Minchin, Dr S. S. Molema, Mr J. S. M. Matsebula, Dr James Moroka, Dr Mbulelo Mzamane, Dr Bill Nasson, A. B. Ngcobo, Suzie Newton-King, Mr D. B. Olmesdahl, Dr Richard Rathbone, Rev. John Rutherford, Chris and Pam Saunders, Heidi Suhr, Kevin and Pippa Shillington, Dr Leon Spencer, Rev. A. Sandilands, Gillian Smith, Mr Graham Stapleton, Bingham Tembe, Dr Stanley Trapido, Professor A. N. Tucker, Nancy Tietz, Dr Werner van der Merwe, Professor E. O. J. Westphal, Professor Charles van Onselen, and Dr Peter Warwick. I am also indebted to Dr Andrew Roberts for his invaluable comments and suggestions upon an earlier draft of this manuscript, and to Ann O'Connor for typing the final version.

There are three people to whom I owe an especial debt: Shula Marks, Director of the Institute of Commonwealth Studies, supervisor of the PhD thesis from which this book emerged, for her invaluable criticism, encouragement and friendship; Andrew Reed, of Rhodes University, Grahamstown, for his generosity in sharing with me the fruits of his own meticulous research on Plaatje's life and career, and for his valuable comments and suggestions upon my manuscript; and to Tim Couzens, of the African Studies Institute, University of the Witwatersrand, doyen of African social and literary history in South Africa. I will never be able to repay the debt I owe him for all he has done to make this book possible, or forget the excitement of the discoveries we shared. He has been both example and inspiration.

◇

The author and publishers would like to thank the following for permission to reproduce copyright material: Macmillan for extracts from *The Boer War Diary of Sol. T. Plaatje: an African at Mafeking* edited by John Comaroff; David G. Du Bois for material from the W. E. B. Du Bois collection at the University of Massachusetts.

Sources of photographs

The author and publishers would also like to thank the individuals and institutions, whose names appear below for permission to reproduce photographs: 1 *Missionsberichte*, 1884, p. 336; 2 Rev. J. Dire (Edenburg, OFS), m/f of records in School of Oriental and African Studies archives; 3 Mr J. L. Plaatje, Kimberley, courtesy Mr Andrew Reed; 4 *Missionsberichte*, 1894, p. 144; 5 Mr J. L. Plaatje, Kimberley; 6 Miss E. M. Westphal, Johannesburg; 7 Author's private collection; 8 Author's private collection; 9 S. M. Molema, *Montshiwa: Barolong Chief and Patriot* (Cape Town, 1966); 10 McGregor Museum, Kimberley; 11 R. Bennett, *Reminiscences of the Cape Telegraphs* (Cape Town, n.d.), p. 35 (courtesy Dr A. Grundlingh); 12 T. D. Mweli Skota, *African Yearly Register* (Johannesburg, 1930), p. 104; 13 University of Witwatersrand, Molema/Plaatje collection, A979/Fcb 8; 14 Africana Library Kimberley; 15 *Diamond Fields Advertiser*, 13 March 1897; 16 University of Witwatersrand, Molema/Plaatje collection, A979/Fca 3; 17 D. D. T. Jabavu, *The Life of J. T. Jabavu* (Lovedale, 1922), frontispiece; 18 *Men of the Times: Old Colonists of the Cape Colony and Orange River Colony* (Johannesburg, 1906); 19 *South African Law Journal*, 1908; 20 Mafeking Museum; 21 University of Witwatersrand, Molema/Plaatje collection, A979/Fa 1; 22 S. T. Plaatje, *Sechuana Proverbs* (London, 1916); 23 University of Witwatersrand, Molema/Plaatje collection, A979/Fb 3; 24 *Men of the Times*; 25 University of Witwatersrand, Molema/Plaatje collection; 26 University of Witwatersrand, A979/Fca 2; 27 J. Comaroff (ed.), *The Boer War Diary of Sol T. Plaatje* (Macmillan, London, 1973), p. 40; 28 Mafeking Museum; 29 Mafeking Museum; 30 D. Taylor, *Souvenir of the Siege of Mafeking* (London, 1900); 31 South African Library, Cape Town; 32 Mafeking Museum; 33 Author's private collection; 34 *Cape Argus Weekly*, 5 Feb 1902; 35 University of Witwatersrand, A979/Fcb 1; 36 *Koranta ea Becoana*, 16 August 1902; 37 University of Birmingham, Chamberlain papers, G9/13, album of photos presented to J. Chamberlain; 38 Ibid; 39 *With Chamberlain in Cape Colony* (Cape Town, 1903), p. 50; 40 University of Birmingham, Chamberlain papers, C9/16, photos taken by Mrs Chamberlain; 41 University of Witwatersrand, Molema/Plaatje collection, A979/Fca 1; 42 Ibid, 43 Ibid; 44 Ibid, A979/Fcb 3; 45 M. Wilde, *Schwarz und Weiss* (Berlin, 1913); 46 S. T. Plaatje, *Sechuana Proverbs* (London, 1916); 47 Ibid; 48 Skota, *African Yearly Register*, p. 253; 49 Ibid, p. 144; 50 University of Birmingham, Chamberlain papers, C9/13, album of photos presented to Joseph Chamberlain at Kingwilliamstown, by SANNC, Feb 1903; 51 *African Yearly Register*, p. 180; 52 Ibid, p. 71; 53 *Abantu-Batho* in the *African Orthodox Church Records*, Mss. no. 0001, Manuscript Collection of Pitts Theology Library, Emory University, Atlanta, Georgia; 54 T. Karis and G. M. Carter (eds), *From Protest to Challenge* (Hoover Inst., Stanford, Cal., 1972), v. 4; 55 *Tsala ea Batho*, 31 May 1913; 56 P. Meiring, *Ons eerste 6 premiers*, facing p. 104; 57 University of Witwatersrand, Molema/Plaatje collection, A979/Fcb 4; 58 School of Oriental and African Studies, Plaatje papers, STP 3/2; 59 University of Witwatersrand, Molema/Plaatje collection; 60 National Portrait Gallery, London, reg. no.

Acknowledgements

3390; **61** University of Witwatersrand, Molema/Plaatje collection; **62** H. H. Johnston, *The Story of my Life*, pp. 470–1; **63** University of Witwatersrand, A979/Fa 3; **64** University of Witwatersrand, Molema/Plaatje papers, A979/Fca 3; **65** Anti-Slavery Society, London, courtesy Mr Jeffrey Green; **66** W. E. B. Solomon, *Saul Solomon: the Member for Cape Town* (OUP, 1948); **67** University of Witwatersrand, Molema/Plaatje collection, A979/Fca 7; **68** Ibid, A979/Fcd 21; **69** Ibid, A979/Fca 8; **70** Author's private collection; **71** University of Witwatersrand, Molema/Plaatje collection, A979/Fcc 19; **72** *Mhudi* (The Lovedale Press 1932 edn); **73** University of Witwatersrand, Molema/Plaatje papers, A979/Fcb 6; **74** Basil Matthews (ed.), *World Brotherhood* (London, 1920), p. 216; **75** School of Oriental and African Studies, Plaatje papers, STP 3/2; **76** Ibid; **77–82** Moorland- Spingarn Research Center, Howard University, Washington DC; **83** Skota, *African Yearly Register*; **84** University of Witwatersrand, Molema/Plaatje collection, A979 Fcb 17; **85** School of Oriental and African Studies, Plaatje papers, STP 3/2; **86** J. S. M. Matsebula, *A History of Swaziland* (Cape Town, 1972); **87** University of Witwatersrand, Molema/Plaatje papers, A979/Fcb 14; **88** Ibid; **89** *Imvo Zabantsundu*, 15 Oct. 1924; **90** Blanckenberg, *Thoughts of General Smuts*; **91** D. E. Neame, *General Hertzog* (London, n.d.), frontispiece; **92** University of Witwatersrand, Molema/Plaatje papers, A979/Fcb 16; **93** S. T. Plaatje, *Diphosho-phosho* (Morija, 1930), title page; **94** Mrs Ramoshoana, courtesy Andrew Reed; **95** *Catalogue of the C. M. Doke Collection of African languages at the University of Rhodesia*; **96** South African Library; **97** *Pretoria, Administrative Capital of SA*; **98** Mrs Mary Plaatje, Natalspruit, SA; **99** University of Witwatersrand, Molema/Plaatje papers, A979/Fcb 11; **100** Ibid, A979/Fcc 14; **101** Ibid, A979/Fcc 2; **102** Ibid, A979/Fcc 18; **103** School of Oriental and African Studies, Plaatje papers, STP 3/2; **104** Ibid; **105** Author's private collection.

Map of Orange Free State and northern Cape in the late nineteenth century, showing its location in present-day southern Africa.

1

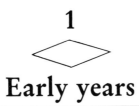

Early years

In the 1870s South Africa was more of a geographical expression than a political entity. It consisted of a sparsely inhabited but remarkably diverse collection of societies, both African and European in origin, linked in a pattern of relationships that ranged from extremes of peaceful interdependence to outright warfare. As yet there was no unified political authority across the whole of the subcontinent. The largest state was the Cape Colony, the oldest area of European settlement, now a self-governing colony of the British empire and equipped with the ordered parliamentary, legal and administrative institutions of the mother country. Outside the colony's few towns most of its inhabitants, black and white, made a living from the land: hunting, herding or cultivating crops.

In the extreme north-west, however, in an area that fell just beyond the northern borders of the Cape Colony, there was a new focus of economic activity: diamonds. Here, the new town of Kimberley had sprung into existence, and thousands of people – of all races and backgrounds, and from both within and beyond the borders of the colony – were drawn in to the area. The novelist Anthony Trollope, who visited Kimberley in 1877, thought it 'perhaps the most unlovely city that I knew', but the wealth it produced had nevertheless given South Africa a new economic importance in the eyes of the outside world.[1] The British imperial government, whose primary concern hitherto had been to administer the Cape Colony as cheaply as possible, now took a new interest in the region; despite the claims of the Boer states of the Transvaal and Orange Free State, Griqualand West (as this region was known) had accordingly been annexed to the British empire.

Neither the Orange Free State nor the Transvaal had the strength to dispute the British annexation of the diamond fields. Both were poor, underpopulated agricultural republics. Gold had yet to be discovered on the Witwatersrand, and the Transvaal in particular had the greatest difficulty in supporting its own bureaucracy and financing the 'native wars' against neighbouring African states in which it was often involved. The two Boer states were the lineal descendants of groups of farmers who had left the Cape Colony in the 1830s to escape the authority of the British in a mass migration known as the Great Trek. Over the next thirty years the British authorities had been, for the most part, prepared to condone their aspirations to independence and to allow the two republics a limited degree of sovereignty. Such a tolerant attitude towards them was not generally shared by the several neighbouring African chiefdoms who claimed the right to use much of the land the trekkers came to occupy, and there had followed a series of often bloody confrontations as these African chiefdoms defended their rights to land which they, too, regarded as essential to their existence.

In the 1870s the largest and most powerful of these African societies remained substantially intact. Through a combination of fierce resistance (using guns, in many cases, acquired with wages earned on the diamond fields) and skilful diplomacy, African peoples such as the Basotho, the Swazi, the Zulu, the Mpondo, the Pedi, had managed to preserve the essential features of their independence: freedom from external control, and continued access to the land they occupied. Other African societies, particularly in the eastern half of the Cape Colony, had been brought under the rule of that portion of the British empire, and had come to both accept and exploit their new circumstances; many Africans, indeed, had taken advantage of the educational facilities laid on by Christian missionaries, and the economic opportunities provided by the markets of the colony, to fulfil the literacy and property qualifications of the franchise and thus to vote in its elections.

Of the Tswana-speaking Barolong people, or nation as they sometimes supposed themselves to be, it would be true to say they fell somewhere between these two extremes of independence from the white man, and adaption to his way of life. The Barolong were scattered over wide areas of what is today the northern Cape, the western Transvaal, the Orange Free State, and parts of Botswana, dependent on their cattle for their livelihood, in some places living within the colonial borders of the day, in some places beyond them. Most were attached to one of four chiefdoms. To the south lay the Seleka Barolong chiefdom of Thaba Nchu, ruled by the elderly Chief Moroka, completely surrounded by the Orange Free State but still nominally in control of its own affairs, though now occupying no more than a fraction of the land it once had. Trollope estimated its population at 6,000, and was struck more than anything else – in assessing the progress of 'civilisation' amongst the Seleka Barolong – by the sight of a 'large double bedstead with mattress' in the house of Sapena, heir to the chiefdom; he felt sure it had 'come from Mr Heal's establishment in Tottenham Court Road'.[2]

To the north lived the Tshidi branch of the Barolong, the most powerful section of the nation, and rather greater in numbers; they were ruled by the imposing figure of Chief Montshiwa, and throughout the 1870s were engaged in contesting with Boers from the Transvaal and Orange Free State for the right to occupy the area around the Molopo river, long regarded by the Barolong nation as their ancestral home. Had Trollope made his way here he would have found the greatest signs of 'civilisation' among the Christian section of the tribe, led by Montshiwa's younger brother, Molema. At that time they actually lived apart from the main body of the Tshidi Barolong, having been sent to found a defensive settlement (against the Boers) in an otherwise uninhabited spot known as 'Mafikeng', or 'place of rocks'. Chief Montshiwa, as it happened, had other reasons for dispatching them to Mafikeng, for he was finding that Christianity, while it had some very practical advantages, was also proving a disruptive influence in the affairs of the Tshidi tribe as a whole.[3]

In the large region lying in between these two main Barolong chiefdoms lay scattered, less coherent groups of people of Barolong origin – belonging to the Rapulana and Ratlou, as well as the Tshidi and Seleka branches of the nation – living on still sparsely populated land now taken over by white farmers, land companies and missionary societies. It was within this region, just inside the northern border of the Orange Free State, on land occupied by one of these missionary societies, that Solomon Tshekisho Plaatje was born.

<><>

The more immediate circumstances of Plaatje's birth are clear enough. It took place during the afternoon of Saturday, 9 October 1876, at a place called Podisetlhogo, on the farm Doornfontein, an outstation of the Berlin Mission Society's main mission at Pniel, which lay some fifty miles to the south-west.[4] Both Plaatje's parents, Johannes and Martha Plaatje, were of Barolong origin and, as their names suggest, both were Christians, and of the Lutheran faith. This latest arrival was their sixth child, all of them boys: Simon, the eldest, had been born in 1855, followed by Andrew, Samuel, Mmusi (Moses) and then Elias.[5]

After his birth, the first recorded event in Plaatje's life was his baptism, which took place a little over four months later. He was taken to be baptised not to the mission station at Pniel, but to the Society's older mission at Bethanie – a considerable journey, this, since Bethanie lay well to the south of Bloemfontein, over a hundred miles away. Johannes and Martha Plaatje had good reason, however, to make the journey, for until recently they had lived at Bethanie themselves, and had left behind numerous friends and relatives.[6] At the same time their decision to make the long journey with a four-month-old baby to enable him to undergo the sacrament of baptism suggests a degree of commitment to the Christian faith quite in keeping with what else is known of their circumstances.

The baptismal ceremony took place at Bethanie on 14 January 1877, and was performed by the senior missionary, by now well advanced in years, the Reverend Carl Wuras. Entry number 795 in the Bethanie mission register records the customary information about the event which had just occurred: the names of Plaatje's parents, and the four godparents symbolically entrusted with care for the child's future Christian upbringing; his date of birth; and the Christian name his parents had decided to give him – Solomon, or Salomo, as recorded in its German form.[7]

But as well as being Christians Plaatje's parents were also Barolong, and it was natural that they should want to give him a Tswana name too – Tshekisho, meaning 'judgement'. The choice of this name was an appropriate reminder of Solomon's biblical associations – Plaatje's mother is remembered as a keen reader of the Bible – but it also possessed a deeper significance. According to Martha Bokako, Simon Plaatje's daughter, and the source of much valuable information on the Plaatje family history, Martha Plaatje had longed for a baby girl, since all her children had so far been boys. When the new arrival turned out to be another boy, however, she was overcome with remorse for having tried to anticipate God's will. Hence she

3

gave him the name Tshekisho, in repentance, and in recognition of the righteousness of God's judgement.[8]

◇

Of his Barolong ancestry Plaatje was to become very conscious, and later in life he took a close interest in this subject. So much so that he once took the trouble to write down what he had found out about it, being the first in his family, so he believed, 'to put memory to paper'. At one time, Plaatje wrote, his ancestors had been kings of the Barolong nation before being dispossessed:

> My ancestry lost the Kingship of the Barolong during or about the years 1580–1600. It passed to the House of a younger brother and descended down to Tau (Lion), who ruled over the Barolong about 1770–1790. Tau is thus the progenitor of the four royal branches of the Barolong: (1) Ratlou (2) Tshidi (3) Seleka (4) Rapulana.
> My mother is a direct descendant of a grandson of the last named from Tau's youngest and dearest wife, Mhudi. Mother, therefore, is a near relative of Chiefs Matlaba of Bechuanaland and Western Transvaal, also of Chief Fenyang, O. F. S.
> My mother and father are both descended from King Morolong. Father from the senior house of the tribe (deposed about 1600) and mother from the junior house which still survives the changing scenes and vicissitudes of time.
> Thus, father and mother are on a common ancestry but 27 degrees apart.[9]

Like every Morolong, Plaatje thus traced his ancestry back to Morolong himself, regarded to this day as the founder of the nation, and believed to have lived in the twelfth or thirteenth century. Although opinions differ as to exactly when he lived, the existing genealogical accounts of the Barolong are largely in agreement on the line of succession, on the identities of Morolong's successors as chief of the nation, and on the claim that they had once lived in the region of the great lakes of Central Africa. Morolong was succeeded by Noto, then came Morara, Mabe, Mabua, Manoto, and then Mabeo, the reign of each chief being associated with a particular human quality, and a step in the direction of claiming the region around the Molopo river as their home.[10]

After Mabeo came Modiboa, the last Barolong chief to preside over a united nation before dissension – a familiar pattern this – led to groups breaking free from the authority of the chief, and moving into the still unoccupied lands that surrounded them. But during the reign of Modiboa, as Plaatje believed, there arose a dispute over the succession which was to have a direct bearing on the male line of descent of his own family. He related the tradition that had been handed down:

> My last royal ancestor was Modiboa. They [the Barolong] got dissatisfied with him and said he was too fond of hunting when they wanted him at legothla [the tribal assembly]. He was not always there and he refused to attend and they went to him where he was camping and hunting and informed him what they would do. This was 400 years ago. They told him if he was

under the impression they were going to do without a chief he was very much mistaken. They returned to the tribe and the tribe decided to have his brother [Tsheshebe] as their chief. They did not cut off his head but they got rid of him.[11]

Figure 1   Barolong genealogy

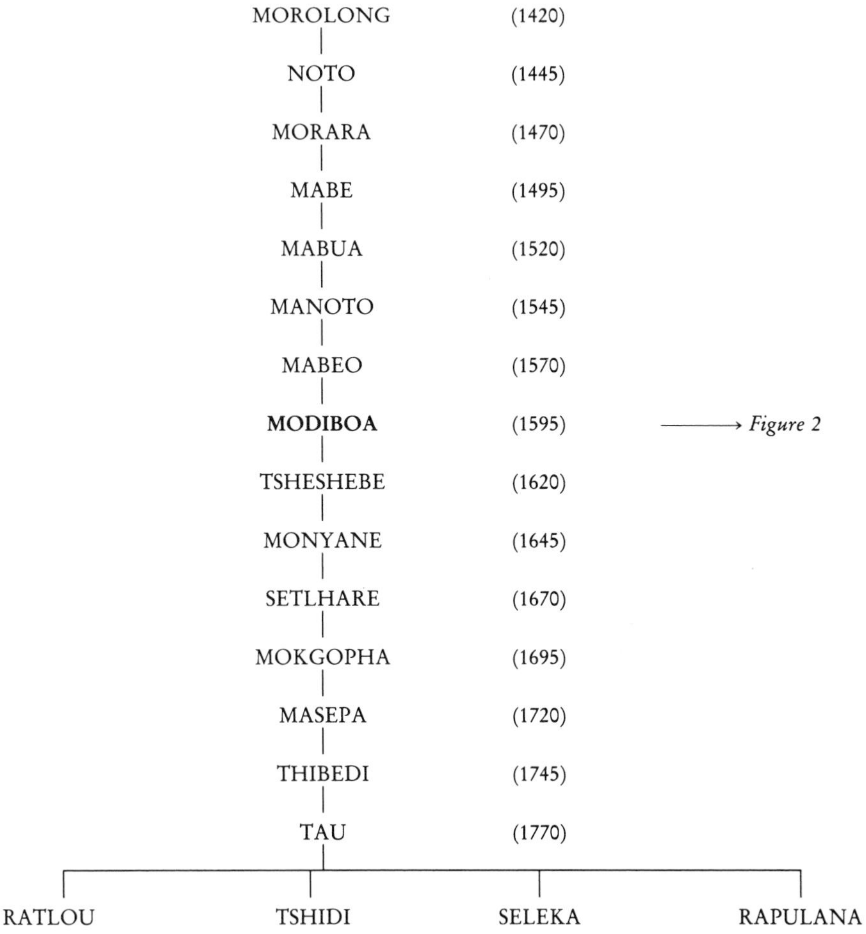

```
MOROLONG        (1420)

NOTO            (1445)

MORARA          (1470)

MABE            (1495)

MABUA           (1520)

MANOTO          (1545)

MABEO           (1570)

MODIBOA         (1595)          ————→ Figure 2

TSHESHEBE       (1620)

MONYANE         (1645)

SETLHARE        (1670)

MOKGOPHA        (1695)

MASEPA          (1720)

THIBEDI         (1745)

TAU             (1770)
```

RATLOU	TSHIDI	SELEKA	RAPULANA

Other accounts of these events vary in their details, and suggest that what happened rather was that Modiboa died whilst still chief, and that Tsheshebe was not actually a younger brother, but a younger son, who triumphed over Mooki, his elder brother, by tradition the rightful heir in the ensuing succession dispute.[12] Martha Bokako had a vivid recollection of these family traditions. In her version, the dispute was between Mooki and Tsheshebe, the two sons of Modiboa. It was Mooki who went out on the hunting expedition, intending to kill some jackals and bring back their skins. He then disappeared for

5

three days, during which time his people gave him up and accepted Tsheshebe as their chief. And when Mooki returned and found out what had happened, he was happy to accept his deposition because, he said, he did not really want to be their chief anyway.[13]

Figure 2   Barolong ba ga Modiboa

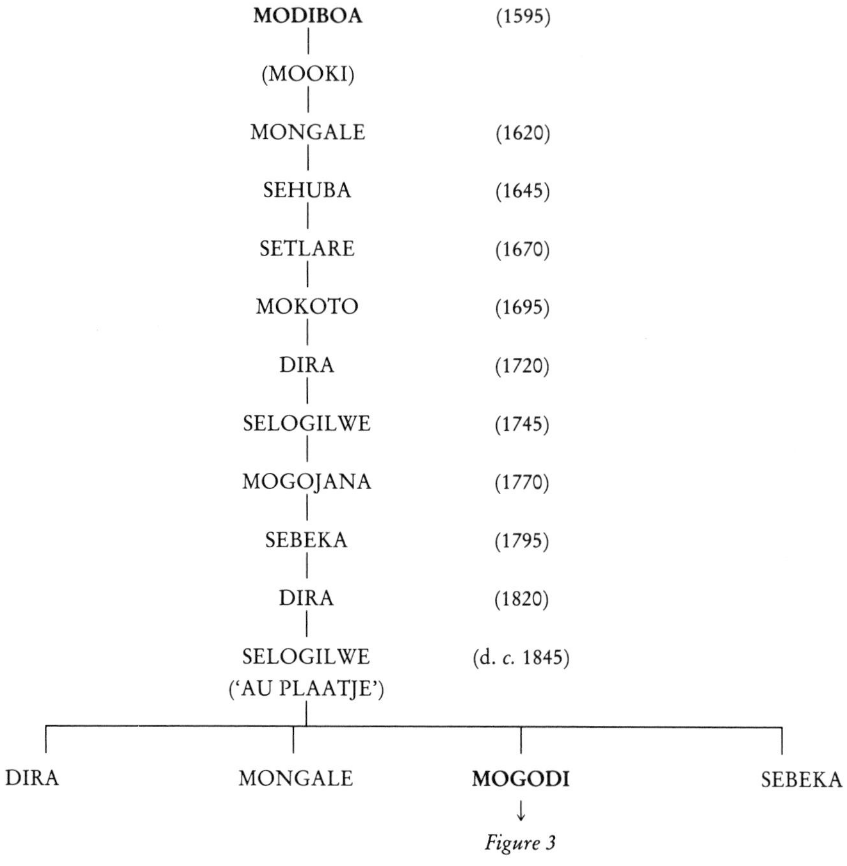

MODIBOA	(1595)
(MOOKI)	
MONGALE	(1620)
SEHUBA	(1645)
SETLARE	(1670)
MOKOTO	(1695)
DIRA	(1720)
SELOGILWE	(1745)
MOGOJANA	(1770)
SEBEKA	(1795)
DIRA	(1820)
SELOGILWE ('AU PLAATJE')	(d. *c.* 1845)

DIRA   MONGALE   **MOGODI**   SEBEKA
↓
Figure 3

The details and personalities involved thus differ in the two accounts, but the central strand is clear: one of Plaatje's ancestors, Modiboa or Mooki, neglected his royal duties in favour of hunting, and as a result his direct descendants were removed from the royal line of succession. These descendants continued to cherish, nevertheless, the memory of this royal ancestry, while those few members of the Barolong people who remained loyal to Mooki and his heirs became known as the Barolong *ba ga Modiboa* (the Barolong of Modiboa), who did not desert the rightful heir of Modiboa. They thereby came to enjoy a reputation for loyalty and reliability. 'It is regarded as a special mark of distinction and reliability,' wrote Modiri Molema, himself of the Tshidi Barolong royal line, 'to be recognised as being descended from this loyal stock,

6

and the Barolong, with their punctiliousness in such matters, are ever ready to accord precedence to their brothers of Modiboa's stock.'[14]

Once the Barolong *ba ga Modiboa* had become separated from the main body of the Barolong, they were able – in Modiri Molema's account of the history of the Barolong – to retain an independent existence, remaining in the Molemane (Ottoshoop) and Mooka-osi (Slurry) districts, while the main body of Barolong settled at Setlagole, 45 miles to the south-west of present-day Mafikeng.[15] For several generations each community lived in peace and prosperity. With the main body of Barolong the line of succession passed from Tsheshebe to Monyane to Sethlare to Mokgopha to Masepa to Thibedi, and then to Tau; with the *ba ga Modiboa*, according to Plaatje's account, the line passed from Mooki to Mongale to Sehuba to Setlare to Mokoto to Dira and then to Selogilwe, who lived in the middle of the eighteenth century.

From the time of the reign of Tau we can be far surer of the actual history of the Barolong, for the memories of those who had lived through these times were recorded in writing by the European missionaries who first arrived in the region in the early part of the nineteenth century. From these and later accounts, based upon Barolong traditions, it is evident that Tau's turbulent reign represented something of a turning point in the history of the Barolong. Tau was an ambitious leader whose territorial designs brought him into conflict with the Batlaping, another Tswana-speaking tribe to the south, and the Koranna, a mixed race of nomadic hunters. Together they proved to be more than a match for Tau's Barolong, many of whom were apparently opposed to his ambitions for conquest and expansion. It was a recipe for disaster: Tau was killed in about 1780, and in the ensuing confusion and dispute over the succession the Barolong broke into four sections – the Tshidi, Ratlou, Seleka, and Rapulana. Thereafter, the Barolong were to retain a strong sense of a common ancestry and nationality, but they lived henceforth in independent chiefdoms, each of them taking their name from one of the sons of Tau.[16] It was from the youngest of these, Rapulana, that Plaatje's mother was descended.[17]

As for the Barolong *ba ga Modiboa*, the male side of Plaatje's ancestry, they were in no position to withstand the attacks of Koranna and Bushmen marauders who flourished in the wake of Tau's defeat and death, and they were scattered among the newly forged divisions of the Barolong, forced to seek refuge and protection that they could no longer provide for themselves, ceasing to exist as an independent entity, comforted only by the memory of a more glorious past. From the time of Tau the *ba ga Modiboa* largely ceased to have a history of their own; we know only that it was with the Seleka branch of the Barolong that they seem to have been predominantly associated.[18]

◇

The early years of the nineteenth century were no less eventful for the Barolong. For now, along with many other peoples, they found themselves caught up in one of the most far-reaching series of events in the history of the subcontinent, the *mfecane* (or 'scattering'), which followed the expansion of the Zulu kingdom to the east. This produced in its wake a dramatic movement of peoples, bringing first the 'Mantatees' (the followers of the Tlokwa chieftainness, Ma Nthatisi) and then the Ndebele (Matabele) under Mzilikazi into the areas occupied by the Barolong. Weakened by their own internal divisions and greatly outnumbered, the Barolong could offer little effective resistance, and fled wherever they could to escape annihilation at the hands of superior forces. Providentially, as it must have seemed to many of them, an unexpected source of protection then materialised – Wesleyan missionaries, with whom the Barolong first made contact in 1822. From that point onwards the history of the Barolong was closely linked with that of missionary endeavour in the region. The main body of the Barolong was first of all associated with the Wesleyan mission at Makwassi (Maquassi), near the present town of Klerksdorp (1822–6); then at Platberg (near present-day Warrenton), where the predominantly Seleka Barolong were joined by Tshidi, Ratlou and Rapulana; and then at Thaba Nchu, an area which the Wesleyan missionaries had succeeded in obtaining from Mosheshwe, chief of the Basotho, where the Barolong from all sections now gathered. In a time of crisis the Barolong nation was once more united.[19]

The Barolong and the Christian missionaries had rather different expectations of this relationship. Essentially, what drew the Barolong to the Wesleyan missionaries at Thaba Nchu was their need for refuge and protection against their enemies. The aims of the missionaries themselves were more far-reaching and complex. Seeking to win adherents to the religion they espoused, they hoped to wean away their potential converts from such traditional customs as polygamy and circumcision, to adopt western styles of clothing and housing, to foster a way of life built upon the virtues of monogamy, hard work, discipline, and regular religious observance. They insisted on Sunday being set aside as a day of rest and worship; they encouraged regular church attendance and the reading of the Bible; and they required the children of families living on mission stations to attend school so that they could be taught the basic elements of the Christian religion, prepare for their confirmation, and learn to read so that the contents of the Bible and prayer book could be made accessible to them.

On the basis of their past experience, missionaries were keen to encourage their adherents on mission stations to settle permanently, abandon their habit of migrating from one place to another, practise settled forms of agriculture, and free themselves completely from the ties of chiefly authority and influence. They preferred, moreover, to be landlords as well as spiritual mentors to their flocks, for control over the allocation and distribution of land greatly increased their chances of making permanent converts.

In their encounters with the Barolong, as with other African peoples, the missionaries at first met with resistance from the chiefs when they tried to introduce these kinds of changes in the lives of their followers. Whilst the Barolong chiefs and headmen valued the protection provided by the missionaries against those who sought to dispossess them of their land and livestock, they were far less enthusiastic about allowing them to work permanently amongst their people, for they posed an obvious threat to their own authority and influence. Many of them, indeed, departed with their people from the orbit of the missionaries when it was safe to do so, and so long as there remained somewhere else to go.

Almost everywhere, the missionaries tended to be most successful in winning the allegiance of those Africans who were in some sense refugees or outcasts: people, in other words, who had nowhere else to go. In the wake of the *mfecane* and in the chaos and confusion that followed, there were, amongst the Barolong, many people in such a position, and for them a continued association with missionaries had very definite advantages.

Amongst the Barolong who gathered at Thaba Nchu during the early 1830s was Selogilwe, Plaatje's paternal great-grandfather, remembered as 'the first Christian in the family'.[20] Since that time, family traditions agree, his direct descendants lived their lives in some form of association with Christian missionaries, albeit of different denominations and in different places, adopting a way of life whose values, beliefs and outward characteristics were to be progressively shaped and influenced by this association. As *ba ga Modiboa*, vulnerable dependents of one or other of the larger Barolong tribes, with no recognised chief of their own, it was perhaps the obvious choice for them to have made. For Plaatje's ancestors, the missionary option was clearly an attractive one.

Selogilwe and his family are believed to have left Thaba Nchu sometime during the 1830s. Before they departed, however, Selogilwe's son Mogodi was married to a woman called Magritta Morwagadi, who gave birth to their first son, Kushumane (Plaatje's father), in 1835, his date and place of birth – Maamuse, or Schweizer Reinecke – being recorded in a prayer book preserved among the Plaatje family to this day.[21] Thereafter their next known place of residence was the Philippolis district. By the time Kushumane was twenty years old he had married Martha Lokgosi (or Motsieloa, as Mrs Bokako believes), of the Rapulana clan, and it was here, on 28 February 1855, that their first son, Simon, was born.[22] The family must have remained in the district for at least four or five years thereafter, for it was also at Philippolis, as Mrs Bokako recalls, that the next two sons, Andrew and Samuel, were born, there being two years between each child.[23]

Figure 3   Solomon Plaatje's immediate ancestry

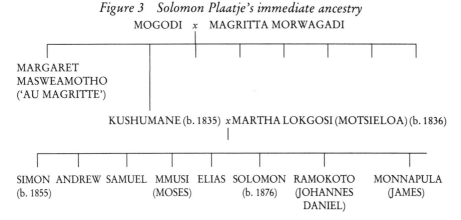

MOGODI   x   MAGRITTA MORWAGADI

MARGARET
MASWEAMOTHO
('AU MAGRITTE')

KUSHUMANE (b. 1835) x MARTHA LOKGOSI (MOTSIELOA) (b. 1836)

| SIMON
(b. 1855) | ANDREW | SAMUEL | MMUSI
(MOSES) | ELIAS | SOLOMON
(b. 1876) | RAMOKOTO
(JOHANNES
DANIEL) | MONNAPULA
(JAMES) |

Philippolis in the 1840s and 1850s was the centre o an independent state governed by the Griqua people, a mixed race who had done much to maintain the balance of power, such as it was, in the relations between the different groups competing for land and power in the region between the Vaal and Orange rivers over the previous twenty or thirty years.[24] Plaatje's parents, grandparents, even great-grandparents, were in all probability part of the Methodist missionary settlement at Philippolis, comprised of a mixture of Dutch-speaking Griquas and Basotho and Tswana refugees, and divided for religious purposes according to the language they spoke. For a while during the 1840s the missionary responsible for the Tswana-speaking congregation was Gottlieb Schreiner, father of the novelist Olive Schreiner, with whom Plaatje was to cross paths on more than one occasion later in life; Plaatje's family, though, seems to have arrived there only after he had departed.[25]

Family tradition has it that it was while living at Philippolis that Plaatje's forebears first acquired the name 'Plaatje'. Meaning 'flat' in Dutch, the name was reputedly given to Selogilwe, Plaatje's grandfather ('Au Plaatje'), by a Dutch-speaking Griqua farmer on whose land they lived; 'Au Plaatje' was supposed to have had a flat-looking head, and the Griqua to have been either unable or unwilling to pronounce the family name of Mogodi correctly. Whatever the exact circumstances of its acquisition, the name stuck and has been retained by one branch of the family ever since.[26]

The fact that 'Au Plaatje' was also referred to – both by Plaatje himself and by Martha Bokako – as 'Rich Old Plaatje' suggests that the family were among the beneficiaries of the period of relative peace and prosperity enjoyed at Philippolis in the 1840s and 1860s.[27] Plaatje himself, writing many years later, had his own family history very much in mind when he wrote: 'Prior to the establishment of the Orange Free State [1854] our forefathers were trading grain for cattle and horses amongst the Griqua of Philippolis, and exchanging wheat for merino sheep among European pioneers around Colesberg and Victoria West.'[28] Martha Bokako, too, believes that the period her grandfather and great-grandfather spent in this district was chiefly notable as one of prosperity, in which they built up the size of their herds and stocks.

Philippolis's existence as an independent state came to an abrupt end in 1862 when the Griqua leaders, threatened by the encroachments of the surrounding Boer state, left the area with their people and trekked to the district of Kokstadt in what became known as Griqualand East, sandwiched between the border of the Cape and Natal colonies. At about the same time, possibly as a consequence of this, the Plaatje family moved northwards to the large mission estate at Bethanie, granted to the Berlin Mission Society some years earlier by the Griqua leader, Adam Kok II. The first definite evidence – one of the entries in the Bethanie mission register – showing the presence of the Plaatje family there is for the year 1867, but they may well have been living there for several years before this.[29]

Bethanie itself had been established as far back as 1834 – indeed it was the oldest mission station in the Orange Free State – but for most of its existence it had been singularly unsuccessful, and the missionaries failed dismally in their attempts to convert the nomadic Koranna people, once the main inhabitants of the region, to a Christian way of life. It was only in the 1850s and 1860s, when there was an influx of Tswana-speaking people (the Plaatje family among them) seeking access to land which was becoming increasingly difficult to find elsewhere, that the mission at Bethanie grew into the kind of settled, prosperous community that was regarded as essential by the missionaries for the spread of the word of God and the creation of truly Christian communities.

This period of consolidation took place under the autocratic guidance of the Reverend C. J. Wuras, who ran the mission according to the maxim 'Pray and labour', and it saw members of the Plaatje family rise to positions of authority and influence in its daily affairs; the ruins of 'Plaatje's Camp', solid stone buildings, testament to this in themselves, can be seen there to this day. Names of members of the family appear regularly in the mission register for the 1860s and 1870s, recording births, deaths, baptisms, and marriages, collective tribute, in their way, to the new way of life being forged by the residents of the mission. The Plaatje family was very much at the heart of this.[30]

Early in 1876, however, Plaatje's parents, Johannes and Martha, probably accompanied by other members of the family, left Bethanie to go and live at Doornfontein, the farm where, later that year, Plaatje was born. Exactly why they decided to make the move is unknown. Possibly it was to assist in the creation of a new Christian community on this outstation; possibly – as Martha Bokako believes – it was because Johannes Plaatje was by this time looking around for larger areas of land upon which to graze his sheep and cattle. It could well have been a mixture of the two, for the co-existence of temporal and spiritual considerations of this nature was at the heart of life on any mission station. Whatever the reasons for the move to Doornfontein, their decision to return to Bethanie early the following year for the baptism of their new-born baby by their former missionary is understandable enough: they had, after all, been very much part of this community at Bethanie, they had contributed to its development, and they would have identified themselves with its values and religious beliefs.

In fact the Plaatje family did not then remain very long at Doornfontein, and within a few years they had moved on again: this time to the mission at Pniel, some fifty miles further down the Vaal river.[31] In all probability their move was precipitated by the decision of the missionaries at Pniel (in 1880) to give up the settlement at Doornfontein because of its remoteness, and because of the apparent unwillingness of its inhabitants – hardly unreasonable in the circumstances – to provide transport on horseback to and from Pniel whenever one of the missionaries required it.[32] Plaatje did not then return to his place of birth for nearly forty years.

<>

So it was at the Berlin mission at Pniel that Plaatje spent, as he later recalled, the 'best and happiest days' of his childhood. Like many mission stations it was ideally situated, set in attractive surroundings on a bend on the south side of the Vaal river, not far from the town of Barkly West. It occupied an area of some three square miles, its northern boundary formed by the banks of the river, which were lined by a row of tall willow and karee trees. The main mission buildings – the church, school building and missionaries' houses – lay close to

11

the banks of the river, just high enough to avoid being washed away by occasional floods. A little further up the river the ground was broken by clumps of rocky outcrops, but most of the estate, irrigated by dams and steam pumps constructed by the missionaries, possessed rich soils which made it suitable for either agriculture or grazing sheep or cattle. The Pniel mission estate was recognised, indeed, as one of the most fertile stretches of land for miles around, and visitors were often struck by its great natural beauty and abundance of flowers.[33]

The mission station had had an eventful past. The land it occupied was once the home of Koranna and Griqua people, then it was claimed by the government of the Orange Free State, and was later annexed as part of the British colony of Griqualand West, itself incorporated into the Cape Colony in 1881. The history of the mission itself extended as far back as 1845, when missionaries were sent from Bethanie, hoping to evangelise among the Koranna who had moved to the region. But as at Bethanie, so the Berlin mission at Pniel failed to build up a permanent, settled community amongst the Koranna nomads, and it barely survived; in the 1860s, indeed, the Pniel mission had seemed to be on the point of closure, and a severe drought forced almost all its inhabitants to leave.[34]

In 1867, however, life on the mission had been transformed by the discovery of diamonds along the banks of the Vaal river, initially on the north side, but soon afterwards on the south side on the land claimed and occupied by the Berlin Mission Society. Thousands of people were drawn to this new scene of activity, and almost overnight there sprung up two new towns – at Klipdrift (later renamed Barkly West), and the town of Pniel itself – to serve the needs of this new digging community. Although the diamond town of Pniel lasted for no more than three years, disappearing almost without trace as the majority of the diggers transferred their attentions to the more fruitful 'dry diggings' further south, the discovery of diamonds nevertheless had a lasting impact upon the Pniel mission. From the missionaries' point of view it was all very much of a mixed blessing: on the one hand it had brought in a great deal of money which the mission was able to extract from the diggers who were charged dues for the right to prospect on their property; on the other, it added to the already formidable task of establishing a godly life amongst the residents of the mission, and it led to a long and very bitter dispute over the ownership of the Pniel estate, claimed by the society on the basis of a grant made to them in 1854 by the Koranna chief, Cornelius Kok. The Berlin Society had thus found itself in *de facto* possession of what was for a while the most valuable piece of real estate in southern Africa, and was fortunate to have been able to retain its title to the land, the matter being finally resolved in their favour, after ten years of anxiety and uncertainty, in 1881.[35]

Although by this time most of the diamond diggers had moved on, the affairs of the mission, in the early 1880s, were nevertheless not causing much satisfaction at missionary headquarters in Berlin. Of the 500 or so inhabitants of the mission, drawn from a wide variety of ethnic groups as was so often the case in mission stations elsewhere in southern Africa, only a handful were regarded as 'serious Christians'; the remainder consisted, so it was reported in 1883, either of people who only called themselves Christians when it was convenient to do so, or those who did not even bother at a pretence of this kind, and who were not surprisingly resentful of the attempts of the missionaries to impose some sort of religious discipline upon them.[36] To make matters worse, there had been some unfortunate problems with the missionaries as well: early in 1881 the Reverend Mecklenburg had to be dismissed for what was described as 'gross carnal sin', and shortly afterwards his colleague, Heinrich Kallenberg, was also relieved of his duties for having committed what was – in the hierarchical and very strict Berlin Mission Society – another cardinal sin, 'severe disobedience to his superior'. Matters were complicated further by the fact that Kallenburg, a very popular figure locally, then set up a rival mission of his own on a neighbouring estate, drawing to it a number of the 'more advanced Christians' from Pniel, who were attracted by the rather less authoritarian regime (with lower dues) over which he presided.[37]

When the newly appointed missionary, Carl Meyer, took over at Pniel in June 1881 he found the work of the mission in a parlous state. Dues were not being paid, the mission school had virtually collapsed, and the spiritual life of the inhabitants – so he reported – had sunk very low. Meyer did his best to re-establish some sort of order and control over life at Pniel, but in the end he did not prove to be up to the task of reconstruction, and a year later he was forced to return to Germany through ill-health.[38] This task fell instead to the Reverend Martin Baumbach, who had been working at one of the society's stations in the Transvaal, also a man who did not enjoy the best of health. He was accompanied by a young apprentice missionary, fresh from Germany, called Ernst Westphal.

It was during this somewhat chaotic period at Pniel that Johannes and Martha Plaatje and their family arrived to join the mission, together with several other Barolong families of the *ba ga Modiboa* clan with whom they had been living. Exactly when they arrived is unknown, but it was certainly not later than the second half of 1881, the date of the earliest mention of Johannes Plaatje's name in the mission records.[39] Additional evidence is provided by a handwritten inscription in the Plaatje family Bible, to which is appended the place and date, 'Pniel, 2nd October 1881', one week, that is, before young Solomon's fifth birthday; and by a sadder entry in the pages of the prayer book set aside for the recording of family information, dated 30 October 1881, indicating that Joshua Plaatje, aged six years old (probably one of Sol Plaatje's cousins or nephews), had been drowned in the Vaal river.[40]

Plaatje never left a proper account of these early years of his life at Pniel. Occasionally, however, he did refer afterwards to isolated incidents he remembered from his childhood, mostly in order to contrast the happy times in which he grew up with those he experienced later. But from these few memories and from a variety of other sources, human and archival, a reasonable impression of the circumstances and surroundings in which he grew up can be formed. Much of the account which follows has thus been pieced together from the records of the mission itself; from the records kept by the Cape Colony's Education Department, which had jurisdiction over the mission school at Pniel which Plaatje in due course attended; from the memories of Mrs Martha Bokako, who grew up at Pniel during the 1890s and 1900s, and lived in the same household as Plaatje; and from the recollections of Erna Westphal, daughter of the Reverend Ernst Westphal.

One thing seems clear enough: that, materially speaking, the Plaatje family were comfortably off. They appear to have owned considerable stocks of horses, sheep, cattle and other livestock, and lived in a large, thatched-roofed stone building which they built on the edge of the estate, at the foot of a ridge which came to be known as 'Plaatje's Hoogte' (or 'Plaatje's Heights'), not far from the main road from Kimberley to Barkly West, which formed the western boundary of the mission estate.[41] They grew vegetables in the grounds around their compound, and most years would probably have had a good living from the sale of stock and produce in the two nearby towns; part of the proceeds then had to go to the mission in return for their right to live there and graze their livestock, payment for the latter being calculated in proportion to their numbers. At a time when many Africans in the northern part of the Cape Colony (as in some other parts of southern Africa) were being evicted from their lands, or having to seek employment elsewhere, the Plaatje family enjoyed a favoured and relatively secure position, well placed to take advantage of the high prices paid for livestock and agricultural produce on the nearby diamond fields. For others it had been very different: three years before the Plaatjes arrived at Pniel, nearby groups of Tlaping, another Tswana-speaking tribe, had resorted to hopeless acts of armed resistance in a desperate attempt to preserve a way of life now threatened by the demands of white colonists.[42] Residence on a mission station provided at least some degree of protection from the worst excesses of this new colonial order.

On occasions Pniel's favoured position provided opportunities for the children who lived there, as well as the adults. One of Plaatje's earliest memories testified vividly to the possibilities which sometimes arose:

> In rainy seasons . . . the river used to overflow its high banks, and flood the surrounding valleys to such an extent that no punt could carry the waggons across. Thereby the transport service would congregate for weeks on both sides of the river until the floods subsided. At such times the price of fresh milk used to mount up to 1/- per pint. There being next to no competition, we boys had a monopoly over the milk trade. We recalled the number of haversacks full of bottles of milk we youngsters carried to those waggons, how we returned with empty bottles and with just that number of shillings. Mother and our eldest brothers had leather bags of gold and did not care for the 'boy's money'; and unlike the boys of the neighbouring village, having no sisters of our own, we gave away some of our money to our fair cousins, and jingled the rest in our pockets . . . we had hardly any use for money, for all we wanted to eat, drink and wear, was at hand in plenty. We could then get six to eight shillings every morning from the pastime of washing that number of bottles, filling them with fresh milk and carrying them down to the waggons . . .[43]

By the time Plaatje wrote these lines (in 1914 or 1915) he had good reason to look back upon his childhood years with fondness and nostalgia, and they were written with the more or less explicit intention of showing how much better things were at that time. Even so, the incident he described had obviously remained in his memory, and his recollections convey a general sense of prosperity and well-being which his family probably did enjoy – even if they suffered, like everybody else on the mission, from the outbreaks of smallpox, cattle disease, the destructive visitations of locusts, and the crop failures that followed insufficient rains, all of which are recorded in the Pniel mission records for the 1880s.

Of his parents Plaatje has left few memories. Almost the only time he mentioned his father was to say that he was 'a cattle farmer', and that 'he thought he knew a lot'.[44] Of his mother, too, he wrote little, but he did remember her telling him of an extraordinary incident she had witnessed in Fauresmith, a small town in the Orange Free State (not far from the mission at Bethanie), in the 1860s. It was apparently the custom for the ox-waggon drivers to give public displays of their skills when they visited the town, but on the occasion which Martha Plaatje witnessed one young driver came to grief in rather remarkable circumstances: whilst displaying his skills, one of the wheels of his waggon hit a boulder and knocked him off balance; as he fell to the ground, a waggon wheel passed over his neck, completely severing his head from his body. To everybody's amazement his body then rose up, ran alongside the moving waggon and cracked a whip at the leading oxen before dropping down stone dead. Fact or fiction, it was not surprising the story remained in Plaatje's mind.[45]

Plaatje's mother was one of several women at Pniel from whom he learnt much in the way of family and tribal traditions, and who taught him his first language, Setswana. 'The best Sechuana speakers known to me,' Plaatje was to write later, 'owe their knowledge to the teachings of a grandmother, or a mother, just as I myself . . . am indebted to the teachings of my mother and two aunts.'[46]

'Au Magritte', or 'Granny Masweamotho', Plaatje's great-aunt (on his father's side), was another of these women who evidently made quite an impression upon him. She was a fund of family history and tradition, and it was from her, so Plaatje recalled later, that he first derived 'complete information' about the details of his own ancestry.[47] When he wrote later of having been 'taught almost from childhood to fear the Matabele', of being frightened with stories of the 'unreasoning ferocity' of their attacks upon the Barolong in the 1820s and 1830s, part of the reason why these stories left such an imprint was that he had very probably heard them from a woman who had either witnessed these scenes of devastation herself, or had been told about them by her parents. It seems reasonable to assume that 'Au Magritte' had a very great deal to do with Plaatje's fascination with the history and traditions of his family and people. His mother, too, was very knowledgeable about the history and traditions of the Barolong, for it was to her, so Erna Westphal remembers, that Ernst Westphal used to turn whenever he needed information on such matters.[48]

Collectively, the Plaatje family occupied a pre-eminent position in the social and religious life of the mission. Together with representatives of a half-dozen or so other families living at Pniel, Johannes and Simon Plaatje in particular occupied positions of responsibility and influence that set them apart in many ways from the other residents of the mission. For at Pniel, as on other mission stations in southern Africa, the maintenance of the authority of the missionaries, in temporal as well as spiritual matters, depended upon the support they received from families like the Plaatjes: it was they who provided the deacons, elders, 'native helpers', the interpreters, the men and women whose job it was to help maintain discipline, to ensure the regular payment of dues, to support the missionaries with help and advice, visit the sick, admonish the weak in spirit – duties which, as the mission reports for Pniel suggest, did not always make them popular with other members of the mission community.[49]

Johannes and Simon Plaatje played a leading part in activities of this kind from 1881 onwards, and became intimately involved in the religious life of the mission community, attending and often helping to organise the daily church services, the Bible and prayer meetings, Sunday schools, confirmation classes, and the great religious festivals that marked out the Christian year. Johannes Plaatje was appointed as one of the two deacons responsible for the Tswana community at Pniel (about 200 persons) in the latter part of 1881, and several months later Simon was made a church elder.[50] Probably it was one of these appointments that inspired the handwritten inscription, taken from *Acts of the Apostles* XX:28, written in Dutch and dated 2 October 1881, which appeared at the beginning of the family Bible. Certainly it was an appropriate reminder of new responsibilities:

> Take heed, therefore, with yourselves, and to all your flock, over which the Holy Ghost hath made you overseers, to feed the church of God, which he hath purchased with his own blood.

With a tradition of Christianity in the family that went back over three generations it is not difficult to see why, particularly with the affairs of the mission in such a state of flux, Johannes and Simon Plaatje should have been given such responsible positions. Somebody who could address the church congregation on 'The Advent of Christianity among the Barolong', as Plaatje's father did in 1883 (he delivered his address in Setswana), or talk to the Reverend Westphal's first 'Tea Meeting' (a popular means of raising money for church funds) about the history of the Pniel mission, was clearly a valuable asset to the two new missionaries.[51] Over the next few years both their names appear regularly on the list of those who attended the monthly church council meetings. Often it was Johannes Plaatje who took the chair on these occasions, and it became the custom, too, for him to say the prayer that closed the meeting. Outside these meetings, his single most important duty was the preparation of candidates for confirmation before presenting them to one of the missionaries for examination.[52]

Simon Plaatje assumed a rather greater degree of responsibility in assisting the missionaries in the more temporal aspects of running the mission. Erna Westphal has a vivid recall of his relationship with her father:

> Solomon's elder brother, Simon, became my father's right-hand man in the management of the many and often very complicated situations not only among the Tswana and others on the Pniel estate, but especially between Europeans and Tswana on the diggings. You see, the diggers were wont to imagine they could act just as they pleased, regardless of whether their acts were legally or morally permissible . . . It was here that Simon showed both wisdom and tact, and father trusted him.[53]

Her account is borne out by the mission records: throughout the 1880s there are frequent references to Simon Plaatje's work in collecting dues from both the diggers and the more permanent residents on the estate, in acting as an interpreter, and as a guide for both Westphal and Baumbach on their visits to the several outstations that lay to the north of the main mission at Pniel.[54] Both Plaatje's father and eldest brother, in short, were very closely associated with the two missionaries at Pniel: the relationship must have impinged on Solomon Plaatje's consciousness as he grew older.

◇

In 1883, or 1884, when Plaatje was seven or eight years old, his family split up. Exactly what precipitated this is uncertain, but it was to have very important consequences for his upbringing and education. What happened, it seems, was that Plaatje's parents, certainly his father, decided to move away from Pniel to go and live at Mayakgoro, some sixty miles to the north (on the Harts river, a tributary of the Vaal), and the site of one of Pniel's main outstations. Johannes Plaatje was apparently keen for everybody to move, but he was unable to persuade his eldest son and his family to come with them. Simon was to spend the rest of a very long life at Pniel, and even at this early stage he evidently felt that he had found a secure niche in the life of the mission community, and he had no desire to leave. But he also insisted, as Martha Bokako recalls, on keeping his younger brother Solomon there with him: even at this age, it seems, the young Solomon had already shown himself to be an exceptionally bright child, obviously likely to benefit from attending the mission school at Pniel; it is possible, indeed, that he had already begun to do this.[55] When his parents and brothers departed for Mayakgoro, therefore, Solomon Plaatje remained instead at Pniel in the care of his elder brother. Henceforth it was to be Simon Plaatje and his wife Gracie who were to be immediately responsible for his upbringing, and instead of his brothers as companions the closest to him now in age was his niece Lydia, just a year younger than himself.

For a while it appears that the move opened up some kind of rift in the family. According to the mission records, when Simon went to visit his mother some time later he found her to be not only unwell, but to have lost all religious faith, blaming her husband for her misfortunes, and wishing to prevent her younger children from going to school.[56] Martin Baumbach was later happy to be able to report that her faith had been regained with a new fervour, but she had evidently gone through a period of great distress.[57] And Johannes Plaatje, though he continued for a number of years to be a deacon of the community at Mayakgoro, and to attend church councils at Pniel from time to time, seems to have gradually grown apart from his attachment to the Berlin Mission Society, and by the late 1880s he was intent on migrating further northwards.[58]

But for the young Solomon Plaatje the immediate consequences of these family upheavals were clear enough: he was to remain at Pniel, to live with his elder brother Simon, and to attend the mission school. This, in turn, was to bring him into close contact with the man who was to be, outside his immediate family, the single most important individual of these years of his life, the Reverend Gothilf Ernst Westphal.

Ernst Westphal was in many ways a remarkable man, tremendously hard-working and self-disciplined, and wholly committed to the life of the mission where he was to spend almost the whole of his adult life. He had first arrived in Pniel early in 1882, aged 26, as an apprentice missionary. Unlike most of the missionaries sent out to Africa by the Berlin Mission Society, who were drawn from an artisan background, Westphal came from a wealthy family in Brandenburg, Prussia. His father had owned a large textile business which Ernst Westphal would, in the normal course of things, have inherited, had not both his parents died very young. He was brought up instead by his uncle, also a wealthy businessman, and when he was old enough joined another firm, owned by a man called Metz. However, his career changed course sharply after he attended a conference of Christian students; he decided to become a missionary, joined the Berlin Mission Society, and then attended the Berlin Seminary for four years, there to undergo the demanding course of instruction which all intending missionaries had to take. When he completed this the society decided that, with his business training and background, Ernst Westphal would be the ideal person to take charge of the administration of the Pniel estate, and to restore some order to the chaotic state of affairs which existed there in the early 1880s. In order to familiarise himself with the diamond business he was first sent to work for several months for De Beers, the large diamond company, in nearby Kimberley.[59]

In the event, the urgency of the situation at Pniel ensured that Ernst Westphal joined the mission much sooner than had been anticipated, and he soon succeeded in improving the financial position of the estate. But Westphal also assumed responsibility (as from 12 April 1882) for the running of the mission school, and here too he quickly made his mark. When he arrived the school was in a sorry state. The school inspector from the Cape Education Department (responsible for the maintenance of standards at the school since Griqualand West became part of the Cape Colony in 1881) paid a visit early in 1882 and reported that 'the general standard of attainment is low', that attendance was poor, and that the school 'had not made the progress that might be expected, owing to several changes of teachers'; he added, though, that 'a new appointment had been made which is likely to be a permanent one', and looked forward to better things in the future.[60] He was proved right on both counts. Under Westphal's guidance and the watchful eye of the Cape Education Department, the Pniel mission school went from strength to strength.

Just how successful Westphal was in this is shown by the enthusiastic report on the school written by no less a person than Dr Heinrich Wangemann, the Director of the Berlin Mission Society, following his visit to Pniel during his tour of southern Africa in 1884. When he examined the pupils he was struck by their keenness, tidiness, punctuality, and discipline (such were the qualities valued most highly), and compared them favourably with children of the same age whom he had seen in schools in Germany. He found that the children at the Pniel mission school, boys and girls, were able not only to relate stories from the Bible, but also to explain their meaning. A few of the older children knew the catechism as well, could read in both English and Dutch, the two European languages spoken in the Cape Colony, and were able to take down dictation and write out on the blackboard what was read to them, making very few mistakes.

Dr Wangemann was pleasantly surprised, too, at the ability of the older children at mathematics, since he had often found this to be a weak point amongst African children in other mission schools he had visited – Westphal's business background and training had presumably been of some advantage here. In geography – the children were taught about both Africa and the Holy Land – Wangemann thought the children's knowledge was 'considerable'; and he concluded his report with the observation that he had never seen a better-run school anywhere in either Africa or Germany. Both Ernst Westphal and his Koranna assistant teacher, Thomas Katz, were commended in the highest possible terms, and the latter was awarded an immediate pay rise (from £18 to £24 per year) in recognition of his contribution to bringing about so satisfactory a state of affairs.[61]

Such was the mission school where Plaatje was to receive most of his education. Without doubt he was fortunate to have been reaching school age at a time when, thanks largely to the efforts of Ernst Westphal, the school had been improved out of all recognition compared to its state several years previously; and to have been taught by a teacher who was evidently capable of recognising a talented pupil and willing to encourage him in his endeavours. At the same time one should not exaggerate what the school could offer. It provided a very basic primary education, strongly religious in content, aiming to equip the pupils who passed through it with the basic skills of literacy and numeracy. Few of the pupils would ever go on to any form of secondary education, only a handful would pass into Standards II or III, and the vast majority would fall at the first hurdle of Standard I. The same would have been true of most other mission schools in the colony, a reflection not so much of any inherent lack of ability on the part of the pupils, but rather the alien cultural environment they encountered in the classroom, and the limited expectations their teachers had of their capabilities.

At Pniel there was an additional complication in the profusion of languages spoken. In a situation where the language of instruction in the school classroom was generally 'Cape Dutch', where the reading and dictation was mostly in English, where the children spoke amongst themselves in Koranna, Setswana, Herero or Sesotho, and where the teachers spoke to one another in German or heavily accented English, it was small wonder that the school children should encounter difficulties; or that the school inspector should comment one year that 'the children seldom remain at school sufficiently long to acquire either English or Dutch well enough to pass the various standards'. Better results, he concluded, would be achieved if the teachers concentrated their energies on one language.[62]

For most of the pupils at Pniel such elaborate linguistic and intellectual demands were clearly too much to cope with. For a handful – the young Solomon Plaatje amongst them – they evidently presented a challenge to which they responded, and it seems likely that Plaatje's remarkable gift for languages developed at an early age. Exactly how old Plaatje was when he first attended school at Pniel is not at all clear, and he never gave any subsequent indication on this himself. Modiri Molema thought Plaatje began school at the age of ten, but this seems rather late and it may well have been before this;[63] photographs of the mission school from around this time show children looking rather less than ten years old, and the school did run a kindergarten class for the youngest children. If any youngster was likely to have attended this, then young Plaatje – given the position of his family in the affairs of the mission – would surely have been among them.

Quite fortuitously, evidence has survived to indicate that Plaatje also received, at quite an early age, some instruction at another school altogether, the Church of England's All Saints' mission school in Beaconsfield, part of the mining town of Kimberley, 17 miles away. The source of this information is a man called David Ramoshoana, a close friend of Plaatje's later in life. In a letter to the press, written shortly after Plaatje's death in 1932, Ramoshoana had this to say:

> In 1886 he [Plaatje] attended the Church of England Mission School, then housed in the little iron building which still stands near the large church building near the town hall of Beaconsfield. Often, when we went past that iron building he fondly remarked that it was in that little house that he learned to spell English words and the rudiments of arithmetic. His teacher, whom he held in high esteem, was the late Reverend H. Crossthwaite.[64]

There seems no reason to doubt David Ramoshoana's testimony; he knew Plaatje very well, and the Reverend Herbert Crossthwaite certainly did run the All Saints' mission in Beaconsfield at this time (he was there between 1884 and 1891). Like Westphal, Crossthwaite was another businessman-turned-missionary, he was equally dedicated to an ethic of hard work, and was remembered by his colleagues as a man who brought to his teaching duties 'the accurate and methodical habits acquired . . . in his life as a man of business'. To his pupils he was known simply as 'Crosbie'.[65] Despite being dogged by ill-health and handicapped by a constant shortage of funds, Crossthwaite managed to provide an elementary education for the 140 or 150 pupils who generally attended his classes each day. They came from an even wider variety of backgrounds than the mission community at Pniel. 'Since our Day School was opened in 1884, when I came,' Crossthwaite wrote several years later,

> we have had over 700 children at one time or another in the school, of both sexes, and varied in race, colour, language and creed. This division, classified in numerical order, would be – Cape Dutch [i.e. Coloured], Bechuana, Zulus, Fingoes, Malays, Indians; and classified in numerical order of creed, would be – Christians of the following communions: Dutch Reformed, Anglican, Wesleyan, Independent, Roman Catholic; and in addition to Christians, Mahommedans, and Brahmin.[66]

It was probably the most polyglot collection of schoolchildren to have come under a single roof anywhere in southern Africa, and it was a vivid demonstration of the social effects of this first phase of South Africa's industrialisation now occurring on the diamond fields.

How it was that Plaatje ever came to attend this school remains a mystery, and neither Miss Westphal, Mrs Bokako or Modiri Molema were aware that he had gone there. It is known, however, that from October 1887 to July 1888 the Westphals themselves lived in Beaconsfield, filling in temporarily for the Reverend Carl Meyer (son of the former missionary at Pniel), who had gone

1 The Berlin mission at Bethanie, Orange Free State, where Plaatje was baptized in January 1877. His parents had lived there until shortly before he was born.

2 Page from the Bethanie mission register showing entry 795, recording Solomon Plaatje's birth and baptism.

3 *Johannes Kushumane Plaatje (1835–96), Sol Plaatje's father.*

4 *Simon Plaatje, Sol Plaatje's eldest brother, with whom he lived at Pniel in the late 1880s and early 1890s.*

5 *A view of the Pniel mission in the early 1890s, showing the church and other mission buildings. To the rear and left of the church is the school building, while the Vaal river can be seen clearly in the background.*

6 *Ernst and Elizabeth Westphal, Plaatje's mentors at the Pniel mission.*

7 *Mrs Martha Bokako, daughter of Simon Plaatje, at Thaba Nchu, September 1980, aged 91. She died in December 1983.*

8 *Certificate recording Plaatje's confirmation at Pniel by Rev. G. E. Westphal, 6 January 1892.*

10 *The Kimberley Post Office. Plaatje began work here on 1 March 1894 when he was seventeen years old, starting on a salary of £72 p.a. He later described it as his 'educational institution'.*

9 *Montshiwa (c. 1815–96), chief of the Tshidi Barolong. One of Plaatje's earliest memories was of being present when he gave judgement in his council in Mafikeng.*

11 *The 'Lovedale experiment': the photograph shows the first African telegraph messengers, all of them educated at Lovedale, who were employed in Kimberley from 1883 onwards. Plaatje followed in their footsteps eleven years later.*

home to Germany on leave.[67] If Ramoshoana is allowed a slight margin of error in his recollection of the year in which Plaatje attended the school – and he got a number of other dates wrong – then it would seem entirely possible that the Westphals decided to take young Plaatje with them to enable him to attend Crossthwaite's highly regarded school, thereby giving him the opportunity, amongst other things, of learning English (and evidently some mathematics) from a teacher who spoke it as a first language. Whether or not this hypothesis is correct, no evidence has survived to indicate what Plaatje, then nine or ten years old, made of the school or its urban surroundings beyond the remarks he made to David Ramoshoana. All that can be added with any certainty is that the experience did not deter him from taking up his first job in Kimberley a few years later.

◇

Most of Plaatje's school days, though, were spent at the Pniel mission, and it was Ernst Westphal, not Herbert Crossthwaite, who played the greater part in his education. After a while Plaatje's normal school lessons were supplemented, so Erna Westphal recalls, by extra tuition from Ernst Westphal's wife, Elizabeth.[68] The daughter of a large landowner in Westphalia, she had been engaged to her future husband before he left for South Africa in 1882, and came out to marry him in 1884, accompanying Dr Wangemann on part of his tour of inspection.[69] Unlike her husband, Elizabeth Westphal had had some experience as a teacher in Germany before joining him at Pniel, and it may have been this that inclined her to take a special interest in the progress of young Solomon Plaatje – more of a challenge for her than the sewing classes for which she also assumed responsibility. Her daughter has related how these extra lessons began:

> I believe Solomon himself came to mother one day. He found her in the kitchen. There was an English lady with her. Solomon stood just outside the door listening. Mother looked up and saw him. She asked him in Dutch . . . what he wanted and he said: 'I want to be able to talk English and Dutch and German as you do.' Mother then recognised him and told him to come to her the next day. That is how his lessons began.[70]

In due course, so Erna Westphal recalls, her mother introduced Plaatje to many of the best-known figures in English literature – Shakespeare and Sir Walter Scott were two names Miss Westphal particularly remembers her mother mentioning. She remembers being told, too, of how Plaatje himself began to acquire some books of his own with the proceeds of some earnings from working as a groom at the Bend Hotel, close to the family home on the edge of the Pniel estate, and one of the main coach stopping-places on the road between Barkly West and Kimberley. At the same time Mrs Westphal took a keen interest in fostering Plaatje's musical talents, teaching him to play the piano and the violin, and training his singing voice. Later in life, when Plaatje presented Mrs Westphal with a copy of his novel, *Mhudi*, he inscribed it 'with the author's *filial* compliments': such was the closeness of the relationship that had developed at Pniel.[71]

21

Plaatje had several memories of his own which probably date from around this time. The most amusing of them concerned the way in which he first discovered what April Fool's Day was all about, when the two missionaries at Pniel fooled Plaatje's class at school with a story about an enormous, but non-existent, snake which they then vainly rushed around trying to find; strict as they were on matters of discipline and religious observance the two men obviously enjoyed a good joke at the expense of their pupils.[72] Another episode which Plaatje remembered might have turned out rather more unhappily. This arose from the year he evidently spent as a herdboy, working for a Dutch farmer named Bacchus, who must have lived near the Pniel mission estate, although how old Plaatje was at the time is unknown. Bacchus was a thoroughly unpleasant character. 'Before I entered his employ,' Plaatje wrote, 'he had sjambokked a Hottentot herd to death,' and it was his practice to try to swindle his employees out of their wages, his method being to accuse his herdboys of losing sheep which he had himself slaughtered, and then refusing to pay them on the grounds that they could not prove him wrong. In due course he tried the same thing with Plaatje:

> Now I had been taught from childhood to calculate and could add up things just as quickly as a Dutchman can count his sheep and you know that that is very fast. On every time that a sheep was slaughtered I used to cut a nick in my walking stick – on the obverse for sheep slaughtered, and the reverse for sheep that died. Now, one evening, just fourteen days before my pay was due, Baas Bacchus counted his sheep as we kraaled them and told me that there were 60 missing and I should find them before my year was up or forfeit my pay. I said, 'Baas, there is no difficulty. I will find them if you will let me come with you.'
> 'Where will you find them?' he asked.
> I said, 'In your pantry, and in your kitchen.'
> I produced my marked stick and said: 'Count those nicks.'
> He counted 61. I told him those were the sheep he slaughtered during my year in service.[73]

The remainder of the story has not survived, but the implication of the remaining words that have ('When my year was up, to the amazement . . .') is that Plaatje did indeed receive the money that was due to him; a triumph, one can assume, for youthful resourcefulness and initiative.

At some point in 1891 or early 1892, when Plaatje was 14 or 15 years old, he was appointed as a pupil-teacher at the Pniel mission school.[74] This involved instructing the youngest children while continuing with his own education; for the performance of these new duties, he later recalled, he was paid the 'princely sum of £9 per year'.[75] Pupil-teachers were used in mission schools throughout the Cape Colony, and provided both missionaries and the Cape education authorities with an economical means of resolving the acute shortage of properly qualified teachers. Nobody pretended that the system was wholly satisfactory, least of all the Superintendent-General of Education. In his report for 1893 he had this to say on the use of pupil-teachers in mission schools: 'Pupil-teachers, in fact, in one class of schools are subsidised pupils; in another they are a cheap form of teaching drudge; in very few indeed are they pupil-teachers properly so called.'[76] But for somebody in Plaatje's position, evidently keen to continue with his education, the advantages of the system, whatever its imperfections, were clear enough: without the prospect of this form of employment he would very probably not have been in a position to stay on at school at all. Most children of his age on the mission would have been expected by now to earn a living either in paid employment or by looking after their family's livestock.

Plaatje's appointment may well have been precipitated by the death, in 1891, of the Reverend Martin Baumbach, the senior missionary at Pniel, who used to assist Ernst Westphal in the classroom, but it was to be some time before another teacher, August Schulz, arrived from Germany to fill the gap that had been left. In between, the school inspector paid a visit and was not too impressed with what he found. The building was 'in the same half-ruined state as on the occasion of my last visit,' the school itself was 'not in a very satisfactory state' since it had had 'no efficient assistant teacher' since Martin Baumbach's death, and there were far too many pupils below standard. When he visited there were 87 pupils present in class, of whom 51 were below Standard I, 18 were in Standard I, 15 at Standard II, and three at Standard III.[77] Plaatje, then 14 years old, was probably one of these three, but he seems then to have been the only one to go and actually meet the requirements. Almost certainly he was 'the boy who passed in the Third Standard' mentioned in the inspection report for the next year, 1893, probably the first pupil at Pniel to achieve this distinction.[78]

Plaatje had one memory of his own of Standard III. Seven years later he was reminded of one of the stories he had had to master in the Standard III *Nelson's Royal Reader*, one of a series of graded English primers used to teach generations of schoolchildren throughout the British empire.[79] The story in question was called 'The Wonderful Pudding', an instructive little tale which sought to demonstrate the number of people involved in all the different stages of producing a Christmas pudding. Several pages earlier there appeared another story, a characteristically Victorian homily against sloth and laziness, which one imagines Plaatje would have read with particular interest. It was called 'The Boy who was Always too Late', and was about the adventures of one Solomon Slow. He was given the name Solomon, so his mother explains, 'Because he is a wise child'.[80]

Whether Plaatje duly succeeded in passing his Standard IV as well, as several accounts have it, is less certain; had he done so it must have been thanks to his special lessons with the Westphals and his own efforts outside class, for there were no Standard IV classes at the Pniel mission school during his time there.

Of his experiences as a pupil-teacher at Pniel Plaatje left no record, but he did leave quite an impression upon his superiors. By the end of 1892 August Schulz, now the second missionary and assistant teacher at Pniel, was referring to him in his reports as 'der bekannten klein Schulmeister' ('the well-known young schoolmaster'), and his responsibilities, according to the mission records, now included the children's choir.[81] Singing and music had always been of the greatest importance in the communal life of the Pniel mission, and Plaatje had evidently learnt quickly with Mrs Westphal's tuition. Perhaps he can be credited, too, with some of the general improvement that the school inspector noted at the end of that year: 'The pupils work very diligently,' he commented, 'and are closely supervised in an agreeable fashion'.[82]

◇

Plaatje continued to live with his brother Simon and his family during the three years he spent as a pupil-teacher at the Pniel mission school. Even on the meagre £9 a year he was paid, he wrote later, he was quite comfortably off since 'my eldest brother not only gave me free board and lodging, but he also bought for me all my clothes, including luxuries, and I rode his horses, using his saddles and bridles'.[83] Plaatje's own parents were rather less settled. They had stayed on at Mayakgoro for some years, but in 1891 or 1892 his father Johannes decided to move on again, and that year was the last that saw his name appearing in the records of the Berlin Mission Society.[84] Leaving children at both Pniel and Mayakgoro, but taking his two youngest sons, Ramokoto (Johannes Daniel) and Monnapula (James), along with him, he now moved to a place called Ditlarapeng in the Mafeking district, just inside the border of the Bechuanaland Protectorate.[85]

Ditlarapeng was one of the so-called Barolong farms, exceptionally good agricultural and grazing land which had been the subject of a long dispute with the Bangwaketse, another Tswana-speaking tribe who lived in the Protectorate. The Barolong claim was finally recognised by the Protectorate authorities in 1892, whereupon the Barolong paramount chief, Montshiwa, had the land divided up into individual farms. He then distributed these to his relatives and followers, and allocated Ditlarapeng to Joshua Molema, his son-in-law and one of the leading Barolong headmen.[86] Molema, in turn, must then have reached some form of agreement with Johannes Plaatje, who may have been living there already, allowing him to reside there with his cattle and other livestock. Johannes Plaatje therefore found himself living under the jurisdiction not only of the British colonial authorities, but of the Tshidi Barolong paramount chief and his headmen. The connection thus established was to prove very significant in Solomon Plaatje's life several years hence.

Plaatje probably visited his father at Ditlarapeng on a number of occasions during the early 1890s. Once, in 1891, he travelled from Mafeking to Setlagole by ox-waggon; he remembered the journey because it took five whole days to travel the distance of 45 miles between the two places.[87] Another memory of Mafeking which must date from around this time is more revealing. Visiting the Tshidi Barolong settlement in Mafeking 'when quite a youngster', he managed to steal into Chief Montshiwa's council and listened, fascinated, to the proceedings of a court case then being heard. The case in question arose out of a man being accused of stealing the affections of another man's wife. What was of particular interest, and the reason why Plaatje later wrote about it, was the way in which the married man had resorted to witchcraft to catch the adulterous couple in the act. As plaintiff, the married man won his case but was then publicly warned by Chief Montshiwa that if he ever employed such methods again he would be severely punished, since they constituted a threat to the well-being of the community as a whole.[88]

Quite apart from the interest of the case itself the memory has a wider significance. For it shows that Plaatje had direct experience, and at an impressionable age, of the functioning of an African chiefdom which still enjoyed a large measure of independence. Witnessing the great Barolong Chief Montshiwa giving judgement in council was an experience far removed from anything Plaatje could have seen at Pniel, for here it was the missionaries who performed such functions and laid down the code of behaviour by which people lived. Plaatje may have learnt much of the traditions and history of his people while living at Pniel, but direct chiefly rule such as he found in operation at Mafeking was something quite different.

Other members of Plaatje's family had fared rather less well than his father. Already Plaatje had lost two brothers – Joshua, drowned in the Vaal river in 1881, and Samuel (the third eldest of the brothers), who had died in 1884, but in 1893 there was another death, that of Elias. His elder brother by two years, Elias had left Pniel with his mother and father when they went to live in Mayakgoro and had then taken a job with a white trader travelling northwards to Mashonaland. He had returned home 'full of experience', according to the mission records, but without having been paid for his services, and with a fever which eventually led to his death in September 1893.[89] Although he and his younger brother Solomon had been living apart for some years they probably visited one another regularly. Elias had taken some of his confirmation classes at Pniel, and the two of them were confirmed together by Ernst Westphal on the same day in January 1892.[90] Plaatje's certificate of confirmation, torn and stained, survives to this day.

◇

Plaatje remained at Pniel for another two years. Then, early in 1894, he left the mission to take up a job as a messenger, or letter-carrier, with the Post Office in Kimberley.[91] According to a surviving fragment of an account which Plaatje left about his departure from Pniel, there had been some discussion amongst both relatives and the Westphals about the possibility of his going on to one of the few colleges of secondary education open to Africans in the Cape Colony, most notable of which was the prestigious Lovedale College in the eastern Cape.[92] Certainly this would have been feasible. Although Lovedale was run by Scottish Presbyterian missionaries it did take in pupils from other denominations if they were considered to have sufficient ability, so there would have been nothing in theory to prevent his admission, and he would not have been the first product of a Berlin mission school to have gone there.[93]

However, raising the fees would have presented some difficulties, and for some reason (according to Modiri Molema) it seems that Plaatje's own father was unwilling to assist. The Westphals, at any rate, 'had something mapped out for me which they could not quite define', so Plaatje related, 'and it came as a bombshell to them . . . when I left the old mission by way of the Cape Civil Service'.[94]

In the circumstances, Westphal's concern – and it was shared by members of his family – was understandable enough. With some justification they regarded the mining town of Kimberley as a den of vice and iniquity, full of pitfalls for the unwary; they were worried, as Plaatje himself said on another occasion, lest 'he should fall an easy prey to the temptations of city life'.[95] But Plaatje was obviously intent on leaving 'the old mission'. With his already proven abilities it was natural that he would want to move on, and not at all surprising that he should have applied for a job at the Kimberley Post Office, an institution well known for providing employment for Africans who had the advantage of a mission-school education. Colonial society, it should be said, did not otherwise offer a great deal in the way of career prospects for even the abler products of its mission schools.

◇

Such was Plaatje's life, so far as it is known, up to the age of seventeen and a half. In many respects it had been a comfortable, almost privileged existence. Compared with the majority of other Africans of his generation who grew up in southern Africa during these years, he had enjoyed security and material comfort, and he was now equipped with the means – an education up to Standard III or IV – of escaping from the unskilled, manual labour that was becoming for so many a necessary part of their livelihood.

Other Africans had grown up in broadly similar circumstances on mission stations elsewhere in southern Africa. When they came together, as they did in places like Kimberley, they were conscious of a communality in experience and outlook that far outweighed either the doctrinal differences of their respective missionary societies, or their tribal or ethnic identities and loyalties. Like those contemporaries, Plaatje had been brought up to accept the values and beliefs of the Christian religion, and – as happened on countless other mission stations – he had been greatly influenced by one particular missionary, in his case the Reverend Ernst Westphal. It was almost in the nature of mission-station life, indeed, that close relationships of this kind should develop (although it was rather less common for missionaries' wives to be quite as influential as Mrs Westphal), and almost certainly the importance Plaatje himself came to attach to individual example and character owed much to his memories of this man.

What probably distinguished Plaatje's upbringing from that of many of these contemporaries was the depth of experience his family and forebears had accumulated in reconciling African and Christian tradition, in forging a distinctive way of life which represented a synthesis of the two. At Pniel, as later, there is nothing to suggest that Plaatje was conscious of there being any irreconcilable conflict between these two fundamental elements of his identity. Being the fourth generation of his family since his forebears first came into contact with Christian missionaries undoubtedly helped to make things easier.

Several more individual aspects to Plaatje's personality and experience are also suggested by what is known of his early life. The fact that he had done so well at school as to outgrow its capabilities speaks for itself. He had then impressed the missionaries with his ability as a teacher, and had displayed a keen interest and talent in music. Almost certainly he had already developed – thanks above all to the example of the Reverend Ernst Westphal – a capacity for hard work which was to be very much in evidence later on in life. And now he had shown, in his decision to leave Pniel rather than wait for the Westphals to work out plans for his further education, a willingness to make decisions of his own, and to find employment for himself outside the confines of the Pniel mission. He was due to start his new job on the first day of March 1894.

2

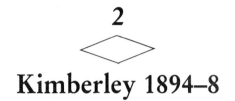

Kimberley 1894–8

Kimberley in the 1890s had changed almost out of recognition from the mining shanty-town that had sprung up so rapidly in the early 1870s. In the early days diamonds were sought by a multitude of individual claim holders; in the chaotic situation that resulted the scene was likened by one observer to 'an insane asylum turned loose on a beach'.[1] But by the 1890s Kimberley was very much a company town, dominated by one great corporation, De Beers Consolidated Mines Limited. Created by the logic of the business of diamond mining as much as by the driving ambition of its founder, Cecil Rhodes, De Beers had first of all bought up the small diggers, then the numerous other smaller companies who were intent on doing the same. Finally, in the late 1880s, Rhodes gained control over his greatest rivals – Jules Porge's French Company, Barney Barnato's Kimberley Central Mining Company, and, in 1889, the Griqualand West Company and the Bultfontein Consolidated Company. With consolidation came control over the selling price of diamonds, tight control and regimentation of the labour force through the newly instituted compound system, and massive profits. By the 1890s the wealth this produced supplied more than half the revenues of the Cape Colony.

These developments in the diamond industry had transformed the character of the town of Kimberley as well. Its population was now much reduced and parts of the town lay almost deserted. Fewer people were needed to work on the mines now that they were under the control of a single corporation, and many of the whites who had come to the diamond fields had been forced to leave the town and seek employment elsewhere. Most of the unskilled work was done by African migrant labourers, cheaper to employ than whites, and more ready to endure the harsh discipline of the compounds. For those whites who remained Kimberley had developed the atmosphere and trappings of a company town, its local institutions now almost as much under the control of De Beers as the mining of diamonds. The 'old roughness', as one distinguished visitor to Kimberley put it in 1894, 'has been replaced by order and comfort'.[2] It was no longer 'an adventure camp, but a town inhabited by intelligent people who read and study'; whilst its public library, in the opinion of another much-travelled observer, was 'one of the largest and best stocked that I saw in the Colonies'.[3] Certainly this was the image Kimberley's city fathers were keen to foster. All were now aware that Kimberley's wider importance had already been eclipsed by the gold discoveries in the Transvaal. Kimberley could nevertheless claim to have seen the development of South Africa's first industrial community; by the 1890s this was displaying distinct signs of maturity.

In addition to the thousands of migrant labourers – many of them from well beyond the borders of the Cape Colony – who were housed in closed, tightly guarded compounds, Kimberley was the home of a larger and rather more permanent population of Indians, Coloureds, and Africans, the last group living in the crowded residential areas (known as locations, and numbered one to four) that had grown up around the four great mines. Mostly they earned a living by small-scale trading, or in servicing the domestic needs of the town's white population, in working for De Beers, the larger trading stores or contractors, or for the Kimberley municipality. Amongst this very mixed group of perhaps 20,000 people was a group of Africans, consisting of probably no more than several hundred, at most a thousand people, who possessed a marketable commodity of a different kind: a missionary education. 'In the townships,' noted the civil commissioner for Kimberley in 1892, 'a considerable number of educated natives are employed. They come principally from Lovedale, and belong to the Fingo or AmaXhosa tribes', and they occupied positions as clerks, messengers, teachers, police constables, interpreters, and the like.[4] These jobs were reasonably well paid, and since the 1870s their existence in Kimberley had been a powerful attraction for the products of mission schools like Lovedale, Healdtown, Morija (in Basutoland), and a handful of others, which provided Africans with the opportunity of acquiring a secondary education. As the civil commissioner pointed out, many of them were of Xhosa or Mfengu origin; that is to say, they were from the eastern Cape, the earliest and most successful field of missionary endeavour in southern Africa, and the region which produced the largest number of Africans with the best educational qualifications. Unable to find suitable employment nearer home, many had made their way to Kimberley in the 1870s and 1880s in search of jobs commensurate with their ambitions and aspirations. The Mfengu in particular, close adherents of the missionary cause, and relatively recent immigrants in any case to the eastern Cape, proved most adept at exploiting the opportunities for employment that the diamond fields provided; they more than anybody were prepared to make a permanent home in this new industrial environment.

In the eyes of Kimberley's mission-educated African community one institution in particular had a reputation for providing employment: the Kimberley Post Office. The General Manager of Telegraphs for the Cape Colony, in his annual report for 1883, explained how this had come about:

the hand delivery [of telegrams] in several of the large towns of the Colony, but especially in Kimberley, threatened at one time to prove an insurmountable stumbling block. The circumstances were so peculiar that it became absolutely impossible to obtain 'white' labour for this purpose. Mere lads were paid at so high a rate of wages by the store-keepers that the Government could hardly enter into competition with them; but even if we had been prepared to pay any price there was a disinclination on the part of the parents in those communities to allow their children to perform so menial a service. On the other hand, a grown-up man combining the requisite qualifications of steadiness, the power to read and write, and willing to perform the duties of a Telegraph Messenger, could not be obtained. The result was that more complaints originated from delays or non-delivery owing to the unreliable character of the staff employed for the purpose than from all other causes put together. In 1880 it occurred to me that the educated Native of the country might with advantage be employed for this purpose and during my annual tour of inspection in that year I discussed the question with Dr Stewart of Lovedale. He at once expressed his readiness to co-operate with the Department as far as possible, but at the same time impressed upon me not to be too sanguine of success. The experiment was tried. A staff of Native messengers, educated at Lovedale and selected by Dr Stewart, was sent to Kimberley in October 1880, and it affords me pleasure to be able to state that from the day on which they took up their duties up to the present, not so much as the shadow of a complaint has been urged against them, and not a single case of non-delivery or delay in delivery has been officially reported to me. The experiment so successfully tried at Kimberley has been followed at East London and King Williamstown. A beginning has been made at Port Elizabeth, and so far the same success has attended it in each case.[5]

Similar circumstances had encouraged the Cape Civil Service to take on larger numbers of mission-educated Africans in several other capacities as well. Government service, as a result, came to be a very highly regarded avenue of advancement in these circles. Most of the positions open to Africans were, it is true, at the lowest levels, but this was readily accepted since it was only recently that Africans had been allowed to occupy even these positions; and it was expected that in time, as they achieved additional qualifications and experience, further progress would be made. 'We are just emerging from barbarism,' wrote John Knox Bokwe, one of the best-known African spokesmen of the day, in 1894, 'and have to find our way, and by degrees gain their [Europeans'] confidence. By and by we shall attain, if one here and there shows capacity for positions of trust and responsibility, and creditably discharge the responsibility.'[6]

By the time Plaatje applied for his job in Kimberley white attitudes towards the employment of Africans in the Post Office had changed considerably. Whereas in Kimberley's boom-days in the late 1870s and early 1880s whites had for the most part been able to find more profitable ways of earning a living than working for the Post Office, by the late 1880s and early 1890s this was no longer the case. Kimberley was far less prosperous, unemployment amongst whites had grown, and there had developed, moreover, an intermittent campaign, led by a clergyman by the name of James Morgan, to replace African telegraph messengers and letter-carriers by whites: 'Surely with so many respectable white men and lads out of employment,' he argued, 'there should be no difficulty in procuring white labour to fill any vacancy that arises. It is the white population who contribute most largely to the revenue of the Post Office,' he continued, 'and I maintain that they deserve a recognition of their just claims in the matter.'[7]

It was fortunate for Plaatje that the Kimberley postmaster, John Henry, was not persuaded to alter his policy of employing Africans as messengers and letter-carriers. He had had good service from his African employees, they were cheaper to employ, and they were also rather better educated than the whites he would have been likely to attract in their place: a liberal attitude towards the employment of Africans may have made him unpopular in some quarters, but it made very good financial sense. Doubtless he was also conscious of the fact that he was unlikely to find amongst the ranks of the white unemployed such loyal, capable and long-serving members of his staff as Alfred Moletsane and Nelson Lindie, both of them employed at the Kimberley Post Office when Plaatje commenced work there on the first day of March 1894. Both men had been part of the original Lovedale 'experiment' and had remained with the Kimberley Post Office ever since. Alfred Moletsane, indeed, had, by dint of what Plaatje described as 'diligence and assiduous application to duty', achieved promotion to the rank of assistant postmaster, the only African amongst the usual complement of twenty Europeans in such positions, earning – like them – a salary of £110 a year.[8]

Nelson Lindie, too, had made some progress in the local Post Office hierarchy, occupying the position, at the time Plaatje started work there, of 'sender-out', responsible for the direction and dispatch of the thirty or so messengers he had under his charge; he would have been, in all probability, Plaatje's immediate superior.

A little more is known about Nelson Lindie because an article about him appeared in the local newspaper, the *Diamond Fields Advertiser*, in March 1895. This is of interest not only for the details it contains of his background and ancestry (he claimed descent from a Xhosa royal family), but also because of what it reveals of the values and behaviour considered desirable on the part of Africans in such positions, and which were obviously necessary for survival, let alone advancement, with employers like the civil service. One essential requirement was an appropriate degree of deference to one's superiors. Thus, Lindie was 'not overbearingly proud of his genealogical tree, but on the contrary is a well-spoken, well-educated native of respectable demeanour, and is as politely mannered as a large proportion of his fellow civil servants of European origin'; he was, moreover, 'to be commended for his extremely creditable record as a private citizen and as a servant of the Government', representing in his own person 'a satisfactory solution of the native problem', and one who was in his 'usefulness and general conduct of life a complete answer to those who are strenuously opposed to native education'.[9] African employees of the Kimberley Post Office – as in other parts of the Cape Civil Service – were clearly expected to be respectable, humble, loyal, polite and do exactly what they were told.

Moletsane, Lindie, Plaatje and their colleagues were also required – in keeping with the high standards that the Cape Colony's postal and telegraphic service prided itself upon – to be efficient and well-disciplined. In return, they expected, and generally received, fair treatment. Such, at any rate, was how Plaatje remembered things some fifteen years afterwards during the course of an interview with the then Minister of Posts and Telegraphs. Protesting on this occasion about the way Africans were being (in 1911) unfairly treated by the post office authorities, Plaatje sought to emphasise his point by providing the minister with the benefit of some of his own recollections of the treatment he and his colleagues had been accustomed to in the Kimberley Post Office in the 1890s. At that time, Plaatje said, minor misdemeanours were punished by a fine of one shilling, and were certainly not used to provide a pretext for their dismissal and replacement by whites. And if all fairness had gone, then so too had standards of efficiency; whereas, Plaatje pointed out to the minister, 'a telegram addressed "Brown, Kimberley" is [today] returned marked "insufficient address" even if "Brown" is well known', in *his* day, Plaatje said, 'when a telegram came for "Robinson, Kimberley", Robinson had to get it or the Postmaster General would know the reason why'.[10]

Discipline may have been strict, but it was fairly applied: white and black alike were subject to the same rules and regulations. For somebody brought up to the discipline of mission station life, it cannot have been too difficult to cope with.

Plaatje left few other memories of the work he did during the period of nearly five years he spent with the Kimberley Post Office. We do at least know that he started on a salary of £72 a year, and that this had risen, by the time he departed in 1898, to £96 a year;[11] that, apart from Nelson Lindie and Alfred Moletsane, his colleagues there also included Joseph Mikwalo, Aaron Nyusa, Simon Sondolo, Hendrik Molschane, David Oliphant, Anthony Makubalo and Herbert Mizine, their names reflecting in themselves a wide diversity in ethnic origin;[12] and that one of the white telegraphists who worked in the office at this time – a man called J. K. Bray – remembered it as one in which everybody was accustomed to 'working at high pressure'.[13] But at least he did not have to face up to the occupational hazards of actually delivering letters or telegrams. Shortly after Plaatje left the Post Office one of his former colleagues, Aaron Nyusa, was awarded £5 damages in the local magistrate's court after being bitten on his hand and shoulder by a dog while delivering a letter to a house in Market Road.[14] Things could be even worse in the neighbouring borough of Beaconsfield: here Theo Binase, well known to Plaatje, requested permission (which was not given) to carry a loaded revolver to protect himself whilst carrying out his duties.[15]

At some point it seems that Plaatje was promoted from the position of telegraph messenger to that of letter-carrier, which was better paid and considered to carry a greater degree of responsibility. But in retrospect Plaatje believed he benefited from his spell of employment with the Kimberley Post Office in other ways. On one occasion later in life he described it as his 'educational institution'; 'An abnormal thirst for knowledge,' he said, showed him that 'no-one was too humble or too young to teach [him] something', whilst 'a keen observation' of what he saw around him 'stood him in good stead so that he was soon able to gain a footing'.[16] There would seem little reason to doubt, therefore, Modiri Molema's contention that Plaatje responded quickly to the demands of the job and the example of the people with whom he worked, and that he acquired a reputation at work as 'a clever young man, who was quick, energetic, who knew his job well, and had good manners'.[17]

$$\diamond$$

In the employment of the Kimberley Post Office Plaatje would have had to conform to the patterns of behaviour expected from so junior an employee. He and his colleagues were expected to know their place, and not to defy the accepted conventions that prevailed in the workplace between black and white. If they failed to do so they not only put their own jobs at risk but also played directly into the hands of those who were opposed to them being allowed to do these jobs anyway – those who believed they formed part of the so-called 'native problem'. But much of Plaatje's time during these years in Kimberley was spent outside his place of work, in the company of friends of his own colour and class, and here attitudes and circumstances were very different. As soon as Plaatje arrived in Kimberley he was drawn into a natural association and friendship with the individuals who made up the town's mission-educated African community, and in time he came to play an increasingly prominent part in the network of social, religious, sporting and political activities which helped give them so distinct an identity. They were in many ways a remarkable group of men and women, and they provided Plaatje with a lively and talented group of friends. Occupying positions as interpreters, clerks, messengers, teachers, and the like, they had created for themselves a communal life which had already achieved – well before Plaatje first came to live in Kimberley – an impressive degree of maturity, sophistication and vitality.

Some members of this community had been there since the earliest days of the diamond fields. John Kosane, for example, a Wesleyan lay-preacher of Mfengu descent, and one-time ox-waggon driver, now a cab-owner, took a special pride in his claim to have been the earliest African resident of the diamond fields, having arrived on the very same day the first diamond was discovered at Bultfontein.[18] The Reverend Gwayi Tyamzashe, a Congregational clergyman, remembered by Plaatje as 'the first ordained black minister I ever saw', was another who had been there since the early days, and for several years, up until his death in 1896, he was a close neighbour of Plaatje's.[19] As a clergyman, he enjoyed an elevated status in the eyes of his community, and along with Kimberley's other African clergyman, the Reverend Jonathan Jabavu, a Wesleyan minister who lived in Greenpoint, he was invariably asked to become president, chairman or honorary member of the many societies and clubs which flourished in the life of this community. The two men assumed, indeed, a natural role as spokesmen for the community as a whole when representations needed to be made to the white authorities over some issue that affected their interests.

Then there were the court interpreters, also very highly thought of in this community. Amongst the longest established of these was Joseph Singapy Moss, a man of Mfengu origin who had first come to the diamond fields in 1879 to take up the position of interpreter in the Beaconsfield magistrate's court, achieved promotion to the Griqualand West High Court three years later, and was now a well-known public figure and a substantial property owner; George Polisa, a resident of No. 4 Location, who started work at the Post Office in Beaconsfield in 1885 before moving on to better things in the Kimberley magistrate's court; and Jonas Msikinya, educated at Lovedale, interpreter and office messenger at the Beaconsfield magistrate's court since 1879, and a member, too, of a prominent local family.[20]

Like the smaller mission-educated communities in other parts of the Colony, Kimberley's African community was bound together by a body of shared beliefs, values and assumptions as well as the close personal ties of friendship, marriage and an often hectic social life. Its members, almost by definition, were committed Christians and regular churchgoers, firm believers in the idea of progress, in the virtues of education, hard work and individual achievement, and they had a warm admiration for the institutions of the Cape Colony and the British empire. Two such institutions in particular they always singled out for special praise: the notion of equality before the law, regardless of racial or any other distinctions; and the non-racial Cape franchise, the right to vote, enshrined in the laws of the colony, and open to any male citizen who possessed property worth £75, or an income of £50 a year, and who could fill in a registration form in either English or Dutch.

It would be difficult to exaggerate the significance of these two constitutional facts in the perceptions of this community: they provided the encouragement to strive towards proving themselves worthy of entitlement to the privileges of 'civilised life' and the means of making a place for themselves in a society which otherwise threw up so many barriers and obstacles; they gave substance to a vision, almost, which sustained them in the face of the discrimination and insults often encountered in daily life – the vision of a common, non-racial society in which merit and hard work, and not race, would determine their position within it. Often this vision was expressed in symbolic terms, above all through expressions of loyalty to the figure of Queen Victoria; her name, and the image of the great white queen, were inextricably associated with notions of justice, progress, and opportunities for education and advancement. For this reason, the African community on the diamond fields believed they had special cause to join in the celebrations for Queen Victoria's Diamond Jubilee in June 1897, and this provided one of those occasions when many of these often unspoken assumptions and associations were made very explicit.[21]

To a greater or lesser degree the members of this community, like their compatriots elsewhere in the Cape Colony, also believed they had a special role and duty in the leadership of their people as a whole. Whilst they were keen as individuals to prove themselves entitled to full citizenship and equal treatment in the life of the colony, their personal ambitions were tempered by an often deeply felt sense of responsibility towards their own societies as well, towards the people they had left behind, as it were, and whose interests they claimed to serve and to represent. For some it appeared as a contradictory and at times a confusing responsibility. On the one hand they were faced with constant pressures to reject and disown many of the features of their own societies in order to 'prove' their worthiness of entitlement to equal treatment with whites. On the other, there was sometimes widespread suspicion of them on the part of their less well-educated countrymen for appearing to do precisely this; it was not always easy to find the right course to steer, socially or psychologically.

But amongst Kimberley's African community in the 1890s there were very few hints of tensions of this kind. The impression rather is one of great optimism and self-confidence. Both locally and nationally there still seemed good reason to be hopeful about the future direction of the Cape's political affairs and the role they seemed likely to be able to play in them. And Kimberley itself was so much of a self-contained society, situated far away from the rural societies from which most of its mission-educated community originally came, that the kind of social divisions that arose between town and country in the eastern Cape simply did not emerge.

Plaatje was probably drawn into the life of this community from the moment he arrived in Kimberley. He was fortunate to have had the ideal introduction into these circles in the person of Isaiah Bud-M'belle, a man whose career and achievements were frequently held up as an example of what it was possible for Africans to achieve. The two young men first met in 1894, soon after Plaatje had begun work at the Post Office, when, so Martha Bokako recalls, Plaatje used to deliver letters or telegrams to the High Court building where Isaiah Bud-M'belle worked as a clerk and interpreter.[22] They quickly became friends, and agreed, shortly afterwards, to share lodgings in the Malay Camp, a racially mixed residential area close to the centre of Kimberley. This part of town was originally occupied by Malay artisans who had come up from Cape Town in the 1870s, but now whites, Africans, and Coloureds lived there as well, and those who could afford it were able to purchase freehold property as they pleased. Several Africans, it is interesting to note, had accumulated substantial property interests in the Malay Camp, Joseph Moss amongst them.[23]

Isaiah Bud-M'belle was then 25 years old, seven years older than Plaatje. Like the majority of mission-educated Africans living and working in Kimberley, he came from the eastern Cape, and was of Mfengu origin, having been born in Burghersdorp in 1870. He had received his education at the Healdtown Institute, second only to Lovedale in its reputation as a college for secondary education for African pupils. Then he taught for a few years at the Wesleyan mission school in Colesberg, studying privately in order to take the Cape Civil Service examinations, then open to black and white alike, passing these successfully at the end of 1893. He was the first African ever to achieve this distinction, and it attracted a considerable amount of comment in the press at the time. He had first come to Kimberley for a holiday over Christmas 1892, and had agreed to fill in for the interpreter in the local police station during his temporary absence. In March 1894, having passed the civil service examination and qualified in English, Dutch, 'Kaffir' (Xhosa) and Sesuto, he was appointed Interpreter in Native Languages to the Griqualand West High Court, the special and circuit courts, and clerk to the Resident Magistrate, and took up his duties in June 1894, earning a salary of £200 a year. It was not long before it was being said that he was one of the best interpreters, black or white, in the colony.[24]

Isaiah Bud-M'belle was also a man of great energy and humour (he often amused his friends by telling them of the occasion when he had been introduced at a meeting as the judge's 'interrupter'!),[25] a talented sportsman and musician, and he soon assumed a leading part in the social and political life of Kimberley's African community; after the two African clergymen nobody was held in higher esteem than he. For he personified so many of the values which this community admired, and he had demonstrated what could be achieved through natural ability and hard work. His profession, too, was highly regarded by mission-educated Africans throughout the colony. Court interpreting was seen as an area in which Africans could make a special contribution to the institutional life of the colony by virtue of their familiarity with their own languages, for few of the Europeans prepared to do work of this kind had a command of these languages – Xhosa, Sesotho and Setswana especially – which matched the command of both Dutch and English possessed by most African court interpreters. Court interpreting was considered to be a highly responsible occupation, moreover, since it was upon these interpreters that depended the proper functioning of the judicial system, and hence the means of providing Africans with access to one of the institutions they valued so highly: the courts of law. To the African court interpreters, in the eyes of their community, fell the task of making a practical reality of the Cape judiciary's claims to give equal treatment to every individual, black or white, in the courts of law. When this interpreting was done, as in Bud-M'belle's case, in the High Court, as opposed to the magistrate's courts, this burden of responsibility was all the greater. Nobody had any doubt that he was up to the task.

Probably it was through Isaiah Bud-M'belle that Plaatje first became involved in the activities of the network of clubs and societies around which the social life of Kimberley's African community revolved. Of these, none was more characteristic of their ideals and aspirations than an organisation known as the South Africans Improvement Society, formed in June 1895, and during the few years of its existence it came to play an important part in Plaatje's life. The society's name is revealing in itself: 'improvement', like 'progress', was regarded as a key concept in these circles, whilst the decision on the part of the twenty members who attended the society's inaugural meeting to call themselves 'South African', rather than 'Native' or 'African', seemed to emphasise an aspiration towards an identity in which nationality rather than race was the defining factor. The society's objects, in the mind at least of its first secretary, Simon Mokuena, interpreter in the Beaconsfield magistrate's court, whom Plaatje remembered as 'perhaps the greatest linguist and orator I ever knew', were equally explicit:

> firstly, to cultivate the use of the English language, which is foreign to Africans.
> secondly, to help each other by fair and reasonable criticisms in readings, recitations, English compositions, etc. etc.[26]

It would be difficult to exaggerate the importance that mission-educated Africans in the Cape Colony in the late nineteenth century attached to a command of the English language, and there was nothing unique in the South Africans Improvement Society's view of the matter. Just a few months later the same point was made in the columns of *Imvo Zabantsundu*, the English/Xhosa weekly:

> The key of knowledge is the English language. Without such a mastery of it as will give the scholar a taste for reading, the great English literature is a sealed book, and he remains one of the uneducated, living in the miserably small world of Boer ideals, or those of the untaught Natives. But besides, in this country where the English are the rulers, the merchants, and the influential men, he can never obtain a position in life of any importance without a command of English.[27]

The point could not have been made more clearly: without good English, employment, 'improvement' and 'progress' would all be impossible. The members of Kimberley's South Africans Improvement Society had every reason, therefore, to take their self-declared objectives very seriously indeed, and Plaatje probably owed a great deal to the society's members and its meetings (they met every second Tuesday at 7.30 p.m. in a room hired from a white organisation) in improving his command over a language in which he was to attain such fluency and power of expression. Certainly he seems to have been one of the regular attenders and participants in the early meetings of the society. He did not, however, contribute a paper or reading at the first meeting; this was taken up with a talk by Isaiah Bud-M'belle, entitled 'My ideas of a debating society', and was followed by the election of office-bearers. But at the society's second meeting, held on 16 July 1895, the secretary reported that Plaatje read out a chapter from *John Bull and Co.*, by Max O'Rell, a recently published book written by a Frenchman (whose real name was M. Blouet), best described as a humorous celebration of the glories of the British empire. Plaatje had not been in Kimberley when Max O'Rell visited the town in 1893, but many of the older members of the South Africans Improvement Society had, and it may well have been the chapter on Kimberley that Plaatje read out. His rendering was by no means perfect: 'his style of reading and pronunciation', so Simon Mokuena thought, 'was fairly criticised', whilst 'the mistakes corrected did not only benefit the reader, but also the other members'.[28]

Such was Plaatje's literary debut. If, on the evidence of the above, it can be considered no more than a modest success, the other members present would probably have been prepared to make some allowance for the fact that he had grown up on a German-run mission station, and not an English one as most of them had done; and that he had received no formal education beyond Standard III or IV, whereas most of them had had some secondary education at Lovedale, Healdtown, Morija or elsewhere. But at least Plaatje's text proved to be a happier choice than that chosen by the previous speaker that evening, Mr Walter Kawa. Kawa's admittedly able recitation from Milton's *Paradise Lost* was not, in Mokuena's opinion, 'highly appreciated by the majority of members, as it was too classical to be comprehended by the average native mind'. What Plaatje made of it was not recorded, but it was clear that Kawa had overstepped the limits of social and literary one-upmanship; for the secretary of the South Africans Improvement Society at least, Milton represented the point at which some doubts could be legitim-ately entertained as to the universality, not to say the comprehensibility, of English culture, something which they generally took for granted.

Plaatje's contribution to the society's meeting a month later was rather better received. Certainly it gave an indication of an early interest that had developed at Pniel, and which was to continue to fascinate him later in life, the essay he read on this occasion being entitled 'The History of the Bechuanas'. 'Being a Bechuana by birth,' it was recorded, with perhaps just a hint of condescension, 'he showed great mastery over his subject.'[29]

At subsequent meetings of the South Africans Improvement Society, debating and musical performances were added to its regular activities. Their proceedings are perhaps worth pursuing a little further because they brought out, very clearly, so many of the aspirations and qualities of the people with whom Plaatje was closely associated at this time; he was younger than they, and much of this must have rubbed off. This is how the motion 'Is insurance a proper provision for life?' proposed by Isaiah Bud-M'belle, opposed by Joseph Moss, was reported:

> It was at this meeting that one could notice that there is much native talent in Kimberley, hidden in the ground and unused. Mr Moss led his side in able manner, and tried to prove that insurance is a mere speculation, and is therefore a risky investment, whilst the other leader proved that it is a poor man's savings bank and a stimulant and encourager to industry. After some heated discussion for both sides by its members, the affirmative side carried the day. In consequence of this debate, many who did not fully understand insurance made proposals to the various companies.[30]

The South Africans Improvement Society could help to familiarise its members, in other words, with the pros and cons of different aspects of what they would have regarded as 'civilised life'; it was not simply the English language with which they were concerned but many of the customs that went with it. On occasions difficulties could arise when conventions of debating procedure ran counter to personal conviction. At a meeting of the society early in 1896 the subject debated was 'Is lobola as practised at the present time justifiable ?' – Walter Kawa for, Henry Msikinya (a teacher at the local Wesleyan mission school) against. Not surprisingly, Msikinya won the debate, but to Walter Kawa must surely go the credit for maintaining a stiff upper lip in what must have been a difficult situation for him: 'It is only fair to state that Mr W. B. Kawa, after having ably led his side, publicly stated that his own personal convictions were entirely against this relic of barbarism.[31]

Perhaps the most striking feature of all about the meetings of the society – and here they reflect the characteristics and qualities of its members at large – is the blend of humour and self-confidence they displayed. These were qualities which Plaatje himself was to show so clearly in the future, but it is evident that in this respect, as in others, he owed much to their example. Their humour arose largely out of the social situation in which they found themselves. They were frequently willing to make fun not only of the 'ways of European civilisation', but of their own aspirations towards them; this situation was, after all, potentially a very rich source of humour. In Kimberley there was no better exponent of this brand of humour than one of Plaatje's friends, Patrick (or 'Pat', as he was known – his full name was Tait Dugdale Patrick) Lenkoane, a long-established resident of Kimberley, originally from Basutoland, who had at one time been in personal service with Cecil Rhodes, then worked as a gardener, but now described himself as a boarding-house keeper.[32] Plaatje remembered Lenkoane as the 'humorous black Irishman', whose jokes and funny stories constituted a genre called a 'Lenkoaniac'.[33] Everybody found him funny. Nearly eighty years after Maud Zibi had first met Lenkoane, the mere mention of his name brought on a big smile: he was, she remembered, 'very, very humorous, oh very humorous – we would all laugh when he came in the room'.[34] And Lenkoane's contributions invariably enlivened the proceedings of the South Africans Improvement Society. On one occasion it was in response to an undoubtedly weighty paper, 'Civilisation and its advantages to African races', read by the society's vice-president, W. Cowen, a West African now living in Kimberley:

It was during the comment and criticism on this essay that the native Artemus Ward, Mr Patrick Lenkoane, said, in his inimitable and humorous manner, 'That the natives of this country have caught hold of civilisation by the tail, and not by the head, and it is therefore dangerous to them'.[35]

When Patrick Lenkoane was around, it would seem, the meetings of the Improvement Society could rarely have been a wholly serious business, and Plaatje used to exchange 'Lenkoaniacs' with friends of his several years after he had left Kimberley. That Lenkoane was found funny by his colleagues is a tribute not only to their willingness to make themselves and their situation the object of satire and humour, but a reflection of their underlying optimism and self-confidence. For Plaatje, Lenkoane, Bud-M'belle and the others, 'progress' and 'improvement' seemed assured, and the future held every promise. They could afford to laugh at themselves now and again. They were very different characteristics from those they were expected to display at their places of work: here any departure from the customary deference was likely to be considered 'cheeky' by their white colleagues or superiors.

◇

If Plaatje owed much to the meetings of the South Africans Improvement Society and to his association with its members for forming and refining many of his ideas on a variety of subjects during these years, there seems no doubt that he also spent a great deal of time in private study on his own. 'Constant reading after office hours', he recalled later, enabled him to develop his knowledge.[36] Most of Plaatje's friends had had some form of secondary education (up to Standards VI or VII), and this must in itself have acted as a powerful stimulus to his efforts at self-improvement. So too was living in the same house as a man like Isaiah Bud-M'belle, who had demonstrated by his own example what could be achieved by this, and it is highly probable that he gave Plaatje every encouragement in the direction of qualifying himself for a career as a court interpreter as well. For by the time Plaatje left Kimberley in 1898 he could read and write in English, Dutch, Sesotho, and Setswana, and speak 'Kaffir' (Xhosa) and German – an impressive range of linguistic accomplishment by any standards.[37] Cosmopolitan Kimberley was the ideal place for such qualifications to be acquired, and to this extent Plaatje was fortunate to have had around him friends and colleagues from so wide a variety of ethnic backgrounds, from whom he could learn and practise his linguistic skills. At the same time such impressive qualifications could scarcely have been achieved without a great deal of hard work and concentrated private study on his own; hard work, though, was something Plaatje was never afraid of.

Upon one aspect of this process of self-education Plaatje did elaborate later in life. It concerned the way in which he had first become really familiar with the plays of William Shakespeare, symbol for black and white alike of all that was of value and excellence in English culture. Plaatje and his friends saw no reason why Shakespeare should not be as accessible to them as he was to their white fellow citizens, who had been taught to believe that Shakespeare was England's greatest playwright. As *Imvo* had said, a failure to acquire such a knowledge of English as would give them access to 'the great English literature' meant 'living in the miserably small world of Boer ideals, or those of the untaught Natives'. Very probably there had been readings from Shakespeare and discussions at several meetings of the South Africans Improvement Society. For Plaatje, at any rate, there developed a particular fascination:

> I had but a vague idea of Shakespeare until about 1896 when, at the age of 18, I was attracted by the press remarks in the Kimberley paper, and went to see *Hamlet* in the Kimberley Theatre. The performance made me curious to know more about Shakespeare and his works. Intelligence in Africa is still carried from mouth to mouth by means of conversation after working hours, and, reading a number of Shakespeare's works, I always had a fresh story to tell.
>
> I first read *The Merchant of Venice*. The characters were so realistic that I was asked more than once to which of certain speculators, then operating around Kimberley, Shakespeare referred as Shylock. All this gave me an appetite for more Shakespeare, and I found that many of the current quotations used by educated natives to embellish their speeches, which I had always taken for English proverbs, were culled from Shakespeare's works.[38]

It was to become a lifelong interest. The performance of *Hamlet* to which Plaatje was referring was one of several Shakespearean performances in the Queen's Theatre, Kimberley, in October 1896, and again in December 1897, by the De Jong-Haviland Company, a touring theatrical company from England, responsible, so the *Diamond Fields Advertiser* reported, for the 'novel and somewhat daring experiment of importing Shakespeare into South Africa'.[39] Mr William Haviland, the leader of the company, told the *Advertiser*, on the occasion of his first visit to Kimberley, that he was impressed by the appeal that Shakespeare had had to European audiences in South Africa. Most of his audiences, indeed, would have been composed almost exclusively of whites but in Kimberley at least there was nothing to prevent Africans from going to the Queen's Theatre, although they were always in a very small minority and their presence there did sometimes give rise to abusive letters in the press. It can scarcely have crossed Mr Haviland's mind that the end product of the imagination he had stirred would be the first published translations of Shakespeare into any African language.

After Plaatje had been a couple of years in Kimberley it is apparent from reports in the *Diamond Fields Advertiser* (a paper which took a relatively enlightened attitude towards the doings of the local African and Coloured population) that he had become almost as active in the affairs of the African community as Bud-M'belle. Perhaps the most striking instance of this – and the growing degree of self-confidence and assurance that went with these activities – was the part he played in the 'social gathering of Africans', fully reported in the *Diamond Fields Advertiser*, which took place on 21 August 1896. The occasion was one of a number of activities which took place that week to provide a fitting send-off to Henry Msikinya and Chalmers Moss (the latter a son of Mr 'Interpreter' Moss), both of whom had secured places at Wilberforce University in the United States in order to continue their education. In view of the importance that was attached to education as a means of progress and advancement, both individual and collective, it was an achievement of which they, their parents, and the community as a whole could be very proud, and it was decided to give them an appropriate farewell. As was customary with important social events of this kind, an organising committee was formed. Plaatje was made its secretary, and was therefore responsible for the arrangements that needed to be made to ensure that the occasion was a success.

And a success it certainly proved to be. Isaiah Bud-M'belle considered that the farewell dinner 'was really an elegant affair in the fullest sense of the word', and found himself lost for words ('in this day of loose adjectives and thoughtless exaggerations') 'to convey that anything out of the ordinary has occurred'. He did feel, though, that since the function 'was carried on in a novel manner, judging it from an African standpoint', the after-dinner proceedings deserved to be reported in some detail, and from the account he wrote afterwards it is clear that Plaatje, still several months short of his twentieth birthday, was much involved. For after Bud-M'belle had taken the chair ('in obedience to the desire of the committee of arrangements'), and letters of apology were read from the Reverends Gwayi Tyamzashe and Jonathan Jabavu regretting their inability to be present 'owing to prior arrangements', it was Plaatje who commenced proceedings with a toast first to 'The Queen and Royal Family', and then another to 'The Acting Administrator'. It must have been quite a moment for him. There then followed a variety of further toasts – to 'Africa', 'Local Black Folk' and 'Our Guests ' – interspersed with musical interludes and songs, African and European, concluded, as was the custom on these occasions, with 'God Save the Queen'. It had been, Bud-M'belle wrote, 'a function long to be remembered', and he ended on a note of thanks to those who had been involved in the arrangements. 'The entire success of this gathering,' he said,

> is due to Messrs Sol T. Plaatje and E. J. Panyane who got up and prepared everything, to Mr T. J. Binase, who gave the use of his fine organ and accompanied most of the songs, and lastly, but not least, Mr Patrick Lenkoane, who superintended the waiting during the evening and seemed to be here, there and everywhere at the same time, arranging the details and looking after the introductions.[40]

Three days later Msikinya and Moss departed for Cape Town on the first stage of their journey to the USA, taking with them the good wishes and hopes of Kimberley's African community. It would be surprising if Plaatje, denied the opportunity of a secondary, let alone a university, education himself, had not harboured some feelings of envy at their good fortune. Chalmers Moss, sad to say, never returned to Kimberley. Two years later news was received from Wilberforce that he had died, 'preparing for his life work', so the Reverend David Msikinya wrote, 'the uplifting of his native land'.[41] Great things were expected from Africans with a university education.

◇

Just a month later, in September 1896, Plaatje was again amongst those who took the initiative in another episode in the affairs of Kimberley's African community, this time involving an approach to De Beers. The company's records tell the story. On 22 September, Mr William Pickering, Acting Secretary at the De Beers head office in Stockdale Street, received a letter from a very select group of African residents of Kimberley, Plaatje amongst them, who had recently formed an African branch of the YMCA. They wanted financial aid towards the construction of a meeting hall, and they had already constituted themselves into a building committee for this purpose. Their letter reminded the company of the number of Africans it had on its payroll ('Your worldwide known company has the honour of being the largest employers of native labour in this country'), and 'respectfully and humbly' put in a plea for 'financial aid towards defraying the necessary expenses connected with the building of and equipping the premises about to be erected in the Malay Camp'. 'We earnestly hope, nay believe, that our request will not be in vain,' ended the appeal, 'as this is the first and only request from the native inhabitants of the Fields to you.'[42]

At the end of the letter, carefully written out in Bud-M'belle's hand, were appended ten signatures, each with an indication in brackets afterwards of their tribal, or racial, identity: T. J. Binase ('Fingoe'), John Cowan ('West African'), R. R. M. N. Gella ('Kaffir'), T. D. P. Lenkoane ('Basuto'), I. Bud-M'belle ('Fingoe'), J. J. Makwalo ('Mpondo'), S. M. Mokuena ('Basuto'), J. M. Ngcezula ('Fingoe'), E. Panyane ('Basuto'), and lastly, Sol T. Plaatje ('Bechuana'). Their wide variety of ethnic backgrounds illustrates graphically the cosmopolitan nature of Kimberley's African community, and the signatories themselves probably hoped that this point would not be lost on De Beers; the more representative they seemed, the greater chance they were likely to have in obtaining a contribution from the company. Perhaps because he had proved himself so successful as secretary of the committee of arrangements for the farewell dinner for Moss and Msikinya the previous month, it was agreed that Plaatje should become 'Secretary *pro tem*' of the YMCA committee, and it was he who wrote a short covering letter to accompany the petition:

Kimberley
22 Sept 1896

Dear Sir,
I have the honour to inform you that I have been directed by the Building Committee of the Native YMCA to respectfully request you to submit the attached letter to the directors of your company.
I have the honour to be
Sir
Your humble servant
Sol T. Plaatje
Secretary pro tem.

Address: Sol T. Plaatje
Malay Camp
Kimberley

W. Pickering Esqre
Acting Secretary
de Beers Coy
Kimberley

It is the earliest letter of Plaatje's to have survived: although it contains one crossing-out – Plaatje had got half-way through the word 'enclosed' before deciding that 'attached' would be more appropriate – it is written in a clear, bold hand and signed with the abbreviated form of his Christian name by which he was now known to his friends.

Later the same day Plaatje evidently had some second thoughts about the letter he had just sent. How, he wondered, were De Beers to reply to his committee's request? He decided to write again:

Malay Camp
Kimberley
22 Sept 1896

Dear Sir,
    When handing that letter from the Native YMCA Building Committee, I accidentally omitted to enclose the attached stamps for communication.
    I therefore most humbly request that you must accept them for the said purpose.
        I am, dear Sir,
           Your obedient servant,
           Sol T. Plaatje

The Acting Hon. Sec.
de Beers Coy
Stockdale St
Kimberley

Plaatje's concern for De Beers' postal budget was considerate, but somewhat misplaced: the company's gross profit that year amounted to over two million pounds and it could well afford to meet the cost of the six one-penny stamps enclosed in his letter. And if he thought that his last-minute intervention was likely to tip the balance in his committee's favour when it came to the directors' decision on their application, or even to bring it to their attention in case it got lost amongst the numerous other appeals for money, he was in for a disappointment: the directors' minutes note simply that the request was 'refused', and Plaatje and his friends got – as he recalled several years later – not 'a brass farthing' towards their building fund.[43] But De Beers did at least return the stamps to him, and therein perhaps lay a little lesson in the realities of life in Kimberley in the 1890s: providing De Beers with stamps with which to reply to letters was simply not done.

◇

There was one further area of activity in which Plaatje made his mark in Kimberley during these years – music. Various forms of musical activity were popular amongst mission-educated Africans throughout the Cape Colony (it being prominent on every mission station's curriculum), but in Kimberley concerts and other musical events seem to have taken place on a more regular and extensive basis than anywhere else. As well as specially arranged concerts held in churches, or on occasion larger venues like the Kimberley Town Hall, some form of musical performance was usual at almost every gathering of Kimberley's African community: meetings of the South Africans Improvement Society, for example, frequently included some form of musical entertainment (Henry Msikinya was particularly active here before his departure to the United States), as did the annual prize-giving ceremonies for the African cricket and rugby clubs; and there had been a mixed and varied after-dinner musical programme at the farewell function for Moss and Msikinya.

But there were also specially arranged concerts, and in these Plaatje often participated. The first such occasion for which evidence has survived was a 'Grand Vocal Concert', held in the Kimberley Town Hall on 22 July 1896, and given by the Wesleyan Native Church Choir. On the face of it it is a little surprising to find Plaatje, a Lutheran, involved in such an event, but his vocal talents were obviously in sufficient demand for strictly interpreted denominational differences to be overlooked. His participation can be seen, moreover, as a gesture on the part of Kimberley's African community against their division on denominational lines, regarded by many of them as akin to the ethnic differences that on occasion also divided them. It is likely, too, that whilst Plaatje would have attended the Lutheran church on Sundays, the far smaller Lutheran congregation was not in a position to organise such elaborate affairs as this 'Grand Vocal Concert'; the majority of Plaatje's friends belonged to the Wesleyan Church, and it was only natural that they should seek his participation for events such as these.

The 'Grand Vocal Concert' was a great success. Plaatje himself was one of the baritone soloists, and sang a piece called 'Chiming Bells'. The *Diamond Fields Advertiser* described the evening's entertainment as 'excellent', commented upon the manner in which the 'very good audience expressed its appreciation of the proceedings by frequent applause', and commended Henry Msikinya upon the 'evident results of the careful training of this choir'.[44]

One of the most striking characteristics of almost every musical event of this kind was the variety of influences – European, African and American – reflected in their programmes: in almost every one of them, Negro spirituals ('Roll, Jordan, Roll'; 'Pickin' on de Harp') jostled for place with popular contemporary European songs ('The Village Blacksmith'; 'The Gendarmes') and Xhosa compositions ('The Kaffir Wedding Song'; 'The Bushman Chorus'; 'Intlaba Nkosi'). Plaatje and his Kimberley friends considered themselves to be the inheritors of all these traditions, and explored with enthusiasm the rich cultural possibilities thus provided. The black American element was particularly strong. During the late 1880s and early 1890s several travelling American coloured troupes visited southern Africa and left a great impression upon both black and white audiences, none more so than the famous Jubilee Singers, whom Plaatje recalled having seen on the two occasions they visited Kimberley while he was there.[45] They held a peculiar fascination for black South Africans, in part because they represented an area of cultural achievement admired as much by whites as blacks, in part because they exemplified the message of educational self-help expressed in the Jubilee Singers' connection with Fisk University in the United States, for which they raised funds. In Kimberley there was a further reason why the black American influence remained so pervasive: Will P. Thompson, one of the leading members of the troupe, and highly regarded as a 'first-rate pianist', fell out with Mr Orpheus Macadoo, leader of the Jubilee Singers, and decided to remain in Kimberley, together with several female members of the troupe, when they visited the town in July 1895. Over the next few years Thompson was much involved in the musical life of the town's African community, his 'invaluable services', so it was reported, always being in great demand.[46]

One of Thompson's enterprises in which both Plaatje and Bud-M'belle participated was a new musical society, called the Philharmonic Society, whose debut took place in the Woodley Street Hall on 19 March 1897. Its programme, so the notice in the *Diamond Fields Advertiser* announced, 'consists of modern part songs, selected solos, the famous Bushman Song, Kaffir ditties, with clicks, the Kaffir Wedding Song, and *Ulo Tixo 'Mkulu* ('Thou Great God') as sung by the first Christian converts among the AmaXhosa Kaffirs, whose name was Ntsikana Gaba'.[47] There were some familiar names among the artistes. The musical director was Isaiah Bud-M'belle, also a baritone soloist, who rendered on this occasion the highly popular 'Close the Shutters, Willie Boy's Dead'. Plaatje himself sang a piece called 'Trusting'. Amongst the bassos was the versatile T. J. Binase (also well known as a cricketer), and H. R. Ngcayiya, a future head of the Ethiopian Church of South Africa.

Plaatje was rather less involved in sport, perhaps the other most important social activity in the life of Kimberley's African community – especially rugby football and cricket.[48] The leading light here, as in so many other spheres of activity, was Isaiah Bud-M'belle, a talented cricketer and rugby player, who organised leagues in both games (with Coloured, Malay and Indian as well as African teams), and whose most enduring achievement was to persuade De Beers to present a silver trophy for the South African Colonial Rugby Football Board. Possibly it had been Bud-M'belle too, who encouraged Plaatje to become, in September 1896, joint secretary of the Eccentrics Cricket Club, one of the two African teams in Kimberley (the other was the Duke of Wellington Cricket Club, or 'Duke' as it was more familiarly known).[49] Fixtures between these two clubs were high up on the social calendar, but there is no evidence that Plaatje ever played the game himself; an upbringing on a German mission station had doubtless put paid to his chances of ever making the grade here, and – unlike Bud-M'belle – he certainly did not possess the physique of a rugby player. Plaatje stood no more than 5ft 2in tall, stocky in appearance but with thin, delicate fingers which looked more suited to a concert hall than a playing field.

<>

Plaatje's involvement in all these activities – from the time of his hesitant debut before the scrutiny of the South Africans Improvement Society to his rather more confident performance at the Philharmonic Society's concert in July 1897 – were an inseparable part of the business of developing and refining the values, the beliefs, the personal qualities that were to sustain him in the more troubled times that lay ahead. At the same time these years which Plaatje spent in Kimberley in the 1890s were of great importance in forming many of his more specifically political attitudes and beliefs. The views held by Plaatje and his friends were shaped by their experience and perceptions of both local and wider colonial political developments. Generally speaking they were strong supporters of the existing political institutions of the colony, and sought not so much to alter them as to secure and protect their own right to participate in them, to do all they could to ensure that they were not discriminated against on grounds of colour. In particular they attached very great importance to the Cape franchise, protested vigorously against the moves that were being made by some white politicians in the 1890s to reduce the numbers of Africans who qualified for it, and exploited to the full the political leverage that their vote gave them. They took a very keen interest, in short, in the political life of the Cape Colony.[50]

The most influential African political leader of his day by a long way was John Tengo Jabavu, brother of Kimberley's Reverend Jonathan Jabavu, and editor of the English/Xhosa weekly newspaper, *Imvo Zabantsundu*. Jabavu was of Mfengu origin and had started *Imvo*, the first African newspaper of its kind, in Kingwilliamstown in 1884, with the financial support of two sympathetic white businessmen, Richard Rose Innes and James Weir. Over the next ten years *Imvo* built up widespread influence among African readers in the colony, enjoying, as Plaatje later put it, 'a kind of monopoly in the field of native journalism'.[51] Each issue of *Imvo* carried a wide variety of news and comment in both English and Xhosa: news of local political and religious developments; information about the progress being made by blacks in the United States and West Africa, always a source of inspiration; detailed accounts written by local correspondents of the social and sporting life of mission-educated communities in the Cape and beyond; numerous articles and editorials advocating temperance, education, self-help, and improvement along the lines pursued by Kimberley's South Africans Improvement Society. Above all, *Imvo* urged Africans to become involved in the political life of the colony through the constitutional means that were open to them, arguing that Africans should be moderate and cautious in their political attitudes and demands, exploit the differences that existed between white politicians in the Cape in order to extract concessions, and place their trust in the various 'friends of the natives' who were sympathetic to their interests. 'Civilised' Africans, Jabavu also believed, had a special responsibility towards their less articulate brethren, and a duty to act as spokesmen for them and to pass on the beliefs and values which they themselves proclaimed: *Imvo*'s guiding metaphor, so its first issue announced, was the hope that it could serve as 'a rope to tow those stragglers to the desired shore'.[52]

Jabavu himself was an able and experienced politician and a skilful behind-the-scenes negotiator. Although his behaviour was shaped by the clear perception he had of the limits to the political influence he was able to exercise, he nevertheless represented a political force of considerable importance in the affairs of the Cape Colony in the last two decades of the nineteenth century, and he did more than any other individual to formulate the political aspirations of a generation of mission-educated Africans. On occasions his name was even bandied about in the Cape House of Assembly. Shortly after the elections of 1894 Cecil Rhodes, Prime Minister of the Cape Colony, was accused in parliament of 'having played Tengo Jabavu' to secure the African vote in Barkly West; it was the kind of comment, widely reported in the press, which served only to emphasise Jabavu's reputation, and the efficacy of the kind of participation in Cape political life that he advocated.[53] Had Plaatje felt the need for an African leader and spokesman with whom to identify, there is no doubt at all that Jabavu would have been the man.

Jabavu's influence was at its greatest around election time when white politicians tended to pay rather more attention than usual to their African constituents. But in Kimberley, as in the other large towns of the colony, there also developed a more continuous tradition of political activity, concerned with local as well as wider colonial issues and personalities. Here, too, great importance was attached to securing the support of 'friends of the natives'. In Kimberley, so Patrick Lenkoane was to recall, the local African community relied for assistance upon what he described as 'a saintly company', consisting of men like Advocate Richard Solomon, Advocate Henry Burton, Samuel Cronwright-Schreiner and Percy Ross Frames: 'a magnificent group', Lenkoane said, 'in whose hands the Natives of Kimberley entrusted their interests', and whose names were 'household words in native circles throughout the length and the breadth of the land'.[54]

In time, Plaatje came to be closely involved in the discussions and deputations that drew Kimberley's African community and these 'friends of the natives' together, and the sympathetic response which he and his colleagues received – and several notable successes in defence of their rights – was to have a lasting effect upon his political thinking. For two members of Patrick Lenkoane's 'saintly company' Plaatje developed a particularly warm admiration. The first was Samuel Cronwright-Schreiner, husband of the novelist Olive Schreiner, who established his credentials amongst Kimberley's African community with a famous and controversial address (later revealed to have been largely the work of his wife) on 'The Political Situation' which he delivered in the Kimberley Town Hall in August 1895.[55] In essence, his address was a fierce attack upon Cecil Rhodes and the capitalist interest he represented, and he accused him of using the Afrikaner Bond, with whom he was then in alliance, for his own purposes, and of maintaining it by 'retrogressive legislation on the Native question'. Although Cronwright-Schreiner did not actually come out with anything very concrete in the way of a more positive 'native policy', his sympathetic comments were nevertheless sufficient to earn the gratitude of, among others, the Reverend Jonathan Jabavu. 'Those of us who knew Mr Cronwright-Schreiner and therefore attended his lecture on the 20th inst.,' Jabavu wrote, 'knew a good word would be uttered against their oppression.' And he went on:

> Few as they are, we believe that men of Mr Cronwright-Schreiner's stamp will some day succeed in emancipating us from slavery caused by such oppressive measures as the Glen Grey Act, the East London and Haarhoff's Dear Bread and Cheap Brandy, and the Strop Bill. It only needs us to move and unite, and raise our voices against such unjust legislation, which aims at lowering the standard of the Queen's beneficent rule.[56]

Jabavu's sentiments would probably have been shared by the other members of the South Africans Improvement Society (of which organisation he was president) who also attended the meeting. Most of them, according to its secretary, were in fact present and the society had to postpone its regular Tuesday evening meeting as a result. It would be very surprising if Plaatje had not been amongst them.[57]

Cronwright-Schreiner's address on 'The Political Situation' had an interesting sequel. It was scarcely to be expected that either De Beers or the *Diamond Fields Advertiser*, which the company owned, would approve of much that Cronwright-Schreiner had to say, and after deliberating for a few days the newspaper came out with a long editorial to counter his arguments.[58] Then, a few months later, De Beers arranged for a further address to be delivered in Kimberley in defence of the Rhodes–Bond alliance. The man chosen for the job was not at that time very well known, but he was somebody with whom Plaatje was to cross paths on more than one occasion later on in life: his name was Jan Christian Smuts, future Prime Minister of the Union of South Africa. Smuts put forward what he described as 'the general principles of a broader political platform as a reconciled basis for both the white peoples of the Cape Colony', and at the time his speech was acknowledged as 'the ablest and clearest exposition yet given of the principles of the Bond–Rhodes alliance'.[59] Subsequent events were to make a mockery of almost every word he spoke.

The other figure amongst Kimberley's 'friends of the natives' for whom Plaatje came to develop both admiration and friendship was Advocate Henry Burton, an able, ambitious and somewhat arrogant young South African-born lawyer who had practised in Kimberley since 1892. Burton was a popular figure in the eyes of Kimberley's African community as a whole because he supported their claims for fair and just treatment: 'he acted on our behalf directly on the platform, in the press and at the bar', so Plaatje was to recall.[60] What Plaatje and his friends particularly appreciated was Burton's willingness to accept briefs from Africans to fight test cases in the courts. This was a strategy in which they placed great faith, and they won several important victories. Most notable of them all was the case of *R. v. Mankazana* which gave them legal protection against the rigours of the pass law legislation, designed to control the movement of African labour, which were embodied in Proclamation 14 of 1872. The point at issue was whether the police were legally entitled to ask any Africans they encountered in the street to show their passes to them, or whether it was necessary for the police to have reason to believe that they had committed an offence before doing so. The African community was prompted to challenge the way in which the police – supported by the local magistrates – had been behaving, because of the growing degree of harassment they were experiencing: according to *Imvo*, prosecutions under this proclamation were 'fast becoming unbearable', particularly for 'the more advanced Natives'.[61] Then, as Plaatje explained, 'This lawless persecution of guiltless black men became so intolerable that the Natives retained Advocate Henry Burton and sought the Higher Palace of Justice.'[62] Mr S. Mankazana, a respectable member of the community (he was chairman of the Eccentrics Cricket Club), was the individual in whose name the case was to be fought.

They won their case. It was heard in the Griqualand West High Court in Kimberley in June 1898, Judge Percival Lawrence ruling that 'it was not enough for a native to have no pass' for an arrest to be made by the police. Several weeks later his ruling was upheld by Judge William Solomon. As a result, respectable, law-abiding Africans like Mankazana, Plaatje and their colleagues no longer had to worry about harassment from the police; whilst the municipality, which had come to rely upon the flow of prison labour that resulted from arrests under the pass law proclamation to carry out the work of night-soil removal, had to employ contractors to compensate for its sudden disappearance.[63]

Plaatje regarded the outcome of the case as a famous victory, and judging from the number of occasions he referred to it later in life it made a deep impression upon him; more than any other single case it seemed to emphasise the part that the courts could play in the protection of African rights, and engaging sympathetic lawyers like Henry Burton was a strategy he was to advocate time and time again. In contrast to the generally 'anti-native' drift of legislation emanating from the Cape parliament during the 1890s (such as the bills which the Reverend Jonathan Jabavu had specified in his expression of thanks to Samuel Cronwright-Schreiner), in the law courts at least there still seemed every prospect of securing justice and redress of grievance. The case illustrated clearly the way in which an older, established tradition of Cape liberalism could on occasion be utilised to enable Africans of this class and background to resist being treated simply as units of labour, subject to what the municipal authorities considered to be the appropriate means of control. Such controls were already in effective operation in the gold-mining areas of the Transvaal, and in the Cape the pressures in this direction were growing all the time. But for the time being at least, Kimberley's African community had demonstrated that these pressures could be successfully resisted. For Plaatje, *R. v. Mankazana* provided a lesson in political and legal strategy which he did not forget.

◇

When the case of *R. v. Mankazana* was heard in the Griqualand West High court Plaatje was nearly 22 years old and had been living in Kimberley for over four years. By now it would have been perfectly clear to the friends and relatives he had left at Pniel that their fears that he would succumb to the 'temptations of city life' had not been realised. Part of the reason for this, so Plaatje reminisced later, was that he always remained very conscious of the hopes they had placed in him. When he was asked, years later, how he, 'a country boy', had managed to keep along the straight and narrow after leaving home, he replied that his 'greatest standby' was 'consideration for the feelings, first of the missionary and his wife, and next his mother and two aunts'. He knew, he added, 'how much it would grieve them if ever he went wrong; and as they thought the world of him, he dreaded to distress them'.[64]

Plaatje's family at Pniel in any case had every opportunity of keeping a watchful eye on his progress, since he used to spend many of his weekends there. Martha Bokako was only four years old when Plaatje left Pniel to go and work in Kimberley, but she had a clear recollection of his visits back home during the few years after that. On some occasions, she remembered, her father Simon travelled the 17 miles into Kimberley on horseback to go and fetch him.[65] Plaatje probably also visited his father at Ditlarapeng – up until his death in September 1896. Earlier that year old Johannes Plaatje had lost all but four of the 150 head of cattle he then possessed, one of the many sufferers in the great rinderpest epidemic which swept across the whole of southern Africa with such tragic consequences, for African societies especially.[66] The loss was perhaps too much for him to bear: he died, so the family prayer book records sadly, far away from his children, and he had to be buried, according to Modiri Molema, before either Solomon or Simon could make the long journey northwards.[67] Later, though, Plaatje apparently did travel to Mafeking in order to sort out his father's affairs, and sold off his sheep and other livestock, and the few head of cattle that had survived the rinderpest.[68]

By then – certainly by the following year, 1897 – another person had come into Plaatje's life: Elizabeth Lilith M'belle, Isaiah Bud-M'belle's younger sister. Elizabeth was several months younger than Plaatje; she had been educated at the Lesseyton Girls' School, receiving what Plaatje later described as 'a much better schooling than he';[69] and she was at that time teaching at a mission school in Steynsburg, a small town some 200 miles south-east of Kimberley, close to her parents' home in Burghersdorp.[70] Plaatje first met Elizabeth M'belle on one of the occasions she came up to Kimberley to visit her brother.[71] As their relationship developed both must have been conscious of the difficulties likely to be encountered with their respective families: he, after all, was a Morolong, she an Mfengu, and it was unlikely that either set of parents would approve of such a liaison. Almost certainly it was this that Plaatje had in mind when, a couple of years later, he wrote of his memory of the 'long and awful nights in 1897 when my path to the union . . . was so rocky'.[72] The problem, as Plaatje was to explain, long after matters had been satisfactorily resolved, was this:

> My people resented the idea of my marrying a girl who spoke a language which, like the Hottentot language, had clicks in it; while her people likewise abominated the idea of giving their daughter in marriage to a fellow who spoke a language so imperfect as to be without any clicks.[73]

The linguistic problem was of course only part of it. Inter-tribal marriages may have been the accepted thing in the cosmopolitan African community in Kimberley, but they were certainly not in either Pniel or Burghersdorp, where Elizabeth's mother and relatives lived. They were strongly opposed to the proposed match, so Modiri Molema relates, and they insisted on burning all the letters Plaatje wrote to her.[74] Predictably, this did not prove to be an effective deterrent, and the couple were duly married by civil licence, parental disapproval notwithstanding, in Kimberley on 25 January 1898, the Reverend Davidson Msikinya (Congregational minister in Kimberley since Tyamzashe's death late in 1896) officiating at the ceremony which followed.[75] This was conducted in a style and manner thought appropriate by Kimberley's African community to the social standing of the young couple (for in the view of this community it was a manifestly suitable match), and it was – like so many of their social functions – a formal and ostentatious affair. Not all of the attention attracted by it was favourable. The following passage appeared in the *Diamond Fields Advertiser* the next day:

> Last evening a couple of 'swagger' looking natives resplendent in bell toppers, morning coats, white waistcoats, light pants, and patent leathers, with a

number of females in holiday attire, were the centre of an admiring group in the Kimberley Railway Station. The rumour had gone forth that they were a couple of Lobengula's sons and certain of his wives, and the passengers and platform loungers were deeply interested in watching Master Lobengula making preparations for Mrs Loben's comfort for the journey, while when one of the princes of the blood royal deigned to take a long drink of water from an old lime juice bottle brought by one of the porters, excitement 'ran high'. Shortly before the train left, the police sergeant on duty at the station 'spotted' one of the 'princes' as an interpreter at a court down colony, while his companion was discovered to be a telegraph messenger. It transpired that the former had come up to the Diamond Fields for the purpose of getting married, and that the buxom dusky lady who had been put down as one of the sharers of the late Matabili monarch's joys and sorrows was in reality a daughter of the people and the bride of the 'got up regardless' interpreter.[76]

Notwithstanding the confusion on the part of the *Advertiser* as to exactly who it was that was getting married, one imagines that both Plaatje and his bride would have been vastly amused by the rumour that the bridegroom was one of Lobengula's sons. Less pleasing, though, was the tone of the report – a sharp reminder of white resentment at black social aspirations, and of the gulf that existed between the exuberant world of their own creation and the attitudes held by the majority of their white fellow countrymen: to them, the obviously well-educated, self-confident group of Africans attending Plaatje's wedding constituted an affront to their sensibilities and – as some at least would have perceived it – in the long run a threat to their livelihoods.

But for Kimberley's African community the marriage of Sol Plaatje and Elizabeth M'belle in a way gave romantic expression to many of their collective hopes and aspirations. They had always stressed the importance of achieving unity amongst themselves, of overcoming the tribal differences and resentments that sometimes stood between them: Plaatje and Elizabeth M'belle, Morolong and Mfengu, were achieving this in a particularly personal way. Family objections were in any case soon overcome. Presented with a *fait accompli*, both sets of 'erstwhile objecting relatives', as Plaatje called them, soon came to accept what had happened – a happy outcome to a romantic affair, and the beginning of what proved to be a very happy marriage.[77]

$$\diamond$$

Plaatje's relationship with Elizabeth M'belle unfolded against a troubled background in the political affairs of the Cape Colony. The catalyst in these new tensions had been the abortive Jameson Raid in late December 1895 and early January 1896. In a conspiracy involving Cecil Rhodes, Prime Minister of the Cape Colony, and a number of other mining capitalists, Dr Jameson had agreed to lead an armed force into the Transvaal, their objective being to take control of Johannesburg, spark off a rebellion amongst the so-called 'uitlanders' ('foreigners'), and replace Kruger's regime with a government more sympathetic to the interests of certain of the mining companies. Despite the elaborate preparations that had been made, the raid was a fiasco: the planned rising of 'uitlanders' failed to materialise, and Dr Jameson and his men were forced to surrender ignominiously to a Boer force at Doornkop, twenty miles from Johannesburg. The abortive raid nevertheless had far-reaching consequences. In terms of the wider southern African political situation, its effect was to generate a new level of hostility on the part of the South African Republic (the Transvaal) towards the British imperial government; with every justification, President Kruger suspected Joseph Chamberlain, the British Colonial Secretary, of at least tacit support for the conspiracy. Political opinion polarised radically in the Cape Colony as well. The Rhodes–Bond alliance, so eloquently explained by Jan Smuts several weeks earlier, was destroyed almost overnight, and Rhodes himself was forced to resign as Prime Minister of the colony. A compromise coalition government was formed under the premiership of Sir Gordon Sprigg, but opinion now hardened on either side of the white racial divide. A pro-British Progressive Party was started, linked to the South African League, an organisation with branches throughout southern Africa and dedicated to upholding British supremacy in the subcontinent. On the other side, the Afrikaner Bond was now solidly anti-Rhodes and pro-Kruger and the Transvaal. The political life of the Cape Colony was transformed.

Against this background the campaign for election to the Cape House of Assembly in the middle of 1898 proved to be a bitterly fought affair. Rhodes himself re-entered the political fray as the leader, in all but name, of the Progressive Party, and much of the electioneering revolved around the question of the future shape of southern Africa as a whole, rather than the more parochial concerns that had hitherto dominated political life in the Cape. The election campaign was also notable for the greatly increased competition amongst prospective candidates for the African vote. For the first time, two opposing political parties now competed openly for African support, and the more perceptive African voters drew their own lessons from observing the way in which both Sir Gordon Sprigg, the outgoing Prime Minister, and W. P. Schreiner, his successor, campaigned personally for African votes.[78] Such developments were welcomed by John Tengo Jabavu, still the editor of *Imvo*. He was, though, no longer in so strong a position as before to take advantage of this new situation. A new newspaper, *Izwi la Bantu* ('The Voice of the People'), had been started up with Progressive support late in 1897 with the forthcoming elections very much in mind, and it succeeded in making considerable inroads into *Imvo*'s political constituency, making great capital out of the inconsistencies that Jabavu's continued attachment to individual 'friends of the natives' produced. For the essential fact about political life in the Cape was that it now had a two-party system. Jabavu's friends and supporters found themselves divided between both parties, or were 'Independents', and it made it very difficult for him to put forward a consistent political line. *Izwi*, by contrast, was fervently pro-British and pro-Progressive.

The general election of 1898 was the first one at which Plaatje – over 21 years old, literate, and with a salary of over £50 a year – was qualified to vote. In Kimberley, as elsewhere, the candidates made some gestures towards their African and Coloured constituents, but there was never any doubt that all four Progressive candidates would be returned with majorities that were anything less than overwhelming; the only opposition they encountered came from two

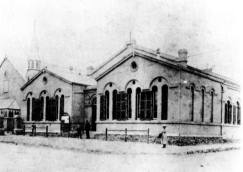

14 *The Kimberley Town Hall and Library in the 1890s, venue of S. C. Cronwright-Schreiner's famous political address in August 1895, also the Wesleyan Native Church Choir's 'Grand Vocal Concert' (in which Plaatje participated) in July 1896.*

12 *Rev. Gwayi Tyamzashe, Congregational clergyman and a leading resident of Malay Camp, Kimberley. Plaatje remembered him as 'the first ordained black minister I ever saw'.*

13 *A group of friends: Sol Plaatje (standing, centre) and Isaiah Bud-M'belle (standing, right), with two unidentified colleagues. The photograph was probably taken in the late 1890s.*

16 Elizabeth M'belle. This portrait was probably taken several years after she and Plaatje were married by special licence in Kimberley in January 1898.

15 Notice announcing the debut of the Philharmonic Society in the Woodley St Hall, Kimberley, 19 March 1897. Plaatje was the soloist for the third item on the programme, 'Trusting'.

17 John Tengo Jabavu, editor of Imvo Zabantsundu ('African Opinion'), in 1896—the leading African politician of his day.

'Friends of the natives'. **18** (left) Samuel Cronwright-Schreiner, husband of the novelist, Olive Schreiner. He impressed the president of the South Africans Improvement Society with his political address in Kimberley in August 1895, and later played a part in Plaatje's decision to become a journalist. **19** (right) Advocate Henry Burton: 'he acted on our behalf directly on the platform, in the press, and at the bar', so Plaatje recalled.

20 The Barolong royal homestead, Mafikeng, as it was in 1890 during the reign of Chief Montshiwa.

21 Wessels Montshiwa, son and heir of Montshiwa, and chief of the Tshidi Barolong, 1896–1903. 'Whoever can interpret for Wessels correctly ought to consider himself a professor', Plaatje wrote of one incident during the siege.

23 Modiri Molema, elder son of Silas Molema, later a well known medical doctor and author. He is seen here at a time when he and Plaatje knew one another in Mafeking in the 1900s.

22 Silas Molema, Barolong headman and respected citizen of Mafeking. As first editor, proprietor and financier of Koranta ea Becoana ('The Bechuanas' Gazette') he made possible Plaatje's career as a journalist.

24 Charles Bell, magistrate and civil commissioner in Mafeking, whose staff Plaatje joined in 1898. Plaatje wrote that he was 'fortunate to have served my apprenticeship [as a court interpreter] under such a man'.

25 Portrait of Sol Plaatje (sitting, centre), with a group of young friends. The figure standing to Plaatje's right is Isaiah Makgothi, from Thaba Nchu, who was to join the staff of Koranta ea Becoana and standing to his left his brother, James. Sitting, on Plaatje's right is Ebie Schieman, a nephew.

independent candidates, and the Afrikander Bond did not bother to put up any candidates of its own.[79] Rather more interest both locally and nationally was generated by the contest for the Barkly West constituency, represented in the House of Assembly for the past seventeen years by Cecil Rhodes. Plaatje had a particular interest in the outcome of this contest not only because the constituency included the Pniel mission station, but also because the main candidate standing against Cecil Rhodes, for the Afrikaner Bond, was Advocate Henry Burton, who only several weeks previously had fought and won the pass law case in the High Court in Kimberley. Had the Bond been represented by some other candidate, Plaatje may well have felt inclined to support Cecil Rhodes and the 'British' party – certainly this was where his friend Patrick Lenkoane, a leading figure in the newly formed local Native Progressive Association, placed his loyalties.[80] But in the circumstances Plaatje's admiration for Henry Burton was uppermost in his mind, and he was the candidate he thought it right to support. This was not a view shared by the Reverend Ernst Westphal, the missionary at Pniel, who was a keen supporter of Cecil Rhodes. 'He sent me,' Plaatje recalled a couple of years later,

> a hot letter going for me for having leanings towards the Transvaal and Krugerism, simply because I sympathised with Adv. Burton during the last election; and he could not be convinced by my reasons that the young QC earned my sympathies not because he was supported by the Afrikaner Bond, but simply because he was a negrophilist and did a lot for us while I was in Kimberley.[81]

Whatever influence Westphal once had over his former pupil, Plaatje was evidently well able by now to make up his own mind on the political issues and personalities of the day.

The Barkly West election also provided a prime example of the new importance that the emergence of a two-party system had given to the African vote. Barkly West had one of the highest proportions of African voters in the colony, and the candidates went to great lengths to solicit African support. Cecil Rhodes personally addressed a number of African and Coloured meetings and deputations, and it was at one of these that he came out with his famous formula of 'equal rights for all civilised men'.[82] On the other side, Samuel Cronwright-Schreiner, seeking to secure the African vote for Henry Burton and his running-mate, resorted to rather cruder election propaganda in a bid to discredit Rhodes on the basis of his Chartered Company's treatment of Africans in Rhodesia.[83] Although in the end Rhodes and his Progressive running-mate were returned with comfortable majorities, Barkly West was one of the most fiercely contested seats in the colony, and it received intensive coverage in the press. Tengo Jabavu may now have found himself outflanked politically, but his longstanding advocacy of African participation in the Cape parliamentary system was never more strongly vindicated. For Plaatje and his friends in Kimberley the elections of 1898 would have reinforced their belief in the importance of participating in the political life of the Cape Colony in the same way that the case of *R. v.Mankazana* had reaffirmed their faith in the Cape's legal system: they had every interest, in other words, in the survival of the existing order, and they could look forward with confidence to being able to play a gradually more influential part in the affairs of the colony.

◇

At the same time as the voters of the Cape Colony, black and white, contemplated the future complexion of their government and House of Assembly, Plaatje was preoccupied with a consideration of a more personal kind: his career. He had by now spent over four years delivering letters and telegrams for the Kimberley Post Office. He had made the most of his opportunities during this period, but prospects for advancement were nil. It was clear that Alfred Moletsane, the only African assistant postmaster, was going to get no further, and it seemed unlikely that any African would again be considered for such a position; the chill wind of racial discrimination was already threatening the careers of African employees in government service. But financially, too, things cannot have been too easy for Plaatje, especially now that he had a wife to support. As even the Postmaster-General was prepared to admit in his report for the previous year, 1897, 'rinderpest, drought and other causes [had] enhanced the cost of living to such an extent that those who are married on small salaries find much difficulty in living in comfort'.[84] Because of the high cost of living in the Kimberley district, all Post Office employees here were granted an increase in the special cost-of-living allowance they had always enjoyed, but those at the bottom of the salary scale would have been little better off.

In all probability Plaatje had been on the look-out for a job as a court interpreter for some time. Quite apart from the improved financial prospects that such a position held out – in the long run if not immediately – he had a keen interest in the law ('as a boy I was tremendously fascinated by the work of the Supreme Court', he once said),[85] and he had been busy qualifying himself for such a position by improving his command of both African and European languages; living in the same house as Isaiah Bud-M'belle must have provided, moreover, the ideal unofficial apprenticeship. So when he heard, probably early in August 1898, that a clerk and interpreter was required at the Mafeking magistrate's court he decided to apply. Such opportunities did not arise frequently, and this particular position had only fallen vacant because of the departure of the previous incumbent, Jan Moloke, following the belated discovery that he had once served a jail sentence for illicit diamond buying.[86] Plaatje's letter of application, preserved in the archives of the Cape Colony's Law Department, reads as follows:

Kimberley
5th August 1898

Application for a vacant situation
in the RM Office, Mafeking

Sir,
    I beg to apply for a situation in the RM court as an interpreter.

54

I have been a teacher at the Pniel Mission Station for three years. I have also been a messenger in this office for nearly five years.

My knowledge and ability to translate and retranslate into the English, Dutch, German, Kaffir, Sesuto and Sechuana languages qualifies me for the position I am applying for.

I can only fill a position in Mafeking by being transferred from here as a resignation would forfeit all of my five years pension. Should you feel pleased to have me transferred from here to your office, I shall do my utmost best [*sic*] to discharge my duties satisfactorily.

> I beg to be,
> Sir,
> Your obedient servant,
> Sol T. Plaatje

RM
Mafeking   Address: Solomon T. Plaatje
                     P.O. Kimberley[87]

Charles Bell, the magistrate and civil commissioner at Mafeking, to whom Plaatje's letter was addressed, may well have known, or known of, the Plaatje family when he held the same position at Barkly West several years earlier. In reply, he first of all requested testimonials, and then, on 12 September, wrote to ask Plaatje to come to Mafeking for a couple of days to see if he measured up to the job. Plaatje found, though, that he could not very easily take all this time off work. He explained the difficulty in an apologetic, slightly anxious, letter that preceded his visit:

> Post Office, Kimberley
> Griqualand West
> September 13th 1898

Sir,
    I have received your message of yesterday's date, and am extremely sorry to inform that pressure in our Department does not permit me to be absent for more than three days, i.e. Wednesday, Thursday, and Friday; which means I will arrive at Mafeking on Thursday morning and leave again on Thursday night (day after tomorrow).
    Hoping that the brevity of my visit will not inconvenience you.

> I am, Sir,
> Your obedient servant,
> Sol T. Plaatje[88]

Bell could hardly object to such an arrangement; indeed Plaatje's apparent commitment to his current duties may well have created a favourable impression. If so, this was amply confirmed in the interview which followed. After testing Plaatje's competence in the range of languages in which he claimed to be qualified, Bell declared him to be 'fairly well educated', 'well suited for the appointment for which he applies', and recommended him for the position.[89]

Plaatje also had the advantage of a good reference from the Postmaster-General in Kimberley, who thought him 'suitable for the position of Interpreter', and added that 'he knows the native languages and is a good English scholar'.[90] Perhaps even more valuable, in Bell's mind at least, was the verbal recommendation Plaatje had obtained from the influential local figure of Silas Molema, the Barolong headman, a younger brother of Joshua Molema. In a place like Mafeking such things counted for a great deal.[91]

Plaatje, in short, had all the right qualifications for the position of interpreter in the magistrate's court in Mafeking. An offer from the Law Department duly followed, and he accepted. The transfer problem was resolved satisfactorily without harm to his pension, but in one respect there was a disappointment: despite the more responsible duties he was to be undertaking, the salary offered was no more than he had been getting at the Post Office in Kimberley, that is to say, £96 per annum. Since the cost of living in Mafeking was known to be higher even than in Kimberley, Plaatje had good reason to feel that he was being somewhat hardly done by, and he must have known that Isaiah Bud-M'belle, now his brother-in-law, was earning more than twice as much. On the other hand, it promised to be a much more interesting job, and prospects for higher earnings in the future were considerably better than they had been in the Post Office.

Plaatje intended to move to Mafeking and assume his new duties at the beginning of October 1898. In the event he did not do so until the end of the month because of illness – the first recorded instance of ill-health which was to be, in one form or another, a fairly regular occurrence over the next four years, and which was to affect him throughout his adult life. Neither Plaatje's own description of his ailment on this occasion ('a serious indisposition'), nor that entered on his doctor's certificate ('fever') give much clue as to its nature.[92] Possibly it was a bout of malaria, something which he was to suffer from a couple of years later, and it may be that this was the reason for the otherwise unexplained 61 days' leave of absence which his civil service record shows him to have taken in the middle of 1897.[93]

A rather more worrying possibility was that he had some form of epilepsy: for about a year later a sharp-eyed clerk in the Cape Law Department noticed – as a batch of papers passed through from the Civil Service Commission – that Plaatje was certified by Dr Hayes, one of the doctors in Mafeking, 'to be suffering from epilepsy'.[94] Whether or not his diagnosis was correct it is impossible to tell, and he may simply have got it wrong; there is no other evidence that Plaatje suffered from this disability either at this time or later in life, and he never subsequently applied for sick leave on these grounds. Indeed, had he done so he would have found himself in some difficulties, for in applying for his new job in Mafeking he had attached his signature to the statement that he did not suffer from 'fits or any other bodily infirmity'.[95]

Whatever the nature of the ailment Plaatje suffered from in early October 1898 it was sufficiently serious to prevent him from beginning his new job when he had hoped. By way of compensation, though, it did enable him to spend his 22nd birthday, 9 October 1898, at home with his wife, Elizabeth. She was now expecting a baby in a month or so, and they had evidently decided that it would be more sensible for her to spend the last weeks of her confinement at Pniel with

Plaatje's family, and to join him in Mafeking only after the baby was born. That they were both able and willing to contemplate such an arrangement suggests that the objections of Plaatje's family to his choice of bride were already a thing of the past. Personal contact had presumably done much to break down the barriers of prejudice that had once coloured their view of Plaatje's bride-to-be.

3

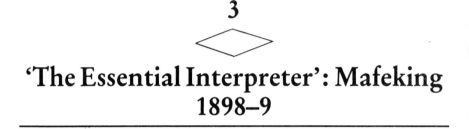

'The Essential Interpreter': Mafeking
1898–9

Plaatje's new job took him into very different surroundings. The town of
Mafeking, his home for the next twelve years, was very much smaller than
Kimberley – it had a population of some 5,000 blacks and 1,500 whites – but it
was nevertheless a place of considerable importance, serving as a railway
junction on the line northwards to Rhodesia, as the administrative capital of the
Bechuanaland Protectorate, and as the market centre for the surrounding
districts of both the Transvaal and the Cape Colony. There were, to be more
precise, two Mafekings: the European township, laid out in 1885 when
Bechuanaland was annexed to the British empire, and the older African
settlement of Mafikeng, founded and occupied by the Tshidi Barolong, and
separated by the railway line from the European township which now shared its
name. Taken together, the two Mafekings constituted the largest concentration
of population for many miles around; within the Cape Colony one had to go as
far south as Vryburg, some 100 miles down the railway line, to find a place which
even approached it in size.

Most European visitors to Mafeking were struck by its sense of isolation.
Colonel Robert Baden-Powell, who had passed through Mafeking several times
en route to Rhodesia during the mid-1890s, considered Mafeking to 'be a very
ordinary looking place. . . . Just a small tin-roofed town plumped down upon
the open veldt',[1] but others were more flattering. Another English visitor, Lady
Sarah Godley, who first saw Mafeking in 1899, wrote: 'it astonished one how at
the end of all these miles, through desolate bush and desert one finds this
apparently quite large place, and civilisation'.[2]

Of the two views Lady Godley's would undoubtedly have been the more
popular with the town's inhabitants: to them there was much to justify this
notion that Mafeking represented an oasis of 'civilisation' along the Cape's
barren northern border, for the town lay on the fringes of the Kalahari desert,
and most of the year it was extremely hot and dusty. Physically speaking, the
township of Mafeking was neatly laid out around two large squares, and it owed
its existence not to the proximity of some precious mineral or metal but to the
fact that it lay astride the most convenient route to the north. Mafeking still
possessed some of the characteristics of the frontier town it once was, but that

frontier, like the railway line which was extended to Bulawayo in Rhodesia in 1897, had now moved on. Mafeking was no longer the end of the line, and even the border of the Bechuanaland Protectorate, of which it remained the administrative capital, now lay – thanks to the annexation of British Bechuana-land to the Cape in 1895 – some 15 miles away.

By 1898, it would be fair to say that the European township of Mafeking had assumed the character of a respectable, settled colonial community. It had been proclaimed a municipality two years previously, and was now equipped with the institutions, societies, sports and social clubs and other amenities thought appropriate to any self-respecting small-town community in the British empire in the late Victorian era. There were four churches, a convent, a hospital, a spacious government square, some tennis courts, a branch of the Standard Bank, a Masonic Hall, a library, a race course, and it was very shortly to acquire its own regular weekly newspaper, the *Mafeking Mail and Protectorate Guardian*, established in May 1899. The biggest employer of labour in town remained the railway (its employees and installations were all housed in what was known as the 'railway reserve'), followed by the numerous trading stores and contractors, most notable of whom was the wealthy firm of Julius Weil and Co., one of whose partners had represented Mafeking in the Cape parliament since representatives were first elected in 1896 (though this did not prevent rumours circulating that the Weil fortune was based on diamond smuggling).

Despite its new-found pretensions the town of Mafeking was hardly comparable in scale or maturity to Kimberley. One anonymous newspaper correspondent, writing for the *Diamond Fields Advertiser* in 1897, remarked that the small wooden market house in the centre of the market square might quite easily be mistaken for the 'municipal broom cupboard', and he was struck, too, by the fact that the Resident Commissioner of the Bechuanaland Protectorate administered the whole of his territory (an area of 220,000 square miles) from offices in a building which was originally built as the Anglican rectory. Perhaps even more pertinent was his observation about the main (Cape) government building where Plaatje was to be working. This, thought the *Advertiser*'s correspondent, 'was not of much architectural pretension', and 'quite inadequate for the purpose required. In one gable end justice is dispensed, in the other – postage stamps.'[3] At least Plaatje would be familiar with what went on in that end of the building.

Just outside the European township of Mafeking, south of the Molopo river, lived two other communities – the Cape Coloureds, who made a living mostly as craftsmen and artisans, or were employed by the railways and the police; and a slightly larger community of several hundred Mfengu, who resided in the so-called 'Fingo location'. Many of them had first settled in Mafeking in 1890, having arrived in the town as members of Cecil Rhodes's famous pioneer column, on its way northwards to occupy Mashonaland for the British South Africa Company. Once they had reached Mafeking, however, the Mfengu contingent refused to go any further, decided to make their home there, and were subsequently joined by their families. Since that time they had grown into a thriving community. Like their compatriots in Kimberley, they were very much a church-going community, they sent their children to the local mission schools, and they tended to regard themselves as both 'civilised' and 'progressive', and considerably superior to the mass of the Barolong who lived nearby. It was among this Mfengu community in Mafeking that Plaatje would find the closest approximation to the kind of social life he had known in Kimberley, although on a much smaller scale.

To the west of the 'Fingo location' lay the far larger Barolong settlement, the *stadt* as it was known. In appearance it was very different from both the European township and the 'Fingo location'. Apart from the church erected by Wesleyan missionaries, most of its buildings – scattered amongst the large boulders from which Mafeking took its name – were round huts with red walls and thatched, peaked roofs, many of them with their own courtyard, and surrounded by high walls. Some of the wealthier members of the Barolong people, however, had built European-style houses for themselves, a visible mark of their superior status within their society. Most of the tribesmen earned an increasingly precarious living from cultivating small plots of land, or tending herds or livestock on the communally held land which the Barolong occupied around Mafeking. But in 1898 the Barolong of Mafeking were in a parlous state. Two years previously they had lost virtually all their cattle (£60,000 worth, the local Wesleyan missionary thought) in the rinderpest epidemic, and since then they had suffered further from the ravages of locust plagues and drought.[4] Now, having eaten or sold off their remaining stocks of sheep and goats to raise money, there was severe famine. Some people, indeed, were reported to be dying of starvation. Charles Bell, the magistrate and civil commissioner, had given up all hope of collecting any taxes that year.[5]

Many of the younger Barolong men had been forced by these desperate conditions to go and work on the gold mines of the Witwatersrand in order to raise some money to provide for themselves and their families. Hitherto, the Barolong of the Mafeking district had been able to support themselves without having to send out very many of their men into such uncongenial and dangerous forms of employment. But early in 1898 labour recruiting agents were seen 'loofing about on foot collecting boys for the mines',[6] the first occasion they considered it worth their while to come to the district. Nothing demonstrated more vividly the manner in which the economic self-sufficiency of the Barolong people had been, within a very short space of time, undermined by rinderpest and the disasters that followed it. Things had not improved when Plaatje came to live there at the end of the year. He had known Mafeking in more prosperous times, and must have been struck by the sad state in which he found the majority of the Barolong people.

Chief of the Tshidi Barolong at the end of 1898 was Wessels Montshiwa, successor to Chief Montshiwa who had died, aged 85, at the end of 1896. The old chief, though dead for over two years, still cast a long shadow over the daily lives of the Barolong of Mafeking. Chief of his people for nearly half a century, he had led the Barolong to their present home in Mafeking in the 1870s, and through a mixture of stubborn courage, skilful bargaining, and a fair measure of good luck, had ensured for his people a measure of control over their land and independence from white rule. Boer forces from the Transvaal, who had laid claim to the land around Mafeking, had attacked and besieged the Barolong settlement on many occasions during the 1870s and early 1880s, but each time the Barolong managed to hold out. Montshiwa had always sought the aid of the British imperial government in his efforts to resist Boer expansion, and in the end his supplications had borne fruit in the dispatch (on the advice of Cecil Rhodes) of the Warren expedition in 1885 and the subsequent declaration of a British protectorate over the area in which the Barolong lived. It was this that led to the establishment of the European settlement of Mafeking alongside which they now lived.[7]

At the time, the Barolong regarded the securing of British protection in this way as a great achievement; without it Montshiwa and his followers would certainly have lost the land they occupied in the Mafeking district, suffering the same fate as many other African communities who fell victim to white settlement and expansion in southern Africa. But British protection had itself led to a gradual diminution in the independence of the chief and his people, and by the mid-1890s the municipal, district and protectorate authorities were all making inroads into the chief's sphere of jurisdiction. The British Bechuanaland proclamation of 1891 had marked one important stage in this process, for this provided for the establishment of proper legal machinery to handle civil and criminal matters, marriages, trade, taxation, and various other functions involved in administering a territory, and it effectively defined and limited the areas in which the Barolong chief was to be permitted to exercise jurisdiction over his people.

With the incorporation of British Bechuanaland into the Cape Colony in 1895 – the protests of Montshiwa and his headmen notwithstanding – these powers had been proscribed still further: the region around Mafeking now became a magisterial and administrative district of the colony, and acquired its own magistrate and civil commissioner in the person of Mr Bell. The establishment of the local bureaucratic apparatus necessary to enable him to carry out his duties was of course what brought Plaatje to Mafeking; his very presence in Mr Bell's office, a welcome opportunity for him, testified at the same time to the existence of the administrative and judicial restrictions which now circumscribed the daily lives of the Barolong of Mafeking.

For all this, Chief Montshiwa had remained an imposing, revered figure and such was the degree of personal authority he exercised that the colonial government at first felt little need to intervene in the internal affairs of his chiefdom, even when it had the power to do so. But his son, Wessels Montshiwa, never looked like making a success of the chieftancy he inherited on his father's death. Quite apart from the difficult political and economic circumstances which prevailed at the time, he was not a popular figure and he lacked the personal qualities to respond to the challenge that faced him. He only became chief because all his elder brothers had been killed fighting in wars against the Boers, and he was largely unprepared for the unexpected responsibility that came his way. In addition, he was unable to read or write, he suffered from continual ill-health (being laid up for weeks on end with gout), was frequently drunk, and was never accorded anything like the respect that had been enjoyed by his illustrious father. Indeed, it was not long before he was hauled before the magistrate for non-payment of debts and charged with 'committing a public nuisance'; such things had never happened in his father's time.[8]

But whatever Wessels' failings as an individual and the intrusions of the white authorities, the institution of chiefly rule remained very much the dominant factor in the daily lives of the Barolong people: neither could detract from the pervasive reality of tribal traditions and custom in the life of this community, and the *kgotla*, the chief's court, remained very much its focal point both geographically and symbolically. It was here that the affairs of the tribe and other matters of common interest were discussed, and it was to the chief that people continued to bring their problems. As Plaatje himself summed it up several years later, 'Anything that crops up, or anything affecting the Natives here, we first advise the Chief about it and ask him to take steps in the matter'.[9] In practice this generally meant referring any such matters to the chief's council as much as the chief himself, but this was a long-established tradition among the Barolong and it had always been the way in which the chief had ruled in the past. The ethos and character thus given to life in this Barolong community was quite different from anything Plaatje had known in Pniel or Kimberley.

When Plaatje moved to Mafeking he went to stay with Silas Molema, a Barolong headman and member of a family who occupied a very special position in the affairs and history of his people, and was soon to play a decisive part in Plaatje's life. Silas Molema was then 48 years old, a younger son of Chief Molema, the founder of Mafeking. The old chief Molema, a brother of Montshiwa and leader of the small Christian community amongst the Tshidi Barolong, had been sent to occupy Mafeking in 1847 as a stronghold against Boer invasion. Thirty years later Molema was joined by Montshiwa and the main body of the Barolong people, and it was only then that it became their main home. Thereafter there was always a somewhat uneasy relationship between Montshiwa and the Molemas and their following, but they had been bound together in a mutual dependence in which the outward forms of unity, at least, had always been preserved: each faction – for this was what they amounted to – was only too conscious that it needed the other, and that disunity would endanger the survival of the Barolong people as a whole.

Even more than their claim to be the original founders of Mafeking and the leading family amongst the Barolong nobility, the Molemas were known for their commitment to the Christian religion, their belief in the power of education, and their conviction that the Barolong must adapt and change in response to the new circumstances that the developments of the latter part of the nineteenth century had created for them. In these changing conditions it was not surprising that it was to members of the Molema family – above all to Israel, Joshua and Silas, the three elder sons of Chief Molema – that the task of negotiating with the outside world would often devolve (for this required the skills of literacy), nor that these same skills would be applied with good effect to the advancement of the interests of the family as well. All these characteristics were evident in the career of Silas Molema. Educated at the Wesleyan Healdtown Institute in the eastern Cape, Silas Molema had become convinced of the importance of extending education amongst his people, and had returned to Mafeking in 1878 to set up a school. He combined this task with the other chiefly duties that he was expected to perform, and regarded it as his duty to use the position he had inherited to spread a knowledge of western ideas among his people. Not that he ever neglected his more traditional functions: the school he ran, so Plaatje recounted later, 'was often interrupted by the several quarrels with the Boers, as the teacher, being a sub-chief, always went on active service at the head of the regiment'.[10]

By the 1890s Silas Molema had also become a large landowner in his own right, harvested his crops with a steam threshing-machine, and had built up an extensive range of business and property interests on both sides of the Bechuanaland Protectorate border. Amongst his properties was a stretch of land at Pitsani, on the railway line just north of this border, known to posterity for the fact that it was from here that Dr Jameson had launched his ill-fated expedition into the Transvaal in 1895. Rather less well known is that in return for the use of his land for training and assembling the raiders, Silas Molema had been promised, in the event of the raid achieving its objectives, further tracts of land inside the Transvaal. As it was, he had not done badly: while the rest of Mafeking nervously awaited retribution from across the border once the raid had failed, Silas Molema had quietly pocketed £300 for his services.[11] It was a typical combination of the man's entrepreneurial instinct and loyalty to the British. Twenty years later he was to look back upon these times with understandable regret: since the time his 'late lamented friends' Dr Jameson and Cecil Rhodes 'had left these parts', he recalled, 'as you know it has been very difficult to get on'.[12]

Silas Molema had also been careful to cultivate a good relationship with many of the other influential white newcomers to the district, and he was highly regarded by Mafeking's leading white residents, private citizens and government officials alike. The manager of the local branch of the Standard Bank, for example, whom he favoured with his account, considered him 'a steady man', and with assets (according to the bank) of nearly £10,000 was obviously one of their more valued customers.[13] Silas Molema got on very well, too, with Charles Bell, magistrate and civil commissioner since 1897, who considered him 'one of the most trustworthy and respectable men in the district'.[14] It was a relationship from which both men stood to benefit. If Bell was successful in gaining the confidence of the Molema family, then half the battle in securing the co-operation of the Barolong in the administration of their affairs by the government was won; without it – given the very limited resources at his disposal – this task would have been infinitely more difficult. And on the Molemas' side there were also very definite advantages to be derived from holding some sway with the magistrate when it came to the finer points of interpreting government proclamations, assessing tax liabilities, granting trading or firearms licences, or the more general business of distributing such patronage as the magistrate controlled. Beneath the respect and friendship that Charles Bell and Silas Molema developed for each other there lay a clear perception by each of the advantages to be gained from the existence of such a relationship.

One expression of this relationship seems to have been the understanding that when any vacancy arose in Bell's office, for which an African employee was required, then it would be up to Silas Molema to make an appropriate recommendation; this was of course what had happened in Plaatje's case when the position of court interpreter had fallen vacant in 1898. Exactly when Plaatje and Silas Molema first met is unknown, but they had probably been known to one another for a few years before then. Plaatje's father, it will be remembered, had lived on one of the Molema family farms until his death in 1896, and it would be surprising if Plaatje himself had not met both Joshua Molema and Silas Molema on one of his earlier visits to Mafeking. Silas Molema had not been slow to recognise the talents and potential of this able (and by Mafeking standards well-educated) young man to the Tshidi Barolong people, and when the opportunity arose to have him placed in so strategic a position as the magistrate's office he took it gladly.[15] His recommendations had obviously helped Plaatje in getting the job, and Silas Molema, for his part, would have been well aware of the potential benefits for the Molema family in having 'their man' so conveniently placed. In the circumstances it can have come as little surprise to anyone living in the *stadt* that when Plaatje moved up to Mafeking he went to stay with Silas Molema's family, well attended by the servants and hangers-on who formed a natural part of the entourage of so influential and progressive a member of the Barolong aristocracy.[16] Socially this was now very much where Plaatje belonged.

Amongst those who looked upon the new arrival with particular interest, albeit from the youthful perspective of a seven-year-old, was Silas Molema's son, Modiri. Looking back on the occasion later in life, he recalled being at first slightly puzzled by the lightness of Plaatje's complexion (lighter even than his own family, renowned for this characteristic themselves), and guessed that he might have been a Griqua or somebody else of mixed race. But he soon took a firm liking to the new house-guest, and he was struck by Plaatje's generosity and lively sense of humour.[17] From these beginnings in 1898 there developed a relationship which in time grew into one of close personal friendship.

◇

Plaatje commenced his new duties at the office of the Mafeking magistrate and civil commissioner on 14 October 1898, evidently recovered from the illness that had detained him in Kimberley for the previous two weeks. In view of Elizabeth's condition – she was at that time nearly eight months' pregnant – his new responsibilities at work were undoubtedly not the only things on his mind. The good news from Pniel came five weeks later: Elizabeth gave birth to a baby boy on 23 November, an event which was duly announced in the appropriate columns of *Imvo Zabantsundu* in its next few issues. Subsequently the baby was christened Frederick York St Leger ('Sainty' for short), after the well-known founder and editor of the *Cape Times*, a man whose liberal views on 'the native question' were evidently held in high esteem by Plaatje and many of the friends he had left behind in Kimberley. Elizabeth did not come up to Mafeking to join her husband, though, until some time afterwards, leaving Plaatje – so he was to recall – to endure a rather lonely Christmas holiday that year.[18]

But their continued separation did at least mean – once these anxieties were over – that Plaatje could devote his energies to getting on top of his new job. On the face of it the work promised to be much more demanding than anything he had been accustomed to in the Post Office in Kimberley, and so it proved: from the records of the Mafeking magistrate's office it is clear the Charles Bell presided over a busy, overworked staff who struggled to keep abreast of the mountain of paperwork which Bell's wide range of responsibilities, as both administrative and judicial representative of the Cape government, generated for them. From time to time Bell applied to the Law Department for permission to take on additional staff to enable his office to cope, but the response was rarely sympathetic; the primary concern of his superiors in Cape Town was to save money, not to make life easy for government servants. Several months before Plaatje arrived, in fact, Bell had put in an unsuccessful plea for a third European clerk, since the two he had were simply not managing. His first clerk (with whom he did not get on) had broken down with 'a severe attack of haemor-rhage, the long hours in the office being too much for him', whilst young Ernest Grayson, who had just joined the office as second clerk, was having to work long hours overtime, simply to get through all that had to be done.[19] One thing looked certain: any new employee could expect to be kept fully occupied during working hours.

When Plaatje joined the office the staff thus consisted of Charles Bell, the magistrate and civil commissioner; Herbert Cowie (when he was well enough), the first clerk and assistant magistrate, who deputised for Bell when he was away on tour in the district, but was shortly to be replaced by a man called William Geyer; Ernest Grayson, the second clerk, fresh from Cambridge, whom Bell considered to be 'gentlemanly', somewhat lazy, 'very slow', but 'has ability if he will make use of it'; and now Plaatje himself, as junior clerk and court interpreter.[20] There was also an office messenger, but a permanent appointment was not made here until a few months later. Then, the person taken on was a man called Patrick Sidzumo, son of a well-known Mfengu preacher who had come to live in Mafeking for health reasons. In 1898 Plaatje and Patrick Sidzumo were both 22 years old, and they soon became close friends.[21]

Of Bell himself Plaatje had the fondest of recollections. He considered himself fortunate, he once said, to have 'served my apprenticeship under such a man', and he always remembered him with affection.[22] In some respects his close association with Charles Bell over the next three years was comparable to his relationship with the Reverend Ernst Westphal during an earlier part of his life, for he learnt – in different ways – a great deal from both men. Then in his mid-forties, and married with a large family, Bell was amongst the Cape Colony's most widely experienced magistrates, having joined the Cape Civil Service nearly thirty years previously. Since then he had made steady, if unspectacular, progress, and before his posting to Mafeking in 1897 had served on the commission set up to try to contain the rinderpest epidemic.[23] In many ways Bell personified the finest traditions of public duty of the Cape Civil Service. When he died in 1908 one of his friends summed up his qualities as follows:

Thoroughness and efficiency were his mottoes throughout life. Under a genial disposition and kindly manner, he retained a firm resolve to see that those under him should do their duty to the public. He was a strict disciplinarian. He had no faith in Civil Servants who amplified red tape regulations or treated the public with indifference. Mr Bell insisted that persons coming to his office on business should receive prompt and courteous attention, no matter what their position in life might be. And he inoculated all those under him with this ideal.[24]

The records of the Mafeking magistrate's office yield another revealing piece of information about Charles Bell: at the time Plaatje joined his office in Mafeking, he had taken no leave from work for over five years. There can be no doubting the sense of duty of such a man.[25]

As well as being a more than usually dedicated public servant Bell was also a popular local figure in Mafeking. He took a very active part in the town's social life; was largely responsible for the establishment of the public library; was always in demand as an after-dinner speaker, and he was the automatic choice as president for Mafeking's numerous clubs and societies.[26] Everybody who met him seems to have been impressed by his lively sense of humour, only superficially hidden beneath a serious-looking face which bore a striking resemblance to that of Cecil Rhodes. In the opinion of one of his colleagues Charles Bell was 'a very clever and amusing fellow',[27] and in time Plaatje came to share exactly the same view. 'Our Civil Commissioner,' he wrote after he had worked for Bell for a couple of years, conferring upon him the highest accolade, 'is a white Lenkoane. His acumen in fixing sarcastic phrases and aptitude in putting comical jokes is beyond description. His mere silence gives him a very ferocious appearance.'[28]

Plaatje was impressed as well by the dutiful attitude that Bell took not only towards his work in general but towards the welfare of the African population (some 15,000 people) for whom he was administratively responsible. Bell believed that it was his responsibility as magistrate and civil commissioner not simply to keep the peace in the district, but to actively promote the well-being and interests of its inhabitants. In contrast to those magistrates who never ventured outside their offices, he pointed out to his superiors on one occasion, 'a Magistrate who individualises himself, obtains a moral control over the people . . . is consequently enabled to mould them into a condition of peace and prosperity and an observance of the laws and the regulations of civilised usage'.[29]

It was the kind of creed with which Plaatje could readily identify, and from the beginning the two men established a friendly, albeit necessarily unequal, relationship. Bell, for his part, was soon impressed with the qualities of his new court interpreter, and he found him a great improvement upon Jan Moloke, his predecessor. Whereas Moloke had not been considered trustworthy and reliable enough to handle office records without supervision, Plaatje was – so Bell was to observe in April 1899 – 'a steady, diligent person', and to be trusted in every respect.[30] Moreover, Plaatje could speak and write Dutch, which Moloke had been unable to do.

Plaatje's duties at work were divided between interpreting in the magistrate's court when it was in session, and attending to the more routine, clerical work of copying documents, typewriting (in which he soon became very skilled), filing correspondence and office records, and translating into English incoming letters written in Dutch and Setswana (Messrs Grayson and Geyer being incapable of understanding either); on occasions, too, Plaatje was entrusted with the rather more responsible task of writing up the civil and criminal record books, theoretically the responsibility of the assistant resident magistrate. Such duties he seems to have mastered without undue difficulty, although his first few entries in the criminal record book do reveal a few crossings out before he came to terms with exactly what was required.[31] Interpreting in court, however, provided a far greater challenge, and there is no doubt that this was the aspect of his job that Plaatje enjoyed doing most.

Few of the court cases which came before Mr Bell were considered very serious; mostly they were cases of petty theft, drunkenness, trespass, committing a public nuisance, assault, causing a breach of the peace, and offences of a similar nature.[32] Two cases (numbers 290 and 291) selected at random from Plaatje's first week at work in October 1898 can perhaps be given by way of illustration. First, there was the case of *R. v.Katje*, described as 'a Hottentot female', with no occupation, charged with being 'wrongfully and unlawfully on or about 19 October at Mafeking, drunk in a public place, to wit, Carrington St'; she was found guilty and fined 7s 6d, or a sentence of five days' imprisonment with hard labour. It was not the first time, nor was it to be the last, that the unfortunate Katje was hauled up before Mr Bell on the same charge. Then came the case of *R. v.Moses Callan*, described as 'a Barolong labourer', charged with 'wrongfully and unlawfully on 18 October 1898 at Mafeking steal[ing] one fowl, the property of George Francis, Market Master': he was also found guilty and got fourteen days' imprisonment with hard labour.[33]

Cases of this nature formed the staple diet of business in the Mafeking magistrate's court, the consequences not of an inherent criminality on the part of the inhabitants of the district but the product, for the most part, of sheer poverty: in 1898 and 1899, in the wake of the rinderpest, this was much worse than before, and it is scarcely surprising that most of those who appeared before the court in criminal session were both poor and black.

Occasionally more serious cases were heard in the magistrate's court. If the gravity of the offence warranted it, Bell would hold a preliminary hearing in his own court and then, if there was sufficient evidence, refer the case to the High Court, where it would either be heard in Kimberley or in the Northern Circuit Court during its next visit to Mafeking – always a welcome occasion for both Plaatje and Elizabeth, since it provided an opportunity to see Isaiah Bud-M'belle, the Northern Circuit Court's interpreter. One such case which was heard in Mafeking before being referred to the higher court is of particular interest, for it could have had very unfortunate consequences for Plaatje. The accused was an African by the name of Joseph Ephraim, from Kimberley; who was caught trying to sell diamonds in Mafeking, a serious offence in view of the strictly enforced legal monopoly which De Beers enjoyed over the selling of diamonds. The hearing took place in March 1899, and it attracted a great deal of interest locally in view of the value of the diamonds Ephraim was trying to dispose of; but for Plaatje the embarrassing, and doubtless very worrying, aspect of the case was that Ephraim had actually been staying in his house, and it was here that the police discovered the diamonds after being tipped off. There was nothing to suggest that Plaatje knew anything about the diamonds and, fortunately for him, Bell was quite satisfied that he was in no way 'acquainted with Ephraim's illicit intentions'. Clearly, though, Plaatje needed to be a little more careful about the kind of people he extended hospitality to – in this case probably the result of an acquaintanceship in Kimberley.[34] Needless to say, had Bell found any evidence that Plaatje knew what Ephraim was up to it would have been a very disappointing end to a promising new career.

By this time, though, Charles Bell had had every opportunity to form an opinion of the character and qualities of his new court interpreter, and he would probably have been very surprised to have found any evidence that Plaatje was involved in any such thing. Already it would have been quite evident to him that Plaatje approached his duties in court with commendable seriousness of purpose, that he was genuinely concerned that justice should be done and be seen to be done, and that he was well on the way to attaining a high level of professional competence. Such impressions are amply confirmed in the account that Plaatje himself wrote about his experiences as a court interpreter in Mafeking. Entitled 'The Essential Interpreter', Plaatje's account, some ten pages long, and as yet unpublished, was written in 1909, seven years after he had left the profession.[35] It contains some vivid descriptions by Plaatje of what he had seen and experienced during the course of his work in the magistrate's court in Mafeking, and provides a revealing picture not only of the attitudes which Plaatje developed towards his work, but of the way in which he responded to the demands that Bell made upon him.

For in interpreting, as in other matters, Charles Bell insisted upon the highest standards. 'Mr Bell informed me,' so Plaatje wrote, 'when I first came into his office, that interpreting in court and interpreting at the sale of a cow were two different things entirely, and that it was as necessary to cultivate the art as to acquire a knowledge of the respective languages.'[36] Plaatje took the words to heart and 'very soon' discovered what he meant. And as he learnt to 'cultivate the art' so he found that Bell's own proficiency in languages (he was fluent in English, Dutch and four African languages) was to prove a source of security and comfort when he was called upon to perform his duties. He continued:

> I always made my translations with a perfect security believing that he could rectify my errors, if any. I cannot express the satisfaction this gave me – always – not only because of the correctness of my renditions but on account of the knowledge that the chances of a miscarriage of justice were *non-est*.[37]

On some occasions, however, Plaatje found himself officiating in cases which required him to interpret in languages with which Bell was unfamiliar. In such circumstances he felt a rather greater sense of responsibility and anxiety, and took even greater care than usual over his translation. He recalled one occasion in particular, when he had to interpret in German and Koranna, languages in which Bell was 'absolutely unversed' and in which he himself was 'less familiar':

> Mr Bell's abilities as a linguist were often the byword with the motley crew [the court audience], and on that morning I found an impression among them that the proceedings had given me the greatest satisfaction since for the first time I was able to exercise a free hand having to perform a role in which I was not subject to criticism, but my mind was working in the opposite direction. It seemed to me that the magistrate, prisoner, prosecutor, and spectators could not really believe that I was doing my best in a difficult position, and

that it was a very good best. As mistakes are very common in these matters, I left no loophole for the slightest error. I took much pains eliciting my facts and getting the deponent to revise his sentences if they contained a phrase of the meaning of which I was not quite certain. This retarded the proceedings in an unmistakable manner and my renditions, usually noted for their expeditiousness, were clearly boring. I felt that it was a tedious performance taking up the time of the court to ascertain minute details which could easily be left unresearched; however, I threw the approbation of the Court and its loafers to the winds and centred my attention in the correct administration of justice only, determined to tell the magistrate so should he remonstrate against me for delaying the court more than is my wont.[38]

It is a revealing account that says much about the kind of pressures that existed in the courtroom (which could all too easily affect the judicial process), as well as Plaatje's own high-minded approach to his work. On this occasion, however, virtue had its reward:

It transpired in the end that this did deserve the approbation of the Court, for in conversation with his worship the mayor, the magistrate expressed his satisfaction with his new interpreter, who, unlike some that he had had, preferred to be understood when he translates and who visibly feels grave and took extraordinary pains when interpreting into and from languages not known to any others, and when he knows that the course of justice depends on him entirely. Others, he said, considered it *infra dig* to invite correction, they seem to fear that patient eliciting of obscure facts will be mistaken for incompetence and are happier if they can easily gloss over mistakes in an inaudible tone. Needless to say I was highly elated at the testimony.[39]

There were several aspects of his work which Plaatje found particularly challenging, amongst them the problem of explaining legal terminology:

My own difficulty when I was still a fresh attaché of the Court was the finding out of the real meaning of most of the least known of forensic phrases, including commitment for trial, and how to express them in the vernacular. I found out that this was too difficult a phrase to render into intelligible Dutch, or any of the native languages, in half a dozen words. A literal translation of it will be beyond the reach of the intellect of a person of mediocre intelligence, so I found the following rendition rather roundabout but more satisfactory because better understood.

Magistrate: 'You are committed for trial.'
Interpreter: 'Kgetse ea gagu yaka e koaliloe e tla romeloa koa mosekising eo mogolo koa Teemaneng, fa a sena go a bala ke ene o tla holeling fa u tla sekisioa Magesetrata, kgona ke Liyoche eo o tla tlang, lefaele gore ga nke u Sekisoa gope' – 46 words to explain 5.

I have often found English prisoners, after being told in this pithy official language, and despite the fact that the phrase is in their mother tongue, that they scarcely understood their fate as they did not know if 'Committed for trial' was something round or square. My translation just quoted would, if retranslated into English, read: 'Your case as recorded will be sent to the Crown prosecutor at Kimberley. After reading it he will see if you are to be tried by the Magistrate, by the next Circuit Court Judge or if you are not to be prosecuted at all.'[40]

The tricky business of cross-examination in three languages was something which caused Plaatje a few problems at first, for this required not only a good command of the three languages involved, but also a detailed knowledge of the procedure, the ability and patience to explain it to a witness or the accused, and of course absolute integrity: the slightest mistranslation, as Plaatje became very aware, could result in the miscarriage of justice. Efficient court interpreting required, indeed, a very high level of skill and application, and it placed a heavy burden of responsibility upon the individual concerned. Plaatje quite clearly relished the challenge. From 'The Essential Interpreter' there emerges an impression of a confident, conscientious and very able young man who responded with enthusiasm to the demands of his work in court, and who believed implicitly in its importance in the proper functioning of the judicial system of the Cape Colony.

At the same time, there were several aspects of the job with which Plaatje was not wholly enamoured: in particular, the related questions of pay and status. On the former, Plaatje believed himself entitled – on the basis of an undertaking made to him by the Postmaster-General in Kimberley – to an additional £1 per month as from the first day of March 1899. He wasted little time in drawing the matter to Bell's attention:

> Office of the Resident Magistrate
> Mafeking,
> 1 March 1899
>
> Sir,
> I beg leave to inform you that according to our agreement with the Postmaster-General, when I joined the service five years ago, my next increase of salary, £1 per mensem, became due on the first Ultimo.
>
> I joined the service March 1st, 1894, at £72 per annum and I was to reach the maximum of £120 per annum March 1st 1901, if I continued.
>
> When I was detached from their Department, to take the appointment here, I was informed that the transfer will in no way disturb this scale, unless it be found expedient to improve it seeing that I was raised from the post of Letter Carrier to that of C.C. and R.M's translator – oral and documentary – in the Native and Dutch languages.
>
> As they seem not to have brought this matter to your notice, at the time of my transfer, I beg the honour to do so with the sincere but humble request that you will be pleased to use such influence as you may be empowered with to have the omission rectified.

I may most respectfully mention that this application claims your first attention as I am the only married member of your staff.

I have the honour to be
> Sir
>> Your obedient servant
>> Sol T. Plaatje

The C.C. and R.M.
Mafeking[41]

Unfortunately for Plaatje, the Postmaster-General, when consulted about the matter, denied that any such promise was made 'by any responsible member of this Department'.[42] And Bell himself, whilst perfectly satisfied with Plaatje's work, did not think he had been working for him long enough to justify an increase; and so he did not get it. Even more galling to Plaatje's sensitivities than an inadequate salary was the question of status. Possessing as he did such a high-minded, conscientious approach to his work, he found it particularly irritating to be ordered about like the most junior office messenger, and not to be accorded the respect to which, he thought, his position entitled him. One incident, related in 'The Essential Interpreter', he remembered clearly:

A messenger from the Resident Commissioner's office called at our office one morning and stated that His Honour needs the services of an interpreter. I went over as soon as my time allowed, and officiated. In due course, I rendered my account for the service to the Imperial Government. Later in the day, I was called by my chief – the Colonial Magistrate – who produced my account, returned in a note from the Resident Commissioner, His Honour expressing surprise that I should claim any remuneration for my service, a claim that was never put forth by any of my predecessors. My chief supported his view and added that as an employee of the Cape Government, I should render my services free as the Cape was bound to assist the Imperial Government whenever necessary. I told him of my inability to appreciate the logic of this contention; that it was monstrous, from my point of view, that I should be called upon to go and adjudicate upon Protectorate cases in the Imperial office, or that any of his subordinates could be ordered to go and do clerical work in the Imperial headquarters, without emoluments, as in that case his staff, and not the Cape Government, would be assisting the Imperial Government; that if the Imperial authorities were to run offices on charity, and other people were giving their services free, I also could go and do my share of free labour; but I could not, I told him, go and render free services to facilitate the work of well paid officers any more than I could afford to work in his office without a salary. I did not press my claim, however, and the matter lapsed.[43]

Plaatje's case may not have been entirely watertight (he would presumably have done the work during office hours rather than in his own time), but his sentiments were clear enough, and when a second request for an interpreter came from the Resident Commissioner's office he declined to make himself available. It gave him no satisfaction whatever to hear, shortly afterwards, that the Resident Commissioner had obtained 'a street boy to interpret "anyhow" ', with predictably disastrous results.[44] Plaatje could be very prickly when he felt that his skills and position were not being accorded the status and recognition they deserved.

◇

On two occasions during 1899 Plaatje found himself before the presiding magistrate in a rather different capacity from usual: as plaintiff in the first, defendant in the second. On the first occasion, 9 June 1899, Plaatje had brought a civil action against one Alfred Ngidi, a local railwayman of Mfengu origin, for the recovery of the sum of 7s 6d which Plaatje had incurred on his behalf. What had happened was this: Plaatje had agreed to hire his musical organ to Ngidi to enable him to use it one Saturday evening at a function in the location, and – since Ngidi did not possess the means of transporting it from Plaatje's home – to hire a horse and cart (from Joshua Molema) on his behalf; it was then arranged that Ngidi would go to Plaatje's house on the Saturday afternoon to pick up both horse and cart and organ. But he never showed up. Plaatje, obviously very annoyed, was kept waiting the whole afternoon, was unable subsequently to recover from Ngidi the 7s 6d he had already paid Joshua Molema for the hire of the horse and cart, so determined to take him to court to try to recover the sum. Judgement, with costs, was duly made in his favour. Perhaps just as satisfying for Plaatje, though, was personally writing out the summons which brought Alfred Ngidi to court, for this now formed one of his official duties.[45] Working as a court interpreter soon made Plaatje aware of the possibilities of the law in the resolution of difficulties such as he encountered with Alfred Ngidi; the law, he had discovered for himself, was an accessible instrument that could be used for civil as well as political purposes, as he and his friends had demonstrated in Kimberley.

But on the second occasion Plaatje was not quite so lucky. This time he was the defendant, having been brought to court by one Joseph Whiffler, a Mafeking storekeeper, for the alleged non-payment of 14s 6d owed for bread, cakes and ginger beer which Plaatje had ordered and had delivered to his home. Plaatje then declined to pay the whole of this amount since Whiffler owed him 9s on a separate account, which Plaatje had tried repeatedly to extract from him. When Whiffler's collector, Mr Mahoney, went on his rounds, therefore, Plaatje's suggestion was that he should pay not the full 14s 6d but rather the balance of 5s 6d. Mahoney, however, was unwilling to agree to such an arrangement, and applied for a writ. In the light of the circumstances of the case, Plaatje, frustrated at having had to wait so long for Whiffler to settle his debt with him, argued that he was 'entitled to the dismissal of the summons with costs', adding in court that he would have paid up 'had the plaintiff not been so precipitous'.[46] Charles Bell, however, did not see things quite in the same light, and judgement with costs was awarded to Joseph Whiffler. Since Plaatje did not thereafter sue for repayment of the 5s 6d he was still owed, he was presumably successful in getting this back.

The two cases are of interest for what they suggest of Plaatje's character, for in both an impression is conveyed of a young man (he was still only 22 years old) determined not to allow any liberties to be taken with him – whether the other party was black or white really did not matter. In the second case Plaatje may have misjudged, in the heat of the moment, the consequences of his refusal to pay the full amount of money demanded by Mr Mahoney, but what had upset him was the *manner* in which it had been demanded: he would have paid up, so he said, had not Mr Mahoney been so 'precipitous'. Obviously, Plaatje was not prepared to tolerate this kind of treatment without protest – just as, at work, he was quick to claim the recognition and remuneration he believed himself entitled to. Clearly, there was a keen sensitivity in Plaatje's make-up to anything he perceived as unfair treatment.

Throughout 1899 Plaatje applied himself assiduously to his work in the magistrate's court, by his own account enjoying it immensely. Occasionally there were lighter moments in the courtroom. On one occasion, recalled many years later, Plaatje walked into the courtroom one morning and to his surprise noticed that the magistrate was wearing a shirt of exactly the same line and pattern as his own. 'I quickly disappeared into one of the anterooms,' Plaatje related, pondering the Tswana adage 'never measure your straw with great places', 'and hid the offending garment before I returned to officiate.'[47]

In addition to performing his normal duties in court, Plaatje was also busy, during the first half of 1899, preparing himself to take a number of the Cape Civil Service examinations, held twice a year in Cape Town and Grahamstown, hoping thereby to qualify himself for a higher salary and promotion to the High Court. His intention was to take the papers in Setswana, Sesotho, Dutch, German and Typewriting – an impressive array, for candidates in these examinations generally took no more than two papers at any one session.[48] These were not the entry examinations for the civil service in which Isaiah Bud-M'belle had distinguished himself in 1892, but the proficiency examinations open to people already employed in government service. In July 1899 Bud-M'belle had gone a step further and taken two more papers – Setswana and Sesotho – and passed both of them. It may well have encouraged Plaatje to try to do the same.[49]

But as the year 1899 wore on, it began to look more and more likely that wider political developments would affect the normal course of the lives of everybody living in Mafeking, black and white. Tension between the British imperial government and the two Boer republics, soon to develop into armed conflict, was increasing steadily. The origins of the conflict may be traced back to the discovery of gold on the Witwatersrand in 1886, and the radical transformation that this brought about in the balance of power in southern Africa.[50] In the years that followed both the mineowners and the British imperial government grew increasingly alarmed at the emergence of a powerful, independent and wealthy Boer state in the Transvaal. The Jameson Raid in 1895 had been an attempt on the part of these mineowners – or at least a group of them – to effect a *coup d'état* and replace the Kruger government with a regime more sympathetic to their interests: it had failed miserably. Since then the greater threat to the independence of the Boer republics had come from the imperial government itself, particularly since the time of Sir Alfred Milner's appointment as British

High Commissioner for southern Africa in 1897. For Milner, an uncompromising figure, confident he enjoyed the full support of Joseph Chamberlain, the British Colonial Secretary, combined an acute awareness of the importance for Britain of control over the world's supply of gold with the conviction that the overthrow of the two Boer republics – by military means if necessary – was essential to Britain's long-term future; he was intent on achieving both objectives, and determined to allow nothing to stand in his way.

By the time Plaatje had moved to Mafeking late in 1898 the hostility between the Boer republics and the British imperial government was beginning to threaten the stability of southern Africa as a whole; the fragile social and political order of the Cape Colony, in particular, already severely strained by the effects of the Jameson Raid, now lay at the mercy of forces over which it could no longer exercise any control. By the middle of the following year, 1899, relations between the republics and the imperial government had deteriorated still further, there was open talk of war, and both sides prepared themselves for military conflict. Although the government of the Cape Colony tried desperately to steer a neutral course, in Mafeking in particular there were understandable signs of anxiety. The town's residents, black and white, whilst well disposed, for the most part, towards the cause of the British imperial government, were acutely conscious that Mafeking, by virtue of its geographical location, was likely to be one of the first places to be attacked in the event of a declaration of war. In addition, the town's association with the Jameson Raid had not been forgotten in the Transvaal, and in August and September 1899 it was daily becoming a more attractive target in view of the large quantities of stores and railway equipment being accumulated there.

For several months the Cape government, fearful of providing the Boers with a pretext to justify invading Cape territory, had refused to allow the nearest imperial military force, led by Colonel R. S. S. Baden-Powell and based in the Bechuanaland Protectorate, to station any of its men in Mafeking. In response, Mafeking's white citizens began to take some secret measures to defend the town by themselves.[51] In the middle of September, though, Baden-Powell decided to risk the displeasure of the Cape government and moved his entire Protectorate regiment into Mafeking from their base at Ramatlabama, and preparations for the town's defence proceeded with a new urgency: a Town Guard was formed, earthworks were thrown up, trenches dug, forts constructed, and inner and outer defensive perimeters were established. Many white women and children now began to leave the town to journey southwards to Kimberley, Cape Town, and – so it was hoped – to safety. Mafeking prepared itself for a siege.

Like Mafeking's white citizens, the Barolong, too, had been growing increasingly concerned as they heard news of the mobilisation of Boer forces on the other side of the border, for there was no way that they could avoid involvement in any fighting, should this break out. As with the whites, there was a long-established pro-British tradition among the Tshidi Barolong, but they were by no means confident of the ability of the British forces in Mafeking to defend them against a Boer attack.[52] Wessels Montshiwa and his headmen repeatedly asked Charles Bell for arms, so that they could defend themselves in time of war, only to be met with 'confident assurances', so Plaatje recalled, 'that the Boers would never cross the boundary into British territory'.[53] Unhappy with these assurances, at the beginning of October 1899 they demanded a further meeting with Bell in the *stadt*, at which Plaatje himself interpreted. It was a dramatic occasion, and Plaatje remembered it clearly:

> The chiefs told the Magistrate that they feared he knew very little about war if he thought that belligerents would respect one another's boundaries. He replied in true South African style, that it was a white man's war, and that if the enemy came, Her Majesty's white troops would do all the fighting and protect the territories of the chiefs. We remember how the chief Montsioa and his counsellor Joshua Molema went round the Magistrate's chair and crouching behind him said: 'Let us say, for the sake of argument, that your assurances are genuine, and that when the trouble begins we hide behind your back like this, and, rifle in hand, you do all the fighting because you are white; let us say, further, that some Dutchmen appear on the scene and they outnumber and shoot you: what would be our course of action then? Are we to run home, put on skirts and hoist up the white flag?'
> Chief Motshegare pulled off his coat, undid his shirt front and baring his shoulder and showing an old bullet scar, received in the Boer–Barolong war prior to the British occupation of Bechuanaland, he said: 'Until you can satisfy me that Her Majesty's white troops are impervious to bullets, I am going to defend my own wife and children. I have got my rifle at home and all I want is ammunition.'[54]

As before, Bell simply proffered confident assurances, and when he communicated the proceedings of the meeting to Cape Town there were simply more of the same. 'The reply from headquarters,' Plaatje thought, 'was so mild and reassuring that one could almost think it referred to an impending Parliamentary election rather than to a bloody war.'[55]

Several days later, on 9 October 1899, Plaatje's 23rd birthday, President Kruger issued an ultimatum to the imperial government, demanding the immediate removal of all imperial troops from southern Africa. With war now a certainty, Chief Wessels and his headmen made another desperate appeal to the Cape government for 'arms and ammunition sufficient for the defence of the town', since, they said, 'we are entirely defenceless'.[56] But their letter went no further than the magistrate's office, and within hours of the expiry of the ultimatum on 11 October the two towns of Mafeking – Barolong and European–found themselves surrounded by a force of several thousand men under the command of General Piet Cronje.

Plaatje laboured under fewer illusions than most as to what lay ahead. Immediately before the outbreak of hostilities he had predicted – in the presence of a disbelieving representative of the imperial government (he did not say whom) – that it would take 150,000 soldiers of the imperial government over twelve months to conquer the Boer republics; such an assessment, in the view of the officer concerned, verged on 'disloyalty', his own estimate being that 50,000 troops 'could within six months have made such a complete business of it as to have almost forgotten that there ever was war'.[57] Time would show whose estimate was closer to the truth.

Over one thing at least Plaatje could feel some sense of relief in the desperate circumstances in which all of Mafeking's inhabitants now found themselves: Elizabeth and St Leger, not yet a year old, were safely out of Mafeking and staying in the comparative security – or so it must have seemed at the time – of Elizabeth's parental home in Burghersdorp in the southern part of the colony. They had left Mafeking on a visit there in August, staying for a few days in Kimberley on the way, and had not returned.[58] From his position in the office of the local civil commissioner Plaatje would have been in an ideal position to offer informed advice on the likelihood of the town being attacked from across the border, whatever reassuring public pronouncements Charles Bell felt it appropriate to make. If Mafeking was indeed likely to be attacked, there was no sense in risking the lives, if it could be avoided, of his wife and young son. Plaatje of course had no alternative but to remain at his post; this time there was not the luxury of choosing whether or not he cared to render his services to the imperial government. They were all in it together.

One communication Plaatje never did receive before Mafeking was cut off: his civil service examination registration papers. He had applied in August to take the papers in Dutch, German and Typewriting (he had wanted to take the papers in Setswana and Sesotho as well, but was evidently told that this would not be possible), intending to sit the examinations in Cape Town in December. Accordingly, the secretary of the Civil Service Commission dispatched the certificates of registration to him on 5 October, but they never arrived.[59] Nor, for reasons which were to become painfully clear, was Plaatje to get to Cape Town that year. 'My intentions,' he wrote later, 'were completely defeated' as 'unfortunately war broke out.'[60] Mafeking was now completely surrounded by enemy forces. The famous siege had begun.

4

The siege and after: Mafeking 1899–1902

The siege of Mafeking was to last until 17 May 1900, 217 days later. During that time Mafeking became the focus of worldwide interest and attention. Its seemingly heroic resistance in the face of repeated onslaughts and apparently overwhelming odds provided one of the few 'bright spots' in a British military campaign in southern Africa which began with one reverse after the other. Mafeking became, in short, the necessary myth of the war, its significance magnified out of all proportion by the need to rally public support for Britain in an imperialist war that desperately needed an image that cast the Boers as aggressors, the British as underdogs. Inevitably, the reality was somewhat at odds with the myth that was created. There was, for one thing, relatively little fighting for most of the siege. After a few skirmishes at the beginning, in which several lives were lost on both sides, the surrounding Boer forces – greatly reduced in numbers after the first few weeks of investment – made no serious attempt to take the town until the following May, when it was evident that relief was close at hand; whilst Baden-Powell, commanding the British garrison with undoubted 'pluck', imagination and no little concern for his own reputation, was quite prepared to sit out the ineffectual shelling to which the besiegers then resorted. That such a course was open to him was due in large measure to the mountain of food supplies and stores which had been accumulated in Mafeking before the siege began, which ensured, for the white population at least, that surrender through threat of starvation was a very remote possibility.

For much of the siege hostilities were conducted by the opposing commanders in a very gentlemanly fashion: they corresponded regularly, accused one another of the heinous crime of arming Africans as combatants (the British military authorities duly provided the Barolong with arms once the Boers had surrounded Mafeking), and agreed to observe Sunday as a day of rest and recreation. On only one occasion did Baden-Powell make a serious assault upon the surrounding forces – a disastrous, ill-planned foray against a well-defended Boer position on Boxing Day, 1899, which resulted in over 50 casualties. Thereafter most of the actual fighting – intermittent sniping, for the most part – took place in the trenches of the brickfields to the south-west of the town where the Cape Corps, composed of members of the local Coloured population, distinguished themselves with both skill and gallantry.[1]

Once the two sides had settled down to the routine of the siege, boredom soon proved to be as much of a problem as the threat posed by Boer shells, although 'Big Ben', the Boers' 94lb siege gun, was always treated with a healthy degree of respect. A surprising number of those inside Mafeking – aware, as one of them wrote, that their town was engaged 'in making history for the British empire'[2] – passed the time by keeping diaries, recording the daily events of the siege with varying degrees of skill and imagination. With one exception the diaries which have survived, some published, some not, were kept by whites: by the war correspondents, the military officers, by residents of Mafeking, male and female. That one exception was Plaatje's. His diary, written in English, came to light some seventy years after it was written, and was first published in 1973.[3] The entries begin on 29 October 1899, two weeks after the siege began, and continue until the end of the following March. Quite possibly Plaatje was encouraged to start writing the diary because so many other people whom he knew had already begun to do just this, including his boss, Charles Bell. Since Plaatje had already been requested to type this out (whether this formed part of his official duties or not is unclear)[4] it must have seemed to him the most natural thing in the world to begin his own diary. What Plaatje then wrote provides not only a detailed record of the siege as he saw it, but also a revealing insight into the mind, the character and abilities of its author.

More than anything else Plaatje comes over from the pages of his diary as a young man of great self-confidence and humour, quite consciously using the diary to experiment with and to practise the obvious literary skills he had now acquired in the English language. In many respects the opening passage of the diary, Plaatje's entry for Sunday 29 October 1899, looking back over the whole of the previous week, sets the tone for much that follows:

> Divine Services. No thunder. Haikonna terror; and I have therefore got ample opportunity to sit down and think before I jot down anything about my experiences of the past week. I have discovered nearly everything about war and find that artillery in war is of no use. The Boers seem to have started hostilities, the whole of their reliance leaning on the strength and number of their cannons – and they are now surely discovering their mistake. I do not think they will have more pluck to do anything better than what they did on Wednesday and we can therefore expect they will either go away or settle around us until the Troops arrive. To give a short account of what I found war to be, I can say: no music is as thrilling and as immensely captivating as to listen to the firing of the guns on your side. It is like enjoying supernatural melodies in a paradise to hear one or two shots fired off the armoured train; but no words can suitably depict the fascination of the music produced by the action of a Maxim, which, to Boer ears, I am sure, is an exasperation which not only disturbs the ear but also disorganises the free circulation of the listener's blood. At the city of Kanya they have been entertained (I learn from one just arrived) with the melodious tones of big guns, sounding the 'Grand Jeu' of war, like a gentle subterranean instrument, some thirty fathoms beneath their feet and not as remote as Mafeking; they have listened to it, I am told, with cheerful hearts, for they just mistook it for what it was not: undoubtedly the enrapturing charm of this delectable music will give place to a most irritating discord when they have discovered that, so far from

it being the action of the modern Britisher's workshop going for the Dutch, it is the 'boom' of the State Artillerist giving us thunder and lightning with his guns.[5]

Plaatje delighted in constructing elaborate musical metaphors of the kind displayed in this passage, and they recur throughout the diary. So too does the rich vein of ironic humour, often self-mocking, evident in the story he had to tell a little later on in his entry for the same day:

After I left Mr Mahlelebe yesterday I came through the gaol yard onto the Railway Reserve's fence. Mauser bullets were just like hail on the main road to our village. I had just left the fence when one flew close to my cap with a 'ping' – giving me such a fright as caused me to sit down on the footpath. Someone behind me exclaimed that I was nearly killed and I looked round to see who my sympathiser was. When I did so another screeched through his legs with a 'whiz-z-z-z' and dropped between the two of us. I continued my journey in company with this man, during which I heard a screech and a tap behind my ear: it was a Mauser bullet and as there can be no question about a fellow's death when it enters his brain through the lobe, I knew at the moment that I had been transmitted from this temporary life on to eternity. I imagined I held a nickel bullet in my heart. That was merely the faculty of the soul recognising (in ordinary post-mortal dream) who occasioned its departure – for I was dead! Dead, to rise no more. A few seconds elapsed after I found myself scanning the bullet between my finger and thumb, to realise it was but a horsefly.[6]

The imminence of the hereafter in conditions of siege was a subject to which Plaatje – appreciating its potential source of humour – was to return later. He was particularly amused at the way in which both sides claimed divine justification for their cause. Thus his entry for 12 November 1899:

We spent this day in church. The pulpit was occupied by Mr Lefenya, who warned his hearers to be very careful in their prayers, and remember that their God was the enemy's God; we, however, have the scale in our favour as we have never raised our little finger in molestation of the Transvaal Government, or committed an act that could justify their looting our cattle and shooting our children in the manner they are doing.[7]

But as well as the humour there were often moments of gloom and despondency too, hardly surprising in view of the circumstances, particularly as time went on. The siege may not have produced – for the whites at least – the unendurable physical hardships that many outsiders were led to believe, but after a while the regular shelling and sniping began to take its toll on life, property and morale. Several of Plaatje's friends, black and white, were killed, as was his horse 'Whiskey' (the best horse in the *stadt*, he thought), victim of a direct hit upon the civil commissioner's stables on 6 February 1900: 'poor creature', Mr Bell commiserated, 'I was so sorry for him. He had not even murmured or done anything of the kind'.[8] And as the months of the siege dragged on with no immediate prospect of relief, Plaatje, like others in Mafeking, came to share the growing mood of pessimism. Like everyone else, he wondered what the imperial government was up to, why relief failed to materialise. 'I am inclined to believe,' he wrote on 3 January 1900,

> that the Boers have fully justified their bragging, for we are citizens of a town of subjects of the richest and the strongest empire on earth, and the Burghers of a small state have successfully besieged us for three months and we are not even able to tell how far off our relief is.[9]

By the middle of February 1900 the situation seemed even more serious. 'The Imperial Government,' Plaatje now complained,

> may be as good as we are told it is, but one thing certain is that [it] does not care a hang over the lives of its distant subjects. It is distressing to hear that Troops are still having a holiday at Modder River, even now after we had been besieged over four months.[10]

There were moments of loneliness for Plaatje as well, felt most keenly on traditional family occasions like Christmas. All things considered Christmas 1899 was not a happy time for him. As well as being separated from Elizabeth and St Leger he was confined to bed with a severe bout of influenza. 'I am not even graced with as little as a congratulatory missive from both of them,' he complained, 'but am nailed to a sick bed with very poor attention – worst of all, surrounded by Boers.'[11] The Christmas celebrations enjoyed by others served only to emphasise the pain of separation:

> Lady Sarah Wilson sent down a collection of toys and sweets for distribution amongst the children of our village. Contented little black faces musing over their gifts reminded me of a little fellow far away, who enjoys whatever he gets at the expense of the comfort of a bewildered young mother, deserving a Christmas box from his father but unable to get it. It squeezed out of my eyes a bitter tear – its course is bitter for I have never felt anything like it since the long and awful nights in 1897 when my path to the union that brought about his birth was so rocky.
> Surely Providence has seldom been so hard on me.[12]

Moments of loneliness such as these would have been very much more frequent had not Plaatje been kept extremely busy throughout the siege with his work, the result both of the extension of the range of his official duties as well as his keenness to take advantage of the other opportunities that came his way. His duties under Mr Bell expanded greatly at the beginning of the siege because the two European clerks, Geyer and Grayson, took up arms with the Town Guard, the civilian militia raised to defend the town, and he therefore took over many of their clerical and administrative responsibilities; and with the declaration of martial law, moreover, Plaatje found himself interpreting in the two new courts that were set up, the Court of Summary Jurisdiction and the Officer's Board Court. Working in the latter he particularly enjoyed, so he noted in his diary on

23 November 1899, because it 'transacts a lot of business in a very short time as evidence is taken by a shorthand writer, which causes one to extremely enjoy interpreting, as you have to fire away without stoppages'.[13] Ever ready to relish a challenge to his professional abilities, Plaatje was delighted also to get himself appointed as the Dutch interpreter to the Court of Summary Jurisdiction. Not that this had been the original intention of the authorities: a white man had first of all been appointed to this position, but 'he being incompetent in Dutch', Plaatje related with satisfaction, 'my services were secured'.[14] Amongst those who came before Plaatje in court, it is interesting to note, was Alfred Ngidi, the Mfengu railwayman whom Plaatje had taken to court before the siege. Now (January 1900) he was found guilty of falling asleep on sentry duty, for which misdemeanour he was duly dismissed; then he got seven days' hard labour after being found guilty of failing to hand over 'Kaffircorn' in line with the new rationing regulations. 'Hard luck on poor little Alfred,' Plaatje commented.[15]

◇

Court interpreting in siege conditions varied considerably from normal practice. Apart from interruptions from shelling (towards the end of the siege the courtroom sustained a direct hit from a Boer shell, fortunately when nobody was present), the conduct of court cases often departed radically from Plaatje's notion of what constituted proper courtroom procedure and decorum. Thus his amused description of one courtroom scene in December 1899:

> A lot of boys of the firm of Julius Weil are suing their employers for wages. Mr Spencer Minchin L.L.B., solicitor (now Lieutenant Minchin, Bechuana-land Rifles) appeared for all the plaintiffs, and Mr J. W. de Kock, attorney (now member of the Town Guard), appeared for the defence. It was a novel court: only the parties concerned looked as usual, but not the court. The plaintiffs' attorney was in military attire; lawyer for the defence, never shaved since the siege, all hairy and dressed in a third-hand suit without a collar, looked more like a farmer than an attorney. Myself in knickerbockers and without a jacket, looked more like a member of the football team or a village cyclist than a court interpreter. All the natives, but one, carried their cases.[16]

Punctuality, as well as decorum, also suffered during the siege. Plaatje was especially concerned about this when he himself proved to be at fault, as happened, for example, on 25 November 1899:

> The Summary Jurisdiction Courts are not as particular as our Divisional Courts about punctuality. Night before last I was warned to be at the office at 7.00 pm. I misunderstood the warning and went to the Courthouse until they sent for me half-an-hour later. Last night I was told to be at the office at 6.15. I misunderstood the time this time and turned up at 7.00. I thought that these warriors would pistol me as this was my second offence but they viewed the matter with total unconcernedness. This morning I turned up 10 minutes late. The shorthand writer was also fifteen minutes late. The Officers, finding me an irresolute, unreliable wobbler, engaged the services of a white man as the

witnesses and prisoners were principally Boers – but the fellow being an amateur interpreter was completely flabbergasted when it came to cross-examinations, and I took his place to immense advantage. This lateness appears to be a disease with which I am affected and I will see it does not occur again as I feel very uncomfortable in consequence.[17]

The contempt that Plaatje invests in the term 'amateur interpreter' could hardly have been more clearly expressed. But, as before the siege, he encountered some difficulty in securing full and proper renumeration for performing these additional duties. In January 1900 the following letter passed between Plaatje and Lord Edward Cecil, Baden-Powell's Chief Staff Officer and elder son of the English Prime Minister, Lord Salisbury.

> My lord,
>   I beg to apply for an appointment to the Courts of Summary Jurisdiction as an Interpreter. As a member of the said Court you will remember that, at its formation, the Staff Interpreter was called on to perform that duty: he being incompetent in Dutch my services were procured, and I have since been the 'unattached' Interpreter of the Courts. I have not previously drawn your attention to this fact for I hoped that you would in course of time remember me as in Colonial Courts Interpreters have the consideration of Heads of Department to a certain extent and are paid at the rate of 4/6 per hour if not permanently attached to the Court, and permanent Interpreters are paid at that rate 'extra', when they are engaged in other than criminal cases, besides their usual salary.
>   I hope your Lordship would remember that except during the week of my indisposition (last Christmas) I have never failed to act to the satisfaction of the Officers of the Court in that capacity; and also bear in mind that, although it would do me an amount of good, it will not hamper the Government in any way if you felt pleased to grant my request.
>   Your obedient servant,
>   Sol T. Plaatje[18]

That last flourish at the end of the letter was entirely characteristic, but on this occasion Plaatje had gone just a little too far. He was severely ticked off by Lord Edward for having presumed to write direct to the Chief Staff Officer, rather than to Mr Bell. In response, Plaatje felt obliged to write a suitably contrite letter of apology (which nevertheless contained a repetition of his request) to his more immediate superior:

> Sir,
>   With reference to the attached paper I beg to state that I exceedingly regret the irregularity and humbly request that you will overlook it and kindly have the matter fixed up satisfactorily. You might kindly mention to the Chief Staff Officer that, if he felt pleased to grant it, such appointment may only be stipulated to interpreting

during each session of the Summary Jurisdiction Courts and such other assistance as I am able to render the staff, without prejudice to my Civil duties, the same as I have been since the commencement of the siege.

Your obedient servant,
S. T. Plaatje[19]

On this occasion Bell, too, might have been somewhat irritated with Plaatje – with some justification, it should be said – at the way in which he had sought to go over his head to a higher authority, but he was far too aware of the value of Plaatje's assistance to him during the siege to make an issue of it (and was probably more amused by the exchange of correspondence than anything else since he took the trouble to preserve the letters amongst his personal papers). For in addition to fulfilling his normal duties Plaatje acted as the vitally important intermediary between the civil commissioner and the Barolong population of the *stadt*; he was responsible for organising, instructing and issuing passes to the 'Native Runners and Spies and those who went out to capture cattle';[20] and he then drew up reports from information taken from them when they returned from their expeditions across Boer lines. One such report which has survived, written in Plaatje's hand and dated 7 November 1899, was probably typical of many:

Morena,
20 Barolongs, under Paul, accompanied 80 troopers of the Protectorate Regiment during the small hours of the morning and went to about 400 yards from the laager down Molopo, from where they maximmed and musketted it. They nearly put down every tent and many of the Boers fled up Lothlakane. By that time a large number of them was returning from the Eastern Camp and our men retreated slowly with only one Trooper badly wounded. It was the wish of the Barolongs to go for no other purpose than capturing their cannon but the whites would not do that. They subsequently discovered that they could have found it very easy indeed if they prepared for it when they started. They were ably assisted by a '7 pounder' from the Refugees Camp. They consider the enemy's loss enormous.
Sol T. Plaatje[21]

Since Baden-Powell's local military intelligence was based almost wholly on reports such as these it would be difficult to exaggerate the importance of the part that Plaatje played in transmitting such information to him; and they conveyed, as Bell acknowledged, an accurate indication of 'what the Native meant', constituting a 'true record of what happened from a Native point of view'.[22] Later on in the siege Plaatje supplemented these reports with more general reports on 'the Native situation' – 'all the doings in connection with Native affairs',[23] as he described these reports in his diary when he started writing them at the beginning of February 1900. There was rather more than a grain of truth in a later observation of Plaatje's that the work he carried out on behalf of the authorities was 'so satisfactory that Mr Bell was created a CMG at the end of the siege'.[24]

Interestingly, several of Plaatje's reports were then published in the columns of the siege edition of the *Mafeking Mail* – anonymously, but evidently with Bell's knowledge and approval, and certainly with that of the press censor who vetted everything published in the paper.[25] They were probably the first writings of Plaatje's to have been published.

During the last few months of the siege Plaatje's range of official duties expanded still further when he found himself responsible, in February 1900, for assisting in arrangements for the departure of large numbers of the African population living within the lines of investment, Baden-Powell's method of resolving the increasingly acute food-shortage problem.[26] 'On horseback all day,' Plaatje wrote on 27 February 1900, 'gathering people together and arranging for their exodus tonight.'[27] A month later he was involved, with two others, in taking a census amongst those who remained. This was not something that the Barolong were very happy about, and many were reluctant to co-operate. In Plaatje's account of the difficulties he encountered there emerge some hints of the potential conflict which always existed between his identity as a Morolong on the one hand, and his role as a civil servant in the employ of the colonial government on the other:

> The people are vexing me exceedingly: one would ask me what I wished to do with the name of the owner of a place, another would object to a repetition of the census as they were counted (registered) twice already during the present siege. Another would say: 'No wonder the present, unlike all previous sieges of Mafeking, is so intolerable for the unfortunate beleaguered people are counted like sheep.' Another would stand at the door, empty herself of the whole of her stock of bad words, then threaten me to 'just touch my pen and jot down any numbers of her family'. The so-and-so![28]

In Plaatje's reaction here it is the voice of the harassed civil servant which comes over most strongly, and there were several other occasions when he felt similar feelings of exasperation in his dealings with his own people. On Sunday, 21 January 1900, for example, he had been called upon to interpret at a meeting with Chief Wessels in the *stadt*:

> This afternoon the Civil Commissioner held a meeting of the Barolongs in the Stadt. Reuter and London *Times* war correspondents were also there. Things went on very smoothly until Wessels commenced to speak. He threw a different complexion on the otherwise excellent harmony which characterised the commencement of the proceedings. He misunderstood, misconstrued and misinterpreted everything said and an undesirable scene ensued.
> I think he took serious exception to the suggestion by the Civil Commissioner that whoever desires to leave the place for the time being should be permitted to do so, as our supply of food is too limited. They both kept on talking, and scarcely gave each other a chance, each expecting me to translate his hot beans first. Whoever can interpret for Wessels correctly ought to consider himself a professor. Fancy having to either make an English speech, or to turn every word of the following half-sensible, broken Setswana parts of sentences and phrases, offered after peculiar intervals, into English:
> 'E' – 'ke a utlwa' – 'ke utlwa sentle' – 'jaka a bua' – 'ke re, morena' – 'a re . . .'

Every one of these sentences causes him to assume a more serious attitude. He will wave to and fro and occasionally change position and chair, or stand up to demonstrate his injured feelings. It is an excellent thing that the CC is so patient or else things could happen that would cause great joy in the Boer laager when they became known there.[29]

Here, Plaatje's sympathies lie very much with Mr Bell. On other occasions, though, Plaatje's criticisms were directed against the authorities themselves for their insensitive handling of relations with the Barolong – particularly the arrangements made for the restriction of grain sales (it was these which Alfred Ngidi had failed to observe): 'from a Serolong point of view', Plaatje thought, 'this whole jumble is more annoying than comforting. For this they may be excused, as the arrangement is in the hands of young officers who know as little about Natives and their mode of living as they know about the man on the moon and *his* mode of living.'[30] Plaatje must have been well aware of the delicacy of his position: he possessed loyalties to both his employers and to his own people, the Barolong, and on occasions such as these they threatened to come into conflict.

Plaatje's obligations to his employers, however, did not prevent him from engaging himself – presumably with Mr Bell's permission – in several other forms of employment, for he also offered his services to several of the war correspondents who had made their way to Mafeking before the siege began. One of those who took him on, after Plaatje had responded to his advertisement for a 'secretary amanuensis', was Vere Stent, the Reuters' correspondent. Over thirty years later Stent recalled the qualities and characteristics of the young man ('an educated native, very rare in those days') who presented himself:

One fine morning I became aware of a very smart, sprucely dressed young native standing to attention before me.
'Well?' said I.
'I hear you need a secretary-typist, sir,' he answered.
'Well, so I do. Is your master one?'
'I haven't a master,' said Plaatje, with a faint smile, 'but I write shorthand and can use the typewriter.' He spoke perfect English and I engaged him at a ridiculously low wage which he named himself and seemed glad enough to get ... I recognised, in my new secretary, an extraordinarily capable assistant. To begin with, he could spell – which I can't and never could. He was quick on the machine ... quick-witted and understanding and quick to pick up and catch a new expression, ask the meaning and derivation of it and add it to his vocabulary. As to what would now be called a liaison officer, between me and my little corps of native dispatch runners, he was invaluable and I find in my diary entries of substantial sums of money paid to him for distribution amongst them.[31]

As well as Vere Stent (who was to become a lifelong friend), Plaatje also worked for several of the other war correspondents, enabling him to 'keep pace with the hard times', as he described it, and to gain at the same time, one imagines, some insight into the world of journalism. He had particular reason to regret the tragic murder of E. G. Parslow, correspondent for the Daily Chronicle, after only three weeks of siege:

> Nothing happened during the day but in the evening my dear friend Mr E. G. Parslow was murdered by Lieut. Murchison – mentioned in the Official Publication yesterday. This murder has not only deprived me of a good friend but it has wrecked me financially. He paid for my little assistance so liberally that I never felt the prices of foodstuffs that [have] reigned here since the commencement of the Siege. The cause of the murder is incomprehensible; but then reasons are hardly tangible.[32]

◇

The entries in Plaatje's diary cease at the end of March 1900. Probably his main reason for not persevering with it was pressure of work, for he was by this time heavily involved in assisting Bell to organise the exodus of both Barolong and non-Barolong Africans from Mafeking, and in implementing the food-rationing arrangements for those who remained. It is also likely that Plaatje was as affected as everybody else by the general lowering of morale, and that in such circumstances he could no longer summon the physical or emotional energy to continue with a diary which he had been keeping, after all, for nearly six months;[33] perhaps, too, the effort involved in typing out Bell's diary, and in writing his regular reports on 'native affairs', simply made it seem less necessary to persist with his own private diary as well.

Amongst the Barolong there was now increasing hardship. Although Plaatje himself had complained in his diary on several occasions in a fairly light-hearted way about the size of his ('European') rations, some Africans in the albeit much reduced population of the *stadt* were by this time dying of starvation. Those of the non-Barolong refugees who remained were in an even worse state. Several days before his last entry Plaatje had this to say in his diary:

> I have not seen my Siege friends (the beggars) today. There were always scores of them every day at the Residency and they were relieved by the soup kitchen. They are made up of the blackish races of this continent – mostly Zulus and Zambesians. They venerate the Civil Commissioner and call me 'Ngwana's Molimo'. It is really pitiful to see one who was too unfortunate to hear soon enough that there was a Residency in Mafeking, and, being, too weak to work, never had a chance to steal anything during the last 6 days, and so had nothing to eat. Last month one died in the Civil Commissioner's yard. It was a miserable scene to be surrounded by about 50 hungry beings, agitating the engagement of your pity and to see one of them succumb to his agonies and fall backwards with a dead thud. Surely those Transvaal Boers are abominable.[34]

Such tragic scenes were not the only cause for despondency. At the beginning of April 1900 Colonel Plumer, in command of the part of Baden-Powell's regiment that had remained outside Mafeking, attempted to break through the lines of investment with a small force, but was repulsed by the Boers with the loss of a dozen men; relief seemed further away than ever. A week later there was further loss of life when a party of 25 Mfengu, out on a cattle-raiding expedition, were lured to their death by two Barolong 'guides' who had sided with the enemy.[35] Many of them Plaatje would have known well. April 1900 brought little cheer to those in Mafeking, black or white.

The siege finally came to an end in the middle of May 1900. Having been satisfied for the previous seven months simply to bottle up Baden-Powell's force inside the town, the Boers, aware of the progress of the long-expected relief column from the south, at last made an attempt to take Mafeking, and launched an attack through the Barolong stadt, passing very close to where Plaatje lived.[36] It did not succeed; Commandant Eloff, who led the assault, was captured; and two days later the besieging forces melted away as the relief column – led by a number of officers who had been involved in the Jameson Raid in 1895 – finally made its way into Mafeking. The welcome they received in the town was dwarfed by the enthusiasm with which news of the relief of Mafeking was greeted by the English-speaking world outside. Extraordinary scenes of national rejoicing were enacted throughout Britain and the British empire, and in due course a new word (maffick: to exult riotously) was added to the English language. Henceforth, Mafeking's seven-month siege made even the town's name a byword for the highest qualities of the British national character. Baden-Powell, instantly promoted to the rank of Lieutenant-General, became one of the most popular heroes of the day.

So ended the siege of Mafeking. As the town gradually got used to the idea of being in normal communication once again with the outside world, as work started to repair the damage it had suffered, as those of its inhabitants who had left the town before the siege began to return to their homes, Plaatje for one could look back upon the episode with every feeling of pride and satisfaction. There is no reason to believe he would not have identified himself fully with the sentiments expressed by Charles Bell as he typed out the final words of the civil commissioner's diary on the office typewriter: 'Although we have suffered many hardships and troubles, we nevertheless all feel proud to think that each individual, both European and Native, has done his utmost to maintain the honour of the British Empire.' Nor is there any reason to doubt that he enjoyed typing out Bell's words of acknowledgement (on the previous page) to his 'faithful interpreter, who shifted about with his typewriter, in order to meet the requirements of the big gun and the Mauser bullets, and varied his accuracy according to the activity of the Boer fire'.[37] For Plaatje had in many ways had a very good siege: he had been fortunate to have avoided injury – though like everybody else he had his collection of 'near miss' stories – and he seems to have suffered little real privation and hardship, thanks to the privileged position he occupied in the service of the government; he had made an invaluable contribution to the delicate business of mediating between the military authorities and the Barolong population in the *stadt*; he had responded with characteristic enthusiasm to the new challenges and responsibilities which had come his way; and he had gained valuable experience in drawing up reports on the 'native situation' for Mr Bell.

Above all he had written a remarkable literary document in the form of his private diary, one of the very few diaries of its kind to have been written by a black South African, and the first to have been published. Judged by any standards it stands head and shoulders above most of the other diaries kept during the siege of Mafeking. Many of its qualities are evident in the passages quoted earlier. It contains some delightful descriptive passages; it reveals a fluency and subtlety in conveying the nuances of its author's moods and feelings; and it is enlivened throughout by an imaginative exploration of the capacity of the English language to express the humour and ironies of life under siege, as perceived from a wholly novel perspective. The sheer quality of writing in the diary is all the more remarkable – although herein lies much of its freshness and originality – when one remembers that it was written by somebody for whom English was not the first nor even the second language he had learnt. Plaatje, it is fair to say, had come a very long way since that flawed performance in front of the members of the South Africans Improvement Society in Kimberley in July 1895.

Whether or not Plaatje told Charles Bell or anybody else in Mafeking about the diary he was writing is unknown. Quite possibly he did not, for he seems to have regarded it very much as a private document, and there is no evidence that he ever tried to get it published, either then or subsequently – though the thought must have occurred to him when a number of the other siege diaries duly appeared in print. Had Charles Bell been given the opportunity of reading it one conclusion would surely have struck him: that it was the product of a very talented individual destined to greater things in life than a career as a court interpreter. Given that its author was a black South African, however, it would not have been easy to say exactly what these greater things were likely to be in a society which provided so few opportunities for those who did not possess a white skin.

◇

Many of the Barolong, Plaatje included, were hopeful that the part they had played in defending Mafeking against the enemies of the British empire would bring them some tangible reward. In the immediate aftermath of the siege there were at least some encouraging signs which suggested they might not be disappointed. Compensation for injury and damage and loss of property was promised by the authorities, and there seemed no lack of official recognition of their contribution to the defence of the town. Charles Bell reported to his superiors that the Barolong had 'rendered invaluable services throughout the siege and defended their posts with energy and courage';[38] Lord Roberts, commander-in-chief of the British forces in South Africa, sent one of his senior officers, Sir Charles Parsons, to Mafeking to congratulate the Barolong leaders and people 'on the successful issue of their courageous defence of their homes and property against the invasion of the enemy';[39] and several months later there took place a moving ceremony – 'unprecedented in the annals of the history of the native tribes in this country', Bell thought – at which a framed address from Lord Roberts was presented to the Barolong chief, headmen and people.[40] For Plaatje, who interpreted at this ceremony, it must have gone some way towards making up for the rather less than gracious (and less than honest) attitude which Baden-Powell had displayed towards the contribution of the Barolong during the siege. Determined to maintain the fiction that it was 'a white man's war', Baden-Powell had neglected to mention in his general orders most of the operations in which the Barolong had been involved, and at the end of the siege he had repeatedly prohibited the *Mafeking Mail* from giving a true account of the vital part the Barolong had played in defeating the final Boer assault upon the town.[41] Black and white alike were critical of his heavy-handed misrepresentations, and Plaatje later went so far as to accuse Baden-Powell of 'coolly and deliberately lying' about the behaviour of the Barolong during the siege of Mafeking.[42]

But the official expressions of gratitude were not accompanied by any immediate material or political rewards. Some promises of land had been made during the siege in order to secure Barolong loyalty, and Plaatje, Silas Molema, and many others elsewhere were hopeful of some wider recognition for the African population generally in the new political dispensation for southern Africa which they looked forward to once the British had completed their victory over the Boer republics.[43] On this last point, however, some patience was certainly going to be needed, for at the end of May 1900 British victory lay two years in the future. For the moment, in the Mafeking district, martial law remained in operation, and the Boers still controlled large parts of the northern Cape.

In the office of the magistrate and civil commissioner, meanwhile, the staff set about tackling the administrative chaos caused by a seven months' siege. Within a month Bell was applying once more for additional clerical assistance, this time to enable him to cope with the extra work generated by two major new responsibilities: dealing with the numerous claims for compensation for losses and damage caused by enemy action, and collecting evidence and information about the activities of the 'suspected rebels', that is to say the Boer subjects of the Cape Colony who had fought with their compatriots from the Transvaal and Orange Free State against the imperial government, so that they could be brought to court and tried for high treason.[44] If anybody in the Mafeking magistrate's office had imagined there would be any let-up in the pressure of work once the siege had ended, such hopes were rapidly dispelled. Not all of them could take it: Ernest Grayson had suffered from 'insomnia' and 'nervous debility' during the last few months of the siege, and he was packed off to England for 'home leave' at the earliest opportunity.[45]

Plaatje's response was to apply himself with customary diligence to these new duties, and he wasted little time in putting in another request for an increase in salary. It was a carefully composed letter with a refined turn of phrase, reflecting perhaps the skills he had developed in his diary, and it must have afforded some amusement both to Charles Bell, to whom it was addressed, and then to the Attorney-General's Office in Cape Town to whom it was duly forwarded. Plaatje began by explaining how his plans to qualify himself for promotion by taking the civil service examinations had been upset by the outbreak of war, and how his studies were thereafter 'adversely affected' by 'the class of shelling we were subjected to for upwards of six months of the siege'. He then proceeded to demonstrate why £96 per annum was quite inadequate for the position he held:

I think it impossible from the very nature of things that a man, dressed in a cord suit of clothes, dwelling in a Native hut and living on mealies and Kafir corn could make a suitable person for the medium of speech, between a Magistrate and a community as we find locally; but I am sorry to say that this is the only mode of living that a man in receipt of my salary can manage to provide for himself and family, without the liability of falling into debts as is often the case.

Nothing can improve an employee much more than recognition of his services, on the part of the Head of his Department, by way of stern encouraging remarks and by way of increase of emoluments. My present salary is £96 per annum. I have been in receipt of this since the beginning of 1897, when I was still a bachelor, and engaged at more inferior duties, in a Post Office. I have now got to perform higher duties, on a better situation, to keep a wife and child as well as an old mother of 60 years at the same salary. This is almost an impossibility in Mafeking, unless one adopts a mode of living, which may render him objectionable to the sight and presence of his senior officers.

In one office in the Colony, we have an interpreter, very well known to me, who does not even know how to read (or much less translate) a Dutch letter, and who does nothing beyond barely interpreting in the Kafir and Sesutu languages, receiving £200 per annum: this ought to be an example that you would be quite within your rights to ask for a substantial increase for your Interpreter, who, besides being a faithful oral and documentary translator in the Dutch and Native languages, does the Office Typewriting and as much of Shorthand writing as is within the requirements of your Office.

To complete the presentation of his case, Plaatje then concluded his letter with a timely reminder of his contribution during the siege:

I have no doubt that up to the present, especially during the trying times we both had to undergo for upwards of six months of the siege, you are aware that I have always endeavoured my utmost to perform my duties to your satisfaction; that you will feel pleased to give my application a favourable recommendation; and I am sure it will be the best incentive to better zeal, in improving myself for duty, in future.[46]

Charles Bell was happy to give Plaatje's request a favourable recommendation (as indeed he ought to have been), and he commended him to the Law Department as 'a painstaking, hardworking man' and 'a thoroughly efficient interpreter' who 'rendered invaluable service during the late siege';[47] doubtless, too, he was more than a little impressed by the comprehensive lecture on how court interpreters ought to be treated by their employers – few requests for salary increases were quite as articulate or forthright as this. Plaatje was duly awarded an increase of an extra £12 a year from the beginning of July – not perhaps the 'substantial increase' he had in mind, but certainly better than nothing at all.[48]

Neither Charles Bell nor his successor, J. B. Moffat, who took his place as magistrate and civil commissioner in November 1900, can have been left in any doubt that their court interpreter was serious in his desire to 'improve himself'; for Plaatje was now preparing himself once again for the civil service examinations he had been prevented from taking the previous December. He intended to take the same papers as before (Dutch, German, Sesotho, Setswana, and Typewriting), and at the beginning of August 1900 he wrote off once again to register himself. In reply, the secretary of the Civil Service Commission had this to say:

> The Commissioners will be pleased to register you again for those subjects [Dutch, German, and Typewriting] at the next December examination upon receipt of your application any time before the end of next month.
>
> You may also take Sesuto and Sechuana if there should be any other candidates for examination in those two subjects, but the Commissioners cannot go to the expense of having papers prepared solely for one candidate.[49]

On the face of it this last ruling seemed rather unreasonable, but there was obviously little point in arguing. What Plaatje may well have done instead was to encourage his friends to apply so that he was no longer the only candidate. For a month later the secretary of the Civil Service Commission received a second application to take the Setswana paper – from Petrus Sidzumo, a brother of Plaatje's friend Patrick (the office messenger in the Mafeking magistrate's office), who occupied a similar position in Vryburg. If Plaatje had encouraged Petrus Sidzumo to register so as to enable him to sit the examination, the tactic was not successful. Sidzumo was informed by the Civil Service Commission that it would not be possible for him to take the paper 'unless there is a candidate for examination in that subject *who takes the whole of the ordinary Examination*' – that is to say, an external candidate applying for entry into the civil service (by this time almost exclusively whites) rather than an existing employee of the civil service seeking to improve his qualifications.[50] The grounds for refusing to register the two applicants for the paper in Setswana, in other words, had changed, a fact Plaatje would presumably have discovered had he compared notes with Sidzumo afterwards. One thing seems clear: the secretary of the Civil Service Commission was simply not willing to go to the trouble or expense of having a paper prepared in Setswana for the convenience of two African applicants, whatever the arguments used to justify this.

So Plaatje was obliged to concentrate his efforts instead on preparing himself for the papers in Dutch and Typewriting (he seems to have dropped the idea of taking the paper in German), and as the time approached he obtained two weeks' special leave of absence from the office to enable him to make the long trip down to Cape Town – his first visit to the city – to sit the examinations.[51] They were duly held, shortly before Christmas 1900, in the new Art School building in Queen Victoria Street, virtually opposite the Cape Parliament buildings.[52] There seems to have been only one other African candidate that year – one David Nqwana, who joined Plaatje in sitting the paper in Dutch. Nqwana also took the paper in Xhosa, his examiner in this being none other than Isaiah Bud-M'belle, who had recently been transferred temporarily to Cape Town.[53] It may well have been with him that Plaatje stayed during the week he spent in Cape Town.

What Plaatje made of the experience is unknown, and he left no record of his impressions of his first visit to Cape Town, or of the examinations he took. But he did have quite an eventful trip back home. He got as far as the railway junction of De Aar, some three hundred miles south of Mafeking, only to be stranded there for four days as a result of a second major Boer incursion into the Cape from across the Orange Free State border.[54] It was a reminder that the war was still far from over, and it contributed in large measure to the extension of martial law right across the colony. For Plaatje the more immediate consequence was that for the third Christmas in succession he found himself separated from Elizabeth and St Leger.

Plaatje was informed of the results of the two examination papers he had taken some weeks later: he had not only passed, but came top in both, heading the list of eight successful candidates in Dutch (these also included David Nqwana), and nine in Typewriting – all of whom, thought the examiner in Typewriting that year, were 'of a much higher class than he had seen before in the Civil Service'.[55] It was quite an achievement.

That, however, was not the end of the story: for when the results of these examinations were published in the government gazette several months later Plaatje was surprised, and obviously very disappointed, to see that his name was not printed at the head of each list. In the list of successful candidates in the Dutch paper he found himself in sixth place, sandwiched between David Nqwana and Robert Kidman; in Typewriting, a little higher up, in third place, between Albertina Centlivres and Alec Robb.[56] Since he had already been informed officially that he had come top of each he wrote at once to the Civil Service Commission to complain, expressing his 'considerable astonishment' at this discrepancy.[57] After all, anybody reading through the published list, seeing that the names were not listed in alphabetical order, would naturally assume that the successful candidates were being listed in order of merit; such was always the practice, indeed, with the entry examinations. Plaatje can hardly have been satisfied with the reply he received: 'the only explanation I can offer', said the secretary of the Civil Service Commission,

> is that in Special Subjects the names of successful candidates are not arranged in any order, nor does it appear necessary to so arrange them. The fact that a candidate has passed in any such subject seems to be sufficient to record, without reference to the position of any other candidate.[58]

Why this distinction between special subjects and the entry examination was made was not explained. One can appreciate why Plaatje was so upset.

So Plaatje was deprived of proper recognition of his achievement, and there was none of the publicity that had accompanied Isaiah Bud-M'belle's comparable performance in 1892. Coming on top of the Civil Service Commission's refusal to allow him to take the papers in Setswana and Sesotho, it would be surprising if it had not made Plaatje feel rather bitter at his treatment. He had been keen enough to want to take the examinations, to secure promotion in the Cape Civil Service, but had been first of all been rebuffed, and then had every reason to feel aggrieved that his achievement was not properly recognised. If the conclusion that one needed a white skin in order to get on in the Cape Civil Service had not previously suggested itself, then now was perhaps the time it did.

◇

Plaatje returned home from Cape Town to a bout of malaria and a great deal of work to get through in connection with the preparation of cases against the 'suspected rebels'. These duties often took him out and about in the district – one such trip to Setlagole being notable for a violent dust-storm which caused him to lose a couple of railway tickets.[59] In most of these cases Plaatje's most important task was to interpret what the Dutch-speaking 'suspected rebels' wished to communicate to the authorities when making their statements; many of them must have been surprised to find themselves dependent upon an African to make themselves understood to the British authorities – and perhaps wondered what such a state of affairs signified for the future political arrangements in southern Africa if the British won the war, as now looked certain. Plaatje was also kept busy in helping to process compensation claims, and his services as an interpreter were very much in demand with Colonel Vyvyan, commander of the British military forces still stationed in Mafeking, and the local Assistant Provost Marshal, in charge of transport – also now under military control.[60] On top of this, Plaatje had to translate letters and notices for them, and assisted in the issue of permits for railway travel; he succeeded, too, in obtaining some extra remuneration for himself, especially necessary, he argued, in view of the high prices for food and other commodities which wartime disruptions were causing.[61]

In other matters the continued presence of the British military forces in the district was rather less welcome. There were often differences between the military and civil authorities in Mafeking during this time, and there was a growing number of complaints from the *stadt* and the Mfengu location about the behaviour of British soldiers – particularly their treatment of African women.[62] Plaatje, too, had particular cause for complaint. Shortly after he had returned from Cape Town he submitted a claim for compensation to the military authorities for damage caused by cattle, owned by the military transport department, which had been allowed to stray onto the gardens around his house (the transport herds had 'replied to my remonstrances with abuse', Plaatje complained), damaging his crops – by no means the first occasion, he added, that this had happened.[63] His claim was unsuccessful: the officer in command of the ox transport department acknowledged that this might have taken place, as Plaatje claimed, but denied liability on the grounds that Plaatje's gardens were badly fenced; he did, however, agree to make arrangements for the cattle to be watered elsewhere in future – for Plaatje's home was close to the Molopo river, and the cattle had evidently trampled through his gardens on the way to it from the main road.[64]

At the beginning of the following month (the first day of April, as it happened) a case was brought before the magistrate's court, sitting in criminal rather than civil session, which probably owed something to the incident described above. The charge was one of criminal assault, and it was laid against 'Solomon T. Plaatje, Barolong Interpreter', accused as follows:

> that on the 19th day of March 1901 and at (or near) Mafeking Native Reserve, in the said District, Solomon T. Plaatje did wrongfully and unlawfully assault one Indalo, a native herd in the employ of the Imperial Government by knocking him to the ground, by tying him with reins, by kicking him while on the ground with his booted foot and by damaging his clothing and other wrongs and injuries to the said Indalo did then and there do.[65]

What truth there was in Indalo's allegations it is impossible to tell. No corroborating evidence was brought forward, it was obviously a question of Indalo's word against Plaatje's, and the case was quickly dismissed in court by William Geyer, the Assistant RM. In view of what had taken place the previous month though, and indeed prior to that, it would not be surprising if some form of altercation *had* taken place, or that it was occasioned by cattle being allowed, yet again, to trample all over Plaatje's gardens; only this time, knowing that he would not get any compensation, he resorted to rather more direct means of expressing his displeasure. Whether or not this version of events is correct, it was the first and last appearance Plaatje was to make as the accused in a court of criminal law.

◇

From the records kept by the magistrate's office in Mafeking for these years a fairly good impression of Plaatje's duties and activities at work can be formed. Of his life outside office hours far less is known. Family responsibilities were certainly one preoccupation, particularly so, one imagines, after the birth of his second son, Richard, in September 1901. But there were signs also of a growing degree of involvement in the affairs of the Barolong people, *his* people. For all Plaatje's education, his employment in government service, his European-sounding name, he was very much a part of this community. Admittedly he was not of Tshidi descent like most of those who lived in Mafeking, but he was of the respected *ba ga Modiboa* line and there was no doubt that he was a trueborn Morolong who clearly enjoyed the confidence and friendship of one of the leading Tshidi families.

In interesting himself in the affairs of the Barolong Plaatje was continuing a well-established tradition, for the Barolong chiefs and headmen had been accustomed for many years to making good use of the educated commoner in the interests of the community as a whole – as indeed had a number of other African communities. Prior to Plaatje's arrival in Mafeking in 1898 the person upon whom they relied, more than anybody else, was a man called Stephen Lefenya. Educated at the Wesleyan mission at Thaba Nchu in the 1850s, Lefenya had occupied the extremely influential position of tribal secretary for the Barolong for some forty years, and he had been well rewarded by Chief Montshiwa for his services. It had been he who was responsible for keeping the tribal records, for dealing with the paperwork generated by contact with the outside world, and for briefing lawyers to represent Barolong interests whenever the need arose.[66] But by the 1890s Lefenya was growing old, and less able to comprehend the world around him. The complexities of the legal and political structures imposed upon the Barolong in the 1890s seemed to suggest the need for somebody who was not only unquestionably loyal to the interests of the Barolong, as Lefenya had certainly been, but who possessed, in addition, the knowledge and expertise to guide them through the mass of laws and regulations which now confronted them. Who better for such a task than Plaatje? Silas Molema would not have been alone in believing that Plaatje, though still young in years, was the ideal person to be groomed for this advisory role, and this had almost certainly been in his mind when he recommended Plaatje for his job in the magistrate's office in Mafeking in the first place. Now, as then, the talents of his young protégé seemed all the more necessary in view of the continued weakness and incompetence of the current Paramount Chief, Wessels Montshiwa.

In part Plaatje's value to the Barolong stemmed from the privileged access he enjoyed to the local representative of the colonial government. Before the siege, to give one example, he was involved in approaching the authorities to try and secure an improved water supply locally; later he provided invaluable assistance in helping some of the Barolong to draw up compensation claims for damage inflicted during the siege (though he later took several of his 'clients' to court when they failed to pay him for the services thus rendered!).[67] More generally, he was in an ideal position to give guidance to the chief and headmen on how best to approach the many issues which arose in their relations with the local authorities, be they magisterial, military or municipal. Given Plaatje's official position, though, and his obligation of loyalty to his employers, it placed him in a somewhat delicate position, and he had to learn to be very careful about the path he negotiated, publicly and privately, between these two potentially conflicting loyalties.

Not that there was always this difficulty. Plaatje's employers could have had no objection to his involvement in organising the presentation, on behalf of the Barolong people, which was made to Benjamin Weil, the local storekeeper and contractor, on the eve of his departure for England in November 1901. Weil was presented by the Barolong chiefs, headmen and people with an elaborate silver shield which carried the following inscription:

Siege of Mafeking
1899–1900
Presented to
BENJAMIN B. WEIL ESQUIRE

Wessels, Chief of the Tribe of the Barolong, as an appreciation of never to be forgotten kindness shown to the Barolong Nation during the Siege of Mafeking and as a mark of respect and esteem on his leaving South Africa

Wessels, Chief
Saane, Balirile, Lekoko, Joshua Molema, Silas T. Molema, J. Motshegare, Headmen
Sol T. Plaatje, Hon. Sec.

To accompany the silver shield, Weil was also presented with an illuminated manuscript, painted in by hand, asking him to accept the shield 'as an appreciation both of your personal qualities, and of the valuable services which you rendered to us during the siege of Mafeking'. At the bottom stands the characteristically bold, confident signature of 'Sol T. Plaatje', obviously responsible for organising the whole affair in his capacity of 'Hon. Sec'. His signature stands in stark contrast to the simple cross made by Wessels, Paramount Chief of the Barolong (and two of his headmen who also could not write) in the space Plaatje had provided. It all seemed to sum up in strikingly visual form the importance of the young court interpreter in the affairs of the Barolong people – as well as providing testimony to the cordial relations existing between the Barolong and one of Mafeking's most prominent white citizens. Plaatje himself would not have forgotten Ben Weil's personal kindness to him during the siege, for on two occasions he had made arrangements for money to be paid to Elizabeth, via an intermediary, when Plaatje, worried that she was 'hard-up', had requested the favour.[68] Such things were not easily forgotten.

In the same month, November 1901, Plaatje was involved in another episode, also arising out of the siege, which in its way revealed as much about his character and beliefs as the presentation of the silver shield said about the part he now played in the affairs of the Barolong people. The episode revolved around the case of *R. v.Maritz and Lottering*, one of the so-called 'treason trials'. Plaatje was of course no stranger to these, having spent a great deal of his time since the siege in assisting the authorities in collecting information and evidence to enable the state to bring the 'rebels' to court. But in this particular case – heard in the Special Treason Court sitting in Mafeking between 6 and 9 November 1901 – Plaatje was called upon in a very different capacity: as witness for the defence.

The facts of the case can be briefly summarised: Maritz and Lottering, both of them citizens of the Cape Colony and hence British subjects, had joined the Boer forces surrounding Mafeking during the siege and taken up arms against the imperial government. The charge against them – which if proved carried the death penalty – was that they had cold-bloodedly murdered an African by the name of Monthusetsi, several miles outside Mafeking. They did not deny that this had happened. However, the case for the defence, ably conducted by Advocate Henry Burton, rested on the argument that in killing Monthusetsi, Maritz and Lottering were simply carrying out the orders given by General Snyman, then in command of the Boer forces surrounding the town, that all Africans leaving Mafeking were to be shot; that they had joined Snyman's forces, and were therefore subject to his orders and commands; and that Monthusetsi had come from Mafeking before meeting his death, was thus an enemy, and that Maritz and Lottering were therefore justified in killing him.

As the trial progressed it became clear that this last point, that Monthusetsi had actually come from Mafeking, which the defence had to prove, was going to be critical. For a while it looked as though the necessary evidence would not be forthcoming. Local feeling in Mafeking against the the two accused 'was very high at the time', Plaatje recalled, due to 'memories of incidents connected with the recent bombardment of the place during the siege'; as a result, 'loyalists were not disposed to assist the defence in finding a loophole'.[69] Local opinion in Mafeking, in other words, saw in this case the opportunity for judicial revenge for what had been inflicted upon the townspeople during seven long months of siege, and by the second day of the trial it began to look as though they would get it. Then Plaatje stepped forward as witness for the defence to make the dramatic statement that he not only knew Monthusetsi as somebody who had lived in the *stadt* in Mafeking, but that he had actually issued him with a pass to go out and raid cattle. The prosecution's case thus collapsed. 'At the last minute of the eleventh hour,' Plaatje remembered, 'Mr H. Burton personally made the discovery that I held the key to the solution of the fateful riddle.' His evidence, he said, 'outraged loyalist sentiment' and turned the case.[70] It was cited in the judge's summing up (he referred to Plaatje as 'a respectable coloured witness . . . about whose evidence there can be no shadow of doubt'), and the verdict (reached, said the judge, 'with the greatest reluctance') was that in killing Monthusetsi Maritz and Lottering had the protection of the law, and had therefore to be acquitted.[71] The accused were thus found not guilty, and were themselves left in no doubt as to whom they owed their lives; although still held in gaol on another charge, they managed to send through to Plaatje 'a verbal message of thanks' for having come forward in the way he did.[72]

If the whites in Mafeking were furious at being denied the opportunity for revenge, feeling amongst the black population was no less strong: it was, after all, one of their people who had been killed. Joseph Gape, a local farmer who lived in the Mafeking Reserve, and a man of some standing, was probably expressing widespread sentiment against Plaatje's decision to give evidence in the case when he wrote about what happened some time later. In his view, Plaatje's intervention amounted to a shameful betrayal of African interests, his evidence a gratuitous reward for 'a pair of the most rancorous Boers who cruelly murdered your countryman'. He went on:

> The three judges, the murderers' advocates and everybody else had given up hope and it only remained for the death sentence to be passed when, at nobody's invitation, you came forward and gave the most undesirable evidence which capsized the whole case, and the fiercest criminals were let loose.[73]

Joseph Gape was inclined to attribute Plaatje's action to a sentimental distaste for the death penalty: he recalled an incident during the siege when Plaatje had apparently sought unsuccessfully to save the life of an African convicted by the British authorities of spying for the Boers – an action that had earned from Charles Bell, so Gape claimed, the observation that all Plaatje had 'inherited from those German missionaries was their absurd benignity and nothing more'. But the treason case in November 1901 was not really comparable: whatever had happened during the siege, Plaatje came forward with his evidence at the trial of Maritz and Lottering not out of compassion for the predicament of the accused, but from the conviction that it was the duty of every responsible citizen to assist in the operation of the judicial process so as to enable justice to be done. He must have been well aware that the evidence he gave in this case was likely to make him extremely unpopular amongst his own people, and in the circumstances it was a courageous thing for him to do. But above all it was, in Plaatje's mind, the right thing to do. And in the long term he clearly believed his people had far more to gain from the protection of a judicial system that operated without fear or favour than one which could be swayed by pressure of public opinion. Nine times out of ten, as he would have known only too well, this was likely to operate to the detriment of the interests of his own people.

Plaatje did not have to wait long to see these views vindicated. Several days later another treason trial was heard in the same court: *R. v. Rinke, Burke, Bruwer, van Rooyen and Moolman*. The circumstances of this case were similar to *R. v.Maritz and Lottering*, but this time there were no grounds for arguing that the killing constituted an act of war, and the five accused were accordingly found guilty and sentenced to death. In passing sentence Judge Solomon, so it was reported in the *Mafeking Mail*, had this to say:

> They, the Court, were satisfied that the prisoners hunted these natives, as if they were wild beasts, and shot them down. It was probable that the prisoners did not at the time, and do not now realise, that in killing these unfortunate natives, the offence was as serious as if those they were killing were white men; but it is necessary that they, and those who think with them, should know that the law does not recognise a difference between white and black. A black man has just as much right to live as a white man.[74]

These words were to stay fresh in Plaatje's memory for the rest of his life: they remained, for him, the classic statement of the moral basis of the Cape's judicial system, and he was to reiterate them on a number of occasions.[75] Judgements such as these, it is clear, served to reinforce his belief and commitment to the Cape's judicial system, to emphasise the value of the rule of law as an instrument for the protection of the lives, the interests, the rights of his people.

◇

For Plaatje himself prospects of advancement within this system were very limited, and comments he made later make it clear that he was becoming increasingly frustrated with the position he occupied. Already, by the end of 1901, there were indications that he was thinking very seriously about a new and more challenging career: one that promised to provide greater scope for the expression of his talents and ambitions; that would enable him to use his abilities more directly in the service of the people amongst whom he lived, and at a time – with southern Africa looking to be on the eve of great political change as the war drew to a close – when they were likely to need individuals like him as never before. Such an opportunity, for Plaatje, presented itself in the form of a Tswana-language newspaper, *Koranta ea Becoana* ('The Bechuana Gazette'), which had appeared – at admittedly irregular intervals – since the end of April 1901.

The origins of this novel venture remain somewhat obscure, and it is by no means certain where the real initiative lay in getting it off the ground. G. N. H. Whales, editor of the *Mafeking Mail*, was definitely one of those involved. He had been editor of the *Mail* since August 1899, and he had made his name during the siege by keeping his paper going under such difficult conditions, and copies of its 'siege edition' were now eagerly sought by collectors. Once the siege had ended it was evident that Whales had no intention of sitting back on his laurels, and there were several new developments. Though still operating under the watchful eye of the press censor, from the beginning of September 1900 Whales published the *Mail* on a daily rather than on a weekly basis as had been the case hitherto; and two months later it was announced that he had acquired proprietary rights in the paper from the Vryburg firm of Townshend and Son, the owners of the *Bechuanaland News*, published in Vryburg, and several other small newspapers.[76]

It may well have been Whales' new financial responsibility for the newspaper he edited that prompted him to seek new ways of maximising revenue from sales and advertising. Whether it was his idea that this might be achieved by starting up a news sheet in Setswana, the language of most of the African population in and around Mafeking, or whether the idea was suggested to him by Silas Molema, or even by Plaatje himself, it is impossible to tell. What is certain, however, is that in its issues of 13 and 20 April 1901 the *Mafeking Mail* contained for the first time several columns of news – mostly about the war, and the details of a case in the local magistrate's court – written in Setswana; and that the following week, on 27 April 1901, there appeared the first number of a single-page news sheet, entitled *Koranta ea Becoana*, written entirely in Setswana, and selling for 3d a copy. According to information at the foot of the page, the news sheet was printed on the *Mafeking Mail*'s press and was both owned and edited by Whales. Whales, however, could neither speak nor read any Setswana, so the composition of the single page of news had obviously been undertaken by somebody else – probably Silas Molema, possibly assisted by Plaatje himself. As an employee of the government, though, Plaatje was explicitly prohibited by the terms of his employment ('Acts, Rules and Regulations of the Cape Civil Service', section III, clause 32, to be precise) from 'becoming editor of a newspaper, or taking any part in the management thereof';[77] any involvement on his part, therefore, had to be kept very quiet or he was liable to lose his job.

The first issue of *Koranta* introduced itself as the first Tswana-language paper to be produced by the Tswana themselves, but it did mention two earlier newspapers in Setswana produced by missionaries – *Mahoko a Becwana* ('News for the Bechuana') (printed by the London Missionary Society at Kuruman, which Plaatje used to read at the Pniel mission), and the more recent *Moshupa Tsela* ('The Guide'), produced by Lutheran missionaries of the Church of Sweden in the Transvaal. A further difference was that *Koranta* was to be a weekly; in this way, so it said, it could be of even greater value to the Tswana people, keeping them well up to date with current affairs, whether they were of the Bamangwato of the Bechuanaland Protectorate or the Seleka Barolong of the Orange River Colony. Every Tswana chief, so it urged, should do his best to popularise the paper among his people and inform them – in a metaphor that obviously reflected the perceptions of its originators – that the sun (enlightenment) had now risen amongst the Tswana people.[78]

After twelve somewhat undistinguished issues devoted largely to the progress of the war there was a significant change in the direction of the affairs of the little news sheet. By the terms of an agreement signed between Whales and Silas Molema on 5 September 1901, for a consideration of £25 Whales sold 'all his rights, title and interest' in *Koranta ea Becoana* to Silas Molema, who would thenceforth 'edit and be responsible for the same as from the next succeeding number to be published, to wit: No. 13'. At the same time, rates for printing were agreed (the initial circulation was to be 500 copies), Whales was to take 20 per cent of advertising revenue, and Molema agreed to indemnify Whales for any action for damages brought against him as a result of anything printed in the paper.[79] For Whales, such an arrangement was perhaps an easier way of making money than retaining personal responsibility – and liability – for the affairs of a paper he was unable to read. For Silas Molema, on the other hand, it offered new possibilities – not so much any great hope of financial gain, but rather an opportunity, through control of a new medium, to foster the education and progress of his people.

That Plaatje was by this time heavily involved behind the scenes is suggested by the survival of the draft of a letter about the proposed agreement with Whales, purported to have been written by Silas Molema, but actually in Plaatje's handwriting. The letter itself, undated but probably composed shortly before the agreement was signed with Whales in September 1901, outlined a programme of gradual expansion, culminating in a paper envisaged as being of about the same size as the *Mafeking Mail*, and with 'about 2 or 3 English columns like *Imvo*'. Meanwhile, said the letter, 'at the present there is only hard work to get Bechuanaland to know the paper'.[80] The mention of *Imvo* is clearly significant: Plaatje, like Molema, had long been impressed by the part *Imvo* and its editor, Tengo Jabavu, had played in the affairs of the Xhosa people. Nothing similar had yet been attempted amongst the Tswana beyond the several missionary-run journals. So *Koranta* in a way inherited a dual tradition: that of its Tswana-language missionary predecessors, mentioned in its first issue; and that exemplified by *Imvo*, the secular vehicle for the expression of African opinion which was now to provide the model for its future development.

Once under Silas Molema's control *Koranta ea Becoana* developed into a more ambitious publication. From the time of its first issue of 7 September 1901 it expanded to two pages, and for the first time began to carry advertisements, mostly inserted by local European dealers and traders in Mafeking, naturally keen to increase their business with a potentially lucrative African market. Over the next few months there was progress in other directions as well. Selling agents were appointed, and circulation began gradually to increase amongst Tswana-speaking people in the Cape, the Orange River Colony, the Bechuanaland Protectorate, and the Transvaal; even in Johannesburg, so one of its readers later recalled, 'it was almost marvellous to see how much the little sheet . . . was in demand out there'.[81] One important step towards financial viability was achieved with the securing of regular notices and advertisements from the various governmental authorities in the area in which *Koranta* now circulated. The Resident Commissioner for the Bechuanaland Protectorate, for example, saw no objection to meeting Silas Molema's request for government notices and advertisements; scribbled in the margin of a letter he wrote about the matter was the comment, 'I do not understand the paper but I presume it loyal and respectable.'[82] This was evidently a view shared by the other governmental authorities, and by issue no. 42, 22 March 1902, *Koranta* was able to announce that it had become 'the only authorised medium for publishing

Government Proclamations addressed to Natives by Colonial, Protectorate, and Imperial Military Authorities'. The regular income that such advertising provided was likely to be essential if *Koranta* was to survive and prosper.

Probably it was towards the end of 1901 that Molema and Plaatje between them took the decision to order a printing press of their own to enable them to develop the paper as they planned, and to escape the increasingly costly and irksome dependence upon the presses of the *Mafeking Mail*. The rates they were charging, Plaatje thought, were 'exorbitant', the printing was often late (up to three weeks, sometimes), and it was generally a 'horrid nuisance' being 'dependent upon somebody else for the issue of their paper'.[83] It was nevertheless a big step to take, and more than one person advised them – as Plaatje remembered – not to 'undertake anything so disastrous'.[84] The printing press and ancillary equipment suitable for their needs cost Molema (for it was he who financed the enterprise) something in the region of £1,000, quite apart from the money that had to be found for renting or purchasing a suitable building from which to operate.[85] There was then a frustrating delay before the press was actually delivered, and by February 1902 Silas Molema was writing to the local commandant in Mafeking asking that the existing weight restrictions on railway transport (the reason for the delay) could be waived so that the plant could be transported without further delay from Cape Town; it was, he pointed out, 'urgently required as the *Koranta ea Becoana* is the only channel through which the truth can be disseminated to the native population of Bechuanaland'.[86]

In all probability the words were Plaatje's: it was he who had typed out the letter, and the indent attached to the letter was in his hand. There could be little doubt now of the extent of Plaatje's involvement in the venture: already it must have been agreed that Plaatje was to edit the paper once the new press arrived. Quite possibly he had been the driving force in the project from the beginning. Such, at any rate, is the implication of a statement he made to a government commission in 1904: 'I just started it as an enterprise,' he explained, 'and one of the chiefs [i.e. Silas Molema] financed it.'[87] Even if this statement was something of a simplification of what had actually happened – quite understandable in the circumstances – it would be surprising if Plaatje had not been, from the beginning, a strong influence, at the very least, in persuading Molema to commit his resources to starting the newspaper.

At the beginning of April 1902, in anticipation of the arrival of the printing machinery from Cape Town, Plaatje and Molema signed a lease with Russell Paddon, a Mafeking storekeeper, for the hire of part of a building in Shippard Street to house the press and offices of the newspaper. In the document recording the agreement Molema and Plaatje are described as 'Proprietors and Publishers of the Koranta ea Becoana/Bechuana Gazette, Mafeking', but 'trading under the style or form of Silas Molema'; and the lease was for two years, commencing on 1 April 1902, the annual rent of £84 being payable in quarterly instalments.[88] A week before signing the document, on 27 March 1902, Plaatje handed in his notice of resignation from the Cape Civil Service, indicating his intention of leaving two months hence.[89] He was committed to a new career.

<>

Plaatje's letter of resignation would have come as little surprise to the magistrate and civil commissioner, now a man called E. Graham Green, who had replaced J. B. Moffat late in 1901. It was nevertheless a matter of considerable inconvenience to him since Plaatje had been performing a great deal of additional work in the office – 'duties of a delicate and responsible nature', Plaatje called them – fulfilling in effect the duties of second and third European clerks; the first being absent on sick leave, the second, a very recent arrival in the office, being wholly inexperienced.[90] During his last few months in the office, indeed, Plaatje managed to completely overhaul its system of record-keeping, obviously determined to end his eight years' service in the Cape Civil Service on a high note, and to leave a favourable impression upon Mr Green – a natural inclination, perhaps, but also a wise precaution from the point of view of *Koranta ea Becoana*'s future prospects. In the hazardous occupation of editing a newspaper Plaatje was likely to need all the friends and good will he could get, and in a small town like Mafeking the attitude of the local civil commissioner was going to be a factor of considerable significance. Certainly Green, like his predecessors, seems to have been pleased with the performance of his clerk and court interpreter, for his confidential report on Plaatje that year recorded 'good' on every count except punctuality, which was only 'fair'.[91] The difficulties Plaatje had encountered on this score during the siege had evidently not been put fully behind him.

Plaatje's ability as a court interpreter and his industry in the office were to be sorely missed. His replacement, Petrus Sidzumo, failed to measure up to his predecessor's high standards and after persistent complaints about bad interpreting in court from the town's two attorneys he was dismissed.[92] Green had high hopes of the man he found to replace him – Ezekiel Bud-M'belle, an elder brother of Isaiah and Elizabeth, but he too was dismissed after only a few months' service, having arrived at the office one day in an intoxicated state and 'quite incapable', Green said, 'of performing his duties'.[93] Court interpreters of Plaatje's ability and character were few and far between.

Whilst it is not difficult to see why Plaatje should have been so attracted by the prospect of a new career as a newspaper editor, exactly when such an ambition was formed in his mind it is impossible to tell. Possibly it was already there by the time he left Kimberley in 1898. Plaatje was by that time well aware of the influence that *Imvo* had built up among the African people generally, the Xhosa in particular, and its editor, John Tengo Jabavu, had visited Kimberley on several occasions whilst he was living there. Plaatje's decision to name his first son, St Leger, after a famous newspaperman, too, suggests, at the very least, a keen interest in the world of journalism, and this must have been further stimulated by the fortuitous contact he then had with the war correspondents in Mafeking during the siege. Later, he also recalled being influenced to 'leave the Cape Civil Service and try journalism' by Samuel Cronwright-Schreiner, whom he had known in Kimberley before the war; presumably the two men were still in touch with one another.[94] But once Plaatje became associated with Silas Molema's *Koranta ea Becoana* it was really only a matter of time and the right opportunity before he committed himself to this new career.

Plaatje's frustration with the Cape Civil Service of course pushed him in the same direction. The difficulties he encountered over the examinations in 1900 and their aftermath were an early indication of what lay ahead, and thereafter it seems he became more and more disenchanted with his treatment. He had served his employers well, but he did not believe that his skills were being properly rewarded or recognised: he wrote later that he thought the £130 per annum he was getting at the time he left was 'a waste of time', and he did not consider the status accorded to the position of court interpreter was at all commensurate to the responsibilities involved.[95] Prospects of promotion and advancement, moreover, now seemed negligible.

Almost certainly there were wider considerations as well. As an employee of the Cape Civil Service Plaatje must have become increasingly conscious of the difficulties of reconciling the loyalties he owed to his employers with his sense of responsibility for the leadership of his people, and he must have been aware of the unpleasantness involved in being party to unpopular acts or decisions on the part of the civil commissioner. From eight years' service to the government of the Cape Colony Plaatje had acquired a wide range of skills and much valuable experience; it was now time to leave and put these assets at the service of a wider cause. Private ambition and public sense of responsibility were at one in pointing him in the same direction.

5

Editor of *Koranta ea Becoana* 1902–5

Five days after Plaatje's resignation from the Cape Civil Service took effect the peace negotiations which had been taking place between representatives of the British imperial government and the Boer republics were finally concluded. To many, the war had appeared to be over nearly a year previously, but it had continued in the form of protracted guerrilla warfare as the Boer leaders held out for peace terms which would have fallen short of total surrender. In the end they were able to extract little in the way of concessions. Lord Milner, the British High Commissioner, was intent on a programme of reconstruction designed to ensure that southern Africa remained forever British and he was determined not to have his hands tied in any way by concessions in the peace treaty; despite the more conciliatory attitude of Lord Kitchener, the British military commander, he got his way. After three years of war, heavy casualties amongst combatants and civilians, and widespread devastation of large areas of the Transvaal and Orange Free State, peace finally returned to the subcontinent.

For many Africans – in the Cape as well as the Transvaal and Orange Free State – the terms of the Treaty of Vereeniging were intensely disappointing. Wartime propaganda had led many of them to expect some form of recognition at least of the political rights of Africans living in the conquered Boer republics, in line with what was already enjoyed in the Cape Colony, and the elevated claims made in the British press and elsewhere that the war was being fought in the interests of true Christianity and an imperial order based on equality before the law and 'equal rights for all civilised men'. Shortly after the war had broken out, for example, Lord Salisbury, the British Prime Minister, had declared: 'There must be no doubt . . . that due precaution will be taken for the kindly and improving treatment of those countless indigenous races of whose destiny I fear we have been too forgetful.'[1] Many other statements in a similar vein had been made, with varying degrees of sincerity. But Clause 8 of the Treaty of Vereeniging disappointed those who had hoped for an immediate improvement in political status: it provided that no decision would be taken on extending the franchise to Africans until after the introduction of responsible government in the former Boer republics. Then, as later, Lord Milner and the imperial government, despite the noble expressions of concern for the interests of the 'native races' which came out from time to time, were in no doubt that the question of extending political rights to Africans should not be allowed to stand in the way of reconciling Boers and English-speaking South Africans to the new imperial order that was to be created for southern Africa. The contribution of black South Africans to the war effort, in other words, was to be without tangible political reward.

In Mafeking, as elsewhere, the signing of the peace treaty was greeted with relief by black and white alike. The town's white business community looked forward to the re-establishment of normal trading relation with the Transvaal, and the Barolong community, too, welcomed the opportunity of being able to rebuild their stocks and herds after the succession of disasters, natural and man-made, of the last few years. The latest to have afflicted them was a well-planned raid by Boer forces from across the Transvaal border on the night of 12 January 1902. Knowing that the British authorities had refused to allow the Barolong to keep their arms after the siege, they had entered the *stadt* and carried off vast numbers of cattle and livestock, and caused a great deal of damage (including, it is interesting to note, £150 worth of loss or damage to the assets of *Koranta ea Becoana* – such, at any rate, was what was subsequently claimed in compensation).[2] The Barolong had been well aware of the danger, and had repeatedly requested permission to carry arms to defend themselves and their property. They were understandably exceedingly bitter when their predictions of a raid were borne out, and 'extremely indignant', as the magistrate reported, 'at the way in which the Boers were able to almost completely devastate the District without the least resistance'.[3] They lost more stock and suffered more damage, in fact, in that one night than during the entire seven months of siege.

Now that peace had come they were determined to secure full compensation, to secure, too, a rather juster measure of recompense than that which they had hitherto received for their losses in the siege. As the civil commissioner, Mr Green, pointed out to his superiors in Cape Town, with reference to the Boer raid, 'it would have been infinitely cheaper to have given out arms'.[4]

◇

Plaatje faced difficulties of a different nature. He had timed his resignation from the civil service to coincide with the expected time of arrival of the printing press that he and Molema had ordered so that he could assume the editorship of the new *Koranta ea Becoana* as soon as it was ready and set up in their new offices. But things did not work out as planned. The printing plant would have had to be ordered from England, and a further delay had then ensued while the necessary permission (in terms of martial law regulations) was obtained to transport it by rail. It took five days to get from Cape Town to Port Elizabeth by rail, but a further two months to travel the distance between Port Elizabeth and Mafeking. Having solicited subscriptions from subscribers and advertisers *Koranta*'s proprietors were understandably very frustrated at being unable to start their newspaper when they anticipated: 'the plant could not have been delayed much longer', so *Koranta* was to announce, 'had we inspanned our ox-waggon and personally went to fetch it'.[5] As it turned out there was to be a delay of four months between the last issue of the two-page Tswana-only version of *Koranta ea Becoana* and the appearance of the first edition from the new printing press.

In between there was one notable event: a performance, on the evening of 23 May 1902, of the Mafeking Philharmonic Society, which Plaatje himself had started up some time after arriving in Mafeking, obviously modelled closely upon the Philharmonic Society in which he had been involved in Kimberley before the war. Their concert was held in the Masonic Hall, Mafeking, and all the proceeds went to the Victoria Memorial Fund, recently set up by Africans in the eastern Cape to try and raise money for educational purposes. As one might have expected, most of the performers, apart from Plaatje himself, were of Mfengu or Xhosa origin. They included James Mpinda, who worked for *Koranta ea Becoana* as a compositor; Miss Linah Nyati, by all accounts the star of the evening with her rendering of 'The Orphan's Waif'; Mr J. K. Mokuena, of Sotho origin, shortly to disgrace himself by attempting to forge the local magistrate's cheque; and Miss E. E. Sampson, a daughter of the well known 'Teacher Sampson', who sang 'Barney O'Hea'.

Plaatje's own performance did not go unnoticed in the columns of the *Mafeking Mail*. He was commended for being 'indefatigable throughout the evening in "bossing up" the show', but in his duet with his wife Elizabeth he was reported to have gone 'shockingly flat'. Overall the evening seems to have been considered a success, the only real complaints being about the high admission prices – seats costs 4s and 6s, which was possibly the main reason for the slightly disappointing attendance. But at least Plaatje had not lost interest in musical matters, and he was evidently keen to recreate in Mafeking some of the more sophisticated forms of entertainment he had enjoyed in Kimberley.[6]

Much of Plaatje's time during the next few months was presumably taken up in making preparations for the launching of the new newspaper. Several offers of employment, he did later recall, were made to him at this time by people who must have heard he had resigned from the Cape Civil Service, but he turned them all down, and was struck, as well, by the low salaries being offered. For all his complaints about what he had been getting in the Mafeking magistrate's office, it was obvious, he wrote afterwards, 'that the Cape Government was not the worst offender in this connection'.[7] At last, early in August, the printing presses arrived and were speedily set up; all was now ready for the commencement of the paper and the opening of the printing works.

So it was against this background that there took place a dignified and well-attended ceremony in Main Street, Mafeking, at 11 o'clock on the morning of 16 August 1902, formally opening the Bechuana Printing Works, as they called themselves, and commemorating the publication of the first number of the enlarged *Koranta ea Becoana*, now in English as well as Setswana, and carrying the additional title of *Bechuana Gazette*. The interest of Mafeking's white community, by no means unappreciative of the advantages that advertising in the new paper could bring to their business amongst the African population, was evident in the presence at the ceremony of the mayor, the town clerk, the manager of the local branch of the Standard Bank (somewhat concerned, one imagines, at the damage the enterprise had done to Silas Molema's bank account), and other local notables (including, so *Koranta* was to report, 'a number of others we had not the pleasure of knowing'). It was unfortunate, however, that the Barolong Paramount Chief, Wessels Montshiwa, and most of his headmen, were unable to be present because they had a prior appointment with Ralph Williams, the Resident Commissioner for the Bechuanaland Protectorate, concerning a land dispute, and the Barolong were represented instead by Chief Lekoko. Whether or not Wessels and his headmen would have come if they had not had this prior engagement is a moot point, but in a way it was quite fitting that it should have been Lekoko who represented the Barolong. He was a friend of Silas Molema, a close ally in local Barolong political affairs, and very much identified with the Christian, 'progressive' section of the tribe: the people, in other words, who could be expected to support and identify with the new enterprise.

Mr E. Graham Green, the magistrate and civil commissioner, had consented to open the new plant, and in performing the ceremony he took the opportunity to say a few encouraging words:

Gentlemen, I have been requested by the Editor of the 'Koranta ea Becoana' to start the new machinery, by which it will in future be printed, with the additional name of 'Bechuanas' Gazette'. I do so with pleasure; and it is very gratifying to see how the Barolong are progressing in being able to publish and print their own paper. I should like those, however, connected with its publication to bear in mind that they have a powerful instrument in their hands, for in no way is the saying that 'the pen is mightier than the sword' more exemplified than in the publication of a newspaper (Applause).

The press, during the past three years, have been greatly responsible for the varied feelings that have moved various classes of the people (Hear, hear), and I do trust that this paper will be published in the interests of truth, justice and charity (Applause). Of truth, that its news may be reliable and verified, before publication; of justice, that it will see that the weak are not oppressed, and that the law is upheld; and of charity, that its personal criticism will be for the public benefit, and not to satisfy the personal feelings of the writer (Applause).

If these principles are upheld, then the paper will certainly be a benefit to the general public and the Natives in particular; and trusting such will be the case, and hoping that it will be successful in every way, I have great pleasure now in starting the paper on its new course (Applause).

Mr Green then started the machine, pulled off one copy and said: 'Gentlemen, this is the first copy of the first number of the 'Koranta ea Becoana and Bechuanas' Gazette.' He then read the English part . . . in a clear voice, occasionally which was punctuated by a hearty Hear, hear.[8]

Further words of congratulation and encouragement were uttered by the Reverends Weavind and Moshoela. Both expressed themselves well satisfied with the degree of progress amongst the Barolong that the launching of the new venture demonstrated. Weavind hoped that the paper would be 'a success from a literary point of view as well as financially', whilst it was left to Moshoela to express the hope that the paper 'would be of service to the Governments and people of this and of the Transvaal and Orange River Colonies, by explaining the laws to the Natives and maintaining a healthy feeling between them and the whites'. Nobody could argue with sentiments of this nature.

It was a unique and impressive opening ceremony which *Koranta* itself described, in its next issue, as 'a success beyond our anticipation', and the blessing of the local civil commissioner seemed to augur well for the future. The occasion was obviously an important moment, too, in Plaatje's life. Still only 25 years old, he now found himself occupying a position of considerable potential influence and importance in the affairs of his people, and with every prospect of making his reputation as a spokesman for them; he really could not have asked for a better opportunity for the exercise of his talents and the realisation of his ambitions.

In assuming the editorship of *Koranta ea Becoana* Plaatje joined the ranks of a select band of black pressmen in South Africa. So select, in fact, that there were at that time only two other black newspapers appearing on anything like a regular basis: A. K. Soga's *Izwi la Bantu*, printed in East London, written in English and Xhosa, and published since November 1897; and the *South African Spectator*, published in Cape Town, and edited by F. Z. S. Peregrino, a talented, if a little eccentric, West African journalist from the Gold Coast, who had lived in both England and America before making his way to South Africa in 1900. One famous name was missing: that of *Imvo Zabantsundu*, still edited by Tengo Jabavu, but closed down by the military censors in August 1901 for expressing allegedly disloyal sentiments. Although *Imvo* was to reappear in October 1902, it was a sad irony that the paper which more than any other had provided the inspiration for *Koranta ea Becoana* should have been suspended when *Koranta* first appeared with Plaatje as its editor.

The editors of these newspapers shared a common perception of their purpose in life: they were the 'mouthpiece' of the community they both served and represented, and they regarded it as their duty to provide in the columns of their newspapers a forum for the expression and formulation of 'native opinion', and the means of conveying aspirations and grievances to the authorities, while asserting at the same time their own claim to its leadership. Plaatje's perceptions of the role of his newspaper, as he was soon to make clear, were no different, and it was not long before *Koranta ea Becoana* was proclaiming its dedication to 'the amelioration of the Native', and its commitment to the four principles of 'Labour, Sobriety, Thrift and Education': all had been plainly evident in Plaatje's career to date.[9]

From the beginning Plaatje was assisted in the *Koranta* office by a permanent staff of at least three or four other people, all of them Africans; no whites, to the surprise of many who found it difficult to believe that the newspaper could be run without white assistance, were ever involved in running it. A year after *Koranta*'s inception its staff was known to have included James (Ramokoto) Plaatje, Plaatje's younger brother, who lived with the family in Mafeking; Isaiah Makgothi, a recent product of Lovedale, and a member of a well-known Seleka Barolong family from Thaba Nchu, who was one of the compositors; James Mpinda, one of the performers in the Philharmonic Society concert in May 1902, who had worked on the *Mafeking Mail* as well as the earlier *Koranta* news sheet; and another man by the name of Henry Mtotoba, described, like James Plaatje, as a 'labourer'.[10] One employee called Salatiele, working at the *Koranta* office when it was formally opened, had not lasted so long: a couple of weeks after this took place he was caught trying to cash a cheque upon which he had forged Silas Molema's signature, and was duly sentenced by the Circuit Court to ten months' imprisonment with hard labour.[11]

Exactly what part Silas Molema played in the day-to-day affairs of *Koranta ea Becoana* once Plaatje was installed as editor is unclear. His financial backing of course remained vital to the success of the venture, but in view of his many other commitments it is likely that he left the running of the office, and decisions over the content of each edition of the paper, to Plaatje: certainly when Plaatje was asked, several years later, who wrote the editorial matter in the paper, he said that he did all of this himself.[12]

The character of the newspaper itself became clear after only a few issues. It appeared at weekly intervals, was often printed on brightly coloured newsprint, carried articles and news in both English and Setswana (in roughly equal proportions), together with letters from readers and a substantial number of advertisements, and it sold at 3d a time. Usually there were eight pages, but this did later vary from time to time, and was eventually reduced to four when the page size was doubled. *Koranta* could be bought direct from the newspaper's office in Main Street, obtained on subscription, or purchased from one of the network of agents living in Tswana-speaking areas of the Cape Colony, the Bechuanaland Protectorate, the Transvaal and Orange River Colony (as the Orange Free State had been renamed by the British authorities).

Probably between one and two thousand copies of each issue of *Koranta* were printed.[13] The large towns of Johannesburg, Bloemfontein, Kimberley, the Seleka Barolong settlement at Thaba Nchu, and Mafeking itself, provided the most concentrated areas of readership, the vast majority of them Tswana-speakers, but there were individual subscribers, black and white, scattered all over South Africa. Several of the latter, indeed, wrote encouraging letters to Plaatje when they heard about the new newspaper, and these were then published in its early issues in August and September 1902. Samuel Cronwright-Schreiner, who had influenced Plaatje to leave the civil service in order to edit the paper in the first place, had further words of encouragement and congratulation, and advised Plaatje 'to get a clear grip of your policy and support it through thick and thin, strenuously, but not racially'. Vere Stent, with whom Plaatje seems to have remained in contact since the siege, also had some words of advice – together with a prediction: 'Steer clear of race hatred and beware of the Ethiopian Mission* which is preaching mischief. Don't abuse white people, and I am sure you will some day be a power amongst your people.'[14]

It was in the nature of these weekly African newspapers that they should reflect very clearly the personalities of their editors. *Koranta ea Becoana* was not an

---

* A form of African religious and political separatism, taking its name from the Ethiopian Church of South Africa, founded by Rev. M. Mokone in 1892.

exception to this general rule. Appearing with impressive regularity after its launching in August 1902, *Koranta* soon developed into a very professional publication, marked by an exuberance, humour and a sense of optimism which sprang directly from its editor. There was an assertiveness, too, equally characteristic of the man, which found expression in the biblical quotation from the Song of Solomon which Plaatje inserted in each issue of *Koranta* – it became, indeed, a kind of personal motto of his:

> I am black, but comely, O ye daughters of Jerusalem, as the tents of Kedar, and the curtains of Solomon.
>   Look not upon me because I am black for the sun hath looked down upon me; my mother's children were angry with me; they made me the keeper of the vineyards; but my own vineyard have I not kept.

Each issue of *Koranta* consisted of a varied mixture, in both English and Setswana, of letters from readers, reports from local correspondents (often the same people as the agents), extracts from the local and international press selected for their interest to an African readership, as well as editorial comment and original articles upon the issues of the day. Plaatje took his information about what was going on in the world from a wide variety of newspapers and periodicals with which he had entered into exchange arrangements; by 1904 these amounted to no less than 61, printed in eight different languages, arriving from other parts of Africa, Britain, America, and Europe, as well as all the main centres in southern Africa.[15]

Amongst the most interesting of these exchanges were the Afro-American newspapers from the United States of America. Plaatje's personal interest in the situation of black Americans, shared by many others in South Africa, black and white, probably dated from his days in Kimberley, but once he was editor of *Koranta* it was not long before he was giving prominence to reports upon the doings of leading black spokesmen and thinkers like Booker T. Washington, principal of the famous educational institution at Tuskegee, Alabama; later, indeed, Plaatje claimed credit for being the first black South African newspaper editor to do this.[16] One of these American exchange arrangements, with John Edward Bruce, editor of a Washington weekly, proved especially fruitful. Nearly twenty years later, Bruce remembered receiving a copy of *Koranta ea Becoana*, only the second copy of an African newspaper he had ever seen, and was struck by the 'virile and well written editorials, its snappy editorial notes and contributed articles which, though brief, were instructive and to the point', and 'then and there decided to get better acquainted with Africa and Africans'. So he wrote to Plaatje to thank him for putting him on his exchange list, 'and to tell him how well pleased I was with his newspaper'. Thus began what Bruce called 'a desultory correspondence' during which they came to know each other 'pretty tolerably well'.[17] None of this correspondence, unfortunately, has survived.

But what of those 'virile and well written editorials' which had so impressed J. E. Bruce? Essentially they fall into two categories: those which commented upon the issues of the day as they affected African interests locally or nationally, and those that offered what amounted to statements of editorial policy and principle. Of the latter, the most striking was the considered statement which appeared under the heading 'Equal Rights' in the third number of *Koranta ea Becoana*, issued on 13 September 1902, and repeated verbatim on several occasions thereafter:

> We do not hanker after social equality with the white man. If anyone tells you that we do so, he is a lunatic, and should be put in chains. We do not care for your parlour, nor is it our wish to lounge on couches in your drawing rooms. The renegade Kafir who desires to court and marry your daughter is a perfect danger to his race, for if his yearnings were realised we would be hurrying on the path to the inauguration of a generation of half-castes, and the total obliteration of our race and colour, both of which are very dear to us.
>
> For this reason we advise every black man to avoid social contact with whites, and the other races to keep strictly within their boundaries.
>
> All we claim is our just dues; we ask for our political recognition as loyal British subjects. We have not demonstrated our fealty to the throne for £.s.d., but we did it to assist in the maintenance of the open door we now ask for, so it cannot be said we demand too much.
>
> Under the Union Jack every person is his neighbour's equal. There are certain regulations for which one should qualify before his legal status is recognised as such: to this qualification race or colour is no bar, and we hope, in the near future, to be able to record that one's sex will no longer debar her from exercising a privilege hitherto enjoyed by the sterner sex only.
>
> Presently under the British Constitution every MAN so qualified is his neighbour's political equal, therefore anyone who argues to the contrary, or imagines himself the political superior of his fellow subject, is a rebel at heart.

It was a political creed which was to sustain *Koranta* throughout its existence, and Plaatje himself for many years afterwards; 'equal rights for all civilised men', equality of opportunity, equality before the law – all were the product of a set of beliefs formed in Plaatje's mind before he even came to Mafeking. But there was an awareness now of the salience of political considerations, of the importance of distinguishing such claims from the aspiration to social equality, which the majority of white men were apt to lump together as one and the same thing. Plaatje was anxious to ensure that the two things were not confused, well aware that during the last few years there had been a great deal of comment in the white press and elsewhere about the effect that the war had had upon African aspirations. For in the popular white imagination that war had had an unsettling effect upon 'the native mind', and any response to African demands for new political rights was met with the spectre of social equality and the question, 'Would you let a native marry your daughter?' Hence Plaatje's concern to disarm this line of argument in the way he does, to adopt the path of caution without compromising his underlying principles. Undoubtedly this strategy owed something to his knowledge of the ideas of Booker T. Washington.

But in the columns of *Koranta ea Becoana* Plaatje also saw himself fighting on another front. If his people were to be justified in their claim for 'equal rights for all civilised men' then they needed to meet the requirements of the second part of this formula; and Plaatje was never afraid to criticise his people in the strongest terms when he considered them guilty of failing to measure up to the recognised standards. A very critical article that he wrote in 1903 on the subject of 'Bogwera' (circumcision rites), recently revived among the more traditionally minded Barolong, was a case in point, and provides at the same time a fine example of his style of writing:

> In some pity we record that during this, the fourth month of the third year of the twentieth century, the Barolong have revived the ancient circumcision rites which had long since gone down beneath the silent power of Christian civilisation. Scores of young men have during the week been taken away from their profitable occupations into the veld to howl themselves hoarse and submit to severer flogging than is usually inflicted by the Judges of the Supreme Court. The fact that in the year A.D. 1903 the sons of Montshiwa can safely solemnise a custom, the uselessness of which was discerned by their father, and which the rest of Bechuanaland has for years relegated to the despicable relics of past barbarism, shows that someone has not been doing their duty. A startling state of affairs is that there are still to be found such a large number of youths who being accustomed to dress like Europeans, and live on three meals every day, and others who have again been living under luxurious circumstances behind shopkeepers' counters and in white men's kitchens, willingly surrender their contentment and volunteer to expose themselves to all kinds of weathers, in the open air, besides the thousands and one other tortures forming part of this ceremony, the nature of which ex-pupils of the weird hedonism are not permitted to tell us.[18]

So as editor of *Koranta* Plaatje saw himself with a two-fold task: to encourage the education and advancement of his people along 'progressive', Christian lines, and to fight, by strictly constitutional methods, with caution and moderation, for their just rights and fair treatment by the white authorities who exercised political power, to ensure that 'native opinion' became a factor to be taken into account in the political future of the country in which he lived.

<><>

Some idea of the influence exercised by *Koranta ea Becoana*'s young editor in the affairs of his people emerges from the part he played in what was to be the first major political campaign in which he was involved: the question of the proposed annexation of the Bechuanaland Protectorate and the Mafeking district of the Cape to the British colony of the Transvaal.

The demand for annexation originated late in 1902 with a group of white traders and businessmen in Mafeking, the product primarily of their dissatisfaction with the high rates of tariffs on goods moving between the two colonies, and their idea was to present a petition to Joseph Chamberlain, the British Colonial Secretary, on the occasion of his visit to Mafeking at the beginning of 1903 during his tour of southern Africa. In order to strengthen their case the originators of the scheme decided to try to enlist some African support, and they duly succeeded in getting some local African chiefs to sign their petition. Plaatje, as it happened, had been away from Mafeking for a few days when all this was done, and he was extremely disturbed to hear the news when he returned home; a great believer in the political and legal system of the Cape Colony, he was horrified at the implications (he said it was 'by far the most appalling information we have heard since the war broke out'), and wrote a strong editorial in the next issue of *Koranta*, pointing out the dangers, which he concluded as follows:

> In the face of the eighth clause of the final peace terms, this action on their [the chiefs'] part is nothing but a terrible leap in the dark and never was there a more flagrant case of wilful political suicide than there is in this movement; and we earnestly trust that for the sake of themselves the Chiefs will see to its early withdrawal before it is too late.[19]

Plaatje's editorial, combined with intensive personal lobbying, proved to be highly effective, and he was delighted to be able to make the following announcement in *Koranta* several weeks later:

> It is therefore with pleasure . . . that we are able to state that the Barolong Chiefs, who previously signed a petition in favour of Annexation, have discovered their mistake, as clearly explained to them in these columns, and they have withdrawn it in time for the arrival of Mr Chamberlain . . . Attempts have since been made to obtain the signatures of the Ratlou Chiefs and headmen in the further ends of the District. Acting on our advice these Chiefs have stoutly refused to associate themselves with the movement and it is right that this should be the case.[20]

Mafeking's whites were understandably somewhat disappointed at the sudden loss of support for their scheme, and Chief Badirile's letter of explanation to the *Mafeking Mail* on the subject must have come as little consolation to them. But at least they were left in little doubt about the influence their adversary now commanded locally. 'The older headmen of the tribe,' Badirile wrote,

> are a number of primitive men who know nothing about South African politics, which appear to be difficult to be understood by the white people themselves; and if anything affecting the welfare of the nation is under consideration we have enlightened men amongst ourselves whom we consult under such circumstances, and their counsel may be relied upon to be better than that of a solicitor, as their interests will also be at stake.[21]

Plaatje had good reason to be satisfied with this outcome. When Joseph Chamberlain did arrive in Mafeking he was presented with a petition requesting him to consider the question of annexation, but it carried no African support, it did not in any case find favour with the Cape colonial authorities, and the Colonial Secretary could safely ignore it; it was the end of the campaign.

The Barolong, however, had several points of their own which they wished to put to Joseph Chamberlain, and they were keen to take full advantage of the rare opportunity afforded by his visit. Plaatje, as one would expect, was heavily involved in the preparations for it. Mr Chamberlain had indicated in advance his willingness to receive a deputation from Barolong, and time had also been allowed in his programme for a visit to the *stadt*. In the circumstances it naturally fell to Plaatje ('as representing the Chief Wessels Montsioa and the Barolong tribe') to brief lawyers in Kimberley to draw up an elaborate petition which they intended to present to him, along with a decorated address of welcome.[22] Contained in the petition were effusive expressions of loyalty to the imperial government, reminders of the contribution of the Barolong during the siege of Mafeking, an affirmation of their wish *not* to become part of the Transvaal, and a request that several of their more pressing grievances be attended to: in particular, that some land around Polfontein, just over the border in the Transvaal, which they had been promised during the siege, should now be handed over; that the substantial war losses compensation which was still due to them should be paid immediately; and that there should be no variation whatever in the terms on which their partial autonomy was recognised when British Bechuanaland was annexed to the Cape in 1895.[23]

Chamberlain arrived in the *stadt* early in the afternoon of 28 January 1903, having spent nearly the whole of the morning in the company of the chiefs of the Bechuanaland Protectorate ('not a picturesque lot', Mrs Chamberlain thought), who had travelled to Mafeking for the purpose.[24] After his party was cheered all the way along the road into the *stadt*, proceedings were commenced by Chief Wessels Montshiwa reciting the address of welcome, which Plaatje then interpreted into English, and it was followed by further expressions of loyalty from Chief Lekoko. Then Mr Chamberlain rose to address the large gathering of Barolong, acknowledging the warm welcome extended to him and the loyal sentiments he had heard expressed. He was full of appreciation, he said, for the loyalty of the Barolong during the late war, and particularly for their behaviour during the siege; unfortunately, however, he could promise nothing on the question of Polfontein; he avoided comment on the compensation issue beyond saying he would look into it; but then gave what was taken as a firm commitment over the future protection of the rights the Barolong people currently enjoyed and recognised under the terms of their annexation to the Cape Colony, which gave them a measure of independence from the jurisdiction of the local municipal and divisional councils. 'I have the assurance of the Prime Minister of the Cape Colony' [Sir Gordon Sprigg, then sitting next to him on the platform], he declared, that these rights 'shall not be altered in the slightest respect.'[25] As Plaatje was to point out later, the assurance seemed doubly secure since it was delivered in the presence not only of the Cape Colony's Prime Minister, but also its Attorney-General and Governor, all of them up there on the platform with him.

Plaatje was delighted with the outcome of Joseph Chamberlain's visit to Mafeking. He had spent almost as much time in the company of Africans as Europeans, he had been persuaded to address the Barolong in their own surroundings in the *stadt*, one of the few occasions during his tour of southern Africa as a whole that he had been prepared to make such a gesture; and he had given an unambiguous public assurance on their future rights and status. Certainly the *Diamond Fields Advertiser* was in no doubt that the Barolong had scored a considerable political victory: on the question of their future status, it said, they had obtained 'the fullest assurances' from the mouth of His Majesty's Secretary of State for the Colonies, while the 'noble stand of the Barolong against the disruption of the Cape Colony, should provide Sir Gordon [Sprigg] with material for an epic'. 'From the Ministerial point of view,' concluded the *Advertiser*, 'they saved the situation.'[26] The notion of half the Cape administration applauding the Barolong to save their embarrassment at the attitude of the whites of Mafeking was one that would have appealed greatly to Plaatje; apart from a not unexpected response on the question of Polfontein and war compensation, things had worked out very well.

Ten days later Plaatje received a more personal memento of Chamberlain's visit to Mafeking: a signed testimonial stating that he had carried out the work of interpreting in the Barolong *stadt* that day 'in a very satisfactory manner'.[27] Plaatje was of course no stranger to high-ranking British military officers – he already had a testimonial from General Baden-Powell and one from Major Goold-Adams (now the Governor of the Orange River Colony) testifying to his valuable work during the siege – but it was not every day that one interpreted for a British Secretary of State for the Colonies. There was one final benefit that arose from his visit. Several weeks later Messrs Mallett and Bowen, the lawyers in Kimberley whom Plaatje had commissioned to draw up the documents to be presented to Mr Chamberlain, wrote to him to take out a subscription to *Koranta ea Becoana*.[28] Clearly they anticipated more business from the Barolong of Mafeking, and knew where they were likely to find it.

◇

During the months following Joseph Chamberlain's visit to Mafeking the war losses compensation question figured prominently in the columns of *Koranta ea Becoana*. Nothing came of his vague undertaking to look into things, and Plaatje wrote several strongly worded editorials complaining about the way in which the Barolong had been treated: the very least the government could do to show its appreciation of the contribution and sacrifices of the Barolong during the siege, he argued, would be to pay full and proper compensation for the losses they had sustained.[29] Plaatje had of course spent a lot of time when still employed in the magistrate's office in Mafeking in dealing with compensation claims; he was very familiar with the intricacies of the whole issue, and was determined not to let the matter drop until the Barolong obtained what was due to them.

Eventually it was decided to send a deputation to Cape Town to press their case in August 1903, when the whole subject was due to come up for discussion in the Cape House of Assembly. The deputation was composed of Chief Lekoko, Silas Molema, Badirile Montshiwa (shortly to succeed his father, Wessels Montshiwa, as Paramount Chief), and Plaatje himself. During the month they spent in Cape Town they enjoyed the hospitality and support of F. Z. S. Peregrino, editor of the *South African Spectator*. From his residence in Newlands they mounted an energetic lobbying campaign amongst politically sympathetic members of parliament. These included Henry Burton, now the member of parliament for Burghersdorp, who was especially critical of the treatment of the Barolong at the hands of the Compensation Commission; and Dr Jameson, well known to Silas Molema at least by virtue of their business arrangement of eight years previously. Although the deputation ultimately failed to achieve its main objective, the participants went about their task with skill and determination. They secured interviews with the Prime Minister and Attorney-General, enlisted the support and sympathy of the *Cape Argus*, and refused to be satisfied with vague promises to look into their grievances.[30] Even the *Mafeking Mail*, usually full of sarcasm when it came to the doings of the Barolong or the comments of *Koranta*, was impressed: 'they exhibited an astuteness', declared the *Mail*, 'that must have called forth admiration from the Premier', and it went on to express its own admiration for the way in which the deputation refused to be fobbed off with a promise by the Prime Minister that he would 'confer with his colleagues and see to it, etc. etc.'[31]

How much the deputation's 'astuteness' was due to Plaatje's guidance is impossible to tell: bearing in mind his recent record it was probably very considerable. The episode was certainly significant in providing valuable experience in developing his skills as a political lobbyist and negotiator at the highest levels of government; few black South Africans, indeed, were to become so skilled in dealing with white politicians. In a striking manner it marked, too, the distance he had come since he was last in Cape Town for those civil service examinations in December 1900, less than three years previosly. As the *Cape Argus* commented at the time, 'the young Barolong editor' of *Koranta ea Becoana* had 'made good use of his opportunities'.[32]

◇

In 1903 and 1904 Plaatje came to be noticeably more concerned with issues which went well beyond the interests of the people amongst whom he lived. From the time of *Koranta*'s inception Plaatje had displayed a keen concern for the rights and well-being of the African population of South Africa as a whole, and he emphasised time and time again that their loyalty during the recent war deserved proper recognition. He was constantly criticising the actions of government bodies of one kind and another, the utterances of illiberal white newspaper editors, the decisions of biased white juries, or commending – by way of contrast – sympathetic white missionaries prepared to make a stand for African rights, or judges prepared to uphold the ideal of equal rights before the law in the face of the pressures of white public opinion.

But during the course of 1903 and 1904 Plaatje's strictures came to be directed much more specifically against the policies and behaviour of the new British administrations of the Transvaal and Orange River Colony, for it was here that the contrast between the hopes engendered amongst Africans during the war, and the reality of its aftermath, was strongest. In the absence of any means of direct political representation for Africans living in these colonies, *Koranta* and its editor came to assume a particularly important role in drawing attention to their disabilities. Plaatje himself, indeed, spent an increasing amount of time travelling in these two colonies, observing conditions and campaigning personally on behalf of Africans who lived there over such issues as their treatment in the courts, on the railways, or the discriminatory practices condoned by the municipality of Bloemfontein and other bodies, often to very good effect.[33] But above all it was the British administration of the Transvaal, devoted as it was to the reconstruction of the colony in collaboration with the mineowners, which became the focus of Plaatje's criticisms. For Africans, one of

116

26 *Portrait of Plaatje taken around the turn of the century.*

27 *Diary of a siege: the first entry in Plaatje's diary, Sunday 29 October 1899.*

28 *The court of summary jurisdiction sentences an African 'spy' to death. Charles Bell and Lord Edward Cecil are sitting at the desk, Plaatje is standing alongside them. 'Myself in knickerbockers and without a jacket', Plaatje commented upon his appearance in another case during the siege, 'looked more like a member of the football team or a village cyclist than a court interpreter'.*

29 Siege administrators. Sitting, right to left: Frank Whiteley, mayor of Mafeking; Charles Bell, magistrate and civil commissioner; Captain Greener, chief paymaster. Plaatje is standing behind, between Bell and Greener.

30 War correspondents in front of their dugout during the siege of Mafeking. Left to right: J. E. Neilly (Pall Mall Gazette), Vere Stent (Reuters), Major F. D. Baillie (Morning Post), J. Angus Hamilton (The Times and Black and White).

31 The Mafeking Mail Special Siege Slip, 16 February 1900. The leading article ('Our Beef Providers') reproduces one of Plaatje's reports to Charles Bell about the exploits of Mathakgong, one of the unsung heroes of the siege.

32 G. N. H. Whales, editor and proprietor of the Mafeking Mail, seen here amidst the chaos in his office caused by a direct hit by a Boer shell. After the siege he published the first numbers of Koranta ea Becoana ('The Bechuanas' Gazette'), Mafeking's first Tswana-language newspaper.

33 Illuminated address presented by the Barolong to Ben Weil, one of Mafeking's leading traders, on the occasion of his departure to England in November 1901. Plaatje's signature can be seen clearly at the bottom.

34 The art school building in Queen Victoria St, Cape Town, where Plaatje sat his civil service examinations in December 1900. He took the papers in Dutch and Typewriting, and came top in both.

35 *The staff of* Koranta ea Becoana. *This photograph was probably taken soon after the opening of the Bechuana Printing Works in Mafeking in August 1902. Plaatje is sitting centre left; Silas Molema (holding a piece of paper) is sitting front right.*

36 *The front page of the first number of* Koranta ea Becoana *to be printed at the Bechuana Printing Works, Mafeking, 16 August 1902. Plaatje was its editor.*

Formulators of 'native opinion'—two of Plaatje's fellow newspapermen. **37** *(left) A. K. Soga, editor of* Izwi la Bantu *('Voice of the People'), published in East London from 1897 to 1909.* **38** *(right) F. Z. S. Peregrino, originally from the Gold Coast, editor of the* South African Spectator, *published in Cape Town from 1900.*

the worst features of this administration was the pass law, now being enforced more vigorously than it ever had been during the days of the South African Republic. 'The benefit of the Pass Law,' Plaatje argued in one editorial,

> is that thousands of useful unoffending black men, than whom His Majesty has no more law abiding subjects, are daily sent to prison, without having done harm to anybody, and they die as regular gaol-birds even though they had never, during their lifetime, dipped the tips of their fingers in the cup of criminality. It is revolting to anyone who comes from districts like Mafeking, for instance, where the jailor has no such snare and where revenue is raised by honest and lawful means. The writer met an inhabitant of this place in Johannesburg last month, who looked at one of the 'blessings' of the Pass Law, and said: 'Well, if this is British, then our colony is certainly not.' Here, no such horrors are licenced, and in no spot on earth do whites and blacks live as peacefully as they do in Mafeking. And we are sure that if there is any Native unrest in existence it is the outcome of the callous and oppressive administration of the Pass Law.[34]

Criticism of the arbitrary behaviour of Native Commissioners and sub-Commissioners in the Transvaal also came to fill *Koranta*'s columns in 1903 and 1904. Plaatje published a number of letters of complaint from those who had suffered at their hands, and he devoted several editorials to the subject. 'All the Natives who write to us from the Pietersburg district,' *Koranta* said in April 1904,

> unanimously declare that they were far better off under the Field Cornets of the late Government than what they are under the sub-Native Commissioners, as we are sure that never was the name of her late Gracious Majesty, Victoria, dragged in the mire like now, when the cruelty of those officials drives it into the minds of the black people, who lost their life and property to establish British rule in their country, that her reign is worse than Krugerism.[35]

Plaatje was only one of many to be sadly disillusioned with the reality of the British regimes in the two conquered Boer republics. There were other incidents which he witnessed which only reinforced his views:

> I was in Johannesburg in the winter of 1904 when the Rand Municipality cleared the Natives to Nancefield, 12 miles away. I saw the misery and hardships which attended the enforcement of the measure, and heard Native viragoes loudly lamenting the fall of Kruger and cursing the new administration, which they termed 'remorseless tyrants' (*batana li-sitlhogo*, lit: 'cruel beasts of prey').[36]

In one institution, though, Plaatje retained confidence – the courts of law. Intimately familiar as he was with the legal system, his response to nearly every instance of injustice he encountered or exposed was to advise those concerned to turn to the law to seek redress of their grievances; nobody, indeed, had a keener eye for the contradictions between the theory and practice of British rule in the new colonies, and the possibilities that lay in the gap in between. For many Africans, of course, the financial obstacles to recourse to the law were too strong a deterrent for them even to contemplate action of this kind, but on occasions it did prove successful. One case in which Plaatje was closely involved concerned the rights of African residents of the Transvaal to purchase land in their own name. Until 1904 this had been prohibited by Native Commissioners on the grounds that the laws of the Boer Republics had prohibited it, and that the law in question had not been repealed. Plaatje, however, had not been convinced; he 'searched the Transvaal Law Book from cover to cover, but failed to find in it a single ordinance prohibiting the sale of land to Natives', and decided to take up the case. The opportunity arose in the refusal of the local Native Commissioner for the Johannesburg district to allow prospective standholders in the new Kensington Township to acquire proper legal title for the plots of land which they had already paid for. 'Acting on our advice,' *Koranta* stated in its issue of 13 April 1904, the majority of them refused to be intimidated by the 'written word of a snow-white Government official that the laws of the country were against us', and Paulus Malaji, Chairman of the Basuto Association in Johannesburg, made a test case of it.[37] It was some months before the case was heard in court, but the decision, when it came, was in their favour. The letter Plaatje received from the solicitors who were involved, informing him of the decision, was, he said, 'the best letter that ever reached us by the Johannesburg mail since the declaration of peace'. Several weeks later one of *Koranta*'s readers composed a praise poem to celebrate the victory.[38]

Within a couple of years of taking over the editorship of *Koranta ea Becoana* Plaatje had built up a reputation as an influential journalist and the spokesman for a far wider body of people than was once the case. If at one time Plaatje had been considered as a representative of the Barolong – and he would always be regarded as their special spokesman – now he was coming to be accepted not only as one who spoke for Tswana-speaking Africans in the various colonies of South Africa in which they lived, but as a man who could now claim a political constituency, and readership for his paper, which extended beyond this.

Several factors had contributed to making this possible: the sense of common grievance engendered amongst Africans by their treatment by the post-war 'reconstruction' administrations in the Transvaal and Orange River Colony; the widespread geographical distribution of *Koranta*'s readership, composed as it was of people living under four different colonial administrations, often living alongside Africans of other ethnic or language groups with whom they now shared a wider interest; above all, perhaps, Plaatje's own attitudes and outlook, founded as they were upon a set of universalist values and beliefs. If one believed in the notions of equal opportunity for all subjects of the British empire, or equality before the law, as Plaatje so often stated in his editorials, then it followed that these had to apply to everybody, Tswana-speakers or not. All these factors combined to ensure that, politically speaking, Plaatje never became a prisoner either of the relatively privileged circumstances of the Cape Colony or of too exclusive an association with the interests of the Barolong, or even the

Tswana-speaking, people. Plaatje's horizons extended well beyond both the *stadt* in Mafeking and the intricacies of Cape electoral politics with which he had grown so familiar in the 1890s.

For these same reasons Plaatje was also very well placed to take the initiative in establishing, late in 1903, a Native Press Association to try to advance the degree of unity and common purpose amongst the African press as a whole. Part of the impetus for this was undoubtedly provided by the fact that, since *Koranta*'s inception in 1902, there had been several new additions to their ranks. In April 1903 the Reverend John Dube, a Zulu, had founded *Ilanga lase Natal* ('The Natal Sun'), published in Ohlange, Natal; in Pietersburg, in the northern Transvaal, Levi Khomo, like Plaatje a former interpreter, now edited *Leihlo lo Babatsho* ('The Native Eye')–the only paper amongst all his exchanges, Plaatje remembered, which he could not fully understand (most of it was written in Sepedi); and in Pietermaritzburg, Natal, *Ipepa lo Hlanga* ('The Paper of the Nation'), closed down in 1901, was now being published once again.[39]

Despite their dispersal in the different colonies and regions of South Africa, and their often considerable political differences, these newspaper editors shared an identifiable sense of common purpose. They all faced the same financial problems, they often addressed themselves to the same issues, they exchanged copies with each other, quoted each other's opinions, rejoiced in their triumphs, sympathised with each others' difficulties. Perhaps above all they were united in a desire to develop and give expression to the idea of 'native opinion', at a time in the affairs of the subcontinent when this seemed a particularly important and worthwhile thing to be doing. Late in 1903 Plaatje, together, it seems, with F. Z. S. Peregrino of the *South African Spectator* (his host, of course, on the Barolong war compensation mission to Cape Town that August), took the initiative in proposing that a Native Press Association he formed to develop and give some institutional form to this existing sense of community.[40] Where the idea came from is uncertain; quite possibly the Association was modelled upon the Negro Press Association in the United States, which Plaatje may have heard about from J. E. Bruce, or one or other of the exchange newspapers he received from the United States. The South African Native Press Association, at any rate, came into existence. Its purpose, so Plaatje said, 'was to improve the press of the Natives generally'. Several meetings were convened, and Plaatje himself, still by far the youngest of these African newspapermen, became its first secretary.[41]

The subsequent history of the South African Native Press Association is obscure; it was in existence a year later, in October 1904, but probably ceased functioning effectively some time during the following year. Its demise was perhaps predictable enough. Political unity remained an elusive goal, and it was certainly no easy task to overcome the practical and financial difficulties of running an organisation representing newspapers from so wide an area. Most of them, in any case, had more than enough financial problems of their own, *Koranta* included. It is nevertheless revealing that it should have been Plaatje who took the initiative in setting up the association, and that his fellow editors should have been ready to accept him in taking such a leading role in its affairs. In several respects the Native Press Association, premature at the time, was a portent of things to come.

Nowhere were the difficulties faced by 'native opinion' greater than in the reaction Plaatje and his colleagues encountered in the white press. Here there was very little sense of community or common purpose whatever. In the eyes of many white newspaper editors in South Africa, particularly outside the Cape, the African newspapermen could generally be lumped together as jumped-up, semi-educated barbarians who ought to know better than express views on current affairs or criticise their superiors. The African newspapermen, for their part, were well able to cope with the disapproval of the white press and a hostile climate of opinion generally, and Plaatje in particular delighted in doing battle with his white contemporaries in the columns of *Koranta ea Becoana*. The Bloemfontein *Friend* – Plaatje christened it 'The Foe' – was a frequent adversary, and its editor not a man accustomed to restraint when commenting upon what he read in African newspapers. The following torrent of abuse, sparked off by several articles complaining of unfair discrimination which had appeared in recent issues of *Koranta*, was typical:

> Now, I hope I have shown these people who will persist in teaching natives what the result is. They decline to accept the fact that they cannot be placed on the same footing with the white man, and it is coming to a nice pass when they refer to white men as 'fellows' and themselves as 'ladies' and 'gentlemen'. Now that the war is over, and the necessity for officers and privates of the British Army chumming with niggers, and – I regret to say – negresses, has passed, it is time for us to bring the native back to the status he was placed in before the war. The first step in that direction would be the suppression of all the nigger papers, for they are spreading a propaganda throughout the country which is the cause of all the trouble in the native question, i.e. the fact that the native is equal to the white man. I am not in favour of slavery, but I think the time has come to place a firm hand on the native and put him in his place, and keep him there.[42]

Such was the climate of opinion in at least some parts of post-war South Africa in which papers like *Koranta ea Becoana* had to operate. Plaatje's response to 'The Foe' on this occasion was rather more dignified: 'Woe betide this country,' he concluded in reply, 'if the farming colonist would be misled by the drift of mischievous penmanship, which is strictly guided by pernicious designs, the outcome of prejudice and misrepresentation.'[43]

The Bloemfontein *Friend* was perhaps the most intemperate of *Koranta*'s opponents (at least until there was a change of ownership late in 1903), but it was by no means alone in taking *Koranta*'s editor to task for exceeding his supposed station in life. The *Natal Witness*, for example, took exception to Plaatje's articles on 'the alleged harsh treatment of natives', accusing both Plaatje and Tengo Jabavu, editor of *Imvo*, of ingratitude towards the British, 'the race to which they and theirs owe everything, and which has fostered, to an almost continental extent, progress among the natives of the sub-continent'.[44] Closer to home was the *Mafeking Mail*. Despite its initial connection with *Koranta*, the *Mail*'s occasional references to the pronouncements of its local contemporary generally varied from the caustic to the sarcastic, and sometimes descended to outright abuse. On one occasion it went further, describing an article Plaatje had carried in *Koranta* on the administration of the Transvaal and Orange Free State as 'seditious', and it quoted with approval some strong comments from one of the Johannesburg papers:

Disloyalty, now-a-days, is the refuge of the ignorant. It has sunk down to the level of a Kaffir pastime. The editor of the Mafeking Kaffir newspaper, 'Koranta ea Becoana', is a studious person who used to interpret at the Magistrate's Court. He got into the habit of thinking during the course of his duties, and a lot of stored up, compressed thought drove him into journalism as an outlet for it. Thinking, however, is a bad thing to get into late in life, if you haven't been used to it before. One is apt to get a wrong perspective, and when he complains of British rule it is an evidence of it.[45]

The *Mail*'s solution to the problem? 'It would be merciful if a little of the cat o'nine tails were applied now.'

Occasionally the white press was more complimentary. Such was the case with the Dutch language newspapers in response to Plaatje's recommendation in an editorial for a reprieve from the death sentence which had been passed on two Boers found guilty of murder by the Griqualand West High Court late in 1902. The case was similar to the one at which Plaatje had given evidence a year earlier, but on this occasion the judge had interpreted the law differently, found the two men guilty and sentenced them to death. Plaatje's view was that in the light of the precedent that had been set the two condemned men were 'strongly entitled to a reprieve', and said so in forthright terms in an editorial in *Koranta*. He thereby earned some favourable comment in the Dutch-language press in the Cape, but predictably, the disapproval of a number of his African readers whose reaction was the same as that of Joseph Gape the previous year.[46] Again, though, Plaatje was not afraid to take an independent line even if it was likely to make him unpopular with many of his own people. Both condemned men were, in any case, duly reprieved.

◇

From the official authorities in the colonies in which *Koranta* circulated the response was generally much less hostile than that encountered in the white press, even though Plaatje did not hesitate to criticise their actions in strong terms when he felt this was necessary. In Mafeking Plaatje continued to enjoy a good relationship with the civil commissioner, Mr E. Graham Green; it was on his recommendation that Plaatje received regular orders for carrying government notices and proclamations in the columns of *Koranta*, and it was thanks to him that he got a useful government contract in 1904 to print 10,000 copies of a Tswana-language pamphlet explaining the purpose of the census that year – valued by Plaatje not simply for the revenue it brought in, but because it was implicit recognition of that intermediary role between government and people which all the African newspapermen sought to fulfil.[47]

Plaatje provided the Cape authorities with a copy of each issue of his newspaper, and they seem to have been read carefully. When the South African Native Affairs Commission, set up to investigate the possibility of devising a common 'native policy' for South Africa, visited Mafeking to take evidence in September 1904, its members made it clear that they were familiar with several of his articles – on the treatment of Africans on the mines, and 'Ethiopianism' – and he was questioned further about what he had written.[48] From time to time, too, Plaatje would send copies of particular articles to the authorities for special consideration – one of them, indeed, a critical article by 'A Native' on the composition of the above commission. Another was on the treatment of Africans on the railways.[49] In response to the latter Plaatje duly received a comprehensive reply from E. Graham Green (instructed by the Secretary for Native Affairs in Cape Town), advising him that 'exhaustive enquiries have been made into the matter represented by you', and that steps had already been taken to prevent a recurrence of the instances of ill-treatment (about which there had been other complaints).[50] In short, the Cape authorities – and this was true of those of the Transvaal and Orange River Colony as well – were prepared to take seriously anything he brought to their attention, and to treat him with consideration and courtesy. It was a very different attitude from that displayed by the white press or white public opinion in general.

On only one occasion during these years was this generally quite cordial relationship threatened. It happened when a letter from Segale, a Tswana chief living in the Transvaal, complaining about British rule in somewhat stronger terms than usual, was published in *Koranta* in August 1903. The authorities took strong exception to the 'disloyal' sentiments expressed, but it turned out that the letter had been published when Plaatje himself was away in Cape Town on the Barolong compensation mission, and they were quite satisfied with a humble apology from Plaatje and a promise that such a thing would not happen again. Apart from generating an enormous amount of correspondence the matter was not actually taken too seriously: 'if I gave currency to every utterance circulated in the "Koranta" ', explained Ralph Williams, Resident Commissioner for the Bechuanaland Protectorate, in a letter to the British High Commissioner, 'Your Excellency would weary of my dispatches'.[51] Whoever it was that deputised in the *Koranta* office when Plaatje was away in Cape Town obviously had a few lessons to learn about where to draw the line between what was acceptable and what was not.

For the most part the colonial authorities were well aware of the value of the African newspapers – at a time of intense official concern over the dangers of 'Ethiopianism' and a 'native uprising' – in providing a channel for the expression of opinion that was far better left in the open than suppressed. For what Plaatje and his fellow newspaper editors advocated in the interests of their people was always strictly along constitutional lines; Plaatje, indeed, was on occasion openly critical of members of the organisation most closely associated with 'Ethiopianism', the African Methodist Episcopal Church (a point which commended him to the Native Affairs Commission). The authorities were not slow to realise, moreover, that the African press could actually function as a useful agency in helping to keep what was a potentially volatile African opinion on strictly constitutional lines in seeking redress of their grievances. Plaatje may have been highly critical of the British administrations of the Transvaal and Orange River Colonies in the immediate post-war years, but it was a criticism which arose from a set of commonly held political assumptions and conventions;

he would not for a moment have associated himself with the 'Ethiopian' fantasies of the white South African imagination, or advocated the kind of armed conflict that erupted in Natal at the time of the Bambatha rebellion in 1906. Plaatje's preferred methods, rather, were reasoned discussion and argument and the presentation of irrefutable evidence, taking advantage of such constitutional channels as existed, resorting to the law courts when they did not.

In the circumstances, therefore, the various governmental authorities in southern Africa were well advised to take a relatively tolerant attitude towards Plaatje and his fellow newspapermen, however irritated they may have been by the strong criticism frequently directed at them. Such, at any rate, was the conclusion of the South African Native Affairs Commission when it reported in 1905: 'the native press', it felt, had 'on the whole proved itself to be fairly accurate in tracing the course of passing events and useful in extending the range of native information'; even if, it felt, 'an infant press could not be expected to be wholly free from mistakes and indiscretions'. A minority of the members of the commission favoured the enactment of some form of legal control over the African press, but the resolutions to this effect were not carried: 'freedom of thought and speech within lawful limits', the report concluded, 'is not lightly to be assailed'.[52] In this space thus permitted did Plaatje and his colleagues carry on their business of informing, educating, criticising. With the future shape of South Africa still to be decided there seemed every reason to make the effort.

By the beginning of 1905 Plaatje could look back on a very successful two and half years as editor of *Koranta ea Becoana*. The paper had appeared regularly, it was read widely, and it carried articles and editorials in the by now characteristically vigorous prose of its editor. In a relatively short space of time Plaatje had emerged as an influential public figure, experienced in dealing with politicians and administrators at the highest levels, regarded as the spokesman not only of the Barolong people but of a much wider, if somewhat ill-defined, African political constituency spread out across the northern Cape, the Transvaal and Orange River Colonies, and the Bechuanaland Protectorate. Few would have denied that Vere Stent's prediction that Plaatje would 'some day be a power amongst your people' had already been fulfilled. For somebody not yet thirty years of age it was a considerable achievement.

At the same time there were several developments that did not augur so well for the future. Politically speaking, it was becoming clear that the British imperial government was intent on reaching a rapprochement with the defeated Boer republics, and was anxious to grant them some form of self-government at the earliest opportunity. In contrast to the high hopes generated during the war years, there now seemed only the remotest prospect that Africans living in the Transvaal and Orange River Colonies would be given any form of franchise at all in the new constitutions that would soon be devised. What Plaatje of course wanted was the extension of the Cape franchise, and it was only after this had been agreed, he felt, that the question of self-government should be considered. 'On this side of the border [i.e. in the Cape]', he wrote in an editorial in *Koranta* in October 1904, 'we have that expensive little asset, the franchise, which to us is worth a Jew's eye. We ourselves are too few to do anything with it, but knowing that we possess it, the Colonists treat our people very well.'[53]

Just as disturbing for somebody in Plaatje's position was the growing consensus in governing circles in favour of policies of segregation as the basis for a uniform 'native policy' throughout southern Africa as a whole. Segregation meant different things to different people, but it had two main underlying elements: separate occupation of land as between black and white, and the provision of separate means of political representation, designed to maintain white economic and political domination in the subcontinent. Whatever the differences between Boer and Briton during the late war, the vast majority of whites were united on this last point. In such a scheme of things, Africans were to provide an adequate supply of labour for white farmers and mineowners, whilst their political aspirations were to be confined to the 'reserves' where most of them would live, and control of affairs of state would remain firmly in white hands. Both considerations were very much part of British plans for a unified southern Africa, and to many it was clear that – in the long run – there could be no place for the non-racial Cape franchise, nor for those Africans who believed, like Plaatje, in the notion of 'equal rights for all civilised men' and who looked forward to playing a progressively more influential role in the future affairs of their country.

In 1904 and 1905, though, the full implications of this growing consensus in the direction of segregation had yet to become clear. For Plaatje there was an altogether more immediate cause for concern: the financial plight of *Koranta ea Becoana*. Its issue of 21 December 1904 had carried the following announcement:

It is with great satisfaction that we are able to tell our readers that we have survived the trial and financial struggle of a most trying year. Indeed, we confess that at one time we have almost felt inclined to throw up the sponge, but here we are at the beginning of the year, alive and kicking.

Those financial difficulties to which reference was made were to be the overwhelming problem with which both *Koranta* and its editor would have to cope over the next few years.

6

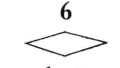

Koranta and after: 1905–10

The fundamental problem faced by *Koranta ea Becoana*, like its African contemporaries, was that its potential circulation, and accordingly its revenue from advertising, was limited by the low African literacy rate: not enough of its potential readership, in short, could read. In view of the low level of missionary activity amongst the Tswana – compared, for example, with the situation of the Xhosa and Mfengu of the eastern Cape – the problem was even more acute for *Koranta* than it was for the two eastern Cape newspapers. Moreover, *Koranta ea Becoana*, unlike *Imvo* and *Izwi*, did not benefit from a subsidy from one of the Cape Colony's main political parties. With a circulation of around a thousand copies per issue it is doubtful if *Koranta* was ever able to cover its cost of production (which of course included salaries for compositors and clerks, as well as for Plaatje himself, as editor); in strictly commercial terms, in other words, there was never much hope that *Koranta* could be a viable concern. It survived only because of Silas Molema's willingness and ability to underwrite production costs – the second of which, at least, was not limitless; and the degree of commitment and determination which all those involved appear to have put into running the newspaper.

Plaatje in particular displayed a remarkable degree of commitment to the newspaper. After a while he, like Molema, began to run up personal debts incurred in raising funds to meet *Koranta*'s running expenses, and he worked extraordinarily long hours to see that it appeared regularly; at one time these amounted, so he recalled on one occasion, to a staggering 18 hours a day, including Sundays.[1] Such determination arose out of a commitment to the view, so he said, 'that our people need a mouthpiece', but it probably also owed something to the realisation that upon the survival of his newspaper depended the survival of his own position of influence as a spokesman for his people. For somebody in his situation, there was no other means of livelihood that would have enabled him to continue to fulfil this role. As he had discovered earlier in life, the options were strictly limited.

In May 1903 Plaatje and Molema had felt sufficiently confident to purchase new freehold premises for *Koranta* (an office and workshop in Main Street, Mafeking), but the following year, 1904, 'a most trying year', was clearly much more difficult. Probably *Koranta* was only saved from going under by a massive £650 loan taken out jointly by Plaatje and Molema in July 1904 from Charles

Wenham, a local trader, which involved mortgaging the entire printing works and paying interest at a rate of 12 per cent a year.[2] Meeting the monthly repayments cannot have been easy, but the indications are that *Koranta* continued to appear with reasonable regularity for most of 1905 – it is impossible to be sure of this, though, since no complete copies of *Koranta* have been preserved after December 1904. But comments in other newspapers reveal clear signs of life. In May 1905, for example, *Koranta* was being accused of displaying disloyal sentiments by a hostile white newspaper; in August there was a report in *Koranta* (of which an extract has survived) of a meeting that took place in the *stadt* between the Barolong and the latest in the succession of distinguished visitors to Mafeking, Colonel Crewe, the Colonial Secretary – Plaatje was again the interpreter; and in December 1905 an article in *Koranta* about education in Natal was being quoted with approval in *Ilanga lase Natal*, which appeared regularly throughout these years, thanks to the support of wealthy Natal sugar barons.[3]

But by early 1906 *Koranta ea Becoana* was in an unhealthy state. From documents left by Silas Molema it is clear that Plaatje and Molema had been forced to contemplate transferring *Koranta* back to the *Mafeking Mail*; and in January 1906 G. N. H. Whales, still the editor of the *Mail*, was indicating to Spencer Minchin, Plaatje and Molema's lawyer, the terms on which he might consider taking the newspaper on.[4] For a while this was averted, and some further funds were raised through issuing shares and taking out further loans. But in May or June 1906 *Koranta ea Becoana* definitely ceased publication.[5] Both Plaatje and Molema had exhausted all sources of credit available to them, and they were unable to repay either the loans they had already taken out, or the interest payments that were due on them. An attempt was made in October 1906 to interest the Bechuanaland Press, the owners of the *Bechuanaland News* and several other small country newspapers, in taking over *Koranta ea Becoana*, but with no success.[6] Then, on 26 November 1906, Molema and Plaatje received a letter from Spencer Minchin informing them that in view of the outstanding debts of their business – the most pressing of which was £200 now due to a Mrs Helen Moroney – 'he had no alternative but to take possession of the Printing Plant in terms of the Bond', and added that he would be 'obliged if you will kindly let me have the key to the building'.[7] It must have been a sad moment for both of them.

But remarkably this did not prove to be the end of *Koranta ea Becoana*. Mrs Moroney was put off for a few weeks, and Spencer Minchin did his best to find ways of avoiding the closure of the newspaper and the disposal of its assets. Minchin was a friend of both Plaatje and Molema, as well as being their lawyer, and he seems to have felt a considerable admiration for the degree of commitment that both of them had displayed in keeping *Koranta* going (at least until recently) in the face of such difficulty, and felt genuinely saddened at the prospect of seeing it go under. Minchin tried first to negotiate the sale of the newspaper to the Barolong paramount chief, Badirile Montshiwa; the attempt failed.[8] But he did then succeed in coming to an arrangement with Whales. Although this was complicated by the fact that Whales himself was in the process of liquidating his own debts by transferring his business to the Bechuanaland Press, some form of agreement was reached, and on 30 January 1907 the

Mafeking Mail announced that *Koranta ea Becoana*, 'the only Sechuana paper published', which had been 'in temporary shade for some weeks', was to recommence 'under new editorship'.[9]

Exactly what happened thereafter, and why it was that Plaatje was either unwilling or unable to continue as editor, remains obscure. There is some indication, though, that there had been some difference of opinion between Molema and Plaatje, the two partners in the business, over the whole question of the paper's future. *Ilanga lase Natal* had this to say in its issue of 1 March 1907:

> We regret to hear of the stoppage of the Becoana newspaper, the Koranta of Mafeking, especially so as that appears to be the result of a disagreement between the persons particularly concerned. The Native people of South Africa cannot afford to let any of their newspapers go by default as probably that would materially affect their progress. How the sad affair came about we do not know, but the fact of a newspaper affecting so large a number of South Africa's natives, coming to a halt, makes us consider what result should there be any repeats of the retrogressive action.

And it continued, in more detail:

> We are glad that the native's old and trusted friend, Mr Peregrino of the *South African Spectator*, came to the rescue, and devoted a special page or two to the Sechuana news; this will help to tide over their difficulties. But we hope that the *Koranta* will soon be alive, and be able to go on into the journalist work with more zeal than ever.[10]

It is impossible to know exactly what had been going on. The report in *Ilanga* obviously conflicts with the arrangements that were being made to secure *Koranta ea Becoana*'s future in Mafeking, and Whales was understandably somewhat surprised when he noticed an announcement in this same issue of the *Spectator* to which *Ilanga* referred. 'I see that in the *Spectator* it is announced that the *Koranta ea Becoana* is combined with that paper,' he wrote to Silas Molema on 19 February 1907: 'What does this mean? I have purchased the copyright of the *Koranta* of you. How does this notice appear?'[11] Molema's reply (if there was one) has unfortunately not survived. One possible explanation is that Plaatje, unknown to Whales, Minchin or even Silas Molema (or at any rate against their wishes), had reached some sort of agreement with Peregrino, who had happened to be in Mafeking in January 1907, to combine the two papers, and that it was this that *Ilanga* had in mind when it referred to 'a disagreement between the persons particularly concerned'. If this interpretation is correct, then it would seem that the difficulties and frustrations of keeping *Koranta ea Becoana* afloat had finally taken their toll on the relationship between the two men whose partnership had sustained *Koranta* from its inception. Silas Molema, it seems, did not share Plaatje's view that an association with the admittedly somewhat eccentric figure of F. Z. S. Peregrino provided the best means of ensuring *Koranta*'s future.

Since no copies of the *Spectator* from this period have survived either, it is impossible to know what form this association took and how long it endured. It cannot, however, have lasted very long, for in April 1907 *Koranta* resumed publication once again, owned now by the Bechuanaland Press, the new owners of the *Mafeking Mail*.[12] According to *Izwi la Bantu*, in its issue of 30 April 1907, *Koranta*'s editor and policy remained as they had been before, so it seems likely that Plaatje had managed to resolve his differences with both Whales and Molema. There were definitely issues on 10 May and 16 August 1907.[13]

◇

The desperate financial struggles that *Koranta ea Becoana* faced during these few years, the labyrinthine possibilities that were constantly being explored in search of ways of keeping it going, must have been, for Plaatje, a source of continued strain and worry, since so much in his life depended upon this. But *Koranta ea Becoana* did nevertheless appear, albeit at irregular intervals, and it continued to address itself to the issues of the day, and to reflect Plaatje's views upon them.

Over one issue in particular during these years Plaatje felt very strongly: the treatment of Sekgoma, a Tswana chief from the extreme north of the Bechuanaland Protectorate, who was involved in a succession dispute, arrested in March 1906 at the instigation of Lord Selborne (Milner's successor as British High Commissioner for southern Africa), and then detained in prison without ever being brought to trial. Plaatje's reaction to the episode almost certainly provided an important ingredient in issues of *Koranta ea Becoana* from March 1906 onwards, and it led him to develop very strong views on the nature of the British administration of the Protectorate – very much part of what he saw as his political constituency. In an unpublished account of the whole affair written in 1909 (when the unfortunate chief was still in prison), Plaatje characterised Sekgoma as 'The Black Dreyfus' (after the French *cause célèbre*) and condemned in the strongest possible terms the judicial and administrative system of the Bechuanaland Protectorate which permitted such arbitrary action to take place. In contrast to the mature legal system of the Cape Colony, Plaatje considered that of the Protectorate to be 'dictatorial', 'a country under the despotic rule of one man, a well-administered country but without any judges and where provincial courts sit in judgement over their own acts'. Lacking the judicial machinery to safeguard the liberty of the subject, 'the protection of the subject in the said Protectorate', Plaatje believed, 'exists in shadow only and not in substance'. The essential problem, he concluded,

> is the absence of a clear Charter of Justice for the protection from their rulers of the inhabitants of that portion of the British empire known as the Bechuanaland Protectorate. This indeed is one branch of the Protectorate administration which calls for immediate consideration.[14]

Plaatje's concern over the manner in which Sekgoma was treated was a typical example of the way in which his political views were shaped by his deep attachment to the judicial system he knew so well from his experiences in the courts in the Cape Colony: as on so many other occasions, his point of departure was the set of principles which underlay the Cape's legal system and the institutions through which they were expressed. Several years later the strong feelings he came to hold on the behaviour of the imperial government in the affair coloured his views on the rather more important political developments that were to culminate in the creation of the Act of Union. Plaatje was rather more conscious than any of his colleagues that the imperial government was just as capable of arbitrary, unjust behaviour towards Africans as any self-governing colony in southern Africa.

One other issue over which Plaatje seems to have felt just as strongly during these years – and which was to assume an even greater significance later in life – was of a rather different nature: it concerned the form of the Tswana language, a matter in which he was always keenly interested. At the time it was a contentious issue because there was no agreed orthography, no commonly accepted convention for representing the sounds of the Tswana language in written form. The only organisations producing books in Setswana were missionary societies, and each had developed its own orthography, differing significantly from one another, reflecting both the different Tswana dialects spoken in the areas in which they operated and the differing European languages (English and German) used by the missionaries themselves. The orthography which Plaatje used in *Koranta ea Becoana* was different again, carefully chosen and developed by him in accordance with his own views, and undoubtedly reflecting his feeling that the Tshidi Barolong dialect represented one of the purest forms of the Tswana language. Although the need to achieve some measure of uniformity was widely recognised, the difficulties that lay in the way of achieving any progress towards this end were immense. None of the interested parties was much disposed towards making concessions to other forms of usage from its own.

The issue became a pressing one, however, when it became known that the London Missionary Society – by far the largest missionary body operating amongst the Tswana – was revising the original Setswana translation (by the pioneer missionary to the Tswana, J. S. Moffat) of the Bible. Along with missionaries from the Berlin and Hermannsburg societies, Plaatje was very concerned at the decision of the LMS to proceed with this without seeking first to ensure some wider agreement over its orthography, and at the end of 1906 he took the initiative, in conjunction with a group of missionaries from the German societies, in broaching the matter with the LMS. The reaction was a hostile one: A. J. Wookey, the missionary primarily responsible for the revision, expressed surprise that the Berlin and Hermannsburg missionaries should 'subjoin the signature of a man who calls himself "Sol Plaatje" '. Plaatje, he went on, was 'the native editor of a not very respectable paper', who 'months ago [had] published a very scurrilous article on the revision and other things'. His 'chief standing as expressed in his paper', he added, 'is not such as to recommend him for the work', and he had been 'supported by those on the press who had attacked and tried to belittle the work of the B.S. itself in Bechuanaland and Cape Colony'.[15]

Plaatje felt very strongly over this linguistic issue, then as later, and was resentful of the policy of the LMS to try and determine the future form of the Tswana language without due reference to native Tswana-speakers like himself. But there was already in existence, as Wookey's comments suggest, an undercurrent of bad feeling between Plaatje and the LMS. On the Society's part, several of their missionaries – in particular the paternalistic W. C. Willoughby, principal of the LMS institution at Tigerkloof, near Vryburg – had come to resent the influence that *Koranta* and its editor had acquired in the area in which it circulated, for the Society had until then been accustomed to a near-monopoly in the provision of education and literature for the Tswana, particularly in the Bechuanaland Protectorate itself. On one occasion, after *Koranta* had reported (misreported, claimed the LMS) some hostile statements made by Willoughby about some of the products of Lovedale, he had dismissed Plaatje's own, very critical comments upon the affair as no more than 'the irresponsible utterances of the youth at the *Koranta ea Becoana* office'; and he took particular exception to the assertive motto that Plaatje carried at the head of every issue of *Koranta ea Becoana*: ' "I am black but comely" was the proud boast,' Willoughby wrote, 'that appeared in heavy type on the front page of every number of a Native newspaper that I often used to read.'[16] Detecting a whiff of Ethiopianism in the whole business, Willoughby had warned a fellow missionary that 'the influence of men like Sol Plaatje will prove harmful to you by introducing the spirit of Ba-Ethiopia even if it does not introduce the people themselves'.[17] Missionaries like Willoughby and Wookey did not find it easy to accept forthright African spokesmen like Plaatje on anything approaching equal terms, whatever the issue involved; in their view, the expression of African aspirations was – for the time being at least – the proper responsibility of the Africans' missionary mentors, not their own representatives.

Plaatje, for his part, had on several other occasions carried articles in *Koranta* that were critical of the shortcomings of the LMS in the educational field, and at a meeting in Mafeking in October 1908 he was reported to have expressed the view that the LMS was a 'pioneer society which had outlived its usefulness' and now 'blocked the way to progress'.[18] With such sentiments being freely expressed on either side it is not surprising that the question of orthography should have been such a contentious one, or that when, in 1910, a conference was eventually called at the behest of the British and Foreign Bible Society to try and resolve the issue, Plaatje should have found himself excluded from it.[19]

<>

Closer to home, in Mafeking, it was inevitable that Plaatje should be drawn into more local controversies and disputes. Throughout the first decade of the twentieth century the Tshidi Barolong were involved in a long-running battle with the municipal and divisional councils over their autonomy and title to land. These were supposedly guaranteed in perpetuity by the provisions of the Annexation Act of 1895, by which jurisdiction over them was transferred to the Cape Colony, and had been publicly reaffirmed by Her Majesty's Secretary of State for the Colonies, Joseph Chamberlain, during his visit to Mafeking in 1903. But this had done little to discourage the local authorities in Mafeking from seeking to extend their jurisdiction over the Barolong. In their view the autonomy they enjoyed was a great nuisance, and it prevented them from administering the district as they thought fit.

One of the main issues over which the two parties came into conflict was the question of dog tax, which the divisional council sought to impose, in 1903, in order to control what the *Mafeking Mail* called the 'numberless mongrels' kept in the Barolong *stadt*. The Barolong challenged the council's legal right to impose the tax, took them all the way to the Supreme Court in Cape Town, and won a famous victory in November 1904: Plaatje had celebrated the occasion with a special 'Dog Tax' number of *Koranta ea Becoana*.[20] The following year the local magistrate attempted to implement the Native Locations Act, a recent piece of legislation designed to give local authorities throughout the colony greater powers over African 'locations'. He, too, was challenged, first of all in his own court, but then in the Supreme Court, and again the Barolong won their case.[21]

But despite these notable legal victories, the Barolong people were nevertheless steadily losing control over their own affairs. On the question of their incorporation into the local administrative district the government simply passed a proclamation to give effect to this. Despite a second trip to Cape Town in 1906 and another interview with the Prime Minister, Dr Jameson, the Barolong representatives could do nothing to reverse this and each year the local authorities made some further inroads (though it was some years before the district council actually managed to collect any dog tax).[22] Along with the chief and headmen Plaatje could do something to delay this process through skilful use of the legal machinery open to them – although it cost them a fortune in legal fees – but they could not halt it. There was an increasing air of inevitability to the final incorporation of the Tshidi Barolong into the administrative structures of the Cape Colony. Success in the court was one thing; the political power to resist government proclamations was quite another.

Within the Tshidi Barolong community matters were scarcely more encouraging. Economically, there was growing poverty and increased dependence upon the earnings of the young men sent out to work on the mines. Politically, Badirile Montshiwa was proving to be even more of a disaster as paramount chief than his predecessor, Wessels. 'Although this man did remarkably well during the first three years [1903–6] of his short reign,' Plaatje recalled, 'he soon after took to drinking and polygamy' and then 'shockingly mismanaged the affairs of the tribe'.[23] F. Z. S. Peregrino, who continued to maintain a close interest in the affairs of the Barolong and now acted as their agent in Cape Town, went even further. He fully endorsed the critical remarks of the local Inspector of Native Reserves, made in 1908, to the effect that Badirile had become a habitual alcoholic and quite incapable of fulfilling his chiefly duties. 'Badirile,' in Peregrino's opinion, was 'a hopeless and abandoned drunkard, being lost to every sense of shame and personal regard and utterly unscrupulous as to the means employed to procure the liquor.'[24] What Plaatje was witnessing, whether he liked it or not, was the disintegration of a once proud and prosperous community. Things had changed dramatically since that first memory of Chief Montshiwa giving judgement in council in the 1890s.

In contrast to this picture of decline and disintegration amongst the Barolong tribe was the social and family life that Plaatje, Elizabeth and their friends created for themselves during these years in Mafeking. For the Plaatje's home, 'Seoding' ('Riverside'), situated in the Molopo Native Reserve and built on land provided by Silas Molema, had become very much the focal point for the social life of the more 'progressive' Africans who lived around Mafeking – like Patrick Lenkoane and his wife, or the Molema, Sidzumo, Ncwabeni, Tyamzashe, Xaba and Samson families, and a number of others. Apart from the Molemas and several Sotho families, the majority of these people were of Mfengu origin; they taught in the local mission schools, worked in the offices of *Koranta* or the local magistrate (as messengers and interpreters), and represented in microcosm, almost, that close-knit community Plaatje had known so well in Kimberley in the 1890s. Over seventy years later Maud Zibi, a product of Lovedale, and between 1905 and 1910 a teacher at the local Congregational mission school, remembered the warm, welcoming atmosphere of the Plaatje home.[25]

In comparison with Kimberley there was much less in the way of organised entertainment for this group of people. How active the Mafeking Philharmonic Society was is unknown, but it certainly did continue to exist, and in July 1908 the *Mafeking Mail* carried a report of a successful concert held in the Wesleyan Church in the Mfengu Location – with a very similar programme to its earlier concert in May 1902, and many of the same participants. Proceeds this time, however, were to go to the Bechuanaland Teachers' Association, one of the highlights of the evening (it was reported to have 'brought the house down') being the duet 'A.B.C.' which Plaatje sang with his wife.[26]

Some other forms of public entertainment were also shared with the white people of Mafeking. In April 1906, however, there did take place one unfortunate incident in this regard, in which Plaatje was directly involved. What happened was this: one Wednesday evening Plaatje and an unnamed friend decided to 'make the acquaintance of Mr Nelson Jackson, the entertainer', and went along to the Town Hall where he was performing. They were let in without difficulty, but after a few minutes an usher came in and requested them to leave since, he explained, the Town Council had passed a regulation forbidding the admission of coloured people to entertainment functions in the Town Hall.

Plaatje complied with the request to leave, but then wrote a long letter of complaint to the *Mafeking Mail* to publicise what had happened, and to draw attention to the existence of the 'bigoted regulation' (as he called it) in question, concluding his letter by quoting from Shakespeare to emphasise his point that Africans were just as entitled to attend these shows as were the whites.[27] The letter was then discussed at the next meeting of the Town Council, and the mayor explained that the council had not in fact passed such a regulation (as the usher had claimed), but rather that it was the lessees of the hall that evening who had decided not to admit coloured people.[28] Unpleasant though it was, what the incident suggests is that black/white relations in Mafeking were generally quite cordial and relaxed. Plaatje had obviously not anticipated being asked to leave the Town Hall on account of his colour, and was very surprised when this happened. He and his friends had presumably attended other forms of entertainment in the Town Hall without this difficulty having arisen before; and it would not have been at all in character for him to have deliberately provoked an incident over a thing like this.

Far more of Plaatje's time was in any case being given to his own family. Elizabeth, or 'Ma-Sainty' as she was often called, had by now given up teaching and devoted herself to the upbringing of the children. After St Leger (Sainty), born in 1898, had come Richard, in September 1901, followed two years later by a daughter, Olive, born in Burghersdorp in December 1903, and then a second daughter, Violet, in 1907. Although the long hours in the *Koranta* office and frequent absences from Mafeking must have limited the amount of time Plaatje himself was able to spend with his young family, there is no doubt that he greatly enjoyed being with them, and watching them grow up. Certainly this is the picture which emerges from a rough, unpublished account, entitled 'With the kids', which he wrote some years later, recalling some of his memories of his children during this time in Mafeking.

Sainty, the eldest child, seems to have fulfilled all his father's hopes. He showed signs of musical talent from an early age, attended the Wesleyan mission school when he was old enough, and soon had a very good knowledge of the three languages which were spoken in the Plaatje household – English, Setswana, and Xhosa. Sainty made good progress at school, and learnt to read without any difficulty. But he was not nearly so quick at mathematics, as one of his father's memories makes clear:

We will never forget his clanger on the morrow of his passing his Standard V with flying colours. He had $4\frac{1}{2}$ sums right, he proudly told his sister to inform us. His disappointment was so intense that one could almost hear him thinking when his sister came back with the retort: Papa wishes to know what about the other half and why all the sums are not wholly right.

Richard, the next in the family, was sent away to live with relatives at Bethanie from an early age – because it was found that the extremely dry climate of the northern Cape did not suit him.[29] But Plaatje's daughter, Olive, soon became a favourite, and he had a fund of amusing anecdotes about her behaviour as a child.[30] One of these indicated quite clearly that she had, like many youngsters of her age, a quite literal understanding of the religious beliefs which obviously formed an important part of her upbringing:

Her cousin Winston died when she [Olive] was three. For months after when she heard of someone's death she would say: 'Oh! What a pity we did not know of it before. I would have gone there and sent a message to Winston. Why doesn't some one come from there and tell us of Winston?' One evening after prayers she asked Mamma whether God has a big house in heaven. On receiving a voice in the affirmative she said: 'I am sure that house must be full of the bread in the Lord's Prayer because wherever you go people are always asking for that bread.'

On another occasion, Olive greatly amused her father with her misunderstanding of the full range of meaning of the Tswana term, *tsheko*, during one of Isaiah Bud-M'belle's visits to Mafeking:

Her uncle used to come to Mafeking with the Circuit Court. They arrived with the early morning train and went to court immediately after breakfast.
Late in the afternoon, Olive asked:
'But what is Uncle doing in town?'

We: 'Working.'
Olive: 'Working at what?'
We: 'Cases' (The Sechuana for a court case is the same as a 'bag').
Olive: 'Are these bags of mealies or bags of corn?'
We roared and Olive continued more seriously:
Olive: 'What is there to laugh at? Surely he is not working at empty bags?'

Olive had been christened after Olive Schreiner, the well-known novelist, sympathiser with African aspirations, and wife of Samuel Cronwright-Schreiner, whom Plaatje had known since they had all lived in Kimberley.[31] It was something young Olive evidently was quite proud of:

One afternoon she went to a Sunday School at Beaconsfield where we were visiting. She was asked for her name which she gave as, 'Olive, Sir'. The teacher wanted the full name and after a little consideration she gave it serene and seriously as 'Olive Schreiner'. Naturally, the class rocked with laughter at the serious yet funny answers of the newcomer.

And it was Olive who inspired Plaatje to write a poem, 'Olive and I', which was published in *Koranta ea Becoana* in November 1907 – not great poetry, perhaps, but a touching record of a day they spent together out in the country around Mafeking:

By the verdant bank of a country spring
Olive and I sat watching a pen of
Kalahari partridges on the wing.
In their Aerial trend they looked peculiarly well off:
They sipped the precious fluid with Elysian nod.
Thus Olive softly: LI THABILE.

O'er the grassy turf 'neath the desert sun
Olive and I walked picking wild flowers,
Up sprang a duiker and commenced to run,
Sprightly and hale he flew and darted across the bowers.
I speedily fired and shattered his back;
The nickel bullet also pierced his vivific pluck.
Said Olive dolefully: E SHULE.

In the western vale of Mahur'take,
Olive and I mused of break-(ing our)-fast,
'Neath the clear rural sky, our meat to take:
Comprising wild fruit, 'morama', a handy repast,
Porridge, winged-game, cocoa beans and cookies,
Displaying her neat set of youthful ivories,
Olive quoth SOTTO VOCE: MONATE.[32]

◇

The obvious enjoyment that Plaatje derived from the company of his children was overshadowed, during the years 1907 to 1909, by the grim struggle to keep *Koranta ea Becoana* in existence and, increasingly as time went on, financial embarrassment of a more personal kind – although even to make such a distinction is to imply a separation between Plaatje's fortunes and those of his newspaper which in reality barely existed. Exactly what happened to *Koranta ea Becoana* after it was taken over by the Bechuanaland Press early in 1907 is not at all clear. Although copies of the newspaper are known to have been published in May and August, it is by no means certain that Plaatje was actually the editor.[33] Indeed, according to a letter written in September 1907 by the civil commissioner, now a man by the name of E. C. Welsh, Plaatje was 'no longer connected' with *Koranta*, 'and in fact left the district some months ago, stating that he was going to German West Africa on a trading trip, and has not yet returned'.[34] A short news item which appeared in *Imvo* the following month offers confirmation of at least part of this: Plaatje, it said, had left for the Kalahari three months previously and was expected back soon, the editing of *Koranta* having been left meanwhile in the hands of Petrus Sidzumo and G. Tyamzashe, a local teacher.[35] *Koranta* did not actually appear, though, after August 1907, and by September Welsh was left with the distinct impression that 'publication of this paper has now ceased'.[36]

Yet two months later – October 1907 – Welsh was obviously surprised to be able to report that it was 'probable that *Koranta* will be published again at an early date', and four days later it did indeed reappear.[37] Plaatje himself – returned now from his 'trading trip' – was probably back in control as editor, for the issue of 1 November 1907 contained an article on the liquor question (later reproduced in the *Christian Express*) which seems to bear the imprint of his views;[38] and that of 15 November carried the poem, 'Olive and I'. Early in January 1908 *Izwi la Bantu*, the paper edited by A. K. Soga in East London, carried an article referring to something that had appeared recently in *Koranta*, criticising those responsible for 'sending forth a feeble cry from the dry marshes against the Queen Victoria Memorialists', the African-run education fund based in the eastern Cape.[39] Soga's metaphor was undeniably an appropriate one. By now *Koranta*'s cry was indeed a feeble one. The issue of *Koranta ea Becoana* to which *Izwi* drew attention must have been one of the last that appeared before it ceased publication once again – the victim this time of Whales's second bankruptcy.[40]

Koranta's demise now looked certain; there was little hope that the remaining assets could be saved from Whales's creditors, and on 9 December 1907 Spencer Minchin advised, not for the first time, that the newspaper's 'plant and buildings will probably have to be sold off by auction'.[41] Minchin did his best once again to interest Chief Badirile in taking over the business but, not surprisingly in view of the chief's condition, he did not succeed. Arrangements were accordingly made for all the assets to be sold off by auction on 28 March 1908.[42] But then, just before this was due to take place, Spencer Minchin himself stepped in with an offer to purchase the plant for the sum of £600, and it seems that this was accepted.[43] And here, for a year, the matter rested. Minchin was either unable to sell off the remains of *Koranta* at a satisfactory price, or (probably this was more likely) simply could not bring himself to do so. Either way, *Koranta* did not reappear in 1908.

In the circumstances it is not at all surprising that *Koranta*'s dire condition, and the debts it had accumulated, should have had serious consequences for Plaatje's own financial position. Just how serious these were emerges starkly from the records kept by his former employer, the Mafeking magistrate: between 1906 and 1910 Plaatje was issued with summons on no less than sixteen occasions for the repayment of unpaid bonds (incurred to raise money for the newspaper) or bills. In some cases these were served on him in his capacity as a business partner of Silas Molema; in others it was as a private individual. Most of those suing for repayment of money owed were general dealers in Mafeking who had supplied him with goods on credit, and had then been unable to secure repayment. The first summons had been for the relatively small sum of £3 13s 6d which he owed to the firm of A. W. and A. E. Fincham for 'goods sold and delivered', but the sums soon began to grow in size until, by January 1908, he was being pressed for payment of £116 to S. Kemp and Co.[44] *Koranta ea Becoana* may have been one of the finest, liveliest newspapers of its day; by the time it collapsed it had left its editor in a desperate financial state.

On two further matters – perhaps not so directly attributable to *Koranta ea Becoana* – Plaatje also found himself in difficulties with the magistrate. The first concerned the question of the 12s per annum hut tax for which all African householders were liable. According to the local Inspector of Native Locations, who was the official responsible for its collection, Plaatje had been 'a habitual defaulter' on payment since 1903, and gave him 'the same trouble every year before he pays his hut tax'.[45] Early in 1907, however, Mr Welsh, the magistrate, felt it was time to issue a summons to try to extract payment from Plaatje for the previous year.[46] For nearly five years Plaatje had dealt with the paperwork for such cases when he was employed in the magistrate's office; now he knew what it felt like to be on the receiving end.

The second difficulty was of a different nature, and arose out of a disagreement over – of all things – a borehole which Plaatje arranged to have dug on his property so as to provide him with a regular supply of water. The work was carried out at his request by a government drill-operator in June 1905, but the operation was not a success. Plaatje's version of events was that the operator refused to drill in the place he wanted, then secured Plaatje's agreement ('much against my will', Plaatje said) to start drilling on another spot, failed to find any water there, tried again in the original place selected by Plaatje, but – 'for reasons which I discovered afterwards were not founded on fact' – ceased drilling here when he had reached 39 feet, 'just when it promised to give satisfaction'.[47] The outcome was that Plaatje failed to get his supply of water, but found himself liable nevertheless for the very considerable expenditure (£90) involved. So he refused to pay; so, too, for a while at least, did several other leading citizens in Mafeking, including J. W. de Kock, Mafeking's member of parliament, also dissatisfied with the results achieved by the government drill-operator.[48] Unfortunately for Plaatje, though, his argument that he could not reasonably be held liable for the whole of this sum (he was prepared to pay part of it) did not impress the magistrate, and by the end of the year (1905) – still refusing to pay the balance of £38 – he was threatened with legal action. Over the next three years a voluminous correspondence then ensued between the magistrate, the Secretary for Public

Works, and the Treasury, as they sought means of either recovering the outstanding debt or accounting for it satisfactorily.[49] Both E. Graham Green and his successor, E. C. Welsh, sent out numerous reminders to Plaatje to pay up, but they were reluctant to actually institute formal legal proceedings since they were well aware that there was virtually no chance of getting the money repaid; in March 1907, indeed, the time when Plaatje was reported to have ceased his connection with *Koranta ea Becoana*, Welsh reported that Plaatje was 'insolvent', and feared 'the amount would not be recovered'.[50] Plaatje's motive in embarking upon his otherwise mysterious 'trading trip' into the Kalahari was undoubtedly to try and relieve this grim financial situation.

◇

Eventually Plaatje was obliged to resort to a rather more uncongenial occupation to try and earn a decent income and keep his creditors at bay: labour recruiting. It cannot have been a prospect that appealed to him, but it remained one of the few legal means now open to him to earn some money. It was an occupation which at least one other African newspaper editor (A. K. Soga) had resorted to when his paper was in difficulties, and Plaatje would have had a very good idea of what was involved since it was a job his friend Patrick Lenkoane had been doing (as an assistant to Charles Goodyear, the local representative of the Witwatersrand Native Labour Association), for several years now.[51]

Plaatje's intention was to act as the local agent of another labour recruiting organisation, the Mines Labour Supply Company, whose speciality was recruiting labour for the coal mines in the Transvaal. But he ran into a number of obstacles right from the beginning. To carry out work of this kind Plaatje needed to obtain a licence from the government, for which he duly applied in January 1909.[52] The licence was on the point of being issued to him when it occurred to Welsh, the magistrate, through whom his application went, that this provided an excellent opportunity to get Plaatje to settle the debt he still owed to the government on the borehole. Welsh's recommendation 'that it might be deemed advisable to decide that the matter might be adjusted before his application for a labour agent's licence can be considered' was accepted, and it was then left to Welsh to resolve the question directly with Plaatje.[53] But Plaatje was in no position to make any payment whatever: there were numerous other debts he owed, and more summons were on the way. Eventually, though, an arrangement was reached whereby the Mines Labour Supply Company would guarantee that Plaatje paid off the money in monthly instalments, and on this condition, early in February 1909, Plaatje commenced work as the 'Bechuanaland Representative', according to the headed notepaper he had printed, of the Mines Labour Supply Company Limited, and advised that all communications be addressed to 'Box 11, Mafeking', so long the post office box number familiar to readers of *Koranta ea Becoana*.[54]

In the event Plaatje's career could not have got off to a worse start. On 12 March, having contracted nine labourers in the Mafeking district for the South Rand Coal Mine, and duly sent them on their way to Johannesburg, Plaatje was informed that when they got to Zeerust, in the Transvaal, they had been intercepted by the police, and turned back by the magistrate there on the grounds that Plaatje's recruiting licence did not extend to the Transvaal itself – a point subsequently upheld when Plaatje complained about the matter to the magistrate.[55] It seems that labourers recruited from outside the Transvaal were only allowed to cross its borders at certain places, and that a 'conducting licence' was also required. The problem was eventually resolved by an agreement that Plaatje would in future send labourers he had recruited in the northern Cape and Bechuanaland into the Transvaal via Fourteen Streams, a village on the Cape/Transvaal border nearly two hundred miles away.[56]

Plaatje's catalogue of misfortunes was extended when the Mines Supply Company went into liquidation several months later.[57] Plaatje then seems to have made arrangements to contract labourers for another organisation, and in October 1909 his licence was endorsed for operation in the Transkei – although whether he actually visited this region for this purpose is doubtful.[58]

One other significant development took place during these unhappy months, which Plaatje may have been involved in: *Koranta ea Becoana* came briefly back to life again. On 30 March 1909 Mr Welsh was undoubtedly surprised to receive a letter from Spencer Minchin informing him that he, Minchin, intended to re-start *Koranta* in a few days' time: the printer and publisher, he explained, would be himself; and the paper was to be 'brought out in the interests of the Bechuana people', issued 'weekly or fortnightly according to demand', and printed and published at the 'old Koranta Building on Erf No. 74, Mafeking'.[59] He gave no indication as to who was to actually edit the paper.

Predictably, Spencer Minchin's venture into the hazardous business of newspaper publishing did not last very long. The first number appeared on 7 April, and was then issued at irregular intervals until the end of May.[60] Prospects of its becoming a viable commercial proposition were negligible, Minchin was obviously unwilling to run up the kind of debts he had seen Plaatje and Molema accumulate, and he decided to call a halt a month later. He disposed of the printing plant, and on 14 June 1909 the following notice – epitaph almost – appeared in the *Mafeking Mail*:

> FOR SALE
> Portion of Erf 74 in the Township of Mafeking, with
> Buildings thereon, known as the KORANTA Offices.
> Suitable for Shop or Dwelling
> For particulars, apply to S. Minchin, Mafeking.[61]

This time there was to be no last-minute reprieve. It was a sad end for a venture that had begun with such high hopes at that formal inauguration in August 1902, nearly seven years earlier. Spencer Minchin had been amongst the guests present that morning to witness the opening of the 'Bechuana Printing Works' and to hear those encouraging words from the then magistrate, Mr Green: he can scarcely have imagined then that he might end up as *Koranta ea Becoana*'s last proprietor.

The year 1909 was the most difficult so far in Plaatje's life: he was heavily in debt, *Koranta ea Becoana* had finally collapsed, and he was encountering one difficulty after another in the far from agreeable task of earning a living as a labour agent. In view of the far-reaching political developments that were now taking place around him as well it must also have been an extremely frustrating time, since he was hardly in a position to make any effective contribution to the debates and activities which they generated. For that year witnessed what was in a sense the culmination of the plans of the imperial government in South Africa since the end of the Anglo-Boer War: reconciliation between Boer and Briton, agreement upon the formation of a unitary, self-governing state, and a coming together of the four colonies in a Union of South Africa which – it was hoped – could be relied upon to preserve the long-term British interests in the subcontinent.

Plaatje had observed and commented upon the moves that had been made in this direction over the previous six years. Now, between October 1908 and February 1909, a convention of representatives from all the colonies in South Africa sat in a number of sessions in an attempt to reach agreement on a constitution acceptable to all of them. On this last objective there was, not surprisingly, much disagreement; quite apart from the divergence of views of how best to reconcile the conflicting economic interests of the different colonies, there was also the difficulty of the franchise. Was the Cape's non-racial franchise to be preserved, or should it defer to the practice of the other colonies and be made the preserve of whites only? Only a handful of whites who attended the Bloemfontein convention argued that the Cape franchise should become the model for that of the union as a whole. Nor was the imperial government in favour of such an idea; the priority rather was to effect a reconciliation between Boer and Briton, and the divergent interests of the different colonies, and this was never likely to be achieved with a franchise based on that of the Cape.[62]

The majority of the population of South Africa – Africans – were not consulted over the arrangements they favoured. The moves being made by white politicians nevertheless provided a great stimulus to political discussions and activity among Africans generally. Towards the end of 1908 a number of meetings were convened in different parts of the country, and they invariably passed resolutions against the colour-bar clauses in the draft South Africa Act (which had emerged from the discussions held by whites), protesting against the failure of the white policy-makers to extend the Cape franchise to the northern colonies. This movement of protest culminated in a 'South African Native Convention', held in Bloemfontein from 24 to 26 March 1909. Further resolutions of protest were passed, the 60 delegates present called upon the British imperial government to intervene on behalf of the black population of South Africa, expressed their support for the extension of the Cape franchise throughout the proposed Union, pressed for more rigorous safeguards to protect their franchise in the Cape itself, and demanded the removal of the colour bar in the Union parliament. They proposed, too, to send a deputation to England to protest about the terms of the draft South Africa Act before it received the approval of the imperial government.

The Native Convention in Bloemfontein was the most representative meeting ever to have been convened by black South Africans, and it was clear to everybody that the threat of Union, and the grave danger perceived therein to their future political status, had created an unprecedented sense of unity of purpose among them. But there were some notable absentees from the meeting, Plaatje amongst them. Exactly what prevented him from attending a gathering where his presence would have been so valuable is unclear. Possibly it was due to illness; more likely, he simply had to stay in Mafeking to try and resolve the more immediate problem then confronting him, of getting the mine labourers he had contracted for the South Rand Coal Mines to their destination, for the dates of the convention coincided almost exactly with the difficulties he was having here. The Barolong of Mafeking were represented instead by Silas Molema, who in fact took quite a prominent part in the proceedings.[63] The other most notable absentee was John Tengo Jabavu, editor of *Imvo*. Although he was to join the deputation to England several months later, early in 1909, he was away on another trip to Europe and he did not get back in time to attend the convention. There were many who thought this was not just a question of bad timing; for Jabavu now found himself somewhat out of step with the new movement for unity, and was fearful that attempts to secure the extension of the Cape franchise northwards would serve only to jeopardise its survival in the Cape. Upon this, of course, his entire influence depended.

Little notice was taken of the representations of the Native Convention, either in South Africa or in Britain. Nevertheless, the holding of the Native Convention was a significant achievement in itself, and Plaatje does seem to have been amongst those who were involved in seeking to capitalise, in organisational terms, upon this admittedly fragile, new-found sense of political unity. For at the meeting of the convention it was resolved that a permanent organisation (of the same name) should be formed. Plaatje was soon to become an office-holder in the organisation, and many of his friends – from the Orange Free State particularly – were already heavily involved; and he was amongst those who attended (he was described in a newspaper report as 'formerly editor, *Koranta ea Becoana*') the second annual meeting of the convention, also in Bloemfontein, in March 1910 – exactly a year after the holding of the original convention.[64] A week later he led a deputation to General Botha, Prime Minister of the Transvaal, to compliment him on his decision to repatriate the last of the Chinese miners who had been imported into the country six years earlier; like most African leaders of opinion, Plaatje had been opposed to this from the beginning.[65]

In the difficult personal circumstances Plaatje faced in Mafeking – with no newspaper, no money, and no obvious outlet for his energies and skills – these political opportunities probably came more as a relief than a burden, a chance, too, to escape from the increasingly limited role as adviser and general secretarial dogsbody for the hapless Barolong paramount chief. Perhaps these same considerations were also a factor in the long essay he wrote, probably around Christmas 1909, on the question of segregation, a subject of growing interest in view of the political opportunity that now presented itself to white politicians to implement segregatory policies across the new Union of South Africa. Plaatje's essay was actually written in response to a competition organised by C. F. Tainton, a prominent pro-segregationist from Johannesburg. Tainton was, not surprisingly, inclined to favour those essays which contained some good words in favour of segregation, and the first three prizes went accordingly to A. A. Moletsane, from Kolo in Basutoland; Cleopas Kunene, from Natal – he shared joint first prize with Moletsane; followed by one E. S. Mbele from the Transkei. Plaatje was awarded third prize, worth £1 10s (which can have done little to relieve his financial difficulties), and his essay attracted the following comments from Tainton:

> Greater care in the arrangement of his arguments would have added much to their value. His paper is a clear but bitter protest against our present native policy and throws much light on the effect of a repressive policy on educated and able members of the Native races.[66]

In fact the arguments Plaatje put forward in his essay – subsequently published in the *Transvaal Chronicle* (a daily newspaper published in Johannesburg), which commented that Plaatje 'hits hard with lumps of truth' – appear to be perfectly well arranged. His central point was absolutely clear: that however desirable or undesirable total segregation was in theory, any attempt to implement it would be quite impracticable. Plaatje conjured up a vision of what complete geographical segregation would mean:

> What a glorious millennium! A city of black folks where Europeans, being excluded, the havoc wrought in the Native territories by attorney's fees will be a thing of the past. With black postmasters, black carpenters, black tax collectors and black shopkeepers, making money! In fact, black everything . . .

But all of this, Plaatje went on,

> is visionary. Has it ever occurred to the thousands of white officials that when the segregation idea becomes an accomplished fact they stand three chances to one of being retrenched? I think it has, and I am satisfied that when the natives begin to move the whites will stop them even if they have to use Martini rifles for the purpose.

For the economic interdependence of black and white, Plaatje went on to argue, would ensure that the complete segregation of black and white was an impossibility. 'Two things only you need give the native,' he concluded,

> and two things only you must deny him. Keep away from him liquor, give him the franchise, and your confidence, and the problem will solve itself to your mutual advantage.[67]

The first recommendation was rooted very much in Plaatje's recent experiences in Mafeking; the second – that Africans should be given the franchise and trust of those who possessed the power to give it – were clearly rooted in Plaatje's wider experience and his commitment to the ideals of the Cape constitutional system. To the extent that the non-racial Cape franchise was preserved in the Union constitution of 1910, Plaatje had reason to feel some sense of optimism for the future; to the extent that it had not been extended to the other parts – provinces as they now were – of the Union, there was cause for concern. Only the future would tell which system, which set of values, which theory of government, gained the upper hand.

Plaatje left Mafeking with his family in May or June 1910. There was little to keep him there. He was no longer able to earn a living as a labour agent since Welsh had not seen fit to renew his licence when it expired in December 1909 (he gave no reasons), and he clearly had to do something to secure a regular income. His financial position was as desperate as ever. In the early months of 1910 several new summons were issued against him, and at the end of April a warrant was issued for the seizure of property and furniture in his house: specifically, a dining-room table, letter press and stand, kitchen stove, bedstead, sofa, mirror, rocking chair and bookcase.[68] This particular debt (for a relatively small sum this time) was duly settled, but the larger ones could not be; it was to be years before Plaatje was free of them.

Plaatje's main reason for leaving Mafeking was that he had now managed to find backers for a new newspaper, to be based in Kimberley, and had probably been involved in discussions and negotiations over this new venture from at least as early as the beginning of 1910, possibly well before this. If Plaatje was to play any meaningful role in the affairs of the new Union of South Africa, now on the point of coming into existence, his chances of doing so were not going to be improved by remaining in a small, still remote town like Mafeking. Kimberley promised to provide a more conveniently situated and appropriate base from which to operate. The beginning of a new era in the political history of South Africa coincided almost exactly with the opening of a new phase of Plaatje's own life.

7

Tsala ea Becoana, Congress and the Land Act of 1913: Kimberley 1910–14

Exactly how this new newspaper, *Tsala ea Becoana* ('The Friend of the Bechuana'), came into existence, or when the idea was first mooted, remains unknown. But the names of a number of the directors of the *Tsala* syndicate are known; and it is clear that much of the impetus, and probably most of the initial capital, came from a group of wealthy landowners from the Seleka Barolong settlement in Thaba Nchu – most notably Chief J. M. Nyokong, head of the Matlala section of the Seleka; Jeremiah Makgothi, an elder brother of Isaiah, who had gone to Mafeking to work in the *Koranta* office some years previously; Chief W. Z. Fenyang, also a man of considerable wealth and local influence, to whom Plaatje was related on his mother's side of the family; Moses Masisi, a wealthy landowner who owned the farm 'Naawpoort' in the Thaba Nchu district; and the elderly Reverend Joel Goronyane, remembered too for his translations into Setswana.[1] All of them were very well known to Plaatje, had contributed in the past to *Koranta ea Becoana*, and had acted as the newspaper's agents. Collectively they were – in social position – to the Seleka Barolong of Thaba Nchu what the Molemas were to the Tshidi Barolong of Mafeking. None of them could have been in any doubt as to Plaatje's experience and ability as a newspaper editor, or of the reputation he had established as a spokesman for the Barolong people.

It is quite likely that the idea of establishing a new newspaper gained momentum during the political deliberations surrounding the calling of the Native Convention in March 1909 and its subsequent establishment as a permanent political organisation, for it was this same group of people who took the initiative in each – Moses Masisi and Jeremiah Makgothi, for example, being Treasurer and Secretary respectively of the Native Convention.[2] Underlying their involvement in each enterprise was a keen awareness of their precarious political position (in relation to the security of their land particularly) and an anxiety to do all they could to ensure that their voice was heard. Denied the means of political representation in the Union, a newspaper remained one of the most effective means open to them to do this, and they would have been responsive to any representations Plaatje might have made on the issue. And he, after all, was desperately in need of a new means of livelihood.

Other members of the syndicate included Thomas Mapikela of Bloemfontein, a wealthy businessman of Mfengu origin, who had been a member of the Schreiner deputation to England in 1909 – he had himself sought to establish a newspaper in Bloemfontein in 1908, so his involvement in the enterprise comes as no surprise;[3] and John Tengo Jabavu, editor of *Imvo*. Exactly how and when Jabavu first came to be involved in the syndicate is unclear, but one important result flowed from this: he undertook to print the proposed newspaper on his press in Kingwilliamstown, despite the difficulties involved in being so far away from Kimberley where, it was agreed, *Tsala ea Becoana* would have its office (at the corner of Brett and Shannon Streets). Jabavu and Co. were actually the first registered proprietors of the new newspaper; however, this arrangement did not last for very long and within a short while the *Tsala* syndicate had taken the place of Jabavu and Co.[4]

For Plaatje the prospect of a return to Kimberley to edit a new newspaper must have been attractive, bearing in mind the difficult state of affairs he had been facing in Mafeking. Although it had been 13 years since he had last lived on the diamond fields many of his old friends remained there, as did Isaiah Bud-M'belle and his family, and the move also brought him much closer to his elderly mother and his elder brother Simon at Pniel. Kimberley itself had not changed greatly since Plaatje had last lived there. If anything, the town's prospects were somewhat bleaker than they had been in his time. The low price of diamonds on the world market had led to a long-term local recession from which the town only began to recover in 1910 and 1911, and it was obvious to everybody that it had been eclipsed still further by the growth of Johannesburg as an industrial centre.[5]

Kimberley nevertheless promised to provide an altogether more satisfactory base than Mafeking from which to run a newspaper, and the surroundings – politically and socially – were, for somebody in Plaatje's position, as congenial as in any of the larger towns of the country. In terms of the wider national political context, too, Plaatje had some reason to be optimistic, and he did not share quite the same degree of pessimism about its likely effects on African political aspirations as many of those who had attended the Bloemfontein Native Convention in 1909. Partly, perhaps, his feelings were influenced by the change in his personal fortunes; things could not have got very much worse for him, after all, in Mafeking in 1909 and 1910. But there were other reasons as well. Like Tengo Jabavu he was inclined to the view that the liberal tradition of the Cape would gradually spread northwards: that the liberalism of the Cape, indeed, could yet prove to be the dominant force in the affairs of the Union.

Plaatje's attitude towards Union had also been strongly influenced by the Sekgoma case and the views that this had led him to develop on the administration of the protectorates – Bechuanaland, Basutoland, and Swaziland. The question of whether or not they were to be included within the Union had been a contentious one. African opinion, broadly, was against this; the general preference was for continued direct rule from Whitehall rather than the uncertainties of incorporation into the Union of South Africa – the devil they knew rather than the one they did not. Plaatje saw things differently. He had witnessed arbitrary imperial rule in the Bechuanaland Protectorate, and did not believe direct imperial rule to be necessarily beneficial. Rather, he believed that the inhabitants of the protectorates would be better off if attached to the Union, for here they had the Supreme Court to which they could appeal against arbitrary misrule. 'In my opinion,' Plaatje wrote, 'the jurisdiction of the Supreme Court alone warrants the change [i.e. the incorporation of Bechuanaland into Union] as it will give to the common people the King's protection in practice as well as in theory.'[6]

It was yet another instance of the way in which Plaatje's experience in the law courts, the views he had developed about the use to which they could be put in protecting African rights, and his confidence in the legal system of the Cape Colony, could colour his political judgement. Within a few years his view of the position of the protectorates would change dramatically: but in 1910 and 1911 Plaatje was optimistic about the prospects that lay before him in the new Union of South Africa.

◇

The first number of *Tsala ea Becoana* appeared on 18 June 1910. With four pages, columns in both English and Setswana, an intended circulation (by the second issue this was claimed to be 'large and increasing') throughout Tswana-speaking parts of the Union and the Bechuanaland Protectorate, and a network of agents to distribute and sell copies, it is not surprising that *Tsala ea Becoana* was taken by many to be *Koranta's* successor – *Ilanga lase Natal*, for example, welcomed its reappearance as 'our old friend "Koranta" resuscitated'.[7] With a familiar balance of advertisements, local correspondents' reports, readers' letters, news items, and editorial matter, the main concern of its early editions was with the new circumstances of Union, with the first general election (held in September 1910), and then with the behaviour of the new government formed by General Botha's South African Party. Plaatje's early editorials were hopeful in tone. He argued that 'Native interests' would be best served if neither of the two major parties (the South African Party and the Progressive Party) achieved overwhelming majorities (thereby rendering criticism ineffective), and that is just how things turned out, although it was not, in practice, very easy to detect much difference in their policies. Plaatje also derived considerable satisfaction from the fact that a number of vehemently 'anti-native' candidates (in both parties) had been defeated, and from the inclusion in the first Union cabinet of several well-known Cape liberals and 'friends of the natives' – F. S. Malan (Minister of Education), J. W. Sauer (Minister of Railways and Harbours), and above all, Henry Burton, as Minister of Native Affairs.[8]

Plaatje had known Burton since the 1890s when both lived and worked in Kimberley, when Plaatje had been so impressed by Burton's willingness to defend African rights in the courts. Later, in Mafeking, Plaatje had found himself interpreting in court cases in which Burton was also involved (*R. v. Maritz and Lottering* most notably), and he saw a lot of Burton thereafter. Burton accepted a number of briefs for the Barolong during the few years after that – in connection with the long-running 'Dog Tax' battle particularly – and he had assisted over such matters as the compensation question as well. The two men seem to have come to know one another well, and they shared a number of common assumptions over the value of the non-racial Cape franchise; both men, too, were steeped in the traditions of the Cape legal system. Plaatje was naturally delighted, therefore, to hear of Mr Burton's appointment as Minister of Native Affairs, and was quick to draw the attention of his readers to their good fortune. He looked forward to the development of favourable 'native policies' and to finding a sympathetic ear for the particular grievances of his own people, the Barolong. 'Well may the Natives . . . congratulate themselves,' said *Tsala* in October 1910, 'that the wonderful year of 1910 [has] brought what promises to be the inauguration of a sound system in the administration of their affairs, under the most sympathetic Minister who ever administered this Department.'[9] Plaatje's close relationship with the Minister of Native Affairs seemed, moreover, to place him in a pre-eminent position amongst his fellow newspaper editors and political spokesmen who were now coming to terms with the new political structures that had been created, and to justify the optimistic views he had expressed earlier about Union providing the means of 'liberalising influences' from the Cape spreading northwards.

Cape liberals were also prominent in the ranks of the four 'native Senators', appointed under the provisions of the new constitution (F. R. Moor, W. P. Schreiner, W. E. Stanford, Mr Krogh) to look after 'native' interests, and here too Plaatje hoped to be able to achieve favourable consideration for his people, especially through W. P. Schreiner with whom he had also had contact in the past. One letter which Plaatje wrote to Schreiner on 17 December 1910, in connection with a visit to Cape Town on behalf of the Native Convention, provides a clear illustration of the way in which he was now going about the task of enlisting influential 'friends of the natives' to his cause, which on this occasion concerned the system of Barolong landholding in Thaba Nchu:

> My dear Sir,
>
> As I will not see you before Tuesday and you will in the meanwhile be seeing the other three Native Senators on my behalf, I think that I should mention to you that I wrote the Rt Hon. J. X. Merriman at the same time as I wrote you and Colonel Stanford, and if you think that his influence will help us you might ask him also to re-inforce us and help us to induce the Prime Minister to see the justice of introducing a short relieving bill.
>
> I was very much struck by the tactics of General Hertzog 20 years back when he addressed a Dutch jury at Fauresmith in favour of two Native prisoners. I was but a youngster then but I will never forget the episode and I have carried with me a warm admiration for the General all these years and I will be very much surprised if he also does not see the justice of our modest request for immediate relief.
>
> With such a combination I am sure we could favourably impress the Rt Hon. the Prime Minister (who knows me) and the Minister of Lands; for it will be a pity, having regard to what has been done for the participators in Bambata's rising, if the law abiding Barolongs of Thaba Nchu cannot get the ear of the government (judging from the *Gazette* I showed you) the Free State Government was anxious to redress.
>
> Yours respectfully,
> Sol. T. Plaatje

P.S. For the present I am not seeing any of my friends about this for if it were voiced abroad the opposition press will make political capital out of it, and do our cause more harm than good.[10]

Letters like this, confidential in tone and written as one politician to another, were one of Plaatje's specialities; he knew exactly the compliments to pay, the names to drop, the tone to adopt. And lest Plaatje be accused of having a rather naive view of General Hertzog, it would be as well to note in passing that he had far less complimentary things to say about the General when writing to Silas Molema soon afterwards.[11] Plaatje was, after all, in the business of politics and was very aware of the fact, his confident tone notwithstanding, that the political weight he carried in the counsels of the Union government depended very much on the personal impact that he was able to make. There were times when it was necessary to subordinate one's real feelings and opinions to the requirements of political expediency.

Even when, in 1911, the policies and behaviour of the Union government began to assume a rather less favourable aspect as far as 'native affairs' were concerned, Plaatje still managed to achieve for himself a very real degree of consideration and attention. One striking example of this took place in December 1911. Following a series of critical articles and editorials in *Tsala* earlier that year, attacking the way in which blacks were coming to be replaced by whites in the civil service, Plaatje managed to secure for himself a series of interviews, and a courteous consideration of his representations, with a number of government ministers and heads of departments. During the week he spent in Pretoria for this purpose he was sympathetically received (twice) by Henry Burton, Minister of Native Affairs, who in turn arranged for him to see Sir David de Villiers Graaff, the Minister of Posts and Telegraphs (who, despite being 'very busy with great matters of State', so *Tsala* reported, nevertheless 'evinced the greatest interest in the representations made'). Thereafter, Plaatje saw J. W. Sauer, Minister of Lands, the Postmaster-General (with whom Plaatje reminisced about his own early days in the employ of that department), the Government Mining Inspector, senior officials from the Department of Printing and Stationery, and Edward Dower, Secretary for Native Affairs, whose department supplied Plaatje – when he went to Johannesburg for the day – 'with an Orderly to facilitate his day's work there'.[12] He came away with promises to investigate all his complaints and to provide him with written replies when these had been completed.

It was not an isolated example. On other occasions Plaatje took up cases of miscarriages of justice he had witnessed in the law courts, often to very good effect. He later recalled several examples which date from this period:

> I once visited a town where there had been insistent complaints against the work of the Circuit Court interpreters. The Court was sitting at the time and I attended in order to verify the facts. I took notes of a very short case, that is, what the Judge said and what the Interpreter said. Two different things indeed; also the prisoners' answers and the interpreters' version; two different things again. On that faulty interpretation a man had got 12 months with hard labour. General Hertzog was Minister of Justice then and Mr Burton

that of Native Affairs. When my letter reached Pretoria, General Hertzog promptly recommended the man's release, after he had served only one month of his sentence.

Again I visited another town where some Natives complained against an Assistant Magistrate. They alleged that in his Court a native litigant stood no chance whatever in an action against a white man. Again I went to take notes, this time of two typical cases, secured a copy of the Magistrate's own records and forwarded them to Pretoria with a covering letter. Again General Hertzog, in his capacity as Minister of Justice, ordered an inquiry at the instance of Mr Burton. That Assistant Magistrate, to his credit, frankly admitted that it was quite possible for a Magistrate to be influenced by the eloquence of clever attorneys with the result that innocent Natives suffered, if they are not legally represented.

Further, that Magistrate promised to be more careful in the future, and so he was.[13]

This was Plaatje in the watchdog role in which he was so effective; always careful to be in full command of the details of the cases he took up, he invariably left a strong impression upon the people he saw. Few people in South Africa, black or white, had the kind of access he enjoyed to senior members of the government and administration. Often, the personal instincts of these ministers and officials were sympathetic to the eminently reasonable representations – put to them in fluent English or Dutch, whichever they preferred – which Plaatje laid before them, either in correspondence or in person. So long as the Cape liberal tradition retained a foothold in the Union government, and so long as no major initiatives in 'native policy' were taken, then Burton, Sauer, Malan, Schreiner, and several others, were prepared to take his representations seriously, and to accept him as a responsible spokesman for his people.

Of course it worked both ways: Plaatje's own influence, and the circulation of his paper, can only have benefited from his readers being able to read detailed reports in the columns of *Tsala ea Becoana* about his meetings with the highest government officials. Such a political honeymoon was not destined to last. It was nevertheless during these first two years of Union that Plaatje enjoyed perhaps the greatest influence and access to the machinery of government that he was to have. 'He had a way particularly his own,' Isaiah Bud-M'belle wrote later, 'of approaching, interviewing, and placing his case before cabinet ministers of all different shades, and other highly placed authorities of English or Dutch extraction – a rare and valuable quality not possessed by other Bantu leaders.'[14] Circumstances were such as to ensure that it was in these first two years of Union that there remained scope for Plaatje's abilities in this direction to produce results.

◇

As ever, there was a stark contrast between Plaatje's growing influence and stature as a leader of the African people in the Union of South Africa and his own financial circumstances, and those of his business. Although *Tsala ea Becoana* managed to come out at weekly intervals for over two years, its finances, judging from the correspondence which has survived, were rarely less than precarious. If cautious

Joseph Chamberlain, Secretary of State for the Colonies, visits Mafeking during his tour of Southern Africa in 1903. **39** *(left) Arriving in town.* **40** *(right) Crowds line the road into the Barolong* stadt, *displaying suitably loyal sentiments. Plaatje interpreted at the meeting which followed.*

41 *Badirile Montshiwa, chief of the Tshidi Barolong, 1903–11. Plaatje thought he 'shockingly mismanaged the affairs of the tribe'.*

42 *Hunting small game was one of Plaatje's few forms of relaxation, and he had a reputation as a crack shot. Here he is shown with the proceeds of one outing. The photograph is undated, but was probably taken around 1905 or 1906.*

44 *(above) Mafeking's African elite c. 1905—probably a gathering of the Philharmonic Society. Plaatje is standing in the middle of the back row, Elizabeth Plaatje is sitting, second from left. The figure sitting on the extreme right is Patrick Lenkoane, 'the black Irishman', displaying the medal he was awarded in 1897.*

43 *Portrait of Plaatje from the same period, holding what looks like a song sheet.*

45 *(below) Plaatje as editor of* Tsala ea Batho *('The People's Friend'). This photograph was taken in 1912, probably during a visit to Cape Town.*

46 *(above left) Chief W. Z. Fenyang (seen here with his wife), and* **47** *(below left) Rev. Joel Goronyane, members of the* Tsala ea Becoana *('The Bechuana Friend') syndicate.*

Founders of the South African Native National Congress in January 1912 (left to right).
48 *Pixley ka I. Seme, prime mover and first treasurer.* **49** *Rev. John Dube, first president.*
50 *Rev. Walter Rubusana, vice president.* **51** *S. M. Makgatho, vice president.* **52** *Saul*
Msane, vice president. **53** *Richard Msimang, who, like Plaatje, investigated and*
documented the effects of the Natives' Land Act.

54 *Dr Abdullah Abdurahman, President of the APO (African Political Organisation).*

Tsala ea Batho.

KIMBERLEY, MAY 31,   1913.

I AM BLACK, but comely, O ye daughters of Jerusalem, as the tents of Kedar and the curtains of Solomon. Look not upon me because I am black, for the sun hath looked upon me; my mother's children were angry with me; they made me the keeper of their vineyards; but mine own vineyard have I not kept.

WE are standing on the brink of the precipice. We appealed to certain Members of Parliament against the suspension clause in Mr. Sauer's Land Bill, and the result of our appeal has been an agreement between Sir Thomas Smartt and the Minister to the effect that the first part of the Bill only be proceeded with. The effect of this agreement is infinitely worse than the whole Bill. In its entirety, there were certain saving clauses, one of them practically excluding the Cape Province from the operation of the Bill. Under the Sauer-Smartt agreement, all these clauses are dropped, and Section I. of the Bill, which prohibits the sale of land between Europeans and Natives (pending the report of a future Commission) is applicable to all parts of the Union, including the Cape Province. Now, then, if this suspension clause becomes law, what is going to happen? It is simply this: That the whole land policy of the Union of South Africa is the land policy of the Orange *Free* State—that misnamed Province which is virtually the Orange Slave State—the blackest spot of the Empire and it will be as difficult to abrogate that suspension as it is difficult to recall a bullet, or.ce fired through someone's head, and resustate the victim. Our object then should be to prevent the pistol being fired off, as prevention is infinitely better than cure. The days of the present Parliament are numbered. Supposing the Boers send Gen. Botha about his business with this suspension among the Statutes of the country, do you think they will allow Genl. Hertzog to repeal the suspension? His Cabinet Members will each have "3,000 solid reasons" to keep it there. Our business is to prevent its getting there.

55 *'We are standing on the brink of the precipice'. Tsala ea Batho, 31 May 1913, three weeks before the Natives' Land Act came into force. Plaatje's editorial was read out to the South African House of Assembly by T. L. Schreiner during the debates on the bill.*

56 *General Louis Botha, first prime minister of the Union of South Africa. He was unable to persuade the SANNC deputation to abandon its plans to appeal to the British imperial government against the Natives' Land Act.*

optimism characterised much of what went into its columns during this period, the same could certainly not be said of the financial foundations upon which it rested. Thus the Reverend Joel Goronyane, one of the *Tsala* syndicate, to Silas Molema in June 1911:

I herewith beg to report that the scheme on the Bechuana Friend is not well carried out since the £250 [that] was borrowed from Mr Masisi was consumed. And that the committee of the *Tsala* which met in January last appointed Messrs W. Z. Fenyang and J. M. Goronyane as Treasurer and Secretary respectively. The object in view being that the agents of *Tsala* may send their subscriptions to them in order that they may pay the Editor, Compositor, etc. You are earnestly requested as an agent of the *Tsala* to speak with the subscribers to send money monthly to the Syndicate. As it required your serious attention any negligence on your part would mean the total ruins of *Tsala*. Your heart and soul in the work would be the only solution to relief [sic] us from the present embarrassment. It is possible that if the money is not paid regularly the manager would abandon the work.[15]

Silas Molema was, of course, not unaware of the problems, and he had probably written numerous letters in the same vein on behalf of *Koranta ea Becoana* during the previous decade. On this occasion, both the 'present embarrassment' and the prospect of 'total ruins' to which Goranyane alluded were somehow overcome, and *Tsala* continued to be published without any hint of these difficulties appearing in its columns and thereby deterring potential subscribers or advertisers. Other letters that have survived reveal Plaatje having to write to Joshua Molema for a loan to keep the paper going, Isaiah Bud-M'belle coming to the rescue to pay the rent on the *Tsala* office, and Plaatje himself having to remind the Thaba Nchu syndicate of the urgent need to pay his own salary for the previous three months.[16]

In addition to having constantly to solicit funds to keep *Tsala* afloat, Plaatje had also to find the means of repaying his own outstanding debts in Mafeking so as to prevent further legal action being taken against him; on a number of occasions in 1910, 1911, and 1912 he wrote to Silas Molema to ask him for loans to avert the issuing of fresh summons, or to secure more time for him to repay his debts. Plaatje did begin to make some progress in this direction through taking on additional work, first as a regular contributor to Vere Stent's *Pretoria News*, his contributions being published regularly under the heading 'Through Native Eyes'; and then as an insurance agent, earning commission on policies he was able to sell to Africans.[17] Life remained, in other words, a perpetual financial battle, and it was only through his own determination to keep *Tsala* from the fate that befell *Koranta*, at whatever cost, that the newspaper kept going. In Plaatje's view it was vital in the interests of both the people he represented and of his own livelihood and career as their spokesman, for *Tsala* to survive; the last few years had brought home to him very clearly that if he had no newspaper, there was little else he could do. Behind Plaatje's steadily growing importance and influence in the affairs of his people there lay an often desperate struggle to support his position, his family, his newspaper.

◇

Towards the end of 1911 the general political outlook began to look rather bleaker. The Cape liberals in the Union cabinet found themselves in an increasingly tenuous position, and the scope they possessed for responding sympathetically to representations made to them by Plaatje and his colleagues was being progressively reduced. It was no longer politically feasible, for example, for Sauer, Burton, Malan or de Villiers Graaff to take action to halt, or even delay, the growing discrimination against Africans in the civil service, and their replacement by whites. It might have been distasteful for Burton, in particular, to see this happening, but to have attempted to do something effective about it would have played directly into the hands of General Hertzog's Afrikaner nationalist supporters, already impatient at the Botha government's pro-British tendencies, resentful at what they saw as his betrayal of the interests of Afrikaner workers and farmers, and now calling for harsher 'native policies' to reflect the reality of the new political balance of power. The presence of the Cape liberals in the first Union cabinet did not for long disguise the fact that an important change in this balance of political power had taken place. The replacement of blacks by whites in various branches of the public services was one outcome of this, and Plaatje – for all his eloquent pleading and the access he enjoyed to government ministers – was ultimately able to do nothing to prevent it. J. X. Merriman, the man Plaatje would have dearly liked to have become the first Prime Minister after Union, could do little to help either: 'What can I do?', he wrote to Plaatje after receiving from him a letter complaining about the dismissal of African waiters in the South African Railways, 'I can only talk and that does not seem to help your people at all.'[18] Plaatje himself could only comment with increasing bitterness upon the passage of such pieces of legislation as the Native Labour Regulation Act, which tightened controls upon African labour; the Mines and Works Act, which reserved certain categories of work for whites, the first time that such a principle was actually embodied in government legislation; and the Dutch Reformed Church Act, which prohibited full African membership. Politically, the northern colonies now predominated in the Union: it was essentially their interests and their traditions to which the first Union parliament gave expression. Afrikaner nationalism was growing in strength the whole time.

It was against this background, and amidst a growing realisation amongst politically conscious Africans in all parts of the Union that there was probably worse to come, that the South African Native National Congress was formed in January 1912. The movement was conceived as an attempt to provide a truly united forum for the representation of African opinion and inerests, a response to the coming together of Boer and Briton in the Act of Union, and a reaction to their own exclusion from any effective representation in the new political structure that had been created. An awareness of the importance of achieving unity of this kind was not, of course, new, and even before the Act of Union some experience in trying to reconcile the immense political and regional differences that existed had been gained in organisations like the South African Native Press Association, in which Plaatje had played a leading part in 1903 and 1904, in the Native Convention held in Bloemfontein in 1909, and then in the formation of a permanent – if not altogether representative – organisation of the same name, which maintained a somewhat discreet existence throughout 1910 and 1911; in this, too, Plaatje had played a part, occupying the position of Assistant Secretary.

It was from the experience of the South African Native Convention that Congress actually emerged, and it is clear that a great deal of discussion and deliberation, in which Plaatje was much involved, had taken place before Pixley Seme, a lawyer trained at Columbia University, USA, and Jesus College, Oxford, who had recently returned to South Africa, was able to issue his now famous clarion call for unity at the end of 1911. Plaatje had been amongst those who attended a special meeting of the executive committee of the convention, held in Johannesburg early in August 1911, which provided Seme with the first opportunity to expand upon his ideas about the need for a more vigorous, more representative, above all a more united political organisation.[19] Later, indeed, Plaatje claimed to have made possible the establishment of Congress by persuading the leaders of the two main Transvaal African organisations already in existence, the Transvaal Native Congress and the Transvaal Native Political Organisation, to set aside their differences and rivalries and co-operate in setting up a single, national political body; there seems no reason to doubt his claim.[20]

Pixley Seme's contribution was that of a newcomer to the political scene, equipped with the training and prestige of an attorney and a strong sense of mission to bring about the political unity of the African people. Several of his colleagues, though, were inclined to regard him as over-ambitious, arrogant and rather hot-headed. One incident in particular seemed to lend weight to their views. Shortly after returning to South Africa Seme had drawn a loaded revolver on a group of whites who took violent exception to his decision to travel in the first-class compartment of a railway carriage (not in itself illegal); he was taken to court for using a firearm in a threatening manner, and found guilty.

In the circumstances Seme was in one sense fully justified in taking the action he did, and had he not drawn the revolver to frighten off his would-be assailants he would undoubtedly have been physically assaulted and probably thrown off the train. Nevertheless, his decision to travel in a first-class railway carriage ('Like all solicitors,' he subsequently explained, 'I of course travel first class')[21] would not have commended him to many of the older-established and more experienced African political spokesmen, far more cautious in approach and always worried about alienating their white sympathisers. This was particularly true of Plaatje, who was always careful to avoid provoking incidents of this nature, still concerned – as he had first shown in that early editorial in *Koranta ea Becoana* in 1902 – to disarm accusations that Africans were seeking social, as well as political, equality with whites. When, nearly two years after Pixley Seme's conviction, Plaatje had reason to complain of his own mistreatment by the white conductor of a tram in Kimberley, his response was not to argue the case on the spot, let alone draw a revolver, but to get off the tram and complain in writing to the manager of De Beers (which owned the tram), pointing out the various ways in which he had always sought to act in such a manner as to avoid any provocation.[22] Clearly, Plaatje and Seme were men of very different temperament and experience, an added complication in itself to the achievement of unity amongst the potential leaders in any new African political movement.

Pixley Seme nevertheless had the very great advantage of being free of any earlier political involvement and associations, and he proved to be the right person to take the initiative in overcoming the obstacles and rivalries which had hitherto kept so many of South Africa's leading black political personalities apart. At the August 1911 meeting and subsequently Seme was able to argue powerfully and eloquently for a new unity and the need for a fresh, more vigorous political organisation that represented the interests of all Africans. Like Plaatje, Seme, closely connected to the Swazi royal family, was acutely aware of the importance of securing the support of the chiefs in any organisation that sought to represent the African people of South Africa, and he knew their financial support was likely to be a crucial factor in its success. Both Plaatje and Seme, and others who were involved in the discussions and negotiations in the second half of 1911, had in mind a movement that would not only unite politically active Africans and their separate organisations in different parts of the country, but also achieve a social unity – of the chiefs, as representatives of traditional forms of authority and influence; of the new generation, or generations, of mission-educated Africans who were now ready to assume the leadership in the political affairs of their people; and the masses of the people who needed to be led. Only by achieving this, Seme argued, could Africans overcome the political disabilities recently confirmed in the Act of Union, and only with such an organisation would they be able to 'make their grievances known and considered', he said, 'both by the Government and by the people of South Africa at large'.[23] With a momentum that combined high idealism with close attention to the thorny problem of reconciling existing political and personal differences, Plaatje, Seme, and their colleagues, moved slowly, during the second half of 1911, towards the establishment of the first united African political organisation in South Africa. In November a further 'caucus' meeting was held, Plaatje was reported to have made a closing speech 'exhorting the members to be united', and it was finally agreed to hold an inaugural conference in Bloemfontein at the beginning of January 1912.[24]

Perhaps partly because the achievement of this unity seemed to many to have been so long delayed (as Seme had pointed out at the November meeting, the idea of a united African political organisation was 'a very old idea'), most of the chiefs and delegates, representing organisations from all four provinces of South Africa (and the protectorates), were conscious that they were attending a conference of historic importance. Seme pointed out in his opening address that it was the first time that 'so many elements representing different tongues and tribes ever attempted to co-operate under one umbrella', and he went on to emphasise the difficulties they faced; the formation of Congress, though, was the 'first step towards solving the so-called native problem, and therein lay the advancement of the dark races who had hitherto been separated by tribal jealousies'. His motion proposing the establishment of Congress was seconded by Chief Joshua Molema, and the two men were followed by a series of other speakers, chiefs and commoners, all urging support. When it was put to a vote – late in the afternoon of Monday, 8 January 1912 – the motion was passed unanimously, and met with loud cheers from all the delegates, who had risen from their seats.[25] Even at the time they were in no doubt that they had taken a vital step forward in the history of their people – equivalent in significance, as many saw it to the achievement of the 'whites only' Act of Union.

The next business in hand – the appointment of officeholders – was a matter of some delicacy, for it was generally recognised that it was of the utmost importance to the future of the organisation to achieve a satisfactory balance between the different regions and people represented. It was widely expected that Dr Walter Rubusana of East London, a Congregational minister, member of the Cape provincial council (the only African ever to be elected to this), formerly president of the South African Native Convention, and already something of an elder statesman in African eyes, would be elected as president of Congress. In fact, the presidency was offered to another clergyman, the Reverend John Dube, who was not actually present at the meeting (having injured himself in a bad fall from a horse), being represented instead by his brother, Charles Dube. Behind this decision lay a desire on the part of the assembled delegates to select at their head as widely acceptable a figure as possible. Since Rubusana was involved in Cape politics both as a Cape provincial councillor and as a longstanding political opponent of the other major Cape African figure, John Tengo Jabavu, his election as president would have been anathema to many Cape Africans and would have made it impossible to attract Jabavu's supporters to the movement. John Dube, a Zulu, was in any case an impressive figure. Ordained as a clergyman by American missionaries in Natal, as a young man he had travelled to the United States to further his education, and, perceiving the parallels between Natal and the American south, came to be strongly influenced by the ideas of the black American educator, Booker T. Washington; so much so, indeed, that in his declaration accepting the presidency of Congress, he indicated that Booker T. Washington was to be his 'patron saint' and 'guiding star'.[26]

Dube was well known, too, both as editor of the English/Zulu newspaper, *Ilanga lase Natal*, and as principal of his own school at Ohlange, near Durban. He was acceptable as president of Congress because the majority of delegates at its inaugural conference wished to emphasise that African political activity would in future no longer be centred in the relatively privileged Cape. And Dube himself seemed to be inspired by this new spirit of national unity, writing on one occasion of 'the great work we have taken upon ourselves as Natives of South Africa to unite together and give up old differences and racial hatreds and tribal quarrels to stand as one man, to speak as a voice of one person, for the interest of all'.[27] Dr Rubusana, therefore, had to be content with the post of vice-president, and the other positions were distributed as follows: Pixley Seme and Thomas Mapikela were to be the two treasurers, Attorney G. D. Montsioa of Pietersburg (northern Transvaal) became recording secretary, and eight of the chiefs, including the Barolong paramount, Badirile Montshiwa, became honorary presidents. Together with the provision in the constitution for an upper house of chiefs, these last-mentioned appointments emphasised the importance that the Congress leaders attached to their support and involvement. Plaatje, perhaps more than most, believed very strongly that Congress was likely to stand or fall on this question, and was reported to have remarked at the time that 'the Natives can never effect anything which is not supported by chiefs': he undoubtedly had his own experiences in Mafeking very much in mind.[28]

Plaatje himself was elected general secretary, a position that was in many ways even more important than that of president. With his many years' experience as a newspaper editor and political spokesman, his clerical experience in the Cape Civil Service, a well-known capacity for hard work (likely to be essential to success in building up any new national movement), and his ability to speak all the major African languages of the country, there could have been little argument that he was an ideal choice for the position. An additional consideration was the fact that he was known to be close to the politically sophisticated Africans of the Cape (the fact that he had a Mfengu wife obviously helped here), without, however, being tainted with their degree of involvement in the party and ethnic rivalries of the eastern Cape. Widely accepted at the same time as a spokesman for Africans living in the Transvaal and Orange Free State, as well as the Bechuanaland Protectorate, Plaatje was seen as the right person to bring to the new national movement the traditions and skills of African political life in the Cape, but to direct these instead to the wider political realities that were now imposed by Union. And more than any other African political leader, Plaatje had acquired the reputation of having ready access to the Union administration; if any of the delegates at Bloemfontein had any doubts on this point, they had only to look at the most recent issue of *Tsala ea Becoana*, which carried detailed reports on Plaatje's series of interviews in Pretoria with government ministers and high-ranking administrators; or to have read an editorial that appeared in *Ilanga lase Natal* several weeks later congratulating him on the good work he had been doing here, concluding that 'South Africans are much indebted to our good friend, Mr Sol Plaatje'.[29]

So it was, as *Tsala ea Becoana* remarked in February 1912, that its editor, 'besides taking a leading part in the movement, has been saddled with nearly the whole of the secretarial work at the instance of the Native lawyers who convened the movement'.[30] Possibly, as this report suggests, Plaatje was somewhat reluctant to take on the task. Knowing the amount of time and work that was likely to be required in getting the SANNC effectively off the ground, he must have given careful consideration to the potentially adverse effects this was likely to have upon his newspaper business. At the same time, it was recognition of the part he had now come to play in the political affairs of his people, and of the talents that suited him so well to the position; it was not an opportunity – or responsibility – that he felt it right to turn down.

The other main business of Congress's inaugural conference consisted of discussing the draft constitution. No agreement, however, was reached over this, the main stumbling block being the question of its financial structure and the size of contributions from the local branches. There was some discussion, too, about the name of the new organisation, and this also proved to be a point of considerable contention. Plaatje's proposal was that it should be 'known by a distinctive name, and a native name for preference', his argument being that there were already in existence so many councils and congresses that an additional name of the same kind would only confuse people further. Although strongly supported by Joshua Molema, the meeting decided by a small majority to adopt the recommendations of the Transvaal organisations represented there that they should be known as the South African Native National Congress. Plaatje clearly felt strongly about the issue, for when the executive committee was authorised (on his own motion) to remain behind and complete the unfinished work and review the constitution, he again urged that Congress's name be changed. Again, though, Plaatje's resolution was defeated – this time by a majority of two, and the name 'South African Native National Congress' was incorporated into the constitution.[31] It was the first, although not, as time would show, the last instance of differences of view between Plaatje and the Transvaal members of Congress.

Agreement was reached, though, on the objects of the organisation, and these were defined as follows:

(a) The promotion of unity and mutual co-operation between the Government and the Abantu Races of South Africa.
(b) The maintenance of a central channel of communication between the Government and the aboriginal races in South Africa.
(c) The promotion of the educational, social, economical and political elevation of the native people in South Africa.
(d) The promotion of mutual understanding between the Native chiefs and the encouragement in them and their people of a spirit of loyalty to the British crown, and all lawfully constituted authorities, and to bring about better understanding between the white and black inhabitants of South Africa.[32]

By no stretch of the imagination could Congress's aims be described as radical. Industrial action was not contemplated as a means of obtaining redress of the growing number of grievances of which its members now complained. Congress hoped and believed that in bringing their complaints to the attention of the authorities through the tried methods of explanation, petition, and deputation, they would be given a fair hearing and their grievances attended to. They resolved now to give added weight to their cause by demonstrating that the new organisation did genuinely represent the African people of South Africa as a whole; to make it impossible for South Africa's white rulers to dismiss their claims, as they so often did, on the grounds that they spoke only for the educated minority.

◇

In practice it was to Plaatje, and to a lesser extent, John Dube, that the main responsibility for building up the Congress movement, and establishing its legitimacy in the eyes of both government and people, devolved. For some months their hope that the government would accept and recognise Congress's desire to act as a kind of consultative body on 'native affairs' seemed justified. Taking up issues that had been discussed at Congress's inaugural meeting, Plaatje travelled to Cape Town in March 1912 (in advance of John Dube and several other Congress office-holders) to arrange meetings with various government ministers, taking the opportunity whilst there to discuss with Dr Abdul Abdurahman, president of the (predominantly coloured) African Political Organisation, the possibilities of co-operation between their respective organisations. This in itself was a development of potential importance, and it brought together two men who were to enjoy a relationship of respect and friendship for many years to come. Of all the Congress leaders Plaatje was the best equipped by temperament and experience to take such an initiative: Kimberley had a long history of co-operation between Africans and Coloureds and Plaatje himself was now an active member of the Kimberley branch of the APO. And, in Plaatje's view, the achievement of unity amongst Africans, however desirable and important in itself, was not something to be achieved at the expense of friendly co-operation with the Coloured people (or indeed of white sympathisers) in their common struggles.

Plaatje therefore arranged a meeting of the executive of the South African Native National Congress with that of the APO at its offices in Loop Street, Cape Town, and the meeting duly resolved that 'there should be closer co-operation between the Coloured and Native races of South Africa', declaring 'that the two bodies should keep in close touch with each other, and discuss matters directly affecting non-Europeans, and where necessary take united action'.[33]

But the main purpose of Plaatje's visit to Cape Town was to meet with government ministers. These meetings also went well. Amongst the matters brought to the attention of J. W. Sauer, the minister responsible, by a deputation composed of Plaatje, Thomas Mapikela, and S. M. Makgotho, one of the Congress vice-presidents, was the question of the treatment of Africans on railways. On this, they managed to secure from him a promise that the matters they had raised would be looked into. The interview was preceded by an interesting exchange that served to illustrate the value both of Plaatje's relationship with Henry Burton, the Minister of Native Affairs, and his experience in handling junior government officials. *Tsala ea Becoana* recounted the story:

The members of the deputation reached the office punctually at 10 a.m., the appointed time, and were ushered with great ceremony into the presence of a clerk who seemed all affability. He told them in courteous terms, that Mr Sauer was too busy to see them, and if they would be good enough to entrust him with the object of their mission he would take it down, and ensure a reply. The Minister, he told them, was too busy to see them, and if they acted on his advice things would be all right. They told him they regretted the Minister was so busy, and if he would be kind enough to tell them when he would see them they would call again.

'No,' said the official. 'Mr Sauer is very busy, and he is not likely to be able to see you for days. Just tell me all about it, and I will see that you get an answer.'

'No,' said our editor, 'we have not come to see you, we have come to see the Minister by arrangement with another Minister, and if he cannot see us we will go back and ask Mr Burton why he sent us at ten o'clock, sharp, to a Minister who is unable to see us.'

It transpired that just at that moment Mr Sauer was expecting the deputation.[34]

That meeting took place on a Tuesday. During the same week Plaatje secured two hearings for a Congress deputation (which included John Dube, just arrived in Cape Town) with the Minister for Native Affairs, one concerned with the issue of passes for women, the other with the so-called 'Squatters Bill', the latest in a line of measures designed to limit the numbers of Africans living on European-owned farms, and an issue that had greatly concerned Congress at its inaugural meeting. If this law was passed, the meeting had felt, the effect 'could only be to turn the native population of South Africa into wanderers and pariahs in the land of their birth'. They were prophetic words. This 'Squatters Bill', however, was dropped during the parliamentary session of 1912, as a result – or so Plaatje claimed later – of Congress's representations on the issue to Henry Burton. Although no such promise was actually made by Burton at his meeting with the Congress deputation, both the Minister and his Secretary for Native Affairs, Edward Dower, had been willing to receive Plaatje, Dube and the other delegates who accompanied them, and discussed the bill with them in some detail. Burton told them, however, that 'those who battle for their rights must exercise patience', and that the last thing the government wanted was 'injustice to the natives'; whilst he was 'prepared to adopt a most reasonable attitude when it is brought up for discussion in Parliament', he saw 'no other way of dealing with the state of affairs', and that something of this sort was 'absolutely necessary'.[35]

That Burton was actually influenced by the deputation's representations on this occasion is very doubtful. Of much greater weight in influencing the government's decision to drop the bill was the opposition of certain white interests (particularly the influential large absentee landlords, who stood to lose most from it), and a speech in the House of Lords in England by Lord Selborne, the former High Commissioner, strongly opposing the proposals.[36] It nevertheless suited both Plaatje and the other Congress leaders, keen to establish the movement amongst their people, to believe that their own representations had been taken into account, and to spread round the idea that this had been so. Certainly on other issues raised by the deputation Burton had responded more favourably. To the request of Plaatje and Dube that the government set up a commission to look at the so-called 'Black Peril', he indicated that he 'quite agreed with the sentiment', and a commission was duly set up; on the subject of 'Natives employed on Railways', he told Plaatje that he 'ought to see Mr Sauer', and arranged the interview referred to above; and to Thomas Mapikela's request that part of the imperial vote of funds that had been 'set apart for the natives in the Orange Free State' should be used for educational purposes, he agreed to 'try and help them' to arrange this.[37] These interviews represented the first direct, official contact between the newly formed South African Native National Congress and the government of the Union of South Africa; on the whole the Congress delegates went home well pleased with their reception.

Plaatje's newspaper business, meanwhile, was encountering one difficulty after the other. Throughout the early months of 1912 *Tsala ea Becoana* managed to appear regularly (despite several changes that were made in its printing arrangements), but with its issue of 8 June 1912 publication ceased.[38] Exactly what happened is unclear, but it can safely be assumed that it was due to an accumulation of financial problems – although it may well have owed something to Plaatje's heavy involvement in the affairs of the South African Native National Congress as well; for most of March, April and May 1912, Plaatje had been away in Cape Town and elsewhere, and it is difficult to believe that these extended absences from the office – whatever the arrangements made to ensure the paper appeared regularly during his absence – were not also a contributory factor to its demise.

But within three months Plaatje was back in business, not only with a new newspaper, *Tsala ea Batho* ('The Friend of the People'), but with a new printing press of his own. The opportunity to acquire this arose from the bankruptcy of a short-lived Johannesburg newspaper, *Motsualle oa Babatsho*, and Plaatje was fortunate to have been able to acquire its press at a good price, and to merge this paper with his. He was heartened to find support for the project in Johannesburg from non-Tswana Africans, who generously provided the £200 that was needed – the kind of gesture that was very much in line with this new spirit of inter-tribal unity epitomised in the formation of the SANNC. At the same time the gesture drew attention to the apparent reluctance on the part of his own Tswana people – or so Plaatje saw it – to support a paper in their own language, fighting for their rights. A letter that he wrote to Silas Molema (the original in Setswana) on 8 August 1912 gives a good indication of the difficulties he still faced and the frustrations he felt:

> Last night – I was surprised to find in the mailbag a letter I wrote and thought I had posted to you from the Transvaal; I don't know how it got there. I had to put the machinery on the train without money. I then passed on to Thaba Nchu where I hope to get some money for railage. I found the gentlemen concerned absent, so I went to Kimberley. It was a wild goose chase I went on.
>
> There are many things that disappoint me. What tore my heart apart was when sympathetic Zulus bought us the machinery for £200 and I realised that the Tswana people are unable to collect money and start their own newspaper. Even the scheme for concerts was arranged by Mr Msimang. People are aiding us! It makes one sometimes feel that there is no good in all this stirring for the rights of the Tswana people.
>
> I have heard very little from home and it is hard to go and arrive there after three months without a penny. It would not be so shameful if the train money had been paid for.
>
> Yours very truly,
> Sol T. Plaatje[39]

The first issue of the new combined newspaper, published in Sepedi as well as Setswana and English, appeared in the middle of September 1912. Its new title, *Tsala ea Batho*, reflected both the union of Tswana and Pedi peoples which the merger was taken to signify, and to symbolise also an aspiration towards a wider unity – precisely what the South African Native National Congress was striving for in terms of political organisation. New offices were also acquired in Shannon Street (soon to become known as the Newton Printing Works) and were formally opened on 7 September 1912, the very day Plaatje's wife Elizabeth gave birth to a son – promptly christened Johannes Gutenburg in celebration of the fact; for the Plaatje family there was thus double reason for celebration that day.[40] Although it was not long before Plaatje was complaining that lack of capital was retarding the growth of *Tsala*, and preventing improvements from being made to the machinery, the newspaper appeared regularly for the next four months; from the point of view of his newspaper business, Plaatje was therefore able to start the new year, 1913, in a mood of relative optimism.[41]

◇

The same thing could no longer be said of Plaatje's view of the wider political prospects faced by the African people, for since the middle of 1912 there had been a number of significant, and from his point of view ominous, developments. Foremost amongst these was the replacement of Henry Burton as Minister of Native Affairs by General Hertzog, whose views on 'native policy' were sufficiently well known to cause considerable alarm to the Congress leadership when the news was announced. At the meeting the Congress leaders had with Henry Burton in March 1912 John Dube, though he can have had no knowledge of the ministerial changes soon to take place, had quite bluntly told Burton, 'What we are afraid of is your successor in office.'[42] His fears proved to be wholly justified. After taking office as Minister for Native Affairs in June 1912, Hertzog busied himself with preparing some comprehensive proposals to deal with the 'native problem' which went a great deal further than the abortive 'Squatters Bill'.

Henry Burton's replacement by General Hertzog in fact marked an important turning-point in the behaviour and composition of General Botha's administration. It signalled the end of a period of relative inaction and lack of direction in the field of 'native affairs', a sharp decline in the influence of the Cape liberals in the government, and the ever-growing strength of Afrikaner nationalism both inside and outside parliament. What optimism Plaatje and his colleagues once had about African prospects in the Union soon evaporated in the face of the government's determination to implement a comprehensive 'native policy' that was acceptable to the country's two most powerful interests: the farmers and the mineowners, maize and gold. One legislative proposal in particular sought to achieve this objective: it was known as the Natives' Land Bill, whose provisions were first made known in February 1913.

The Natives' Land Act of 1913 (as it duly became) was one of the most important pieces of legislation in South African history, and one of the central events in Plaatje's life; over the next four years, indeed, its course was largely shaped by his response to the legislation. When the provisions of the bill were first made known, the effect was to confirm the worst fears of the Congress leadership about the direction in which official 'native policy' was going. The Natives' Land Act was important above all for introducing into the legislation of the Union the principle of territorial separation, or segregation. Its central provision was to deprive Africans of the right to acquire land outside their existing areas of occupation, and to prohibit whites from acquiring land within these areas, now defined as 'Scheduled Native Areas'. Few Africans at the time objected strongly to the principle of territorial segregation *per se*, provided it could be implemented in a reasonable and equitable manner, and provided it did not also entail acceptance of giving up any political or constitutional rights. At the same time, few had any illusions about the possibility of either condition being met, and many would have shared the views Plaatje had expressed in his prize essay on the subject of segregation in 1910. These views seemed to be fully vindicated with the publication of the Natives' Land Bill, for it was clear from this that there was in practice no possibility whatever of territorial separation being implemented in anything like an equitable manner, whilst the debates in parliament suggested that the logical corollary to the bill – in the minds of some, at least, of its supporters – was the phasing out of the Cape franchise.[43]

Under the terms of the bill, only 7.3 per cent of the total land surface of the Union was to be set aside for African occupation, patently inadequate to support a population that was four times the size of the white population. To meet this objection, a commission was appointed under the provisions of the bill to find and purchase land for African occupation to add to what had already been set aside – consisting largely of the 'reserves' already in African occupation, and nearly all of them very overcrowded. Under the chairmanship of Sir William Beaumont, a former administrator of Natal and a Supreme Court judge, the commission was charged with completing its investigations and presenting its report within two years. In the intervening period though, before the commission reported, Africans were to be barred from purchasing land except from other Africans, or in existing reserves where, as Plaatje was to point out, this could not be done anyway since most land here was held communally, not individually.

Neither the idea of territorial separation nor the wider philosophy of segregation which underlay and served to justify the Act were of course new. Certain provisions of the Natives' Land Act gave expression to recommendations of the South African Native Affairs Commission of 1903–5, and in a very real sense the Act actually implemented – somewhat belatedly, it is true – one of the major objectives of British imperial policy as formulated during the reconstruction period. The implementation of this grand design, though, formed only part of the objectives of the Natives' Land Act. Other provisions it contained, as well as the hasty manner in which it was pushed through the House of Assembly, reflected the response of General Botha's administration to the acute political pressures that were, in 1912 and 1913, coming to be exerted upon it, particularly from white farmers in the Transvaal and Orange Free State, whose demands for state intervention on their behalf had been becoming more and more insistent. The legislation they got went further than anything that had been proposed in the past, and it threatened to have particularly drastic consequences in the Orange Free State. Here, the system of 'sowing on the halves' (widespread in the province since the Anglo-Boer war), whereby Africans living on white-owned farms gave half of their produce to the white landowner in exchange for the seed and the right to farm the land, was made illegal. What many white farmers in the Free State now wanted was not a share of the produce of 'squatters' living on their land, but their labour, and on the best terms possible. Capitalist farming had, for a variety of reasons, become a much more attractive proposition than hitherto, but depended upon an adequate supply of cheap labour. This the Natives' Land Act – by converting African producers in these areas from peasants into farm labourers – aimed to provide.[44] The segregationist ideology in which the Natives' Land Act was framed, and with which it was justified, barely disguised the manner in which these provisions expressed the new-found political power of the white farmers, mobilised under the banner of Afrikaner nationalism, in the politics of Union.

◇

Plaatje's reaction to the Natives' Land Bill, once its provisions became known, was one of shocked disbelief. He felt it particularly because it appeared to be aimed specifically at an area he knew so well: the Orange Free State, province of his birth. Like many of his colleagues, Plaatje had been lulled into something of a false sense of security, politically speaking, by the lack of direction in 'native affairs' during the first two years of Union. Possibly, too, his own success in building relationships with government ministers and administrators – even if he did recognise the tenuous foundations upon which they were built – had created an illusion of influence in government circles that for a while disguised the highly vulnerable position in which the African people and their leaders found themselves in the period after Union. Neither Plaatje nor any of his colleagues in the leadership of the South African Native National Congress were properly equipped to respond effectively to so momentous and drastic a piece of legislation as the Natives' Land Act of 1913. They had been brought up to believe in notions of gradual progress and advancement. Setbacks they had certainly experienced in their adult lives – at Vereeniging in 1902, the Act of Union more recently – but the ideal persisted. Nothing prepared them for an Act such as this: it struck at the heart of their belief in a common society, at their conviction that, ultimately, a shared sense of decency and humanity, between black and white, rulers and ruled, would protect them from measures such as that now before them. What could they do but respond in the terms and with the methods to which they had been so long accustomed?

But as Plaatje for one was quick to realise, the Natives' Land Act – by far the greatest threat yet faced by the South African Native National Congress – did at least provide the opportunity to mobilise the movement in a way that no other issue had yet done.[45] Unlike many of the earlier issues with which Congress had been concerned – travelling on railways, or employment in government service – the Land Act threatened the interests and well-being of virtually every section of the African population. It thus provided an opportunity to cement that social unity which Seme had talked of when calling Congress's inaugural meeting, a sense of unity founded in an identity of interest so strong that the government could not overlook it.

Plaatje himself was in the forefront of organising African opposition to the Land Act. From the time of its passage in June 1913 until his departure from South Africa as a member of a Congress deputation to England a year later it was to be the overwhelming preoccupation of himself personally, of his newspaper, and of the South African Native National Congress as a whole. Congress's response from the beginning was to concern itself not with the principle of territorial segregation which the Land Act claimed to embody, but with the effects it was likely to have. Its first move, after the provisions of the bill first became known at the end of February 1913, was to call a meeting in Johannesburg which appointed a deputation to go to Cape Town to protest to the government about the harm that would follow if the bill became law. Plaatje himself was not able, for financial reasons, to travel with his deputation, which went in May, but was present at the special July meeting which was convened to hear its report. The delegates had, so Dr Rubusana related, four interviews with J. W. Sauer, who had recently succeeded Hertzog as Minister of Native Affairs, and further sessions with other members of parliament. Their protests had made no impact whatever, and even their clear willingness to compromise had failed to elicit the slightest response. Lord Gladstone, the High Commissioner, a keen supporter of General Botha's government, offered no hope either. Plaatje had written to him earlier, requesting that he withhold his assent to the bill until he had heard the 'native view'. To this, Plaatje recalled, 'His Excellency replied that such a course was not within his constitutional functions'. John Dube again approached him after the Act had become law, with a request for an interview to inform him of 'the nature of the damage that the Act was causing among the Native population'. He received exactly the same reply.[46]

As the Congress leaders feared, the effects of the Land Act, once it had come into operation on 20 June 1913, were immediate and devastating. They were discussed at the July meeting of Congress, which heard from delegates from all four provinces of their observations of the way in which white farmers were taking advantage of the new law to rid themselves of unwanted tenants, or forcing away others who refused to accept arbitrary demands for their labour. Plaatje himself, on the journey from Kimberley to Johannesburg, came across some of the worst effects of the Act, witnessing scenes that were to remain with him for the rest of his life. He set out from Kimberley in the first week of July in the direction of Bloemhof, on the Transvaal side of the Vaal river, and had found there, barely three months after the Act had become law, a large number of African families with their stock, who had travelled from the Free State, thinking that the Land Act was only in operation in that province. Travelling by bicycle, Plaatje encountered many of these evicted families on the road. On the boundary of the Hoopstad/Boshof districts of the Free State, not far from his place of birth, he described what he saw:

> We passed several farm-houses along the road, where all appeared pretty tranquil as we went along, until the evening which we spent in the open country, somewhere near to the boundaries of the Hoopstad and Boshof districts; here a regular circus had gathered. By 'a circus', we mean the meeting of groups of families, moving to every point of the compass, and all bivouacked at this point in the open country where we were passing. It was heartrending to listen to the tales of their cruel experiences derived from the rigour of the Natives' Land Act. Some of the cattle had perished on the journey, from poverty and lack of fodder, and the native owners ran a serious risk of imprisonment for travelling with dying stock.[47]

Having heard Plaatje and other Congress delegates tell of their experiences of the effects of the Land Act, Congress resolved to appeal directly to the King, to the British parliament and, if need be, to the British public, to secure the removal of this iniquitous piece of legislation from the statute book. Since the passage of the Act of Union the constitutional position was that legislation passed by the South African parliament had still to be ratified by the imperial authorities, and then to receive the royal assent. In practice, these constitutional requirements were regarded in official circles as purely formalities, and only in the most exceptional circumstances was the imperial right of veto throught likely to be invoked. When the legislation in question owed so much to British policies evolved during the reconstruction period in any case, it seemed certain that the attitude of the imperial government–quite apart from the niceties of the constitutional position–would be one of warm support for General Botha's government. It was upon his shoulders, after all, that hopes of maintaining British influence in southern Africa now rested. Most of the members of Congress, even if they did not see things quite in these terms, seem to have been well aware that the prospect of persuading the imperial government to refuse its assent to any piece of South African legislation was remote in the extreme. An appeal to the imperial government was, though, the only constitutional option open to them, and they decided to take it.

For what alternative was there? The idea of some form of strike action was indeed raised at this meeting by several delegates from the Transvaal, but they were in a small minority, and easily outvoted. Plaatje was strongly against the proposal. He had an instinctive distaste for any action of this kind, and at the July meeting had personally drafted a resolution 'dissociating the natives from the [white miners'] strike movement' after this idea had been put forward, and he took strong issue with several prominent Transvaal Africans who later on in the year argued in favour of abandoning the deputation and resorting to strike action instead.[48] Although Plaatje, like his colleagues, had few illusions about the chances of securing an imperial veto on the Land Act, he was in a large majority in believing that it was essential to exhaust every constitutional option that existed. 'Let our delegates tell the Imperial Government that we have appealed to the highest authorities in South Africa,' Plaatje wrote,

> and both our appeals, and the church's representations on our behalf, have been ignored; and let the Imperial Government inform our delegates that His Majesty's kingship over us ceased with the signing of the Act of Union and that whites and blacks in South Africa can do what they please; then only will we have the alternative, and I too will agree that we had better have a general strike, and 'damn the consequences'. Till then I will maintain that the consequences of a strike are too serious, and the probable complications too dreadful, to contemplate.[49]

Once it was decided to send a deputation to England an emergency committee was set up to raise the necessary funds. Then Plaatje, accompanied by Dube and Makgatho, travelled to Pretoria to convey these decisions in person to the new Minister for Native Affairs, F. S. Malan. Malan attempted to dissuade them from proceeding with their plan to send a deputation to England, but had no concessions whatever to offer them in return. Nor did the minister's words inspire any confidence in the prospect of any alleviation in the sufferings being caused by the Act. He advised the three of them to wait until the Beaumont

Commission reported, 'as it was rather too early to judge an Act which has been in operation only one month', and wait until there were 'cases of real suffering'. Plaatje asked for a definition of the word 'suffering'. 'If the evictions of all the families he had already told the Minister about did not amount to "suffering",' he said, 'then what did the word mean?'[50] It was difficult for Plaatje to believe that F. S. Malan, a man with a reputation as 'a friend of the natives', a product of the Cape, shaped by so many of the traditions and ideals as himself, could have displayed so callous an attitude.

Bitterly disappointed at Malan's attitude – for Plaatje continued to hope against hope that a personal appeal to the human nature of those in power would cause them to relent – he travelled back home to Kimberley with his colleague from Thaba Nchu, J. M. Nyokong, by way of Vereeniging, Kroonstadt, and Bloemfontein. In all three places he addressed meetings about the Natives' Land Act, collected further evidence of its effects, and appealed for funds to enable the deputation to travel to England.[51] At the beginning of the next month, September 1913, he set out on another tour to investigate the effects of the Act in other parts of the Free State, and found many more examples of what he had seen during those first few weeks in July: African families wandering from place to place, refusing to accept arbitrary conversion from peasant to labourer but unable to find anywhere else to go and live. Many of them had congregated around Ladybrand in the hope of being able to cross the border into Basutoland (where the Act did not apply), whilst many of those who actually lived in the area had been given notice to quit. The only advice Plaatje could give them was that they should travel to Thaba Nchu the following week and listen to an address from Edward Dower, the Secretary for Native Affairs, who was travelling around the country advising on the implementation of the Land Act; and to seek the Governor-General's special permission to continue to live on their farm, as was provided for in Section 1 of the Act.[52]

Plaatje himself travelled to this meeting. He soon discovered that Dower had no relief whatever to offer. In his first speech, to the astonishment of the thousand or so people present, Edward Dower failed even to mention the Natives' Land Act. When he finally did address himself to the question he gave no indication whatever that the government was prepared to compromise in any way. He explained that the Natives' Land Act, through introducing the principle of territorial segregation, was in the best interests of the African population, and advised those present to do one of three things: become servants; move into the 'reserves' (he did not specify which he had in mind – there were none in the Orange Free State); or sell their stock for cash. He concluded by stating that in the Orange Free State, unlike the other provinces, there was in actual fact no provision for special cases being made through application to the Governor-General. This concluding statement, Plaatje reported, 'settled the minds of those who had expected from the Government any protection against the law, and the disappointment under which the meeting broke up was indescribable.'[53]

◇

In November 1913 Plaatje undertook yet another major tour of investigation into the working of the Act, this time to the eastern Cape. While other Congress leaders were collecting evidence and raising funds for the deputation to England in other parts of South Africa, nobody as yet had been doing this in the eastern Cape. Plaatje agreed to undertake the mission. Although there was some confusion in legal circles as to whether the Natives' Land Act was applicable in the Cape – since its provisions impinged upon the landholding qualifications for the franchise, itself entrenched in the Union constitution – Plaatje nevertheless found that some white farmers were taking advantage of the situation to rearrange their relationships with their African tenants in the same way as was happening elsewhere.

Plaatje's other objective during this tour was to meet and discuss with two prominent individuals who had previously expressed their support for the Natives' Land Act. The first of these was James Henderson, Principal of Lovedale, Plaatje's first port of call. Here he found that Henderson's views were 'based on second-hand information', and that he had little real knowledge of the Land Act and what it was about. Plaatje then took advantage of the opportunity to air his views in Lovedale's influential journal, the *Christian Express*, which duly contained the long letter he wrote in order to express his view of the purpose and effects of the Act: 'a carefully prepared, deliberate and premeditated scheme,' he said, 'to compass the partial enslavement of the Natives.' What Plaatje went on to say can have left nobody in any doubt whatever about the impact which his observations of the effects of the Act had had upon him:

> I shall never forget the scenes I have witnessed in the Hoopstad district during the cold snap of July, of families living on the roads, the numbers of their attenuated flocks emaciated by lack of fodder on the trek, many of them dying while the wandering owners ran risks of prosecution for travelling with unhealthy stock. I saw the little children shivering, and contrasted their condition with the better circumstances of my own children in their Kimberley home; and when the mothers told me of the homes they had left behind and the privations they have endured since eviction I could scarcely suppress a tear.[54]

What Plaatje saw in the wake of the passage of the Natives' Land Act remained in his mind for the rest of his life; it generated in him a sense of anger and betrayal far deeper than anything hitherto, a feeling of disbelief, too, that fellow human beings could be so callous about the consequences of their actions. It was almost as though there was a sense of responsibility on his own part for having misjudged government ministers, many of whom he knew quite well by now – the men responsible for the passage of such inhuman legislation. Plaatje's response to the Land Act seems to have given him a deeper, more emotional sense of identity with the people he represented than had existed before.

The second person, after James Henderson, whom Plaatje wished to see was John Tengo Jabavu, editor of *Imvo*, who lived in Kingwilliamstown. The Natives' Land Act was the point at which South Africa's two leading black newspaper editors finally parted company, and in circumstances that were both tragic and bitter. Jabavu had been one of Plaatje's childhood heroes, a man whose career and position had provided him with example and inspiration, never far from his mind when he first became a newspaper editor himself. Thereafter, despite their differences in age, the two men had become good friends. Jabavu had become godfather to Plaatje's daughter Olive, in 1904, and on several occasions had stayed with Plaatje and his wife while visiting Mafeking and Kimberley.[55] Jabavu had then been involved with Plaatje in the establishment of *Tsala ea Becoana*, his company had printed the paper for over a year, and Plaatje himself had taken over the editorship of *Imvo* for a month during Jabavu's absence in Europe late in 1911. Taking place as it did at a time of intense discussion over forming a new, united political organisation, this last move in particular seemed to symbolise the new spirit of co-operation amongst African political leaders in South Africa; it had looked as though Jabavu, at last, might be persuaded to lend his support to this new movement for unity.

In 1913, though, Jabavu came out in favour of the Natives' Land Act, the only African politician of any significance to do so. After so many years of involvement in the politics of the Cape Colony, Jabavu found himself tied – after Union – to the policies of General Botha's government, for three shareholders in Jabavu's company were now cabinet ministers. His closest association was with J. W. Sauer, one of his oldest political allies, and the man to whom fell the task of introducing the Natives' Land Bill in the House of Assembly. The measure broke both men. Sauer was reported to have been in tears after introducing the bill in the House of Assembly, justifying his decision to do so on the grounds that Africans would get something much worse if he had not done so. 'Why,' Dr Rubusana had asked him, 'did you not resign in protest?' 'Because,' replied Sauer, 'your position would have been infinitely worse.'[56] Several weeks later Sauer died, his death hastened, as many saw it, by the anguish of having to introduce a piece of legislation that went against all he had stood for in a long and distinguished political career. Jabavu, though, continued to support the measure. In doing so, he met with almost universal criticism from Africans inside as well as outside the Cape, and he rapidly lost what remained of a reputation built up over so many years. Given the position he had taken, this was virtually inevitable; it was rendered all the more so, however, by Plaatje's determination to challenge him directly over the issue.

Plaatje reached Kingwilliamstown on 3 November, carrying with him an invitation to address a meeting there about the Natives' Land Act. Jabavu, whom he called upon before the meeting was due to take place, refused to see him, and did not attend the meeting. Several days later *Imvo* carried a very disparaging report about the meeting, and Plaatje responded with an invitation to a public debate about the Land Act. Jabavu failed to accept the challenge. Details of the whole episode were widely publicised in the press – African and European – at the time, and contributed further to the eclipse of Jabavu's political reputation.[57]

The episode perhaps illustrated more clearly than anything else the ambiguous legacy of a Cape tradition to the politics of Union. Plaatje's ideals and political philosophy were rooted in the Cape quite as much as those of Tengo Jabavu; as John Dube once remarked, very aptly, 'if Mr Plaatje had had his own way, he would have torn up the Union constitution and re-enacted the old Cape constitution'.[58] But Plaatje was able to emerge as a national political leader and spokesman after Union because, unlike Jabavu, his vision, his political constituency, was a wider one, and he was not at the same time tied to the interests and structures of the Cape. In the process of forging a national African movement there were some sad casualties: Jabavu was the most notable amongst them. At such a critical moment in the history of his people, Plaatje was not prepared to allow sentimental attachments of the past to stand in the way of what he saw as his clear political duty. He had seen too many of the drastic effects of what he was by now describing as 'the Plague Act' to feel able to extend any degree of sympathy to a man he had once so admired: the very closeness of their association in the past seemed only to emphasise the sense of betrayal which Plaatje clearly felt. By the time Jabavu acknowledged his error of judgement several years later his reputation was in tatters. Posterity has yet to redeem him.

$$\diamond$$

Throughout late 1913 and early 1914 Congress's campaign to collect funds for the deputation to England continued apace. In February 1914 a further conference was called to discuss the South African government's response to their representations, to ratify their decision (if no satisfactory assurances were forthcoming from Pretoria) to send the deputation, and to elect its members. The conference was originally meant to take place in Johannesburg, but the venue was changed to Kimberley at the last minute because of the martial law regulations (imposed as a result of a white miners' strike) in operation in the Transvaal.[59] After all the travelling he had been doing over the previous months it must have been some relief for Plaatje to have the conference in his home town, and the delegates received there the kind of reception which they would not have expected in Johannesburg. De Beers assisted in various ways, and the proceedings of the conference were opened by the Bishop of Kimberley and Kuruman, one of a substantial body of churchmen in South Africa who had considerable sympathy for Congress's case on the Natives' Land Act.

The conference's deliberations were then transformed as a result of a telephone call which Plaatje received from the local magistrate, informing him that he had received a telegram from Edward Dower, the Secretary for Native Affairs, which read as follows: 'Leaving tonight for Kimberley to attend the Native Congress. Inform Plaatje.' The effect of this surprising piece of news, which Plaatje then conveyed to the assembled delegates, was to raise their hopes that the government was, at last, preparing to make some concession to them over the Land Act, for no government representative of his standing had ever accepted one of the routine invitations to attend its meetings which Congress had always sent out. At last, it seemed, the government was showing some public sign of taking Congress seriously. The meeting therefore decided to postpone the election of the deputation until after Dower's arrival in the hope that he would make an announcement that would render it unnecessary.

Not for the first time Dower's message came as a great disappointment. During the course of a long speech he argued the case for territorial segregation, emphasising that more land had been promised and that the Act of 1913 should therefore be seen simply as a first instalment. At several points his arguments brought forth disbelieving laughter from his audience, and he aroused a visible resentment with his criticism of some Congress leaders for 'beating the air' and his description of the idea of a deputation to England as 'a huge mistake'. Dower had been sent to Kimberley, it became clear to everybody in the crowded hall, to try and dissuade Congress from proceeding with its plan for the deputation, but with absolutely nothing to offer in return.[60]

Although Dower succeeded in sowing some seeds of dissension by revealing that the crown had already been advised by the British government to give its assent to the Act, a large majority of the delegates were in favour of proceeding with the deputation (for which the sum of £1,353 19s 5d had now been raised), and five delegates were elected by the executive committee to accompany John Dube, the President, to England. Plaatje, with thirteen votes, topped the poll, followed by S. M. Makgatho (9), Saul Msane (6), W. Z. Fenyang (3) and T. M. Mapikela (3).[61] It was a clear enough reflection of the esteem in which Plaatje was held by his colleagues on Congress's executive committee: more than anybody else he had devoted himself over the past months to travelling the length and breadth of the land to investigate the effects of the Land Act, and to bring his observations to the attention of all those who would read and listen. The South African Native National Congress now prepared to take its case overseas.

◇

Plaatje's contribution to the formation of the South African Native National Congress at the beginning of 1912, and then to its early development, and above all the leading role he took in its mobilisation in response to the Natives' Land Act, culminating in his election as a member of the deputation to England early in 1914 – these developments provide the overwhelmingly important thread in Plaatje's life during these two years. But Plaatje was not of course a professional politician in the sense that this provided him with a living. Throughout these years Plaatje remained editor of his newspaper and in charge of the business that published it; this was in itself a very demanding task, and would have been more than sufficient preoccupation for somebody less committed to the political affairs of his people than he.

Tsala ea Batho had not only survived, but prospered. It had appeared without a break from September 1912, and at the end of the following year, 1913, could look back with some satisfaction at this achievement – even if, politically speaking, things had been extremely depressing:

> Three native papers have ceased publication during 1913, but we are still here to tell the story. It is not through any valour on our part, as much as through the liberality of advertising firms throughout South Africa, who stood by us when our natural customers, the native peasants of the 'Free' State and Transvaal, were driven from pillar to post under the cruel provisions of an unprecedented law, and could not send us any money.[62]

The disruptions caused by the Natives' Land Act may have adversely affected the number of paid-up subscriptions that Plaatje received, but *Tsala's* coverage of the Act, which dominated its columns from mid-1913 onwards, brought it a degree of influence greater than either *Koranta ea Becoana* or *Tsala ea Becoana*. Not without justification, *Tsala* claimed to be the 'most accurately informed Native newspaper in South Africa', and by 1914 it carried regular reminders of a number of notable 'scoops' it had achieved – news of the death of J. W. Sauer, for example, 'a whole week before any other Native newspaper'; it had published news of the return of Dr Abdurahman as a member of the Cape provincial council 'simultaneously with the daily papers'; and it gave 'the first news to the natives of the result of the Tembuland election; although one of the defeated candidates is an editor [Tengo Jabavu, editor of *Imvo*, who had stood in the Tembuland provincial council election], his defeat became known to the *Tsala* readers four days before it appeared in his paper'.[63] *Tsala*'s circulation had, moreover, risen (by the beginning of 1914) to 4,000;[64] and on one occasion one of Plaatje's editorials on the Natives' Land Act was read out by T. L. Schreiner in a debate in the South African House of Assembly.[65] Despite the debts with which *Tsala* continued to be saddled, it succeeded in establishing itself, in other words, as an important and influential newspaper, providing Plaatje with exactly the independent platform that he wanted.

At the same time Plaatje's name and views were becoming increasingly well known to white readers as well. The *Pretoria News* had carried his articles on current affairs since the beginning of 1911 (the series would prove a success, Vere Stent thought, 'if only we can persuade the more rabid negrophobes to adopt a moderate and sensible attitude'), and on occasions these were reproduced in other newspapers as well, particularly the *Cape Argus*.[66] Amongst both black and white in South Africa Plaatje had become perhaps the most widely-read black journalist of his day.

Plaatje was well aware that both his reputation and livelihood depended on being in control of his own newspaper business. The viability of this, in turn, depended very much upon his own constant attention to its affairs. For this reason the possible consequences of his absence overseas as a member of the Congress deputation to England must have been something that occupied his thoughts between February (when he was elected a member of it) and May 1914 when the deputation eventually departed; and it was clearly a concern for the future of his business that led him to offer his resignation ('owing to pressure of work', so it was reported) of the secretaryship of Congress at the time of the February meeting in Kimberley.[67] Plaatje was, though, persuaded to reconsider his decision and he stayed on as secretary until the time of his departure to England.

Plaatje's family life had also suffered greatly as a result of his heavy involvement in the affairs of both Congress and his newspaper, and possibly this was in his mind as well when he offered his resignation as secretary of Congress. Particularly since the passage of the Natives' Land Act in June 1913 Plaatje had spent an enormous amount of time away from home on his travels around the country. But even when he was in Kimberley – the family were living now in a house in Shannon Street – he inevitably spent most of the time working in the newspaper office, in the library at home, or attending meetings in town. 'Working from 8 a.m. to midnight and often till later than 3 a.m. next day (with only short intervals for meals), and 5 or 6 hours sleep in 24 hours,' Plaatje himself wrote of this time, 'we cannot have the same time we formerly devoted to the children';[68] and with all these commitments it is small wonder that Elizabeth was reported to have commented on one occasion, early in 1914, that the only time she enjoyed the company of her husband was when he was unwell and laid up in bed.[69] Presumably the same was true for the children as well. St Leger, the eldest, now doing well at Lyndhurst Road Native School (and probably already thinking of a place at Lovedale), was old enough to understand the reasons for his father's heavy involvement in political affairs. But for Halley, named after Halley's Comet which appeared at the time of his birth in 1910; for Violet, born in 1907, the 'accredited chatterbox of the family', and for Olive, six years old when they had moved to Kimberley, and still very much a favourite child, Plaatje's long absences from home must have been more difficult to understand. When he *was* around, Olive, at least, was determined to claim as much of his attention as possible. Thus one of Plaatje's memories:

> As she [Olive] passed on in years from 6 to 7 our work was increasing in leaps and bounds. I had not the same amount of time to devote to the children and Olive's attentions became almost burdensome. She would walk in just when we could not afford to be interrupted and gently stroke us.
> [Plaatje:] 'What can we do for you, dear?'
> Olive: 'Have a cup of tea.'
> [Plaatje:] 'No thanks, dearie, very busy just now.'
> Olive: 'But it is made by me, Pappa.'
> [Plaatje:] 'Well, let's have a cup.'[70]

Persistence was a quality Plaatje very much admired!

Amongst the happy family memories of this time there was a sad one: the death of Plaatje's youngest child, Johannes, born on the day the new printing office was opened in September 1912. Unlike the other children, he never recovered properly from an attack of whooping cough that Christmas, and died in January 1914 – a family tragedy which affected Plaatje deeply and left, as he was to write later, 'an indelible gap . . . in our domestic circle'.[71] W. P. Schreiner and Vere Stent were among those who sent letters of condolence when the news was announced.[72]

Whatever reservations Plaatje may have had about leaving both his family and newspaper business, he was nevertheless committed to travelling to England with the Congress deputation, and spent much of his time between February and May 1914 in collecting further funds to finance the trip and, together with Richard Msimang, in gathering further information about the effects of the Land Act to lay before the British public.[73] He took the precaution, too, of obtaining testimonials from the mayors of Kimberley and Mafeking, and the secretary of De Beers: all three were happy to provide glowing references, Ernest Oppenheimer, the mayor of Kimberley, testifying that Plaatje was 'a much respected member of the native community'.[74] As the time for the deputation's departure approached, Plaatje wrote a letter to his old friend Henry Burton, now Minister of Railways and Harbours:

Kimberley, 7 May 1914

My dear Sir,

I have received notice to leave for England next week with the deputation of the S.A. Native Congress. I am altogether ignorant of the necessary permits and passports required by one to leave the Province for foreign countries. I would be so glad were you to kindly secure for me the requisite official documents so that I be fully armed with the necessary authorities when I leave.

My Cape Town address is 119 Loop St. Apologising for thus encroaching upon your valuable time,

I remain, Dear Mr Burton,

Yours very respectfully,

Sol T. Plaatje

I will, if all is well, reach Cape Town on Friday morning a day before the steamer sails.[75]

In fact Plaatje did not need any form of passport to travel to England, so there was no need for Burton to take action on his behalf. It is nonetheless revealing of the nature of Plaatje's relationship with Henry Burton that he should have chosen to write to him about the matter, his current ministerial portfolio notwithstanding.

By the time Plaatje actually reached Cape Town there had been several quite interesting developments. John Dube, the President of Congress and the leader of the deputation, had been the first to arrive there, his intention being to submit the final Congress petition to the South African parliament before the deputation took it with them to England to submit to the imperial government; he was told, however, that it would take at least a month for the petition to be heard and considered by Parliament – which meant that it would be impossible for the deputation to be in England by 16 June, the date by which, in terms of the provisions of the Act of Union, the King could still disallow any South African legislation. Dube also took the opportunity, once he had arrived in Cape Town, to get in touch with J. X. Merriman, to find out his views on the deputation, and if possible to secure some introductions to people in England, but also to reassure him that his primary personal interest still lay with his educational institute of Ohlange, and not in political agitation; he found himself, he said, in a rather 'delicate position', and did not want his true motives to be misunderstood.[76]

Merriman was not at all in favour of the idea of the deputation to England, and when he met Dube he did his best to dissuade him from going – having in the meantime communicated privately with the Prime Minister, General Botha, over the matter.[77] Merriman's view was that Dube was by no means wholeheartedly behind the proposal himself, but that he was 'associated with some hot heads' from whom it was difficult to dissociate himself. 'Bechuanas, I suppose,' Merriman said. 'Yes,' apparently, was Dube's answer. There can be no doubt as to the identity of the principal 'Bechuana' they had in mind: Plaatje, the only 'Bechuana' among the elected delegates. 'The impression was left on my mind,' Merriman concluded from the meeting, 'that Dube sees he is in the wrong boat and would be glad if he could get some pretext for getting on dry land

171

again.'[78] Merriman was by no means the only person to have formed such an impression. Edward Dower, the Secretary for Native Affairs, had seen Dube a few months earlier and thought he had managed to persuade him not to proceed with the deputation, and had evidently communicated his views to the Prime Minister. 'I have reason to believe,' so General Botha informed J. X. Merriman, 'that Dube is in the horns of a dilemma'; his 'better judgement' convinces him of the 'unwisdom' of appealing to the imperial government, 'yet he has pledged himself to the Native contributors [to the fund] to proceed to England', and found it difficult to escape from this commitment.[79]

Whatever private doubts Dube had about his mission to England he was not persuaded to abandon the idea. Several days after meeting Merriman he saw General Botha, accompanied on this occasion by Dr Rubusana, who had by this time arrived in Cape Town. The Prime Minister did his best to dissuade the two men from proceeding with their mission, but was prepared to offer no concession whatever: parliament, he said, simply could not suspend the operation of the Land Act as they requested. At the end of the meeting Dube agreed to 'consult with his colleagues', who were due to arrive in town that day, and a further meeting with the Prime Minister, for the whole deputation, was arranged for the next day.[80] Plaatje's arrival seems to have stiffened Dube's resolve, but the government was still unwilling to make the slightest concession: 'If I went to Parliament now with a Bill to amend the law,' Botha told the delegates during the second meeting, 'they will think I'm mad.'[81] 'The lengthy official arguments,' so Plaatje summed it up, 'so far from promising relief to the native sufferers under the Lands Act, may be summed up in five short words: "Give up going to England".'[82] Later the same day they also met Lord Gladstone, the Governor-General; his attitude was precisely the same. There was now no alternative but for them to depart for England as planned.

All these last-minute meetings and discussions, whilst they did not in the end affect the decision of Congress to send a deputation to England, are nevertheless of considerable interest. It is clear that John Dube, the leader of the deputation, had severe doubts about the wisdom of proceeding with it at all, and only did so because in the end he was left with no way out – in contrast to Plaatje who, of the five delegates, gave the appearance of being the most determined. Such a display of disunity scarcely boded well for its future conduct.

Perhaps the other most significant point to have emerged was that the government was actually rather more concerned about the impact that the deputation might make in England than it ever admitted publicly (although even General Botha went on record as saying 'they might succeed in arousing a certain amount of public sympathy in England').[83] This had been implicit in Edward Dower's attendance at the February meeting of Congress in Kimberley, and it was what lay behind the considerable amount of time and effort the Prime Minister personally spent in trying to dissuade the delegates from going to England. It was certainly not the done thing for a Prime Minister of South Africa to be seen to be requesting interviews with black South African politicians. The use of J. X. Merriman as an intermediary meant that no such impression was created publicly, but from the correspondence between the two men it seems that General Botha was very glad of the opportunity to meet John Dube and the other delegates for this purpose.

One other precaution was taken by the government: Mr A. P. Apthorpe, a senior member of the Native Affairs Department who had been closely involved in monitoring the implementation of the Natives' Land Act (he had been present at the meeting at Thaba Nchu in September 1913), was now preparing to board the next ship to England with a brief to do everything possible to counter the arguments of the Congress delegates and to neutralise any impression that they might succeed in creating there.[84]

After addressing a public meeting in the City Hall, Cape Town, on 15 May, the members of the deputation duly departed – Dube and Rubusana on 16 May, Plaatje, Mapikela and Msane on the *Norseman*, which sailed the following day. All five of them would have had ample opportunity to ponder the hostile editorials which appeared in the two Cape dailies on the 16th.[85] Their principal objective, so Dube had explained to General Botha, was 'to bring the facts of their grievances to the notice of the English public with a view to bringing influence to bear on the British government, and then lodging their protest through His Majesty's Ministers with the King, and asking the King to exercise his powers by disallowing the Act'.[86] They now had until 16 June to bring their case to the attention of the King (which did not give them a great deal of time), but constitutional niceties of this kind were really not of very great significance: none of the delegates had any real hope that their stated objectives would be fulfilled. They nevertheless felt, with varying degrees of commitment, that they were fulfilling a responsibility that had been thrust upon their shoulders, and that it was important – if nothing more – to exhaust the constitutional options that were open to them. On the whole they would not have much cared to contemplate what happened next.

Most of the delegates also had several more personal objectives in mind as they prepared to leave South Africa. While John Dube hoped that the trip might provide the opportunity to raise money for his school in Natal, Plaatje hoped to be able, once he had arrived in England, to press the claims of the Barolong in the matter of several outstanding land claims, and to this end he took with him a letter of authority from the Tshidi Barolong paramount chief and headmen, clothing him 'with all the power to fully represent the Barolong Nation in England'.[87] He hoped also to be able to raise some money for his newspaper – its debts by now accumulating alarmingly – and for financing educational and community work in Kimberley, in which he had always taken a keen interest. Beyond this there seems to have been what was probably at this stage no more than a half-formed ambition: the notion of visiting the United States of America. He would have been well aware that such an opportunity as he now had was unlikely to present itself again, at least not for a long time.

All this was of course subordinate to the overriding priority in travelling to England: to present the case of the South African Native National Congress, representing the African people of South Africa, against the Natives' Land Act of 1913. Plaatje anticipated being away for no more than five months.[88] It was nearly three years before he saw his wife and family again.

8

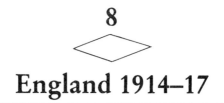

England 1914–17

Plaatje's voyage did not begin auspiciously. Even before the *Norseman* sailed he got a splitting headache, and was forced to retire to his cabin. When he woke up, feeling much better, the ship had sailed out of Cape Town and he was just able to catch a last sight of the African coastline receding slowly into the distance. Not having travelled by sea before, Plaatje had some worries about seasickness, and these were not eased by his noticing the way in which Thomas Mapikela and many of the other passengers were 'croaking and squirming' during the first night of the voyage. He shuddered, so he wrote afterwards in a somewhat amused tone, 'in anticipation of the impending onslaught on an inexperienced greenhorn like myself'. But his anxieties were soon allayed:

> Just at this time a rugged-looking veteran of the seas came on deck and asked how I fared. It was with a sigh of relief that I listened to his, to me, interesting conversation, especially that part of it (which was afterwards over-corroborated), wherein he assured me that, having survived the first day and night, I need no more expect any trouble from seasickness. I felt like a discharged prisoner, and prepared for my work with an extra freshness and security.

In the same account of the voyage Plaatje elaborated upon the work he had in mind, and how it occupied him for the remainder of the voyage:

> I am compiling a little book on the Native Land Act and its operation which I hope to put through the press immediately after landing in England. It keeps me busy typewriting in the dining-room all forenoons and evenings; the afternoons I spend on deck, making notes, etc. With such a regular daily programme I can afford to sympathise with our fellow passengers who are always very busy doing nothing. Their inertia must be well-nigh maddening and, as I see the heavy loads of time hanging down their weary necks, it is to me strange that they can stand it so long. I think that the reason why three of them got fainting fits is that they have nothing else to do; but I will be sorrier for them when, after landing, they endeavour to re-attune themselves with the normal life of toil.

So accustomed had Plaatje become to working almost every hour of the day that it had become almost second nature to him, and he could see no reason whatever to abandon the habit aboard ship. Rather, he considered the three-week voyage to be an ideal opportunity to complete the book about the Land Act that he was writing, and regarded the inactivity of his fellow passengers with a mixture of incomprehension and contempt: he simply could not contemplate a life without work.[1]

The reaction of Plaatje's white fellow passengers to the presence of three black men on board the ship was for the most part a favourable one. Many were Australians, with whom Plaatje seems to have got on very well. Inevitably, the voyage was not without its 'incidents' involving white South Africans. They found it difficult to accept with equanimity Saul Msane's pre-eminence at the game of chess – he took on some of the white passengers one after the other and beat the lot of them – and could not easily repress their resentment at his good fortune in winning a sweepstake to which all had contributed. The average white South African was not well equipped to cope with such a sudden change in treating those who, under 'normal' circumstances, would have been regarded as 'cheeky Kaffirs' to be kept firmly in their place. For some, the demands of civilised intercourse aboard ship with people like Plaatje, Msane and Mapikela were a distinct strain.

Seventeen days after leaving Cape Town the *Norseman* called in at Teneriffe, in the Canary Islands. It was, Plaatje said, the first time he had stepped on soil that was not British, and he was intrigued to hear a language spoken – Spanish – which he had not heard before. But overall he was not greatly impressed by the place. He complained of the high postal charges he had to pay to send letters back home, and like many visiting passengers, before and since, his predominant recollection was of being fleeced at every opportunity by souvenir sellers and tourist guides.[2]

Several days later, after a violent storm in the Bay of Biscay which irritated Plaatje because it prevented him from working for two days, the *Norseman* arrived in Plymouth, and most of its passengers (Plaatje, Mapikela and Msane included) boarded the special train to London. Plaatje was impressed by the speed of the journey: while South African Railways were capable of doing the journey from Kimberley to Mafeking in 12 to 14 hours, Plymouth to London, exactly the same distance, took just four hours. It was a similar reaction to that of almost any colonial citizen visiting 'home' for the first time, and Plaatje's first impressions of London – sweltering in an exceptionally hot summer – were in much the same vein. He was struck above all by the crowds of people, the traffic, the London policemen, and, when he had a chance to. go there, the Houses of Parliament. But few other colonial citizens could have come up with the anecdote that arose in relation to the question of accommodation in London. For he was reminded once again of the Tswana adage 'never measure your straw with great places', which had come to mind some fifteen years previously when he had walked into court to find the magistrate wearing the same shirt as himself:

This Sechuana adage troubled me again when I arrived. I was booked to put up at the Buckingham Hotel, in the Strand; in an hour's conversation at the station, I noticed that some friends repeatedly confused my address with a more august residence of that ilk, and I promptly changed quarters and accepted one of several invitations to stop with friends in the suburbs, which is very welcome, as it is a relief to get out of these moving crowds of an evening after a full day.[3]

◇

Once they had all got together the deputation soon got down to work. Friends and sympathisers had already been active on their behalf. John Dube, the leader of the deputation, had received a letter of welcome at Teneriffe from the Anti-Slavery and Aborigines' Protection Society, suggesting that they get in touch immediately after arrival, and promising assistance in organising their campaign and arranging interviews with the Colonial Office and other organisations and individuals that the deputation might wish to see. Dube might have been slightly puzzled at the tone of the letter he received from John Harris, the society's organising secretary, or had some reservations about the wisdom of the request that they should 'say nothing to the press until we have had an opportunity of discussing matters', but it was nevertheless reassuring to hear of 'the deep sympathy of our Society in your efforts'.[4] The Anti-Slavery and Aborigines' Protection Society was, after all, the leading humanitarian pressure group in England concerned with colonial matters, and an experienced and seemingly influential organisation whose support was likely to be of great assistance in preparing their campaign and providing them with access to the people they needed to see.

Once all the delegates had arrived in London a meeting to 'discuss matters' was arranged and John Harris outlined to them his views of how they should proceed with their campaign. Again he stressed the importance of not talking to the press or seeking any publicity until after they had met Lord Harcourt, Secretary of State for the Colonies. Although this went against the instincts of Plaatje and Dube especially – both of them newspapermen and well aware of the power of the press in gaining publicity for their cause – they were nevertheless prepared to accept the advice of a man who gave every impression of being an experienced and professional lobbyist who had their best interests at heart. But over two other issues they were less than convinced. Harris's view was that since there was absolutely no chance whatever of the Colonial Secretary disallowing the Natives' Land Act, it would be better for them to express their support for the principle of territorial segregation, provided it could be 'fairly and practically' carried out, and to concentrate their efforts upon securing some minor improvements in several of the provisions of the Act. Against their better judgement the Congress delegates were therefore persuaded to sign a document (drawn up by Harris) for presentation to Lord Harcourt, with whom an interview had now been arranged; far from requesting that the Land Act be disallowed, this contained instead the proposition that General Botha's policy of segregation should be given formal and public approval by the imperial government, 'or better still form the basis of an understanding as a native policy by the Imperial and South African Governments'.[5]

Like a number of whites in South who were concerned with the 'native question', Harris supported the principle of segregation because he believed it provided a guarantee against total dispossession, something he had seen so often in other parts of Africa – particularly in the Congo, the area he knew best; he regarded the Natives' Land Act, therefore, as an essentially progressive measure, defective not in principle but in some of its details.[6] It is perhaps a little surprising in retrospect that the delegates were prepared to append their signatures to such a document – and they quickly came to regret having done so – but the pressures upon them were strong, and Harris made it clear that the prospect of an interview with the Colonial Secretary depended upon them doing so. And to have refused would have alienated the one organisation whose support seemed essential to their campaign.

The second question discussed at their meeting related to the land question in Rhodesia, in which Harris appeared to be a good deal more interested. He outlined to the five members of Congress his plans for initiating a legal case at the highest level against the British South Africa Company, to challenge its rights to any title to land in Rhodesia. Since Harris sought to take up the case in the interests of Rhodesia's African population (who had in no way authorised him to do this), he believed that the Congress delegates could provide him with the authorisation he felt would be useful to him. He therefore asked the delegates if they would not mind signing a document giving power of attorney to a firm of lawyers, Messrs Morgan, Price and Co., to represent the interests of the African population of Rhodesia.[7] Again, the delegates were persuaded to sign, even though Plaatje said at the time, so a friend of his recalled, 'none of them were qualified to do this – neither being Natives of Rhodesia, nor possessing any mandate from the Natives of that country'.[8] Again, the five Congress delegates were very much in the hands of Harris and his organisation, and they could not risk jeopardising at this early stage his support for their campaign in England.

After a frustrating delay of several weeks (during which time, Plaatje was told by several friends, 'the Right Honourable the State Secretary is still awaiting instructions from General Botha before deciding when, where and how to meet the deputation of the Native Congress'),[9] the Colonial Secretary agreed to see them at the end of June 1914. John Harris had wanted to come along as well, but the Colonial Office, who generally regarded his society as an irritating and interfering nuisance, did not see the need for this, and advised him that his presence would not be required.[10] This was to prove of some significance. Freed from Harris's influence and supervision, the delegates, speaking in turn, took the opportunity to express their views on the Natives' Land Act in much stronger and more forthright terms than Harris had prescribed. Despite the earlier document that they had been persuaded to sign by him, they made it clear that they sought not the approval of the imperial government for a policy of segregation, but an investigation into the effects that it was having, and the suspension of certain clauses of the Act; or, in the words of one of the Colonial Office officials who was present, 'they clearly asked for certain impossibilities which they did not ask in their written demands'.[11]

It came as no surprise to any of them that Harcourt was unwilling to accede to any of their demands, written or spoken. South Africa was now a self-governing dominion, and General Botha's government was held in high esteem by the imperial authorities: Lord Harcourt had no intention of causing him the slightest degree of embarrassment. He felt that an undertaking to guarantee a promise of General Botha's that Africans would be awarded more land under the provisions of the Land Act would be 'insulting'; that 'any attempt on the part of H.M.G.' to intercede informally on behalf of the delegates with General Botha 'would be inconsistent with the responsible Government which has been granted to the Union of South Africa'; and he could offer the delegates absolutely nothing to take away from their meeting with him.[12] Plaatje's description of the meeting told a familiar story:

> Mr Harcourt made no notes and asked no questions at the interview accorded to our deputation. He listened to how desperately we resisted the passing of the law; how the Government ignored all our representations, and those of all the churches and missionary bodies on our behalf; how we twice applied to Lord Gladstone for opportunities to inform him of the ruin which is wrought by the law among our people; how Lord Gladstone wrote in each instance saying it was 'not within his constitutional functions' to see us. To all this Mr Harcourt replied with another 'assurance of General Botha' that 'we have not exhausted all South African remedies before coming to England.'[13]

Lord Harcourt did at least agree to 'consider' the delegates' request to 'pay their respects' to the King. 'Consider' in this case meant referring the request back to the South African government; predictably enough, they were not in favour of the idea. Whilst General Botha indicated that his government did 'not wish to press objections to the request of the Native Deputation presently in London for permission to pay their respects to His Majesty the King', both he and Lord Gladstone, the Governor-General of South Africa, were in agreement that 'no useful purpose will be served if audience is accorded to these Natives by His Majesty and suggest for the consideration of the Right Honourable the Secretary of State for the Colonies that the result might be the establishment of an inconvenient precedent for the future'.[14] Since the King's personal secretary had already indicated that His Majesty 'presumed there will be no necessity for him to receive this Deputation, which does not seem to be a representative one' (the King was more accustomed to receiving visiting African royalty in traditional regalia), such an indication was more than sufficient.[15] In view of the King's attitude, it was perhaps just as well.

John Harris was somewhat peeved at the outcome of the interview. As he pointed out to the Colonial Office afterwards, it was with a fear that the delegates might not confine themselves to the points that appeared in the document he had prepared for them that he had suggested that he and several other representatives of the society might accompany them to the interview. Harris had done all he could to use his society's influence, so he said, 'in the direction of securing a modification of their original programme and an abstention from public agitation pending the exhaustion of every constitutional means open to them', and he was clearly disappointed to have secured no recognition in this from the Colonial Office.[16] Harris was now left with little alternative but to accede to the increasingly impatient demands of the delegates to seek publicity for their cause (and in particular to respond to attacks made upon them by the London weekly, *South Africa*). His efforts now were directed to ensuring that the delegates created the right impression in the press and upon public platforms with a view to influencing the Colonial Office vote in the House of Commons, due to take place in the middle of July, which would at least enable their grievances to be raised and placed on official record. This, Harris told Dube, was 'your last chance of doing anything effective . . . when that is over you can do nothing more in the country at present'.[17]

In the three weeks that remained before this vote was to take place, therefore, the five delegates embarked upon a spirited – if somewhat belated – attempt to bring their case to the attention of the British public. A printed statement of their grievances – *The Natives' Land Act of South Africa: an Appeal to the Imperial Parliament and Public of Great Britain*, drafted by Plaatje – was prepared and distributed, letters were written to the press, interviews were given, and a variety of meetings were addressed by one or more members of the deputation; these included gatherings held under the auspices of various church bodies, a meeting at the House of Commons with some members of parliament, and several evening receptions held in the homes of their small band of sympathisers.[18] The response was on the whole very favourable. Plaatje in particular was gratified by the amount of sympathetic coverage given to their case in the press (he himself was interviewed on one occasion by the *Westminster Gazette* and wrote an article for the *Daily News*, the leading Liberal newspaper), and by the unequivocal support extended to their cause by the Brotherhood movement, an interdenominational religious organisation whom the members of the deputation were introduced to at the beginning of July. They subsequently attended a meeting of the London Federation of the Brotherhood movement at Bishopsgate on 14 July, and were invited to address a number of other meetings held under the auspices of the movement elsewhere in the country.[19] For Plaatje, their success in gaining support of this kind only confirmed his view that they should have embarked upon this from the beginning, and paid rather less heed to Harris's demands for restraint. Comments made by Mr Will Crooks, a Labour member of parliament and a member of the Brotherhood movement, were especially encouraging. 'I was considerably surprised,' he said after listening to public addresses by Msane and Rubusana, to a crowd of over 3,000 people,

> to find our South African brothers on the platform; but, after all, they have done more good here this evening than they have done at the C.O. The problem with which they are associated is a very difficult one, as they must well know. They have to win over the people of this country, and, after all, listening to their statement here this evening, I am inclined to think they will succeed in their task.[20]

Clearly, there was far more sympathy for their cause on public platforms than in the hostile corridors of power of the Colonial Office.

The sympathetic response achieved at the hands of the press and on public platforms did not influence the outcome of the Colonial Office vote in parliament. But it did give Sir Albert Spicer and Mr Percy Alden, two sympathetic Liberal MPs whom the delegates had met earlier, the chance to raise the question of the Natives' Land Act in the House of Commons, and to request the Colonial Office to 'raise the question of the hardships being inflicted by it with the Prime Minister of South Africa'. Lord Harcourt's reply was little different from the one he gave the Congress delegates a month earlier: he refused to contemplate taking any action, repeated his statement about the constitutional position, and drew the attention of the House to the recommendations of the South African Native Affairs Commission of 1905. Far from being a recent piece of Dutch-inspired legislation, he emphasised, the Natives' Land Act of 1913 had a respectable English ancestry and was in the best tradition of British colonial policy; sadly, that was perfectly true. But at least the Congress deputation had ensured, via the two MPs they had seen, that a statement of their case now formed part of the official record of the British parliament: that, in itself, was some reward for their efforts.[21]

For a few weeks thereafter the delegates continued with their campaign of public agitation, but with a growing realisation of its pointlessness. John Dube, the leader of the deputation, had already returned home to South Africa, promising to hold meetings there in order to raise further money to support the deputation's work and their families back home in South Africa.[22] He had been keen to return home anyway. Of all the delegates, Dube had been the least committed to the idea of sending over a deputation in the first place on the grounds that it was unlikely to achieve anything worthwhile, and he now had several somewhat more delicate personal matters to attend to; he had thus returned home soon after the meeting with Lord Harcourt.[23] After the Colonial Office vote had taken place the remaining delegates began to lose heart as well. They felt they had achieved as much as they were going to, money was rapidly running out, and there were disturbing signs of personal differences developing among them.

Then, in early August, they were rapidly overtaken by a series of events which they could not possibly have foreseen when they left South Africa in May: it began with the assassination of the Austrian Archduke Ferdinand in the obscure Balkan town of Sarajevo, and ended with all the major European powers being at war. Britain was the last to become involved, but on 4 August 1914 declared war on Germany in fulfilment of treaty obligations to France and Belgium. At the time these events unfolded the campaign being mounted by the Congress delegation was already beginning to lose its momentum, and they consequently provided a not unwelcome pretext for calling it off and returning home. John Harris and a number of others were quick to point out the difficulties of continuing with the campaign at a time when public opinion in Britain was likely to be focused exclusively upon the war, and when a display of unity within the empire would also be a vital requirement.[24] Several days later a cable was in any case received from John Dube urging the delegation to come home immediately, and reporting the outcome of a meeting of the South African Native National Congress held in Bloemfontein during the first week in August. Learning, half-way through its deliberations, that war had broken out between Britain and Germany, Congress had resolved 'in view of the situation . . . to hang up native grievances against the South African Parliament till a better time and to tender the authorities assistance'.[25] A display of loyalty, the meeting had concluded, was the most effective gesture Congress could make; for those in London it provided good reason for a respectable termination to a campaign in England that was fast running out of steam.

Rubusana, Msane and Mapikela accepted immediately that they should call off their campaign and return home. Plaatje, disappointed amongst other things that the outbreak of war between Britain and Germany also ruled out his plan of visiting Berlin (headquarters of his old missionary society), seems to have accepted this too, albeit rather more reluctantly. He was nevertheless keen to stay on for a while longer to complete and publish the book he had been writing, to fulfil a number of speaking engagements, and also to try and resolve the matter of the Barolong land claim in the Bechuanaland Protectorate which he had already taken up with lawyers. A letter he received from Elizabeth several weeks later may well have inclined him in the same direction. She had written urging that he should not leave England until he was 'sure that the track was clear of German ships', and he had taken this to mean that 'they may know something that we do not quite know here'.[26] But the problem now was that none of the delegates had the money to pay for their passages back to South Africa. They had expected Dube to send this over, but in his cable he had indicated that because of the declaration of martial law in South Africa he could not hold any meetings to raise the necessary funds.[27] Plaatje for one felt Dube had left them all in the lurch: 'It now amounted to this,' he wrote, 'that we must now look about and find the wherewithal to return home. Dr Rubusana volunteered to approach some friends, borrow money, and get us out of the tangle.'[28]

What happened thereafter was to be the cause of lasting bitterness. Rubusana was successful in negotiating a loan from the London Missionary Society, but only under strict conditions. According to Plaatje, the arrangement was as follows:

The Wesleyan Society would guarantee half, the Aborigines Protection Society one quarter and the London Missionary Society (who are also guaranteeing one quarter) were to act as Treasurers, book and pay our passage for us; (2) pay our board and lodging, until our steamer sails on September 17, to the landlords if the latter would draw up weekly accounts and send them to the L.M.S. (3) We must leave England within a given date in September, by a certain boat – the *Borda* – and (4) during our stay we must not approach any other friends for assistance; (5) we must not speak to any other African friends (goodness knows who they are).[29]

These conditions were imposed, so it transpired, at the instigation of John Harris, anxious now to pack the delegates back home to South Africa and fearful that if they stayed any longer they would become both a financial burden and a political embarrassment for his society. Whilst Mapikela, Msane, and Dr Rubusana were themselves keen to return home immediately, and duly accepted these conditions, Plaatje was not. He described what happened next:

When we got to the L.M.S. offices I told them on hearing this that I would never borrow money under such degrading conditions, with the added pleasure of having to repay it when I get back. Having come here to protest against bondage I could not very well go and sign away my liberty by undertaking not to speak to certain people and not to be at certain places at certain times. Moreover, I said I would never ask my landlady to make her accounts and ask someone else to pay my board and lodging. I had no objection to their booking my passage but as for the rest the money must be paid into my hands and not to the landlady if I am going to repay it. In any circumstances I would not take such money from anybody. They (the L.M.S.) played me another trick which is too long to mention here, and I am beginning to understand now why native deputations . . . always start so well and then end in smoke immediately afterwards. It must be that they always get hard-up and borrow money under stop-gap conditions.[30]

Plaatje then went to see John Harris to try and get these conditions altered, but to no avail – hardly surprising since they had been his idea in the first place. On this occasion Plaatje lost his temper, and stormed out of Harris's office, determined to have no more to do with a Society which, he was now convinced, had sought to sabotage the efforts of the deputation from the moment of its arrival in England.[31]

Plaatje felt so strongly about the conditions John Harris was seeking to impose, not only because they were personally humiliating – which they certainly were to somebody of Plaatje's sensitivity to such things – but because it was his intention to stay on in England to continue with the campaign for a while longer, and above all to get his book published. It was obviously not easy to tell exactly how long this would take, and he did not want to be pressured to return home to South Africa by a certain date. In a sense, though, the argument over the loan, and Plaatje's refusal to accept Harris's conditions, were probably as much a pretext to justify his own desire to stay on in England as a reason in itself – for it happened to provide a convenient justification for his decision to go against the cabled instructions of John Dube, President of Congress, the advice of his fellow delegates, all of them keen now to return home, and indeed the resolutions of the meeting of the South African Native National Congress at the beginning of August.

For the fact of the matter was that Plaatje was determined to fulfil his mission, the outbreak of world war notwithstanding. Of all the Congress delegates he had been the most committed to the deputation's work in England, and from the beginning he had been motivated by a strength and depth of feeling against the Natives' Land Act which had impelled him to extraordinary efforts in his campaign against it from the moment the legislation first became known in February 1913. Plaatje did not believe Congress had had a fair opportunity to present its case in England, and he was quite ready – indeed probably welcomed the opportunity – to continue with the campaign alone.

Plaatje's conviction that Harris had sought to undermine the work of the Congress deputation from the beginning was one reason for his view that this opportunity had been denied them. Another was his discovery, quite by chance, of the presence in London of Mr A. P. Apthorpe, the senior Native Affairs Department official who had been sent over to counter their efforts. Late in July Plaatje had visited the popular Anglo-American Exhibition at White City in west London. Amongst the crowd of visitors he happened to see Mr Apthorpe, which naturally surprised him, especially since they had met in Bloemfontein shortly before Plaatje left South Africa in May, and discussed the deputation's intended visit to London; Apthorpe had given no indication on that occasion that he was planning to travel to London as well. When Plaatje approached him at the exhibition he claimed to be there on 'a holiday trip'. It was hardly convincing. Plaatje's suspicions as to the true purpose of his visit were confirmed a year later when the expenses of his visit were accounted for in a published government blue book, revealing, as Plaatje later wrote, that Mr Apthorpe was over not on a holiday 'but to counteract our propaganda at Downing St and to deny, in the name of the Union government, that the Land Act had hurt a single Native'.[32] What Plaatje probably never knew, although he may well have suspected it, was that Apthorpe had also been along to the Anti-Slavery and Aborigines' Protection Society, as well as the Colonial Office, and had succeeded in making quite an impression upon John Harris. Undoubtedly his visit helped to influence Harris's attitude towards the deputation and its cause.[33]

<><

Before the other three delegates – Msane, Rubusana, and Mapikela – departed in the middle of September there was another unseemly row over funds: Rubusana and Mapikela, it seems, objected strongly that Plaatje, by now 'penniless', should be given £20 (which had just been received from South Africa) to enable him to further the work of the deputation. When Plaatje bade them farewell at St Pancras Station on 17 September Mapikela did at least promise – although it was clear he did not believe Plaatje was doing the right thing in staying – to try and get Congress to send him some money for his eventual passage home.[34] Not that Plaatje can have held out too much hope on this score; he was now very much on his own.

Over the next few months Plaatje persevered with his programme of public lectures and meetings, and was particularly encouraged by the response he encountered outside London: it seemed to confirm his view that there was a great public reservoir of sympathy there to be tapped, even though the war had become such a preoccupation in people's minds. Early in October he travelled to Wales to fulfil a number of engagements, and was delighted with the response:

> I spent a very happy week in Wales at the beginning of the month, among exceptionally kind Welsh people who took me for a pleasure trip to Cardiff and showed me round that interesting town and port. At Abertillery I addressed, in the Pavilion, the largest audience I ever spoke to, and all these P.S.A. [Pleasant Sunday Afternoon] gatherings promise to pay earnest attention to the cause of the South African Natives after the war.[35]

But Plaatje's financial position was desperate. He found himself in constant difficulty when it came to paying the weekly rent to his landlady (a Mrs Timberlake), at 25 Carnarvon Road, Leyton, one of London's eastern suburbs. But he was at least fortunate in his choice of lodgings. Mrs Timberlake was a kindly lady and did not press him over the sums he owed, and she showed great kindness when he began to suffer from the extreme cold of the winter of

1914–15–'a dark, dreary winter of almost continuous snowflakes, cold, mud, and slush', he called it. As he wrote in February 1915:

> I have been seriously troubled by colds and damp during the winter, but its severity has been modified by the exceptional kindness of the people with whom I am living. I am afraid I will never be able to repay the painstaking manner in which they have carried me through this winter.[36]

Several of Plaatje's letters from the last months of 1914 have survived, and they reveal an increasingly despondent mood on the score of finance. Even Ben Weil, the man to whom the Barolong had presented the silver shield back in 1901, now living in London, could not be persuaded to part with more than £1 10s, and he insisted upon repayment at the earliest possible opportunity. By the time Plaatje wrote to the Barolong chief, Lekoko, on 12 December 1914, his position was even worse. It was becoming difficult, he said, to look his landlady in the eye in view of the money he owed her, and he appealed for help:

> Please help, Morolong. I sometimes even regret having ever come over here all the way from home to these foreign countries. The seed of fighting for the land, and of stopping the Union from the Protectorate, that I have sown; the only trouble is that I can't get my way back home. I am in a very difficult situation, and it seems to worsen every day. Right now I owe £13 for board and lodging for the past few months, and I will not be able to come back home even if the money comes. I'm terribly stuck in the quagmire. Please help me, my Chief, before I go even deeper beyond redemption.[37]

Whether or not Plaatje ever got anything from Lekoko is unknown. The chances of his responding positively would perhaps have been better had Plaatje managed to see General Baden-Powell in connection with the Barolong land claim, as Lekoko had requested, but his efforts in this direction had not been successful. Plaatje had hoped to meet Baden-Powell at the funeral of Lord Roberts (who died in November 1914), and had written to him requesting a ticket to enable him to attend. When Baden-Powell only responded after the funeral had taken place, Plaatje was convinced he had been trying deliberately to avoid him. But as he explained to Lekoko, Baden-Powell, whatever his status as the hero of the siege of Mafeking, was in no position of influence when it came to political decisions affecting any part of the empire.[38]

Gradually Plaatje's circumstances seem to have improved. He earned both money and publicity for his cause by writing articles for the *African World*, a weekly journal with offices in Fleet Street which was addressed primarily to those with an interest in government, industry and commerce in Africa. Editorially, the *African World* was of a more liberal persuasion than *South Africa*; it had presented a more favourable account of the cause of the Congress deputation when its members first arrived in London (it carried, indeed, a photograph of them); and late in 1914 its editor, Leo Weinthal, commissioned Plaatje to write some articles for them – mostly obituaries of prominent Africans who had recently died. One of these obituaries, however, was of a white South African called Allan King, a close friend of Plaatje's ('the best white friend in

South Africa I ever had', he wrote), who had been killed during the Boer rebellion which broke out shortly after the outbreak of the First World War.[39] This article – together with another that Plaatje wrote entitled 'The South African Coloured Races and the War' – evoked a lively response in South Africa itself. *De Volkstem*, the Dutch-language newspaper, took particular exception to the anti-Boer comments it contained, and demanded that such material should in future be suppressed by the censor; the *African World*, for its part, responded with an editorial in defence of the free expression of opinion, and continued to publish Plaatje's articles.[40] In South Africa the effect of the episode, taken up by the African press, was only to publicise the work Plaatje was doing in England. It was clear he was not entirely forgotten.

Plaatje's difficulties during these months were also greatly eased by the support, moral and probably financial as well, extended to him by a circle of friends and sympathisers who were now beginning to gather around him. Closest of all was a group of women of solidly middle-class background who had some prior connection or interest in South Africa or African affairs, and who were drawn to Plaatje through their sympathy for his cause, an admiration for his determination to succeed in the task he had undertaken, and a keen enjoyment of his lively company. Perhaps the most formidable of this group of women was Mrs Georgiana Solomon, widow of the late Saul Solomon, one of the great figures of the Cape liberal tradition in the nineteenth century, and a man who ranked high in Plaatje's pantheon of distinguished 'friends of the natives'. In fact Plaatje was well acquainted with several other members of the Solomon family. He was a great admirer of one of Georgiana Solomon's nephews, Judge William Solomon, the man responsible for that court judgement in Mafeking in 1901 which had left such an impression upon him; and he had also known another of her nephews, Richard Solomon, Attorney-General of the Cape during Plaatje's term of appointment as a court interpreter, and it was probably after him that he had named his second son, Richard Solomon Sebeka.

Georgiana Solomon herself had lived in England since her husband's death in 1892, and had devoted her life to a variety of liberal and radical causes before throwing herself with characteristic enthusiasm into the women's suffragette movement. She had participated, at the age of 68, in the famous march upon the House of Commons in 1909, chained herself to the railings, was arrested, and then spent a month in Holloway prison.[41] A committee member of the Anti-Slavery and Aborigines' Protection Society as well, she shared with Plaatje a very deep attachment to the ideals of Cape liberalism, and a common frustration with the position each shared in the societies in which they lived – she as a woman having to live with sexual discrimination in England, he as an African suffering from racial discrimination in South Africa. Plaatje had met Mrs Solomon shortly after arriving in England (she held a reception for the delegates in her home in Hampstead), and he became thereafter a regular visitor to her home, where she lived with her daughter Daisy, also a proud veteran of Holloway prison from the campaign of 1909. Later, Plaatje visited Saul Solomon's gravestone in Eastbourne, Sussex, and arranged for a local photographer to take a picture of him standing in front of it – in a pose of homage, almost, to a lost creed of Cape liberalism.[42]

A similar bond of friendship grew up between Plaatje and several members of the Colenso family, in particular Mrs Sophie Colenso, a daughter-in-law of the famous South African bishop. All five Congress delegates had been invited to 'Elangeni', the family home in Amersham, some 25 miles outside London, soon after arriving in England, and after the others had departed Plaatje became a regular and eagerly anticipated visitor.[43] He spent a number of weekends at Elangeni in 1914 and 1915, and enjoyed relaxing here from his campaign of public engagements, finding friendship with people who shared a knowledge and deep interest in South Africa with common views on race and colour – a relationship inconceivable in South Africa itself where such familiarity would have been frowned on by black and white alike.

Others in this circle of friends were Betty Molteno, daughter of another famous Cape statesman, Sir John Molteno, the first Prime Minister of the Cape Colony; her brother Percy Molteno, member of parliament for Dumfriesshire, and his family;[44] and Jane Cobden Unwin, wife of the publisher T. Fisher Unwin, who also had a longstanding interest in African affairs. She, too, was a committee member of the Anti-Slavery and Aborigines' Protection Society, was involved in the suffragette movement, and saw herself as an upholder of the liberal ideals of her late father, Richard Cobden, in the same way as Georgiana Solomon consciously upheld those of her late husband. Plaatje often met her at her home in Adelphi Terrace, just off the Strand in London. Years later he spoke of his memory of 'her crown of beautiful white hair', and recalled that he used to worry that he would be suspected of rudeness, 'for only with great difficulty', he said, could he keep his eyes off it! Another in this close circle of friends was Alice Werner, a lecturer in African languages at King's College, London, and an extremely able linguist whose interest in South Africa was largely the result of her friendship – sustained in a regular correspondence – with Harriette Colenso, the best-known of the bishop's daughters, who had remained in Natal.[45]

There were other friends of course: William Cross, Her Majesty's Collector of Taxes in the London borough of Ealing, in west London, whom Plaatje had met through the Brotherhood movement, and often used to visit at his home at 69 Shakespeare Road, Hanwell;[46] and various members of London's substantial African and Afro-American community, some of them associated with the *African Times and Orient Review*, a journal run by Mohammed Duse Ali, an exiled Egyptian nationalist. Among these was F. Fredericks, a lawyer from Sierre Leone, whom Plaatje later described as 'a personal friend of mine'.[47] In Scotland, which Plaatje visited for the first time in August 1914, and again several times thereafter, there were two rather more familiar African faces: Modiri Molema, Silas Molema's son, who was now in Glasgow studying medicine; and James Moroka, a descendant of the Seleka Barolong Paramount Chief, Moroka, doing the same thing at Edinburgh.[48] But it was the old white South African families – the Solomons, Moltenos, Colensos – whom Plaatje saw most regularly. He was always welcome in their homes, they were eager to hear news from Plaatje's wife and family in Kimberley, and they provided him with support and encouragement to continue his campaign; above all, to accomplish his most important task – the completion and publication of his book on the Natives' Land Act.

◇

Plaatje's original hope, as he wrote on the voyage to England in May 1914, was to complete and publish 'the little book' he had been writing 'immediately after landing in England'. Things had not, of course, quite worked out like that. Plaatje had found himself far too busy with the work of the deputation during the few months after his arrival in England to get it finished, and he was keen in any case to expand it from being simply a book on the Land Act into something rather larger, which included an account of the work of the deputation itself. With the outbreak of war in August 1914 Plaatje decided that, if he was to be successful in arousing British public opinion, then he had to link his cause to the wider struggle in which the British empire was now engaged; essentially, to emphasise the loyalty of the African people to the cause of the British empire, and to argue on these grounds – as well as the wider ones of justice and humanity – that his people deserved relief from such oppressive measures as the Natives' Land Act. As he heard news of the Boer rebellion in South Africa following the outbreak of war, Plaatje perceived in this further ammunition for his argument, and the means of contrasting 'African loyalty' with 'Boer disloyalty'. All these developments needed to be incorporated and written up, and inevitably Plaatje found himself with a far larger task on his hands. He did not therefore manage to complete it nearly as quickly as he had once hoped.

But the other reason for the delay was a thornier one: the question of funds to pay for the printing and publication of the book. Plaatje quickly discovered that no printer or publisher in London was prepared to take on the book without a substantial cash payment in advance. Of those he had approached by the beginning of November 1914, Longman, Green and Co., the London school book publishers, were the most expensive, wanting £120 to print 1,000 copies of the book, whilst Edward Hughes and Co., who had printed the deputation's pamphlet several months previously, were the cheapest – they wanted £87. All of the publishers he approached wanted a down payment of £50 before they would even embark upon the work of typesetting and printing.[49] Plaatje simply did not have this kind of money, and there seemed little immediate prospect of his being able to collect it together; he was struggling indeed for money to pay his rent and subsistence. The obvious source of funds would have been the Anti-Slavery and Aborigines' Protection Society but given what had taken place between Plaatje and John Harris there was clearly no prospect of a contribution from this quarter.

Plaatje appealed, therefore, to the Barolong paramount chief, Lekoko, for the funds he required. Writing to the chief late in 1914, he explained his dire predicament, emphasised what a tragedy it would be if his book was not published in view of all the work of the deputation, and pointed out the ways in which the book could assist the cause of the Barolong nation. Should Lekoko provide the funds to make possible the book's publication, Plaatje went on, it would be a matter of pride to the chief and his descendants that he, paramount chief of the Barolong, made possible the first book to state the case of the African people to South Africa as a whole; it might cause some jealousy amongst other African people, he added, but it would do much for the Barolong, and special attention could be given in the book to the land claims of the Barolong, and to the story of their contribution to the defence of Mafeking during the siege. Finally, Plaatje asked, could the chief send him his photograph – together with a copy of the address presented to the Barolong by General Roberts in 1900 – so that both could be reproduced in the book?[50]

Whether or not the chief actually sent any money is very doubtful, for this was not acknowledged in the book when it was eventually published, nor was his photograph included (although it did contain the text of Lord Roberts's address). Plaatje nevertheless persevered with writing the book in between his speaking engagements, and was much encouraged by the response of people to whom he showed parts of it. Writing to Mrs Colenso in February 1915, in response to a letter of hers, he had this to say:

> I too must apologise for delaying so long with my answer, but you will understand my situation when I give you my programme only for this week. On Tuesday I was invited to go [to] Dartford, Kent. The following Sunday I go to Southall and so forth.
>
> In the meantime I am working hard at my book, which I hope to place in the printers' hands this very quarter. Each one (and I must say they are competent to judge as they have themselves written books), each who has seen a chapter of the book I am writing raises hopes in me: they say if the rest of the book is like what they have seen, it must sell well. Let us hope so, for the sake of the cause.[51]

Plaatje wrote the last chapter of his book over the Easter holiday, 1915, and managed to get his manuscript off to the printer soon afterwards. The London firm of P. S. King and Co., publishers of a number of Africa-related books over recent years, had agreed to do the work, and Plaatje had evidently raised sufficient money to persuade them at least to embark upon the typesetting.[52] By May 1915 he had galley proofs back from them, and these were shown to a number of people for comment and suggestion: again the response was encouraging – Alice Werner, William Cross, Dr Theo Scholes (an old West Indian author doctor living in London whom Plaatje knew) all wrote to congratulate him.[53]

Rather less encouraging, though, were the views of Sir Harry Johnston, the eminent (if a little eccentric) one-time explorer, colonial administrator, linguist, and writer, now living in very active retirement in Sussex, whom Plaatje had asked to write an Introduction for the book. Plaatje knew that Sir Harry was generally sympathetic to his cause, and the two men had met for the first time in the middle of August 1914 when Plaatje, accompanied by Saul Msane, had travelled down to the south coast to visit him. Their meeting had gone well, and Sir Harry had been most impressed by his two visitors ('immensely helpful' in his work on Bantu languages, intellectually 'many grades above the average white man in South Africa', 'charming in their manners').[54] Probably Plaatje had discussed with him the book he himself was writing, and it may well have been on this occasion that Sir Harry had agreed to write an Introduction for it. At any rate, Plaatje sent him a set of galley proofs to have a look at in May 1915.

But the response was not quite what Plaatje anticipated. Sir Harry had a number of objections, and said he would only write an Introduction if changes were made; otherwise, he said, 'if I was to write anything at the present moment it would of necessity criticise your presentation of the case so severely that it would nullify its purpose'. Some of Sir Harry's points were sensible ones – his suggestion, for example, that it was a mistake to entitle the book *The European War and the Boer Rebellion*, which seems to be what Plaatje had in mind at the time; others – his notion that Plaatje should substitute the word 'Negro' for 'native', for example, much less so. He felt, too, that Plaatje ought to remove a lot of the quotations and generally 'pull the whole work together'; once all this had been done, he said, he would have another look through it at page-proof stage and then write the Introduction.[55]

Plaatje was somewhat upset ('greatly exercised', as Alice Werner reported) by the letter he received from Sir Harry, and he decided, with Alice Werner's encouragement, to do without his Introduction.[56] Even if he was prepared to accept some of Sir Harry's criticisms, it was really too late to make the extensive changes he insisted upon, and to do so would only have entailed additional expense, which Plaatje was in no position to meet. He was experiencing great difficulties, indeed, in paying what he already owed to the printer. By the middle of June 1915, as Plaatje explained in a letter to Philemon Mosheshoe, an old friend in Mafeking (recently retired from his position as gaol warder), the situation was again getting very serious:

> 16 June, 1915
>
> My dear Moshosho,
>
> Thank you for your encouraging letter, altho' I sometimes think that I am doomed. The Printer is threatening already and man if I and that Printer fall out: the cause of the Natives will be irretrievably doomed.
>
> I have written to the Chief just a week after I wrote you and I also telegraphed. If nothing is done by the time you get this please do your best. Things are serious. I have always refrained from trying to borrow money, believing that I will reserve such for this most crucial time; but all I get are promises to push the sale of the book, but no aid to release it and as far as I can see the fewer people you confide with your hardupishness here the better for yourself because when you are hard-up they all shun you. That is why they stuck to me like glue all the time and offered to help me because I never complained.
>
> I address more meetings now and everywhere its WHERE IS THE BOOK? And what a howling shame for the scheme to miscarry after they hear that I have been correcting proofs. Then the Natives can give up appealing to anybody with their grievances for the collapse of the scheme now would be a serious calamity. PLEASE do your best, man. Glad domestic affairs are somewhat easier with you.
>
> Goodbye,
> Sol T. Plaatje[57]

From the tone of the letter – even if it was calculated to convey a sense of crisis in the hope of eliciting funds – it is obvious that there was a note of desperation about the way Plaatje now felt, a realisation that all his efforts could come to nothing, that even the book to which his energies were now directed might still never be published. Mosheshoe wrote back to say that he had taken up the matter with Lekoko, and that he seemed interested; Lekoko was, however, suffering from ill-health and could only attend to the matter when he was better.[58] Plaatje did not meet with much more success in London. Mrs Solomon did her best to raise a loan to pay the £60 that was now required by the printer, but she did not succeed either. Then, in July 1915, came the worst news of all: Lekoko, Plaatje's chief hope for the money, far from making a quick recovery from his illness, died before doing anything about it; the prospect of his book being published in the foreseeable future began to look more and more remote.

At this point Alice Werner came to the rescue – or such, at any rate, was her intention. With the printer refusing to proceed further with the production of the book, she agreed to launch an appeal, and sent out a circular letter to as many possible sympathisers as she could think of. In this she explained the circumstances that made the appeal necessary, stressed the loyalty of black South Africans in the war, and ended with the surprising assertion that it was 'of the greatest importance that Botha should be supported in the just and generous native policy to which I believe him personally to be inclined, though many of his supporters make his position difficult in this regard, so I understand'.[59] Although the appeal did bring in sufficient money to satisfy the printer for a while, it was, to say the least, an unfortunate way to round off her appeal, and rather surprising in view of the fact that she had read proofs of most of Plaatje's book by this time, and must have been familiar with his views. Whatever her reasons for making such a statement, the result was to further complicate the business of getting the book published, for a copy of her letter in due course found its way into the hands of John Harris, organising secretary of the Anti-Slavery and Aborigines' Protection Society. Knowing Plaatje's views and the likely contents of his book, Harris was furious at what he regarded as an attempt to raise money under false pretences, and he immediately jumped to the conclusion that Plaatje had deliberately misled Alice Werner as to its contents – quite unjustifiably, since she claimed to have already read the section of the book which actually dealt with General Botha's attitude.[60] Consequently, Harris set about advising potential contributors against donating money towards the book's costs of publication, and took every opportunity to cast doubt upon Plaatje's character and integrity – suggesting, in particular, that Plaatje had been living off funds collected specifically for the book's printing costs; again, as Alice Werner was eventually able to demonstrate to Harris, this was without foundation.[61]

In John Harris Plaatje had a determined enemy. The two men had not met since Plaatje stormed out of that meeting in August 1914, but he now seemed intent upon preventing Plaatje's book from being published, fearful, among other things, that Plaatje would have harsh words to say about his society. What both Plaatje and several of his friends were also concerned about was the possibility of Harris seeking to influence P. S. King and Co. (who also printed much of the pamphlet material put out by the Anti-Slavery and Aborigines' Protection Society) against him: 'were Mr H. to get on the track of the printer', Alice Werner commented, 'he would do something to complicate matters'.[62]

Plaatje's relationship with P. S. King and Co. remained in a delicate state for the remaining months of 1915, but by the end of the year he had raised some more money and prospects generally looked more encouraging. He was accordingly in quite a cheerful frame of mind when he wrote to Mrs Colenso, from Stockton-on-Tees in Yorkshire, on 28 January 1916:

Many thanks for your kind letter and cheque enclosed. I received your previous letter just when the troubles were at their worst and I am not surprised to hear that I forgot to thank you for the article on the late Dr Washington. I must thank you for it and also for the picture of his military successor of whom I have never heard before; but I pity a man when he has to succeed so successful a worker.

My troubles here have considerably abated since the New Year. I have already paid the printer £27, only £5 of which is borrowed and the binding of the book is now in progress.

I have told Miss Werner that I wish to dedicate it to Miss Harriette Colenso for her good work to our people. Of course, she approves.

I am among Yorkshire people here addressing Brotherhoods and Sisterhoods nearly every afternoon and evening. They are simply fine and sing much better than the people of the south, both men and women. From here I am going straight to Sussex.

You will be agreeably surprised to learn that I have successfully fulfilled Mr Sonnenschein's conditions and that he has agreed to publish my proverbs and that I got him to improve the terms considerably in my favour so that my outlook is much brighter than in 1915.

I have already sold 42 books here besides 9 of the proverbs tho' both the books are not out yet. It is a promising prospect and the Yorkshire people are wildly enthusiastic with me and my question. The weather is ideal, brilliant sunshine! Compared with London they are suffering a severe drought.[63]

At the time Plaatje wrote this letter the actual publication of his book still remained over three months away, and inevitably there were further financial hurdles that had to be overcome. But as he indicated in his reference to 'Mr Sonnenschein' and his agreement 'to publish my proverbs' there was good news on another front as well, a happy culmination of Plaatje's endeavours in a different form of activity, one of several more literary, or linguistic, pursuits that had also greatly preoccupied him throughout 1915.

◇

Plaatje's collection of proverbs – duly published in 1916 by Kegan Paul Ltd with the title *Sechuana Proverbs with Literal Translations and their European Equivalents* – had its origins in Plaatje's longstanding interest in the forms of the Tswana language, combined with the opportunity provided by his presence in England to spend some time in compiling as many Tswana proverbs as he could think of – 732 being the final total.[64] Quite apart from anything else it was a remarkable feat of memory, for there is no evidence that Plaatje had embarked upon collecting together these proverbs before he left South Africa. He received a good deal of assistance and encouragement from Georgiana Solomon (to whom the book is dedicated), Alice Werner, and also from William Cross; his copy of the book contained Plaatje's handwritten inscription recalling the 'helpful hours at 69 Shakespeare Road during 1915–1916',[65] and the three friends obviously helped a great deal on the 'European equivalents' side. For the original Tswana proverbs Plaatje was entirely on his own. He also added to the collection an explanatory Introduction, revealing much of the seriousness of purpose he brought to a task which – in the context of the circumstances in which the book was actually compiled – he probably regarded almost as a form of relaxation, an escape from the more arduous business of addressing meetings and trying to raise money to see *Native Life in South Africa* through the press.

Plaatje had some interesting things to say in this introduction. His main objective, he wrote, was 'to save from oblivion' the wealth of proverbial expression of the Tswana people, a task which had been undertaken for a number of other African languages, but not, until now, for Setswana. At the same time Plaatje was also concerned to point to the significance of the proverbs themselves: their wealth and variety, he believed, demonstrated fully the qualities and capacity of a language that was 'fully equipped for the expression of thought'. The fact that he was able to demonstrate so many close parallels between the proverbs he had collected and proverbs in a variety of European languages was also something to which he drew attention. In Plaatje's mind this served only to demonstrate the universality of cultural phenomena. What Plaatje was saying, in other words, was that the Tswana language was as good as any other, and entitled to full recognition of this fact – something which his friends in London might have accepted without difficulty, but which many people in South Africa would not. To this extent, Plaatje was conscious that his collection of proverbs was a statement of the cultural worth and integrity of his native language – not so different from the wider political statement he was still struggling to get into print in the form of *Native Life in South Africa*: in a sense both were part of a larger whole, a way of life which Plaatje was seeking to defend on two fronts simultaneously, cultural and political.

The second Tswana-language project which had also preoccupied Plaatje throughout 1915 and into 1916 was his work with Daniel Jones, a lecturer at University College, London, and already recognised as one of the foremost phoneticians of his day, in carrying out a comprehensive phonetic analysis of the Tswana language. The two men had first met early in 1915 when Plaatje visited the Phonetics Department at University College in the company of Alice Werner's sister, Mary. At that time Plaatje had, he said, no more than a 'vague acquaintance' with phonetics, and he was struck by the practical demonstration he was given. Thinking of its applicability to Setswana, he saw at once that the science of phonetics provided a means of recording and preserving its correct pronunciation, something about which he had long been concerned.[66] Daniel Jones, for his part, was fascinated by the Tswana language, about which he at that time knew absolutely nothing, and saw in Plaatje the opportunity to carry out a phonetic survey of what was to him an unusual and largely unexplored language. Surprisingly enough, nobody, as yet, had actually carried out a proper phonetic analysis of any African language. The outcome was that Plaatje and Jones agreed to embark upon what was likely to be a lengthy task, and from May 1915 through to September 1916 they had 'constant meetings', totalling, in Jones's estimation, between 100 and 120 hours.[67]

This arrangement was doubly welcome for Plaatje because of the regular income that these sessions provided; together with his earnings from the *African World* they became, so he said in one interview, one of his main sources of income.[68] The results of these sessions were duly published in 1916, under joint authorship, with the title *A Sechuana Reader in International Phonetic Orthography (with English Translations)*. It was widely accepted as a pioneering work – particularly for its recognition of the importance of tones in the structure of Setswana – but it was also a highly technical piece of linguistic research, and there was never really much chance that the book would ever become popular, as Plaatje hoped, amongst missionaries and others working in Tswana-speaking areas.[69] But his collaboration with Daniel Jones nevertheless gave Plaatje, quite apart from much needed income, an interest in phonetics that he was to retain for the rest of his life, and the satisfaction, too, of knowing that it was his own pronunciation of the Serolong dialect that now constituted, as it were, the official phonetic record.

There was one further literary venture with which Plaatje also became involved during the course of 1915: Professor I. Gollancz's *Book of Homage to Shakespeare*, published the following year to commemorate the 300th anniversary of Shakespeare's death.[70] Plaatje probably met Professor Gollancz, a professor of English literature at King's College, London, through Alice Werner, also a lecturer there. Since the purpose of the volume was to bring together a collection of essays on Shakespeare from all over the world (in practice, as one reviewer was to note sourly, from 'us, our allies and neutral states'),[71] it was not altogether surprising that Plaatje, with his keen interest in Shakespeare, should have been asked to contribute. This he duly did. In his contribution, three pages long and entitled 'A South African's homage', Plaatje told of how he had first encountered Shakespeare, how Shakespeare impinged upon his romance with Elizabeth in 1897 (he recalled that he had been reading *Cymbeline* at the time), and why it was that Shakespeare's plays continued to have such an attraction for him. Some recent experiences in London served only to underline the reasons for this:

> It is just possible that selfish patriotism is at the bottom of my admiration for Shakespeare. To illustrate my meaning let me take a case showing how feelings of an opposite kind were roused in me.
>
> I once went to see a cinematograph show of the Crucifixion. All the characters in the play, including Pilate, the Priests, and Simon of Cyrene, were white men. According to the pictures, the only black man in the mob was Judas Iscariot. I have since become suspicious of the veracity of the cinema and acquired a scepticism which is not diminished by a gorgeous one now exhibited in London which shows, side by side with the nobility of the white race, a highly coloured exaggeration of the depravity of the blacks.
>
> Shakespeare's dramas, on the other hand, show that nobility and valour, like depravity and cowardice, are not the monopoly of any colour. Shakespeare lived over 300 years ago, but he appears to have had a keen grasp of human character. His description of things seems so inwardly correct that (in spite of our rapid means of communication and facilities for travelling) we of the present age have not yet equalled his acumen.

The film then being shown in London, to which Plaatje referred, was *The Birth of a Nation*, based on a book called *The Clansman*, notable – notorious in Plaatje's view – for its glorification of the activities of the Ku Klux Klan in the American south. Plaatje had been horrified when he first saw this film, and together with Georgiana Solomon (who on at least one occasion publicly harangued cinema audiences about the iniquity of the film) and Mrs Jane Cobden Unwin had registered their protest with the British Home Secretary. Athough they did not succeed in getting it withdrawn, they were at least promised that it would not be exported to South Africa.[72] Plaatje's preference for *Othello* was understandable enough.

Plaatje's concluding passage in 'A South African's homage' is of special interest:

> It is to be hoped that with the maturity of African literature, now still in its infancy, writers and translators will consider the matter of giving to Africans the benefit of some at least of Shakespeare's works. That this could be done is suggested by the probability that some of the stories on which his dramas are based find equivalents in African folk-lore.[73]

In all probability Plaatje had already embarked upon the work of translating Shakespeare into his own tongue, Setswana; at the very least, it is clear that the idea had occurred to him.

According to one report – a newspaper account of a Brotherhood meeting which Plaatje addressed in Stratford-upon-Avon, Shakespeare's birthplace, late in 1916, at which he was introduced as 'a well-known Shakespearean scholar' – Plaatje's involvement in the *Book of Homage to Shakespeare* extended beyond the role of contributor to that of 'joint editor'.[74] Although no recognition of this appears in the book itself, Plaatje may possibly have undertaken some of the more routine editorial work on the volume for Professor Gollancz, and he would certainly have welcomed the money that any such employment would have brought in to pay for his subsistence, and help finance what remained very much his top priority: the continuation of his political campaign, and the publication of *Native Life in South Africa*. In no way did his work for Daniel Jones, the compilation of his book of proverbs, his contribution to the volume celebrating Shakespeare, divert him from these tasks.

◇

Plaatje had continued to hear regularly from Elizabeth since arriving in England. She had kept him supplied with the South African newspapers he needed to write up recent political developments there for his book (her assistance in this respect was gratefully acknowledged in *Native Life*), and obviously kept him fully abreast of more domestic developments as well. With some financial support from Isaiah Bud-M'belle she seems to have coped well with Plaatje's absence, at least for the first six months or so that he was away. Certainly this was how Plaatje portrayed things in a letter to Mrs Colenso in February 1915:

> I continue to hear from home every week. I thought when I left that my wife would manage very well, but she has surprised me in steering safely up till now, seeing that in our estimates before I left, we had provided for a five months' absence, and did not calculate that there would be a war, and a general retrenchment of income and an increase in cost of living.[75]

In one recent letter Elizabeth had also commented, somewhat philosophically: 'it is strange that we should be separated each time there is a war'. Neither of them was ever likely to forget the last occasion this had taken place.

But news from home was not always so reassuring. One blow, perhaps half expected, was the news that *Tsala ea Batho* ceased publication in July 1915. Isaiah Bud-M'belle had done his best to keep the paper going in Plaatje's absence, and managed to do so for over a year, but in the end the effort proved too much; it must have always been an uphill struggle, and when wartime shortages in South Africa produced a 700 per cent increase in the cost of newsprint, publication had to be discontinued; there was no chance of increases of this magnitude being absorbed by an enterprise that lost money at the best of times.[76] Plaatje could only hope that he would be able to restart the paper when conditions were more favourable.

More bad news was to come at the end of the year. Shortly before Christmas, 1915, Elizabeth's mother died; then, on Christmas eve, Isaiah Bud-M'belle was informed that his position as Interpreter in Native Languages in the Griqualand West High Court was to be abolished forthwith, and that the Public Services Commission could find no other position for him. It was a cruel, abrupt end to a distinguished career in the civil service of both the Cape Colony and the Union of South Africa: he was widely regarded as the finest court interpreter of his day, and he had numerous testimonials to this effect from a host of distinguished High Court judges.[77] But it was a clear enough statement on the part of the South African authorities of their view of employing black South Africans at such levels in the civil service. In Kimberley especially many would have remembered the high hopes that Bud-M'belle carried on his shoulders when he qualified for entry into the Cape Civil Service over twenty years previously.

Plaatje, six thousand miles away in England, would probably have heard the news early in 1916. Sad as the news was it would surely have come as vindication of his determination to stay on in England to get *Native Life in South Africa* into print. For it brought home in a very personal way the grim reality of the situation of able, well-educated black South Africans such as himself. If Plaatje had ever entertained any doubts about leaving what at the time seemed a secure career as a civil servant, they must now have been swept away. Bud-M'belle, for his part, stoically accepted his fate and began to think about making a career for himself elsewhere.

Shortly afterwards, though, Plaatje received some much more encouraging news from home. He explained in a letter to Mrs Colenso at the beginning of April 1916:

> God is so merciful that he has sent me a reward for the thankless sacrifice I am making for my fellow natives. My boy has succeeded in capturing the ONE and ONLY little scholarship which is open to our people in South Africa and he left on March 5th for Lovedale FREE of charge. This is a considerable relief to me in the financial tangle awaiting my arrival in South Africa for which I thank the boy's boldness and Providence for inspiring him.[78]

St Leger had certainly won his scholarship to Lovedale, but in one respect Plaatje was misinformed. There were in fact two scholarships open to Africans hoping to go to Lovedale, and the other was won by a boy called Z. K. Matthews from the same Lyndhurst Road school in Kimberley. Since Plaatje and Bud-M'belle had between them done much to revive the school's fortunes since they both joined its committee in 1910, this double triumph was something for both of them to savour, and for Bud-M'belle it perhaps came as some consolation in view of his recent dismissal. He then accompanied both children on the 500-mile journey to Lovedale at the beginning of term, which happened to coincide with the formal opening of the nearby Fort Hare University College, the first post-secondary educational institution in South Africa to be open to black Africans. Certainly it was an encouraging piece of news for Plaatje in his struggles in England.[79]

◇

Plaatje's great objective in his mission to England was finally achieved with the publication of *Native Life in South Africa* in May 1916, reward at last for his untiring struggles since arriving in England two years previously, and a notable victory, so he wrote later, after '11 months fighting Harris who was battling to suppress "Native Life" in the press'.[80] *Native Life in South Africa Before and Since the European War and the Boer Rebellion*, to give it its full title, had grown into rather more than 'the little book' Plaatje had originally envisaged, and it now ran to over 350 pages – good value for its modest price of 3s 6d. The book consisted of an account of the events leading up to the passage of the Natives' Land Act, the effects it had when implemented, the campaign mounted by the South African Native National Congress to secure its repeal, the story of the deputation to England and the reception it received, and an account of several historical episodes illustrating the loyalty of African people in South Africa to the cause of the imperial government. Without doubt the most striking chapters of the book were those in which Plaatje described his own observations of the effects of the Land Act during the journeys he made in South Africa in 1913 and 1914.

Native Life in South Africa was formulated as a direct and often highly emotional appeal to the British public to right the wrongs being done to the African people of South Africa; to secure, above all, the repeal of the Natives' Land Act. It was an appeal that Plaatje justified not simply by reference to the constitutional responsibilities which Britain still retained for South Africa, but upon the fact that his people shared with the British public a common humanity: natural justice and Christian belief alike demanded their intervention. Throughout the book Plaatje was concerned to demonstrate this common humanity, and to argue that as loyal subjects of the British empire his people were entitled to fair and decent treatment. He was also very conscious of the difficulties caused by the image which his people had in the eyes of the majority of the British public: 'This appeal', he wrote,

> is not on behalf of the naked hordes of cannibals who are represented in fantastic pictures displayed in the shop-windows in Europe, most of them imaginary; but it is on behalf of five million loyal British subjects who

shoulder 'the black man's burden' every day, doing so without looking forward to any decoration or thanks.[81]

Throughout *Native Life* Plaatje was at great pains to present his case in terms which would be meaningful to an English audience. In trying to convey what the Natives' Land Act meant, for example, he likened its operation to an imaginary decree of the London County Council; he evoked memories of Daniel Defoe's *Journal of the Plague Year* by comparing the effects of the Land Act to those of the plague; he quoted Oliver Goldsmith's poem 'The Deserted Village' to emphasise the parallels between the evictions that followed the Natives' Land Act with those same consequences that followed the enclosures in England over a century ago. It is possible, too, that Plaatje had in mind William Cobbett's *Rural Rides*, published nearly a hundred years earlier, more than any other book the record of the destruction of an independent English peasantry through the enclosures in the early nineteenth century. Plaatje believed that what he had witnessed in the wake of the Land Act was the destruction of a black South African peasantry, and he was aware of the similarity in historical process; moreover, the personal, nostalgic technique Plaatje uses in describing what he saw bears a striking resemblance to that of Cobbett.

One constant theme that recurs throughout the book is the war and its relevance to his arguments. In the circumstances this was hardly something that Plaatje could have avoided. What he does, though, with considerable skill, is to turn a potential obstacle to any consideration of his case into a central argument in his favour: he emphasised the loyalty of his people to the cause of the imperial government in both past and present conflicts, arguing that this entitled them to 'fair play and justice', and relief from the 'tyrannical enactment' of 1913. In contrast, Plaatje stressed, stood the behaviour of the Boers, the instigators, as he argued, of the Land Act itself, and the people responsible for the political disabilities of his people, and for rising in rebellion at the outbreak of the First World War; the African population, by contrast, was loyal to the imperial cause, and their representatives – the South African Native National Congress – had resolved at their meeting in August 1914 to 'hang up their grievances' for the duration of the war.

Overall, *Native Life in South Africa* was a powerful and sustained polemic, shrewdly cast in the terms and language most likely to appeal to the conscience of a nation at war, and the first book-length statement of the grievances of the African people of South Africa by one of their own leaders. Its significance was appreciated by at least some of the reviews it received in the English press. The *Birmingham Post* was amongst those impressed by the strength of Plaatje's case:

It is a serious case, well and ably put, and the evidence embodied in it is very disquieting. Here at any rate is a book which makes the native agitation intelligible and may conceivably have an influence on future events in South Africa – and at home, for by no legal fiction can the Imperial power dissociate itself from responsibility for Native affairs.[82]

Other reviews took a similar line, many of them commenting on how remarkable it was that a book such as this could have been written by an African.

Even the journal *South Africa*, so scathing of the Congress delegation in 1914, had some kind words:

> There is the spice if not the charm of novelty about this book. It was written by a South African native and he holds strong views on some recent public questions. He occasionally expresses himself well and forcibly, and it is all to the good that South African publicists should have the advantage of reading the opinions of a native observer when dealing with legislation affecting his race.[83]

Perhaps even more surprising were the positive words that came from such a journal as *United Empire*:

> Mr Plaatje has marshalled his facts with considerable skill. He sets forth the case of his countrymen with energy and moderation. His conclusions seem to be warranted by the information at his disposal, and the facts he adduces seem to bear but one interpretation. And lastly, in the existing circumstances, he is fully justified in appealing to the court of public opinion.[84]

Even if the war had inevitably placed all else in the shade, Plaatje had every reason to be gratified by the generally favourable response which his book received in England. Not every review or opinion was of course favourable. 'Delta', in the *African World*, complained that the title of the book did not accurately reflect its content, that it was too long and in places 'melodramatic and childish', and full of 'unjust and illogical' generalisations; overall he sympathised with Plaatje's case, but thought that 'all real sympathisers with Mr Plaatje and his friends' would wish he had presented it 'with more dignity'.[85] Olive Schreiner was another of those who were not so sympathetically disposed towards *Native Life in South Africa*. Now living in London, and a close friend of Betty Molteno, she had seen Plaatje from time to time over the previous two years, but she disapproved of what she had heard about the book on pacifist grounds: 'You know, I am a pacifist,' she wrote to Georgiana Solomon, 'and from what I hear he [Plaatje] advocates the natives coming over here to help kill.'[86] She had evidently not, however (at least when she made this statement), read the book; as Mrs Solomon elucidated: 'O.S., by the way, seems more taken up with Dutch than natives, just now.'[87]

Georgiana Solomon succeeded in eliciting a rather more substantial response to *Native Life in South Africa* from a man she still considered, their differences in political viewpoint notwithstanding, an old family friend: General Botha, Prime Minister of South Africa. Mrs Solomon would doubtless have shown the General's letter to Plaatje, and he would surely have been intrigued by what he had to say:

Pretoria, 31 August 1916

Dear Mrs Solomon,
    I have received your letter dated the 21st July, 1916, and the book 'Native Life in South Africa' by Mr S. T. Plaatje. Please accept my thanks.

The contents of your letter and your appeal on behalf of the Natives have made a deep impression on me and I am grateful for your kindly opinion of myself.

As regards Mr Plaatje's book I need only say that an opinion held by any man and constitutionally expressed is entitled to respect, however much one personally may differ from it, and the book will certainly not in any way adversely influence my Government in its dealing with the Natives of the Union. On the contrary, I welcome any criticism honestly given and the book may be of value in giving publicity to views, possibly held by a section of the Native community, which may perhaps be in conflict with those held by other sections of the Union's inhabitants; and where differences of opinion exist, full and free discussion is most desirable.

Mr Plaatje, however, is a special pleader, and, consciously or unconsciously, in his book he has in my opinion been somewhat biassed in his strictures on the Government in regard to the Natives' Land Act: he has exaggerated incidents which tell in his favour and suppressed facts that should be within his knowledge which would show the honest attempts made by the Government to avoid the infliction of hardship in carrying out a principle which, you must remember, was sanctioned by the Legislature.

In conclusion, I should like to say that whatever mistakes we Europeans may make in working out the destinies of Whites and Blacks in South Africa, I am convinced that in the hearts of the majority there is a sincere desire to do justice to the Native Races in our intercourse with them, and however wide individual views may differ as to the methods to be taken to ensure that Whites and Blacks shall be peaceful and contented residents of the Union and loyal subjects of the Crown, it is certain that with the existence of such a desire that result must inevitably ensue – although to impatient souls progress towards this ideal may at times be slow and halting.

I am sending you a pamphlet by Sir W. H. Beaumont, Chairman of the Natives' Land Commission which I think will interest you.

With kindest regards,
Yours very sincerely,
Louis Botha[88]

Plaatje did not of course accept General Botha's arguments, but the generally moderate and reasonable tone of his comments would have confirmed his view that the General's chief failing was his weakness in resisting the more extreme demands of Afrikaner nationalists, to whom he attributed the brutal excesses of the Natives' Land Act. Despite the harsh comments Plaatje made about General Botha in *Native Life*, he had always got on well with him during their meetings in the past. They had conversed in Dutch, and at this level of personal contact – particularly when talking to politicians in their native tongue – Plaatje had always been able to find some common ground with people who in public felt constrained to castigate one another as political enemies. It was, indeed, one of his great attributes, and did much to sustain his faith in human nature and a continued hope for a change of heart on the part of South Africa's white rulers.[89]

General Botha's views on *Native Life* stand as an epitome of reasonableness and moderation when compared to those of the man whom Plaatje by now considered to be 'the South African government's most sturdy defender'–John Harris, 'the Organising Secretary of the so-called Aborigines' Protection Society'.[90] Having done his best to prevent the publication of *Native Life*, Harris now sought by every means at his disposal to discredit the book and its author, and sent a stream of articles to the daily and periodical press in England, supporting the policies of the South African government in glowing terms, and fiercely denouncing *Native Life* for its 'grotesque misrepresentations' and 'almost deliberate untruths'. In one of these articles, in the influential *Journal of the Royal African Society*, he argued that 'the attitude adopted at the moment by the natives' constituted 'by far the most formidable difficulty in relation to General Botha's native policies', and that such attitudes had 'just received most unfortunate emphasis by the publication of a book which shows that even now there is an intelligent, well-educated native who either cannot, or will not, grasp plain facts'. *Native Life in South Africa*, in Harris's view, was 'not merely full of the most unfortunate inaccuracies, but upon capital issues the distortions and misrepresentations are of such a nature that they can only do serious harm to the cause of the natives'.[91]

Despite his antipathy to Plaatje (and in private he was even more vituperative), Harris was nevertheless obliged to admit that it was not just Plaatje who constituted the problem: 'It cannot be overlooked,' he acknowledged, 'that at the present time the natives as a whole are against General Botha's policy.'[92] It was an extraordinary position for the organising secretary of the 'so-called Aborigines' Protection Society' to have got himself into.

Plaatje's differences with John Harris were only intensified by the publication of the Report of the South African Land Commission (the Beaumont Commission) shortly after the first edition of *Native Life* itself came out.[93] This was the commission which had been set up under the provisions of the Natives' Land Act in order to find further areas of land for African population. As both Plaatje and other African political leaders had predicted, the commission had been unable to find any substantial areas of land for this purpose, and its recommendations were in any case soon to be rejected by the South African parliament. Whilst Harris preferred to find reason for encouragement in the report, on the grounds that it offered further guarantees on the principle of segregation, Plaatje was fiercely critical, and took its findings as complete vindication of what he had been saying over the last three years.

In a postscript which he was able to have added to the second batch of 500 copies of the first edition of *Native Life in South Africa*, Plaatje subjected the report to a detailed scrutiny, and left his readers in no doubt as to the depth of the deceit that he believed to have been perpetrated: 'I must say,' he wrote, 'that until this Report reached me, I never would have believed my white fellow countrymen capable of conceiving the all but diabolical schemes propounded between the covers of Volume I of the Report of the South African Land Commission, 1916, and clothing them in such plausible form as to mislead even sincere and well-informed friends of the Natives.' Fearful of the ultimate consequences for the future of South Africa if such policies were not altered, Plaatje again appealed to British public opinion to 'stay the hand of the South African Government, veto this iniquity and avert the Nemesis that would surely follow its perpetration'.[94]

With the publication of this analysis of the Beaumont Report, Plaatje's differences with the Anti-Slavery and Aborigines' Protection Society widened further. He was furious at the way in which Harris sought not only to undermine his own campaign in England, but also to ignore the clearly expressed resolution of the South African Native National Congress's annual meeting in 1916 against the Land Act, concentrating instead on a statement in an accompanying letter from Richard Selope Thema, taken out of context, to the effect that Congress was not opposed to the principle of segregation *per se*, provided it could be equitably implemented.[95] Harris translated this into support for the principle of the Natives' Land Act, and argued – using carefully selected parts of Selope Thema's letter to support his case, while ignoring the rest of it – that what was therefore required was not a repeal of the legislation, but simply a modification of some of its provisions. Harris had then written back to Selope Thema to congratulate him on adopting this position, contrasted it with the impression Plaatje was creating in England, and then proceeded to exploit Selope Thema's letter, in Plaatje's opinion, 'with the energy of a politician in the interests of our opponents'.[96]

Then, in August 1916, the Anti-Slavery and Aborigines' Protection Society, at Harris's instigation, passed a resolution expressing its approval of the principle supposedly embodied in the Natives' Land Act, and welcoming the Report of the Beaumont Commission.[97] The resolution was opposed vociferously by Mrs Solomon and Mrs Unwin, Plaatje's two allies on the committee, but they could not prevent it being adopted. Harris himself was duly commended in an approving letter from the South African Department of Native Affairs.[98]

◇

Had the reaction of John Harris and the Anti-Slavery and Aborigines' Protection Society been typical of the response Plaatje encountered during the time he spent in England there would have been little motive for him to have continued with his campaign. In fact his confidence in the existence of an underlying reservoir of sympathy for the cause of his people was immeasurably strengthened as a result of the time he spent in England. Above all this was due to the support and encouragement he had found at the hands of the Brotherhood movement. His first contact with the movement had been in July 1914 when, in the company of his fellow Congress delegates, he visited the organisation's headquarters in London. For Plaatje it was the beginning of what was to become a long-lasting association, and one that was to be of considerable importance over the next few years of his life. At that time, July 1914, Plaatje and his colleagues were glad of the support of any organised body, particularly one that claimed – like the Brotherhood movement – a membership of 600,000, and which was prepared to commit itself so unequivocally to their cause, and to provide speaking platforms throughout the United Kingdom.

Founded in 1875 by John Blackham, a Nottingham printer, the Brotherhood movement was an inter-denominational religious organisation which in practice drew most of its support from members of the nonconformist churches. Its main form of activity was holding 'PSAs' ('Pleasant Sunday afternoons'), Sunday meetings which were devoted to religious and educational instruction; and its members were united above all by an evangelical zeal to promote the practical implementation of Christianity in everyday life. 'The Brotherhood,' said Arthur Henderson, President of the movement, 'must help not only the spiritual part of life, but also in social matters. They should always help the downtrodden, showing the brotherly feeling which was portrayed throughout the life of Christ.'[99] Drawing most of its support from Britain's lower middle class, the Brotherhood movement was a national organisation, was linked to a similar organisation for women, and enjoyed the support of a number of Liberal and Labour members of parliament. Without doubt it was an organisation of considerable importance.[100]

Plaatje had been highly gratified by the initial response of the Brotherhood movement, and after the departure of the other Congress delegates addressed a great many meetings under its auspices. In time, he developed close personal relationships with several individuals connected with the movement (notably Mr William Cross, who was chairman of the Southall branch), and he became closely identified with its aims and beliefs. It is not difficult to see why the movement was attractive to him. The product of a mission-school education, Plaatje had sought throughout his life to ensure that his basic Christian beliefs were applied in the political and social affairs of the country in which he lived; now he found that such a concern was at the heart of the beliefs of those associated with the Brotherhood movement in England. He was a great believer, moreover, in the emphasis upon inter-denominationalism which was so central to the Brotherhood movement's existence, for in South Africa he had long been critical of the divisions within the Christian churches and missionary societies, and had often expressed concern about the effects that this had had in dividing his fellow-countrymen from one another. Plaatje's contact and association with the Brotherhood movement did much, indeed, to restore his belief in the power of Christianity to work for social and political justice, and to bring about individual, moral change in people's outlook and attitudes; only with this, Plaatje believed, could a more just social and political order emerge.

Sharing convictions of this kind, Plaatje established an easy rapport with his Brotherhood audiences. His meetings were invariably well-attended, and often well-reported in the local press. From accounts in such papers as the *Leighton Buzzard Observer* ('South Africa's patriotism in the war'), the *Hastings and St Leonards Observer* ('Loyal dark Africa: native speaker at Hastings Brotherhood'), the *Northampton Daily Echo* ('Black man's pleas: coloured speaker at the Men's Own'), it is clear that Plaatje succeeded in making a deep impression upon his audiences, amusing them with the humorous stories he told, arousing indignation with what he told them of the treatment of his people.[101] Essentially the arguments were those he put forward in *Native Life in South Africa*, but he had a knack of tailoring them to the particular character of the audience he had before him, and making use of news of any developments in the war which could be used to add weight to his case; particularly notable amongst these was the recruitment, in mid-1916, of a South African Native Labour Contingent for non-combatant service with the Allied army on the Western Front. What better illustration of African loyalty to the British empire could there be than this?

In all, Plaatje addressed a total of 305 meetings during the two and a half years he spent in England, half of which took place under the auspices of the Brotherhood movement, the majority of the others being sponsored by other church organisations. This worked out at an average of nearly one meeting every three days. Given the other difficulties and commitments which he faced, and the ill-health from which he seems to have suffered (especially during the cold weather), it was an achievement of almost epic proportions. Single-handed, Plaatje had done more than anybody before to convey to the British public a knowledge of the conditions in which his people lived in South Africa.

<><

Plaatje continued with his lecturing campaign right up until the time he departed from England for South Africa in January 1917. Recognition of his efforts over the previous two and a half years was provided in the form of a farewell reception for him, held at a Fleet Street hotel on 10 January 1917, which brought together many of the friends and supporters he had gathered around him since his arrival in England. The most welcome outcome of the reception was the decision on the part of Plaatje's band of sympathisers to form 'a committee to watch over native interests', to carry on, in effect, Plaatje's work now that he was departing for home, 'to keep in touch with native affairs in South Africa', and 'especially to watch the workings of the Land Act'. As Alice Werner explained, the 'Anti-Slavery and Aborigines' Protection Society seem to have their attention occupied in other directions; moreover, they do not take quite the same view as to the gravity of the situation caused by the Land Act'.

Alice Werner became the committee's secretary *pro tem*.[102] Amongst the committee's other members were Georgiana Solomon and Jane Cobden Unwin, both of them on the point of being thrown off the committee of the Anti-Slavery and Aborigines' Protection Society because of their continued opposition to the line their society had taken over the Land Act; and Sir Richard Winfrey, a member of parliament, active in the Brotherhood movement, who had just been made Parliamentary Secretary for Agriculture in Lloyd George's government. Sir Richard's association with the committee was a cause for concern to John Harris, who was very upset at seeing 'a responsible Minister of the Crown' becoming involved in it, and he 'did not see how it was possible for a Minister to take such an attitude in view of the obligations he had accepted'.[103] The committee was an altogether appropriate legacy for Plaatje to leave behind him, and a promising-looking body to continue the work he had begun.

Two weeks later – on the eve of his departure – Plaatje was presented with an illuminated address by the Brotherhood Federation, a further token of its appreciation of the work he had done. 'We, the undersigned, officers and members of the National Brotherhood Federation, England,' it declared,

> desire to mark our appreciation of the excellent services rendered by you on behalf of our coloured brethren in South Africa. The 150 speeches at

Brotherhood and Sisterhood and PSA meetings which you have addressed during your two and a half years' stay in our midst have brought home to us the grievous wrongs under which the natives of the Union are labouring. We shall not forget your able advocacy of your people's cause, and at the close of the war we shall do all we can to help you to regain that freedom and justice to which as loyal British subjects your people are entitled. The Brotherhood Movement has no colour bar. To us all men are brothers, and we hold out to them the right hand of fellowship. We rejoice at the spirit of Brotherhood that you have manifested in the course of your campaign in England, and we wish you all success in the continuance of your noble work in the service of Christ, the cause of humanity, and on behalf of your people, to whom we send our fraternal greetings.[104]

The address was signed by the leading members of the Brotherhood Federation, together with William Cross (on behalf of the Southall Men's Own Brotherhood) and Sir Richard Winfrey – recognition of Plaatje's achievements in Britain, and encouragement, too, to continue to press for attention to be given to his cause as soon as the war came to an end.

Plaatje sailed from Plymouth on 27 January 1917. He had remained in England for much longer than he had originally intended, but over the course of the previous two and a half years he had achieved (in the face of acute financial difficulty, ill-health, and the opposition of an organisation he might reasonably have expected to have afforded him every encouragement and assistance) his main objectives of publishing his book on the Natives' Land Act, and conducting a one-man campaign to bring the grievances of his people to the attention of the British public. In addition he had made a substantial contribution, almost as a diversion, to the development of Tswana language and literature, although there were of course far fewer people to appreciate the significance of that work. Plaatje had also won a great many friends. It remained to be seen whether his efforts would bear fruit at the termination of hostilities; whether, indeed, the South African government could be persuaded to alter in any way the policies with which it now intended to complement the Land Act of 1913.

9

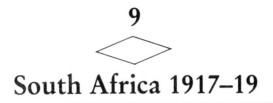

South Africa 1917–19

On account of wartime conditions the voyage home to South Africa, aboard the SS *Galway Castle*, took rather longer than expected – 29 days instead of the usual 17. Not that there was much likelihood of Plaatje wasting the time he spent aboard ship. Whereas in 1914 he had busied himself with writing the first drafts of *Native Life in South Africa* (which, he noted, now received a 'cordial reception' amongst his fellow passengers), on this return voyage much of his time was occupied in translating Shakespeare – more particularly *Julius Caesar* – into Setswana.[1] It was by no means a total preoccupation. Also aboard the *Galway Castle* was a group of 23 members of the South African Native Labour Contingent, who were being invalided back home to South Africa after service in France.[2] Plaatje was naturally interested to find these men aboard the same ship, and keen to hear about their experiences, particularly as a number of his own friends and relatives in South Africa had joined the contingent. He found, however, that the attitude of the white (South African) non-commissioned officers towards him was far from friendly, and within a week he was served with notice not to visit the men on the voyage. Their opposition was only overcome after an appeal to the ship's captain, and with the support and assistance of two white missionaries who were also on the ship. Together, they succeeded in attending to the needs of the men of the Native Labour Contingent, and were eventually able to hold religious services for them.[3] For Plaatje it was a reminder of the attitudes he could expect to encounter on his return home.

Also aboard the *Galway Castle* was a black missionary, the Reverend Herbert A. Payne, accompanied by his wife, Bessie, travelling to South Africa to join an American Baptist mission in the eastern Cape. Both had enjoyed Plaatje's company during the voyage, but the Paynes had expressed to him their fear that – despite the assurances to the contrary which they had received at the South African High Commission in London – they would be prevented, on racial grounds, from disembarking when they arrived in Cape Town. Their fears proved to be justified. Because of the secrecy surrounding the movements of all wartime shipping there was nobody there to meet them, and it was left to Plaatje to take up their case when the Immigration Department informed them that they could not disembark. Plaatje succeeded within a couple of days of arriving in Cape Town in reversing this decision, appealing personally to Sir Thomas Watt, the minister concerned, J. X. Merriman, Advocate William Stuart and then to

General Botha himself (all of them conveniently at hand because parliament was in session). This was a tribute both to his ability to negotiate his way through to the highest levels of government, and at the same time an encouraging sign of recognition of his continued influence as a representative of his people, and a reflection of a reputation that was now considerably enhanced as a result of the publication of *Native Life in South Africa.*[4] General Botha was, besides, keen to enlist Plaatje's support in recruiting more Africans to join the Native Labour Contingent to fulfil his commitment to the imperial war effort.[5] To reverse the decision of the head of the Immigration Department was a small price to pay for Plaatje's active support in the recruiting campaign. It was one of those little triumphs that Plaatje remembered.

If Plaatje's success in the Payne incident seemed to offer some small encouragement that the government might prove more open to rational argument, the new legislation he found being discussed in the House of Assembly served only to confirm his worst fears about the direction of wider questions of policy. 'On landing at Cape Town,' he wrote to Mrs Cobden Unwin, 'I found, besides other difficulties, that a horrible bill was before Parliament to confirm all the horrors of the Land Act. This meant hard work just from the moment of landing.'[6] The 'horrible bill' to which he referred was in fact the Native Administration Bill, and Plaatje's characterisation was apt enough. The bill in effect represented the official response to the Beaumont Commission's report, accepted its recommendations about the division of land into areas of African and European occupation and proposed to take the principle of segregation a stage further by separating the administration of the one from the other. In the so-called 'Native areas' there was to be a uniform system of administration, and it was proposed that the Governor-General would legislate by proclamation, advised by a permanent commission headed by the Minister of Native Affairs. Provision was also made for the establishment of councils to encourage African involvement in strictly local affairs, and several proposals were put forward to separate the administration of justice in 'European' and 'African' areas.[7] Taken together, the provisions of the bill amounted to yet another nail in the coffin of the old Cape ideal, for so Plaatje saw it, of a common society, and he was particularly concerned at the threat to prohibit access by Africans to the Supreme Court; together with the Cape franchise, he saw this as a crucial bulwark in the defence of African rights. Both were once again under threat.

When Plaatje arrived in Cape Town the bill was being given its first reading, but it soon ran into opposition in the House. Whilst J. X. Merriman, Sir Thomas Smartt, and several others, spoke out against the bill from the premises of the old liberalism of the Cape, they were now joined by members from Natal who believed that too much land from their province was being set aside for African occupation. It was a curious alliance, and as ever the professions of concern for African interests masked a variety of interests and viewpoints. But one thing was clear: the bill was going to have a stormy passage in the various stages it needed to go through before it became the law of the land. One other recent development had an important bearing on the debate on the Native Administration Bill in parliament: the decision of the Supreme Court in the case of Thompson and Stilwell *versus* Chief Kama, the effect of which was to render inapplicable certain provisions of both the Natives' Land Act and the Natives' Administration Bill on the grounds that these interfered with the qualifications required for the Cape franchise, entrenched constitutionally in the Act of Union.[8]

Encouraged by this Plaatje remained in Cape Town for two weeks to try and rally support against the bill, both inside and outside parliament, staying with his old friend Dr Abdul Abdurahman at his house in Loop Street, just a few minutes' walk from the House of Assembly. Even before he was reunited with his wife and family Plaatje had launched himself straight into the political affairs of his people.

When Plaatje did eventually complete the final leg of his journey home, by train to Kimberley, it was to return to a warm welcome from both the African people of Kimberley and his family. Elizabeth, St Leger, Halley, Olive and Violet were all there, and, so Plaatje informed Mrs Unwin, in good health. But the 'financial tangle' he had anticipated a year earlier was indeed a serious one. Both Isaiah Bud-M'belle and Simon Plaatje, still living at the old Pniel mission, had helped Elizabeth out during Plaatje's absence, but the South African Native National Congress had not made any contribution, and Plaatje himself had accumulated a debt of nearly £500 to finance his campaign in England.[9] *Tsala ea Batho* had not appeared since the middle of 1915, but at least the printing machinery had escaped the claims of his creditors. 'Mrs Plaatje,' so he wrote to Mrs Unwin, 'turned her house into a workshop, it has not appearance of a home. In fact, she shoved the machinery on one side and is doing ironing on my counter in the office also, until I can make a start with the paper.'[10]

◇

Despite his efforts over the ensuing months Plaatje was never able to raise the money to get *Tsala ea Batho* going again, though for well over a year he continued to call himself 'Editor, *Tsala ea Batho*'. But this did not deter him from reassuming as energetic a role as ever in political affairs, as the two weeks he spent in Cape Town before going home would suggest. During the few months after his return to South Africa Plaatje's reputation and influence as a national political figure reached new heights. Amongst the African people he returned to something of a hero's welcome. 'Now let it be known,' announced *Ilanga lase Natal*,

> that Mr Plaatje has performed the part of an intelligent and energetic champion for the cause of our peoples. In him we have an elder brother whose loving service it will be well for all of us to know. He comes among us once again. Let us show that we are not so dull as not to recognise his value as one of our leading men who can be trusted with the burden of a poor and suffering nation; he is one of whom Britishers of all kind are proud.[11]

A number of other laudatory letters appeared in the African press to similar effect, and praise was heaped upon him at the many meetings he addressed to tell people about his experiences in England, and to urge them to continue the fight against the Native Administration Bill. 'Mr Sol T. Plaatje, as a fearless defender and leader of his people,' so a leaflet advertising one of these meetings said, 'has a wonderful and thrilling message, almost romantic, for the people of this country. The very interesting career of his 2½ years of campaign at an absolute sacrifice is worth the gratitude of his people.'[12] Perhaps the most enthusiastic reception was that extended to him at a special welcome in his home town of Kimberley at the end of March 1917. The meeting, well attended by Africans, Coloureds, and even a few whites, began, in the best traditions of African society in Kimberley, with a variety concert, and was followed by several speeches of appreciation, and the reading of telegrams (including one from John Dube, President of Congress) from those who had been unable to attend; the Reverend C. B. Liphuko 'referred interestingly to Mr Plaatje's life work and more particularly to his activities in England, in the course of which he had proved himself a hero', and similar sentiments were expressed by the Reverend P. E. Kuze who had met Plaatje in England in 1916 en route to Philadelphia, USA. He had seen, so the *Diamond Fields Advertiser* reported,

> some of the hard work he had put in, by speaking and writing, to enlighten the English people as to the conditions of the natives in this country. He urged him to come home, but found him on his return from the United States 'still at it'. He admired him for his devotion to the cause of his people, and wished him every blessing in his unselfish work.[13]

Plaatje himself was in good form that evening. Replying to the speeches, he conveyed to the meeting the greetings he took with him from the Brotherhood movement and his band of sympathisers in England, told the meeting of some of his experiences abroad, and launched into a fierce attack against the Union government's Native Administration Bill, by now entering its second reading in the House of Assembly. Congratulating Kimberley's African population for having lodged their own protests against the bill, Plaatje concluded by saying – to loud applause and cheering – that 'if he could do anything to help them to combat those legislative evils he would not hesitate to do so'. For a while Plaatje could forget the serious financial plight in which his two and a half years' absence had left him: his sacrifices were, at least in Kimberley, both realised and appreciated.

Plaatje's reputation amongst his people was considerably enhanced by the publicity given to *Native Life in South Africa* in the South African press, especially after the book and several of his own speeches were mentioned on several occasions in the House of Assembly during the debates on the Native Administration Bill. 'Last month,' Plaatje informed Mrs Cobden Unwin on 18 May 1917,

> a Boer member – Colonel Mentz, Minister of Lands – referred to it [*Native Life in South Africa*] as a 'scurrilous attack on the Boers'. A chorus of English members promptly defended it so vehemently that even in the subsequent days when the book was quoted by English members during the debates not one had the nerve to attack it again. I will not be surprised if the redoubtable Mr H[arris] makes capital out of the fact that a Boer member – a cabinet minister – attacked my book, and will say nothing about the unanimous defence of the phalanx of English members, including Mr James Henderson

of Durban (who called it 'a triumph for native education'), and Mr Van Riet, K.C., of Grahamstown, the only Dutch member who is a Unionist.

The debates have brought forth orders from all over South Africa.[14]

Not that views on the bill currently before the House of Assembly were wholly a matter of English/Afrikaner divisions: 'Sol Plaatje, and other natives,' so one English-speaking supporter of the bill claimed, 'were already endeavouring to spread the belief that the Boer was the oppressor of the natives'; in his view, however, this was 'wholly unfounded in fact'.[15] It was evident that when it came to securing agreement between Boer and Briton over a uniform 'native policy', Plaatje was regarded as a very unfortunate influence. Certainly this was the opinion of the Inspector and Protector of Natives in Kimberley, clearly somewhat nervous about the possible effect of Plaatje's activities locally. Native Life in South Africa, he thought, was 'in a sense an able exposition of the case against the proposals originally laid before Parliament'; whilst 'the language of the book is often exaggerated, and there are unsuitable innuendoes concerning Lord Gladstone, General Botha, and the Secretary of Native Affairs', he acknowledged that 'the undercurrent of the book is an endeavour which appears to have had a considerable measure of success, to create dissension between English and Dutch, arising from differences of tradition between the races with regard to the treatment of Native matters'.[16]

Other white commentators in South Africa appreciated the importance of Native Life and the significance of the impact it was making. One anonymous review ('from a correspondent') which appeared in the Johannesburg Star early in June 1917 suggested that the book was 'of unusual importance' and 'well worth reading' because it 'called attention to the scandalous way in which natives were treated under the Land Act', and went on to make several other interesting points:

> Recently several references have been made to the work in the Legislative Assembly, by speakers criticising a proposed new Land Act. In reply General Botha and his supporters said that the book was 'scurrilous', 'miserable', etc., but it was noticeable that none of them ever denied the accuracy of its statements or questioned the authenticity of the details. The author has done his best to call attention to a great and crying scandal, and it is unfortunate that space is insufficient for us to recapitulate some of the happenings mentioned by him.

The Star's correspondent was also alive to the longer-term implications of what Plaatje had to say in Native Life:

> It only needs this sort of thing to be persevered with, for the natives to become generally disaffected, and eventually to combine against us. Up to the present this has been prevented by tribal jealousy, but 'adversity makes strange bedfellows' and this may soon be altered.[17]

As if to underline this point about 'disaffection' and the influence that Plaatje now enjoyed, some consideration was in fact given in government circles to prohibiting him from addressing a series of meetings on the Rand that he planned in June. After the Prime Minister himself had been consulted, however, it was agreed not to do this on the grounds that the effect would only be to increase the sense of grievance amongst the African population, and provide Plaatje himself with further ammunition with which to criticise the government. Plaatje was thus able to address the meetings as he had planned.[18]

◇

Plaatje's own protests against the Native Administration Bill during the eight weeks or so after his return to South Africa complemented the efforts of the other leaders of the South African Native National Congress, John Dube and Richard Selope Thema particularly. During Plaatje's absence overseas the organisation had – for the first two years after the outbreak of war – largely refrained from any criticism of the South African government as a demonstration of their loyalty to King and empire in their hour of need, in the hope that there would be some sort of political recognition of this loyalty afterwards. It was in this spirit that the Reverend Walter Rubusana had offered, after his return from England in 1914, to raise 5,000 black troops and accompany them to German South West Africa, which the Union had undertaken to invade. The offer had been refused by General Smuts on the grounds that the war was one between white men only.[19] Despite this, the Congress leaders were nevertheless prepared to assist the Native Affairs Department to recruit 24,000 Africans as labourers for the campaign, and when General Botha later agreed to provide the imperial government with a Native Labour Contingent for the war in Europe, they were also prepared to lend their support to the recruitment campaign – again in the hope that such a demonstration of loyalty would produce some sort of political reward.[20] Although recruiting for the Native Labour Contingent had not so far been as successful as the government had hoped, it would have been very much worse had not the Congress leaders been persuaded to co-operate.

At the end of 1916, however, Congress had ended its period of self-restraint in attacking government policy by passing strong resolutions, in terms similar to those used by Plaatje in *Native Life in South Africa*, in denunciation of the Report of the Beaumont Commission; and in February 1917, while Plaatje was en route back home, an extraordinary meeting was called in Pretoria to discuss the Native Administration Bill. In a crowded and very hot corrugated-iron hall the bill was discussed clause by clause, and the delegates heard the local Native Commissioner's exposition of its provisions and objectives. 'The opposition to the land provisions of the Bill', so Mr Barrett reported back to the Secretary for Native Affairs, 'was very marked, and while sentiments of loyalty were freely expressed words were not minced in denouncing the Government's proposals'; and even he professed sympathy for Congress's opposition to some parts of the bill, duly conveyed by the meeting in the form of a resolution, proposed by John Dube, requesting the South African government to postpone the bill until a year after the end of the war, and in the meantime to repeal the Natives' Land Act of 1913.[21] It failed to deter the government from launching the bill on its passage through the House of Assembly.

When Plaatje returned to South Africa at the end of the month, the South African Native National Congress had thus responded with resolutions of protest against the Native Administration Bill, and further discussion and action was planned for the next annual general meeting, due to be held in Bloemfontein in May 1917; by this time, it was hoped, it would be known whether or not the bill was to become law. But Congress faced other difficulties besides an unsympathetic and unresponsive government, intent on passing legislation to which they were opposed. Behind the façade of unity it was becoming increasingly evident that the movement was now racked by personal differences amongst its leaders, and between the representatives of the constituent organisations that made up the national movement. There had been some very unfortunate irregularities in relation to the funds that had been raised to pay for the deputation to England in 1914 (about which there was a considerable correspondence in the African press), and the constitutional problems of the relations (and financial obligations) of the different branches of the Congress movement had never been satisfactorily resolved. Pixley Seme, indeed, was considered by many to have imposed his own constitution upon the movement in 1915 without proper discussion with the other members of the executive, and in such a way as to strengthen his own hand against the President, John Dube.[22]

The conduct of the deputation in England had been a further cause of tension and jealousy. John Dube was regarded by the other members of the deputation – Plaatje included – as having let down the cause by returning to South Africa early and then failing to provide sufficient money for the others to return home. Between Saul Msane and John Dube in particular the differences seemed irreconcilable: together with Pixley Seme, Msane launched repeated attacks upon Dube's leadership in the columns of the Congress newspaper, *Abantu Batho* (started shortly after the formation of Congress in 1912), which -Seme at that time controlled.[23] The fragile spirit of unity that had been achieved at the time of the campaign against the Natives' Land Act, it now seemed, had all but gone.

Behind all these unseemly personal differences, though, lay several truths which were to assume the greatest importance over the course of the next two years. The first was that the Congress leaders, having apparently exhausted the constitutional options open to them, were simply unsure of which way to turn. Almost without exception, they were unable to conceive of any convincing alternative to the tried methods of appeal and rational argument, methods which now seemed, more than ever, to be ineffective so long as they possessed no means of constitutional leverage, no means of deflecting the government from the policies on which it was set. At the same time there were signs that the Congress leaders were losing touch with the new, urban African population, concentrated heavily in the Transvaal, and much increased in size as a result of the growth of new industries during the war. To this emerging African working class, the immediate reality of wages and urban living conditions, rather than such issues as the Native Administration Bill, was a far higher priority. But with such issues the Congress leadership – drawn for the most part from an older generation who in turn drew their support from the rural, chiefly societies – had not seriously concerned itself. The scene was set for dramatic developments in African political life.

So it was against this background that Plaatje, along with the other Congress leaders and delegates, made his way to Bloemfontein in May 1917 in order to attend Congress's fifth annual general meeting. At the head of the agenda was the Native Administration Bill, which had by now been referred to a Select Committee; as at the Pretoria meeting in February, it was roundly condemned. Plaatje, his reputation untarnished by the public bickerings that had been taking place amongst the Congress leaders, made the opening speech, reiterating his opposition to the Native Administration Bill, and criticising the remarks that General Smuts had made during the course of his much publicised 'Savoy Hotel' speech in London ten days earlier.[24] It was, however, Plaatje's speech on the same subject at an evening reception, held during the course of the three-day meeting, that aroused the greatest controversy, and it was reported in a hostile manner by the *Rand Daily Mail*, not a newspaper generally noted for its sympathetic attitude towards African aspirations. 'The interesting part of the South African Native National Congress at present sitting in Bloemfontein,' said the *Rand Daily Mail*,

> was not the formal proceedings of the opening ceremony, but the speeches at a concert in the evening, where Sol Plaatje, the well-known native orator, politician and journalist, made a vicious attack on the Government, and practically sounded the tocsin of a black v. white propaganda. . . . In a most amazing speech on the Natives' Land Bill, which was loudly cheered, Sol Plaatje said: 'They talk of segregation. It is a segregation where the blacks with a population of nearly 6,000,000 souls are forced to be content with 12,000,000 morgen, while the whites have 120,000,000 morgen.' He alleged that the whole object of the bill was to erect huge reservoirs of servile labour for the Boers. The natives would have to come out of their little segregation plots or starve there. Economic conditions would force them to come out, and their labour would be sold at a cheap rate. They would be semi-slaves. The speaker said that his father and grandfather had helped to tame the Free State. 'I am of this province,' he continued, 'and are we going to allow a Dutchman from Worcester to dictate to us where we shall live and how we shall exist?' Just as the moment when the Empire wanted the absolute, united support of all its peoples the Government of the Union had introduced the most contentious measure ever placed before a South African Parliament.

And on Smuts's 'Savoy Hotel' speech – one of the General's few statements on the subject of 'native policy' – Plaatje was reported to have had this to say:

> The speaker attacked General Smuts for his speech in London on the native question. General Smuts, he said, had done more harm to recruiting for the native labour battalion by that speech than it was possible to realise. General Smuts had practically given the Empire an ultimatum. He had also said that he hoped no government would ever arm the blacks in South or Central Africa. Was this the way to talk of a loyal section of the people who were giving their all in this war – making the supreme sacrifice in this struggle? If it had not been for the black troops in France, who had perished in their tens of thousands in Europe, there would be a different story to write about the war. Was the

57 *Teaching staff and committee of the Lyndhurst Road Public School, Kimberley, 1913. Plaatje is in the back row, third from right; Isaiah Bud-M'belle, secretary of the committee is in the back row, extreme right; Modiri Molema, recently arrived as a teacher, is sitting in the front row, extreme left.*

THE SOUTH AFRICAN
NATIVE NATIONAL CONGRESS.

SPECIAL CONFERENCE

HELD IN THE

St. JOHN'S HALL, KIMBERLEY,

FEBRUARY 27th to MARCH 2nd, 1914,

IN CONNECTION WITH THE NATIVE LANDS ACT, 1913.

President: REV. J. L. DUBE.

Sr. Vice-President: MR. S. M. MAKGATHO.

Treasurer: MR. P. KA I. SEME, B.A.

Junior Treasurer: MR. T. M. MAPIKELA.

Hon. Secretary: MR. SOL T. PLAATJE.

Organising Committee of Protest against the Lands Act:

W. F. JEMSANA (*Chairman*).	R. G. PHOOKO.
ELKA M. CELE (*Treasurer*).	D. D. TYWAKADI.
D. S. LETANKA.	D. MOELETSI.
R. W. MSIMANG.	M. D. NDABEZITA.
H. D. MKIZE.	H. SELBY MSIMANG (*Hon. Sec.*)

S. MSANE, *Organiser.*

58 *First page of programme for the special conference of the SANNC, Kimberley, February–March 1914, called to discuss the Natives' Land Act. Plaatje was elected a member of the delegation to England.*

59 *The South African Native National Congress delegation to England, June 1914. Left to right: Thomas Mapikela, Rev. Walter Rubusana, Rev. John Dube, Saul Msane, Sol Plaatje.*

BROTHERHOOD AND EMPIRE.

COME AND HEAR

MR. SOLOMON

T. PLAATJE

ON

"Aspects of Life in South Africa,"

AT THE

NEW ENGLAND P.S.A.,

Sunday, July 18th, at 3.

Chairman, SIR R. WINFREY, M.P.

Mr. Plaatje is a native of Bechuanaland, Editor of a South African weekly native newspaper, and a member of the native deputation which came to England to place the grievances of natives before the Colonial Secretary.

YOU MUST HEAR THIS INTERESTING SPEAKER

W. B. Pickering, Electric Printer, Bridge street, Peterborough.

60 *Lewis Harcourt, Secretary of State for the Colonies, who met the SANNC deputation in London in June 1914. 'At the interview', Plaatje wrote afterwards, 'he took notes of nothing, and asked no questions. On every point he had "the assurance of General Botha" to the contrary'.*

61 *'Brotherhood and Empire': leaflet advertising Plaatje's address to the New England PSA, Peterborough, 18 July 1915.*

62 *Sir Harry Johnston, explorer, administrator and 'African expert', whom Plaatje and Saul Msane visited in August 1914. He found them 'immensely helpful' in his work on Bantu languages. Plaatje hoped he would write a foreword for* Native Life in South Africa.

63 *(left) Lekoko Montshiwa, chief of the Tshidi Barolong (1911–15), whom Plaatje hoped would finance the publication of* Native Life in South Africa.

64 *(above right) Portrait of Plaatje at his writing desk. This photograph appeared as the frontispiece to* Native Live in South Africa, *published in London in May 1916.*

65 *John Harris, of the Anti-Slavery and Aborigines' Protection Society. Throughout the period he was in England, Plaatje thought, 'the new Boer policy of the Union had no better defender than Mr J. H. Harris, the Organizing Secretary of the so-called Aborigines' Protection Society'.*

66 *Georgiana Solomon, widow of the Cape statesman Saul Solomon. She was one of Plaatje's staunchest supporters during his time in England.*

67 *Homage to the ideals of the Cape. Plaatje is standing at the grave of Saul Solomon in the Ocklynge cemetery, Eastbourne, Sussex. The photograph was taken in 1916.*

68 *Daniel Jones, head of the Phonetics Department, University College, London, with whom Plaatje collaborated in the work for* A Sechuana Reader, *published in 1916.*

memory of those blacks and that of the Indians to be insulted by this Minister? He went on to say that the black man of Africa had stood by the Englishman in this struggle. He was sure that that wonderful sense of British justice would not fail them in this terrible struggle in South Africa. It was strange that the Bill was only supported by the Dutch section of Parliament. The natives' loyalty to the King and the Empire should not be forgotten, and they must not be allowed to be robbed of their heritage by the Boers.[25]

They were sentiments which clearly expressed the feelings of those attending the meeting, and resulted in due course in further attention being paid to Plaatje in the House of Assembly. G. A. Fichardt, for example, representing a rural constituency in the Orange Free State, took Plaatje's speech as ammunition for attacking recruitment in the Native Labour Contingent, to which he was strongly opposed. 'He [Fichardt] referred to a recent speech by Mr Sol Plaatje at Bloemfontein,' so the *Cape Times* reported, 'as indicating the spirit created by the new policy.' It was a curious way of looking at matters, and General Botha – deprecating the fact that 'Sol Plaatje had said this or that' – had little difficulty on this occasion in countering his arguments.[26] But it all tended to confirm, in African eyes, Plaatje's stature as a leader and spokesman for their cause.

As was to be expected, Congress passed formal resolutions condemning both the Native Administration Bill and General Smuts's 'Savoy Hotel' speech, the latter being considered 'an insult to the natives'. The Native Administration Bill was still being considered by a Select Committee (due to present its report in June), but a good deal of time was also spent in discussing ways of raising funds to enable the movement to continue its campaign against the legislation. Plaatje found himself on a committee charged with raising money for a special fund with which to launch a new campaign of agitation.[27]

But the most dramatic events of Congress's annual meeting that year took place on the final day of the proceedings, and arose out of discussions about correspondence between the executive and the Anti-Slavery and Aborigines' Protection Society in England. When John Harris's letter to Richard Selope Thema, acknowledging receipt of the resolutions of the Pietermaritzburg conference in 1916, and praising his attachment to the principle of segregation, was read out it produced, so Plaatje wrote in a letter to Mrs Unwin, 'an outburst of indignation'. He continued:

Delegates wanted to know when, where, and under what circumstances Congress 'adhered' to the policy of separation.

I tried to point out that the whole thing could be rectified by writing a letter to the Society. I pointed out further that the Secretary of the Congress made the same mistake as I did, that is, mistaking Harris for a friend and thus became less guarded in his expressions he relied on the sympathy of a real sympathiser with the Boer policy – but Congress would not be appeased. They denounced Mr Dube for laxity in his management, which made possible the sending out of clumsy correspondence calculated to compromise the cause. The result was that both Mr Dube and Secretary resigned on June 3rd and until June 23rd Congress had neither Head nor Scribe. They asked me to assume its leadership but I pointed out that the

213

deterioration of my business during my enforced absence in England made the idea utterly impossible.[28]

In actual fact there was rather more to this affair than appears from Plaatje's account. There had certainly been some confusion within the Congress movement in attempting to differentiate between the theory and practice of segregation, and John Harris of the Anti-Slavery and Aborigines' Protection Society had clearly worsened matters in attempting to get Dube and Selope Thema, the secretary, to commit themselves to approval of the principle of segregation for use in his campaign against Plaatje in England. It was equally apparent, though, that the issue of correspondence with the society was also being used as a pretext to get rid of John Dube, the increasingly unpopular president, the moving spirits in this, it seems, being Saul Msane, Pixley Seme and Alfred Mangena. Richard Selope Thema, the secretary, who had actually written the supposedly compromising letter, was informed quietly that it was Dube's resignation that was required, not his, and that he could remain on as secretary if he so wished. Out of loyalty to his president, however, Selope Thema decided to step down, thereby precipitating the break-up of the executive, and Dube, aware that a majority of Congress delegates were against him, finally accepted this fact and did likewise.[29] It seems unlikely that Plaatje was party to any of this (although he must have been well aware of the divisions within the Congress leadership), since Msane and Seme would surely have taken the trouble to approach him before the meeting to see if he was willing to assume the presidency. The meeting duly passed a resolution 'strongly and emphatically' denying that Congress 'at any time ever approved of the Natives' Land Act, its policy or principles, expressed or implied', and added:

> This Congress, having already recorded its thanks to Mr Plaatje and appreciation of his services since the commencement of the struggle, accepts the reference to him, contained in the Society's letter of March 29th, as a further tribute to his work.[30]

After the mismanagement of the funds collected for the deputation to England Plaatje seems to have been the one individual figure within the Congress leadership who still commanded almost universal popularity and respect, and many were saddened that he was not willing to accept the position. S. M. Makgatho, president of the Transvaal branch of Congress, was the compromise candidate who became president three weeks later (his position was confirmed at elections at the end of the year), but he seems to have commanded the confidence of neither the Dube nor Msane factions. Congress was thus seriously weakened by its internal divisions at a time when it needed, more than ever, a strong and united leadership. Plaatje did agree to become senior vice-president, but this was as much as he was prepared to take on.

Why did Plaatje refuse the offer of the presidency of Congress? The most pressing consideration was undoubtedly the reason he gave to Mrs Unwin in his letter to her – that 'the deterioration of my business during my enforced absence made the idea utterly impossible'. Anxious both to get his own financial affairs onto some sort of even keel, and to re-start his newspaper, *Tsala ea Batho*,

Plaatje did not believe he could take on the presidency of Congress as well without jeopardising his prospects in this direction. But Plaatje's ambitions, it is clear, did not lie primarily in political leadership for its own sake. In February 1914, it will be recalled, he had offered his resignation as secretary of Congress for similar reasons. Plaatje seems to have believed, rather, that he could render his greatest service as an individual spokesman, free from the duties of leading the South African Native National Congress.

Possibly the sense of bitterness he felt at the failure of Congress to support either his family or himself during his absence in England strengthened this feeling; certainly it made him even more wary of incurring financial obligations on behalf of the organisation if he was unable to meet them from any other source. Without a viable newspaper business, or any other regular source of income, this he was clearly unable to do. It was a great honour for Plaatje to have been offered the presidency of Congress, but there seems to have been no doubt in his own mind that he had to turn it down: 'there are only sixteen working hours in a day', he wrote later, 'and I could not possibly find the time to earn my living while trying to lead the unwieldy masses'.[31]

◇

With no end of the war in sight Plaatje travelled extensively in the countryside of the northern Cape, Orange Free State, and the Transvaal in the ensuing months of 1917. Few of his letters survive for this period and no copies of the Congress newspaper, *Abantu Batho*, have been preserved to throw light on his activities in any detail. But sufficient information can nevertheless be found to provide an albeit fragmented picture of Plaatje's campaign against the impending legislation with which his people were still threatened, and his continued investigations into the effects of the Natives' Land Act – continuing where he had left off, in a sense, in 1913 and 1914. 'I have taken upon myself,' he wrote in September 1917,

> as far as is humanly possible in this wide country, to enlighten the natives, who know absolutely nothing about the prohibitions and restrictions embodied in the new bill. They need no information on the Natives' Land Act which has, since 1913, made its provisions felt in an unmistakeable manner.[32]

In June 1917, shortly after the Congress annual general meeting, Plaatje was, for the first time in his life, arrested by the police. He described what happened in his letter to Mrs Cobden Unwin:

> I was arrested in Johannesburg last month and charged with infringing half a dozen of the multifarious regulations by which natives are surrounded in this country, which constitute Mr Harris's 'growing spirit of justice'. I deposited a £5 bail, asked for a postponement till the fifth instant [July], and prepared an elaborate defence that was likely to bring before the Courts these official outrages upon Natives. The authorities presumably discovered the publicity in store for their numerous pinpricky rules and regulations for when I appeared on July 5th to answer their peccadilloes, they failed to put

in an appearance and the case was dismissed. I am now proceeding against them for wrongful arrest.[33]

As ever, Plaatje was well aware of how the courts could be used to his advantage. What subsequently happened in this particular case is unknown.

But most of Plaatje's time during these winter months of 1917 was spent in travelling in the countryside of the Orange Free State and the Transvaal. He found that the effects of the Natives' Land Act were no less dramatic than on his earlier journeys around the same countryside:

> 37 families in the Pretoria district will be evicted this month, 21 families in Potchefstroom district, and more round Heidelberg. I am only referring to those I have met. Of course some of them will become servants, others will give up country life and flock to the cities where this law [the Natives' Land Act] is not in force, while others will leave the Union altogether; but nobody cares for them.[34]

After two months' travelling around the Orange Free State in districts where the Act had had particularly drastic consequences in 1913 and 1914, Plaatje had more horrors to report:

> I have seen men who prior to 1913 rented land or ploughed on shares and gained from 500 to 1,600 bags of grain each year. Under the tender mercies of 'the gift bestowed upon them by their friend Mr Sauer' they have been reduced to servants and limited to the production of only a dozen (sometimes less) bags for themselves and the remainder for the landowner and, in addition, they have to render unpaid labour to the landowner for the right to stay on part of the land they formerly occupied by ploughing on shares.
>
> Taking advantage of the same law other landowners have likewise changed the status of their former Native tenants who used to pay 33⅓ per cent of the produce in lieu of wages. They are now permitted to cultivate small patches on condition that they plough for the master during four or five days in the week before ploughing one or two days (in some instances only half a day) in the week for themselves. The Natives have besides to render unpaid labour with their families for the privilege of grazing a few cows.[35]

Elsewhere, Plaatje told of the deserted churches and farms he came across, of the reduction of once prosperous African farmers to little more than impoverished labourers. On one occasion, on his 41st birthday, 9 October 1917, Plaatje returned, for the first time since he was a small child, to his place of birth – Doornfontein, in the north-eastern part of the Orange Free State. He discovered that the land was now owned by a man called Karl Woolf, a German subject whose movements had been restricted in accordance with wartime regulations. In the circumstances it struck Plaatje as grimly ironic that he, a loyal citizen of the British empire, should now be legally prohibited (under the terms of the Natives' Land Act) from purchasing the land upon which he had been born, while its present owner and occupant was the subject of a nation with whom South Africa was at war.[36] Plaatje intended to relate all he had found on his travels in 1917 in a new book, a successor – or 'companion volume', as he put it – to *Native Life in South Africa*; collecting information for it was one of his main objectives in this further round of travelling.[37]

Until the end of 1917 Plaatje combined his self-imposed task of investigation and 'enlightening' with assisting in recruitment for the South African Native Labour Contingent. Like the other Congress leaders who had earlier on in the war agreed to lend their support to the scheme, Plaatje hoped that such a display of loyalty would provide a strong argument – both inside and outside South Africa – to back their demands for political and social rights; and General Botha, it will be remembered, had done his best to persuade Plaatje to lend his support to the campaign, having told him, so Plaatje said, that 'this would help the native people better than any propaganda work in which he should engage'. Apart from the general hope Plaatje placed in the efficacy of such a display of loyalty, he seems also to have perceived in the whole issue a means of keeping alive the differences between Boer and Briton (the very existence of the Native Labour Contingent was strongly opposed by the Afrikaner nationalists), and thus to help prevent agreement over a common 'native policy' – a strategy implicit in *Native Life*, and very much part of his campaign against the Native Administration Bill throughout 1917. As Plaatje put it, in the context of recruitment for the Native Labour Contingent, 'the people who did not wish them to respond to the call were the same people who were responsible for their grievances. By neglecting to answer the call they were therefore siding with their oppressors'.[38]

If these arguments made sense in terms of Plaatje's political strategy it was evident that they were not always accepted by potential recruits, who did not come forward in anything like the numbers the South African government had hoped. Few Africans were prepared to draw such fine distinctions between English and Afrikaners, and many were instinctively suspicious of any scheme that had the backing of the South African government, even if the recruiting was being carried out, technically speaking, on behalf of the imperial government. People who attended recruiting meetings were quite entitled to ask why they should co-operate in any way with a government which was at that very moment considering legislation that further threatened their interests. Quite apart from a natural fear of the unknown (which can have only been confirmed with news of the sinking of the troopship *Mendi* in February 1917 with the loss of over 600 members of the Native Labour Contingent), many Africans simply did not trust any government-sponsored scheme. And, as Plaatje himself pointed out on several occasions, speeches such as that made by General Smuts at the Savoy Hotel in London in May 1917 only acted as a further deterrent to success in the recruitment campaign.[39]

Early in 1918 the South African government in any case suspended all further recruitment to the Native Labour Contingent. It was becoming increasingly difficult to attract further recruits without resorting to direct compulsion, and, as Nationalist opposition to General Botha grew, the whole scheme was becoming more and more of a political liability. To this extent Plaatje's view that the Native Labour Contingent was an issue capable of being exploited in the interests of keeping alive differences between English and Afrikaner was perhaps quite justified.

<><>

But the war itself dragged on, and well into 1918 there seemed to be no end in sight. Increasingly it began to look as though any effective initiative on the part of the African political leadership would have to wait until the end of the war, or at least until the middle of 1918–the date to which the government had postponed any further legislative action on the Native Administration Bill. For Plaatje and his fellow Congress leaders this decision (taken in July 1917) did at least provide some sort of respite, and it gave him an opportunity to try and resurrect his newspaper.

From early 1918, however, one of Plaatje's main preoccupations was his attempt to establish the Brotherhood movement in his home town of Kimberley. He had returned home to South Africa in 1917 in a mood of keen appreciation for the support that the Brotherhood movement had extended to him during his stay in England, and he intended–if and when the opportunity presented itself–to start up a branch in Kimberley and, in time, elsewhere as well. The idea attracted him for a number of reasons. As part of an international movement, Plaatje hoped that interest–and above all funds–could be generated overseas (especially in England), and channelled into schemes to further the progress of Africans living in Kimberley, and then in other parts of South Africa. In a sense, indeed, Plaatje saw this as a form of missionary work, but with the very significant difference that it was to be carried out not on behalf of one or other of the missionary societies or church denominations that operated in South Africa, but on behalf of a Christian organisation whose whole *raison d'être* was to challenge the validity of these denominational divisions. This was one of the reasons why Plaatje had been so attracted to the Brotherhood movement in the first place: he had always been very concerned about the effect of religious divisions amongst his own people–quite as serious, as he saw it, as the tribal divisions which were still such an obstacle to the achievement of political unity.

In a way the Brotherhood movement was a counterpart to the South African Native National Congress: whilst Congress was the vehicle to represent the political interests of the African people, and to encourage the achievement of a greater degree of political unity amongst them, the Brotherhood movement, in Plaatje's mind, had the potential of overcoming religious divisions, and at the same time fostering progress in social and educational life: all were essential to the well-being of his people. Undoubtedly, too, Plaatje saw in the possibility of establishing the Brotherhood movement in South Africa the means of providing some secure organisational basis for his own activities and aspirations, never more desperately needed in view of the financial plight to which he returned in 1917.

Preoccupied as he was for most of 1917 with more urgent political activities, Plaatje had to set aside his plans for the time being. In January 1918, however, returning to Kimberley from a trip across the Transvaal and Orange Free State (there had been a meeting of the executive committee of the South African Native National Congress to attend in Bloemfontein just before Christmas) Plaatje noticed that demolition work had just begun on an old tram shed, owned by De Beers and situated on the edge of the Malay Camp. It struck him at once that the shed, if it could be saved from demolition, would provide an admirable meeting hall, suitably converted for the purpose, for Africans in the town, and the material foundation, as it were, for the launching of his Brotherhood movement.

He therefore approached the company, contacting Mr E. C. Grimmer, the general manager, with whom he was on friendly terms, and then, on his advice, wrote a formal letter of application:

15 March 1918

Dear Mr Pickering,

I saw Mr Grimmer at De Beers Offices today with a native request that De Beers Co. should kindly donate the old Malay Camp Tram Shed, on the Alexanderfontein track (now partly demolished) so that we may fit it out as an Assembly Hall for the Natives of the Diamond Fields. He was very sympathetic and, as he was on the point of leaving for the coast, he advised me to meet Mr Williams next week before the shed is further dismantled. He also suggested that I write and request the kind co-operation of some friends of the Natives on the De Beers Directorate, asking them to support the application when it comes before the Board.

At present the Natives have NO place of meeting. All the Native public meetings in Kimberley are churches of particular denominations who cannot be very well blamed for refusing to let them for secular purposes. If this prayer be successful, the Hall will be the property of all Natives, of any Church or no Church – and only the drunken and the rowdy will be barred.

I have also written to Sir David Harris. In 1914 I mentioned the project to him and Mr Oppenheimer, then Mayor. They expressed very encouraging views, but the idea which had already taken shape was hung up by the war. Should you feel pleased to say a word to the Board in favour of the application, it will only be typical of your numerous acts of generosity to the inhabitants of the Diamond Fields, irrespective of race or colour or creed.

I remain, My Dear Sir,
With kindest regards,
Yours very respectfully,
Sol T. Plaatje[40]

It was the kind of letter Plaatje was well practised in writing: appropriate in tone and style, altogether more professional than the similar request made by him and his friends back in 1895, and over the next few months he wrote several more in similar vein as he continued to lobby for support. On this occasion De Beers decided to accede to Plaatje's request; on 9 May 1918 he received a letter from the company informing him that the directors of De Beers 'have now agreed to let you have the use of the building for the purpose mentioned, at an annual rental of 1/–, during the Company's pleasure and on the understanding that you will pay all rates and taxes of whatever description that may be levied on the said building and ground during your tenancy, which this year amount to £29 3s 4d, and that you keep the building in a good state of repair'.[41] In addition, De Beers agreed to replace the windows that had already been removed from the building, and in due course also provided a cheque for £100 as a contribution towards the costs of improvements.

Plaatje was understandably delighted at the outcome of his request, reward as it was for his skilful and persistent lobbying, always one of his great strengths. But De Beers' generosity over the issue was not simply a matter of Plaatje's persuasive powers, considerable as these were, nor of a wholly altruistic desire to meet the wishes of the local African population. As Sir David Harris, another of the directors whom Plaatje had approached, wrote to the De Beers secretary: 'If possible, I think it good policy to help the natives in the direction suggested by Plaatje'.[42] It was 'good policy' because it provided De Beers with a convenient and relatively inexpensive means (the shed was valued at £573 6s), as Plaatje did not hesitate to point out, of 'enhancing their (the natives') loyalty to De Beers as a generous employer of labour'.[43] Underlying the decision, too, was a growing concern in the boardrooms of De Beers and other mining houses on the Rand at the mounting industrial unrest in the early months of 1918. Although this had so far been confined to the Rand, the spectre of an increasingly radicalised black working class, resorting more and more frequently to strike action, was a very worrying one. The gift of the old tram shed to Plaatje, acting on behalf of Kimberley's African population, was very much a product of their concern to discourage the spread of industrial unrest to Kimberley.

Plaatje was not unaware of the factors which impelled companies like De Beers to acts of generosity of this kind, and was quite prepared to draw attention to them to encourage the company to make the decision he wished. At the same time there was a clear realisation on Plaatje's part that his success in persuading De Beers to donate a hall to the African population could be used to his own very considerable advantage locally to reaffirm a position of leadership and influence which no longer seemed to be unchallenged. In part this seems to have resulted from the fact that he had spent so much time away from Kimberley in recent years, devoting himself to issues of national importance that did not always seem to bear directly on the needs of the majority of Kimberley's African population.

But there were also signs of a growing dissatisfaction with the methods he advocated, with a style of leadership that, to many, was no longer appropriate to the needs of the majority of the people. For in Kimberley, as in other urban centres, it was becoming increasingly clear that the interests of the black working class were not the same as those of the ministers, the teachers, journalists, interpreters, and others, who claimed the right to represent the African people as a whole. Plaatje himself was strikingly frank about this in one of his letters to De Beers over his negotiations for the tram shed: 'Let me add, Sir, at the risk of being too personal, that there is a belief among some of the native population here that I am in the pay of De Beers – employed to keep them quiet.'[44] Plaatje's appeal to the company was thus in a sense an appeal for assistance in restoring his own position of influence locally as well as an opportunity for De Beers to respond in a way that 'enhanced their reputation as an employer'. It was an opportunity for both to prove, as it were, that they could deliver the goods.

There were further signs that Plaatje's influence locally was not what it had once been when some opposition was expressed to his proposals to form a 'Native Brotherhood' committee to take over the management and running of the hall, to decide, in effect, what it was to be used for. Plaatje had put his proposals to a series of meetings held in the Kimberley 'locations' in June 1918, announcing publicly De Beers' decision to donate the old tram shed for their use, and outlining in detail the purpose and nature of his proposed Brotherhood committee. Although Plaatje acknowledged, so the *Diamond Fields Advertiser* reported, that 'one or two friends think that the hall should be under the control of certain individuals among us, and kept distinct from any specific organisations', he was nevertheless able to gain public support and approval of his scheme, and a building committee, with himself as chairman, was duly elected in order to raise money to convert the hall into a usable meeting place for Brotherhood meetings, and for use as an additional classroom for the overcrowded Lyndhurst Road Native School.

The proposal to form the Native Brotherhood proper ('upon the lines of the P.S.A. Brotherhood Movements and Sisterhoods of England, and the Fraternité Societies of France and Belgium') was also carried, its committee *pro tem* being that of its building committee.[45] By July 1918 this committee had been properly established as 'The Diamond Fields Men's Own Brotherhood' and its officers included Plaatje himself as president; Mr Arthur Tsengiwe (of the Beaconsfield Post Office) as vice-president; a European, Dr J. E. Mackenzie, as treasurer (Plaatje's doctor since the 1890s); and Mr L. Mashoko, Mr T. D. Mweli Skota; Mr G. M. Motsieloa, and Mr T. G. Diniso, holding other positions.[46] The Brotherhood's headed notepaper also gave a 'London address' – that of Mr William Cross, of the Southall Brotherhood, an indication of the importance Plaatje attached to the link with the Brotherhood movement in England.

◇

The public meetings which accompanied the launching of the Brotherhood movement in June 1918 were dwarfed, however, by the celebrations which surrounded the formal opening of the Brotherhood hall in August, for by the time this took place De Beers' gift had come to assume a rather more than purely local significance. The reasons for this are to be found in the rapid escalation of industrial and political unrest on the Rand in the intervening months, culminating in a successful boycott of mine stores by African workers and a series of strikes for higher wages to meet the wartime increases in the cost of living.[47] A matter of serious concern for both the government and the mining houses, this unprecedented degree of unrest was also beginning to produce increasing tension – complicating the divisions that had emerged in 1917 – within the South African Native National Congress. An influential section of the Transvaal branch of the movement had aligned itself with the demands of the strikers, and supported the methods to which they resorted to try and achieve them. None of the other regional branches of the movement was prepared to go so far, preferring to rely upon traditional methods of representing grievances to the authorities and concerned that this new militancy represented a threat to the legitimacy of their own leadership and the channels of communication with the authorities upon which they relied.

There had been further signs of this growing polarity at Congress's sixth annual conference, which Plaatje attended, at Bethlehem, in the Orange Free State, at the end of March 1918. The 'old guard' had nevertheless managed to retain control, S. M. Makgatho's presidential address being concerned very much with the issues that had been debated in 1917, and with such international questions as the fate of the German colonies once the war had come to an end. Plaatje, Makgatho had also pointed out, had been making 'big sacrifices on behalf of his down-trodden countrymen and women', and had proved himself a 'farsighted champion in the interests of the people he represented'.[48]

On the Rand industrial and political unrest nevertheless continued to grow over the next few months, and was greatly exacerbated as a result of a harsh sentence passed in court on 12 June by the Johannesburg magistrate, T. G. Macfie, upon 152 African strikers employed by the Johannesburg municipality's sanitary department. Congress immediately launched a campaign for the prisoners' release, but the question of what form this was to take brought out very clearly the differences that now existed within the movement. Whilst Plaatje, Makgatho, Isaiah Bud-M'belle (now secretary of Congress) and several others sought to negotiate in the traditional manner with the government to secure the quashing of the sentence (Plaatje, indeed, drafted a petition to the Governor-General calling for the release of the prisoners), the more radical leaders of the Transvaal branch of Congress turned the campaign to release the prisoners into a demand for an all-round wage increase of 1s a day, and threatened a general strike from 1 July if this demand was not met.[49] To the relief of the mining houses, and indeed to many of the Congress leaders, the government ordered the release of the prisoners, the Supreme Court reversed the magistrate's decision of 28 June, and a commission of enquiry was appointed to look into the strikers' grievances: the immediate crisis was thus defused. The general situation remained tense, however, and for several of the Congress leaders – Saul Msane and S. M. Makgatho in particular – their position remained one of great difficulty, propelled as they were along a course that was not of their own choice or making, yet concerned that they would lose all political credibility among their people if they dissociated themselves completely from strike action. The differences between the Transvaal branch of Congress and the national executive were greater than they had ever been before.

The executive meeting of the South African Native National Congress which took place in Bloemfontein at the beginning of August 1918, which Plaatje attended, was not, surprisingly, a stormy affair, but by virtue of their majority on the provincial congresses of the Cape, Orange Free State, and Natal, the moderates prevailed over the ten delegates from the Transvaal. Resolutions were duly passed 'respectfully requesting' the Union government to 'make an urgent appeal to employers throughout South Africa to alleviate this distress by giving their native employees a rise of at least 1s per day per worker of all various classes and grades' (as opposed to threatening strike action), and thanks were expressed to the government for ensuring the reversal of the sentence passed upon the strikers by the chief magistrate of Johannesburg.[50] And there was one further resolution:

The Executive of the South African Native Congress, in session at Bloemfontein, on August 2nd 1918, having been informed that H.E. the Governor-General, at the instance of the Rt Hon. the Prime Minister, is going to lay the foundation stone of the proposed Assembly Hall for Natives at Kimberley – a present from De Beers Company – desire to record its congratulations to our brethren of the Diamond Fields on their good fortune and appreciation of the generosity of the De Beers Company which we feel certain will go far towards removing the causes of friction between White and Black in South Africa.[51]

Circumstances in the country at large had ensured that Plaatje's success in persuading De Beers to part with an old tram shed had now assumed a significance far beyond what any of the parties can have imagined; something was obviously up if it was to be formally opened by 'H.E. the Governor General at the instance of the Rt Hon. the Prime Minister'.

<><

The opening ceremony, when it took place a few days later on the August bank holiday, was chiefly notable, as the Bloemfontein SANNC resolution anticipated, for the presence there of Lord Buxton, the Governor-General of South Africa. On several other occasions Plaatje claimed that this was the direct result of a letter he had himself written to the Prime Minister, and this may well have been the case – another example, if it be true, of that curiously close, highly ambivalent, relationship Plaatje had with the old Boer general.[52] Preparations for the ceremony had involved Plaatje in a great deal of work and correspondence. He was anxious that the affair should get the maximum amount of publicity so as to emphasise the material and political benefits that could be obtained from sympathetic white companies, and to draw attention to his own part in persuading De Beers to make the donation; he was also determined to take full advantage of the presence in Kimberley of so many distinguished (and wealthy) visitors to raise as much money as possible to pay for the conversions that needed to be made to the building, and to this end he devised a scheme whereby visitors to Kimberley on the day of the opening ceremony would pay for specific bricks to be used in the work.

Everything went off very well on the day. As befitted an occasion graced by the presence of His Majesty's highest representative in South Africa, it was attended by all of Kimberley's local dignitaries, and suitably loyal speeches were made by the magistrate, G. J. Boyes, by Plaatje himself, by Mesach Pelem – once a resident of Kimberley himself – representing the South African Native National Congress, and then by the Governor-General. As was to be expected, he took the opportunity to urge Africans in Kimberley not to take such precipitate action in attempting to redress their grievances as African workers on the Rand. He emphasised, indeed, the need for everybody to bear with their grievances while the war was still in progress, and urged his African audience to have every confidence in the commission of enquiry then being conducted into the unrest by J. S. Moffat; as he explained, the fact that Mr Moffat was 'the grandson of the great missionary, Dr Moffat, who was loved by the natives so much . . . showed at all events that the Prime Minister and the Government and Parliament are anxious to meet the natives as far as they can in regard to matters affecting them'.[53]

This was, to say the least, a somewhat arguable assessment of the purpose of the Moffat Commission and the circumstances that led to its appointment, but the stone-laying ceremony (the stone was actually laid by Mrs Grimmer, wife of the De Beers general manager) was hardly the occasion for this to be debated in any detail. Plaatje, as much as De Beers and the South African government, was anxious that the whole affair should be remembered as an example of the harmonious relationships between black and white that it was possible to achieve through the kind of methods to which he was committed. Certainly Plaatje himself was in no doubt as to the significance of the affair, as he had already made very clear in a letter to De Beers several days before the stone-laying ceremony actually took place:

> I beg to explain the cause of my delay in answering your letter of the 1st inst. I had to attend the Native Congress at Bloemfontein to prevent the spread among our people of the Johannesburg Socialist propaganda. I think you are aware of our difficulties in that connection since Mr Pickering, writing to me on an entirely different matter, ended his letter thus: 'For God's sake keep them (natives) off the labour agitators.' The ten Transvaal delegates came to Congress with a concord and determination that was perfectly astounding and foreign to our customary native demeanour at conferences. They spoke almost in unison, in short sentences, nearly every one of which began and ended with the word 'strike'. It was not difficult to understand the source of their backing for they even preceded the Congress and endeavoured to poison the minds of delegates from other parts. It was only late on the second day that we succeeded in satisfying the delegates to report, on getting to their homes, that the Socialists' method of pitting up black and white will land our people in serious disaster, while the worst that could happen to the whitemen would be but a temporary inconvenience. When they took the train for Johannesburg, at Bloemfontein station, I am told that one of them remarked that they would have 'converted Congress had not De Beers given Plaatje a Hall'. This seems intensely reassuring as indicating that Kimberley will be about the last place that these black Bolsheviks of Johannesburg will pay attention to, thus leaving us free to combat their activities in other parts of the Union. Only those who saw the tension at this Congress can realise that the building discussion of this hall of ours came at just the right time for South Africa.[54]

Even allowing for a degree of colouring to suit its recipient, this is nevertheless a very frank and revealing letter which says much about the remarkable transformation that had taken place in African political life in South Africa in so short a space of time, and the position that Plaatje and a number of other Congress leaders now found themselves in. It was quite clear that that sense of national political unity that had inspired the formation of Congress six years previously, and had sustained it in its campaign against the Natives' Land Act in 1913 and 1914, had now disappeared, replaced instead by the political and ideological tensions produced by fast-growing socio-economic cleavages within the African population as a whole. In a way Plaatje had successfully exploited these tensions to his own ends, taking advantage in a skilful manner of the intense concern about the unrest on the Rand felt by both the Prime Minister and De Beers, and using this to launch his Brotherhood movement on a much more secure physical and financial foundation than would otherwise have been the case. But it was a difficult and dangerous game to be playing, as the example of

Saul Msane, one of the members of the Congress deputation to England in 1914, demonstrated most vividly. Throughout 1917 and 1918 he had sought to retain his influence with both the authorities and the radical Transvaal branch of Congress, of which he was president, but in the end, as the two grew further and further apart, he found the task impossible. His conservative instincts got the better of him, he came out publicly against strike action in June 1918, and was rewarded with the epithet 'Isita sa Bantu', or 'Enemy of the people'; it was the end of his political career.[55]

Plaatje himself was fortunate to be based in Kimberley and to have had other sources of influence and support, and there was always less danger that his reputation would suffer so total an eclipse. But the writing was nevertheless clearly on the wall. In future neither Plaatje nor his colleagues on the national executive of the SANNC could claim to be wholly representative of the aspirations of the African people of South Africa. Tribal differences and divisions, regarded for years as the great stumbling block to the achievement of political unity, henceforth took second place to those that accompanied these growing cleavages along lines of class. Within no more than six years of its foundation Congress had been all but torn apart by forces which its founding fathers can scarcely have imagined possible.

◇

The winter of 1918 brought with it some more immediately personal difficulties for Plaatje and his family. As though symptomatic of the troubled times in the country as a whole, in the very midst of Plaatje's hectic preparations for the visit of Lord Buxton to Kimberley he received a telegram from Lovedale informing him that St Leger had been involved in a student riot in which windows had been broken and furniture smashed, and was in serious trouble and in imminent danger of being expelled. Lovedale wanted Plaatje to go down there immediately, presumably to use his influence to calm the students down, but with Lord Buxton due in Kimberley in a couple of days' time this was obviously impossible.[56] Exactly what happened at Lovedale on this occasion is unclear, but the disturbances may well have been inspired by the industrial and political unrest on the Rand. Riots amongst the students at Lovedale were by no means infrequent occurrences, and on other occasions were sparked off by the poor food served to them – indicative, as they perceived it, of the second-class status in society which African students were being prepared for. Nothing could have been calculated to distress Plaatje more than the possibility of his eldest son being expelled from Lovedale. He had wanted St Leger to have the opportunity of receiving the good secondary education he had never had himself, and his ambitions for him had been more than realised when he won that scholarship in 1916. Now it all hung in the balance through St Leger's alleged participation in the riot.

It must have come as a very great relief for Plaatje to hear, several days later, that St Leger's punishment was not expulsion, but two weeks' extra work. When he left Lovedale in December that year he took with him a certificate which testified that his conduct had been 'very good', so it seems that no lasting damage was done to his school career.

But there were other domestic difficulties. While St Leger's fate hung in the balance, Olive, now thirteen years old, tripped over in the house when carrying a kettle of boiling water, and scalded her arm. It was a very painful accident, and she was unable to go to school for several weeks afterwards.[57] Almost as soon as she had recovered from this Kimberley was struck by the worldwide influenza epidemic. It was the first inland centre in South Africa to be affected, and its inhabitants suffered dreadfully: it was estimated that some 40,000 people were stricken by the virus in the Kimberley district, and over 4,000 died. Conditions were worst in the mining compounds and in the crowded African locations, but many whites died as well. Men and women were reported to be simply dropping in the streets, and instructions were issued by the local authorities that households in which the entire family were stricken should hoist a red flag in a prominent position so that help could be summoned; inevitably, comparisons were drawn with the Great Plague of London.[58]

Many of Plaatje's friends and relatives in Kimberley and elsewhere died during the epidemic, and his own immediate family did not escape unscathed. At one stage during October 1918 Elizabeth and all the children (with the exception of St Leger, away at Lovedale) were laid down by the epidemic, and for Plaatje, recently returned from a visit to Basutoland, it was for several weeks a full-time occupation simply looking after them all at home.[59] Eventually Plaatje too caught the virus, and it was with him and Olive, the elder of the two daughters, that the consequences were to be the most serious. In Plaatje's case, the influenza caused what he later described as an 'oppressive heart disease'. Its immediate effect was to lay him up in bed for several weeks, but after that one doctor after the other pronounced his condition to be incurable. Adding as this did to a long history of ill-health, always aggravated by constant overwork, it meant that Plaatje was to live the rest of his life in the knowledge that he possessed a weak heart, likely to worsen suddenly and without warning. None of the doctors he consulted over the next couple of years was able to offer any degree of encouragement.[60]

At the time of epidemic, though, Olive's condition was equally worrying. She had contracted the virus after attending selflessly to the needs of other sufferers, and then became, in Plaatje's words, 'literally shrivelled up by rheumatism', about which the doctors could again do little. There was a sad sequel to this. Unable to recommend any other form of treatment, the doctors advised Plaatje to take her to Aliwal North where there were some hot springs which, it was hoped, would help alleviate her suffering, and where Plaatje himself once used to swim for pleasure, rather than medical necessity, in the days before Union. Following the doctor's advice, Plaatje took Olive to Aliwal North, but when they arrived he was informed that, despite her condition, she would not be allowed to take to the water on account of her colour; it was now for whites only.[61] Few incidents brought home to Plaatje in so tragic and personal a manner the direction in which his country was going. Just as when he had visited his birthplace the previous year only to find it owned by a German subject, so now the memories of a more civilised past served only to make the oppressive reality of the present so much more difficult to accept. The incident provided a very unhappy postscript to a perception that struck Plaatje forcibly at the time of the epidemic: the capacity of whites and blacks to rediscover a common humanity in the face of an epidemic which, if it did not strike at everybody equally, nevertheless did not pay heed to the distinctions of colour and status that governed everyday life in more normal circumstances.[62]

◇

Armistice Day, 11 November 1918, was signalled in Kimberley by long-drawn-out blasts on the De Beers Company's hooters. Over the next few days the town celebrated both the ending of the war with Germany, which had claimed the lives of several hundred of the town's inhabitants of all races, and the passing of the influenza epidemic. For Plaatje, recovering from his illness, it was a time to consider once again the wider political and constitutional position of the African people of South Africa. Like many of his colleagues in the ranks of the South African Native National Congress Plaatje had long looked forward to the end of the war in the hope that a further appeal to the imperial government would result in some form of intercession on their behalf with the Union government. He was not alone in believing that a second deputation might prove more fruitful than the first. There was a feeling that the Congress deputation of 1914 had been prevented by the outbreak of war from achieving its objects, and that it would therefore be a mistake not to try to capitalise upon the impression it had begun to make in England. It was Plaatje himself, of course, who had done most to convey Congress's case to the British public during the two and a half years he had spent over there, and he had taken back with him expressions of support from several seemingly influential sources and organisations. The fact that the Brotherhood movement had presented Plaatje, on the eve of his departure from England in January 1917, with a formal address committing itself 'to do all we can to help you to regain that freedom and justice to which as loyal British subjects your people are entitled', was taken by many of the Congress leaders to suggest that there was a reservoir of support which could be tapped in England.[63] Even more significant was the fact that the memorial contained the signature, amongst others, of Sir Richard Winfrey, at that time a minister in Lloyd George's government, which seemed to suggest that even within the British government they might well elicit support and sympathy for their cause.

In Plaatje's own view of the question of a second deputation there was an element of ambivalence. The period he had spent in England had left him with no illusions about the magnitude of the task which any deputation, himself included or not, would face. Set against this was the question of the political alternatives. If he came out against a second deputation the effect would inevitably be to encourage support for those who were urging – in the still tense climate of political and industrial unrest – that direct industrial action was now the only method left to the SANNC in seeking to remedy the grievances of their people. To this Plaatje remained firmly opposed. More positively, he probably shared some of the optimism that had been generated by the war speeches of Lloyd George and the American President, Woodrow Wilson, which made much of the rights of 'small nations' and notions of 'self-determination', and talked of the need for a just settlement to ensure peace for the future.[64] While neither statesman had the British colonies or dominions in mind when talking in these terms, the arguments their speeches contained could easily be extended, and the

227

African press in South Africa, reduced now to just three newspapers, *Abantu-Batho*, *Imvo*, and *Ilanga*, had been quick to point out the implications for the position of Africans in South Africa.

Similarly, for Plaatje and a number of his other colleagues it now seemed the appropriate time to claim the political rights to which the 'loyalty' of their people, and their contribution to the imperial war effort, entitled them to. This had been one of the central arguments of *Native Life in South Africa*, and since that had been written several other items could be added to the argument – above all the contribution of the Native Labour Contingent to the imperial war effort, and the apparent recognition of the justice of African claims in South Africa in a speech made by King George V to members of the contingent in France in 1917, in which he had said that they, like the rest of his troops, were 'fighting for the liberty and freedom of my subjects of all races and creeds throughout my Empire'.[65] In addition, Plaatje had been in regular contact with the friends he had left behind in England – Mrs Solomon, Mrs Unwin, William Cross, the Colensos and the others who had formed the committee to watch African interests in South Africa after his departure. The committee had been active – on one notable occasion Mrs Solomon had challenged General Smuts at a public meeting in London about his remarks in his Savoy Hotel speech – and had kept alive the cause of the African people of South Africa.[66] From several of the people associated with the committee Plaatje received letters urging him to return to England as soon as possible now that the war was over.[67]

The question of sending a second deputation to England was discussed at the special meeting called by the president of the SANNC in Johannesburg in the middle of December 1918. Opened by the mayor of Johannesburg, loyal resolutions were duly passed expressing thanks and congratulations to the imperial government on the successful outcome of the war, and both *The Star* and *Cape Argus* were moved to devote lengthy editorials to the significance of the strength of African national sentiment which they took the holding of the meeting to signify.[68] They reflected, too, a growing conviction in church, business and government circles that something had now to be done to defuse the apparently growing strength of African political organisation, and both papers took the opportunity to draw the attention of the authorities and their readers to the need to devote rather more care and caution to the development of 'native policy' than had been the case hitherto.

The meeting itself was largely taken up with discussion on a draft memorial for presentation to the Governor-General, for transmission to the King, and then with the question of sending a deputation over to England.[69] The part that Plaatje himself played in this is not clear since no detailed reports of the meeting have survived, but there was no doubting the comprehensiveness of the document that was discussed and eventually adopted. Prefaced by a lengthy reminder of the loyalty of black South Africans during the recent war, and of the lofty statements of allied war aims, the memorial reviewed the sad history of 'native policy' since the Act of Union and requested that the imperial government revise the South African constitution 'in such a way as to grant enfranchisement of natives throughout the Union'; only in this way, the memorial claimed, could Africans gain 'a voice in the affairs of the country, and have full protection so as to check reactionary legislation and unpopular one-sided laws'.[70] Having decided in principle that a deputation should be sent to England, it was then agreed that a total of nine people, two representatives from each province, and the president, should go.

Plaatje was amongst those who were elected to the deputation, but his reactions, notwithstanding the unanimous desire of the meeting that he should be among the delegates, were mixed. In a letter written to Silas Molema on 20 December, the last day of the meeting, he commented with some bitterness at the way Congress now expected him to participate in a second deputation after all the sacrifices that the first had entailed. The organisation had failed to contribute to the ruinous expenses of his campaign in England, and he was reluctant to commit himself to a similar undertaking all over again; as he reminded Silas Molema, he had lost his newspaper business as a direct result of his enforced absence overseas, and he concluded: 'Unless they give ME only £1,000, I am going nowhere. Once bitten, twice shy.'[71]

But Plaatje was persuaded to go. Probably he realised more than anybody that his experience in England between 1914 and 1917 was likely to be vital to its success; as S. M. Makgatho, Congress's president, said, 'only common sense should guide us to send [Plaatje] back, now that the war is over' in order to ask his friends and supporters to redeem their previous promises to him.[72] Over the next few weeks and months, therefore, Plaatje was drawn into the preparations being made to raise money to support a new campaign overseas. As he did so two new possibilities emerged. The first was the idea that, in addition to presenting its case to the imperial government in London, the deputation should also travel to France where, as it now became known, the post-war peace conference was to be held. Support for this idea grew rapidly in Congress circles when it also became known that the Afrikaner nationalists, led by General Hertzog, intended to present their case at Versailles and to argue that the right to national self-determination entitled them to secede from the British empire. Congress, in effect, wanted the exact opposite – a reassertion of imperial control – and felt that if the Afrikaner nationalists were to be represented at the Versailles Peace Conference, then so too should they. It was therefore resolved that the deputation should endeavour to present their case in France as well.

The second new possibility was that the South African Native National Congress should also be represented at the proposed Pan-African Congress, news of which probably reached South Africa in January 1919. This was being convened in Paris the following month by Dr W. E. B. Du Bois, the well-known black American scholar and politician who had, over the past twenty years, led the struggle for black American civil and political rights. It was Du Bois's abiding belief that the struggles of black people everywhere were inseparable from one another, and it was his intention to build upon the foundations laid by others in order to bring together representatives of African, West Indian and Afro-American political organisations to develop this sense of unity and to strengthen their case in the achievement of political progress and emancipation. Despite opposition from the American government, Du Bois succeeded in organising his Congress in Paris; he hoped to present it as a rival to the Peace Conference at Versailles, and to draw attention to the rights of black people as the leaders of the victorious allied powers redrew European and colonial boundaries.[73]

The South African Native National Congress, however, was not amongst those organisations represented when Du Bois's Pan-African Congress assembled in Paris between 19 and 21 February 1919. The notice given was too short, and Plaatje and his colleagues were in any case making very slow progress in raising money to enable the deputation to set off to Europe. Within weeks of the special meeting in December, indeed, it was realised that the idea of sending a total of nine delegates was far too ambitious and expensive. That this was not the only difficulty became clear when Plaatje and Richard Msimang, another member of the executive of the SANNC, formally presented their memorial to the Governor-General, Lord Buxton (for transmission to the imperial government), in Cape Town at the beginning of February. Writing to Silas Molema to tell him what transpired, Plaatje spoke of his fears that this deputation was likely to leave for England in an even greater state of disarray than its predecessor in 1914. When he arrived in Cape Town – sent down there at the instance of S. M. Makgatho, the president – Plaatje got the distinct impression that Richard Msimang resented his presence there, and there then followed an unseemly wrangle over the precise contents of the memorial.[74]

Plaatje had been prepared to sail from Cape Town immediately after this, and passages for himself and three other delegates had already been booked on the *Durham Castle*. But the money to pay for them could not be raised in time.[75] At the beginning of March two delegates, Richard Selope Thema and L. T. Mvabaza, managed to get away on the *Voronej*, but Plaatje, by now appointed leader of the deputation, was unable to accompany them. It was several months before he raised the money he needed.[76] The government refused to allow funds to be released from the so-called Barolong Fund to finance the deputation, but in the end Plaatje's friends in Thaba Nchu – Goronyane, Fenyang, Nyokong, and the others, many of them former members of the *Tsala* syndicate – somehow found the money. Writing on 14 March 1919 Plaatje was happy to be able to report that this group of friends had agreed to pay off all his old debts in England.[77] As he continued to seek further sources of funds, it at last began to look as though he would be able – somewhat belatedly, it is true – to join the other delegates.

◇

Whilst preparations for joining the deputation were Plaatje's overwhelming preoccupation during these early months of 1919, he was able to make some further progress in building up his Brotherhood movement in Kimberley. Like the rest of Kimberley, the work of the movement had been severely disrupted by the influenza epidemic in the latter part of 1918. This had caused, amongst other things, the death of Mr Lucas Mahoko, one of the officials of the organisation, and of Mr Lindsay, the architect responsible for drawing up the plans for the conversion of the tram shed into a proper assembly hall. Despite its half-completed state, regular weekly meetings were nevertheless held, all of them well attended, and a further step forward was taken with the formal dedication of what was now known as the Native Brotherhood Institute by the Rt Rev. Wilfrid Gore-Browne, Bishop of Kimberley and Kuruman.[78] For Plaatje, the bishop's presence, along with that of a number of other local dignitaries, demonstrated how much better industrial and race relations were in Kimberley than on the Rand, for immediately before attending this ceremony Plaatje received news from the Rand of a new wave of 'unrest', mounted police having charged a crowd of anti-pass demonstrators, causing several deaths and a large number of injuries.[79] The coincidence of these events served only to emphasise for him the importance of achieving 'brotherhood' between individuals and races, of helping to overcome the explosive tensions of the immediate post-war era through moral and religious, as well as political, change.

By May 1919 Plaatje had still been unable to effect his departure, having failed in his attempt to get a passage on the *Llanstephan Castle* the previous month as he had hoped.[80] However, the delay did at least mean he could attend the SANNC's annual meeting in Queenstown between 6 and 9 May, during the course of which remarks made by S. M. Makgatho on Plaatje's work over the last few months–he had been occupied in investigating some shootings in the Orange Free State–again earned the attention of the South African House of Assembly;[81] and it enabled him to consider at perhaps greater length than he would have wished his plans when overseas. That these were not likely to be confined to representing the interests of his people before the imperial government was revealed in a letter he wrote to Dr W. E. B. Du Bois, the organiser of the Pan-African Congress:

Kimberley
19 May 1919

Dear Dr Du Bois,

It is a great pity I have not been able to get to Paris in February. It is all owing to the backwardness of our race–a backwardness that is intensified by our tribal and clannish differences. However, I take this opportunity to thank you in the name of our people for the wide ground covered and the success up to date. I feel certain that much more would have been effected had you any information about the semi-slavery extant in South Africa.

I am leaving in a fortnight for London with the Congress deputation work. Please send me a reply to 69 Shakespeare Road, Hanwell, London W. Mr F. Fredericks, your Ass. Secretary, is a personal friend of mine.

I have not received any a/c of books sent from London to the *Crisis* for sale. However, I had the benefit of the *Crisis* for a year. Please continue it to South Africa and send me another to S. T. Plaatje, 69 Shakespeare Road, Hanwell, London W. in addition to the one already sent to Kimberley.

It is a howling pity we did not meet. My paper had to be suspended owing to the war prices–paper alone went up 700%. I hope to restart the *Tsala* next year. But to broaden my outlook I wish to visit the United States before returning. Do you think that a well-arranged tour could pay expenses? I will rely on your kind advice. Kind regards.

Yours very faithfully,
Sol T. Plaatje[82]

What Du Bois's advice was on this last point is unknown, but the knowledge that Plaatje should have left South Africa for a second time with the hope of being able to visit the United States should come as no great surprise. He had, after all, hoped to visit the United States in 1914, and since then he had become, if anything, even more conscious of the relevance of the experience of black Americans to the future of his own people than he had before; *Native Life in South Africa*, indeed, contained several quotations from Du Bois's writings. And if, as seemed likely, the prospect of constitutional changes in South Africa along the lines he would have wished were to be disappointed once again, then the lessons that black America had to offer assumed a new relevance. Quite apart from this, Plaatje was also hopeful of being able to raise funds for his Brotherhood movement in America. As if he needed any reminder of his requirements in this direction, he had recently received several letters from De Beers drawing attention to the alarming accumulation of unpaid rates and building bills on the new hall.[83] It was difficult ever to escape from this constant shortage of funds.

It was therefore with ideas of a rather more far-ranging nature than his colleagues in the SANNC perhaps realised that Plaatje finally left Kimberley on 6 June 1919 so as to reach Cape Town to board a ship due to sail the following Wednesday, 11 June. Before leaving he had got the president and treasurer of Congress to agree to pay Elizabeth £6 a month for as long as he was away. He was accompanied on the voyage by J. T. Gumede, a Congress delegate representing Natal. However, Gumede's travelling documents had not come through from Pretoria as expected, and it was only after some urgent last-minute negotiations with the authorities in Cape Town that the difficulty was overcome, thanks this time to Plaatje's success in persuading F. S. Malan, then the Minister of Native Affairs, to intercede on his behalf. 'That Boer helped us a lot,' Plaatje told Silas Molema, 'because if it were somebody else he could have delayed deliberately until the ship sailed leaving us behind.'[84] Malan also promised to see if anything more could be done to release funds held by the government in the Barolong Fund for use by the deputation. On this note of official co-operation – strikingly similar to that which he had encountered on his return to South Africa in February 1917 – Plaatje departed for the United Kingdom to assume the leadership of the Congress deputation. Whether he was likely to receive such sympathetic attention when it came to presenting their case in London remained to be seen.

10

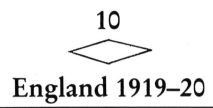

England 1919–20

Richard Selope Thema, Levi Mvabaza, and Henry Ngcayiya, the Congress delegates who had sailed from Cape Town in March, had acquitted themselves creditably since arriving in London. Despite their relative lack of experience in work of this kind, they had soon found accommodation for themselves in Dulwich, South London, and managed to secure an interview with Leo Amery, the Under-Secretary of State for the Colonies, on 8 May 1919. They had achieved this not through the Anti-Slavery and Aborigines' Protection Society, which had not been officially informed about the deputation, but through the good offices of W. P. Schreiner, now the South African High Commissioner in London. Schreiner was himself no stranger to deputations of this kind, for he had led the deputation which travelled to London in 1909 to protest about the colour-bar clauses in the draft Act of Union. Now he found himself on the other side of the fence. Although he now accepted the viewpoint shared by both the Colonial Office and his own government that the imperial government had no right to intervene in the internal affairs of a self-governing dominion, and that the decision of Congress to send a deputation to London was a misguided one, he was at least prepared to arrange an interview for the delegates at the Colonial Office: without his help they would very likely not even have achieved this.[1] They had arrived just in time; several weeks later Schreiner died.

Leo Amery was never likely to do anything other than rehearse the official line to Selope Thema and Mvabaza when they put to him the points contained in the memorial adopted by Congress at its special meeting in December 1918. In reply, so the minutes of their meeting recorded, Colonel Amery

> fully acknowledged the loyalty shown by the natives, but could not help regretting that the leader of the deputation had indicated that this loyalty might be diminished. He pointed out that it was not possible to alter the South African [sic] Act. His Majesty's Government was not prepared to do so, at the request of any section of the population of South Africa; if they were to do so it would probably make the position of the natives worse, and not better. He enlarged upon the nature of Responsible Government, and urged that the educated native should work patiently within the limits of the constitution of the Union, a constitution which being British necessarily contained within itself the power of development.[2]

Privately, though, Amery was somewhat more concerned over the likely consequences of South African policy than he was ever to admit publicly; he believed trouble would arise in South Africa, so he wrote in his diary, 'possibly very much sooner than we have generally thought'.[3] But the Colonial Office as a whole was very careful to ensure that all its dealings with the deputation were constitutionally quite correct. A good deal of correspondence was generated over the whole issue, and in the unsettled post-war period there was a distinct awareness in official circles of the need to avoid action that might provoke any expression of 'disloyal' sentiments or activity in any part of the empire. There was a concern, too, to try to avoid creating the impression that the African deputation was treated with any less consideration and courtesy than that sent over to Europe by the Afrikaner nationalists.

It was this last factor that seems to have decided the Colonial Office against refusing passports for the delegates, when they applied, to enable them to travel to France to see the British Prime Minister, David Lloyd George, then attending (along with, among others, Generals Botha and Smuts) the Versailles Peace Conference.[4] Whilst Selope Thema and Mvabaza failed to make the propaganda coup at the conference that Congress had hoped, or to attend Dr Du Bois's Pan-African Conference, which had ended well before they arrived in Europe, they did at least extract a promise from Lloyd George that he would see them after his return to London.[5] With this the two men had returned to London, and set about publicising their cause – addressing meetings, distributing leaflets and other publicity material, seeking to enlist the support of influential individuals and organisations to pave the way for the more comprehensive programme that would be possible once Plaatje and Gumede had arrived.

◇

Such was the situation which Plaatje and Gumede – having busied themselves on board ship with preparations for the campaign – found when they arrived in London at the end of June. One of Plaatje's very first engagements was to attend the funeral of W. P. Schreiner, whom he had long regarded as a political friend and ally.[6] Apart from the personal sadness that Plaatje felt about Schreiner's death, it was also something of a blow to the hopes of the deputation in London, for Plaatje had probably hoped that his relationship with Schreiner might have been turned to good advantage in opening doors that might otherwise have remained closed. But the more immediate priority was the question of accommodation. On this score, though, Plaatje was happy to be able to report success in a letter of greeting to Mrs Colenso on 17 July:

> 13 Highbury Terrace
> London N.
> July 17 1919

Dear Mrs Colenso,

   I am so sorry that the work kept me at such a high pitch, going at top speed, that I am only just able to communicate to you the greetings of myself and family. The position was intensified by the difficulty of obtaining lodgings, which are unobtainable in London.

However, I am glad to have heard before of the family of Gebuza, through my friend Mr Gumede who came with me. After considerable trouble we have managed to secure lodgings and we are comfortably, though expensively, accommodated here.

The apartments are not so good as what I had at Acton [in 1916] but the place itself is very nice, facing Highbury fields on the opposite side to where Mr Chalk used to be. I will look in one day and find out if he is still there. Moreover, with the bus and tram fares doubled, it is very convenient in that respect as one can get to the City at 2d and to Tottenham Court Road too at the same fare.

I do sincerely trust that you are keeping well and that the dear daughters of Gebuza are all making the home sweeter with their cheerful instruments, including the best of all music – the music of the human voice.

Hoping to see you in not so very far a time.

Ich bin und bleib mit herzlichen grusse

Ihren Hochachtungsvolle

Sol T. Plaatje[7]

It was from the imposing surroundings of 13 Highbury Terrace, a fine Georgian terrace building constructed in the year of the French revolution, that Plaatje commenced his campaign. And it was not long before he had a chance to meet the Colensos and the other friends and supporters from his previous visit – at a drawing-room reception at Georgiana Solomon's home at Hampstead a week later, attended by, amongst others, Olive Schreiner, who commented afterwards: 'How well Mr Plaatje and all the delegates spoke!' For Mrs Colenso it was an inspiring occasion. She was 'enormously impressed' by the 'splendid addresses' given by Plaatje and the other delegates, all of whom were there, and the meeting passed a unanimous resolution to convey to the Prime Minister – via the member of parliament, Dr G. B. Clarke, who chaired the meeting – a request that he fulfil the promise he made in France and grant the delegates an interview; Dr Clarke then wrote a personal letter to the Prime Minister to this effect.[8] Plaatje's only regret at the outcome of the meeting was that with the large number of people present, and the shortage of time, he was unable to greet Mrs Colenso in the appropriate manner. He wrote to express his regret the following day: 'It pained me very much, especially after we came over, to have been separated not alone by war but by distance and the dislocated post – then to meet yesterday and part again like prisoners of war, without exchanging a single word.'[9]

Support for the deputation's cause in London's liberal drawing-room circles, thanks largely to Plaatje's activities between 1914 and 1917, was assured. He nevertheless detected a wider current of sympathetic opinion than had been the case during his first visit. He derived considerable encouragement, too, from the exchanges that took place in parliament at the end of July, when, as in 1914, the colonial vote came before the House of Commons for debate. The most impressive speech came from Mr Spoor, a Labour front-bencher, who spoke of 'the existence of a definite tendency' since the Act of Union, 'to eliminate and destroy the rights of the natives', and urged the imperial government to 'exercise every power they have got in order to restore to the natives [of South Africa] the conditions which existed before the Act of Union'.[10] Supporting speeches came from Henry Cavendish Bentinck, a Conservative back-bencher who had served in the Anglo-Boer war, whom Plaatje had first met in 1914; from Captain Ormsby Gore; and from Colonel Wedgewood, who claimed that what then existed in South Africa was 'only a very thinly veiled slavery'. But even Wedgewood, sympathetic though he was, could only urge that the imperial government should dissociate itself completely from what was going on in South Africa.

In reply to all these speakers Colonel Amery simply told a thinly attended House what he had told the Congress delegates in May: namely, that the imperial government was bound to a policy of non-interference by the principle of responsible government, and that 'with a certain measure of faith in these matters' a solution to the 'very difficult problem of the relationship between the races' could be found – the stock official response, in other words. In reply to a final question from Henry Cavendish Bentinck, Amery did acknowledge, though, the effectiveness of Gandhi's intervention on behalf of the Indians in South Africa. This was a man, Amery said, who 'by his own personality, his persistence and his courage got much further in the solution of the problem of the Indians in the Transvaal than any official representations could have done'.[11] What Plaatje, sitting in the visitors' gallery, made of these remarks is unrecorded. Given the importance he always attached to individual example, they may well have acted as a spur, a challenge almost, to make him more determined than ever to continue with his campaign. He was not, after all, short of the qualities to which Amery drew attention.

Plaatje derived some encouragement from the exchanges which took place in Parliament. For this reason the financial problems the deputation was now facing, less than a month after his arrival, were of particular concern. These he outlined in a revealing letter written – from outside London – to Chief W. Z. Fenyang at the beginning of August:

> Fairly Grange
> Longfield, Kent
> 2 August 1919
>
> My dear Fen,
>
> I am sending you the Report of our case in Parliament. It confirms what I wrote in my last letter, namely that the English people this time are more amenable to reason than they were the last time.
>
> For instance: the Government assured members that the Colonial vote will not be taken for a week. Then they took it suddenly on a Wednesday while they were unprepared for it and most of our supporters were away. Yet the few who were present made a bold stand.
>
> But I am very unhappy on the score of finance. It will cripple the whole movement and bring it to nought. When I arrived here I found that I could not get freedom of movement unless I paid part of the old accounts so I disgorged £54 and at least £200 is wanted immediately. It meant that I handed over everything – pocket-money included,

and I am now standing between two fires – the old debts and my present expenses. I have been to arrange two meetings at Reading where I had three days with Kgoatlhe's friends and I have come to address two meetings here in Kent to get further resolutions sent to Parliament. Bo Thema le Mvabaza are doing good work. I send them to places that are easy to manage (if I am engaged) but not out of London because there is no money. Our hope is in the country – not London – and this scarcity of money is helping the Boers, because we can't go out and strike out.

Mr Makgatho promised me £100 here in London and I laid my plans in anticipation of it. But now that I am here I hear nothing from him. As soon as English people find out that I have no money there will be a terrible set-back because they will consider me a d . . . fool if after what I endured in 1914–17 I came penniless again.

Life here is infinitely more costly than last time and if one shows any hesitation he loses his few friends and they are not so easily picked up again. The other delegates are disgusted for I brought no money; and they are losing all heart in the campaign. The fact that I (their so-called leader) am penniless drives them more desperate and I hope that something could be done to get say £300 partly for old debts and partly for the present campaign. The position is really serious and I am beginning to tremble that the deputation will soon be disgraced – after which we will NEVER AGAIN manage the Boer. We have to strike out *now* or *never*.

Please help or we are undone. When I left S.A. I spoke with Mr Malan. He promised to see into the question of the Barolong money at Mafeking – since then I have not had a word from home tho' three mails came after me.

All these things make me feel very desperate and I tremble that the fight will be lost through lack of funds just when we are thinking of holding the reins.

What do you think?

Please send me a line

    Kind regards,

      Plaatje

Another thing – Makgatho and Pilane promised to pay Ma-Sainty £6 a month. Please find out if they are doing it and drive them to it as you have a more serious undertaking here.[12]

Despite Plaatje's growing mood of desperation on the score of finance he and his colleagues nevertheless achieved considerable success in their campaign over the next few months, and they began to widen the support for their cause. As was to be expected they got no further joy from the Colonial Office. By virtue of a private letter of introduction, Plaatje did manage to secure a meeting for himself and Gumede with Colonel Amery in the middle of August, but the outcome was no different from his earlier meeting with Selope Thema and Mvabaza in May. 'I told him [Plaatje] very much as I had told the previous deputation,' Amery reported, 'that we were not prepared to go back beyond Union and that was our answer to Hertzog and if Hertzog had his way and the Act of Union went, things would be much worse than they are today.'[13]

But outside the Colonial Office the response was much more promising. From the time of their arrival the deputation had been given much encouragement and support from London's increasingly vocal black community. Their cause was given wide coverage in the *African Telegraph*, which also distributed much of their publicity material – most notably a pamphlet entitled *A Summary of Statements made to the 'African Telegraph' by the South African Delegation*, which was circulated with copies of their memorial to the King, together with printed copies of subsequent correspondence with Lord Milner, now the Secretary of State for the Colonies. The black community also held a number of functions in their honour, the best attended of which seems to have been a musical reception organised by the 'Coterie of Friends' in West London in the middle of August.[14] In these circles Plaatje and his colleagues were sure of the fullest encouragement and sympathy in their campaign, and for Plaatje particularly, hoping as he did to travel on to the United States, these meetings also provided a source of valuable contacts and information.

But the public interest in the deputation's cause extended well beyond natural sympathisers such as these. To the support of London's black community, and that of the Brotherhood movement, was added, in August and September 1919, that of the Free Church Council, part of the women's suffrage movement (thanks largely to Mrs Solomon), the Independent Labour Party (this after what Plaatje called 'a long and tedious round of negotiations and constant application'), the Union of Democratic Control, and the Church Socialist League.[15] This was hardly the British establishment, but it was nevertheless quite an impressive array of support, and the meetings which Plaatje and his colleagues addressed under these and other auspices were often given wide coverage in the daily and weekly press.[16] Many of these meetings, at the suggestion of the speaker, then sent resolutions of protest to the Colonial Office and to the Prime Minister. That adopted by the Abney Brotherhood in Stoke Newington, north London, on 17 August 1919, was typical of many that arrived at the Colonial Office:

> This meeting of the Abney Brotherhood, having heard the statement of Mr Sol T. Plaatje, of Kimberley, on behalf of his fellow countrymen, protests against the disabilities imposed upon the South African natives by the Union government, as contrary to the spirit and traditions of English government, and urges that prompt representations should be made by the Colonial Secretary, to secure their removal.[17]

Throughout the English autumn of 1919 Plaatje addressed meeting after meeting, sometimes as many as three a day. His programme for 9 October, his 43rd birthday, was perhaps typical. Describing his experiences in *The Clarion*, a journal published in Cape Town, Plaatje wrote that on this day he had addressed a 'drawing room meeting at Kensington' in the morning, the National Liberal Club in the afternoon, and a Brotherhood meeting at St Michael's hall, Clapton, in the evening. The afternoon meeting was undoubtedly the highlight of the day. Reported in the leading daily liberal newspaper, the *Manchester Guardian*, as well as in the new London weekly, *West Africa*, Plaatje considered this meeting the 'most exciting since we came here', largely because of the opportunity it gave him to demolish 'a South African Jew who styled himself "bosom friend of General Smuts" and warned the English people against offering any sympathies to Kaffirs'. With the wholehearted support of the meeting, Plaatje had little difficulty in ridiculing this gentleman's ill-informed remarks. 'He fled,' so Plaatje recounted, 'when the meeting manifested its enjoyment of this rejoinder at the coward's expense, he did not stop to hear the end, but quickly took his hat and sneaked out of the place.'[18]

Despite the desperate shortage of funds Plaatje did on several occasions venture outside London and the home counties, sometimes accompanied by one or other of the delegates, but usually alone. His visit to Tyneside, in the industrial north-east, was a particular success:

> Last Saturday evening at Sunderland-on-Weir I addressed the biggest crowd I have ever faced. The Victoria Theatre, I am told, has a seating capacity of 4,000, and it was packed to suffocation. Just that afternoon I had addressed another crowd at Newcastle, and reaching Sunderland just over a $\frac{1}{2}$ hour before the time, we found the hall surrounded by policemen turning the crowds back as there was no room inside. A very good thing the advertisements mentioned that the speaker was black as our party would not have been admitted. The meeting actually started 20 minutes before the time as there was nothing else to wait for. Their MP, Sir H. Greenwood, was also present with Lady Greenwood and they simply could not believe that such barbarities were possible: but I followed them up with documentary proof of the South African tyrannies exactly as published by the Government's own departmental printers.[19]

Such a response was always encouraging. But with so heavy a programme of engagements it is hardly surprising that Plaatje should have begun to complain, as he wrote to Mrs Colenso on 12 September, of 'being frightfully overworked', or that several of his friends should have noticed how tired he was beginning to look.[20] Moments of rest and relaxation were confined to the occasional weekend visit to Elangeni, the Colenso's family home, or concerts in London. One such occasion was made possible by Plaatje's friendship with Mr George Lattimore, the black American manager of the Southern Syncopated Orchestra, a highly popular Negro jazz band then playing in London – Plaatje found them '*very* sympathetic to their South African brothers'. It was in their company, too, that Plaatje spent the evening of the first anniversary of Armistice Day, 11 November 1919, at the 'Great Peace Dance' at the Albert Hall. The occasion proved to be a spectacular success, and Plaatje was struck by the overwhelming applause extended to the Southern Syncopated Orchestra by all those present – in contrast, he noted, to the rather restrained reception given to the European orchestra which was also playing.[21]

At the end of September 1919 there took place a thoroughly unpleasant incident which complicated the difficult financial situation Plaatje faced, threatened to upset the relations between the Congress delegates, and occupied a great deal of Plaatje's time and attention over the next few months which could have been far more profitably spent on the campaign itself. The incident occurred aboard the Union Castle liner, the *Edinburgh Castle*, docked at Southampton, which Richard Selope Thema, Henry Ngcayiya and Levi Mvabaza, accompanied by another black South African student, Mdani Xaba, had boarded in order to return home to South Africa. The first three men were by now anxious to return home, having been in England since May, and both Plaatje and Makgatho, the Congress president (with whom he had been in contact), felt that the deputation's fast diminishing funds could be better expended in supporting himself (Plaatje) and Josiah Gumede, to enable the two of them to continue with the campaign by themselves. Just before the ship was due to sail, however, an irate crowd of demobilised South African soldiers aboard the ship threatened to throw the four men ashore because they objected to them occupying third-class cabins, while they – because of the acute shortage of shipping accommodation at the time – were obliged to sleep in hammocks and separated, in many cases, from their wives who were travelling with them. Union Castle officials just managed to prevent the men being physically ejected, but in order to prevent a riot they nevertheless felt they had no alternative but to take the four men off the ship in the interests of their own safety. This they duly did, and the four men had to return to London, without their baggage, to wait until another passage could be obtained for them.[22]

The whole affair generated a great deal of publicity and hundreds of pages of agitated correspondence and telegrams between the Colonial Office, the South African High Commission in London, the Native Affairs Department in Pretoria, the Anti-Slavery and Aborigines' Protection Society, and, not least, Plaatje himself, as leader of the deputation.[23] As the delegates contemplated legal action, and a question was asked in the House of Commons, the most urgent matter to be resolved was who was to be responsible for the living expenses of the four men while they awaited a further passage back to South Africa. The South African High Commission in London intervened with the offer of a temporary loan – to be administered via the Anti-Slavery and Aborigines' Protection Society – but on the understanding that it would in due course be repaid by the South African Native National Congress, who, it was assumed, would ultimately be able to claim compensation from either the Union Castle shipping line, or the South African authorities, whoever it was that ultimately accepted liability. But from the start matters were complicated by the fact that, firstly, of the four men ejected from the ship, only two of them, Selope Thema and Mvabaza, were actually Congress delegates, Xaba being a student who had been studying at Edinburgh University and happened to be going back at the same time, while Ngcayiya, though he was president of the Ethiopian Church of South Africa, was in actual fact representing Africans from Rhodesia, and was not a properly elected representative of the deputation. Secondly, the South African High Commission in London had used a remittance of £200, sent to them by S. M. Makgatho, president of Congress, for forwarding on to Plaatje to support the work of the deputation, and to pay for the subsistence of the four men who had been ejected from the *Edinburgh Castle*.[24]

Plaatje, his hands of course full with the work of the campaign, had thus to become involved in trying to recover the money so that it could be used for the purpose for which it had been sent, and to this end was obliged to spend a great deal of time composing letters and visiting the offices of both the Anti-Slavery and Aborigines' Protection Society and the South African High Commission in London.[25] Since the High Commission was, as Plaatje saw it, in effect withholding the means to enable him to carry on his campaign against the South African government, it is scarcely surprising that his frustration at the situation should have on one occasion given way to anger. 'On previous occasions,' reported Mr Blankenburg, the first secretary at the High Commission, after one of Plaatje's visits to his office in the middle of November, 'Mr Plaatje exhibited much calmness and good reason; on this occasion he appeared to be very "warm" and most strongly protested that as Xaba and Ngcayiya were not delegates, they should not be aided out of the £200 provided by Congress.'[26] It was an unenviable situation for Plaatje to be in: he now found himself dependent for funds upon the indulgence of a representative of the government against whose policies he had come to England to protest.

Ngcayiya, Mvabaza and Xaba were eventually found berths on the RMS *Briton*, which sailed from Southampton early in December, and there was no repetition of the *Edinburgh Castle* incident. Richard Selope Thema, the other Congress delegate, decided at the last minute to stay on in England to assist Plaatje and Gumede with the work of the deputation, hoping that he might also find the opportunity to embark upon some course of further education.[27]

Despite the difficulties and embarrassment caused to all the Congress delegates by the *Edinburgh Castle* incident, their extended stay in England did at least mean that when the British Prime Minister, David Lloyd George, was at last persuaded to see a Congress deputation, Mvabaza, Thema and Ngcayiya were able to join Plaatje and Gumede for the interview. In many ways it was surprising that this took place at all, and it seems to have been Plaatje's connection with Arthur Henderson and Dr Clifford, two Brotherhood men who enjoyed some personal influence with the Prime Minister, which made it possible.[28] Until then, despite Lloyd George's promise made in Versailles, there had been no response whatever to the frequent reminders the delegates had been sending to the Prime Minister's office, and Plaatje for one would have well appreciated that the idea was not likely to be looked upon with favour, to say the least, by either the Colonial Office or the South African High Commission in London. When Lloyd George did finally agree to see the delegates, Henry Lambert, first secretary at the Colonial Office, was understandably concerned that the Prime Minister should be 'very carefully advised as to what his reply should be'; and he summed up the Colonial Office viewpoint with the advice to Philip Kerr, Lloyd George's private secretary, that 'the less said to this Deputation by the Prime Minister the better'.[29]

Underlying Lambert's attitude was the unstated fear that the delegates were quite capable of making a strong impression upon the Prime Minister. In the event it proved to be very well founded. The interview took place late on the afternoon of Friday, 21 November 1919, in a committee room at the House of Commons. The deputation was led by Plaatje, and it included, apart from the South African delegates, several leading figures in London's black community, among them Mr Eldred Taylor, of the *African Telegraph*, and Mr T. H. Jackson, editor of the *Lagos Weekly Record*, who happened to be in London at the time.[30] The meeting began with Levi Mvabaza summarising the historical background to their predicament; he enumerated in detail the discriminatory legislation that had been passed since the Act of Union, illustrating one of their complaints by showing Lloyd George a selection of passes which the delegates had brought along with them: 'Let me have a look at them,' Lloyd George said, 'I have never seen them.' Anticipating the Prime Minister's likely response to their representations, Mvabaza concluded by stressing that it was no use him urging them to seek to remedy their grievances by constitutional methods, for the means to do so simply do not exist.

Then it was Plaatje's turn to explain to the Prime Minister how desperate their position had become. Frances Stevenson, Lloyd George's shorthand secretary and mistress, was on hand to record the proceedings:

> MR SOL PLAATJE: I am very sorry we have to weary you with our African difficulties, but if we were to speak till tomorrow morning we would never succeed to enumerate them all. As a matter of fact we have been to the Colonial Office with these troubles, and they told us we had better go and settle our affairs in our own country. But what footing have we got in a country where we cannot even buy or hire a house? They could logically advise us to go and fight our case in Scotland or in Wales for there at any rate nobody will prevent us from hiring or buying a house if we have the money. We may point out that we foresaw all the troubles that my friend [Mvabaza] has been trying to explain, at the time the Union Constitution was passed limiting the franchise to white people only. The basis and circumstances are not clearly understandable to people on this side of the Atlantic. But we clearly foresaw everything at the time so our people sent a deputation over which was supported by some of the brainiest white people in South Africa.

After Lloyd George interrupted to ask if General Hertzog supported Congress's case (such was his ignorance of South African affairs), Plaatje then went on to detail the legislative measures directed against the African people which had been enacted since the Act of Union – the Natives' Land Act, the discrimination in education, taxation, employment. 'Why do they do these things?' Plaatje asked:

> Because being voteless we are absolutely helpless. Sir Thomas Smartt and other members like the Right Honourable J. X. Merriman have protested against these things again and again but their arguments take no effect. Great Britain, with whom our fathers bargained in the earliest days to come and take our country under her protection, has thrown us away. The people who rule in South Africa are the followers of General Hertzog and all Great Britain tells us is that she has nothing to do with it. And our object in coming over is to let the facts be known to the British public and to enlist the sympathy of the Prime Minister in these matters. We don't expect the Prime Minister to go over there and catch General Smuts by the scruff of his neck and say, 'You must relieve these people or I will knock you down!' What we want done is simply in a constitutional manner. It is useless to go and tell our people that

the home Government is absolutely powerless – even when we are oppressed. It would be useless to tell them that since they know that when the natives of the Belgian Congo were oppressed the people in England raised their voices against it, and the Foreign Office in this country communicated with the Belgian Government with the result that the natives' condition in the Belgian Congo was so ameliorated that white men from our part of Africa who have been to the Belgian Congo have returned and said it was impossible to make money in the Belgian Congo because the Belgians did not allow the white man to exploit the labour of the natives as they are allowed to do in South Africa. You did that for the natives under a foreign flag. It is rather hard lines on the millions of native people whose only crime is that they are not loyal to the local rulers of the country, but that they are loyal to the British flag which out there is called a foreign flag. If in these circumstances you leave these people to the mercy of their oppressors their lot is going to be difficult indeed, and it would be difficult to convince them that the Allies have not lost the war because they heard that the Allies were fighting for the protection of oppressed nations. If ever there was a case which called for protection it is the case of the natives in South Africa who are told that they have no right to buy or lease land in their own country.

Plaatje ended his appeal on an emotional note. He told the Prime Minister of the personal humiliations of the restrictions that existed in his country; of the regulations that would now prevent his son from working in the Kimberley Post Office where he himself had begun his career; of what had happened at Aliwal North when he took his daughter there to try and find a cure for her rheumatism. 'These things,' Plaatje concluded,

> are not confined to particular provinces of the Union, but are spreading all over and it is becoming unbearable for natives to live in some parts of the country. Our only request is, in view of the fact that you have ameliorated the lot of the Belgian natives under a foreign flag, and at the instance of Lord Harding you successfully intervened in favour of Indians who appealed against the operation of an Act passed by the Union Parliament of 1913, you should consider us in the land of our fathers. The native has no place to go to. Our one crime is not that we want to be the equals of the Dutch but that we are loyal to a foreign flag, the Union Jack. If it offers us no protection then our case is indeed hopeless.[31]

It was just the kind of oration that was likely – indeed calculated – to impress David Lloyd George. If the responsibilities of office had somewhat dimmed his earlier radicalism, Lloyd George remained one of the great orators of his day, and his sympathies were easily aroused. It was almost as though Plaatje, with his eloquent and very personal declaration about the injustices suffered by his people, had touched a sensitive chord that brought back to the old Welsh radical his own more youthful tirades against the injustices of British society twenty years earlier. Plaatje's use of the term 'land of our fathers', title of the Welsh national anthem, was surely a quite deliberate ploy on his part to evoke such a response from the Prime Minister.

Plaatje and his colleagues succeeded beyond their expectations. In reply, Lloyd George repeated to them the constitutional position, but he told them that he had listened 'with some distress to the story you have told of restrictions which are imposed upon you in your native land'; that he thought their speeches had been 'very clear and able and temperate', and that they had presented their case 'with very great power'. 'You have said enough', he concluded, 'to convince me that it is certainly a case which ought to be taken into the consideration of the South African government and I shall certainly take the earliest opportunity of presenting the whole of the facts to General Smuts.'[32] They were the kind of words and sentiments which Colonial Office officials, even in their unguarded moments, would never have uttered. Henry Lambert's concern about how the Prime Minister might react, in other words, was more than justified. Plaatje himself thought Lloyd George had been 'greatly shocked' by what he had heard; Eldred Taylor thought he looked 'visibly moved' and spoke afterwards of being struck forcibly by 'the sincere feeling' exhibited by the Prime Minister.[33]

On the question of communicating with General Smuts, now Prime Minister of South Africa, Lloyd George was as good as his word. In two remarkable letters to the General, filed away as 'secret' in the Colonial Office files, he wrote at considerable length to express his concern at the 'deep sense of injustice' which the Congress delegates had so effectively conveyed to him:

> They evidently felt that the existing pass system operated very unjustly in a large number of cases. They were sure that some recent Land Act passed in the Union Parliament deprived the native population unjustly of its land and tended to reduce them to the position of wanderers in the country of their birth. They further were convinced that there was a larger and powerful section in South Africa who were bent on emphasising the colour line, and in preventing the education and advancement of the native population.

One other grievance Lloyd George particularly drew attention to:

> They said that they had repeatedly been told that they ought not to ventilate their grievances outside South Africa and that they ought to secure their reforms by constitutional means at home. But, they asked, what was the use of calling upon them to obey the law and observe constitutional methods in their agitation for betterment and reform if they were given no adequate constitutional means for doing so? If this is a correct statement of the facts it seems to me a very powerful point.

Lloyd George continued with a warning about the general stirring of black nationalism across the world ('which affects us all', he said), and suggested that Smuts might care to see the deputation upon their return to South Africa:

> I was greatly impressed by the ability shown by the speakers. They presented their case with moderation, with evident sincerity, and with power. It is evident that you have in Africa men who can speak for native opinion and make themselves felt, not only within their country, but outside. I am sure you will be impressed by them, and I am equally sure that you will be able to

69 *Portrait of Plaatje by L. Caswall Smith, an Oxford Street photographer, taken late in 1916.*

70 *Plaatje's eldest son, St Leger (sitting), and Z. K. Matthews, at Lovedale College, 1916. Both won scholarships from the Lyndhurst Road Public School in Kimberley.*

To the Memory
of
OUR BELOVED OLIVE
one of the many youthful
Victims of A SETTLED SYSTEM
and in
Pleasant Recollection of her
life work, accomplished, at the
age of 13, during the
INFLUENZA EPIDEMIC
This Book is Affectionately Dedicated

" *Death wounds to cure—we fall, we rise, we reign,*
Spring from our fetters, fasten in the skies.
Where blooming Eden withers in our sight :
Death gives no more than was in Eden lost :
The King of Terrors is the Prince of Peace. "

71 and 72 *Plaatje's daughter Olive, to whom he dedicated his novel* Mhudi *(right). She was badly affected by the influenza epidemic in 1919, and died two years later while Plaatje was in America.*

73 *South African Native National Congress deputation to England, 1919. Top row, left to right: R. V. Selope Thema, J. T. Gumede, L. T. Mvabaza. Bottom row, left to right: S. T. Plaatje, Rev. H. R Ngcayiya.*

74 *David Lloyd George, the British prime minister, who received Plaatje and his colleagues at the House of Commons on 21 November 1919. He told them they presented their case 'with very great power', and had 'listened with some distress to the story you have told of the restrictions which are imposed upon you in your native land'.*

75 *Photograph of Plaatje used by the Canadian authorities for the passport issued to him in Ottowa, December 1920. This enabled him to travel to the United States in January 1921.*

COME AND HEAR

Mr. SOL

PLAATJE
Of Kimberley, South Africa

Gives thrilling account of the condition of the Colored Folk in British South Africa.

A Touching Message well and luridly told

The story has gripped nearly a thousand audiences in England, Scotland, Canada & U.S.A

IT WILL THRILL YOU

Bethel A. M. E. Church
West 132nd Street, bet. Lenox and 5th Aves.

Sunday, March 13, 11 a. m.
THE BLACK MAN'S BURDEN IN SOUTH AFRICA

Friday, March 18th, 8 p. m.
THE BLACK WOMAN'S BURDEN IN SO. AFRICA

Interspersed with Quaint African Music sung in his own native tongue

Free Will Offering for Brotherhood Work among the South African Tribes

ADMISSION FREE
COME EARLY AND AVOID THE CRUSH!!

Dr. MONTROSE W. THORNTON, Pastor

76 *'A touching message well and luridly told': poster advertising Plaatje's campaign in New York, March 1921.*

Black Americans in Plaatje's campaign in the United States 1921–2 (left to right). 77 *J. E. Bruce ('Bruce Grit'), editor of the* Negro World. 78 *Marcus Garvey, President of the Universal Negro Improvement Association.*

Black Americans in Plaatje's campaign in the United States, 1921–2 (left to right). **79** *Dr W. E. B. Du Bois, editor of the* Crisis *and founder of the National Association for the Advancement of Colored People.* **80** *John W. Cromwell, lawyer, former newspaper editor and leading figure in the American Negro Academy.* **81** *Jessie Fausset, novelist and NAACP official.* **82** *Robert Moton, Principal of the Tuskegee Institute, Alabama.*

remove the impression which seems to rest there at present, that they cannot get people in authority to listen to them with sympathy.[34]

It was, to say the least, a surprising letter to have been written from one Prime Minister to another, and it was hardly something that General Smuts can have expected. Then Lloyd George repeated many of the points he had made in a second, unofficial letter, marked 'Private and Confidential' and 'for your private eye', again urging the General to do what he could to meet their legitimate grievances. And he went on to make an interesting comparison:

> I was further impressed by the fact that it is evident that among the natives of South Africa there are men possessed of very considerable oratorical gifts. The contrast between the case made by these black men and by the Deputation headed by General Hertzog was very striking. They are evidently capable, not only of rousing their people, but of rousing public feeling in other countries. I am told that many of them have been going about the country lecturing at Labour Party meetings and Brotherhood meetings, and that they have produced some effect. It was originally proposed that the Deputation should be introduced to me by Arthur Henderson, Secretary of the Labour Party, and Dr Clifford. I refused to agree to this because it looked like mixing up South African politics with British politics, but it shows that they have been able to secure the sympathy of people of power and influence in this country.[35]

Lloyd George went on to elaborate upon the growing threat of 'Bolshevism' and 'Garveyism' to 'not only the British Commonwealth, but the whole existing structure of society', evidently concerned that unrest in South Africa could have much wider implications. And he concluded by stressing once again that General Smuts should see to it that something was done: 'If they do suffer under disabilities,' he said, 'and if they have no effective mode of expression it is obvious that sooner or later serious results must ensue.'

General Smuts's reply, when it came, was predictable enough, and for the most part simply reiterated the points made in the reply which the South African Native National Congress had received in response to their original memorial drawn up in December 1918: Congress was not a representative organisation; the claims of the delegates were 'more specious than true, and largely amount to *suggestio falsi*'; his government was working on what he described as 'improved machinery for voicing the needs and interests of the Natives'; and the delegates should in any case have availed themselves of such constitutional means as were at their disposal in South Africa before seeking to publicise their case outside by 'distortion and exaggeration'.[36] The General, it is clear, was very irritated by the seriousness with which the British Prime Minister had taken the complaints of the Congress deputation, and did not much care to be lectured on what he should or should not do about it. What he made of the contrast Lloyd George drew between the Congress deputation, headed by Plaatje, and the Afrikaner nationalist deputation, headed by General Hertzog, is unknown; that comment would have caused political uproar in South Africa had it been made public.

It is a pity that Plaatje could never know of this correspondence that passed between the two Prime Ministers, for in a way it was a remarkable exchange. Plaatje had always believed in his own ability to appeal successfully to the most highly placed individuals, and Lloyd George's reaction to their interview was striking, indeed spectacular, confirmation of this. At the same time the fact that the Prime Minister could do no more than write a worried letter or two to General Smuts demonstrated very clearly the limits to the effectiveness of personal appeals of this kind. Even the sympathy of the British Prime Minister could not alter the fact that Britain shared, by virtue of her colonial position, a common stance with South Africa, the inheritance of many years of careful policy development in 'native affairs' and imperial policy generally.[37] The people Plaatje really needed to convert in Britain were the hard-headed officials of the Colonial Office, and there was never any prospect of this. Plaatje's victory was to have secured, in the face of opposition from the Colonial Office, an interview with the British Prime Minister, and then to have so impressed him with the strength of their case that he was prepared to take up the matter with General Smuts. In the circumstances that was achievement enough, and the Colonial Office officials were horrified; but it was as far as it could go. Plaatje had taken the technique of personal appeal to its furthest limits. It was a moment when one of his great strengths as an individual, and the fundamental weakness of the position in which he so often found himself, stood clearly revealed.

◇

Levi Mvabaza and Henry Ngcayiya departed for South Africa shortly after the interview with Lloyd George, but Plaatje, Gumede, and Thema, encouraged in no small measure by the Prime Minister's words to them at the conclusion of the meeting, remained to continue their campaign of public agitation.[38] During November and December 1919 Plaatje managed to obtain an interview with the Archbishop of Canterbury; he gave a long interview, published in the Independent Labour Party's *Labour Leader*, with a young but already very experienced left-wing journalist called Fenner Brockway, who was particularly struck by the 'gentle refinement about his features' and the 'fire of passionate indignation against the wrongs committed upon his race'; and he compiled and printed a pamphlet entitled *Some of the Legal Disabilities Suffered by the Native Population of the Union of South Africa and Imperial Responsibility*, notable for its attempt to draw attention to the so-called Byles Resolution of 1906, a noble statement of imperial responsibility for the interests of the 'native races' who were without representation in the legislative assemblies of the colonies in which they lived.[39]

Interestingly enough, Plaatje seems to have written this pamphlet at the suggestion of his one-time enemy, John Harris, secretary of the Anti-Slavery and Aborigines' Protection Society – a matter of some irony in view of his energetic attempts to suppress and denigrate *Native Life in South Africa* in 1916. It is not entirely clear how this rapprochement came about, but it is evident that John Harris's views on the South African situation had altered somewhat since Plaatje was last in the country. With the emergence of several new organisations associated with the *African Telegraph*, he seems to have at last come to realise that his uncritical support for General Botha's policies was moving him further and further away from progressive currents of opinion, and that something had to be done if his society was to play any meaningful role in colonial affairs.

On Plaatje's side, as well, his antipathy towards Harris had begun to mellow somewhat. Despite not having been informed about the decision to send a deputation over to London, Harris's attitude had not been unfriendly when they arrived, and he had earned Plaatje's respect through his assistance and support in the *Edinburgh Castle* affair.[40] But more than anything what drew the two men together was the realisation that they could simply not afford to ignore each other – Plaatje because of the desperate financial situation in which the deputation found itself, Harris because of the risk of losing all credibility to his society's claim to have at heart the interests of 'the native races' of South Africa or anywhere else. Despite all that had taken place during Plaatje's first visit to England, the two men were drawn back to one another, in other words, by the awareness of their mutual dependence. Whereas Harris had considered *Native Life* to be full of 'distortions' and 'misrepresentations', Plaatje's new pamphlet, he said, was 'excellent'; there was even talk of his society assisting in its printing costs.[41]

Plaatje spent most of December 1919 travelling, lecturing and addressing meetings in Scotland, and found the opportunity to meet up once more with Modiri Molema, now close to completing his studies at Glasgow University.[42] Plaatje's campaign in Scotland went very well. After discussions with the Independent Labour Party and the Union of Democratic Control, he had managed to secure their backing for the campaign, and it was under their auspices that most of his Scottish meetings were held.[43] This fact emphasised, perhaps more clearly than anything else, that it was increasingly in left-wing circles that Plaatje was able to enlist sympathy and support for his cause – one of the most noticeable differences, indeed, with his campaign of 1914–17. It produced some ironies that Plaatje would have appreciated. Whereas in South Africa he had been vigorously opposed to the spread of the methods and doctrines of the socialists and communists amongst his own people in South Africa, in England, and even more in Scotland, it was now precisely in these circles that he was able to elicit the most sympathetic response. But the paradox did not bother him unduly, and he enjoyed the times he spent up north:

> I had great times in Scotland [he wrote to Mrs Colenso at the end of December]. There is much to do there if it could be revisited. Great times among the Socialists and U.D.C. members. Shared one Edinburgh meeting with Mrs Helen Crawford, the Socialist speaker. We stayed in the same hotel and sat till LATE exchanging views. I have learned MUCH from her while she thinks I have taught her a lot.[44]

Plaatje knew better than anybody that he was in no position to be choosy about his friends and allies. Even so, it was ironical that he should have been acclaimed by *Forward*, the journal of the Scottish Independent Labour Party, as 'probably the first black lecturer to appear on the Socialist platform in this country'; and it would have been interesting to know of his reactions to the following piece of advice which appeared in *The Workers' Dreadnought* ('For

Revolutionary Socialism, the ending of Capitalism and Parliament, and the substitution of a World Federation of Workers' Industrial Republics'):

> The South African deputation has been well received by many sections of the labour movement. It will travel round the country addressing enthusiastic meetings, and finally it will return to South Africa, if it is wise, to build up the International Socialists, a solid organisation of black and white working together, without distinction of colour, race, or creed, to wrest power from the capitalists and to establish the African Soviets.[45]

At the end of December 1919 Plaatje returned, tired out, to London and spent the New Year recuperating in the company of the Colenso family in Amersham. Physical exhaustion was at last beginning to take its toll. Even before embarking upon his gruelling Scottish tour Alice Werner had commented 'poor Plaatje is nearly worn out', and the few days he spent at Elangeni provided some much needed rest.[46] Here he could relax in friendly company, a substitute of sorts for his own wife and family in yet another year spent away from them. There were long discussions over the affairs of the deputation and many other subjects, and conversations that alternated between English, German and Zulu as though this was the most natural thing in the world – all in an atmosphere in which the great Bishop Colenso, though dead now for nearly forty years, was almost a living presence. Elangeni provided for Plaatje an escape to a world in which he fitted easily, enjoying the company of people of comfortable means, sharing common values and attitudes to race, religion and politics. He appreciated the 'kindness and intelligent love', as he described it, which he found at Elangeni; the 'exquisite music' Mrs Colenso's daughters played, 'the cozy coteries at meal times', 'the alfresco promenades to, from and through the beautiful grounds of Elangeni'.[47] The Colensos, for their part, delighted in Plaatje's lively company, 'his unfailing humour and his irresistible laugh'.[48] He seems to have reminded them of a South Africa that existed in their imagination as much as their memories; his letters were eagerly read, commented upon, and then sent on to Harriette Colenso in Natal – it is thanks to her that several of them have survived.

But the few days Plaatje spent at Elangeni to see in the new year, accompanied on this occasion by both Gumede and Selope Thema, provided no more than a brief respite from an arduous programme. They maintained the momentum of their campaign during January and February 1920 and continued to attract large audiences, especially outside London; in the third week of January, for example, Plaatje attracted a record audience to a meeting of the Portsmouth Brotherhood.[49] It seems to have been to the Brotherhood movement, indeed, that Plaatje now began to devote the greater part of his attention. He had found considerable encouragement during the International Brotherhood Congress which he had attended in London in September 1919. It had been an impressive gathering, attended by delegates from the Brotherhood movement from many parts of the world, and his own address had been warmly received. More than that, he had also been elected a member of the business committee of the

International Federation, and had been involved in drafting both the new constitution and the 'Brotherhood Challenge', a stirring document calling upon nations and individuals to unite to construct a post-war world of peace and brotherhood.[50]

The International Brotherhood Congress had also provided Plaatje with the opportunity to try and raise support and interest for the work of his own Brotherhood organisation in Kimberley, whose mounting debts and difficulties he would have been kept informed about in letters from home; and to solicit contributions towards another scheme upon which he had already done a great deal of work – translating the Fellowship Hymn Book, used by the Brotherhood movement, into Setswana and several other African languages.[51] Plaatje had already translated the hymn book into two African languages (Setswana and Xhosa) by the time he arrived in England in 1919, and at the Brotherhood Congress he received a number of definite promises (or so they appeared at the time) to finance their printing and publication, especially from the Canadian delegates who took a particular interest in his work.[52]

But probably foremost in Plaatje's mind all this time was the notion that if he was to fulfil his ambition of travelling to the United States of America, then the most likely way in which this was going to be made possible was through the help and support of the Brotherhood movement. S. M. Makgatho, president of Congress, was keen that Plaatje should carry the SANNC's campaign to the United States, but was in no position to provide the money to finance the trip. He had been unable, indeed, to repay sums of money advanced to the delegates in the early months of 1920 by the Anti-Slavery and Aborigines' Protection Society once the original £200 sent by Makgatho had been used up.[53] The Brotherhood movement, by contrast, seemed to hold out far more promise, particularly in view of Plaatje's success in making some valuable contacts among the many American and Canadian delegates who had attended the International Congress, and it was probably on this occasion that the idea of undertaking a lecturing and speaking tour in America under the auspices of the Brotherhood movement was first mooted.

Whatever had been agreed, it is clear that during the early months of 1920 Plaatje was actively preparing for his visit to North America. Even before this, however, he had written several letters to prominent black Americans to inform them of his intentions. Amongst them was his old correspondent, John E. Bruce, now working as a journalist in New York, who promised to do all he could to help Plaatje when he arrived there; Bruce then wrote to John W. Cromwell, another well-known figure in black American circles who lived in Washington, and was at that time president of the American Negro Academy, asking him to 'get in touch with him [Plaatje] immediately and take charge of him when he visits Washington as he hopes to do in May next'.[54] Cromwell, to whom Plaatje had also written separately, duly replied with a very helpful letter. These were just the people whose support Plaatje would need if his projected visit to the USA was to be a success, and the warmth of their initial reaction must have come as a great encouragement.

Towards the end of March 1920 Plaatje's arrangements for his proposed visit to North America had advanced sufficiently for him to take steps towards acquiring the travel documents he needed to enable him to enter the United

States. It was the beginning of another long battle. Plaatje's hope was that the United States consul in London would be prepared to issue him with the passport he needed in order to enter the country, but things did not prove to be quite so straightforward. When he went along to the consul's offices for this purpose on 24 March he was informed that clearance from the South African government would first of all be required (also that he would have to meet the expense of the telegrams that were then sent in order to arrange this).[55] The South African authorities did not reply immediately. Unknown to Plaatje, his request was dealt with at the highest level and was ultimately brought to the attention of the Minister of Native Affairs, F. S. Malan. His view, communicated to the United States' consul in Cape Town and thence to London, was that 'whilst not desirous of encouraging the enterprise in any way', he nevertheless 'did not wish to throw any obstacle in the way of Mr Plaatje'.[56]

Within a few days the South Africans had changed their minds. Their High Commission in London, much involved over the past months in the financial plight of the three Congress delegates who still remained in England, indicated that they were not in favour of Plaatje's proposed visit to the United States, and reported that the British Foreign Office 'would prefer a definite request whether the endorsement is to be granted or refused'.[57] In the circumstances this was likely to produce only one outcome, and Plaatje was duly informed that the passport could not be issued to him. In all probability the initial hesitation over the question was due to the fact that F. S. Malan, whom Plaatje had met on a number of occasions, was rather better disposed towards him than was his Secretary for Native Affairs, Edward Barrett. Three years previously Barrett had described Plaatje as a man 'likely to become a troublesome professional agitator', and Plaatje himself remembered with some annoyance Barrett's opposition to his plans for his Brotherhood hall at the time of the Governor-General's visit to Kimberley in 1918.[58] Barrett was not the first permanent secretary to have been irritated by Plaatje's influence – tenuous as it was – with the minister to whom he was responsible, but on this occasion he got his way.

The reasons Barrett advanced for refusing Plaatje a passport are of some interest. It was his view, first of all, that 'Plaatje's lectures will no doubt consist of mendacious attacks upon the Union Government', and he had before him some press clippings from several newspapers and journals reporting meetings that Plaatje had been addressing in London – all of which underlined for him the achievements of the Congress deputation to England, confirming, as Lloyd George was writing to General Smuts at this very moment, that they were men 'capable not only of rousing their people, but of rousing people in other countries'. And like Lloyd George, Barrett was concerned about the 'mischievous activities' of Marcus Garvey's Universal Negro Improvement Association, based in the United States but already spreading to every part of the world (including South Africa) where people of African descent lived: 'If Plaatje proceeds to the United States,' Barrett thought, 'he is pretty certain to link up Native activities here with this American organisation.'[59]

Barrett advanced two further reasons why Plaatje should be denied a passport: firstly, that he had heard from Kimberley that Plaatje's presence was required there by the authorities so as to sort out the 'financial affairs of the "Brotherhood" founded by him which are seriously out of order'; and secondly, that Plaatje, together with his co-delegates in England, 'are a constant source of embarrassment on account of their many difficulties'. It was these latter two considerations that Barrett felt it would be more politic to stress in justifying his government's desire to prevent Plaatje from visiting the United States: 'I think,' he concluded, 'that the passport might be refused and the reason might be alleged that apart from other considerations the financial difficulties already encountered show that the overseas peregrinations of political natives are likely to create trouble for themselves, embarrassment to the government and perplexity to responsible societies in the countries they visit.'[60] A telegram was accordingly sent in these terms to the South African High Commission in London to inform the American consulate and the British Foreign Office of the South African government's decision.

Quite possibly the Americans would have reached the same decision independently. They too had good reason to be concerned at the rapid growth of Garvey's Universal Negro Improvement Association, and had they consulted the current files of the intelligence gathering agency attached to the London consulate – busy at that time in monitoring the activities of American socialists in England – they would have found a report there of a meeting held under the auspices of the Independent Labour Party which Plaatje had addressed, during his Scottish tour, on 12 December 1919.[61] In the circumstances the American authorities can have hardly wished to encourage Plaatje's visit to the United States either, if this was the company he kept: a socialist would have been unwelcome, a black socialist doubly so.

The decision of the government to refuse Plaatje a passport must have come as a great blow, and it seems likely that he seriously considered returning home to South Africa. Certainly it was the wish of the South African Chamber of Mines that Plaatje should do this, for they had approached him in London at about this time to try and persuade him to assume the editorship of a new weekly newspaper they proposed establishing – what became *Umteteli wa Bantu*, or the *Mining Sun*. On at least one occasion, it seems, representatives of the Chamber of Mines entertained him at a concert of the Southern Syncopated Orchestra with this end in view.[62] The idea for such a newspaper actually originated in 1919 with a request from a group of conservative African political leaders in the Transvaal – Saul Msane and Isaiah Bud-M'belle amongst them – for support from the Chamber of Mines for a newspaper which would provide an alternative voice to *Abantu-Batho*, the Congress newspaper which was controlled by the radical Transvaal branch of the movement. Their original approach was not successful, however, and the Chamber turned down their requests for support.[63] But in the early months of 1920, following a massive black miners' strike that February, the Chamber of Mines – more specifically its Native Recruiting Corporation – decided to take the initiative in launching a newspaper with the objective, as they put it, of dispelling 'certain erroneous ideas cherished by many natives and sedulously fostered by European and Native agitators, and by certain Native newspapers'.[64]

251

The problem then was who was to be the paper's editor: since the Native Recruiting Corporation was doing its best to disguise its own association with the new venture, and to present the newspaper as a genuine organ of African opinion, an African editor was clearly a *sine qua non*. Saul Msane, it seems, had wanted to edit the paper when the idea was first mooted, but he died at the end of 1919.[65] The Native Recruiting Corporation then approached Plaatje – obviously an ideal choice if he could be persuaded to accept, and just the right man to establish the legitimacy of the new paper with its prospective readership. Exactly what Plaatje's response was is unknown. Presumably he gave the NRC some reason for encouragement, for when the first number of *Umteteli wa Bantu* appeared in May 1920 it carried the names of Plaatje and John Dube on the editorial masthead. But whether he at any point seriously intended to assume the editorship of the paper is much less certain, and had he really been keen to do so the Chamber of Mines' representatives in London would surely have paid his passage back to South Africa. Probably from the first Plaatje had serious reservations about the idea. Although he was, in a general way, favourably disposed towards both the mining houses and business interests generally – regarding the difficulties facing his people as being caused by a hostile government – he was all too aware of the danger that too close a relationship with them would destroy his own political credibility amongst the African people, not all of whom shared his view of the potentially progressive nature of the mining houses. Whatever degree of editorial freedom Plaatje was promised on the new paper, the fact remained that it was owned by the mining industry, and was to be run in their interests and not in the interests of the African population on whose behalf Plaatje still claimed to speak: they could not always be expected to be in harmony.

There were other considerations that disposed Plaatje against returning to South Africa to assume the editorship of *Umteteli wa Bantu*. These he explained in a letter written to Silas Molema from London in August 1920:

> I have also been asked to go to Johannesburg and print a new newspaper. But I don't care to go to Transvaal where people have no voices and do not count among members of Parliament. Today, everybody knows that I have got a vote in Parliament, on the School Board, in the Divisional Council, and in the Town Council; if I go to Transvaal all that is finished. You can only help me with one thing when I arrive home. I will tell Mr Taberer [Director of the Native Recruiting Corporation] that my people would not allow me to go and write in mixed languages. They want us to work on a special Setswana newspaper like the Basuto and Ndebele. If you could save me just that way, everything will come right and we will resuscitate the *Tsala* again.[66]

Plaatje was only too aware of how painful it would be to uproot himself and his family and move to Johannesburg, which of course he would have to do if he took up the position that was on offer; elsewhere in the same letter, indeed, he referred to Johannesburg as 'that hell'. As the letter also makes clear, he still cherished the hope of being able to restart *Tsala ea Batho* in Kimberley even though it was now five years since the last issue had been published. Plaatje's decision not to take up the editorship of *Umteteli wa Bantu* – attractive as the offer must have been financially – proved to be a wise one. Several months later he was to learn of the unethical measures which the management of *Umteteli wa Bantu* were using to try and put *Abantu-Batho* out of business.[67] Plaatje could never have been a party to this and have retained at the same time any degree of political credibility. He did well, in short, to decline the editorship of the newspaper, and from August 1920 his name was removed from the editorial masthead.

◇

While *Umteteli wa Bantu* was being launched in Johannesburg in May 1920 Plaatje was still in London, living now at 43 Tavistock Square, Bloomsbury. Selope Thema and Gumede were still in England (though Selope Thema was on the point of returning home), and the three of them had persisted in their attempts to raise support and interest in their cause. Plaatje had not given up hope of being able to get over to America, but he was worried about both the gloomy news he received from home about the difficulties of his Brotherhood movement in Kimberley, and the more immediate task of supporting himself in England: 'I nearly died of hunger and the Thaba Nchu people came to my rescue on each occasion,' he told Silas Molema.[68] He was able to make a little money in doing some further work on Setswana with Professor (as he now was) Daniel Jones at University College. On at least one occasion, too, he visited the London School of Oriental Studies, where Alice Werner now worked, meeting for the first time the famous West African educationist, J. E. K. Aggrey, then on his way from America to Africa as a member of the Phelps Stokes Education Commission.[69] And he travelled up to Scotland again, visiting Modiri Molema in Glasgow on the very day the young doctor's first book, *The Bantu Past and Present*, was published. Plaatje was full of praise for the book, and greatly enjoyed reading it:

> God only knows where you raked up these stories; and they are so humorously put that often when I took it up after working tired and late and lie down about midnight it has kept me roaring with laughter some-times till the small hours; and I have felt lonely since Mr Cross took it away. By the way I have asked him and Mr Dennet, also Miss Werner, to try and review it in some paper where they can squeeze it in with a hope of an acceptance.

The long delays that Modiri Molema had experienced before the book was published brought back memories of his own experiences with *Native Life in South Africa*, and the reception he anticipated for it:

> Again, I must congratulate you on your patience. I had to wait 11 months fighting Harris who was battling to suppress *Native Life* in the press and the waiting was unbearable; and I can appreciate your ordeal having to wait three whole years for paper. My only regret is that this book will excite the jealousies of the very Bantu for whose benefit you have laboured thus unselfishly for the book is BIG. Other tribes will maliciously belittle

your efforts while the 200,000 Barolongs will offer you their lip loyalty instead of recommending the book to possible buyers.[70]

Plaatje had also been greatly preoccupied with his own writing during these few months in the middle of 1920. In his letter to Silas Molema, Modiri's father, at the end of August he had this to say:

> I am still busy writing two books. One is a novel–a love story after the manner of romances; but based on historical facts. The smash-up of the Barolongs at Kunana by Mzilikazi, the coming of the Boers and the war of revenge which smashed up the Matabele at Coenyane by the Allies, Barolong, Boers, and Griquas when Halley's Comet appeared in 1835–with plenty of love, superstition, and imaginations worked in between the wars. Just like the style of Rider Haggard when he writes about the Zulus.
>
> I have just finished this book and it is looking for a publisher. Now I am finishing the political work something like *Native Life* which will bring the native troubles up to date. I do not know how I will dodge hatred when I get there.[71]

The second of these books–the 'political work something like *Native Life*'–was never published, and the manuscript, sadly, has never come to light. But several things can be said about Plaatje's intentions. It seems likely, first of all, that the idea of writing a follow-up to *Native Life* had been in his mind since the book was first published in 1916, and that one of his main objectives in his extensive travels in the rural parts of South Africa in 1917, 1918 and 1919 had been the collection of new material to incorporate into it.

There are, however, two specific pieces of evidence which provide some further indication as to the contents of the book Plaatje had in mind. The first is a letter he wrote to the Administrator of Southern Rhodesia, Sir Drummond Chaplin, in April 1919, two months before he departed for England.[72] Essentially, it was a request for information on laws relating to the African population in Southern Rhodesia, and was prefaced by an offer of congratulations to Chaplin for having just written a pamphlet demolishing some of the claims that had recently been made by John Harris as part of his campaign against the Rhodesian Chartered Company. Plaatje wanted this information, so he told Chaplin, as he was writing a 'companion volume' to *Native Life in South Africa* in which 'some mention would be made of Mr Harris's Society'. Plaatje intended, it can be assumed, to include some account of his battle with Harris and the Anti-Slavery and Aborigines' Protection Society in the book, presumably in order to contrast Harris's support for the policies of the South African government with his campaign against the Chartered Company in Rhodesia, which Plaatje considered to be completely misguided; not only because matters were so much worse in South Africa, but because Africans in Rhodesia, living under Chartered Company rule, in fact enjoyed rights and privileges denied to their compatriots living in the Union. In view of the subsequent rapprochement that took place between Plaatje and Harris in 1919 and 1920, however, Plaatje may well have decided to drop this idea–and this was possibly a reason for the delay in completing the manuscript (if indeed this was ever achieved).

The second piece of evidence which reveals something of Plaatje's intentions for this 'companion volume' is rather more substantial: a notebook containing some ten pages of handwritten notes and passages of what was almost certainly intended to be a section of this book. Although in very rough draft, these pages amount to a systematic account of the discriminatory laws then in operation in South Africa, broken down province by province. Plaatje's starting point here was the pamphlet he had written at the end of 1919, *Some of the Legal Disabilities Suffered by the Native Population of the Union of South Africa and Imperial Responsibility*, and in the notebook some of its pages, heavily annotated, have been pasted in where they could be used. One of his paragraphs on the Orange Free State was typical of what Plaatje wrote:

> In the Orange Free State a native is only tolerated when he works for a white man. Even if he works to the satisfaction of his white master he cannot even live in town. He cannot own freehold property and he cannot trade. Under exceptional circumstances some natives may mend boots or make bricks for themselves but for this special permission they are required to pay a special fee of 1/– per month which is not required of any white bootmakers. He cannot even run a School for native children without breaking the law, unless he is a servant in the employ of a White missionary.

After several pages in similar vein Plaatje then went on to pose himself the following questions:

> Where do these natives come from? That they should be subject to a law unheard of in the annals of the Empire of a man being by law denied the right to purchase landed property in this interesting Province?

And he proceeded to answer the question thus:

> Let's go to the beginning. In the year 1830 the Barolongs of Moroka had crossed over from Bechuanaland into a place called Platberg. It is just on the border of Griqualand West, Transvaal and Free State but it is in OFS property. The people had during the Matabele depredation met the Rev. Mr Broadbent, a Missionary sent by the Wesleyans among the Bechuana and after a few days at Platberg (at Motlana's pitse), as it was then called, decided that the place was unhealthy and many of the Barolongs were dying. So a movement was made to Basutoland and Chief Mosheshwe, the founder of the Basuto nation, gave the newcomers a refuge in his territory.[73]

There then follows a five-page account of the subsequent history of the Barolong: the attacks of the Matabele, the friendship between Chiefs Moroka and Mosheshwe, the arrival in 1834 of the Boer voortrekkers, their military alliances with the Barolong, the defeat of Mzilikazi, the subsequent proclamation of the Orange Free State.

It is precisely this series of historical events which provides the setting for the other manuscript Plaatje was working on at this time – the 'love story . . . based on historical facts', as he called it in his letter to Silas Molema, subsequently published, ten years hence, with the title *Mhudi: an epic of native life a hundred years ago*. Although a fuller examination of this must await a later chapter, it is well to note at this point the apparent connection between *Mhudi* and this intended 'companion volume' to *Native Life*. Both were written at the same time, and parts of each appear in draft form in the same notebook. And whilst it is not possible to establish exactly how each developed in relation to the other, it does seem reasonable to assume that the question Plaatje posed for himself – 'Where do the natives come from, that they should be subject to a law unheard of in the annals of the Empire of a man being by law denied the right to purchase landed property in this interesting Province?' – provided something of a starting point for him in *Mhudi* as well; the essential difference being that he chose here the form of a historical novel with which to explore his theme. More speculatively, perhaps it is possible that the success he felt he had achieved in this had something to do with the fact that the political book he was then writing has disappeared so completely. If it was completed no evidence has survived to suggest that Plaatje ever tried to get it published, in contrast to the constant efforts he was to make over the next few years on behalf of both *Mhudi* and his translations of the Fellowship Hymn Book. Perhaps Plaatje simply felt he had said what he wanted to far more effectively in *Mhudi*.

◇

While Plaatje was at work on these two books he was also much involved in the affairs of his Brotherhood movement. By September 1920 a South African Bantu Brotherhoods Committee had been formally established, with Sir Richard Winfrey as its chairman, Irma Colenso as secretary, and William Cross as treasurer. A welcome boost to the committee's funds and prospects was given by a successful benefit concert, given in London on 6 September by the still popular Southern Syncopated Orchestra at the instance of G. W. Lattimore, its manager, with whom Plaatje had evidently remained on good terms. Whether the proceeds were to go to help relieve the mounting debts of the Lyndhurst Road Native Institute back in Kimberley, or towards supporting Plaatje's own mission in England, is not clear. The journal *West Africa* carried a sympathetic report of the evening's proceedings:

> I am glad to hear that West Africa was strongly represented at the benefit concert given by the Southern Syncopated Orchestra on Monday evening at Kingsway Hall in aid of the South African Native Brotherhoods. Prince Oluwa of Lagos sat in the front row with his secretary (Mr Macaulay) and others. The programme, vocal and instrumental, was delivered with a sprightly rendering and a good swing. The singers, who were in excellent voice, had a great reception. During the interval Mr W. B. Dixon, of Leighton Buzzard, thanked the management on behalf of the Bantu Brotherhoods Committee. Mr Sol Plaatje, who seconded on behalf of the Native Brotherhood and Sisterhood, said no place stood in greater need of brotherhood ideas than his homeland, the Union of South Africa.[74]

'West Africa' was particularly well represented at the concert that evening because of the recent arrival in London of a delegation from the National Congress of British West Africa (of which both Chief Oluwa and Herbert Macaulay were members), there to demand a greater share in the government and administration of the several British colonies from West Africa which they represented.[75] Plaatje hoped they might be able to provide some further financial assistance, and he duly enlisted the support of Robert Broadhurst, president of the London-based African Progress Union, then lobbying on the delegation's behalf. Broadhurst accordingly wrote to Herbert Macaulay on Plaatje's behalf to solicit a donation, adding that 'if the Delegates would grant an interview to Mr Plaatje he would willingly give an exposé of the case and what opposition he has experienced both in South Africa and recently in London in advancing the Cause of Africans' – almost certainly a reference to Plaatje's difficulties in obtaining a passport. But their approach was not successful.[76] The London Committee of the NCBWA considered Plaatje's case at its meeting on 8 October, but felt unable to assist:

> The Secretary was authorised to inform Mr Broadhurst that this Committee has its duties prescribed by the West African Constituents and cannot interest itself in the contents of Mr Broadhurst's letter save that it regrets to learn of the financial difficulties of Mr Plaatge [sic] and is entirely in sympathy with the native disabilities in South Africa.[77]

Pan-African solidarity, as Plaatje discovered, had clearly defined limits when it came to matters of finance.

Somehow or other, probably with the help of the Colensos and Moltenos, Plaatje nevertheless succeeded in raising the money he needed to pay for his passage across the Atlantic.[78] For despite the passport difficulty he had encountered back in March and April, he had not abandoned the hope of making this trip (although he did not mention it in his letter to Silas Molema on 25 August 1920), and at the end of September he again applied for a passport. This time he went straight to the South African High Commission in London, only to be told once again by the High Commissioner, Sir Edgar Walton, that this could not be granted to him. If Plaatje's account of the interview (drawn from a CID report of a meeting he addressed three years later) is to be relied upon, it was a stormy affair in which Plaatje emphasised his intention of going to America anyway.[79] What he did not tell the High Commissioner was exactly how he intended going about this. For he had found that whilst it was impossible for him to enter the United States without a passport, the Canadian authorities did not insist upon such a document as a precondition of entry.[80] And once in Canada he hoped it would be rather easier to obtain the documents he needed to take him into the United States. He had been in contact with members of the Canadian Brotherhood Federation, and it had been agreed that he would, for a while at least, lecture and speak under their auspices.[81] They were useful, indeed essential, friends for Plaatje to have, and they had the additional advantage of providing a cloak of respectability to satisfy overinquisitive customs and immigration officials who may have had some doubts about what Plaatje really intended to do, or what else he intended to do, in North America.

Loaded up with several hundred copies of *Native Life in South Africa*, his *Sechuana Proverbs*, and his pamphlet on *Legal Disabilities*, all of which he hoped to be able to sell, and several unpublished manuscripts which he hoped to get published, Plaatje finally sailed from Liverpool, bound for Quebec, on 22 October 1920.[82]

What had he achieved during this second visit to the United Kingdom? Obviously, the stated objective of the Congress deputation – the reassertion of some form of imperial control over South Africa – had not been achieved: there was never any prospect that it would be. But it should not be concluded from this that the deputation's mission had been a failure. As no less a person than the British Prime Minister had acknowledged, Plaatje and his colleagues had succeeded in making a very considerable impression upon British public opinion; they had seen to it that the question of South Africa's policies towards the African population had been raised and discussed in the House of Commons; and they had deeply impressed the Prime Minister himself. That this could achieve so little for their cause was a reflection not upon the conduct of their campaign – for in the circumstances it was remarkably successful – but the underlying nature of the relations between Great Britain and South Africa.

Plaatje now prepared to take this campaign, singlehanded, to North America. Through the friends he had made and his connections in the Brotherhood movement he had raised the money he needed to get himself over to Canada, and had not been deterred by the opposition to his plans on the part of the South African authorities. If anything this seems to have acted as a spur, to have convinced him of the need to take his campaign to another continent, to inform yet more people of the iniquity of what was going on in his own country. At the same time he had just managed to complete a second political book and a historical novel, the first to have been written by any black South African. Given the lamentably poor resources at Plaatje's disposal it all amounted to a remarkable achievement, tribute to great persistence and force of character. It was as though he was driven on by a restless urge to set an example both to his own people and to those who denied them the right to live as decent, civilised beings.

11

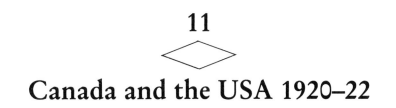

Canada and the USA 1920–22

Writing to Betty Molteno several weeks after he had arrived in Canada, Plaatje described the voyage as 'dark, wet, and foggy'. When he disembarked he was surprised to encounter a language problem:

> Landing at Quebec I was amazed to find that outside the Immigration Offices (where some of the officials speak very imperfect English) I could not get anyone to understand the plainest English question. The population, I am told, is 94% French. Young and old, I could almost always tell beforehand how everyone would answer me, viz: 'Nose-peak Ingless'.

It was not the only problem he encountered upon arrival, for there was an unfortunate misunderstanding over the arrangements made by the Canadian Brotherhood Federation:

> The Brotherhood telegraphed to a friend at Quebec from Montreal to meet me when the steamer arrives. When he reached the wharf I had already left, taken my baggage to the Rly station and was sightseeing in the city. Marvellous Roman Cathedrals and huge Presbyterian edifices in Canadian cities. Poor Mr and Mrs Henderson at Montreal were meeting the evening trains in which they had asked their Quebec friend to book me; but I did not leave Quebec till midnight and reached Montreal early next morning and put up at an hotel where some people speak English.[1]

Plaatje was nevertheless delighted with the warmth of the reception he encountered at the hands of the Canadian Brotherhood Federation, first of all in Montreal where he spent two weeks, and thereafter, until the end of January 1921, in the city of Toronto where the federation had its headquarters. He was fortunate to have arrived in Canada at a time when the Canadian Brotherhood movement had achieved, albeit for a short period, a position of some influence in the religious and social life of the country.[2] Founded in 1894, the Brotherhood movement in Canada drew its strength and support, as in England, from the nonconformist churches, and preached the same message of social concern and Christian involvement in the social, political, and industrial life of the country. The Canadians had provided one of the largest delegations to the International

Brotherhood Congress which Plaatje had attended in London in September 1919, and were well represented, too, in the second world congress (which Plaatje had hoped at one time to attend) held in Washington the following May. Their involvement in the World Brotherhood Federation was very encouraging as far as Plaatje was concerned, and during the two months he spent addressing church and Brotherhood meetings he succeeded – in a way that was by now familiar – in making a considerable impression. One observer had this to say of one of the gatherings he addressed after arriving in Toronto:

> I once heard him preach to a congregation of about 1,500 white Canadians. Except for occasional ripples of laughter (when he taps a vein of his irresistible humor even at the pulpit) he held them spellbound for 45 minutes, and at the close some said they could have stood another hour of his eloquence. His discourses are a revelation to people who had expected nothing but cannibals from Africa.[3]

Plaatje, too, was well pleased with the response of his hosts in Toronto:

> I have been in the City of Toronto at the Brotherhood Headquarters for over a month now. Have spoken and preached at several halls and preached to a number of Methodist and Baptist Congregations. Last Sunday I had in my audience Mr Justice Coatsworth of the Supreme Court. He and his family came to shake hands and congratulate me on my sermon. I went to dinner with his son.
>
> The Brotherhood promise that if I would continue to speak for them they would make an allowance next February to the World's Brotherhood Conference in London and that when disbursements are made they would strongly recommend my South African work to the World Committee for liberal treatment.[4]

Even more hopeful from Plaatje's point of view – bearing in mind his plans to take his campaign south to the large black populations of the cities of the United States – was the overwhelming warmth of the reception he was given by Toronto's own black community. One of the most influential local black figures, Arthur C. Holder, an official in the Toronto branch of Marcus Garvey's Universal Negro Improvement Association, has left a striking account of the impact Plaatje made during his stay in the city. 'It is true,' he acknowledged,

> that Toronto has had some distinguished Afro-American visitors like the late Booker T. Washington, Rev. C. T. Walker, Rev. A. Clayton Powell, the Hon. Marcus Garvey and other bright stars in the Negro firmament of science and art; but they came and went before many Torontonians had had a chance of meeting them intimately. Hon. Sol Plaatje has been with us now over eight weeks, and in that time he has revealed to us the true inwardness of African character and predilection. His humor, benevolence, good form and catchy conversation have earned for him a place in the hearts of many of us.

Again, it was Plaatje's oratorical abilities on the platform that left everybody impressed:

> But you need to hear him on the platform to understand that our western troubles are nothing compared with the sufferings of the lot of the persecuted South African Negroes. To hear Mr Plaatje on that subject – the subject of his great work – is to be convinced that the man is not out on his own but called by a higher power as well as by the votes of his people to be the Frederick Douglass of the oppressed South African slaves of today.

The personal qualities that Plaatje displayed were also highly appreciated by Toronto's black community. 'How did he grip our hearts?' asked Arthur Holder:

> When he gets a number of invitations to dinner on the same day, he takes the first one to hand and asks the others to take another occasion. He will not turn down a colored family for the sake of a grand time with a great white family at Hillcrest or Rosedale. If he is to give any preference it will rather be in favor of a poor black family in narrow apartments where he feels sure his presence is needed more; and he enjoys a conversation with the aged colored women and the kiddies, as thoroughly as the gay company of bright young ladies.
> Within a week after landing in the city he left the sumptuous hotel where he was placed by the Canadian Brotherhood, and asked Dr Thomas, the UNIA President, to find him apartments in a colored household. And whenever the whites needed him they sent their automobiles to fetch him there.[5]

Plaatje felt that the welcome extended to him in Toronto by both black and white communities held out great hope for the success of his long-hoped for visit to the United States. 'I have very pressing invitations,' he wrote after six weeks in Toronto, 'from Chicago, Pittsburgh, Detroit, and New York,' and he felt that 'the enthusiasm of the smaller Coloured Communities of Montreal and Toronto is an index of what one may expect below the line'.[6] He had, in addition, on one occasion spoken on the same platform in Toronto as Marcus Garvey, president of the UNIA, when he visited the city.[7] It seemed likely to be a connection of very great value in giving him access to the immense support which Garvey enjoyed amongst Afro-Americans in the great cities of the United States.

Plaatje's progress on his American tour was nevertheless threatened by two very different factors. One was his health. Although detailed evidence of Plaatje's condition is lacking, it is clear that the heart trouble he developed during the influenza epidemic in 1919 continued to be a great worry, and none of the doctors he had consulted in South Africa or England had been able to do anything to improve matters, or even, it seems, to make a satisfactory diagnosis. When he consulted a heart specialist in Canada the prognosis was even more pessimistic: 'Your heart leaks so badly,' he was told, 'that we cannot help you. All we could do is prescribe something to ease the pain, while matters take their course.' Five years later Plaatje commented that this 'seemingly brutal frankness was altogether superfluous, for I had already been convinced that the end was not far off.'[8] When Plaatje wrote these words he had made an apparently complete recovery, so it may be that this was something of an overstatement of the seriousness with which he viewed his condition at the time. But even allowing for this, the obviously precarious nature of Plaatje's health adds a new dimension to his determination to persevere with his tour. How far he told his wife of the seriousness of the situation will never be known: none of the letters he wrote home to her have survived.

The other consideration that threatened to upset Plaatje's plans for visiting the United States was the fact that he did not as yet possess the passport he needed to enable him to cross the border. Finding a solution to this problem was one of his major preoccupations after arriving in Toronto. There appeared to be two main possibilities: the first was that his friends in the Canadian Brotherhood Federation, some of them apparently men of considerable standing locally, would be able to pull a few strings with the Canadian authorities and persuade the department concerned to issue him with a Canadian passport, endorsed as necessary; while the second was that Dr W. E. B. Du Bois, whom Plaatje had already written to over the problem, would be able to exercise such influence as he possessed with the American government to the same effect. Du Bois did his best in this direction but to no avail. He wrote confidentially to the Assistant Secretary of Labour in the American administration, whom he evidently knew well, to see what could be done to enable Plaatje to enter the country, explaining that 'We American Negroes would very much like to see and talk with Mr Plaatje,' and reassuring him that Plaatje was 'in no sense dangerous or even radical'.[9] Anxious to reinforce such an impression, and keen to encourage Du Bois to further efforts on his behalf, Plaatje then wrote to Du Bois as follows:

> 405 Kent Buildings
> Toronto, Can.
> 19 December 1920

Dear Dr Du Bois,

Many thanks for yours of the 16th inst. I thought you did not appreciate in full the stringency of the immigration laws. That's where the S.A. authorities are sure they have the measure of me. From my one month's experience here I feel certain that my people will never regret my visit to the States if I could get there. Will the following help you?

I have with me translations of Shakespeare's 'Merchant of Venice' and 'Julius Caesar', and 'Comedy of Errors' which will be very readable to the South African Natives. Let us say you want to print them in the States and also an American edition of 'Sechuana Proverbs with English Translations' and *nobody in the U.S.A.* could see Native MSS through the press. Hearing that I am in Canada you wish me to come and see them through. Will that assist us somewhat through the mesh of regulations? After which I will return to Canada.

Trusting that your efforts will be successful.

I remain yours very sincerely,
Sol T. Plaatje

P.S. I am mailing some 'Native Life in South Africa' for which there have been some enquiries. They are two dollars now.[10]

Even with such a respectable pretext to justify Plaatje's entry into the United States – revealing in itself about the progress he had by now made in translating Shakespeare into Setswana – it is unlikely that Du Bois could have ever achieved the desired objective. Further pressure in this direction, indeed, was just as likely to lead to further contact between the American and the South African authorities, and if this happened there could be no doubt about the outcome. A few days before Christmas 1920, however, the efforts of Plaatje's Canadian Brotherhood Federation friends finally bore fruit, and he was issued with a full passport by the Canadian authorities. Plaatje duly informed Du Bois of the good news:

With reference to your yeoman efforts to get me to the U.S. I hasten to inform you that a second string to my bow has just responded.

The Canadians have succeeded in obtaining a passport for me to go to the United States. It now remains for you to 'cease fire' as they say in military signals, 'the enemy has surrendered'. If the efforts you are making at the White House are not relaxed they might fish out more information and just know enough to enable the enemy to stop me at the border for I won't be through with Canada until about the 25th January.[11]

The issue of this Canadian passport was quite an achievement, and a notable victory over the South African High Commission in London and the Native Affairs Department in Pretoria; fulfilment of his long-standing desire to travel to the United States now seemed in sight. This note of optimism was sustained by the success of Plaatje's last few weeks in Toronto. Apart from selling over 400 copies (at $2 a time) of *Native Life in South Africa*, Plaatje had secured a promise from the Canadian Brotherhood Federation of no less than $7,000 to cover the cost of publishing his African-language translations of the Fellowship Hymn Book; and from Toronto's black community he received an equally generous send-off at a rally-cum-concert to bid him farewell on 24 January 1921.[12] Held under the joint auspices of several local black churches and the Toronto branch of the Universal Negro Improvement Association, this 'vast assemblage gathered to do him honour', and was reported to have provided 'tangible evidence of the new spirit of race consciousness among colored Torontonians' and to have been an outstanding success. And whilst Toronto's black community, which numbered no more than several thousand people, could hardly have been expected to match the $7,000 promised by the Brotherhood Federation, they nevertheless launched an appeal to raise $1,500 to purchase a pipe organ for Plaatje to take home for his Brotherhood Hall in Kimberley: 'all this to a man', so the *Negro World* (organ of the UNIA) reported, 'who landed two months ago at Quebec, knowing nobody in Canada, without a friend and without even a passport, as this was refused him by the South African Government – truly a remarkable achievement'.[13]

Although neither gift ever in fact materialised, Plaatje never forgot the warmth of his reception in Toronto, and over the next few months he was to uphold it as an example for other communities to emulate. He addressed final meetings of the

UNIA and Brotherhoods on 31 January 1920, and crossed the border at the Niagara Falls the following day, having acquired a US entry visa at the American consulate in Toronto several days previously.[14] In view of the fears he had expressed earlier in his letter to Du Bois, Plaatje must have felt some nervousness at the prospect of the border crossing, but he went through without any difficulty. Had he delayed his stay in Canada very much longer it might have been a different matter, for just eleven days later the South African High Commission in London discovered – probably from the columns of the *Negro World* – that Plaatje had arrived in Canada and intended visiting the United States. It would have afforded Plaatje considerable amusement and satisfaction to have been able to read the agitated letter, marked 'urgent', that was dispatched from the South African High Commission to the Chief Passport Officer, London, on 12 February 1921, requesting information on how Plaatje might have got over to North America; and even more, to have seen the Chief Passport Officer's reply, explaining that Plaatje had not applied for a British passport, but that 'the government of Canada does not insist upon persons proceeding to Canada being in possession of passports'.[15] Of this fact the South African High Commissioner had hitherto been unaware. But for Plaatje, crossing the American border was a triumph to savour.

◇

Plaatje's first port of call in the United States was the city of Buffalo, in New York State, just over the border at Niagara. His reception there was all he could have wished for. Staying with Dr Kakaza, an African doctor from the eastern Cape who had qualified in the United States and was now practising in Buffalo, Plaatje had intended to address one meeting in the city, to spend several days relaxing and sightseeing, and then to move on to New York. So successful was his first meeting, though, that he was obliged to repeat it every evening he was there. 'My first American meeting,' he wrote afterwards, 'was crowded and it was painful to see for the first time in my life people turned away by the hundreds unable to hear me for lack of standing room. The Pastor told me he never saw his Church so crowded since 1906 when Booker T. Washington spoke there.'[16] That comparison Plaatje would have appreciated, and it must have raised his spirits a great deal for the prospects of his American trip.

Plaatje arrived in New York at a time of great ferment in the life of its black community. Concentrated above all in the overcrowded district of Harlem, New York's black population had grown rapidly during the war years, partly in response to deteriorating economic conditions in the agricultural south, partly, as in South Africa, to meet the new demand for mostly unskilled labour that wartime economic and military activity had generated. Many new black immigrants were drawn in, too, from Central America and the Caribbean islands. Amongst the arrivals from the British West Indies was one individual who had made a particular impact – Marcus Garvey, the charismatic president and driving force of the Universal Negro Improvement Association. Arriving in New York from Jamaica in 1916 Garvey proclaimed the 'redemption of Africa', he possessed a vision of achieving unity amongst black people everywhere in the world, and he promised to restore a pride in being black for people who had little else. With his great gifts as an orator and organiser, Garvey succeeded in building up, in a remarkably short space of time, the largest mass movement amongst Afro-American communities before or since. Linked to one another by its newspaper, the *Negro World*, the UNIA established branches in every part of the world where black people lived, and the new spirit of pride and hope it created caused ripples of concern from the White House to Downing Street. When Lloyd George pointed to the dangers of Garveyism in his letter to General Smuts after seeing Plaatje's deputation in London he was expressing a concern widely felt in ruling circles about the potential threat that the movement posed to 'the existing structure of society', more particularly the British empire, in the troubled post-war years.[17]

New York provided Garvey with a massive base of support, and it was here that he made perhaps his greatest impact. As unemployment, harsh economic conditions and a profound disillusionment replaced the cautious progress and optimism of the war years, Garvey's message of hope and solidarity was adopted enthusiastically by tens of thousands of blacks living in the city. The most visible symbols of this new resurgence were the headquarters of the UNIA in Harlem, an impressive building known as 'Liberty Hall'; and the *Yarmouth*, a steamship which Garvey had purchased in 1919 to provide the means – physical as well as symbolic – of linking Afro-Americans in different parts of the world. Throughout 1920 support for Garvey's movement had grown apace, its success marked by a massive convention, attended by delegates from all over the world, held in Liberty Hall at the beginning of August 1920, which drafted an ambitious 'Declaration of the Rights of the Negro Peoples of the World'. For many, the UNIA seemed the answer to the hopes and prayers of generations of oppressed and downtrodden blacks.

Whatever reservations Plaatje may have had about Garvey's populist style, or the extravagant, bombastic tone of his oratory, the success of his movement and its influence in the life of New York's black community was undeniable. Plaatje would have had some reason, moreover, to believe it might be turned to his advantage. Central to Garvey's message was his emphasis upon the unity of black peoples, and a fervent interest in Africa – the conditions in which African people lived, and a fascination with the achievements of their past. On both these things Plaatje hoped to capitalise in order to arouse support and sympathy for the people he represented, and to raise money for his Brotherhood work in South Africa.

Plaatje was fortunate, too, to have the friendship of John E. Bruce, his old journalist friend, who, unlike Dr W. E. B. Du Bois, had recognised in Garvey and his movement a positive force for the progress of America's black community, and had – along with a number of other black American intellectuals of the older generation – supported his campaign; Bruce, indeed, became one of the editors of the *Negro World*. Bruce and Plaatje had corresponded and exchanged newspapers over the years, and Plaatje had written to him from both England and Canada to keep him informed of the progress of his plans for his American visit – news of which had then appeared in the columns of the *Negro World*. Bruce was, in short, a most valuable contact for Plaatje to have had in New York in giving him access to UNIA platforms and providing introductions, and the two men seem to have got on very well from the moment they first met. Bruce was pleased to hear from Plaatje, amongst other things, that a review he had written of *Native Life in South Africa* in an American newspaper several years earlier had produced a number of orders for the book, and that dozens of other people had referred to it when purchasing copies of *Native Life* at public meetings Plaatje had addressed subsequently. A few months hence Bruce was writing that 'this Plaatje man from Kimberley . . . has gotten closer to me than any African I have ever known personally', with the exception only of his 'late, lamented friend, Edward Wilmot Blyden', the famous West African writer.[18]

Bruce was able to help Plaatje in one other respect as well. Shortly after Plaatje arrived in New York Bruce gave him the address of a German-American doctor, George Sauer, who successfully treated his heart condition where all others had failed. After treatment from Sauer, Plaatje later wrote, 'I never felt the pains in the heart that were such a handicap in my work and made life almost intolerable.'[19]

Plaatje arrived in New York without any fixed plans as to the length of his stay, intending that this should be determined by the nature of the response and support he found.[20] In the event he remained for three months, until the beginning of May 1921, hoping – as he wrote to Mrs Colenso a couple of weeks after arrival – 'to turn my wild goose chase into a financial success'.[21] By the end of these three months it had become evident that he was not going to achieve the degree of 'financial success' he had once hoped for – perhaps he even half-expected this from the start – but he did succeed in making a very considerable impact on black opinion. Throughout February and March the *Negro World* carried reports of the many meetings Plaatje addressed in the city, most of them in churches (usually belonging to the African Methodist Episcopal Church) and private residences. Two of his meetings – he spoke on the 'Black Man's Burden in South Africa' and 'The Black Women's Burden in South Africa' – were at the Bethel AMEC church in West 132nd Street, the very place where, three years earlier, Garvey's own inspired address had effectively launched the UNIA in America. 'Come and hear Mr Sol Plaatje, of Kimberley, South Africa,' urged the bill posters advertising these meetings; 'Gives a thrilling account of the conditions of the Colored Folk in British South Africa. A Touching Message well and luridly told. The story has gripped nearly a thousand audiences in England, Scotland, Canada and the USA. It will thrill you.'[22] Other addresses Plaatje gave were enthusiastically reported. Three weeks before the two Bethel AMEC meetings, Plaatje addressed the Brooklyn branch of the UNIA – attended, according to the *Negro World*, 'by a large audience . . . the isles and hallway were packed to capacity [and] our distinguished visitor held the audience spellbound'.[23]

By far the largest audiences Plaatje attracted, in New York or elsewhere, were the packed meetings (six altogether) he addressed at Liberty Hall, which seated over 6,000 people; many thousands more were able to read the verbatim reports of his speeches in the columns of the *Negro World*. On the first occasion, the day after he arrived in New York, Plaatje and Garvey spoke together on the same platform. The *Negro World*, interpreting Plaatje's account of conditions in South Africa in its own idiom, was full of enthusiasm:

To hear this native of our motherland tell, in splendid English, with rounded periods, and in a coherent, logical, and delightful manner, of the needs of the South African people, and of the greatness of the African Continent, is worth anybody's while. It is instructive as well as entertaining, and no one can hear his message without becoming imbued with a desire as ardent and as enthusiastic and as great as even Garvey himself, in the cause of the redemption of this wonderful homeland of ours and as the only hope we, as a people, have for our salvation and that of posterity.[24]

Plaatje was careful to present what he had to say in terms he knew would appeal to his audience – flattery for 'His Excellency' Marcus Garvey, enthusiasm for 'the new spirit of race consciousness which is gripping the Negro throughout the country' – and he urged his audience, at considerable length, to emulate the example of the white man, when it came to supporting causes in which they believed, and in maintaining unity amongst themselves; unless this could be achieved, Plaatje argued, 'the redemption of Africa will be delayed until we can be a little more trustful and a little more loyal to one another'. At the end of his speech, as on other occasions, he drew attention to the copies of *Native Life in South Africa* and several other pamphlets which he had for sale, the proceeds of which he was using to help finance his campaign.

A week later Plaatje had the opportunity to make a further address at Liberty Hall, again sharing a platform with Marcus Garvey, and he returned for a third time over Easter, at the end of March. On this last occasion, Plaatje spoke once more of the need for solidarity amongst black people everywhere; he told of his own work in South Africa in furthering the work of his Brotherhood movement; and he appealed for financial aid to support it. As was appropriate for the occasion, he was at pains to present his work in this direction as almost an extension of the UNIA in South Africa, preparing the ground, as it were, for the ultimate 'redemption of Africa':

A little while back I found it was impossible to organize the natives in South Africa, unless you can get them to forget the past, to remember that there should be no distinction between any of the tribes; that they should forget their tribal differences, forget that there is a Basuto or a Zulu, and combine and unite their resources, and they should unite and organize. But you cannot organize a people unless you have got places like this [Liberty Hall] where you can gather them together and tell them the facts. It is the organising of these places that I am after. It has pleased God to reward my efforts to such an extent, in this direction, that at Kimberley I had already got a sort of a Liberty Hall, where they gather together every Sunday afternoon. I got information from them while I am here, and they are fascinated by this gospel of the brotherhood of the natives, so that a Negro in one town is recognised as a brother in the other towns. But they have no facilities; they have no meeting places, and it is my endeavor to raise funds during my present trip, to raise money to enable me to get back and start another hall, the same as at Kimberley, at Bloemfontein, and erect building after building, first in one town and then in another.[25]

And Afro-Americans should support such schemes, Plaatje argued, since they could afford to do so whilst his own people, because of the low wages and lack of opportunities for them to earn money, could not; so that – as Plaatje concluded in a Garveyite flourish – 'when the time comes, and you . . . feel you have to make a rush for a jumping off place, you will know that there are people on either side calling you'.

As was very clear on other occasions, it was one of the advantages of Plaatje's Brotherhood work that it could be presented in so many different forms, depending on whether the audience he was addressing was black or white, South African or American, religious or secular. The directors of De Beers, for example, had been given a very different version by Plaatje of what his Brotherhood work was about, and they would no doubt have been horrified to hear him describe the hall they had given to him in 1918 as 'a sort of a Liberty Hall'. Plaatje's English friends, too, though they must have had some awareness of the constraints under which he operated, and the guises he had to adopt, would doubtless have been somewhat perturbed by Plaatje's language as well, and it is significant that his contact with the UNIA formed no part of the account of his visit to the USA which he afterwards wrote for them. But whatever concessions Plaatje made to Garveyite rhetoric it seems that the financial support he received from the UNIA audiences fell far short of his expectations.[26] Whilst the success of Garvey's movement had created a great interest in Africa from which Plaatje undoubtedly benefited when it came to attracting people along to his meetings, when it came to giving money the fact remained that he was not representing a South African branch of the UNIA, and that it was to the UNIA that those who came to the meetings gave such financial support as they could afford. Since so many of those attracted to the UNIA were very poor, there was generally precious little left over for any other cause.

Probably there were other factors that lay behind Plaatje's disappointment on this account. One of them he alluded to at the beginning of his Easter address at Liberty Hall when he referred to 'certain dubious remarks which were current in respect to his African nativity'. The reason for this, he explained, 'is because you have read from your childhood literature concerning South Africa and you are told about swarms of cannibals and gorillas that infest the African forests'.[27] In New York, in other words, Plaatje had come up against those same barriers to comprehension that he had so often found in England; so conditioned were American blacks to an exotic image of Africa – which Garvey had in some respects only encouraged – that they doubted the identity of anybody who failed to correspond to the stereotype. It was an irony that Plaatje might have appreciated himself had it not been for the serious consequences such ideas were likely to have in his efforts to raise money.

<><

When he arrived in New York Plaatje had set up a small 'South African Bantu Brotherhood Mission' committee, enlisting the support of Ellen Wood, who had once worked as a nurse in Kimberley, and was the sister of Mrs Fawcus in whose house (in 135th Street, Harlem) he was staying.[28] Its purpose was to regularise the collection of funds and to provide an American headquarters for this organisation when he himself was outside New York. Plaatje's idea was that all funds collected in the interests of his Brotherhood organisation should be sent here, whilst he sought to support himself and – as far as he was able – his family in South Africa, from the proceeds of the sale of his books and pamphlets. Here it seems he did achieve at least a measure of success. The most substantial book Plaatje had on offer was of course *Native Life in South Africa*, now selling at $2 a time. How many copies Plaatje succeeded in selling is unknown – a considerable number he gave away in return for hospitality – but it was favourably received in the Afro-American press, and it made a great impact upon at least some of Plaatje's friends in the black American community. John E. Bruce, for example, wrote that 'if it doesn't make your blood boil, you are not of African descent'; Booker T. Washington's widow read it 'with a great deal of interest'; while John W. Cromwell, writing to Bruce shortly before Plaatje arrived in the United States, had this to say:

> I told you I would not review 'Native Life in South Africa' by S. T. Plaatje, but I have been looking through it and reading much of it, to such an extent that it and the message of the messenger have impressed me to no little degree. It is a very sad story indeed which is told in this wonderful book by this very talented man, who comes here at a most auspicious moment to let the American people know of the conditions under which the Natives are now laboring in South Africa. I had not the slightest idea that such harrowing details could be told . . . Plaatje will render a great service in his lectures throughout the U.S. as he has done in this wonderful book that displays such genius as well as literary brilliance. I thought I knew something of South Africa heretofore, but this book reveals the depth of my ignorance.[29]

Later in the year, Plaatje arranged with W. E. B. Du Bois for his journal, *The Crisis*, to bring out an American edition of *Native Life in South Africa* (the price now increased to $2.50), an indication at least that the copies of the book Plaatje had brought over from England had been sold out.[30]

Also being sold by Plaatje were copies of his *Sechuana Proverbs* (good value at $1 each), and four pamphlets: an American edition of *Legal Disabilities*; two new pamphlets entitled *The Awful Price of Native Labour* and *Repressive Land Laws of British South Africa*, of which no copies appear to have survived; and a fourth, entitled *The Mote and the Beam: an epic on sex relationships 'twixt white and black in British South Africa*, all four pamphlets advertised as being available from Plaatje's New York address, from J. E. Bruce (who lived further along West 131st Street), and from Young's Book Exchange ('The Mecca of Literature pertaining to Colored People'), also in Harlem.

The Mote and the Beam, selling at 25 cents a copy, was undoubtedly the most successful of the pamphlets in terms of raising money, for by the time Plaatje left the United States in 1922 he claimed to have sold over 18,000 copies.[31] A twelve-page discourse on the hypocrisy of white South African attitudes towards the question of sex across the colour bar, its purpose, as Plaatje explained to potential buyers at one of his meetings, was to expose the fallacy of the white man's claim 'that the Negro is such a low down scoundrel that he cannot trust him with his wife behind his back'.[32] In many ways it is a curious little pamphlet, and unlike anything else Plaatje wrote. A large part of it is devoted to refuting a letter sent by a South African woman to the English press when Plaatje was in England in 1920, and this may well have been when he actually wrote it – possibly as a chapter, or part of a chapter, for the political book he was at that time working on. Whether this was the case or not, *The Mote and the Beam* certainly struck a sensitive chord, judging from its sales, amongst the black American public.

The only sour note was struck by Hubert H. Harrison, contributing editor to the *Negro World*, who reviewed *The Mote and the Beam* in April 1921, his complaint being directed not against its content ('On the whole *The Mote and the Beam* is a nifty little pamphlet'), but the fact that he thought 25 cents for eleven pages was rather too expensive, and 'not a regular business proposition'.[33] Harrison's comments were of no great significance in themselves, and they cannot have had too drastic an effect upon sales, but they did produce a response from Plaatje – published in the form of a letter in the *Negro World* three weeks later – which throws some interesting light both upon the progress of his campaign, and how he perceived its underlying purpose. What Plaatje objected to was Harrison's description of *The Mote and the Beam* as 'a business proposition', and he expressed his concern that Harrison and other prominent black American leaders had 'failed to grasp the inwardness of my mission here'. He went on:

> Let me say again, Sir, that I am not here on business. I have travelled 9,000 miles purely in aid of the most oppressed Negroes of the world. I would gladly have stayed at home and earned $15 per week, like H. H. H., although I would have had to work all the week and a good deal harder for it; but the natives I represent are so oppressed they could not, even if they would, pay $15 or any other sum – worked they ever so hard. But, if anywhere, at one time, somebody had not left home, hearthstones and travelled to the Southern slave plantations in the face of the bitterest hostility on the part of the slave owners; or if, a hundred years ago, someone had not travelled to the South African wilds and made incredible sacrifices on our behalf, neither H.H.H. or I would be able to write. Somebody did it for us, so why not I for the black millions who lie so helplessly at the mercy of the South African Boers?
>
> If we were any other race but Negroes, the heavens would long since have resounded with a diaposan of war from our deliverance; but, because we are Negroes, clever penmen of our complexion stigmatize the efforts on our behalf as 'a business proposition'.[34]

Behind the rhetoric one can detect a growing frustration on Plaatje's part as he gradually abandoned his hopes – exaggerated as they might have been – that a massive response to his appeals from the black American public would enable him to return in triumph to South Africa with funds to finance the expansion of his Brotherhood movement across the country. It had failed to materialise, and Plaatje was naturally upset when influential men like Hubert Harrison cast aspersions – intentional or not – upon the nature and purpose of his visit. At the same time there is a hint in Plaatje's letter, not simply a matter of rhetoric, of that profound sense of individual mission which was so central a part of his make-up, and which sustained him – along with his humour and fortitude – through the difficulties he constantly faced in his campaigns and travels.

◇

By the time Plaatje's letter was published in the *Negro World* he had left New York to continue his campaign in Boston, Massachusetts, remaining in the city for most of May 1921. Whilst there, he attended, amongst other things, a public meeting to celebrate the banning by the city authorities of the *Birth of a Nation*, the notorious film of the reconstruction period which he had first seen in London, and the focus of strong opposition from black communities since it was first released in 1915.[35] Thereafter he made his way to Atlantic City, New Jersey, and it was from here that he wrote on 22 June to Dr Du Bois accepting an invitation to attend the annual meeting of the National Association for the Advancement of Colored People.[36]

The two men – Plaatje and Du Bois – had met for the first time several months earlier when Plaatje arrived in New York, and it must have been clear from the outset that the erudite, scholarly doctor was much more to Plaatje's liking than the flamboyant figure of Marcus Garvey; Du Bois's style of leadership was, moreover, far closer to the kind of approach Plaatje himself preferred to use, and they evidently got on well. Besides inviting him to attend the annual meeting of the NAACP, Du Bois had also agreed to publish a new edition of *Native Life in South Africa*, and invited Plaatje to attend the next Pan-African Congress which he was planning to hold in Europe in July and August that year. Having missed the first congress in 1919, Plaatje was keen to attend as South African representative, but as ever there was the usual financial obstacle. Du Bois in fact wrote to S. M. Makgatho, president of the SANNC, in April, to 'impress upon [him] the necessity of having South Africa represented at the Conference'; and to try to persuade him to provide Plaatje with the £100 or so that would enable him to travel to Europe. Plaatje had told him, Du Bois added, 'that as he was rather hard hit financially by the last two deputations to England he was unable to undertake any further expense on behalf of the native congress'; but that if Congress could finance Plaatje's journey and attendance, 'it would be much cheaper than sending somebody else out especially from South Africa'.[37] Du Bois seems never to have had a reply to his letter.

A couple of months later – resigned to being unable to travel to Europe himself – Plaatje conceived the idea of asking Walter White, a colleague of Du Bois's in the NAACP who was intending to travel to the conference, to read out an address on his behalf. 'Wait till you get to Paris,' Plaatje advised White, 'then stage an auspicious occasion when the best reporters are present to send it all over the world. The secret of the success of British policy in South Africa has been the suppression of the truth.' White agreed to undertake the task and to give Plaatje's speech 'as wide publicity as possible'.[38]

Plaatje's speech to the NAACP conference in Detroit, in the meantime, was very well received. He was brought on as a last-minute replacement for President King, of Liberia, who failed to arrive, and made a great impression upon the assembled delegates with his account of conditions in South Africa. One of Bruce's friends who was there wrote afterwards that he 'covered himself with glory' with a speech 'which was marvellously phrased, powerful in argument, convincing in thought, eloquent in delivery and satisfying in effect'.[39] Bruce was not at all surprised to hear about it: Plaatje had this extraordinary ability to impress any gathering he addressed, every individual he met.

Plaatje was probably still in Detroit when he received tragic news from home: the death of his daughter Olive in the middle of July 1921. Having contracted rheumatic fever during the influenza epidemic in 1918 she had – despite the incident at Aliwal North – recovered her health sufficiently to attend the Indaleni Training Institution in Natal to train as a nurse. Once there, however, her precarious health worsened, and it was decided that she should return home. According to her travelling companions she was well enough to begin the journey, but when waiting in Bloemfontein for the train connection to Kimberley her condition deteriorated rapidly. During the three hours' wait for the train she was prohibited from entering the 'whites only' waiting-room, and not allowed to lie down on one of the seats on the platform, also reserved for whites. Whilst still waiting for the train to arrive she died.[40] Whether she would have done so if she had not been made to suffer from so heartless an application of South Africa's laws of segregation can never be known; quite probably, if her condition had been that serious, she would. But for Plaatje, 9,000 miles away in the United States and without the means to return home, the news of the circumstances of her death added a bitter twist to what would in any case have been a profoundly sad event for him. Olive occupied a treasured place in his thoughts and affections, and the news of the circumstances of her death – coming on top of the incident at Aliwal North, which had perhaps contributed indirectly to it as well – remained a source of bitterness with Plaatje for the rest of his life. 'The South African way of life' which Plaatje had devoted his life to fighting, had never intruded upon his private, family life in so tragic a manner. In Plaatje's life, the political battles he fought were very personal affairs.

Olive was buried at Bloemfontein several days later. Her more enduring memorial, however, was to be *Mhudi*, her father's as yet unpublished novel, dedicated to 'the memory of our beloved Olive, one of many youthful victims of a settled system, and in pleasant recollection of her life work, accomplished at the age of 13, during the influenza epidemic'. Few people who picked up the novel and read its dedication can have had any idea of the depth of meaning that Plaatje invested in the phrase 'a settled system'.

Had Plaatje possessed the means to return home after receiving news of his daughter's death he would probably have done so: certainly it inspired his friends in Thaba Nchu to make another effort to raise funds for him, although not, it seems, with very much success.[41] Plaatje had been away by this time for over two years, and as ever felt his absence from his family very keenly. He stayed on, though, to continue his campaign in the United States and, thanks to Dr Du Bois, was able to make his voice heard at the Pan-African Congress in Europe as well. Du Bois himself had decided to read out Plaatje's typewritten address at the Paris session of the Pan-African Congress, announcing only (thus it was reported in the press) that it came from a 'South African Native

Propagandist now touring the States, but deciding to remain anonymous for the present'.[42] It was one of the most impressive speeches Plaatje had written: a fluent, powerful account of the discrimination and oppression suffered by his people in South Africa, fiercely critical of the pass laws, above all the Natives' Land Act–'by far the most outrageous of the monstrous crimes that characterised the South African Parliament's crusade against law-abiding natives'. In the second half of his speech, anticipating what he imagined was likely to be a major theme at the congress, Plaatje went on to consider who he believed to be responsible for the oppression of his people: not the capitalists, he said, but a government that legislated 'at the behest of a relentless white league of lawyers, overseers, mechanics, and what not, who style themselves "The Labour Party of South Africa" '. It was a significant change of emphasis: at one time Plaatje regarded the Boers as the arch-villains of the South African stage; now they were joined by the white working class and their allies. But his solution to the problem was the familiar one, from which he never departed: 'the extension of a reasonable franchise to all taxpayers irrespective of colour'. He concluded his address with an appeal to the delegates to do all in their power to ensure that South Africa was not given a League of Nations mandate to rule over German South West Africa.[43]

Plaatje's address did not go unnoticed in South Africa itself. The *Cape Times* carried a long report on the conference, confused Du Bois's reading of Plaatje's address with his own 'Manifesto to the World', discussed on the same day, but nevertheless considered both to represent 'a rampant propagandism emanating from the least representative quarters and directed unmistakenly against European governments'; and the *Christian Express*, picking up the *Cape Times* report, made similar disapproving noises, condemning the manifesto of 'The South African Native propagandist now touring the United States who desired to remain anonymous' as having 'dealt in agitator's stock phrases, catch words, and generalities, and sweeping denunciations, ignoring the progress being made in South African Native Affairs'.[44]

◇

At the time Plaatje's address was being read on his behalf in London, Plaatje himself was preparing to move on to Chicago. Another of the cities with large black populations from which he had received a 'pressing invitation', Plaatje was entertained after his arrival here by prominent members of the local black community, staying with Dr Mary Waring whom, so the *Chicago Defender* reported, he had previously met in England.[45] An elaborate musical occasion was put on at the 'Grace Lyceum' to accompany Plaatje's talk on South Africa, he was the guest of honour at a theatre party to see the popular black actor, Charles Gilpin, in Eugene O'Neill's *Emperor Jones*, and he was given the hospitality of the columns of the (anti-Garveyite) *Chicago Defender*, the largest-circulation black newspaper in the United States. Under the headline 'South Africa in grip of British Jim Crow rule: editor tells how British kill Natives' (hardly a headline Plaatje would have chosen himself), he again took the opportunity to tell of conditions in his own country and to appeal for funds to support his Brotherhood work. Describing the violence that had occurred in a strike in Port Elizabeth late in 1920, Plaatje presented what he was trying to do as the only effective antidote:

> Fortunately, there are better and safer means of overcoming such legislative enactments and administrative tyranny. We are doing it by the native brotherhood, whose forte is the power of combined action. We do it through community service and social work and night school for adults. I started this work at Kimberley in 1918, and it has already proved such a blessing that other centers are calling me to help them to do likewise. It is for the extension of this work I am appealing for financial assistance to build halls not in Kimberley, where it is in full swing already, but at Bloemfontein, Pretoria, etc; and anyone in sympathy with a downtrodden people striving for the fuller life cannot do better than communicate with Attorney J. A. Scott, 3710 Prairie Avenue, or R. L. Simmons, 3524 Michigan Avenue.[46]

On leaving Chicago Plaatje travelled to Washington DC to take advantage of a long-standing invitation from John W. Cromwell – with whom he had been in regular correspondence – and to attend (and address) a 'Conference of Fundamentals' organised by the so-called Committee of Seven, representing seven of the major black American organisations. The aim of the conference was to publicise the grievances of black people, in the United States and elsewhere, by presenting the International Armaments Conference, in session in Washington at the same time, with 'a petition which sets forth the economic, political, civil, and educational disabilities of the coloured people in the country and the conditions of the coloured people in foreign lands'. Its promoters claimed that it was a 'Race meeting' which 'would go down in history as one of the most far-reaching towards inspiring race pride, race loyalty, and race confidence in the accomplishment of political, economical, educational, and civic justice ever held'.[47] Exaggerated claims, certainly; for Plaatje it was simply another opportunity to add to the hundreds of meetings he had by now addressed in the United States, and he was delighted by the reception he received in Washington. He wrote to Cromwell afterwards:

> Boston Young Men's Christian Association
> 316 Huntingdon Avenue
> Boston 17, Mass.
> 28 XI 1921

Dear Mr Cromwell,

Just a line to let you know how deeply thankful I am to you for the nice introductions you gave my mission to Washington and the good people of the capital.

I am deeply indebted to you. I had a splendid run thru' Philadelphia and N.Y. and am preparing to get back to Washington Sunday after next.

I shall take the liberty when I reach N.Y. to send ahead my bale of books if you can find a place in a corner of your basement somewhere. I shall address them to you and send them per American express.

I am keeping well and have much to be thankful for. Kindest regards to Mrs Cromwell and yourself.
Ever Yours,
Sol T. Plaatje[48]

Whilst in Boston on this short return visit Plaatje participated in an 'African Pageant', held in the city's Symphony Theatre. He particularly remembered the extremely severe weather at that time: there had been a heavy fall of snow, followed by a blizzard, which had derailed some trains and brought down telephone lines, and when he walked to the theatre on the evening of the performance, in a light drizzle, he found on his arrival that he could not close his umbrella because the raindrops had frozen it up. In view of the cold he was all the more surprised to find the theatre, which could hold 3,000 people, was already completely full.[49]

Plaatje was soon back in Washington as he promised, and addressing more meetings. Their tenor generally differed sharply from the Garveyite gatherings he had addressed in the UNIA's stronghold, New York, for Washington's reputation in the Afro-American world was that of an older established, more prosperous community; it was one of the homes, indeed, of the black middle class, many of whose members were products of the pre-eminent black university, Howard University, in Washington. John W. Cromwell, a former newspaper editor, lawyer and teacher, now in his mid-70s, was very much a leading figure in these circles, and it was at his invitation that Plaatje attended, during this second visit to Washington, the 25th annual meeting of the Negro Society for Historical Research, held at Howard during the holiday between Christmas 1921 and New Year 1922; the journal this organisation published, so Plaatje thought, was 'one of the best quarterly magazines in existence'.[50]

Over the next couple of months Plaatje moved on to Baltimore and then Philadelphia.[51] Here he stayed with the Rt Rev. J. A. Johnson, head of the AME Church, and was presented with a piece of apparatus that was later to play quite a large part in his life: a portable movie projector, worth $420, suitable for showing 35mm educational films.[52] By March 1922 he was back in New York again, this time with a new address – 243 West 128th Street – but now confined to bed for six weeks with neuritis and rheumatism. By the end of the month he was well enough to write an informative letter to Mrs Colenso at Elangeni to tell her of his progress:

I must apologise for my long silence. It is all due to sickness and overwork.
I have not had much success financially but have almost recovered my health at the hands of a very good German-American doctor. It is such a pity that I couldn't stop with him a long time. I had always to go away to earn money to pay board, lodging and travelling expenses, which are very high in this country. Had I the chance to remain in New York under his treatment for three months at a stretch, I could by now have been a new man physically; but circumstances are always beyond our control.[53]

In the same letter Plaatje went on to describe some of his impressions of what he had seen and learnt in the United States. During the latter part of his sojourn it is clear that his determination to take in as much information as possible, which he could usefully apply when he returned to South Africa, had become his primary concern. The desire to 'broaden my outlook', as he had told Du Bois in his letter to him back in 1919, was one of his objectives from the beginning, but after perhaps a year or so in the United States, as it became evident that his hopes of financial salvation for his Brotherhood organisation were not going to be realised, this objective began to assume a greater importance. As long as he was in a position to support himself, the pursuit of this end could provide a lasting benefit (and justification) for his long absence overseas. 'Besides my health,' he told Mrs Colenso, 'the trip has been of very great educational value and I have stored up an immense amount of knowledge; which ought to be very beneficial to my work at home in South Africa.' Certainly Plaatje's general impressions of what he had seen of black life in the United States – the comparison with South Africa always uppermost in his mind – were enthusiastic:

> It is dazzling to see the extent of freedom, industrial advantage, and costly educational facilities, provided for Negroes in this country by the Union government, the government of the several states, by the municipalities and by the wealthy philanthropists. Those who die and those who remain alive continually pour their millions of money towards the cause of Negro education; and it is touching to see the grasping manner in which Negroes reach out to take advantage of the several educational facilities. And oh, the women! They are progressive educationally, socially, politically, as well as in church work, they lead the men.
>
> It is very inspiring to get into their midst, but it is also distressing at times and I can hardly suppress a tear when I think of the wretched backwardness between them and our part of the empire, as compared with other parts. I cannot understand why South Africa should be so God-forsaken, as far as her political and industrial morality is concerned. No wonder they are always flying at each other's throats; and what a terrible amount of blood they shed during this month. It seems to me that the Whites in South Africa are yearly becoming more savage than the Natives.[54]

◇

If the great disappointment of Plaatje's trip to the United States was his failure to raise funds in support of his Brotherhood work, another regret was to have been unable to find a publisher for his novel *Mhudi*. Since arriving in the United States Plaatje had approached Macmillan, Harper Bros., Scribners, and Harcourt, all well known American publishing houses, but all had declined it.[55] This must have been particularly disappointing as in many ways it seemed quite an auspicious time for an African writer seeking to publish his work. René Maran's *Batouala*, for example, a novel written by a native of Martinique (an island in the Caribbean) and set in French colonial Africa where he had spent much of his life, was published in French in 1921, and had been something of a literary sensation, winning the much sought after *Prix Goncourt*; an English edition was published by the American publisher Thomas Selzer in 1922.

Batouala was not an isolated example of Afro-American literary activity, and in America there were the stirrings of an intellectual renaissance, centred in Harlem, amongst America's black community – in literature, poetry, music, and art.[56] Many of the leading figures associated with this Harlem Renaissance, as it was called, Plaatje had met and come to know well during the time he had been in the USA; with several – Dr Du Bois, the novelist Jessie Fausset, the poet James Weldon Johnson – he had corresponded. Probably he had discussed with them his own novel, and his hopes for its publication, seeking to take advantage of the fact that 'Negro Literature' was now both fashionable and being published. But he failed in his search for a publisher. Exactly what reasons he was given are unknown, and the archives of the publishing houses Plaatje mentioned provide no clues; it may well be that it was simply not considered 'exotic' enough. At the beginning of February 1922, having despaired of placing the book with one of the established publishing houses, Plaatje approached one Walter Neale, of the Neale Publishing Company, who wrote back with a glowing report upon his manuscript, a sales estimate of 20,000 copies, and the proposal that Plaatje should pay him $1,500 to handle it. Encouraged at last by a positive response, but highly suspicious of Neale's exaggerated sales forecast, Plaatje wrote to Du Bois for advice:

> Bearing in mind what you told me that there were publishers and publishers, do you think that Mr Neale's eulogy of this MS and his rosy forecast of the probable sales are worth the paper they are printed upon? '$5 for a novel' seems to me a clever dodge on his part to get $1,500 out of me. Supposing his extravagant expectations are realised, 25% royalty seems very small after I paid the initial printing cost plus the labour, anxieties and expense of authorship.
> My reason for asking your advice in the matter is that if there is anything in his glowing forecast I could try and borrow the $1,500.
> Do you think his appreciations are genuine?[57]

Du Bois' reply, which can have come as no great surprise, was that he thought Neale's claim was 'an out and out lie'; that there 'isn't one chance in a hundred thousand of a book like yours reaching a sale of 20,000'; and that if Plaatje was going to spend $1,500 he could use it to print and bind the book himself 'and not pay Neale a cent'.[58] It was sensible advice, and Plaatje did well to avoid any further dealings with Neale: another prominent Afro-American figure who had signed a contract with Neale several years earlier had come to the conclusion that the man was 'a wilful and deliberate fraud'.[59] Possibly, though, Plaatje had another motive in writing to Du Bois as he did. By presenting him with a favourable report on his book Plaatje may well have been seeking to interest Du Bois himself in adding *Mhudi* to the titles published by *The Crisis*, the journal with which he was associated. Du Bois, however, did not come up with an offer and Plaatje failed to interest any other publisher in his book during the rest of the time he remained in the United States. Even less surprisingly he was unable to interest anybody in his Tswana translations of Shakespeare.

In his letter to Mrs Colenso in March Plaatje had indicated that he intended leaving the United States to return to England in May 1922. It was not to be. After a further visit to Boston over Easter, he embarked instead upon a tour of the southern States, something that he had long hoped to undertake but which was by now looking a rather remote possibility because of his shortage of money.[60] In the event the trip was made possible by a grant of $100 from the Phelps Stokes Fund in New York. Plaatje was happy to be able to report that Dr T. Jesse Jones, the director of the fund, was 'intensely interested in my mission', and the money was given to him, he said, 'on condition that I visited Tuskegee, which was just what I was anxious to do'.[61] Founded in 1909 from the proceeds of the will of one Miss Caroline Phelps Stokes, the committee spent its money on promoting educational development amongst Afro-Americans and Africans. More recently it had been responsible for organising an education commission to survey colonial educational policies in Africa. One of the members of this commission was the West African, J. E. K. Aggrey, whom Plaatje had first met in London in 1920, and saw again in New York in late 1921 or early 1922, and it may well have been on Aggrey's recommendation that Plaatje received a favourable consideration from the Fund at its headquarters in New York.

Whether this was the case or not, Plaatje departed from New York early in May 1922, stopping to address several meetings (including the seventh annual session of the National Race Congress in Washington, where his contribution was described as 'an eye opener') on his way south, then visiting the Hampton Institute, Virginia.[62] Six days later he was writing to Jessie Fausset to apologise for having left New York without being able to see her, and informed her of the progress of his tour: 'I have spent a useful and strenuous time since I left you. Saw Hampton and other colleges and universities in Atlanta, Ga; all of them inspiring, and the young people went wild over my message.'[63]

More than any of the other colleges and universities Plaatje visited, though, he was impressed by Tuskegee which he reached a few days later, having written previously to announce his intended time of arrival. Founded by Booker T. Washington, Tuskegee was far and away the best known of the black educational institutes of the American south, and over the years it had provided Africans from all over the continent with the opportunity to acquire an education denied to them in their own countries. In accordance with Washington's philosophy, Tuskegee concentrated its efforts on building up the practical skills of its students, for it was only in this way, Washington believed, that the economic and social regeneration of Afro-Americans (and Africans) could be achieved; only then, he argued, would it be practicable to lay claim to the political rights to which his people, as any other, were entitled. Founded in part upon what Washington had perceived to be a necessary compromise with dominant white interests in the American south (Plaatje would have well appreciated the position here), Washington's philosophy had, over the past ten or fifteen years, come under attack from those—most notably W. E. B. Du Bois and his NAACP—who sought first the political kingdom. Under Washington's successor, Robert Russa Moton, Tuskegee nevertheless maintained its pre-eminent reputation, and Plaatje was one of a long trail of visitors who were deeply impressed by what they saw there. Much of Plaatje's life had been devoted to fighting for the political rights of his people in South Africa, but he was always conscious of the need to provide his people with the skills that would facilitate their progress economically; and as far back as 1903 and 1904, it will be recalled, he had himself publicised Booker T. Washington's ideas in the columns of his old newspaper, *Koranta ea Becoana*. Things had changed greatly since then, but Plaatje was in no doubt that his people in South Africa could benefit from the lessons he might learn during his short visit to Tuskegee.

Plaatje formed an immediate rapport with the principal, Robert Moton. The two men were to correspond intermittently over the next ten years, and in time Moton's portrait came to adorn the wall of the living room of Plaatje's home in Kimberley. As far as Tuskegee itself was concerned, what particularly impressed Plaatje was the amount of money that was being channelled into Tuskegee by white philanthropists: when he saw the books in the accounting department he was staggered to find that its budget for the previous year had been 1½ million dollars. This sum was on a wholly different scale from the sums of money he had sought, or received, for his Brotherhood organisation. As if to emphasise the point, a couple of months later he heard that Tuskegee had been left a further million dollars by a white benefactor from New Jersey.[64]

Plaatje's letter of thanks to Dr Moton's secretary, written from St Louis, Missouri, leaves little doubt about the impression that his brief visit to Tuskegee had made on him:

> I have no words to adequately express my gratitude for the kind reception accorded me by the Principal and everybody at Tuskegee with whom I came in contact. I never felt so sorry to leave a place as I did when I had to turn my back on your great institution yesterday. Please convey my thanks to the Principal.[65]

Plaatje took with him from Tuskegee a promise to provide him with several movie films, showing various activities at Tuskegee, which he intended to show upon his return to South Africa. With the portable movie projector he had been given in Philadelphia he hoped to be able to convey to a wider audience in South Africa something of the lessons that he felt could be learnt from the experiences of the black people in the United States, and a means of passing on – in as accessible a way as possible – that sense of inspiration that Tuskegee had given him. Robert Moton's generous offer to provide several reels of Tuskegee, including one of the unveiling of the statue of Booker T. Washington in April 1922, a month before Plaatje visited the Institute, was therefore more than welcome. A similar, but rather vaguer, promise had also been made by the Hampton Institute.[66]

◇

After a circuitous, zig-zag trip northwards from Tuskegee, Plaatje spent his last few weeks in the United States in the city of Chicago, staying on this occasion with Ida Wells Barnet, one of the best known black women leaders of her day, only recently recovered from a serious illness.[67] There was the usual round of meetings to address (he gave the 'Black Man's Burden' talk at the Unity Club on 25 June), but before he departed a permanent committee was formed by a group of local black dignitaries who had been impressed by Plaatje's work, and who wished to support it after he had returned home.[68] An attorney, James A. Scott, in whose house the meeting to set up the committee took place, became its chairman, and Dr Mary Waring the chairman of its executive board. They duly constituted themselves as the Chicago branch of the South African Bantu Brotherhood Committee, declared their intention of doing all they could 'to assist Sol Plaatje in his great work in South Africa', and made preparations for a 'mass meeting' on 23 July to bid Plaatje farewell.[69] It was the occasion of Plaatje's final address in the United States, his subject being 'Native Conditions in South Africa'. Amongst his audience, and one of the musical performers in the 'Special Native African program' which was put on, was a 29-year-old medical student from Tembuland, in the eastern Cape, struggling through the long period of study needed for qualification at the School of Medicine at Marquette, Milwaukee, some 50 miles north of Chicago. His name was Alfred B. Xuma, later to become president-general of the African National Congress of South Africa.[70]

Several days later Plaatje crossed the Canadian border, and spent a month in Canada before sailing from Montreal to Cherbourg, France, thence to Southampton, at the end of August 1922.[71] If he had hoped, whilst in Toronto, to try to extract the money promised to him by the Canadian Brotherhood Federation to finance the printing of his Fellowship Hymn Book, he would have been disappointed. During his absence in the USA the federation had almost completely collapsed, and Plaatje probably never received a cent of the $7,000 dollars that had been promised to him on the occasion of his first trip to Toronto.[72] Awaiting his arrival in Montreal was the gift of a typewriter from the Corona company, some medicines from Dr Sauer in New York, and some further educational films that he had somehow obtained from Mr Henry Ford (founder and head of the Ford Motor Company), whom he had met personally, to supplement the promises from Tuskegee and Hampton. But he was annoyed to find that some spectacles which he had ordered from a coloured doctor (Dr Scott) he had seen in Chicago had not been sent as requested. Since they had been paid for, Plaatje was understandably upset that Dr Scott had not done as he had requested: 'Truly our folks in America are the limit!' he wrote to Alfred Xuma, almost a year later, still not having received the glasses.[73] Whatever was wrong with Plaatje's eyesight, though, it was not sufficiently serious to prevent him, after he had boarded the RMS *Antonia* on 29 August 1922, from commencing a Tswana translation of *Othello* to occupy himself during the voyage to England.[74]

◇

So ended Plaatje's mission to North America. In many respects it amounted to a remarkable achievement. Even getting over there in the first place required a great deal of persistence and ingenuity; the financial obstacles, together with the opposition of the South African authorities, would have defeated anybody less determined than Plaatje to succeed. And once there, at meeting after meeting, conference after conference, Plaatje conveyed to more people than anybody before him a knowledge of conditions in his country from an African point of view, impressing one audience after the other through his ability as an orator, his natural warmth and humour, his transparently sincere commitment to the cause of his people. But to what end? The people he convinced were far removed from the corridors of power. However sympathetic they were, there was nothing they could do for him in political terms, and for the most part they were not in a position to offer much assistance financially. The vast majority of the Afro-American population in the USA, after all, had more than enough problems of their own to worry about.

It was a tribute to Plaatje's forceful personality that he was able to make the impression he did, but once he had gone it quickly dissipated. Promises of financial support for his work were always more forthcoming than hard cash, and they were easily forgotten once Plaatje himself was no longer around. Even the special committee set up in Chicago on the eve of his departure soon collapsed. Plaatje's campaign was far too heavily dependent on his own strength of personality and physical presence, in other words, to leave much of a permanent impression once he had departed.

What Plaatje himself derived from his experiences in North America is more problematic. When he arrived it was with a realisation that the prospects of political intervention in the affairs of his country from outside had now all but disappeared, but he felt it was important nevertheless to publicise his case amongst the black population of North America. As well as the financial support for his Brotherhood work that he hoped would be forthcoming, he believed that the experiences and example of the life of this community would provide lessons which he could usefully apply in his own country. It was this desire to learn, to collect information on almost every aspect of the life of America's black community, that was his overwhelming preoccupation during the latter part of his visit. From his observations what impressed him perhaps more than anything else was the success – amidst the lynchings and grinding poverty that many black Americans suffered – of the American black community in building itself up through self-help in education, business, and social and religious life; and in attracting the assistance of powerful and wealthy white benefactors.

From comments he made later, contrasting the attention paid by the government and other institutions to black American leaders with that generally given to their counterparts in South Africa, it is evident, too, that in the United States Plaatje saw in the careers of men like W. E. B. Du Bois, John W. Cromwell, and Robert Moton, the kind of role which, in other circumstances, he would himself have played. This constant awareness of the contrast with South Africa, through which his entire experience in the USA was viewed, led him to paint an almost rose-tinted picture of conditions in that country, but the inspiration it provided was nevertheless real enough. What remained to be seen was whether what he had learnt could help him to play any meaningful role in the affairs of his country. As he himself pointed out time and time again, black Americans did not suffer the same political and legal disabilities with which black South Africans had to live.

12

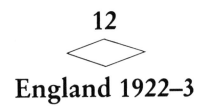

England 1922–3

After 'a most delightful cruise across the ocean with a lot of Canadians whose behaviour made the voyage very pleasant', Plaatje arrived back in England on 21 September 1922, hoping to return home to South Africa a few months after that. But as had now happened so often, things did not quite work out as planned, and in the event it was to be a frustrating – and at times very depressing – period of over a year before he was able to leave: 'circumstances', as he had written to Mrs Solomon a few months earlier, 'are always beyond our control'. Never was that statement more true than now.

Plaatje's main reason for staying on in England, instead of going straight back to South Africa, was to try to raise money to print his African-language translations of the Brotherhood hymn book. He had been trying to achieve this, off and on, since 1919, but he was really no closer to this than he had been then, for none of the many promises of money he had been made for this purpose had actually materialised. It is clear from the efforts that Plaatje devoted to the project that he saw the hymn books as being of great importance to the growth of his Brotherhood movement in South Africa, and as a foundation to its religious life that was every bit as essential as the physical structures – the halls and meeting places – which he had been trying to raise money for as well. In a way these hymn books seem to have assumed an almost symbolic importance in Plaatje's mind: it was as though he felt he now had to bring something concrete back with him to South Africa, something to show for his long absence from home, something to justify the energies he had thrown into trying to build up his Brotherhood movement.

When Plaatje arrived in England, shortly before a general election, there were more immediate difficulties that had to be overcome before much progress could be made in raising money for the hymn books. Some of these he alluded to in a letter to Betty Molteno shortly after his arrival:

I wish the Government had selected a better time to stage a general election. I can see nobody; and my educational films from Henry Ford are held up at the Customs House. The one from Booker T. Washington's School (which shows his work and the activities of his students, including the unveiling of his monument last April, attended by many American millionaires and their families, to say nothing of the thousands of Negroes) is held up at Dover and they threaten to send it back if I don't at once pay some international nonsense. It seems a pity that foreigners should give me moving pictures free gratis and for nothing – worth thousands of dollars – for the education of British subjects and then the British Government give me all this trouble.[1]

These battles with the customs authorities continued for some months to come, complicated by the fact that the customs authorities first of all consented to let Plaatje show his films in England, then changed their minds. As to the elections, Plaatje was no mere observer, for he offered his services to one of the prospective Liberal candidates, none other than John Harris, still secretary of the Anti-Slavery and Aborigines' Protection Society, now standing for the Camberwell constituency in South London. Writing to Mrs Colenso, Plaatje described why he did so: 'You know, I am no personal friend of John H. Harris, but the position he occupied and the loyalty of his wife impelled me to go and offer them my assistance.'[2]

What Plaatje really had in mind in offering Harris his assistance must remain a mystery. Partly, perhaps, it was a question of being able to forgive and forget their earlier battles in the interests of achieving parliamentary representation for a man who could be expected to raise colonial – and possibly South African – issues in the House of Commons. Perhaps, too, Plaatje hoped that his offer of assistance to Harris, especially if he was elected, might encourage him to take an interest in his Brotherhood cause and open a few doors for him in return. As ever, Plaatje could not afford to be choosy about his friends in the situation in which he now found himself, and the bitter personal battles that had taken place between them were now, after all, over five years old. Both were willing to forget their past differences.

Not that Plaatje's assistance in electioneering actually proved sufficient to get Harris into the House of Commons. Harris had set himself 'the very difficult task of winning North-West Camberwell for real Liberalism and progress'; he fought his campaign on 'the application of Christian principles to political life' (Plaatje would not have quibbled with that); but he finished at the bottom of the poll.[3] Plaatje nevertheless considered his assistance had been of some help: 'It proved more valuable than I expected,' he wrote, 'and he [Harris] knows that I got him a number of votes; but he had very poor agents. I doubted if anyone could win with such amateurish canvassers. I was sorry but not surprised when he was defeated.'[4]

Plaatje did find some grounds for satisfaction in the outcome of the election. His letter to Mrs Colenso contained a typically humorous account of his reactions:

Wasn't it a foggy election, but I think that on the whole we came splendidly out of the fog. Everybody seems to be satisfied. The Tories because they are in power. The Labourites because they have doubled their strength; the Liberals have also doubled their number and Lloyd George thinks he had not been entirely obliterated. Was there ever an election that gave such widespread satisfaction?

I was intensely interested in half a dozen candidates and all but two have come in with smashing majorities. Sir Richard Winfrey beat his opponent by

1,777. Dr Salter beat them by 2,325, as for MOREL his victory was as smashing as the effects of a 75 mile Krupp gun. Fancy kicking down to the bottom of the poll – Winston Churchill of all people in the world! I am glad to find that both Tories and Liberal papers are agreed that no election result was so sensational.[5]

◇

Even when things were more settled after the election, and people whom Plaatje wanted to see were more readily accessible, he made painfully slow progress in raising money for the hymn books. Nor was it any easier to find ways of earning a living than it had been during his previous visit to London. As before, there were a few pounds to be made from writing for the *African World* and *South Africa*, and in assisting students of African languages at the School of Oriental Studies. He had some further sessions with Daniel Jones at University College, and also did some work with a South African student called G. K. Lestrade, who was studying Setswana.[6]

Employment of a different kind was provided by the visit to London of a deputation from Swaziland, which arrived in England in January 1923. The deputation was led by the Swazi king, Sobhuza II (a one-time classmate of St Leger's at Lovedale); it included Pixley Seme, moving spirit in the formation of the South African Native National Congress in 1912; and it had come to London to lay its case in the complex land-concessions issue before the Colonial Office. As befitted the long obsession of the British press and public with African royalty (they were much less interested in educated commoners), Sobhuza's presence in London was given a huge amount of publicity, and while Dr Manfred Nathan, his chief legal adviser, negotiated with the Colonial Office over the complexities of the land question, the young king saw the sights of London, attended numerous functions, and was ultimately accorded a half-hour audience with the English King, George V.[7]

In much of this Plaatje was involved, acting as a guide and adviser for the deputation on their various engagements. He appears in several of the photographs that were taken of the deputation when it came to London, and he made himself responsible for the introductions at a number of the functions its members attended – one at Mrs Solomon's house in Hampstead, another at a meeting of the (predominantly West African) Union of Students of African Descent.[8] Plaatje could not disguise from the deputation the desperation of his own position. According to Chief Mandananda Mtsetfwa, one of the deputation, Sobhuza's response, when Pixley Seme reported Plaatje's financial plight to him, was to say: 'Of course, we must help him. He is one of us.'[9] But what, if anything, was done for him is not clear.

With the departure of the Swazi deputation at the beginning of February 1923 Plaatje once again concentrated his energies on the task of fund-raising for his Brotherhood hymn books. William Cross, of the Southall Brotherhood, was the treasurer of the committee that had been set up, and did what he could to assist Plaatje in his task; the response, though, proved to be extremely disappointing, and the prospects of raising the £862 required by the Aberdeen University Press (from whom a quotation had been obtained) began to look more and more remote.[10] Plaatje continued to address meetings to try to raise money, and secured a number of promises of financial support; as ever, only a handful materialised. Plaatje's letter to Betty Molteno on 27 February 1923, written from his lodgings at 101 Lambeth Palace Road ('cheaper and smaller quarters', he said, than those he had previously been occupying in Tavistock Square) reveals a growing pessimism over the whole project:

Dear Miss Molteno,

It was interesting to learn that Mrs Plaatje had written to thank you for your abiding interest in our work. If ever we 'put it over the top' no one should have contributed so much towards its success as your good self.

The flight of time and the slow response to our efforts on behalf of the hymn book are giving me much concern. I have long over-stayed my time and the work is suffering on account of my absence. Again, it is essential that I should correct the hymn proofs and verify the metres before I leave for no one can do the native corrections, if I sailed before the book went to print.

Is it not possible to find some benevolent sympathiser, who could advance our Committee with £300 so that the printer may go to work while we prosecute our appeal? The Committee could guarantee the return of the loan and arrange the refund. Their efforts would be largely supplemented by the sales of the hymn book.

I have discussed the matter with Mr Cross and he feels that some such arrangement is necessary if I am to return to my family and to the work among our people, where I am already long overdue. Unfortunately, few people in this country are interested in South Africans. It is all the East Indies, the West Indies, and West Africans. Apparently, they have no time for the suffering toilers of the land where the gold and diamonds come from – if they only knew the truth!

Could you possibly think of a way out?

Yours respectfully,
Sol T. Plaatje[11]

Several weeks later, writing to Mr Holsey, Robert Moton's Secretary at Tuskegee, with whom he had been corresponding about the difficultites he had been having with the customs authorities over the films from Tuskegee, Plaatje expressed similarly gloomy sentiments:

Perhaps you will be surprised that I am still in England. So am I and so are my folks in South Africa. Of all the things I have ever undertaken nothing has worried me so much as the task of finding the money to print the Native Hymn Book and tonic solfa tunes for our Community Services in S. Africa. The task of translating the metres into African was child's play compared with the job of finding the money.[12]

Although in another letter of the same date Plaatje indicated that 'there are hopes that by the end of April there will be a way out for the Hymns and tunes to the printers' hands', the real truth of the matter was that prospects of success were remote, and they were not improved by the somewhat unhelpful attitude adopted by the National Adult School Union which owned the copyright of the Fellowship Hymn Book.[13] Plaatje nevertheless possessed a remarkable capacity to keep his spirits up in the very difficult–and often embarrassing– circumstances in which he now found himself. As ever, the easygoing relationships he enjoyed with the Solomons, the Colensos, the Moltenos, did much to prevent him from becoming too despondent. A number of his letters to them from this period have survived, and they give a good insight into his state of mind, at least insofar as he was prepared to reveal it in correspondence with these friends of his. One letter to Mrs Colenso was particularly informative:

101 Lambeth Palace Road
London SE1
May 24 1923

My dear Mrs Colenso,
I received your letters and was very glad to hear from you all. I do sincerely trust that you will plead with my Favourite to pardon me. On the night of that beautiful concert I came home and started a letter, thanking my Favourite for the beautiful concert that she and her two sisters gave us on that splendid Beethoven night at Mortimer Hall. The people sitting around me were visibly affected. Observing their emotion, I said, 'Who would believe that these great musicians are three country girls, straight from the farm!'
The remark was whispered round, 'Are they country girls?' I said, 'Yes, they have been feeding the chickens and the cows today and from here they are going straight to Buckinghamshire to trim the cabbages.' 'I thought,' said one, 'that they were regular stage performers in the West End' – Would you believe me, Mrs Colenso, I am so frightfully overworked that I was never able to finish that letter.
Then I had two attacks of neuritis. These illnesses do not advance my work at all; and, after each spell, the accumulation of work does not improve my health.
I have to thank you very much indeed for the trouble you took in reference to my novel. And if the manuscript is not printed it will be in spite of your efforts. Nobody could have done more than you did; but these publishers are not of our way of thinking.
When Miss Irma comes to town, won't you please ask her to meet me for a lunch at any tea room not far from her railway station. It would afford me such great pleasure to talk, if only for half an hour, about Elangeni. It should also do my heart good, for once in my life, to offer a cup of something to Gebuza's daughter whose family have so often tendered me their unreciprocated tokens of friendship.
I continue to hear from Mrs Plaatje and the children. They are much troubled about my long absence and I sincerely hope my efforts will succeed to effect my get-away. If only the summer and

better weather will bring health and enable us to move about and get something.

With kindest regards to all MY FAVOURITES and your good self.

I remain, Dear Mrs Colenso,
Yours very respectfully,
Sol T. Plaatje.[14]

<>

Towards the end of June 1923 Plaatje wrote that he was 'so immersed in the sailing efforts that I have very little time to work', and seemed all set to depart home, having with great reluctance accepted that there was no immediate prospect of raising the money to print his hymn book.[15] But then there came an unexpected offer of paid employment which promised to ameliorate his financial position, which he decided to accept, even though this meant delaying his departure. The offer came from George Lattimore, former manager of the Southern Syncopated Orchestra whom Plaatje had first met in London in 1919. Lattimore specialised in bringing black American bands and stage shows to London, and now had a permanent lease on the Philharmonic Hall in Great Portland Street in London's West End. In July 1923 he was planning to put on something a little different – a wildlife film, based on footage shot by a zoological expedition, led by Prince William of Sweden, which had travelled to Central Africa several years earlier. Hoping to cash in on the recent popularity of other films of this kind, Lattimore employed Plaatje to assist in preparing the film for commercial presentation, and to devise a live theatrical sketch to illustrate the film, and entertain the audience while the reels were being changed in the interval.[16]

Plaatje had been doing this work for a couple of weeks when he wrote to Mrs Solomon:

> 53 Tavistock Square
> London W.C.1
> August 2 1923

Dear Mrs Solomon,

The situation is somewhat changed. I have just signed a contract for a month's job at £10 per week which ought to solve my sailing difficulties by taking me out of the uncertainties of charity. It is a strenuous work preparing my inexperienced team. But when we settle down to the programme I hope to have easier times for then actual work will be but half an hour afternoons and half an hour each evening. And if the play is a success, we are booked to the end of September so that I can now definitely say I will be sailing in October.

Could you please do so kindly and let me have that copy of the novel back. From next week I want to try some other publishers with it. Mr Stanley Unwin wants £75 if he is to handle it.

I had promised to be home by July and these postponements are very depressing. I hope however that this time we are on something definite. I get lugubrious letters from home, they wonder if I am ever coming home. I do sincerely trust that your health is profiting by the holiday at Auld Reekie. How I long to see her green hills once more.

For the more expeditious performance of my work I have had to change quarters. I am now back again in Tavistock Square in a more spacious room, where rest is possible besides the green square. And every part of the city is so easily accessible to this place.

Kindest regards to Miss Solomon and yourself,

Yours very respectfully,

Sol T. Plaatje[17]

The letter probably cheered Mrs Solomon up a little; the day before she had written to a friend that 'Mr Plaatje's lonesome struggle and forsakenness painfully affects my spirit'.[18] Plaatje did not, though, have any further luck in finding a publisher for *Mhudi*: nobody was prepared to risk taking it on.

'The Cradle of the World', as the production was called, opened at the Philharmonic Hall on 9 August. Plaatje professed to be optimistic about its prospects, and was impressed by the technical quality of the film. So, too, for the most part, were the critics, although there was much less unanimity over its actual presentation – 'rather slavishly adapted to the convention that is now so familiar', said *The Times*; the same paper also complained that the sub-titles were 'more than usually irritating', and 'written with a mixture of flippancy and condescension which is decidedly out of place'.[19] Opinions were mixed, too, about the theatrical sketch for which Plaatje was responsible, and in which he also took a part. *South Africa* gave the most detailed account:

> During the interval a number of educated natives from East, West, and South Africa appear in a short sketch. They include Mr Sol Plaatje, the South African native author, who takes the part of Chief Dumakude, and sings a war-song. It is a welcome change, after seeing so many tribes on the screen, to see some Africans in the flesh. To those of us who are acquainted with the wonderful part-singing of the South African natives, the four choruses at the Philharmonic Hall leave something to be desired, as they hardly give effective support to the soloists. But the sketch as a whole is a lively one. Assegais describe circles in the air while the warriors recite their martial deeds. Miss Gupta dances to the pace of an expert tom-tom beater, and draws loud applause which earns for her a beaded necklace from the Chief. Two men subsequently fight over her in a wild scrimmage, during which spears fly and crash against the shields; and one wonders what would happen were the fight between 20 natives instead of only two. The boat song at the end of the picture is more effective and reminiscent of the rhythm and harmony of the South African native vocalists. Those interested in foreign lands will enlarge their knowledge by spending an afternoon or evening at the Philharmonic Hall.[20]

Rather briefer, and more critical, were the remarks that appeared in London's other major African journal, the *African World*: 'the theatrical scenes', it said, 'in which various grotesquely attired natives headed by our old friend, Mr Sol Plaatje, as a Chief, could, we think, be well dispensed with'.[21] The *African World*'s critic surely had a point. Although there is no record of Plaatje having actually said as much, he must have been acutely aware of the paradox implicit in the *African World*'s comments. For here he was, an 'educated', 'civilised' "native" ', come to England to seek support for the cause of his people on the basis of their shared humanity and Christian faith, now employed to project exactly the image that he had devoted so much of his life to fighting. A few months earlier he had told a meeting of the Union of Students of African Descent in London that he had been struck, when he was in the United States, by the 'extraordinary misconceptions' in currency about the African people. Many Americans, he said, supposed them to be 'a kind of baboons running about wild', and that it was therefore of the greatest importance to spread a sound, informed knowledge of African institutions and people.[22] But the harsh fact remained that Plaatje was simply in no position to turn down the financial opportunity that the show presented to him, and there was very little else he could do to earn any money. In the centre of the empire, Africans were expected to be of the traditional variety: witness, most recently, two photographs of King Sobhuza in *South Africa*, one – in which he was in traditional dress – given the caption 'natural'; the other, next to it, in which he was dressed in conventional western attire, had the epithet 'unnatural'.

'The Cradle of the World' did not prove to be a financial success, and it came off after a month. But, as ever, Plaatje took full advantage of any new opportunity that presented itself. One of these he explained in a letter to Mrs Solomon:

> I learnt a lot during the month and came in contact with people I otherwise would never have met – the greatest thing was to get acquainted with some film folks; and while I have educational films about Canada, West Indies and the United States, I was departing with nothing about England. Now I have found a man who gave me decent lengths about the Queen and King attending the races, the Prince of Wales visiting Indian schools, including his unveiling of his grandfather's monument at Calcutta, Lord Allenby entering Jerusalem during the war and a couple of incidents showing the London crowds.[23]

Another opportunity provided by 'The Cradle of the World' enabled Plaatje to put his musical talents to good use:

> My work at the Philharmonic Hall brought me in contact with a different world. It gave me the facility of dictating our traditional music to the Director of the orchestra at the London Coliseum and he arranged some beautiful orchestration for it. When the Philharmonic Band played these melodies to illustrate some of the pictures on the screen, except for their weird repetition, they were scarcely distinguishable from the works of great European masters; and in my own songs I found the harmony of the English orchestral accompaniment very thrilling and opening up a new vision. Anglo-Africans, like Mlle Dumas and Dr Colenso, who heard my songs, informed me they could understand every word of the Sesuto and Zulu phrasing through the

strains of the orchestra and the explosive clicks, which were to them a new thing on the concert platform.[24]

Recalling these same experiences some years later, Plaatje compared the great advances that had been made in the emergence of a distinctive Afro-American style of music in the USA, with the situation of black music in South Africa. The few weeks he spent working on 'The Cradle of the World' convinced him, though, that black South African music, if encouraged and nurtured, had enormous potential for development as well. Clearly, Plaatje's own musical talents deserved a better forum than that provided during the interval of the short-lived 'Cradle of the World'.

◇

Plaatje's association with George Lattimore at the Philharmonic Hall may well have provided the introduction to people in the gramophone recording world, which led in due course to a visit to the Zonophone Company's recording studios at Hayes, Middlesex, on 16 October 1923 to record three discs, Zonophone nos. 4167, 4168 and 4169.[25] The first contained two hymns sung by Plaatje in Setswana; the second contained two traditional songs in Hlubi and Xhosa; while the third was also in Xhosa – a hymn on one side ('A Band of Hard Pressed Men are We'), and an arrangement of John Knox Bokwe's 'Kaffir Wedding Song' (which Plaatje used to sing back in Kimberley in the 1890s) on the other; on all three records he was accompanied on the piano by Sylvia Colenso. At the end of the first side of the second record, though there is no indication of this on the record label, was Plaatje's rendering of 'Nkosi Sikelele Afrika', widely accepted amongst Africans in South Africa as their national anthem, and associated particularly with the South African Native National Congress ever since it was sung at that inaugural meeting in Bloemfontein in 1912. It seems to have been the first time this anthem was recorded. Much had happened since 1912, but few of Plaatje's countrymen would have denied that it was wholly appropriate that this first recording should have been sung by a man who had done so much to bring the organisation into existence and to fight its earliest campaigns, whatever the nature of their subsequent association or the state of the organisation now.

Even before these recordings were made, George Lattimore had very generously promoted a concert in aid of Plaatje's Brotherhood work, and made the Philharmonic Hall available to him for this purpose free of charge. Details of the event, which took place one Sunday afternoon at the end of August, were reported in the journal *West Africa*, and revealed the magnitude of the task Plaatje still faced in collecting funds to enable his hymn book to be printed: £800, it was reported, was still needed. The presence of three members of the spectacularly successful Afro-American production of 'Dover Street to Dixie', then showing at the Piccadilly Pavilion, who gave their services free of charge, helped attract a good audience, but the proceeds cannot have made very much of an impact upon the sum required.[26]

No sooner had this concert taken place than arrangements were begun for another one: not in aid of Plaatje's Brotherhood work, but in honour of Plaatje himself. It was due to take place on his 47th birthday, Monday 9 October 1923, and it was the occasion on which his friends and supporters had decided to bid him farewell, for he had now definitely decided to depart later that month, regardless of the fate of his hymn books. Predictably these last few weeks were rather hectic. He wrote a letter to Mrs Solomon a few days before the concert was due to take place:

> 53 Tavistock Square, W.C.
> Sunday [8 October 1923]
>
> Dear Mrs Solomon,
> You find me on your return from Scotland, in the hard work of preparing for Tuesday's concert. It was painful to come to the door on Saturday with tickets and then run off to Amersham without even waiting to pay my respects and tender to you my greetings. It is going to be a continuous run till this concert is over. It is so difficult to obtain good artistes and their accompanists. Then there are so many things to print and to pay and so many stringent Government regulations to comply with before permission can be obtained to run a Charity show – What between the hall, and Mr Cross at Hanwell, and the Customs authorities at Camden Town, whose requirements and payments are insatiable, to say nothing of my customary drudgery, I really wish these days had 36 hours instead of 24.
> I am so sorry you came from Scotland too late to see our picture. Many people came to see us, among them Mrs Knight-Bruce, who knew you in your old colonial days. I thought she was very old for I saw her nearly 40 years ago when I was a child, but she is remarkably young. She was immensely pleased with the film and promised to bring some friends to the concert.
> Very glad to send you just a line of greeting. Among our artistes will be Miss Coleridge-Taylor (the great composer's daughter), a former member of the Jubilee Singers, one black American baritone, and, of course, the Colensos.
> Kindest regards. Hope to have a little time just after the Concert.
> Yours very respectfully,
> Sol T. Plaatje.[27]

Plaatje managed to gather together an impressive collection of artistes, black and white, and participated in the concert himself, singing two of the songs that he recorded for Zonophone – 'Lead, Kindly Light' and 'Singa Mawele' (in Xhosa). Mr W. B. Dixon, of the Leighton Buzzard Brotherhood, chaired the evening's proceedings, made a short address during the interval, and extended to Plaatje the heartiest congratulations on his birthday. In response, Plaatje made a few humorous comments about other 'October babies' of note in South African history (Kruger, Rhodes, Milner), and – in a touching ceremony – was presented with a laurel wreath by Mrs Sophie Colenso; it was this moment, more than any other, that Mrs Solomon, prevented from attending the function because of illness (she was now nearly 80 years old) regretted having missed. In the view of the journal *South Africa*, the large audience present 'eloquently testified to Mr Plaatje's popularity'.[28]

At the end of the month Plaatje finally departed for South Africa, many months later than he had hoped when returning from the United States a year previously, and years later than he could have imagined would be the case when he had left South Africa at the head of the South African Native National Congress deputation to England in 1919. Despite his efforts to 'take himself out of the hands of charity' in raising the money to pay his passage, in the end he had to rely on Mrs Solomon's assistance. She was a relative of Lord Kylsant, Chairman of the Union Castle line, and through him was able to get Plaatje a second-class berth for the price of a third-class one; very probably the Moltenos helped as well, for Percy Molteno (Betty Molteno's brother) had married into the Currie family, the managers of the company, and was by now closely involved in the affairs of the Union Castle Company himself. Since Plaatje did not have the money to pay for even a third-class berth, Mrs Solomon undertook to guarantee Plaatje's promise of payment in Cape Town once he arrived there.[29]

With such an arrangement the Union Castle Company were satisfied. In fact they owed Plaatje a favour. Six years earlier they had been most appreciative of his intervention on behalf of the Reverend and Mrs Payne, the two black Americans who were refused permission to disembark from the SS *Galway Castle*; had Plaatje not succeeded in persuading General Botha to reverse the decision of the Immigration Department, the Union Castle Company would have had to transport both of them back to London, and at the company's expense.

After a final round of farewells Plaatje sailed from Southampton, bound for Cape Town, on 26 October. A day later the South African High Commission in London cabled Pretoria to announce his departure, suggesting that what they called his 'full agitation schemes' should be 'kept under observation'.[30] They had not forgotten the way they had been outsmarted three years earlier.

<><

On the morning of Plaatje's departure, the journal *South Africa* published a long interview with him, and commented at some length upon what he had to say in an accompanying editorial. Plaatje did not actually say a great deal that was new or at all surprising: he contrasted conditions in South Africa with what he had seen in the United States, indicated that what he had seen over there had made 'a profound impression' upon his mind, and he was very critical of several new pieces of legislation in South Africa – in particular the Urban Areas Act of 1923, which in his view added still further to the disabilities imposed upon the African people. The editor of *South Africa* was not wholly impressed. Whilst on the one hand he considered Plaatje to be a man of sincerity and 'a living (and eloquent) example of the potentialities of the South African Native, being himself a scholar, writer, and very pleasant company', on the other he was broadly in sympathy with the South African government's policies of segregation; he thought that the progress of 'native life' should always be 'within native capacity and in keeping with the pace of his evolution, skill and intelligence'.[31] Not all Plaatje's brothers, he said, were as gifted as he.

In a way these remarks went to the heart of the dilemma that now confronted Plaatje. In a society in which a philosophy of segregation was becoming increasingly accepted in ruling circles, what role was there to be for a man who rejected entirely the arguments upon which such ideas rested, and who had yet been forced to accept that within the limits of the constitution there was nothing further he could do to bring about peaceful political change? Plaatje hoped that what he had learnt in America would at least enable him to play a part in the affairs of his people in the increasingly industrialised, urbanised society in which they now lived. But was this a realistic hope? He had now been away from South Africa for nearly five years, and much had changed. There were many other unresolved questions. Would there be any place for him even among his own people? Who, indeed, could he now consider to be his own people? Was his Brotherhood movement, in which he had placed so much hope, simply an anachronism, the product of a vision that no longer had any relevance to the realities of South Africa in the 1920s? And how, to return to harsh practicalities, was he to earn a living?

13

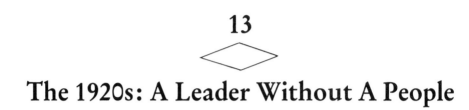

The 1920s: A Leader Without A People

Plaatje disembarked in Cape Town on Monday, 12 November 1923, having preoccupied himself during the voyage in completing his translation of *Othello* into Setswana. On arrival, his most pressing problem, as ever, was a financial one. Unable to raise his passage money from friends in Cape Town, he did at least manage to persuade the Union Castle Company to allow him some extra time for this, and he had also to leave his bioscope films in storage in Cape Town to give him some time to raise the customs duty.

Once in Kimberley, his joy at returning home after so long an absence was tempered by the straitened circumstances in which his wife and children – less St Leger who now had a job in De Aar – were living. At some point during his absence overseas his home, 14 Shannon Street, had had to be sold off to raise money for his family's subsistence, and they were living instead at 32 Angel Street, owned by Isaiah Bud-M'belle, who had moved to Pretoria.[1] Plaatje's letter to Mrs Solomon, written a month after landing at Cape Town, made light of what must have been in reality a serious situation:

> Since landing I have been to Kimberley and had a family reunion of about three weeks. My children were living on next to nothing; but they looked as trim and healthy as others who eat three times every day – if not better. Truly 'men shall not live by bread alone'. Most of our furniture was sold and my credit pledged up to the hilt with grocers, butchers and cloth dealers and I must say creditors have been very patient with them. Now they will get restless since I have come back.[2]

Elizabeth Plaatje was not quite so well. Her eyesight had deteriorated to the extent that she was no longer able to read or write at night, and there had simply not been the money to go and see an eye specialist. And for Plaatje himself there was little immediate prospect of being able to restart his newspaper business, for during his absence the *Tsala ea Batho* printing press had also been sold off – the fate of the *Koranta ea Becoana* press over ten years previously.

Plaatje's Brotherhood movement in Kimberley was also in a sad state of disarray, and its chief asset, the Lyndhurst Road Native Institute, had now passed out of his control. The committee he had left behind in 1919 had been unable to keep up payments for municipal and provincial rates, and Plaatje himself, for all his efforts overseas, had been unable to assist. By the end of 1922 these debts had accumulated to nearly £600. Aware that such sums were unlikely ever to be recovered, De Beers had agreed to a proposal from James Swan, treasurer of the committee, that the terms of the original agreement relating to the hall be altered so as to vest control of its affairs in a new committee, which would give a firm undertaking to pay the rates and taxes that were required. To this De Beers agreed and wrote off the existing debt.[3]

Plaatje himself seems never to have been consulted about this. Whilst the new arrangement meant that he was released from a large debt for which he was personally liable, it also meant that he now no longer had control of the affairs of the institute. What made this so much more difficult to accept was the fact that this action had been initiated by a man whom he had himself installed as treasurer of the Brotherhood committee.[4] All in all it was, for Plaatje, a sad state of affairs to find upon his return, and it seemed to emphasise more than anything else the consequences of the failure of his mission overseas to put the Brotherhood movement onto a secure financial footing, and to put into jeopardy his own local position of leadership and influence. As he was soon to find out elsewhere, it was by no means the only instance of the way in which whites were now beginning to assume control in the field of 'native affairs'. Plaatje came up against the same difficulty when he sought to promote the Brotherhood movement in Johannesburg some weeks after his return home. He held several meetings, public and private, with this object in view, but met with little response. Here, even more than in Kimberley, white liberals and churchmen were tightening their grip upon urban African affairs, and they had no wish to encourage a movement that was independent of their control. As one Methodist churchman on the Rand commented, neither he nor his colleagues looked kindly upon such a movement as Plaatje's because 'it is urging people to a Christianity without the Church'.[5] Plaatje's longstanding complaints about the effects of denomination-alism, so central to his adherence to the Brotherhood ethic, were amply justified.

◇

Plaatje's displacement from the affairs of his Brotherhood in Kimberley, and the opposition he encountered in Johannesburg were part of a wider pattern, and his own experiences were not unique. Essentially they are to be explained by the social and political changes that had taken place in South Africa during the years of Plaatje's absence overseas, for what had taken place here had serious implications – amongst other things – for the role that Plaatje and other African leaders could now expect to play in the affairs of their people.

Plaatje had left South Africa, it will be remembered, at a time of intense political and industrial ferment amongst the African population. While he and his colleagues on the deputation to England were seeking some form of imperial intervention, the South African government, and other influential mining, business and church circles, were seeking other means of defusing a tense situation, the seriousness of which was dramatically underlined by the strike of black miners early in 1920. Several elements of this response were now enshrined in the statute book, most notably in the Native Affairs Act of 1920. Whilst this piece of legislation was the product of a line of thought that went back to the South African Native Affairs Commission of 1903–5, and was conceived as a successor to the abortive Native Administration Bill of 1917, at the time it was passed through the House of Assembly it was presented (particularly by General Smuts) as a means of meeting what was widely believed to be one of the main causes of discontent, the lack of any recognised channel of communication between Africans and the government. As General Smuts had explained in his letter to Lloyd George after his interview with Plaatje and his colleagues in London, the Native Affairs Bill (as it was then) was designed to provide the consultative machinery which would in future render such expeditions as that of the Congress deputation to Europe quite unnecessary.

The Act created a permanent Native Affairs Commission (which did not include any African members), designed to represent African interests and advise the government on matters of policy; established local district councils in which Africans were to be represented; and provided for a regular 'Native Conference', composed of chiefs and other African leaders selected by the government, to whom legislation on 'native affairs' was to be submitted for discussion and recommendation. The Act fell far short of the demands which the Congress deputation took with them to Versailles and London, but it nevertheless established, for the first time outside the Cape, the principle of consultation between Africans and the government and was for this reason welcomed by a number of Congress leaders. Whilst the Act was criticised for not going far enough, and because it was seen as a step towards phasing out the Cape franchise (although for the time being this was left untouched), many in the Congress movement saw it as a step forward that promised to provide them with a platform, and some degree of the recognition and legitimacy from the government which they had long been seeking. If the legislation was in part intended to separate the African political leadership from an increasingly coherent and volatile black working class, in part it succeeded precisely because so many African political leaders had become very nervous about such an association when it grew more difficult for them to control. Richard Selope Thema was perhaps the best representative of this viewpoint. He had left Plaatje in England in June 1920 and arrived in Cape Town just as the Native Affairs Bill was completing its passage through the South African House of Assembly. His view was that it vindicated his mission to England and seemed to him to suggest that the government was not, after all, completely deaf to the demands of the people he claimed to represent.

The response of the government was not an isolated one, and this same concern to defuse African political and industrial discontent was echoed in other circles as well. Most notable was the Chamber of Mines, heavily involved in financing and promoting church- and missionary-inspired moves in the direction of inter-racial co-operation and consultation. Amongst the institutions to arise out of this nexus were the so-called Joint Councils, established in 1921 and 1922, which sought to minimise racial friction through involving 'responsible' African leaders in consultation and discussion with sympathetic whites. As with the Native Affairs Act, the unspoken promise to African political leaders was a degree of recognition and legitimacy in exchange for dissociating themselves from African workers and the use of the strike weapon as a means of remedying their grievances. The Joint Councils – established first on the Rand, and then in many other towns throughout South Africa – owed much to American ideas on racial co-operation introduced into South Africa by American missionaries on the Rand, and to the visit of the Phelps-Stokes Commission between March and June 1921: Plaatje would have heard all about this from Aggrey – a member of that commission – after his return to America.

The Joint Councils were funded heavily by the Chamber of Mines because they furnished a means of dampening down political and industrial discontent. The newspaper *Umteteli wa Bantu*, run by the Native Recruiting Corporation, was regarded in much the same light. Despite having failed to attract Plaatje from England to be its editor, *Umteteli* had built itself up into a well-produced and widely read newspaper, published weekly in English and several different African languages, providing an effective platform for the formulation and discussion of 'responsible' African opinion.

◇

Plaatje's own views on these and other developments were expressed in a series of three articles, widely commented upon, which he wrote for the *Diamond Fields Advertiser* shortly after returning home. They provide an interesting indication of his views on what he now found in South Africa after over four years' absence. Economically, he thought Africans had been hardest hit by the prevailing economic depression, and by the continued effects that he perceived, as he travelled around the countryside during the few weeks after his return to South Africa, of the Natives' Land Act of 1913, which he held to be largely responsible for the growing influx of Africans into the towns – a point he was to make again and again over the next few years. What he saw happening in the towns, though, gave him some cause for optimism. 'The better class of people,' he wrote, 'on the whole seem to feel that these restrictions have gone far enough, and they are looking for a way out of the dilemma', and he went on to comment favourably upon the efforts that the mines, the municipalities and the churches – in particular American missionaries like Ray Phillips – had been making to ameliorate conditions for the African population.[6]

With the state of African political and social life Plaatje was less impressed. The African press, he thought, no longer possessed the vitality it once had, and his observations led him to the conclusion that 'except to a limited extent in one or two instances', 'the native press' had almost ceased to fulfil the function it once had – giving expression to 'native opinion' and acting as 'interpreters of European thought and translators of Government policy'.[7]

Nor was Plaatje much impressed by the state in which he found the South African Native National Congress (renamed the African National Congress in 1923). Certainly his views of the organisation were coloured by the sense of bitterness he felt at its failure to support either his family or himself during his mission overseas, but to any observer it was transparently clear that Congress was nothing like the force it once was. The older generation of leaders, the original founding fathers like John Dube, Pixley Seme, and the Reverend Walter Rubusana, were now preoccupied with other issues and no longer played much of a part in its affairs; several others, Saul Msane for example, had died, in his case discredited. Effectively, Congress – as a national organisation with any claim to express the aspirations of the African people of South Africa as a whole – was dead. The industrial and political discontent of 1918–20 had brought to a head the differences between the more conservative branches of Congress and the radical Transvaal branch, but since then many of those who had been in the forefront of African politics had found a niche with one or other of the organisations sponsored by the Chamber of Mines or the churches. Congress had only briefly represented the hopes and aspirations of the Witwatersrand's growing African workforce, and by 1923 this could no longer be said to be the case. Increasingly, its place was being taken by a new organisation, the Industrial and Commercial Workers' Union, led by an immigrant from Nyasaland, Clements Kadalie. Founded in 1920, the ICU, as it was known, was the first mass African trade union in South Africa, and it had already left a deep imprint upon African political life; for many, its success seemed to suggest that organisation along industrial rather than national lines was now the answer.

Plaatje's first impressions reflected the new complexities of the general situation in South Africa to which he returned. What he saw around him was a country coming to terms with the fact that it was being transformed into an industrial society, with all the stresses and strains that this brought with it; black and white alike were in the process of making their adjustments to this situation. New structures had been created, new loyalties had emerged. Whether in these changed conditions Plaatje would be able to reassume the position of leadership he had once occupied in the affairs of his people, or whether he could find a niche for himself in the more complex society which South Africa now was – these questions remained to be answered.

◇

Plaatje returned to Cape Town at the end of January 1924. He had a number of reasons for making the visit, the most urgent being to collect the bioscope films that he had been obliged to leave in Cape Town when he first arrived, and to pay off the passage money he owed to the Union Castle line. 'It was,' he wrote to Betty Molteno, 'a difficult task trying to raise the wherewithal to pay the Union Castle for my ticket and release the films from the Customs'; but with the help of friends and sympathisers in the city, most notably Stephen Reagon, a well known Coloured spokesman, he managed both, and was able to enjoy a few days relaxation with Elizabeth, who came down to Cape Town with him for a short holiday – her first visit to the city, and the only time she had seen the sea in nearly thirty years. While they were in Cape Town they took the opportunity of visiting Henry Burton, now a minister in the Şmuts government. The 'warm reception' (as Plaatje described it) which he and Elizabeth received from Henry Burton and his family was a tribute to the survival of a kind of friendship – evident in Plaatje's relationship with several other old Cape families – which had been possible in the old Cape Colony, but which seemed almost out of place in the harsher climate of the 1920s.[8]

298

After a few days in Cape Town Elizabeth returned home to Kimberley, but Plaatje himself remained to attend to various matters of a more political nature. Apart from addressing meetings in and around the city he spent much of his time at the House of Assembly, observing proceedings from the gallery, lobbying members on matters bearing on African interests, and writing to the press to seek to influence opinion against 'anti-native' legislative proposals. In particular, he spoke out against the injustices of 'Mr Nixon's Immorality Bill', and against 'the irrelevant and extraordinary views' of Dr Visser, MP for Vrededorp and Chancellor of the Exchequer, on the extent of the African contribution to the exchequer; he criticised General Hertzog's comments upon Africans during discussion of the Women's Franchise Bill; and he played a vigorous part in the behind-the-scenes lobbying in favour of one piece of legislation of special interest to him and his old friends in Thaba Nchu, the Barolong Land Relief Bill, which aimed to bring some degree of legal recognition to Barolong land tenure in Thaba Nchu, and which eventually became law in the following parliamentary session.[9] Plaatje left the House of Assembly in little doubt that an articulate spokesman for African, and Barolong, interests was once more back upon the scene.

Amongst Plaatje's many appointments during this visit to Cape Town was one which took place in Marks' Buildings, Parliament Street, on the morning of 3 April: it was with the Prime Minister, General Smuts, then just two days away from a disastrous bye-election defeat which precipitated his resignation and the holding of a general election.[10]

That the two men should have been willing to see one another is interesting in itself, and understandable only in terms of the transformation of South African political life during the period of Plaatje's absence overseas. For a great deal had changed since that troublesome correspondence with Lloyd George after his interview with Plaatje and the other members of the SANNC deputation in November 1919. Since then, Smuts had replaced General Botha as Prime Minister and leader of the South African Party; he had found common cause with the old Unionist Party (which was dissolved, its members joining the SAP) to meet the growing strength of the Afrikaner nationalists, led by General Hertzog; and he presided thereafter over a government which seemed every bit as responsive to the needs of the mining industry and the imperial connection as the Milner regime in the aftermath of the Anglo-Boer war. As though to prove these new-found credentials, he had shown no hesitation whatever in putting down the white miners' strike in 1922 with all the force at his disposal.

In the light of these changed circumstances Plaatje's view of the General was understandably very different from what it had once been. For he now saw in General Smuts and the South African Party the only effective means of resisting the political influence of the two groups of people he believed to be most opposed to the interests of the African people: the Afrikaner national- ists, to whom he attributed the most oppressive pieces of legislation since Union, and who were now the most fervent advocates of policies of segregation; and the white working class, seeking the protection of the colour bar in employment, and a guaranteed place for their labour, at the expense of

African workers, in the mining industry. Both groups were now united in an electoral pact.

In short, Plaatje now believed that General Smuts and his South African Party were people with whom he now felt there was sufficient congruence of interest to enable them to do business; whilst General Smuts, for his part, his government in an increasingly sticky position politically, would not have been averse to talking to somebody who might be able to sway African voters towards the SAP in those Cape constituencies where they still possessed the balance of power.

Although no actual record of Plaatje's meeting with the Prime Minister has survived, circumstantial evidence, together with a subsequent letter Plaatje wrote on the subject, would suggest that he took the opportunity during the meeting to explore the possibility of financial support from the SAP for the resuscitation of his newspaper, *Tsala ea Batho*;[11] and that he made it clear that in return he would do all he could to deliver African electoral support for the SAP – something which could certainly not be relied upon as a matter of course in view of General Hertzog's recent success in attracting African and Coloured support with some well-judged, but exceedingly vague, policy statements.

Whatever consideration General Smuts gave to Plaatje's overtures, the general election was upon them before anything could be done. Plaatje himself then threw himself into electioneering on behalf of the SAP. English-language newspapers in Cape Town and Johannesburg, as well as the *Diamond Fields Advertiser* in Kimberley, all carried strong articles by Plaatje urging their African readers, where they had the vote, to cast it for the SAP. While pointing to the generally creditable record of the Smuts government in the field of 'native affairs' (it being election time, some of the less creditable aspects of this were not mentioned), he castigated General Hertzog and the nationalists in the strongest terms, held them responsible for the Natives' Land Act of 1913, and condemned their proposals to abolish the Cape franchise. 'If the Nationalists are to attain power in the next election,' so Plaatje concluded one of these articles, 'let them get it by the votes of the Europeans, but let no coloured person be responsible for the orgy of tyranny that is to follow their ascendancy.'[12] In the columns of *Umteteli wa Bantu*, too, Plaatje spoke out strongly against the Labour/Nationalist Pact on the eve of the election, his particular concern being to discredit the allegations that a meeting of the African National Congress at Bloemfontein had advised Africans to vote for the Pact. This had actually happened, but the meeting had been highly irregular, and took place in the absence of any senior Congress leaders.[13] It had nevertheless sowed much discord and confusion, and demonstrated the state of disarray which Congress was now in.

Plaatje played a more direct part in the election campaign on the diamond fields in mobilising African voters for the two SAP candidates in Kimberley, Sir David Harris and Sir Ernest Oppenheimer, chairman of De Beers. He knew both men well, and had every interest – personal as well as political – in seeing them elected. Whatever the difficulties Plaatje now faced with the affairs of the Lyndhurst Road Native Institute, he never forgot that it had been Sir David Harris who had been primarily responsible for getting the board of De Beers to hand over the old tram shed to him in the first place. He had also had many dealings with Sir Ernest Oppenheimer in the past, and he must have been aware that Sir Ernest's election as a member of the House of Assembly (he was standing for the first time) could well strengthen the prospects of gaining SAP support for resuscitating *Tsala ea Batho*. Whatever thought Plaatje gave to such considerations, he was certainly full of praise for Sir Ernest at an election rally of African voters in No. 2 Location, Kimberley, on the evening of 6 June, two weeks before polling day. The *Diamond Fields Advertiser* was understandably generous in its publicity for the occasion: 'I feel certain we are going to win this election,' Plaatje declared in his speech introducing Sir Ernest to his prospective voters,

> and there is only one thing you want to do as a tribute to Sir Ernest and that is to return him with a big majority. There is no doubt about his return, but we want the biggest majority in the Union. We will give them such a result on the 17th that they will say, 'This is what No. 2 Location did' (Loud cheers).

Sir Ernest, sitting next to Plaatje on the platform, was in fine form at well, and he earned loud applause for his criticism of General Hertzog's segregation schemes and his declared intention of removing the Cape franchise:

> I hear an attempt has been made to fool you, went on Sir Ernest. You have been told under this segregation policy you are going to have your own native Parliament (laughter). I suppose you will be drawing lots as to who is going to be your Prime Minister (more laughter). I am sorry to disappoint you, because General Hertzog said a few days ago at Potchefstroom he is going to give you proper Councils in these areas when you are segregated, but he has one condition, and that is that even these Councils must be under European supervision (A voice, 'Oh'). So you see, even Mr Sol Plaatje cannot be Prime Minister (laughter). I am quite sure none of you will risk the loss of your votes by putting General Hertzog in power. ('No', and applause)[14]

It was all good electioneering stuff, even if some doubts remained in the minds of those present as to the security of their votes under a new government headed by General Smuts; in reality it was a question of choosing the lesser of two evils. As was customary, the meeting concluded with the singing of 'God Save the King' and 'thunderous salvoes of cheers for Sir Ernest'. Two weeks later, to nobody's surprise, both he and Sir David Harris were elected to parliament with large majorities as the members for Kimberley and Beaconsfield respectively. But overall the South African Party was now in a minority: it won only 53 seats against the Nationalists' 63 and Labour's 18, giving the Pact a parliamentary majority of 28. General Smuts lost his seat, and so too did a number of well-known politicians with whom Plaatje had worked closely in the past – notably Henry Burton, F. S. Malan, and Advocate Will Stuart, formerly the member for Tembuland.[15] To Plaatje's dismay, a government was now formed from the two parties – the Afrikaner Nationalists and the Labour Party – whose interests he believed to be in direct opposition to those of his own people. The political future, not to mention the unresolved personal dilemma that he faced about how it was that he was to make a satisfactory living, seemed, in the immediate aftermath of the Pact election victory, deeply discouraging. It looked to be only a matter of time before General Hertzog would proceed with his much publicised schemes to 'solve the native problem', implement the comprehensive schemes of segregation that he had put to the electorate (admittedly in somewhat vague terms), and proceed to abolish the Cape franchise. It was not a political future Plaatje could contemplate with any degree of optimism.

◇

In the months following the election Plaatje did his best to solicit support for the newspaper he so desperately wanted, but with no apparent success. Then, in January 1925, he wrote to General Smuts for assistance. From the tone of his letter it is clear that he assumed the General was familiar with his plans:

> I am sorry to say that I have not been able to make any headway with the mining advertising requisite for the resuscitation of my paper. The Chamber of Mines seems willing; but such matters are controlled by their Native Affairs Department – the Great Native Recruiting Corporation – and they are not disposed to advertise; but I think they only require some one to determine and express the advertising value and possible party gains. Sir E. Oppenheimer is sympathetic but advised me to wait till the beginning of this year when he will occupy a higher position in the Chamber . . . You should be doing a party stroke and incidentally benefiting the Natives if you took an early opportunity to remind Sir Ernest Oppenheimer to push the matter and strengthen his hands with any of the mining kings who have the authority to issue the word that would give us the annual financial vote.[16]

General Smuts duly agreed to talk to Sir Ernest about the matter as Plaatje requested, but since his plans to resuscitate *Tsala ea Batho* depended upon support from the Chamber of Mines as well it is not altogether surprising that the paper never materialised. For the Chamber, more particularly the 'Great Native Recruiting Corporation', as Plaatje called it, ran its own newspaper, *Umteteli wa Bantu*, and they can have had little desire to see a competitor. They had tried hard enough, after all, to kill off *Abantu-Batho*, and though they had not quite succeeded in this, support for another paper, even if it was unlikely to pursue such a radical line as *Abantu-Batho*, was never a very real possibility.

Plaatje's plans for resuscitating *Tsala ea Batho* nevertheless reveal much about the changed circumstances in which he had now to operate. In the past, as editor of *Koranta ea Becoana* and later *Tsala ea Batho*, he had an independent platform, supported by a group of Africans who valued his services as a spokesman and who could afford to subsidise his newspaper. Now things were different. Not only was the money no longer there, but there seemed less point in even supporting a spokesman like Plaatje; in the current political circumstances there was simply less scope for him to influence the actions of the government than there had been before.

But where did this leave Plaatje himself? He really had no alternative but to try and exploit such space as was still left to him by the political realignments of the last four years, and to make such accommodations as were necessary. At the same time he had to retain his credibility and independence as a spokesman for African interests. Accepting the editorship of *Umteteli wa Bantu* was not, in

Plaatje's view, consistent with this; but it was consistent to negotiate for political and financial support from the SAP and Chamber of Mines to support a newspaper over which he had editorial control.

After the general election Plaatje also undertook several extensive tours in the Orange Free State, the Transvaal and the eastern Cape, including the Transkei, to familiarise himself once again with the conditions in which Africans now lived in the country, to tell audiences of his experiences overseas, and to show the films he had brought back with him, with such difficulty, on his bioscope apparatus. In many ways this 'Plaatje bioscope', as it was known, was something of a curiosity and, as with so many of his activities, undertaken with a mixture of motives and objectives. Plaatje saw the main purpose of these film shows as educational. Judging from his letters and the publicity material he circulated, the centrepiece was invariably the film he had acquired from Dr Moton, showing the work of the Tuskegee Institute. A leaflet advertising the show in Bloemfontein on 26, 27, and 29 September 1924, for example, urged people to 'roll up and see the Coloured American Bioscope, direct from Chicago, Ill., USA', and billed as 'its principal feature, Booker T. Washington's School, Tuskegee, and her thousands of young men and women students at Drill and Manoeuvres', and in smaller print there followed the statement: 'The Immigration Department will not permit any Foreign Negroes – not even the Jubilee Singers, beloved of our forefathers – to land in the Union. You can only see Coloured Americans on the screen.'[17]

Plaatje seems to have met with his most enthusiastic response, and his largest audiences, in the smaller country towns where films of any kind were a novelty, where Africans were refused admittance to European-run cinemas or when he showed the films to captive audiences, such as those at leper asylums. There was no doubting the warmth of the reception he met, for example, when he visited the West Fort Leper Asylum in Pretoria late in August 1924. Thus the *Pretoria News* report of the occasion:

Mr Sol Plaatje, Kimberley, visited the West Fort Leper Asylum on Friday evening, and treated the inmates to a bioscope display of the scenes and people he visited in Canada and the United States. To meet the tribal distinctions between the several members of the large audience his talk was delivered alternately in Sesotho, Zulu, and the Taal. In this polyglot talk the aid of Mr Germond and Mr I. Bud-M'belle, of the Native Affairs Department, proved very helpful.

The programme started with the Islands of the St Lawrence (the great river by which Mr Plaatje entered the American continent in October 1920), and embracing America, it finished with an interesting display of the city and people of Havana, Cuba. None of the pictures, however, evoked so much enthusiasm as the work and drills of the students of the famous Tuskegee, Booker Washington's great institution in Alabama. At the close, the visitors were loudly cheered, and asked to 'come again with the pictures'.

Between the pictures the gathering sang hymns and gave the entertainment the character of a Church service. Mr Duncan, the official in charge, received the congratulations of the visitors, who were greatly impressed with the cleanliness of the place, as well as the good behaviour and apparent contentment of what the lecturer described as the 'most orderly Native crowd in the Transvaal'.[18]

The programme was typical of many of the meetings at which Plaatje showed his films. But in the larger urban centres his show was not nearly so popular. Several months earlier he had arranged a showing in the spacious Ebenezer Hall in Johannesburg, but less than a hundred people turned up, and Plaatje's promised 'assistants' failed to put in an appearance.[19] In the locations of other larger towns Plaatje wrote that he experienced considerable difficulty in attracting sufficient people to cover his expenses, let alone make some sort of a profit.[20]

It is not difficult to account for the unpopularity of the 'Plaatje bioscope' in the larger industrial towns. For to many Africans who lived and worked there, there must have been something strangely old-fashioned about what Plaatje was trying to do – in paradoxical contrast to the novelty of the equipment he used to convey his message. To those who had been involved in the great political and industrial upheavals of the past few years Plaatje's message of educational self-help and moral improvement must have been difficult to comprehend. Of what relevance could such ideas be in a country which placed restrictions over almost every aspect of their lives, and where the only solution in sight seemed to be to exploit their collective rather than their individual strength? Yet Plaatje himself never lost this belief in individual uplift, and it had clearly been strengthened by his experiences in America. Like many men who had risen from humble backgrounds, he saw no reason why others should not through similar force of character and personality overcome the obstacles in life as he had done himself. Admittedly, the restrictions Africans faced now were much greater than when he had first entered public life, but that simply called for a greater effort to be made. For what were the alternatives? To do nothing? To try and bring about a revolutionary transformation of society, as several small political groups in South Africa were now advocating? Plaatje could accept neither.

So Plaatje sought with his bioscope to pass on what he had learnt overseas, to implant the seeds of inspiration and motivation wherever he went, to give hope where there was only despair. The show was far more popular among children than adults, and those he put on for them, charging half price or less, were always much better attended; in these young minds he was always likely to leave a more lasting impression, as several of those youngsters will today testify, and it is clear that he derived great satisfaction from being able to do this. 'I have been round a good deal with my films,' he wrote to Robert Moton, in September 1924. 'With the poverty of the natives it is a profitless job: but when I see the joy, especially of the native kiddies, at sight of the thrilling drills of Tuskegee and my explanatory remarks enabling them to enjoy that which I have witnessed and they cannot, it turns the whole thing into a labour of love.'[21]

Plaatje's bioscope served other purposes as well. It provided him with the means of financing his travelling in the rural areas of South Africa, of investigating social and economic conditions in the rural areas of the Cape, the Transvaal and the Orange Free State. For here was his real constituency: things might have changed greatly in the towns and cities, but in the countryside the pace of change was slower. Here Plaatje still remained in a position to make a contribution to the life of his people, and here too his authority and reputation, the memories perhaps of his great campaign against the Natives' Land Act, gave him a measure of influence that he no longer enjoyed amongst the urban population.

◇

Plaatje's first year back in South Africa thus saw him involved in a variety of enterprises and activities. He had reminded the country once again of his status and ability as a public figure and spokesman but was unable, as yet, to speak from the position that he so desperately wanted – that of editor of his own newspaper. To lack of progress on this front were added several other disappointments. He had hoped to meet up with Dr Jesse Jones and Dr Aggrey, both of whom were travelling through South Africa on a second Phelps-Stokes Education Commission, 'to enlist the material sympathy', as he put it in a letter to Robert Moton at the end of September 1924, 'in the publication of our Native Fellowship hymnal still in the press through the lack of a few hundred pounds'. After nearly seven years and countless promises in his search for funds to publish these translations, Plaatje had still been unable to raise the money he needed. A note of pessimism ran through much of the rest of Plaatje's letter as well. Whilst conditions had improved somewhat for Africans living on the Rand, he said, in most other areas they were worse than ever. 'Johannesburg,' he wrote, 'is only a speck in British South Africa':

> Away from the beaten track and far from the reach of enlightened sentiment in these terrible times of drought, locusts, and dwindling wages, the lot of the South African native is not enviable. Since 1883, statisticians claim, South Africa never knew a drought like the one we have endured during the past ten years. Sometimes you have to call on a poor family in order to offer some Christian sympathy only to hear such a tale of woe as would force you to part with your last half a crown even if your family depended on it.
>
> To the whites, the Government not only offer relief but they are pressing public bodies to fire their native labourers. If they are displaced by white men the Treasury grants them from 3/– to 5/– per white man for poor relief in order that the latter should get 7/– or 8/– per day where his black predecessor (now thrown in the streets) got 2/– or 3/–.[22]

Few letters that Plaatje wrote, however, were without some expression of optimism to offset the gloom and despondency around him, and this one was no exception. In Kimberley, he said, whilst 'every Department of our work is tottering, thanks to the acute economic depression', the Lyndhurst Road School was still flourishing because, 'Thank God, the Kimberley School Board pays the Teachers', the only school board to do so in the whole of South Africa; elsewhere, teachers in schools for Africans were paid for by the churches, the missionary societies, or the parents of the schoolchildren.

Plaatje derived some encouragement, too, from the fact that despite the change of government, he still felt he retained some influence with members of the new Nationalist administration. For this reason, he wrote in the same letter, he felt confident that should Dr Moton consider visiting South Africa (as he had thought of doing several years earlier), then he would be able, with the help of 'my Boer friends in the Ministry', to 'get General Hertzog to reconsider and rescind the ban' which the Nationalist government had imposed as soon as it had come into office – just as, so Plaatje recalled, he had persuaded General Botha to allow the Paynes into South Africa back in 1917. He then went on to explain to Dr Moton, as one black man to another, just how, with the right kind of approach, this sort of thing might be done:

> The Boers are very mean in some things, for instance one of them may be as good as gold and a millionaire but yet never part with a shilling to a native cause but he is very obliging with his accommodation to certain Natives if it costs him no money.
>
> There are places so hostile to the English and their Imperial rule that even General Smuts as Prime Minister never visited them for fear of being hissed off the platform for his loyalty to England; but I always manage to get by, taking good care however to hold my hat in my hand all the time, even when, to the bewilderment of local custom, I am invited in by the front door. Our Boer 'crackers' are worse than Southerners. Only yesterday, a son of a Boer Senator and a cousin of a Crown Minister (member of General Hertzog's Ministry), brother of a Judge of the Appellate Division of the Supreme Court of South Africa, said to me: 'Man, your politics are putrid: too full of Smuts. But we like you as you are the only Kaffir who writes our language as beautifully as the other cheeky Kaffirs write English'.
>
> The forgotten point of course is that when English missionaries were pushing their language into the bucolic minds of unlettered natives, the Boer Church was too bigoted to teach the cursed descendants of Ham.

Thus a black South African to a black American on how to adopt the guises required by 'local custom': Dr Moton, like his predecessor Booker T. Washington, would have understood fully. The anecdote sums up, in a way, the essence of Plaatje's style, exploiting to the full his personal qualities to carve a niche for himself where by rights none really existed. He was always careful to keep open the channels of communication, even with people to whom he was, politically speaking, strongly opposed.

This same concern lay behind the short letter he wrote to General Hertzog in October 1924, enclosing a newspaper cutting describing one of his recent bioscope shows which he felt 'certain will interest the human side of your work in the Ministry of Native Affairs'; and expressing his thanks, on behalf of the Barolong, for his refusal to allow 'pressure of other work and political differences' to stand in the way of passing the Barolong Relief Act, which had been introduced during the previous parliamentary session.[23]

Strange as it would perhaps have seemed to many who read or heard Plaatje's fierce denunciations of the General and his policies on other occasions, he then ended his short letter with an expression of 'best wishes'. There is no reason to doubt that they were well meant. Plaatje was never quite able to bring himself to believe that even his greatest political opponents were inherently evil, whatever the consequences of the policies they advocated. It was as though there was always a separation in his mind between the cause people stood for and their essential human nature, and in this he never lost faith. Although there was undoubtedly an element of political expediency in this as well, Plaatje never gave up believing that men like General Hertzog might one day see the errors of their policies and views, or that he was himself capable of persuading them to do so. Hence the importance of maintaining good personal relations with them.

At the same time Plaatje was careful to keep in with those on the other side of the party political spectrum. Three months later he was writing to General Smuts to congratulate him on his 'signal success as leader of His Majesty's Opposition both in Parliament and in the country', and wished him 'greater success in the New Year'.[24]

◇

At the end of 1924 Plaatje broke his tour of the eastern province to attend two conferences: the third annual 'Native Conference', held in Pretoria, and convened under the terms of the Native Affairs Act of 1920, which he attended as an observer rather than as an official (nominated) delegate; and a Joint Councils Conference, in Johannesburg, in which he took a rather more active role.

The Joint Councils Conference was organised by Dr J. D. Rheinallt Jones, a lecturer at the University of Witwatersrand and one of the moving spirits in the Joint Council movement. It was a characteristic manifestation of the burgeoning interest in 'race relations' on the part of the white liberals and churchmen, and took place in a building which itself came to symbolise this whole philosophy – the newly opened Bantu Men's Social Centre in Johannesburg. In Plaatje's view any progress that could be achieved through inter-racial cooperation of the kind represented by this conference was welcome, and it had his support. But already in the paper he read to the gathering on 'The treatment of natives in the courts' he gave some indication of his reservations about the effects and scope of work of this kind. As he was to stress time and time again over the next few years, far too little attention was devoted to what was going on the rural areas – in relation to the administration of justice just as much as the pernicious effects of the Land Act of 1913 – and he urged the Joint Councils to extend their activities into the countryside.

He had another warning as well: that Africans should be prepared to fight their own battles, and not to rely wholly upon European sympathisers such as those now involved in the Joint Councils. Plaatje had lived much of his own life according to this principle, and in his address to the meeting he referred back to his own record to illustrate the point, enumerating several of his own successes in securing ministerial intervention in cases of injustice arising from discriminatory treatment in the law courts. Fifteen years ago, he said, 'there was no welfare association . . . we had here instead of a Joint Council what was known as "The University of Crime", and anyone interested in this kind of work had to finance it out of his own pocket like a hobby of his own'. In this there was more than a hint of a feeling of resentment on Plaatje's part at what he now saw happening, for this new European domination of the business of 'race relations' threatened to displace African leaders such as himself from any meaningful role in the affairs of their people. 'Most white men,' he concluded, 'are interested in us because they are after our goods. Other white men are interested in us because they want to save us from exploitation but the best protection would be to stimulate the Natives' own interest in native life.' Plaatje did not find it very agreeable to have to watch well-funded Europeans assuming the mantle of self-appointed advocates of the interests of his people, and as time went on he was to grow steadily more bitter at this process of displacement.

There were also very clear indications in Plaatje's remarks at the conference of what was to become another insistent theme of his over the next few years: criticism of his own people for their failure to take sufficient interest in their own affairs, to measure up to his own high standards of public service and leadership. To illustrate the point he gave several examples from his recent experiences. One arose from his visit to Cape Town at the beginning of the year, and concerned the implementation of a recent piece of legislation, the Natives' Urban Areas Act of 1923:

> Mr Mtimkulu [also present at the conference] will remember that early this year I attended a meeting of the Cape Peninsula Native Welfare Association where they read assurances from the Government that the Native Urban Area Act was not being enforced. I was the only native in the gathering who knew that, and was worrying, because, on that day 40 Natives were fined in a suburban Police Court and 12 more in the City Magistrates Court and ordered to go and live in the Location. The following week some of them were back again in court charged with overcrowding the location. Delicately and single- handedly I pulled some strings and brought the Chief Magistrate and the Town Clerk together on their behalf. We shall never get better treatment in the Courts or outside if we show so little concern in the misery of our fellow men.[25]

A further example Plaatje gave to illustrate what he called 'native indifference to native needs' was taken from the official Native Conference he had attended just a few days earlier. A government spokesman at the conference had stated that Africans paid about two or three shillings per year in indirect tax, but not one person there spoke up to contradict what Plaatje, attending the conference only as an observer, readily saw was a quite unjustifiable claim, and based on a system of assessment whereby receipts for certain taxes were quite wrongly attributed solely to whites. 'If the Natives,' Plaatje concluded, 'leave white people to fight our battle for equal treatment and equal recognition inside or outside the Courts I am afraid we shall continue to pay taxes and the Treasury will keep on mailing the receipts to white people.'

◇

While Plaatje grew increasingly critical of the shortcomings of his own people the more publicly expressed threat they faced was from General Hertzog's proposed legislative solution to the 'native question' which dominated the government's approach to 'native affairs' throughout the 1920s. Hertzog had made much of his longstanding plans for a comprehensive scheme of segregation to solve the 'native problem' at the time of the general election in 1924, and it had proved popular with the white electorate – particularly as it was linked with

84 A group of Africans and Afro-Americans, probably taken in London, 1922–3. Plaatje is standing in the top row, extreme left.

83 A. B. Xuma, later President-General of the African National Congress, whom Plaatje met in Chicago in July 1922.

85 The theatrical sketch which formed part of 'The Cradle of the World' at the Philharmonic Hall, London, August–September 1923. Plaatje is centre stage, holding a spear.

86 *The Swazi land delegation to London, 1923, which Plaatje joined in an unofficial capacity. Seated, left to right: Benjamin Nxumalo, Mandenanda Mtsetfwa, King Sobhuza II, Prince Msudvuka Dlamini, Pixley ka I. Seme. Standing, left to right: Amos Zwane, Loshina Hlope, Sol Plaatje.*

87 *Plaatje and unidentified friends in England, 1922 or 1923.*

Zonophone Records

BY

SOL T. PLAATJE.

The following Records have been made by Mr. Sol. T. Plaatje, who is well known to the South African Natives for his publications and lectures in connection with the Brotherhood movement, which he founded among them.

He has travelled widely in order to further the interests of this object, and lectured in many places during his visit to Europe and North America.

ZONOPHONE RECORDS

Double-sided 10-inch **3/6.**

4167	Hark 'tis the Watchman's Cry .. (Hymn in Sechuana)	..	Sol. T. Plaatje Piano acc. by Miss Sylvia Colenso
	Lead Kindly Light (Hymn in Sechuana)	..	" "
4168	Pesheya Ko Tukela (Across the Tugela)	"	"
	Singa Mawela (We are Twins)	..	" "
4169	A band of hard pressed men are we .. (Hymn in Si—Xosa)		Sol. T. Plaatje with Piano acc.
	The Kaffir Wedding Song (J. K. Bhokwe) (Sung in Xosa)	..	"

Manufactured by

THE GRAMOPHONE COMPANY, LIMITED,

FOR

THE BRITISH ZONOPHONE COMPANY, LIMITED.

88 *Leaflet advertising Plaatje's three Zonophone records, recorded at Hayes, Middlesex, in October 1923.*

Sol. Plaatje's Travelogues

and

Coloured American Bioscope,

direct from Chicago, Ill, U.S.A.

First class animated pictures of The Royal Family, London crowds, Canadian, West Indian and American Scenes. Also **BOOKER WASHINGTON'S GREAT SCHOOL** in Alabama, with thousands of **TUSKEGEE STUDENTS** at work and Drills. African and Foreign Sceneries. Great success in Pretoria, the O.F.S. and the Rand and East London. Independent Church, Brownlee Station, King Wms. Town at 8 p.m., Wednesday, 22nd October and at the Wesleyan Native Church, King Wms. Town, 8 p.m., Friday, 24th October. Admission 9d. Reserved seats 1/-.

F. Y. Plaatje, Pianist; Sol. T. Plaatje, Operator and Lecturer.

89 *The Plaatje bioscope: an advertisment from* Imvo Zabantsundu, *15 October 1924.*

90 *General Jan Christiaan Smuts, Prime Minister of South Africa 1919–24, leader of the South African Party in opposition in the 1920s and 1930s.*

91 *General J. B. Hertzog, Prime Minister of South Africa, 1924–39, and architect of segregation.*

92 *Plaatje addressing a meeting at the time of the visit of the Prince of Wales to South Africa in 1925.*

proposals to exclude Africans from certain occupations in the urban areas. It was not long before the new administration put its proposals before parliament. In deference largely to the Labour half of the Pact, the first bill to be introduced, early in 1925, was the Mines and Works Amendment Bill, known more generally as the Colour Bar Bill, its objective being to legalise the industrial colour bar.

Over the next two years – until the Act finally became law in 1926 – this Colour Bar Bill, at its various stages through the House of Assembly, was the subject of one article after the other which Plaatje wrote for the national press, adding his voice to that of other African spokesmen, church leaders, European 'friends of the natives', and – when it suited them – that of General Smuts and the South African Party. The first stages of the campaign against the bill were coordinated by Dr Rheinallt Jones on behalf of the Joint Councils – it was very much a sign of the times that it was they who took the initiative – and Plaatje was one of many to add his name to a distinguished list of protestors who signed a petition for presentation to the Prime Minister in May 1926.[26] Plaatje in fact travelled down to Cape Town during the first stages of the bill's passage through the South African legislature (the degree of parliamentary opposition meant that it had finally to go before a Joint Sitting of the Senate and the House of Assembly) to offer such assistance as he could to Rheinallt Jones, but to no avail.[27] Plaatje was often able to achieve concessions where others failed on issues over which individual ministers had some discretionary powers, but on questions of national policy such as this his voice counted for very little. Even the combined opposition of the South African Party and the Chamber of Mines (which financed the extra- parliamentary opposition) was powerless with the Pact government in control of a majority in the Houses of Parliament.

General Hertzog was to encounter rather more difficulty with his plans to extend territorial and political segregation. Plaatje had vigorously denounced Hertzog's somewhat vague formulations at the time of the general election in 1924, but it was not until over a year later that his proposals surfaced in any more concrete form. They did so in a famous speech at Smithfield in November 1925, and the Prime Minister took the opportunity of elaborating further at the annual meeting of the Native Conference in Pretoria early the following month. Having received an official invitation to attend the conference Plaatje was therefore amongst the 50 African delegates, or nominees as they really were, who listened to the Prime Minister describe in somewhat greater detail what he had in mind. Addressing the delegates in Dutch, Hertzog laid before the conference, in essence, four interdependent bills – the Coloured Persons Rights Bill, which proposed to remove Africans from the Cape common roll; the Representation of Natives in Parliament Bill, which provided for seven European MPs (with reduced status and voting powers) to be elected by chiefs, headmen and other prominent Africans nominated by the Governor-General; the Union Native Council Bill, designed to formalise the existing Native Conference by establishing a council of 50 members, 15 of whom were to be elected by the Governor-General in similar fashion to the above; and the Native Land (Amendment) Bill which provided for making available additional land for African occupation as a *quid pro quo* for the loss of the franchise.[28]

What the Prime Minister had on offer, in effect, was this: more land, and a limited degree of indirect, separate representation in the House of Assembly, in exchange for the removal of the Cape franchise. Not one of the delegates present expressed himself in favour of the package on offer, and speaker after speaker, Plaatje amongst them, spoke out against any attempt to remove Africans from the common roll in the Cape. 'The idea that the Cape Natives should surrender their present franchise to obtain seven European representatives in the Union Parliament,' Plaatje emphasised,

> was absolutely unacceptable. Experience had shown the value of the Cape franchise in making friends for Natives in the House of Assembly. It was very observable how faithfully those members whom their votes had helped to place there had supported native interests – notably on the question of the colour bar.[29]

Plaatje's entire political career and ideals had been founded on an appreciation of the value of the Cape franchise: on this there could be no question of compromise.

There was considerable discussion, however, over the three other bills which the delegates had before them. Plaatje welcomed the Prime Minister's proposals to make more land available for African occupation as a step in the right direction, provided that this did not imply acceptance of the bill abolishing the Cape franchise. But this of course was the crux of the matter: the Prime Minister had made it clear that he regarded the bills as interdependent, and that they were to be considered and debated as such. The conference, while discussing each one in detail one after the other, found itself unable to accept this proposition, and ended by passing a resolution requesting the Prime Minister to remove the difficulty confronting them by enabling them to take each one separately. It was as far as they could go. If the Prime Minister had expected African approval for the abolition of the Cape franchise in exchange for what he had on offer he had miscalculated badly. Plaatje and his colleagues certainly appreciated the Prime Minister's willingness to address them personally and formally lay the proposals before them, even if he was – in terms of the constitution – under no obligation whatever to take any notice of what they said. Most of them, indeed, were flattered that General Hertzog had taken the trouble to do this, for it suggested that their attendance at the conference, denounced in more radical circles, might not be a wholly fruitless exercise. But even this group of people – representing as they did the more conservative elements in African political life, and all of them present by government invitation, not elected – would never compromise over the Cape franchise. It was the most effective means of political leverage they had, and they all knew it.

Also presented to the conference delegates was another part of the government's legislative programme, the Native Affairs Administration Bill, strongly condemned by Plaatje here and on many other occasions before it finally became law (after passing through several Select Committees) two years later. Although not presented as one of Hertzog's four interdependent bills, the Native Affairs Administration Bill was nevertheless an integral part of his general programme of segregation, it took up the themes of his abortive Native

Administration Bill of 1917, and it embodied a firm commitment to the notion of 'retribalisation': that is to say, the administrative refurbishing of African traditionalism, providing official government backing and authority for the institutions of tribal rule.[30] The bill aimed to create a separate system of courts to administer African law in the rural areas and to extend to the other provinces of the Union Natal's system of recognising and incorporating the chiefs into the system of 'native administration', giving them far-reaching powers over their own people and recognising in law such elements of traditional practice as 'lobola', or brideprice. For Plaatje this all amounted to a reversion to tribalism, it encouraged the survival of polygamy, and it proposed to remove many ordinary Africans from the ultimate protection of the law. Like the proposal to abolish the Cape franchise, the Native Affairs Administration Bill threatened one of his most cherished principles: equality before the law. He therefore found the bill quite unacceptable, and made his views very plain both at the conference itself and in the press in the weeks and months that followed.[31] What saddened him, too, was the fact that at the conference, packed as it was by government-nominated chiefs, the bill predictably had some appeal to chiefs anxious to strengthen their powers. It threatened to drive a wedge between such educated leaders as himself and the traditional leaders of the African people; yet another element of Plaatje's once coherent and united political constituency was now threatened.

Hertzog's four bills came before the next session of the Native Conference a year later in more or less the same form. Again meeting in Pretoria, but this time addressed by the more jovial figure of Tielman Roos, the Acting Minister of Native Affairs, the conference proved to be even more acrimonious than its predecessor. Tielman Roos began by rehearsing the provisions and objectives of the bills in the same way that General Hertzog had done before, Professor D. D. T. Jabavu (Tengo Jabavu's eldest son) proposed a vote of thanks to him for his attendance, and Plaatje seconded in a long speech which Roos interpreted as a speech of complaint rather than of welcome.[32] Impasse on the issue of the interdependence of the Hertzog bills (as they were now known) was duly reached on the second day, and the conference very nearly broke up as the delegates sought to avoid any action that might be taken as indicating their acceptance of the disfranchisement bill. Eventually, after much toing and froing between the conference room and the Prime Minister's office, the delegates were persuaded to stay on and discuss the other bills, but only for speaker after speaker to emphasise their opposition to the government's insistence upon their interdependence.

The highlight of the discussions that followed, in the opinion of Professor Jabavu, was Plaatje's speech on the subject of the Land Bill. Plaatje, said Jabavu, 'probably commands greater authority than any other single native individual in the country to speak on the subject', and his speech was 'admirable for its collation of arguments against the bill'.[33] Again, Plaatje's point was not that Africans did not need more land – he knew better than anybody how desperately they did – but that the loss of the franchise was too high a price to pay. He illustrated the point with a widely quoted metaphor: 'When a Dutchman wants to trap a jackal,' he said, 'he gets a beautiful piece of mutton and puts poison in it, but the jackal usually walks round and round the meat and does not take it.'

Were they to accept the bait of the land they were offered, and give up the franchise, said Plaatje, then they would prove themselves to have less sense than a jackal. They should accept neither the principle of the Land Act, which excluded Africans from acquiring land in 87 per cent of the Union, nor the sacrifice of the Cape franchise along with it.[34]

Resolutions were duly framed to give expression to these sentiments, and passed unanimously by the delegates. It was the last time the government sought African approval for the Hertzog bills; men like Professor Jabavu, Richard Selope Thema, above all Plaatje himself, were far too experienced politically to allow themselves to be used in this way. And if the government had hoped to divide African opinion over the issue by splitting it along regional lines, then they failed here as well; it was for Plaatje a matter of considerable satisfaction that foremost in the defence of the Cape franchise, apart from himself, were Africans from the two northern provinces. Such a 'will to deny oneself for the sake of another', Plaatje wrote afterwards, 'is my idea of progress of civilisation', and the expression of 'a noble spirit on the part of the Northerners which does them credit'.[35] No African wanted to be remembered for being willing to exchange the Cape franchise for the paltry substitutes the government had to offer. If it was to be forced upon them, then so be it; but never let it be said it was done with their approval and agreement. The government itself seems to have recognised the futility of trying to secure African approval for these measures, for the Native Conference was not summoned again for another four years.

◇

Plaatje spoke with such authority on the question of land ownership, as Professor Jabavu had said, not only because of his great campaign against the original Natives' Land Act over ten years previously, but also because he had spent so much of his time over the three years since his return to South Africa in travelling around the countryside, seeing at first hand what was happening in the rural areas, intervening where he could to fight a case of dispossession, acting as a one-man advocate, almost, for Africans living in these areas. Sometimes Plaatje took his bioscope on his travels – particularly after he had been able to supplement his programme with some further educational films from the Hampton Institute in the United States and had been able to acquire (with the assistance of De Beers) a portable generator which enabled him to take the apparatus to remoter areas where there was no electricity.[36] On other occasions Plaatje simply travelled around to watch the Circuit Courts in operation, as he had often done before, reporting upon the frequent miscarriages of justice that he witnessed – especially in cases of white juries sitting in judgement over fellow whites accused of crimes against blacks – and seeking to obtain some form of redress.[37] It was a point he had emphasised in his address to the Joint Council Conference at the end of 1924 in the light of his observations over the previous few months; he had come face to face, he said, with cases that 'seemed hopelessly incredible even in this land of discrimination'. What he saw subsequently served only to convince him further of the need to keep a close watch over the horrors that were being perpetrated in the name of the law.

Plaatje still believed that the law stood as the true guardian of individual liberty. But now he was convinced of the need to replace trial by jury, in cases involving violence between black and white, with trial by judge alone, or by judges and assessors. He raised the point, indeed, at both Native Conferences, presenting Tielman Roos, on the second occasion in 1926, with details of a number of cases where there had been blatant miscarriages of justice as a result of biased white juries, and he emphasised the need for some action to be taken.[38]

At the same time Plaatje continued to report upon the evictions that were still taking place under the terms of the Natives' Land Act of 1913, often returning to this subject in the meetings he addressed, the articles he wrote for the press, seeking the whole time to draw attention to what he believed – in the mid-1920s as much as in 1913 of 1914 – to be the most iniquitous piece of legislation ever passed in South Africa. Now, as then, Plaatje saw it as his particular task to speak out on behalf of the 'inarticulate natives of the rural districts of the Union'.[39] As the years passed he became more and more critical, not only of the impact of government policy and legislation upon African life in the countryside, but at what he saw as the lack of concern of Africans living in the towns to the condition of those who lived in the countryside; in one newspaper article, indeed, he accused them of 'callous indifference to their own flesh and blood'.[40] Plaatje, more than any other individual African figure of the time, enjoyed a reputation as the spokesman for the interests of Africans struggling to make a living in South Africa's countryside.

Above all, Plaatje's platform during these years, and his means of earning a living, was the press; not his own newspaper, for he failed to raise the money or support to re-establish *Tsala ea Batho*, but the columns of almost all the major English-language newspapers of the day – the Johannesburg *Star*, the *Pretoria News*, the *Cape Times* and *Cape Argus*, the *East London Daily Dispatch*, the *Diamond Fields Advertiser*, and *Umteteli wa Bantu*, the newspaper published by the Chamber of Mines. Literally hundreds of Plaatje's articles appeared in these newspapers, often under the familiar headline 'Through Native Eyes'. More than anybody else, Plaatje became known as the pre-eminent spokesman for moderate African opinion. His articles ranged widely over many different aspects of African life in South Africa; they were notable for a characteristic style that combined strong moral indignation with meticulous documentary proof for the points he wished to make; and often they were enlivened by personal recollections of his own experiences where they bore upon the subject he had chosen to write about. By now Plaatje's writings made quite acceptable reading for educated white opinion in South Africa. This was not wholly a product of their intrinsic quality and Plaatje's reliability over deadlines. As a result of the political realignments of the 1920s Plaatje's own political views, seen in terms of the party politics of the day, were sufficiently close to those of the SAP-supporting English-language press for him to be given the freedom of the columns of their newspapers without any great risk that he would upset their readers. Both the *Cape Times* and the *Cape Argus*, for example, supported the maintenance of the Cape franchise – at least so long as the SAP was likely to need

African votes to get back into power – and along with the other English-language newspapers were hostile to job reservation and the colour bar in industry, both of them subjects, together with the long-running constitutional progress of Hertzog's 'Native bills', on which Plaatje frequently wrote.[41] On occasions his pieces were accompanied by some additional editorial comment commending what he had to say to the consideration of those readers who were not altogether convinced of the need to have the views of the 'well-known native publicist' expressed in their daily newspaper.[42]

Many of Plaatje's articles on the political developments of the day arose from his personal observations from the gallery of the House of Assembly in Cape Town which, in the mid-1920s, he made a point of trying to visit at least once a year. In so far as it could be said that there was ever an African parliamentary correspondent, then it was without doubt Plaatje who filled the part – 'Parliament and Natives' was a frequent headline over his contributions to the press. When he was unable to be in the House himself, Plaatje relied upon the daily press for information on political developments, and always made a point of reading carefully any official government publications that related to the subjects with which he was concerned. Often, indeed, he managed to refute arguments from government spokesmen (over such matters as the extent of the African contribution to the exchequer in taxation) with information and evidence derived from the government's own published sources; this way he could not be countered with allegations that his arguments were based on unsound evidence. Many of his articles referred his readers to particular government publications, and in time he came to build up a large library of blue books, select committee reports, Hansards and the like at his home in Kimberley.

Not everything Plaatje wrote was directly political in content. Sometimes he treated interestingly historical subjects, usually as a result of investigating the historical background to some topical issue. On several occasions, for example, he was led to look into some episodes of missionary history to demonstrate the missionaries' contribution to African 'civilisation' in order to counter the arguments, put forward by some to the left of the political spectrum, that the Christian missionaries had succeeded only in helping to dispossess Africans from their land, offering them religion instead – as a 'dope'. Plaatje, by contrast, always remained loyal to his missionary mentors.[43] Other articles he wrote took the form of travel writing, reporting upon his observations as he travelled around the country: hence, for example, two articles entitled 'Native life at the alluvial diggings', published in all the major white newspapers in mid-1927, following his visit to the Lichtenburg diamond diggings.[44]

Perhaps the most striking of all the forms of Plaatje's writings in the white press were the obituaries he wrote. Many were of the great figures of Cape liberalism who were passing away – J. X. Merriman, J. W. Jagger, Sir William Solomon, Sir Percival Lawrence, men whom Plaatje had known in happier times, and who represented for him the values and ideals of a great tradition.[45] In mourning their deaths, he was eulogising the passing of an era very different from the harsher times in which he now lived: an era in which the actions of individuals seemed to count far more than they did now; when he had enjoyed a fruitful association with men willing to recognise and accept him as a spokesman for 'native opinion'; when South Africa was not yet trapped in the segregationist orthodoxies of the 1920s. Above all, perhaps, these obituaries reflected the importance Plaatje always attached to the role of individual character and leadership: he recognised in the lives of these men an example for others to emulate. The same conviction had guided his own actions. Plaatje had always believed that even the most severe disabilities and disadvantages could be overcome through sheer force of character and hard work, and that this was the example he had to set to his people.

If such attitudes suggested a man whose ideas were being overtaken by the realities of the times in which he lived the same was also true of the content of much of what he wrote on current affairs in the 1920s. For Plaatje was not well equipped to understand the dynamics of the complex industrialised society which South Africa had now become. His political ideas were formed out of a combination of Christian belief and Victorian liberalism (his views on individual character of course very much a product of this), grafted onto a powerfully felt sense of responsibility for the leadership of his people. But these ideas had done nothing to halt a government intent on implementing a social and political order which went against everything in which he believed; whilst the notion that there was such a thing as a coherent, undifferentiated community of African interests was becoming increasingly untenable in a divided, industrialised society.

On social and economic issues Plaatje could never really come to terms fully with what was going on around him. He continued to regard the countryside as the 'natural environment' of the African people – a phrase he used on a number of occasions – and he always regarded the members of the urban African working class as essentially displaced rural cultivators. 'Failing anything better', Plaatje was to tell a government commission in 1931, 'the principal industrial centres should have a reserve where an overworked Native or miners' pthisis victim could mind his own goat and spend the evening of his life under his own vine and fig tree.'[46] In spirit, Plaatje was a man of the countryside, not the city, and it often showed in his writings; he sought the restoration of an old regime, not the creation of a new order.

A further consequence of Plaatje's outlook was that he was inclined to attribute to political actions or legislation social and economic consequences which were in reality the product of wider processes of change. This was true above all in relation to the Natives' Land Act of 1913, about which he often wrote in the 1920s, invariably in the strongest terms. 'To me,' he wrote on one occasion, 'it remains the most Draconian piece of legislation ever conceived, and it is responsible for the wholesale moral and economic degradation of our people in the country – including the high mortality of black babies.'[47] There was of course more than an element of truth in this, but it was not the whole story: overcrowding in the towns certainly owed something to the effects of the Land Act in the countryside, but it was part and parcel of a wider process of industrialisation which Plaatje found very difficult to comprehend.

<><>

When Plaatje addressed himself to an African audience it was generally in the columns of *Umteteli wa Bantu*, the weekly paper financed by the Chamber of

Mines, which throughout the 1920s appeared without a break (in contrast to *Abantu-Batho* which struggled desperately to keep afloat). Whilst *Umteteli* was regarded by some Africans, and certainly by the South African Communist Party, as simply a tool of the mining industry, the line it took was a relatively liberal one. Its editorials advised against support for strike action as a means of redressing grievances, and precious little criticism of the mining industry ever appeared in its columns, but it did support the retention of the Cape franchise and its extension to the northern provinces; it opposed the Hertzog bills, and it was strongly against the colour bar in industry, and hence opposed the Mines and Works Amendment bill. For *Umteteli* the villains of the South African political stage were not, as the South African Communist Party would have it, the mining capitalists, but overpaid white workers who possessed the political means to force the government to concede to their demands for a guaranteed place, protected by the colour bar, in industry; Afrikaner nationalists who demanded state handouts to subsidise inefficient farmers at the expense of the mining industry; and a Pact government that represented a cynical alliance of the two.

Because these were the views shared by a considerable number of African public figures, Plaatje included, *Umteteli* did command a wide readership and influence among educated Africans, and with the resources of the mining industry behind it it was a very well-turned-out newspaper, each edition packed full of news and features, and containing material in a variety of African languages as well as in English. Ultimate editorial control, as most people were well aware, nevertheless remained with the Chamber and it was this that led Plaatje to reject on probably more than one occasion the offer of the editorship. He valued his independence far too highly to be willing to subject himself to restrictions of this kind.[48]

But Plaatje did write fairly regular letters and articles for *Umteteli* throughout the 1920s, and in many ways they are the most interesting of Plaatje's extensive writings from this time, for they reveal, in a way that his articles in the European press often did not, a great deal about the personal as well as the political frustrations which he now felt. Many of the topics he chose to write about were the same, but in addressing himself to an African audience he became increasingly critical not only of the government for its totally unsympathetic attitude to African aspirations and representations, but of his own people for their failure to unite, to support their political leaders, to demonstrate that collective strength of character and integrity that he believed was so vital to their well being. He did not mince words in condemning the 'lethargy', 'fickleness' and 'wanton indifference' of many African people; the increasing incidence of alcoholism he saw around him; the failure of delegates to conferences or congresses to prepare their arguments properly; the growing spirit of jealousy he now perceived amongst his people. With shortcomings of this kind, he often argued, it was hardly surprising that African political and social life was in such a sad state.[49]

Along with this there also developed, in Plaatje's mind, a much more personal note of bitterness and frustration, which comes through very clearly in these writings in *Umteteli*: above all on the subject of leadership, a much debated issue in its columns throughout the 1920s. This is what he had to say in February 1928:

It would be impossible for any one to lead a train that is disinclined to follow. Natives as a race recognise only one leader, namely, their hereditary prince; and there being so many chiefs, all independent of one another, individual leadership even by one of royal blood, is impracticable. A man may be a genius but the Native population will regard him very much like a clever actor on the stage – to be admired, not followed. This admiration – like the popularity of a new jazz tune – will last until its novelty has worn off, when the people look for fresh excitement in the shape of a different 'leader'. But, be he ever so faithful and self-sacrificing, they will desert him at the first sound of the call of the tribal chief, even if the latter implied nothing but a tribal chief and clannish tyranny.

I have always forestalled this fickleness by declining any position they offered me, such as the presidency of the Native Congress, preferring to serve – not lead – the sufferers among them, whose name is legion, and let the rest take care of themselves. The failure is not on the part of the leaders of whom we have had several of outstanding ability; the fault lies with the Native masses who by nature object to follow one who is not their tribal chief.[50]

There were many other statements from Plaatje in the same vein, and it is evident he recognised clearly that his own influence was no longer what it had once been. He also became very sensitive to criticism, particularly when it came from those who claimed he was too closely associated with the interests of the South African Party. On more than one occasion he spoke out against the presumptuousness of 'the younger generation' to hold forth on such subjects as 'leadership', 'character', or 'sacrifice', and pointed rather to his own record in the service of his people to demonstrate his independence from any political party, or to the nature of the sacrifices he had made. Replying to 'Enquirer' (Archibald M'belle, a nephew of Isaiah Bud-M'belle) in October 1928, he reminded *Umteteli's* readers of the campaigns he had fought in England and America, and concluded:

Much has been written lately about Native lack of leadership. We of my generation cannot go on working, lobbying among younger politicians and paying the cost. I know, however, that a number of young men (and women too) are willing and able to take over the burden; but what encouragement is offered to them to shoulder the thankless task, when busybodies who pay nothing and do less for the cause can stay at home and sow apples of discord among the Native masses by imputing unfounded motives and generally misrepresenting such voluntary sacrifices?[51]

Having dedicated his life to the cause of his people, Plaatje not unnaturally felt very bitter when aspersions were cast on his integrity, when people failed to appreciate the value of what he had done in the past. Now, more than ever, he thought he deserved better of his people.

Many others joined this debate on the nature of 'leadership' in the columns of *Umteteli*. There was little agreement about the nature of the problems, or what needed to be done. The variety of views expressed reflected above all the frustrations of several generations of African spokesmen, or would-be spokesmen, unsure – many of them – on whose behalf they could really claim to be speaking. They thought they were the leaders, but who were the people? Once, things had been much clearer; but that spirit of political unity, that sense of national feeling which had emerged so strongly at the time of the campaign against the Natives' Land Act, was very much a thing of the past. Then, Plaatje and his colleagues in the SANNC could justifiably claim to represent the African people as a whole. Now that was clearly not the case, and Plaatje's own public arguments with 'Enquirer' and 'Resurgam' revealed that even his own – once authoritative – views were now by no means universally accepted.[52]

But it was not simply that the relationship between these African leaders and their political constituency was so much more ambiguous and tenuous than before. In addition, these men were faced, on the one hand, with an unsympathetic government, deaf to their representations, determined to implement its policies of segregation and retribalisation, with not a care for their careers or aspirations. And on the other, they now found that even that small space still left to them was being occupied by the new breed of white liberals and 'friends of the natives' – the 'self-styled native experts', as Plaatje called them on more than one occasion – who had moved into the 'race relations' business, who controlled *Umteteli* and the Joint Councils, who possessed the resources denied to the Africans whose place they were taking. It was small wonder, in such circumstances that 'leadership' should have been such a contentious and widely debated issue; that men like Richard Selope Thema, Pixley Seme, and many others should have resorted to drink as a means of escape from the impossible position in which they were in; that African political organisation as a whole should have deteriorated to such an extent in the 1920s.

◇

In Plaatje the effect of this growing disillusionment – for he shared it too – tended not to despair but to a renewed emphasis upon the need to set an example of individual service, to be more vigilant than ever as the Pact government pushed its legislative programme through parliament, to reiterate time and again that Africans must fight their own battles. Above all he emphasised the need for moral regeneration. Nowhere was this more evident than in a new form of activity in which he became involved in the middle of 1927 – temperance work on behalf of the Independent Order of True Templars, or the IOTT. A committed teetotaller, Plaatje had long been concerned with the temperance issue. As a youngster he had witnessed in Kimberley the devastating effects that alcoholism could have on a people wrenched from the countryside to employment on the mines and in the towns; in Mafeking he had seen successive Barolong chiefs fall victim to its effects, and always supported calls for the total prohibition of sales of drink to his people. Later, in Kimberley, he used to attend the annual licensing sessions to argue against the extension and renewal of liquor licences. As time went on he became even more concerned about the issue. When he returned from England and America in 1923 he had been shocked at the 'orgy of drunkenness' he encountered in Johannesburg, and he continued to regard it – whatever the other reasons or mitigating circumstances put forward – as ultimately a question of moral failure on the part of those involved. Many of his articles in *Umteteli* over the next few years singled out alcoholism as one of the primary reasons for the deterioration of the life of his people. Over practically no other issue, indeed, did Plaatje feel so strongly.

Plaatje's actual involvement in the affairs of the IOTT began in June 1927 when he was appointed Special Deputy ('A High Mogul of the Order', as he described it in a letter to Robert Moton) to the head of the movement, the Right Worthy Templar, J. W. Mushet, with a special brief to establish new branches of the organisation in the Transvaal, Orange Free State, and eastern Cape.[53] Mushet was an old friend of Plaatje's. A wealthy Cape Town merchant and philanthropist, married to T. L. Schreiner's daughter, he was one of a dwindling band of old Cape liberals who continued to play a part in South African public life in the 1920s, and he succeeded Schreiner as head of the order.[54] Mushet personified an older, more congenial Cape liberal tradition, willing to countenance support and co-operation with like-minded Africans on terms of greater equality than was true of most of the new breed of 'friends of the natives' on the Rand. The obvious point of comparison in Plaatje's life was with the Brotherhood movement, and he was attracted to the IOTT for very much the same reasons as had, over ten years previously, drawn him towards the Brotherhood movement. For like the Brotherhood movement, the IOTT was an inter-racial organisation which Plaatje upheld as an example in microcosm of what South Africa could be;[55] and it held out the prospect of financial support, with few strings attached, to enable him to travel around the countryside, as he had done in the past, investigating and reporting, at the same time as he was furthering the aims of the movement itself. As with so many of Plaatje's projects, there was no single reason for his involvement; he was drawn to the IOTT by a mixture of both practical and moral considerations.

Promoting the work of the IOTT and setting up new branches occupied a great deal of Plaatje's time during 1927 and 1928. That is not to say he withdrew from the other forms of activity in which he had been involved. The government called no more Native Conferences, so this platform was denied to him, but he continued to write regularly for the press, and grew more and more concerned at the implications of the Native Administration Bill which the government was intent on bringing to the statute book. In May 1927 he took the trouble to write a long personal letter to the Select Committee, then engaged in refining its details, to express his views – in his capacity, he said, 'as member of the last Annual Statutory Conference at Pretoria, nominated thereto by unanimous decision of the rural natives of Griqualand West on the invitation of the Prime Minister, and on behalf of the other tribal and detribalised Natives unofficially represented in various capacities by me'. It was a clear statement of his feelings about the proposed legislation:

> The importance of this vital Bill is that, unlike any other measure of its kind, it will, when enacted, effect some drastic changes in native life not only politically but even socially. Its aim is to put all natives under the same native law. One could no more draw up a single code for all the tribes than fix the same speed limit for Adderley Street, Cape Town, and the highways of the Karroo; and one cannot but foresee trouble in any attempt to apply the same social code to the Bapedi (under whose tribal laws it is permissible for a native to marry his first cousin) and the Tembus under whose tribal laws it is an

319

abomination, purged only by death, for a native to marry a blood relation, however distant.[56]

The Native Administration Bill also provided one of the main subjects of discussion at a conference which Plaatje attended in Kimberley in June 1927, a month later. Organised by Dr Abdurahman, still president of the APO, and held in the Kimberley City Hall between 23 and 25 June, it was the first 'non-European conference' to have been called, and was attended by over a hundred delegates representing a wide range of African, Coloured and Indian organisations. Its aim was to secure 'closer co-operation among non-Europeans of all sections in British South Africa' – one of the few concrete steps to have been taken in this direction since Plaatje had initiated talks between the executive of the South African Native National Congress and the APO back in 1912. Plaatje was much involved in procedural matters once the conference had opened, and it was appropriate that it should have been he who moved the opening resolution: 'that the interests of South Africa can be best served by (a) closer co-operation among the non-European sections of South Africa, and (b) closer co-operation between Europeans and non-Europeans'.

A variety of matters of common interest to 'non-Europeans' was then discussed during the conference. From Plaatje himself there were contributions on familiar themes. Welcoming the delegates to the city of Kimberley, he spoke highly of the European, Indian and Coloured communities but had rather harsher words for 'the Kimberley Natives', about whom he regretted he could not do the same; they 'had better opportunities and educational facilities' than anywhere else, he said, 'but they made little use of them', and he expressed the hope that the conference 'would wake them up'. On the Native Administration Bill, too, Plaatje reiterated his criticism. Before moving a resolution to this effect (it was carried unanimously), he pointed out that if the bill was to become law 'the police could march into that Hall and arrest the whole conference, under the sedition clause, because it was called without the permission of the Governor-General'.[57]

The conference was considered to be a success, but it could do nothing to secure any relief from the disabilities from which both Africans and Coloured people suffered. Both Dr Abdurahman and D. D. T. Jabavu, in the closing speeches, spoke hopefully of the historical importance that the conference would one day assume, but this was in the long-term, not the short-term. It was 'a vain hope', so Plaatje wrote to Robert Moton the day before the conference opened, to believe that it could do anything at all to avert the 'drastic laws, most barbarous in character', which parliament was intent on putting onto the statute book, for what they lacked was political power. No wonder Plaatje began his letter to Moton by saying 'the struggle for life in South Africa is so grim that I could scarcely remember whether I owe you a letter or the other way round'.[58]

<>

Once the Native Administration Act became law in September 1927 the defence of the Cape franchise once again became Plaatje's overriding concern – in the press, in lobbying politicians in Cape Town, in ensuring that as many Africans as were qualified for the franchise in the Cape were actually registered. In the early and mid-1920s Plaatje had retained a degree of albeit guarded optimism about the possibilities that lay in the consultative machinery established by the government in the 1920 Native Affairs Act, and he had been willing to participate in the new structures that had been created. By the late 1920s his attitude had changed. The government itself had demonstrated its contempt for the whole notion of consulting representatives of the African people, even those it had nominated itself, by completely ignoring the views expressed at the 1926 Native Conference, and by refusing to call it thereafter; as a result, a number of measures affecting African interests were passed during the few years after this without any official Native Conference ever having a chance to discuss them. Even the conduct of the Native Affairs Commission, supposedly composed of 'friends of the natives', proved to Plaatje and many others to be a great disappointment. During the last Native Conference held in 1926 Plaatje's view was that this commission, 'instead of supporting the natives, interpreted to the natives the government point of view and pressed for its adoption'. Over the next two years the commission's support for the government had been expressed even more clearly. It became, as Plaatje wrote on several occasions, nothing more than 'the political branch of the Native Affairs Department'.[59]

Plaatje's reaction to the failure of the Pact government to take seriously the whole notion of consultation with Africans was twofold. It convinced him, further, of the dangers of relying wholly upon Europeans, even those who claimed to be 'friends of the natives', for the representation of African interests: 'only one person', he said time and time again, could truly represent their views, 'and that was the native himself'.[60] And it convinced him, more than ever before, of the need to defend, at all costs, the Cape franchise. He saw more clearly than anybody that it was the existence of this franchise which, despite the changed conditions of the 1920s, gave African spokesmen like himself some degree of leverage in the House of Assembly, some influence in the deliberations of the South African Party. It was, therefore, as a fervent defender of the Cape franchise that Plaatje spoke out most often in the late 1920s – against European 'sympathisers' who would have Africans adopt a more flexible attitude to the various alternative forms of representation that were being suggested, and be prepared to trust to General Hertzog's good faith; against people like Horatio M'belle, another of Isaiah Bud-M'belle's nephews, who believed him to be in the pocket of the South African Party; against Coloured voters inclined to take seriously General Hertzog's promises of differential treatment from Africans. It was the reason, too, for his involvement in the affairs of the Cape Native Voters Association, whose vice-president he became in 1927, and under whose auspices he played a characteristically energetic role – particularly on the eve of the provincial elections in 1928 and the general election of 1929 – in mobilising Cape voters behind the South African Party, and in countering the efforts of Nationalist Party agents to prevent African voters from registering. Protecting the Cape African franchise involved far more than composing eloquent articles for publication in the English-language newspapers.[61]

For a short while, too, Plaatje became involved once again in the affairs of the African National Congress, having rejected many appeals to do so over the previous few years. He attended the 17th annual conference of the ANC in

Bloemfontein at the beginning of April 1929, and was responsible for drafting a reply to General Hertzog's notorious 'Black Manifesto' (which reiterated the premier's determination to proceed with the abolition of the Cape franchise). Plaatje's document condemned the General for describing 'the native people as something evil and subversive of European civilisation', and for making 'an authoritative appeal . . . to the racial passions of all white people to unite in their suppression, and so create and perpetuate strife and friction between black and white in the Union of South Africa'.[62] Plaatje and his colleagues of the old guard at the Congress meeting were denounced as the 'tools of the Capitalist oppressors and exploiters' in the columns of the Communist Party's newspaper, the *South African Worker*, and accused of dominating the proceedings of the conference and making decisions 'in the name of the African masses'; but even the Communist Party—shortly to be muzzled by the 'sedition' clause of the Native Administration Act—decided to put up candidates for what it called 'the Parliament of the ruling classes'.[63]

To nobody's great surprise the Pact government was returned to power at the general election in June with an increased majority for the Nationalist Party, which gave it overall control in the new parliament. Plaatje and his colleagues could only look forward to the grim prospect of a renewed assault upon the Cape African franchise. The political future looked gloomier than ever.

◇

The general election of 1929 drew to a close another phase in Plaatje's life, which had begun with his return from England and America at the end of 1923. He had returned home having been forced to accept that there was no longer any prospect of outside intervention in the affairs of South Africa, and had applied himself instead to working within the structures that now existed. With his travelling bioscope he had done his best to convey something of the sense of inspiration he had himself derived from his visit to the United States. He had failed in his attempt to resuscitate his old newspaper, *Tsala ea Batho*, but he had written extensively on the issues of the day in both black and white newspapers, and he had sought to exploit white party politics in his own cause. He had done all he could to foster that moral regeneration which he considered to be the only way out of the deteriorating social, economic and political circumstances in which the African people now found themselves.

But for all Plaatje's efforts, and through force of circumstances well beyond his control, he was now much less of an influence in South African public affairs than he had once been. It was no longer at all clear on whose behalf he spoke, and his involvement in such organisations as the IOTT seemed only to emphasise his isolation from any meaningful political constituency. The IOTT gave him some sort of platform and a means of livelihood, but it could provide no substitute for the chasm that now existed. The more he criticised the failings of his own people, the more he emphasised the need for individual uplift, the more lonely and isolated did his own predicament appear.

In such circumstances Plaatje's decision to turn his mind to other things, to devote himself far more systematically than before to the preservation of the language and literature of the Tswana people, appears wholly understandable.

Over the next few months this was to become his main preoccupation. It was to provide the overwhelmingly important theme of his life over the next couple of years.

14

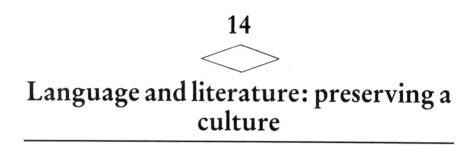

Language and literature: preserving a culture

Plaatje had always displayed a keen interest in the language, history and cultural traditions of the Tswana people. Setswana had been the first language he had learnt, and he had grown up, like others of his generation, to combine without very great difficulty a love for both the traditions he had heard from his family, and the religion, language and values of the mission community where he grew up. Thereafter, he had always responded with enthusiasm whenever called upon in any way to debate the value and nature of this Tswana inheritance – whether this was when regaling the predominantly Xhosa and Mfengu members of the South Africans Improvement Society in Kimberley in the 1890s with an account of 'The history of the Bechuanas', entering the fray with the missionary societies over the proper form in which the Tswana language should be represented in writing, or, when time and opportunity arose, in embarking upon the task of translating Shakespeare into Setswana.

But given Plaatje's political and journalistic commitments from 1902 onwards it is not altogether surprising that it was only during his stay in England during the First World War that he had found the opportunity and encouragement to spend some time in analysing and recording several elements of the Tswana language, and to see through to publication his *Sechuana Proverbs* and *Sechuana Reader*. He had been very clear about his objectives in writing these two books – the preservation of the proverbs, in the first instance, by committing them to written form; and in the second, the preservation of what he saw as the correct and original pronunciation of the Tswana language through the application of the principles of phonetics. Plaatje considered both to be under threat from the spread of 'European civilisation' in southern Africa, and in the interests of the cultural integrity of the Tswana-speaking people he considered it his duty to do whatever he could to arrest this process. Perhaps paradoxically, Plaatje's translations of Shakespeare, undertaken largely during his travels overseas, were very much part of this as well.

By the 1920s Plaatje was, if anything, more concerned than ever over the state of the Tswana language and its meagre literature. He himself no longer possessed a newspaper of his own with which to perpetuate and develop a tradition of writing in Setswana, and Tswana literature, such as it was, consisted of a handful of religious books printed by the various missionary societies working amongst the Tswana. At the heart of this unsatisfactory state of affairs was the unresolved orthographic problem. Each of the four missionary societies working in Tswana-speaking areas had developed their own orthographies, and over the years had been unable to reach agreement over the best means of representing the sounds of the Tswana language. Plaatje himself regarded none of these orthographies as satisfactory, and as editor of *Koranta ea Becoana* and *Tsala ea Becoana* had always used a further version of his own. For a while it seemed that the so-called '1910 orthography', product of the initiative of the British and Foreign Bible Society, might gain acceptance, but these hopes proved to be short-lived. Plaatje's own efforts to promote the use of the International Phonetic Alphabet in his *Sechuana Reader* had not succeeded either, for its refusal to compromise accuracy for simplicity had severely limited its practical value: the *Sechuana Reader* had been a pioneering scholarly effort, but the Tswana people, according to one of Plaatje's friends, always regarded it 'as a strange book in a strange spelling', and it never became popular.[1]

The unsatisfactory state of written literature in Tswana was also underlined – in Plaatje's mind more than anybody else's – by the progress that was being made in the other vernacular literatures of southern Africa. Although Setswana had been one of the first Bantu languages to be committed to writing in the early part of the nineteenth century, and had been very fortunate in the quality of the linguistic and translating work carried out by the first missionaries working amongst the Tswana people, it had, by the 1920s, been far overtaken by work that had been done in other languages, particularly in Xhosa and Sotho. For both these languages the problems of orthography had been, for the most part, overcome, and in each language Xhosa and Sotho writers had progressed a long way beyond the purely religious, didactic works that still, in the 1920s, constituted the bulk of published literature in Setswana. Apart from Plaatje himself, indeed, no native Tswana-speakers had written, or at least published, any books in their own language.[2] Xhosa and Sotho, by contrast, had produced widely known writers like S. E. K. Mqhayi and Thomas Mofolo, whose novel, *Chaka*, published in 1925, had met with immediate acclaim, and was soon to be translated into English. For Plaatje, the effect was only to emphasise the extent to which Tswana had fallen behind. It possessed, in the 1920s, no literature beyond Plaatje's own compilations and a limited amount of religious and didactic material, an inadequate dictionary, no commonly accepted means of representing the language in writing, and no mission press that was either able or willing to publish anything other than its own denomination's religious material. The closest approximation to Lovedale or Morija amongst the Tswana was the London Missionary Society's institution at Tigerkloof, but this was severely handicapped by lack of funds; it used an orthography not accepted by the other missionary societies; and such publications as it produced were based uncompromisingly upon the Tlaping dialect. In the past Plaatje had been very critical of the society's generally poor performance in the field of education; he saw no reason now to change his opinion.

Plaatje was especially conscious of the need to provide suitable reading matter in Setswana for the schools for he saw clearly that unless the language was taught properly here there was a very real danger that it would fall into disuse and ultimately disappear. He was not entirely alone in being so concerned over this. His views were shared by his fellow Tswana scholar, David Ramoshoana, a close friend, who taught at the Lyndhurst Road Native School in the late 1920s, and who was secretary of the Brotherhood movement in Kimberley, and the two men used to have frequent discussions about the state of the Tswana language during Ramoshoana's regular visits to Plaatje's home at 32 Angel Street.[3] Both would have been in agreement with the views of Peter Sebina, a teacher living in Serowe in the Bechuanaland Protectorate, who was moved on one occasion to express his dissatisfaction to the education authorities at the way in which books written in Sesotho were being recommended as reading matter in schools in Bechuanaland because there was simply nothing suitable in Setswana. 'Bechuana children,' he complained, 'are not Basuto children, nor are English children French children. Their colour may be the same, but not their languages. That means our children have to learn to read Sesuto (not by easy stages), and very often taught by a teacher who is himself ignorant of what he professes to teach.'[4]

Plaatje's fear that Setswana would simply fall into disuse or become so distorted as to lose its identity was deeply felt. He was always conscious of the example of Koranna, one of the languages spoken on the Pniel mission station where he had grown up, but by now well on the way to extinction, like the Koranna people themselves: it had been an extraordinarily rapid process. But there was also an equally dramatic example of the reverse, of what could be done to rejuvenate, to create even, a language from seemingly inauspicious beginnings. That example was Afrikaans. 'The Dutch-speaking people of South Africa,' David Ramoshoana wrote, comparing Afrikaans to Setswana, 'have pulled their Afrikaans – a baby among languages spoken in the Union – out of the fire and have launched it as one of the most important languages in the half- continent by writing it in newspapers, magazines, and books. Their ablest writers contributed articles, etc., and thus fixed its literary efficacy, and so it now faces the world as a cultural language.'[5] Both Plaatje and Ramoshoana were committed to the view that this same kind of effort needed to be devoted to Setswana.

Plaatje's intense concern for the condition of Setswana was also linked to some wider considerations. For in part at least it represented a response to his increasingly pessimistic observations of the effects of social and economic changes upon the lives of his people – the lawlessness, alcoholism, the break-down of parental control, a growing disrespect for authority. Plaatje attributed much of the responsibility for this to moral failure on the part of those involved, but this in turn he believed to be a consequence of the weakening of the constraints upon individual behaviour which had once been imposed by the bonds of tribal society. 'Tribal organisation,' Plaatje had written in 1924, commenting upon changes he perceived upon returning home to South Africa from overseas, 'has undergone a marked deterioration during the last five years, and nothing appears to have replaced the disintegration.'[6] What he witnessed over the next few years served only to confirm this view, and much that he wrote during the 1920s emphasised this theme of disintegration in all spheres of the communal life of the African people.

Although Plaatje never stated it explicitly, there seems little doubt that he saw the preservation of the Tswana language and culture as a means, if not of reversing this process of disintegration, at least of providing the means of cultural regeneration, to enable the Tswana people to resist the consequences of what he saw happening to them. Only then could they feel pride in their customs and traditions, and only with a knowledge and pride in their native culture could that process of moral regeneration – of which Plaatje spoke so often – be set in motion. Instinctively, Plaatje looked to the past for the means to resist the consequences of the social and economic changes taking place around him. Just as he continued to regard the countryside as the 'natural environment' of his people, so did he regard the culture of this rural environment as something that had equally to be preserved.

Probably, too, there was a more personal element in Plaatje's renewed concern with literature in Tswana in the late 1920s – a feeling that it provided an area of endeavour where he could yet make a unique contribution, free from the frustrations and restrictions that were by now so much a part of his various other activities. The re-election of the Pact government in June 1929 may well have been the final catalyst. What now could be done to prevent General Hertzog from proceeding to abolish the Cape franchise as he had promised, from turning South Africa into the wholly segregated society upon which he seemed intent? Whatever the precise connection in Plaatje's mind between the general election of June 1929 and his involvement in the provision of Tswana literature for schools, he devoted himself to this task in the months following the election in a way he had not done before.

◇

The greatest problem for Plaatje lay not in actually writing the manuscripts – by 1929 he had several in hand – but in raising the money to get them printed. According to a letter he wrote in November 1929, he had the following manuscripts ready: translations of Shakespeare's *Comedy of Errors*, *Julius Caesar* and *Much Ado about Nothing*; a book with the title 'Traditional Native Folk Tales and Other Useful Knowledge'; and a new, enlarged, edition of his *Sechuana Proverbs*. Judging from the printers' estimates which Plaatje had been sent, £123 was needed to pay for the Shakespeare translations, £205 for the 'Traditional Native Folk Tales and Other Useful Knowledge' (both these estimates coming from the Morija printing press in Lesotho), and £57 18s was required for the new edition of the *Sechuana Proverbs*.[7] Progress in raising these substantial sums had been painfully slow. Between August and November 1929, when fund-raising efforts had been launched under the auspices of the Brotherhood movement in Kimberley, only £41 was raised – a fraction of the sum required to print a sufficient number of copies of all the books he had prepared. In the middle of November 1929, therefore, Plaatje decided to write to De Beers to ask for help. It was the kind of letter he was by now well practised in composing, and it bore the familiar Plaatje style. He began by explaining to the Secretary of De Beers the desperate need of schools in the area for suitable Tswana reading matter; he went on to elaborate upon the work he had been doing recently in preparing this; and offered what he hoped would be an appealing explanation for his committee's lack of progress in collecting the money themselves:

327

It may perhaps be well to explain IN CONFIDENCE why our Committee, which undertook the task last August, should thus far only have managed to raise £41 towards the printing of books that should be ready first thing after New Year. I may say in explanation that the officers of the Brotherhood are the leading social workers among Native Communities in Kimberley and outside, and since the elections last June and July our difficulties have been exceptional and varied. To mention a few, the Pact vendetta against Sir E. Oppenheimer was launched by enemies of native welfare by sowing systematic dissensions among natives in the surrounding locations. It taxed our resources physically, mentally and financially to defeat their aims and keep the native vote intact. Again, besides our regular work we have had our hands full combatting and trying to keep the Communist movement outside Kimberley; this has been a stupendous task since Mr Bunting came here last September and left his agents here to spread his communistic propaganda. Just about the same time our Brotherhood undertook to organise a farewell token of respect for Sir David Harris; this ambition is soon to fructify: it has already taken the shape of a native hand-made kaross, suitable for an old gentleman.

I mention these confidential incidents only to show that while I was proceeding with the work of compiling these books, the Committee were not idling; and if outside meddlers had only left us undisturbed the raising of funds would have kept pace with the edition of the books.[8]

It was the kind of argument calculated to appeal to the directors of De Beers, appealing to the same instincts that had led the De Beers directors to respond so positively to his request for the old tram shed eleven years previously. But then the political and industrial situation was rather more tense, and the donation of a meeting hall for Plaatje's Brotherhood movement was more likely to have some beneficial effect. Now matters were not quite so serious. Sidney Bunting, chairman of the Communist Party of South Africa, was certainly a nuisance, but he had not had a great deal of success in Kimberley, and the government was in any case armed with the necessary legislative powers to deal effectively with such people. In the circumstances it would have been very difficult for Plaatje to have persuaded the De Beers directors that a donation to the cost of printing Tswana school books would have contributed to this end. Their reply to Plaatje's request, when it came, was – in short – no.[9]

Of the books which Plaatje indicated he had ready for publication in 1929 only one of them, *Diphosho-phosho*, his translation of *The Comedy of Errors*, did he succeed in getting printed and published. Probably the reason he concentrated his fund-raising efforts upon *Diphosho-phosho* was that it was the shortest of the Shakespeare plays which he had translated, and therefore cheapest to print. Funds came from several sources: sympathetic churchmen in Kimberley and Johannesburg; a wealthy Indian trader, Mr M. Sammy; Mrs W. Allan King of Pretoria (widow of the man killed in the Boer rebellion of 1914, whom Plaatje once counted as his best white friend), and her sister-in-law, Mrs King Botha. Plaatje was very disappointed at the lack of response to his appeal for funds from the Tswana people, the people who would actually read and use the book. As he pointed out in the Preface to *Diphosho-phosho*, he had imagined there would be a ready response to his appeal for funds to publish anything in Setswana since there was, so he believed, such a demand for this. But even when he appealed for a loan of £30, to be repaid within three months of publication with the proceeds of sales, Plaatje elicited no response. If this was the attitude on the part of the Tswana, he wrote, then it was hardly surprising that literature in the Tswana language was in such a state.[10]

Notwithstanding these difficulties, *Diphosho-phosho* (literally, 'Mistake upon Mistake') was duly printed by the Morija mission press in July 1930; it was a modest 52 pages long, came in a soft brown cover, and cost 2s 3d. On the title page, and in a newspaper interview Plaatje gave when the book came out, it was stated that *Diphosho-phosho* was to be the first of a series of Shakespeare translations under the general heading of *Mabolelo a ga Tsikinya-Chaka* ('The Sayings of William Shakespeare'), and that *Mashoabi-shoabi (The Merchant of Venice)*, *Matsepa-tsepa a Lefela (Much Ado about Nothing)* and *Dincho-ncho tsa bo-Juliuse Kesara (Julius Caesar)* were shortly to follow.[11]

Diphosho-phosho was the first published translation of one of Shakespeare's plays into any African language, and it attracted a considerable amount of publicity. The editor of the *Diamond Fields Advertiser*, Mr Simpson, was characteristically generous in his recognition of Plaatje's achievement, and devoted an entire editorial in one issue to emphasising the wider importance of Plaatje's 'valuable services in saving from extinction some of the rich profusion of the Sechuana language'.[12] The Johannesburg *Star* carried a report of an interview with Plaatje on the same subject, during the course of which he had some interesting points to make about the problems he had encountered in carrying out the work of translation. 'It is only natural,' he said, 'that the translator must experience great difficulty in finding the equivalents for some of Shakespeare's phrases, in which case he has to rely on the general sense of the passage to render the author's meaning in the vernacular, and that has been my difficulty.'[13] However, as he also pointed out, his experience as a court interpreter and editor of a bi-lingual and tri-lingual newspaper had stood him in good stead, and he had by now accumulated a great deal of experience in rendering intelligible to one another two languages constructed around such different concepts and linguistic forms. During his days as a court interpreter in Mafeking, he had become accustomed to devising ways of explaining English legal terms like 'committed for trial' into Setswana in a way that made sense to a bewildered prisoner in the dock. It was rather less of a problem for him to deal satisfactorily with statements such as that of Antonio in Act 4, Scene 1, 'I do obey thee till I give thee bail' – which Plaatje renders as '*Ke utlwa; ke tla ya nau go tsamage begaetsho ba tla go nthelolola*', literally: 'I understand; I shall go with you till my kindred come home to ransom me.'[14]

In the opinion of the handful of people who were in any sort of position to pass judgement upon the quality of Plaatje's translation, *Diphosho-phosho* was a great success. In the view of one African living in the Bechuanaland Protectorate, who wrote to Plaatje to compliment him upon his achievement, *Diphosho- phosho* was 'the first Sechuana book that really speaks Sechuana'. Another (unnamed) African, from the Cape, had this to say: 'Since the death of Robert Moffat and Canon Crisp, the Sechuana language never received such wonderful justice at the hands of a translator as you devoted to it in *Diphosho-phosho*.'[15]

The two university experts on Setswana, Professor C. M. Doke at the University of the Witwatersrand and Professor G. P. Lestrade of the Transvaal University College, Pretoria, were also impressed. Doke thought that *Diphosho-phosho* was 'remarkably good', and was particularly struck by the many examples of Plaatje's 'magnificent wealth of Tswana vocabulary'.[16] Lestrade, whom Plaatje had taught in London in 1923, was in agreement. He compared *Diphosho-phosho* to Tiyo Soga's Xhosa translation of *Pilgrim's Progress*, and considered both works to be 'veritable treasure-houses of the linguistic riches of their respective languages, and show to a remarkable extent their authors' felicity for grasping not merely the language but the thought of the European originals and expressing that thought in idiomatic and vigorous prose'.[17] Both men were impressed by Plaatje's success in matching the puns, the epigrams, the colloquialisms, the distinctive tone of Shakespeare's language in *The Comedy of Errors*.

Nobody was in a better position to appreciate Plaatje's achievement in *Diphosho-phosho* than David Ramoshoana, who had by now left the Lyndhurst Road school to take up another teaching job in Hopetown. He expressed his views on the book in a letter to *Umteteli wa Bantu* early in October 1930:

> Last month I read in the press that the Morija Printing Works had just issued a Shakespearean translation by Mr Sol Plaatje of Kimberley. A group of us, Bechuana working along the Orange River, decided to order a copy and see how Shakespeare's old story had been rendered in our mother tongue. We have come to the conclusion that it is a gratifying success. The translator not only demonstrated his remarkable ability in English and complete mastery of the Sechuana language – a rare thing in these days – but he has also shown a clear understanding of the author's aims. Mr Plaatje has rendered the entire story in a language which to a Mochuana is as entertaining and amusing as the original is to an Englishman.
>
> As far as I know, the translation is the first attempt to introduce Shakespeare to Bantu readers in the vernacular, and the translator has kept alive the sportive tenor of the play without distorting the author's ideas in any way, and without corrupting Sechuana idioms. The book is not rendered into that disagreeable and grating mess which is characteristic of certain books presented in Sechuana garb which yet remains foreign; on the contrary, Shakespeare has inspired Mr Plaatje to bring into bold relief the etymological beauties of his mother tongue. It was Mr Plaatje's good fortune to act as Court Interpreter for years in Bechuanaland. He would otherwise have found the task beyond him, for there are practically no dictionaries in this language to which one can resort for enlightenment in a work of this kind.
>
> When reading 'Diphosho-phosho' one feels as if one were reading the language of a Mochuana who happened to live in England. The pleading, or defence, of Aegeon before the Ephesian Court; the jokes, the treatment of servants and language in which they were ordered about, are very similar to the ways of the Bechuana of the last century. This is one of the features which make Mr Plaatje's translation so pleasant and entertaining.[18]

Of the quality of Plaatje's translations in *Diphosho-phosho*, his skill in expressing

Shakespearean English in fluent Tswana prose, there can be little doubt; the few people in a position to make an informed assessment were agreed that Plaatje's work set entirely new standards, and constituted a uniquely valuable contribution to a language whose very survival was under threat. But in the minds of both Plaatje and Ramoshoana there was another consideration to translating Shakespeare into Setswana. Ramoshoana expressed it as follows:

> Many Englishmen hold the belief that Shakespeare's language and ideals are far above the intellectual scope of Africans and they defy translation into any African language because, they argue, European and African tongues, notions, and outlook, differ so irreconcilably that Shakespeare's elevated ideas must remain to the African an impenetrable mystery, even to those who have secondary training. It will be well for such sceptics to see how successfully a self-educated man has translated Shakespeare's 'Comedy of Errors' into Sechuana. On seeing 'Diphosho-phosho' they will revise their conclusions and change their opinions.[19]

Such a concern to vindicate the claims and status of Setswana had always been in Plaatje's mind from the time he had first considered translating Shakespeare. Shakespeare was always the supreme symbol of all that was of value in English civilisation and culture: in Kimberley in the 1890s, when Plaatje first came to know Shakespeare well, that was in itself reason enough for him and his fellow members of the town's African intelligentsia to be attracted to Shakespeare's plays, even if the language did pose a few problems. But what struck Plaatje thereafter, as he came to know the plays better, was not how different Shakespeare's cultural universe was from that inhabited by the Tswana, but how many parallels and similarities there were. In his contribution to the *Book of Homage to Shakespeare* in 1916 he had this to say:

> It is to be hoped that with the maturity of African literature, now still in its infancy, writers and translators will consider the matter of giving to Africans the benefit of some at least of Shakespeare's works. That this could be done is suggested by the probability that some of the stories on which his dramas are based find equivalents in African folk-lore.[20]

Once Plaatje embarked upon the work of translation himself (mostly on board ship during the long sea voyages he made over the few years after writing these lines) he discovered his prediction to be correct. This fact was perhaps not so surprising: for here was a dramatist writing of a pre-industrial world in which the themes – of kinship, superstition, ambition, fate – had a clear resonance with what he knew of the traditions of the Tswana in general, the Barolong in particular. Even the dominant tradition of Plaatje's own family forebears – the memory of having been dispossessed from a rightful claim to the Barolong kingship – had obvious Shakespearean parallels, which must have struck him.

So for Plaatje the act of translation was both natural and appropriate, in no way a contrived, artificial exercise. In demonstrating this fact, and the capacity of Setswana to comprehend and express Shakespeare's meaning, Plaatje was conscious at the same time of asserting its claim for recognition and preservation.

Much the same thing had been in his mind when compiling his collection of proverbs.

Plaatje's views on this were by no means universally accepted, particularly among whites. For by the time *Diphosho-phosho* was published in 1930 the kind of cultural synthesis and experimentation that had come so naturally to Plaatje and his friends in Kimberley in the 1890s now appeared to be distinctly old-fashioned – at odds, indeed, with the sentiments that now prevailed in political, literary and academic circles in South Africa. In this contemporary climate of broadly pro-segregationist opinion, the very act of translating Shakespeare would have been regarded, at best, as misdirected effort; at worst, as a presumptuous statement of interest in the higher forms of a culture that no African had any business to be concerned with. Even amongst those whites who could have been most expected to welcome Plaatje's initiative some reservations were expressed. Clement Doke, for example, who was more aware of the importance of Plaatje's work in Setswana than anybody else, whilst he was full of admiration for the quality of translation, nonetheless wondered whether 'other types of literature are not at present much more urgently needed in Chuana than this', and expressed the hope that 'the Department of Native Education will give a clear lead to Chuana readers as to what type of literature is of immediate urgency'.[21] Whatever that department would have recommended, it would certainly not have been Shakespeare.

One other person whom Plaatje knew, Stephen Black, editor of the *Sjambok*, a short-lived literary magazine published in Johannesburg, had other objections:

> I suggested to Plaatje the other day that, instead of wasting his time on translating Shakespeare, he should translate something which contains humanity, the one quality of which Shakespeare is entirely devoid. I then asked Plaatje why he had not translated Daniel Venanda [written by W. C. Scully, the recipient of this letter], and he has not yet replied. What in God's name the Bechuanas want to read Shakespeare for I don't know, unless it is that they want to feel more like worms than ever. Shakespeare, to my mind, is literature only, poetry only, and therefore untranslatable, because poetry is as much in the music of the poet's words as in any thought or ideas. This is very trite, but I can never understand why people want to translate Shakespeare.[22]

Plaatje's reply to Stephen Black, if there was one, has not survived. But he would have disagreed with almost every point Black made. Plaatje had his own very good reasons for being interested in Shakespeare; he admired Shakespeare precisely because he found in him a humanity that transcended boundaries of race and colour in a way that so many later English writers conspicuously failed to do; he believed that many of the themes with which Shakespeare was concerned, far from making the Tswana people 'feel more like worms than ever', actually had a very direct resonance with the traditions to which they had been brought up; and in the act of translation he had sought not to reproduce directly the poetic qualities of Shakespeare's language, but to match it and thereby demonstrate the qualities of his own language in its richness of tone, vocabulary and wealth of expression. Few people alive possessed the command of both English and Setswana that would have enabled them to appreciate to the full

Plaatje's success in translating *The Comedy of Errors*. In South Africa, if Stephen Black's reaction was at all typical, there were not very many more who had much sympathy with his reasons for even attempting such a task.

Plaatje never succeeded in raising the money to print and publish his other translations of Shakespeare, and only his translation of *Julius Caesar* was preserved. After his death, the manuscript was acquired by Clement Doke, who passed it on to Professor G. K. Lestrade, and he then edited it for publication in the University of the Witwatersrand's Bantu Treasury series in 1937.[23] Although Professor Lestrade had to do a considerable amount of work on the manuscript to prepare it for the printers, and to convert it to a new orthography, it was evident too that this was a work of high quality. One reviewer, W. Eiselen, commended Plaatje's 'marvellous command of the Tswana language, his easy flow of diction and his instinctive choice of the appropriate word', and he felt that the translation was 'a fine piece of work, and one which has captured much of the dramatic force of the original'. Nobody, Eiselen concluded, had realised more than Plaatje the importance of developing African languages from the literary basis laid by the missionaries, and he more than anybody else had 'set out single-handed to teach his countrymen that there was a literary future for Tswana'; Plaatje, he said, 'had been deeply impressed by the genius of Shakespeare, and he tried to do what no other African had yet attempted, to give a translation of Shakespeare's works'.[24]

Tragically, only fragments of the other Shakespeare translations which Plaatje claimed to have completed – *The Merchant of Venice, Much Ado about Nothing*, and *Othello* – have survived. Amongst these fragments, too, is a page of translation of another play which Plaatje had at least embarked upon – Romeo and Juliet, of which several pages of Act I, Scene I survive.[25] In May 1930, two months before *Diphosho-phosho* appeared, Plaatje wrote of 'completing arrangements' with Longman, Green and Co. over the publication of *The Merchant of Venice* and *Julius Caesar*.[26] No evidence has survived to indicate what went wrong at the last minute, but almost certainly the two plays were casualties of the still unresolved orthographic problem. There were hopes at exactly this time that orthographic agreement on Setswana was in sight, and Longman, Green and Co. were one of several publishing houses ready and waiting to exploit the new market in Tswana school books which now looked like presenting itself. But when it became clear that such hopes were premature these plans were abandoned; there was never any chance that Longmans or any other publisher would take the financial risk of publishing in an orthography that did not command general acceptance among Tswana-speakers, of whom there were relatively few in any case.[27] Plaatje was therefore thrown back upon his own resources to try and raise the funds he needed to pay for printing the books himself, in whatever orthography he chose to use. It is one of the many tragedies of South African literature, albeit one largely unrecognised, that he never managed to achieve this.

Plaatje's new, enlarged edition of his *Sechuana Proverbs* similarly failed to find a publisher, but here at least almost the whole of the typescript has survived. It added a further 400 proverbs and sayings to the 732 that appeared in the original edition – ample vindication of Plaatje's assertion in 1916 that there were 'many unrecorded proverbs' which he had not at that time heard of. Plaatje collected many of these new proverbs on his travels during the 1920s, particularly on the occasions when he visited the remoter parts of the Bechuanaland Protectorate; in this, as with much of his other work in Setswana, he received a great deal of assistance from David Ramoshoana.[28] On occasions, even his friend Michael van Reenen, who lived directly opposite his home in Angel Street, Kimberley, though he knew no Setswana, was able to assist by suggesting English equivalents to several of the new proverbs which Plaatje came up with. Over fifty years afterwards he remembered pondering hard over one proverb which Plaatje mentioned to him – '*Ere u bona ngonne rra u tshabe, ere u bona ngoana mma u eme*' / 'When you see father's son, run; when you see mother's son, stop' – before concluding that 'Like father, like son' was the nearest English equivalent he could think of.[29]

Taken together, Plaatje's two collections, published and unpublished, constitute a unique compilation of Tswana proverbial sayings, many of which would not otherwise have been preserved. Plaatje regarded these proverbs as one of the richest forms of cultural expression in the language, and considered them to encapsulate the particular traditions and accumulated folk-wisdom of the Tswana people. They covered a wide range of subjects. Many, as Plaatje himself noted in the original edition of the *Sechuana Proverbs*, 'originated on the pastures or the hunting fields', just as these same historical circumstances had given Setswana its greatest wealth of vocabulary and idiom as well. The proverbs therefore embody the experience of a people traditionally dependent upon the tending of cattle and the hunting of wild game for their livelihood. Cattle, central to the way of life of the Tswana people, figure prominently. To take just three examples:

'*E mashi ga a itsale*'
'A good milch-cow does not always bear itself' (i.e. bear a calf that grows up to be a good milk-yielder) (no. 117).

'*Go noa tse di choca, tse di dinaka dia faralala*'
'Only hornless cattle can reach the water, the horns will not permit the others to enter' (where 'hornless cattle' represent 'people without encumbrances') (no. 203).[30]

– and, from Plaatje's projected new edition, the superbly expressive

'*Choana ea kgosing, u e thiba ke molato u e feta ke molato*'
'A heifer from the Chief's cattle-fold, drive it along and you are guilty, leave it alone and you are guilty'.[31]

Many of the proverbs concern wild animals in some way or another, often drawing comparisons between their behaviour and characteristics and those of human beings: thus '*Nkoe go lacoana di mebala*' / 'Spotted leopards lick each other' (similar in sense to the English proverb, 'Birds of a feather flock together').[32] In some cases, the thrust of a proverb is to warn against allowing certain characteristics of animal behaviour to intrude into human behaviour, or to warn against over-confidence or recklessness–as in '*Moleleka kgama ea mariga o e leleka a chotse kobo*' / 'He who chases an antelope in winter must do so carrying a cloak'.[33] Other proverbs comment more directly upon various aspects of human behaviour–on relations between men and women, father and son, or the obligation of hospitality, or the nature of chiefs and chiefship. This latter topic, indeed, was the subject of a great variety of proverbs in both of Plaatje's collections. The following examples are drawn from the unpublished addendum:

'*Bogosi bo botlhoko, ke ntho e e sa phungoeng*'
'Chieftainship, like an unbroken abscess, is painful'

'*Bogosi mosima oa phiri*'
'Chieftainship is like a wolf's den'

'*Kgosi ga e tsaloe*'
'A chief is not always born'[34]

One of the characteristics of the collection of which Plaatje was aware was the fact that they were in some cases contradictory. As he wrote in the Introduction to the first edition:

The whole truth about a fact cannot always be summed up in one pithy saying. It may have several different aspects, which, taken separately, seem to be contradictory and have to be considered in connexion with their surrounding circumstances. To explain this connexion is the work of a sermon or essay, not of a proverb. All the latter can do is to express each aspect by itself and let them balance each other.[35]

In fact, there were potentially conflicting tendencies even in Plaatje's own view of the proverbs in his native language. On the one hand, he was struck by the degree of congruity between proverbs that he found in Setswana and those from other languages, English in particular, when he started looking for equivalents; hence his decision to include in the *Sechuana Proverbs* not only their literal translations but also, where possible, their equivalents from other languages. But on the other hand, as the passage quoted above makes clear, Plaatje believed that the full meaning and import of the proverbs could only be properly appreciated with a knowledge of the 'surrounding circumstances', the particular context, in other words, which gave rise to them. The point comes out very clearly in the stories Plaatje included in his *Sechuana Reader* in 1916, for a number of these take the form of explanations of the origin and meaning of particular proverbs and sayings–'Take care that you don't mourn the hartebeest and the hide', 'The ratel is suspicious about the honeycomb', 'Bulging cheeks are a characteristic of the cat family', 'Alone I am not a man; I am only a man by the help of others', and 'The mother of the child is she who grasps the knife by the blade'.[36]

Taken out of context, Tswana proverbs, as any other, could be almost meaningless, the literal translation or equivalent no more than a pale reflection of the wealth of meaning and associations known to native Tswana-speakers. Of this vital need to avoid creating artificial divisions between the different cultural forms of his native language Plaatje was acutely aware: it was at the heart, indeed, of the wide-ranging work he had done in all the different areas upon which he was engaged, the translations, the dictionary, the folk-tales and praise poems as well as the proverbs themselves. It was for this same reason – an intense concern for the interdependence of the cultural forms of his language – that Plaatje could not stand idly by when the very form of the language itself came to be, during these same few years, the subject of renewed debate and discussion.

◇

Nothing at all has survived of the book which Plaatje described as 'Traditional Native Folk-Tales and other Useful Knowledge' in his letter to De Beers in 1929, and variously described by him thereafter as 'Bantu folk-tales and poems – traditional and original', 'a volume of Native fables and traditional poems in the vernacular', and 'my book of folklore'.[37] Although apparently completed and ready for publication there is very little evidence to indicate even what the volume contained. That it was a substantial piece of work is suggested by the fact that the original estimate Plaatje obtained from Morija amounted to £205 as against £123 for three of his Shakespeare translations; very probably this had included the 'Chuana–English glossary' and 'minute explanatory notes' mentioned by Plaatje in a letter to Professor Doke in August 1931, which he afterwards decided to abandon for reasons of cost.[38]

The terms Plaatje used in referring to this book suggest that it was composed of a mixture of the kind of folk-tales he used in his earlier *Sechuana Reader* – indeed these may well have been incorporated into it – and a new collection of Tswana praise poetry. Quite fortuitously, a list of these Tswana praise poems which Plaatje had collected is to be found in the papers of the late Z. K. Matthews, St Leger Plaatje's contemporary at Lovedale, who afterwards went on to become principal of Fort Hare University College. Z. K. Matthews had taken a close interest in the work Plaatje had been doing in this field, and several years after Plaatje's death carried out some anthropological field work amongst the Barolong people, interesting himself in the collection of traditional Tswana praise poetry which he, like Plaatje before him, perceived to be one of the richest forms of Tswana cultural expression.[39] Whether or not Z. K. Matthews ever saw Plaatje's typescript of the book is unknown, but he did make out a list (in his own hand, but under the heading 'Plaatje's collection') of thirty praise poems, giving the name of the chief or other subject of each one; the tribal group from which they originated; the number of lines they contained (these ranged from ten to a hundred); and the name of the informant.[40] Four of these were of Bangwaketse origin; four were Bahurutse; one Rapulana; three Bagatla; eleven Bamangwato, and nine Barolong. Among the last-mentioned, in which Plaatje would have taken a particular interest, was one praise poem to 'moruluganyani', that is to say, 'The Writer', or 'Editor' – Plaatje himself; and three to the great Barolong chief, Montshiwa.

Plaatje's collection of praise poems has disappeared virtually without trace. All that was ever published of this genre were two extracts of praise poetry which appear in a short biographical sketch of Chief Montshiwa, which Plaatje wrote for inclusion in T. D. Mweli Skota's *African Yearly Register*, published in 1931. It seems reasonable to suppose that these extracts were drawn from the three praise poems to Montshiwa which Plaatje intended publishing in his volume. The first of them bore tribute to Montshiwa's involvement in the execution of Bhoya, the Matabele tax-collector whose killing in 1830 resulted in a fierce onslaught upon the Barolong, and provides the point of departure for the historical novel Plaatje had written in London in 1920:

Re kile ra ineelela dichaba,
Ra ineela, ka lecogo, merafe;
Seja-Nkabo a sale mmotlana,
A sale mo tharing eaga Sebodio.
Jaana ke mmonye a tlhatlosa motho lekgabana
A mo pega ncoe ja Ga-Khunoana tlhogo
A nale mmaba, a ea go bolaoa,
Seje-Nkabo-a-Tauana.

Too long we've bent the knee to foreigners,
To long we've yielded the arm to strangers;
Montshioa, at that time, was still a baby
Astride the back of his mother, Sebodio.
Now have I seen him lead a man up hill;
Leading him up to the crest of Mount Kunana;
Conducting a foeman up to his kill,
Seje-Nkabo, the son of Tauana.[41]

The second piece of praise poetry about Montshiwa which Plaatje reproduced testified to his reputation as a fearless hunter and lion-killer – 'One of the few Bechuana,' Plaatje wrote, 'who would follow a wounded lion straight into the thicket.'

Mogatsa Majang, tau ga di kalo!
Tau ga di kalo, moroa Mhenyana.
Ga di ke di bolaoa leroborobo,
Di ba di etsa dipholofolo tsa gopo,
Di ba di edioa pitse tsa gopo,
Lekau, ja Gontse-a-Tauana!
Tau di bolaoa dile thataro,
Lefa dile pedi dia bo di ntse.

That's not the way to kill lions,
O husband of Majang!
That's not the way, O offspring of M'Henyana!
Lions should not be butchered by the score
Nor like hunted animals at the chase;
Lions should not be slaughtered in such numbers,

To litter the field like carcasses of dead Zebra,
O descendant of Gontse, son of Tauana!
Six lions at a time are quite enough
For, even two at a time are not too few![42]

Plaatje had a clear appreciation of the uniqueness, the richness of idiom, the vital importance of the survival of cultural forms such as these if the Tswana language was to be preserved. He did all he could to get his collection into print; but he never succeeded.

◇

Of the other work in Setswana upon which Plaatje was engaged in the late 1920s and early 1930s the most ambitious was his compilation of a new dictionary. His commitment to this task sprang from an anxiety to preserve from extinction the wealth of Tswana vocabulary, and his dissatisfaction at the glaring inadequacies of the existing 'official' Tswana dictionary, first compiled by the Reverend J. Tom Brown in the 1870s, and updated in several editions since then. Although Plaatje had accumulated, according to Professor Lestrade, 'a large amount of new material for a dictionary', this too has been lost.[43] However, some indication of Plaatje's motives for embarking upon this project, and the progress he had made in it, does emerge from several documents that have survived. One of these was a report (unfortunately incomplete) he drew up upon the research he had been doing, probably dating from 1930, and almost certainly addressed to a research committee at the University of the Witwatersrand, from whom he gained (thanks to Professor Doke) some degree of financial support:

> The need for a revised and considerably enlarged Sechuana Dictionary came into prominence in the course of my search for old stories and untranslated proverbs. It attracted the cooperation of Mr D. M. Ramoshoana, a studious English–Sechuana scholar. Between us we have rescued and translated over 400 words. With financial encouragement we can compile another 2,000 Sechuana words but it will require careful investigation in the interior of Bechuanaland where speech is less influenced by European ideas, so as to avoid the errors and omissions in Brown's Dictionary.
>
> In this connection I may mention that Professor Jones of University College, London, has recently brought out a pamphlet illustrating 'The Tones of Sechuana Nouns'. It may interest you to know that Professor Jones, writing alone in London, has in his little brochure 126 Sechuana nouns not included in Brown's big Sechuana Dictionary (the official Dictionary of that language), and he has rendered correctly 30 other nouns which appear but are mistranslated by Brown. One wonders how many untranslated words the Professor would have given us, supposing he had dealt with all the nouns and perhaps the verbs too.
>
> The pamphlet referred to was reviewed by Dr Doke in the Journal of Bantu Studies. In that review the Doctor credits me with having collaborated with Professor Jones. This needs correction, for I have not seen Mr Jones since I last left London in 1924 [sic]. Moreover, I knew nothing about his work until

a couple of months back when he sent me some copies. I have noticed only three words that are wrongly translated by the Professor. This is creditable compared with the 'howlers' within the covers of the official Dictionary and the distance from which the Professor wrote – in England, all by himself.

It may be justly asked why some Missionaries working among Natives can make such glaring mistakes when writing the languages . . .[44]

Plaatje spoke further of the pressing need for a comprehensive Tswana dictionary in the interview he gave to *The Star* at the time of the publication of *Diphosho-phosho*:

> In the absence of a reliable dictionary some doubtful passages had to stand over pending verification from some old natives. 'Not the least of my difficulties,' said Mr Plaatje, 'was the lack of a reliable Sechuana dictionary. Students of this language have often referred to such dictionaries only to find that the best of them itself is in need of improvement and enlargement.'[45]

Once *Diphosho-phosho* was published there was an even greater demand for such a dictionary. Plaatje had made a point of using archaic and little-known Tswana words in *Diphosho-phosho*, and once the book was in circulation he received a number of requests for a new dictionary from people who simply did not know their meaning, and had no means of finding it out. A year later, in August 1931, he wrote to Professor Doke (the only letter of Plaatje's to have survived in what must have been a considerable correspondence) to report upon the progress he had made in compiling this new dictionary, and to request further financial assistance. By this time it was evident that the '400 words' of Plaatje's earlier report had now exceeded even the 2,000 he had previously anticipated he might find:

> I have since met Mr Ramoshoana. Like myself he has no intention of dropping our research. Naturally without support we can devote to it very little time.
>
> Most people are not aware of the wonderful range of Sechuana vocabulary. I think Archdeacon Crisp was the only writer who put that fact on paper.
>
> Sechuana is the only South African language with a distinct word for cock, bull, stallion, ram, goat ram, springbuck ram, duiker and steenbok rams, koodoo bull, buffalo bull, eland bull, etc. Even in Xhosa, it is *inkunzi* this, *inkunzi* that and *inkunzi* the other.
>
> Your little support enabled us to collect 3,000 untranslated words. Fresh discoveries show that we have only scratched the fringe. The changed life made the use of certain words unnecessary in certain parts which are current in other localities. Without a dictionary the language is apt to be spoken in patches.
>
> Anything you could do therefore to facilitate our movements and accelerate our research with financial aid of some kind will hasten the provision of a badly needed dictionary.
>
> Since my translation of Shakespeare enquirers from North and South asked me for a dictionary. It will be the same when my book of folk lore appears.

Shortage of funds makes impossible the insertion of Chuana–English glossary or minute explanatory notes.[46]

Whether or not Plaatje was successful in this appeal for further funds, and how much more progress he was able to make in collecting new words, is unknown. All that has survived of his work on this dictionary is his annotated copy of the 1925 edition of Brown's Tswana dictionary. Plaatje's handwritten comments and insertions in this, however, are of considerable interest, and reveal more of the reasons for his dissatisfaction with the existing compilation. His remarks in the frontispiece sum up his impressions of the dictionary as a whole: 'Object of this Dictionary appears to be Quantity, not Quality'; and 'Hundreds of meaningless words, some of them wrongly translated, no end of duplications such as *makgala-mashaba*, *makgoa-makhoa*, the right and the wrong'.[47] Another part of the Preface to the Dictionary – concerned with the differences between the Tswana dialects – is crossed out with a bold line, and Plaatje has added the words 'Very misleading' in the margin. And on the blank page opposite the first page proper of the dictionary he wrote the following:

The Se-Ruti is not only affecting Sechuana speech but [unclear] Sechuana outlook in every respect. For instance, since Missionaries first translated the names of the Native 'Moons', we find few old natives who know of the 13th month, and even they say the 13th name is interchangeable with one of the 12.[48]

'Se-ruti' was not an original dialect of Setswana, but the name used by Plaatje and others to describe Setswana as spoken by European missionaries, and as here embodied in Brown's dictionary. Plaatje had made a similar point in his Introduction to the *Sechuana Reader* back in 1916 when arguing the case for phonetic spelling as a means of preserving the true pronunciation of his language; and he said it again in his Introduction to *Diphosho-phosho*, stating here that the desire to preserve the true forms of his language from what the missionaries were doing to it was one of his reasons for writing that book in the first place. This passion to preserve was at the heart of his work on the dictionary as well: it was not simply the pronunciation of his language that was being distorted; the words themselves were being lost.

◇

Closely bound up in all Plaatje's pioneering work in Tswana and his struggle to get what he had written into print was his involvement in a battle over the written form of the language itself. Plaatje was all too conscious of the tragic effect that the lack of agreement on orthography had had upon the development of writing in Setswana, and that it had been this more than anything that made it impossible for him to find commercial publishers for his own work. But he also had very strong views on the particular form of orthography that was most appropriate to give proper expression to the Tswana language, and difficult as it was for him to find the funds to print what he had written, the fact that he was paying the printers himself did at least mean he could decide upon the

MABOLELO A GA TSIKINYA-CHAKA

(The Sayings of William Shakespeare)

....

DIPHOSHO-PHOSHO

(Comedy of Errors)

✤

A fetolecoe mo puong ea Secoana
ke
SOL. T. PLAATJE
Morulaganyi oa "Diane tsa Secoana le Maele a Sekgooa."
(Sechuana Proverbs and European Equivalents)
P.O. Box 143, Kimberley, South Africa.

✤

MABOLELO a maŋoe a ga TSIKINYA-CHAKA

MASHOABI-SHOABI,

MATSAPA-TSAPA A LEFELA,

DINCHO-NCHO TSA BO JULIUS KESARA,

Le Buka tse diŋoe gape.

✤✤✤

MORIJA PRINTING WORKS.

93 Title page of Diphosho-phosho *(literally, 'Mistake upon Mistake'), Plaatje's translation of Shakespeare's* Comedy of Errors—*the first African-language translation of any of Shakespeare's plays to be published.*

94 David Ramoshoana, friend and fellow Tswana scholar. They shared an intense concern with the preservation of the Tswana language and its literature.

95 *(top left) Clement Doke, Professor of African Languages at the University of the Witwatersrand, Johannesburg—he provided Plaatje with some financial support for his work on the Tswana language.*

96 *(top right) Stephen Black, editor of* The Sjambok. *He believed that Plaatje was wasting his time translating Shakespeare into Setswana. 'What in God's name the Bechuanas want to read Shakespeare for I don't know, unless it is that they want to feel more like worms than ever.'*

97 *The Earl of Clarendon, Governor-General of South Africa, who visited Kimberley in November 1931. After hearing Plaatje speak he announced that he 'was not altogether sure that he could not have learnt a lesson from Mr Plaatje in the speaking of the English language.'*

98 *Plaatje at the wheel of his 14 h.p. Renault. Left to right: Miss Tutu Kosani, Mrs Elizabeth Plaatje, Mrs Z. Mahabane, Plaatje (in car), Mrs Henry Mashuku.*

99 *(right) Plaatje sitting outdoors at his typewriter, probably in the garden of his home at 32 Angel St, Kimberley. The child standing next to him is unidentified, but is not one of his own children who were now much older.*

100 *(below) 'The rhythm girls', led by Violet Plaatje (seated, centre).*

101 *(right) Richard Plaatje, Plaatje's second son, employed as an interpreter in the magistrates' court in Kimberley, early 1930s.*

103 Portrait, 1932—the last surviving photograph of Plaatje to have been taken before he died.

102 Left to right: Westerfield Ncwabeni, Violet Plaatje, Halley Plaatje, at the Barkly West Show, 4 August 1930.

104 The large crowd attending Plaatje's funeral in the West End cemetery, Kimberley, 22 June 1932.

105 Memorial tombstone in Kimberley erected three years after Plaatje's death, unveiled 13 December 1935.

orthography he favoured – as he had done when editing his own newspapers, and as he did now with *Diphosho-phosho*. In the Introduction to *Diphosho-phosho*, indeed, Plaatje was at great pains to explain and justify the orthography he had chosen to use, for it differed in two major respects from the various other missionary orthographies. He used, first, the letter j, so as to be able to distinguish between such words as *nyalela* (marry my daughter), and *njalela* (give me some), and to provide a more accurate form of representing the pronunciation of words like *bojang* (grass), *mojaki* (migrant labourer) and *dijana* (dishes).[49]

But secondly, and more controversially, Plaatje believed that it was necessary to supplement the 26 letters of the Roman alphabet with additional characters from the International Phonetic Alphabet in order to represent accurately the sounds and tones of Tswana pronunciation where this could not be done by a single Roman character, or any combination of them. In *Diphosho-phosho* Plaatje therefore introduced the phonetic characters ɛ, ŋ and ɔ in order to distinguish differences in pronunciation and tone in words in which the other orthographies made do with e, ng and o respectively. For often, Plaatje pointed out, the failure to make these distinctions could produce confusions in meaning: thus *mme* could mean either 'but' or 'mother', unless the latter meaning was signified by the phonetic symbol ɛ (*mmɛ*); and *botlhoco* could mean either 'illness' or 'want', unless the second meaning was signified by the use of the phonetic symbol ɔ (*Botlɔkɔ*).[50] Plaatje's interest in phonetics had originated in his contact with Daniel Jones in London in 1915; it is clear that he still felt every bit as strongly about the value of the phonetic script in preserving the true pronunciation of his language as he did then.

Plaatje's orthographic preferences and phonetic innovations did not please everybody. One M. M. Kendle, writing to *Umteteli wa Bantu* in December 1930, and again two months later, was of the opinion that *Diphosho-phosho* had 'deplorably digressed from the Sechuana orthography at present in vogue';[51] and Clement Doke, whilst appreciative of the book's other qualities, thought it was 'a pity' that Plaatje had introduced 'his own modified orthography', thereby adding 'yet another to the many diverse methods in which Chwana is written'.[52] From the District Commissioner in Serowe, Bechuanaland, the reaction was one of slight puzzlement: he wrote to Plaatje to compliment him upon *Diphosho-phosho* soon after it appeared, but commented that he found the orthography 'a little strange'. In reply, Plaatje said this was not altogether surprising since most educated Bechuana with whom the DC had had contact would have written to him in English, and he pointed out that 'since the several Se-Ruti orthographies are officially accepted as Se-Cwana, you have in all probability never really seen an indigenous Sechuana spelling'.[53]

Similar reactions to Plaatje's phonetic orthography were expressed elsewhere in the Protectorate. In 1931, H. J. Dumbrell, Director of Education in Bechuanaland, agreed to include *Diphosho-phosho* in the new school syllabus for the higher secondary grades – as an 'experiment' he said – but it was not long before he, too, was receiving criticism of the book on the grounds that it used a 'weird' orthography.[54] In a report to the Resident Commissioner Dumbrell did indicate that he would try to see Plaatje to find out if 'in the interests of the B.P. he would sacrifice his orthography to our wishes, in the interests of Native

Education'.[55] What the outcome was – if Dumbrell did indeed take up the matter with Plaatje – is unknown: since the Protectorate authorities were in a state of confusion as to what their own preferences were on the orthographic question in any case, in all probability nothing at all happened. It would not, however, have been a matter over which Plaatje would have been keen to compromise.

In fact it seems that Plaatje was keen to *extend* the use of the phonetic script in the orthography he used, for late in 1930 he applied to the London-based International Institute for African Languages and Cultures (via his old friend Professor Daniel Jones, a member of its executive committee) for a grant to enable the Morija Press to purchase phonetic type for his 'book of folklore and poems written in Tswana'. Submitting Plaatje's request to the committee, Professor Jones indicated that the total cost of providing the new phonetic type amounted to £36 – a substantial sum which must have covered the cost of a considerable number of additional phonetic characters, on top of the characters ε, ŋ, and ɔ used by Morija in the printing of *Diphosho-phosho* several months previously. A grant of £10 was duly recommended by the committee, subject to the approval of its Director, Professor Westermann, but there is no way of knowing whether this sum, or a further £5 which Jones had obtained from the Phonetic Association, ever reached Plaatje or the Morija Press.[56]

In retrospect it seems tragic that Plaatje's insistence upon the phonetic script as the only acceptable means of preserving the true pronunciation of his language should have helped delay the appearance of his collection of folk-tales and praise poems, with the ultimate result that they were lost entirely. It was clearly an issue over which Plaatje was not prepared to compromise if he could possibly avoid it, although he must have realised that a collection of this kind so heavily reliant upon the phonetic script could not be used readily in the schools; it would surely have been regarded, like the *Sechuana Reader*, as just another 'strange book in a strange spelling'. But Plaatje's insistence upon using it suggests that in his own mind the act of preservation itself had become his over-riding priority: that if his collection of folk-tales and poems were worth preserving at all, they had to be recorded, read, and spoken in what he regarded as the proper manner. Whatever happened to the Tswana language in the future, then here at least, with the phonetic orthography, would be a permanent record of how Plaatje believed it should be.

◇

Plaatje's insistence upon the use of his own orthography, the introduction of phonetic script, his own desperate efforts to get his work in Setswana into print all formed part of an often lonely struggle to preserve what he saw as the true forms of the Tswana language. But there was another dimension to this struggle as well: a far more public campaign over the question of Tswana orthography – fought out at conferences, meetings, and in the columns of the press – in which Plaatje was involved at the same time as he was doing so much of his writing and fund-raising. His principal opponents were no longer the missionary societies with whom he had had to contend in the past, but two new groups of people who had now interested themselves in the orthographic question: the university academics and government officials, potentially far more formidable.

The new-found interest of both these groups in this issue of the orthography of African languages (for it was not just Setswana) was a relatively new phenomenon, and it had diverse origins. It owed much to the growing consensus in governing circles in both the British empire as a whole, and in South Africa itself, in favour of policies of indirect rule or segregation (in its South African form); and a concomitant realisation of the contribution that academics – the anthropologists and linguists in particular – could make to the accumulation of specialised knowledge about the customs, languages and traditions of indigenous peoples: knowledge that was perceived to be necessary if these forms of government and control were to be successfully implemented.[57] In South Africa, these developments found institutional expression in the creation of several academic chairs in Bantu languages and 'Bantu studies' (and a journal of the same name, founded in 1921), a process considerably accelerated by the reaction to the massive political and industrial unrest amongst Africans in the aftermath of the First World War; confronted by the spectre of a militant African working class, one response in ruling circles had been to channel money into academic disciplines that could yield information about how African societies worked and how, ultimately, they could be controlled.[58] It was part, indeed, of that wider process of adjustment in ruling circles in South Africa that led to the formation of the Joint Councils, the setting up of *Umteteli wa Bantu*, the provision of officially constituted means of consultation for Africans in the Native Affairs Act of 1920.

Not that this growing interest in the workings of African societies was a purely South African phenomenon. At a time when 'indirect rule' had come to be elevated to something approaching a theory of imperial government in Colonial Office circles in Britain, several new institutions began to concern themselves with similar issues. Two such institutions were of particular importance: the School of Oriental Studies, later the School of Oriental and African Studies, where Plaatje's old friend, Alice Werner, now lectured and, in 1926, the International Institute of African Languages and Cultures (presided over by the chief exponent of indirect rule, Lord Lugard), followed by the founding of its journal, *Africa*, in 1928. From the Institute's inception, one of its primary concerns was with the possibility of standardising the orthography of African languages – initially on a regional, linguistic basis, but ultimately with the more ambitious objective of standardising linguistic forms for the entire continent.[59]

From Plaatje's point of view these developments were something of a mixed blessing. On the positive side, this new interest in African languages and cultures at the South African universities provided some hope that his own language, Setswana, would no longer be consigned to the general neglect and lack of interest in academic circles that had prevailed hitherto; and it held out the possibility, too, of financial support and encouragement in his own work in this area. By the late 1920s this did indeed materialise. Through Professor Clement Doke, of the University of the Witwatersrand, he obtained funds to support his work on his Tswana dictionary, the collection of new proverbs, praise poems and folk-tales, and encouragement in his work of translation. Doke was alive to Plaatje's unique qualifications for work of this kind – which he could carry out far better than any European – and did his best to channel some money in Plaatje's direction. As a result, Plaatje was undoubtedly able to carry out far more research and writing in these fields than would otherwise have been possible: 'your little support', he wrote to Doke in August 1931, telling him of what he and Ramoshoana had been doing, 'enabled us to collect 3,000 untranslated words'.[60]

But there was another aspect to this new-found interest of the white establishment in South Africa in African languages and cultures: a determination to standardise the orthographies of the different African languages spoken in the Union and the protectorates, and against this Plaatje soon came to stand in equally determined opposition. Encouraged by the publication, in 1927, of the International Institute of African Languages and Cultures' pamphlet, *A Practical Orthography of African Languages*, a group of government officials – from the Department of Education and Native Affairs – initiated a series of discussions with university academics, Clement Doke included, with a view to achieving a measure of orthographic standardisation amongst the African languages of South Africa. These discussions took place under the aegis of a newly formed body called the Union Advisory Committee on Bantu Studies and Research, whose very existence demonstrated this new relationship between government policy and academia; and in July 1928 it appointed a sub-committee (known as the Central Orthography Committee) in order to 'take charge of the question of reform in the various orthographies'. This body then appointed further sub-committees for the various language groups, including one for the so-called Sotho–Pedi–Tswana group.[61]

In principle Plaatje was in favour of orthographic reform. On numerous occasions he had pointed to the tragic way in which Setswana had suffered from the failure of the missionary societies to agree upon a unified orthography for the language, and nobody was more concerned about this than he; his own work, moreover, would probably have been published years ago if such agreement had been reached. But he was totally out of sympathy with the moves being made in the direction of standardisation under the auspices of the Central Orthography Committee, because it was clear that its principal concern was with achieving a uniform orthography, not for Setswana but for a larger Sotho–Pedi–Tswana language group, and beyond that, all the other African languages in South Africa. For Plaatje the threat this posed to the integrity of Setswana was quite unacceptable. His great fear was that once Setswana was linked with these larger language groups – and after that with Xhosa and Zulu as well – then Setswana, spoken by little more than half a million people and with virtually no literature of its own, would be forced to accept orthographic conventions that were foreign to it; that this would lead in practice to a distortion of its true pronunciation; that its unique qualities, and ultimately the language itself, would disappear. Having failed to unify its own orthography, Plaatje believed, Setswana would hardly be in a position to resist the imposition of 'foreign' symbols and conventions; pure Setswana, distorted enough already by the missionaries and the influence of other languages and cultures, African and European, would cease to be a living language.[62]

Plaatje was nominated to the Sotho–Tswana–Pedi language group sub-committee, and attended its first meeting in Pretoria in February 1929, together with Professor Lestrade, the convenor; Dr Eiselen; the Reverends Schwellnus, Baumbach and Ramseyer; Mr Franz, the secretary; and two other Africans,

Motiyane and Mangoela. During the course of the meeting it became clear that Plaatje's views differed sharply from most of those present, above all in relation to the question of which system to indicate pronunciation should be adopted. On two occasions Plaatje proposed the use of phonetic characters to express sounds which could not be expressed directly by the Roman alphabet, but on neither occasion could he find a seconder.[63] Instead, the meeting as a whole voted by a majority of seven to one to adopt the use of diacritics – accents and stress marks, to be placed over letters of the Roman alphabet. These, Plaatje believed, both disfigured and misrepresented the language, and were in no way an adequate or accurate means of representing the subtleties and variations in the tone and pronunciation of his language.

Very little progress at all was achieved at the meeting and its report was in any case rejected by the Central Orthography Committee, whose view was that the lack of unanimity displayed at the Sotho–Pedi–Tswana sub-committee indicated that 'the time is not yet ripe for unifying the orthography of the three languages'; that it seemed most unlikely that Sotho would 'fall into line with the other two in the near future'; and it therefore recommended that separate district sub-committees should be set up for Pedi and Tswana.[64] When nominations were made for the Tswana sub-committee Plaatje's name was not amongst those put forward, so he did not, therefore, attend its first meeting in October of the same year – 1929. When the Reverend P. Motiyane, who was there, questioned why Plaatje had not been invited, pointing out that 'he [Mr Plaatje] had been on the previous committee in February and had been a great help', the chairman, Professor Lestrade, replied that 'Mr Plaatje had not been reappointed by the Central Orthography Committee'. Motiyane then expressed the view that Plaatje should have been reappointed, and attempted to raise the matter again at the end of the meeting.[65] But it was to no effect; Plaatje never again attended any of the numerous orthography committees and sub-committees that sat over the next few years.

Just who was responsible for deciding that Plaatje, far and away the leading Tswana scholar of his day, should not have been reappointed to this sub-committee is unclear. Its effect, however, was to confirm all Plaatje's anger and resentment about interference in his own language by people he believed had neither the right nor the qualifications to decide upon its future form of spelling. Plaatje's description of the second meeting of the Tswana sub-committee in February 1930, which agreed to incorporate a number of the proposals of the Pedi committee, left little doubt about his feelings:

Ten Europeans and two Natives met at Pretoria over a year ago; most of the former knew nothing of Sechuana, while the two natives appear to have been selected by virtue of their outstanding qualifications, viz. (a) neither of them ever wrote a Sechuana book or pamphlet; and (b) neither of them ever lived in Bechuanaland or in districts where the unadulterated Sechuana is spoken. Two missionaries on the committee have done some work in the language and have translated its folklore for English and German magazines; but care seems to have been taken so as to constitute the committee that, should they and two natives stand together and contend for any given point (as indeed they did more than once) the four of them would have to face a phalanx of eight

Europeans whose sole purpose was to vote for the new spelling, whether or not they understood what they were voting upon.[66]

Plaatje was appalled by the orthography which was agreed upon and ratified by the Central Orthography Committee. He believed that the proposal to replace the letter c by tš would cause endless confusions, and he felt that the decision to use diacritics and circumflexes made writing Setswana 'irritating and cumbersome', and disfigured its appearance. 'Some one at Pretoria,' he said,

> appears to have come across orthographic hieroglyphics and fallen head over heels in love with them. We admit that any man is entitled to his fads; but what right has he to embody his notions in our language? Anyone with a taste for diacritical hieroglyphs should incorporate them in his own language, not in ours.[67]

Beyond the differences of opinion over the details of orthography Plaatje made the point time and time again that these self-appointed academics and government officials possessed neither the expertise nor the right to decide the future form of a language which was not their own, and to seek to impose it without adequate consultation with those who were going to be most affected by the proposed changes – the Tswana people themselves. 'Personally,' Plaatje wrote,

> I have nothing but the highest respect for the sound learning of University professors. I yield to no one in my admiration for their academic distinction and high scholarship. The only trouble with the professors is that they don't know my language, and with all due deference, how could a string of letters behind a man's name enable him to deal correctly with something he does not understand? Only one man is capable of determining the spelling of this language. That man is the Native.[68]

This ran directly counter to the predominant view shared by the professors and government officials involved in the orthography committee – as expressed on one occasion, for example, by Professor Lestrade: 'It is simply not done,' he said, 'to consult people who are not expert in these matters, e.g. the natives.'[69] As Plaatje said elsewhere, the whole orthography scheme carried 'the hallmark of true South African ideals, according to which anything of the kind must be evolved by white experts'.[70]

It is not difficult to see why Plaatje felt so strongly over the question, for what he was encountering here was what had already happened elsewhere: the white man was taking over, assuming the right to take decisions that affected the lives of the African people, displacing men like himself who believed that such initiatives rightly devolved upon him and his fellow African spokesmen, leaders of the African people. In the late 1920s Plaatje had made a conscious decision to devote himself to the preservation of the Tswana language and the creation of a literature, and for this task he possessed unique qualifications. But now these white academics and government officials, in an enthusiasm for orthographic unification that matched the commitment many of them felt to comprehensive solutions to 'the native problem', claimed the right to decide even the future form of his native language. It denied Plaatje the right to interpret yet another area of the life of his people – one of the few areas, indeed, that were now left to him. At every opportunity that presented itself he made his views clear in the strongest possible terms.

In fact Plaatje's outspoken campaign against the proposals of the Central Orthography Committee contributed in no small measure to the growing movement of opposition to the new orthography once the government sought ways and means of actually implementing the changes. In the hope that the education authorities of the Bechuanaland Protectorate, the Cape, Orange Free State, and Transvaal provinces, would accept and implement the new orthographies, a conference was held in Bloemfontein in November 1931 to discuss the appropriate administrative action to be taken.[71] But the delegates could not agree. In the Cape and the Bechuanaland Protectorate the authorities were somewhat more responsive to African and missionary opinion over the question than were the theoreticians of the Central Orthography Committee, and already it was clear that there was very strong opposition to the proposals; African teachers' organisations and the different missionary societies, whatever their differences over the finer points of orthographic usage in the past, now found themselves united in condemnation of the proposals from Pretoria. The unanimous resolution (almost certainly drafted by Plaatje) passed by a conference of the Northern Districts Union of non-European branches of the South African Teachers' Association, held in Kimberley in October 1930, seems to have been typical of sentiment in Tswana-speaking areas:

> This Union, after considering the innovations proposed by the Orthography Committee of Pretoria, which intends to create a uniform spelling for all the languages of Africa, is of the opinion that from the point of view of the Sechuana-speaking sections of the Bantu race the proposals are unduly cumbersome; that the complicated and unnecessarily numerous diacritical signs will occasion useless waste of time and space and, compared with the missionary orthography, at present in vogue (which is phonetically simple and easy to learn), this Union feels that the Phonetic proposals will constitute a hindrance rather than an encouragement to the study of the vernacular.[72]

The missionary societies were equally critical. They saw no reason why they should depart from the orthographies they had been using for years, particularly the largest of these, the London Missionary Society. Quite apart from the confusion likely to be caused by its introduction, they had large stocks of books in their existing orthography which they would ultimately have to replace, at considerable expense to themselves. And the education authorities, too, once they became aware of the extent of opposition that existed, refused to commit themselves to implementing the proposals. In the Bechuanaland Protectorate several conferences were held in order to sound out local opinion, and it soon became clear that to try and enforce the new orthography would cause chaos and much bitterness; the authorities there decided instead to concentrate their efforts on the urgent task of finding an orthography acceptable in Bechuanaland itself, and not to wait until final agreement amongst all the authorities covering Tswana-speaking areas of South Africa had been reached.[73] Even this more limited objective, though, proved to be beyond them.

The Cape authorities also concluded that to seek to implement the new proposals in the face of the opposition that existed would be ill-advised, and so too did the Orange Free State authorities.[74] But by that time it was evident that there was simply not enough support for the scheme to have any chance of success, and amidst much chaos and recrimination between local and central government authorities the entire scheme was shelved.

Plaatje at least, as one of the most articulate and vocal opponents, could take some satisfaction in this outcome, but it nonetheless left the future of Setswana as a written language in as much doubt as ever. For the time being Plaatje's native language had been preserved from the attentions of the 'would-be reformers of Bantu languages', but agreement on a more satisfactory and generally acceptable orthography seemed further away than ever before. In so far as this related to Plaatje's own efforts to create a written language for Setswana, and to raise the money to publish what he had been writing, the net result was to throw him back once again upon his own resources. The publishers who had been waiting eagerly in the wings for agreement to be reached soon lost interest and transferred their attentions to more assured markets. For Plaatje the task he faced remained as great as ever.

15

◇

Mhudi

'After ten years of disappointment,' Plaatje informed his old friend, Georgiana Solomon, in May 1930, 'I have at length succeeded in printing my book. Lovedale is publishing it. I am expecting the proofs any day this week.'[1] The book to which Plaatje referred was *Mhudi*, the title of the manuscript he had completed in London in 1920, and somewhat modestly described at the time as 'a love story after the manner of romances . . . but based on historical facts'.

The Lovedale Press was certainly not the leading international publishing house which Plaatje had once hoped would take on his book, but after 'ten years of disappointment' and numerous rejections from publishers in England and America – 'circumstances beyond the control of the writer', so Plaatje described them – he was well pleased to have been able to come to terms with them over it. The Lovedale Press's decision to publish the book is attributable to the arrival at Lovedale, the previous year, of a new chaplain by the name of R. H. W. Shepherd. Up until then, the Lovedale Press had concentrated almost exclusively on publishing books and pamphlets, mostly in English and Xhosa, for religious and educational purposes. Shepherd, though, possessed a somewhat broader view of the literary responsibilities of a mission press, and believed that Lovedale should also concern itself with the provision of more general reading matter for the African population. Within a short time of his arrival at Lovedale he was taking a very active role in the affairs of the press, became convenor of the Press Committee in 1930, Director of Publications in 1932, and was thereafter – for better or worse – one of the most influential figures in the development of African literature in South Africa in the 1930s and 1940s.[2]

The possibility of the Lovedale Press publishing *Mhudi* was raised when Plaatje himself once visited Lovedale. Shepherd recalled the occasion later: 'Into the writer's study came one day an African, Sol T. Plaatje. His object was to talk of a novel in English for which through eight years he had been seeking a publisher. Its title was *Mhudi: an epic of South African native life a hundred years ago*.'[3] Plaatje's mission was successful, and a contract was duly signed in March 1930: it provided for a first edition of 2,000 copies, to be sold at 5s 6d each, with a 10 per cent royalty payable when 700 copies of the book had been sold. Considering that the overseas publishers Plaatje had approached had wanted him to make a prior payment to them if they were to publish *Mhudi*, the terms must have appeared satisfactory to him, and the price of 5s 6d per copy –

for a hard-cover book that was likely to run to over 200 pages – not so high as to deter his potential readership.[4]

Further evidence of Shepherd's personal interest and involvement in seeing *Mhudi* through to publication is to be found in the preface (dated August 1930) which Plaatje wrote for the book, which concludes with an acknowledgement of Shepherd's assistance, along with that of Michael van Reenen, in 'helping to correct the proofs'.

Even though *Mhudi*'s publication had been delayed for ten years, it was nevertheless the first book of its kind, in English, to have been written by a black South African. It was this fact which prompted Plaatje to offer a few words in justification and explanation at the beginning of the book: 'South African literature,' he noted, 'has hitherto been almost exclusively European, so that a foreword seems necessary to give reasons for a Native venture.' He went on:

> In all the tales of battle I have ever read, or heard of, the cause of the war is invariably ascribed to the other side. Similarly, we have been taught almost from childhood to fear the Matabele – a fierce nation – so unreasoning in its ferocity that it will attack any individual or tribe, at sight, without the slightest provocation. Their destruction of our people, we are told, had no justification in fact or in reason; they were actuated by sheer lust for human blood.
>
> By the merest accident, while collecting stray scraps of tribal history, later in life, the writer incidentally heard of 'the day Mzilikazi's tax collectors were killed'. Tracing this bit of information back, he elicited from old people that the slaying of Bhoya and his companion, about the year 1830, constituted the casus belli which unleashed the war dogs and precipitated the Barolong nation headlong into the horrors described in these pages.[5]

The slaying of Bhoya, unrecorded in any of the written histories of the time, provided Plaatje with his point of departure for the book, and it is against this historical background of South Africa in the 1830s that Plaatje develops the action and the characters. There follows a dramatic account of the brutal destruction of Khunana, the Barolong capital, and an introduction to the two main characters, Mhudi and Ra-Thaga. Thereafter the scene shifts to the court of the victorious Matabele king, Mzilikazi. As his people celebrate their victory, Gubuza, commander of Mzilikazi's army, utters one of the prophetic warnings that build up an atmosphere of suspense and impending doom, predicting that the Barolong would not rest until they had their revenge.

Mhudi and Ra-Thaga, meanwhile, meet one another in the wilderness, fall in love, and after several encounters with lions, meet up with a band of Koranna, and join them in the hope of discovering the fate of the rest of the Barolong people. Ra-Thaga then has a narrow escape at the hands of Ton-Qon, a Koranna headman who is intent on taking Mhudi as his wife, but the couple hear that the survivors of the massacre at Khunana, together with the other branches of the Barolong nation, have now gathered and made a new home in Thaba Nchu.

They set out to find them, and arrive to a joyous reception from Mhudi's cousin Baile, each amazed to find the other alive. Soon their arrival is eclipsed by that of another group of newcomers, 'a travel-stained party' of Boers travelling northwards from the Cape Colony, who are offered hospitality by Chief Moroka, the senior Barolong chief at Thaba Nchu. In due course, a friendship develops between Ra-Thaga and De Villiers, one of the Boer trekkers, and after much deliberation, and the dispatch of a spying expedition, the Barolong and Boer leaders decide to form a military alliance, and attack the Matabele.

The Matabele, for their part, prepare themselves for the onslaught; as they do so, a bright comet appears in the sky above them, an omen of defeat and destruction prophesied many times before by their witchdoctors and seers. In the battle that follows, the combined forces of Boers, Barolong and Griqua (also enlisted as allies) prove more than a match for the dispirited Matabele forces, and their triumph is joyously celebrated. In the opposite camp Gubuza brings news of the defeat of his army to the king, and advises him to 'evacuate the city and move the nation to the north'. Only in this way, he said, mindful of an earlier prophecy, could the complete annihilation of the Matabele nation be averted.

From the tragic scene of the court of the defeated Matabele king the action returns to Thaba Nchu, where Mhudi has been left behind whilst her husband is away with the army sent out against the Matabele. It is not a situation she can long endure: having a premonition of an injury to Ra-Thaga, she decides impulsively to make her way to the allies' camp, setting out alone on the hazardous journey. On the way there she encounters Umnandi, the former wife of Mzilikazi, forced to flee his court as a result of the machinations of her jealous rivals, and they arrive together in the allies' camp. Mzilikazi, meanwhile, prepares to move northwards, bitterly regretting his failure to heed the warnings and prophecies that had been uttered so often before: 'I alone am to blame,' he acknowledges, 'notwithstanding that my magicians warned me of the looming terrors, I heeded them not. Had I only listened and moved the nation to the north, I could have transplanted my kingdom there with all my impis still intact – but mayebab'o – now I have lost all!' Then, in one of the most powerful passages of the book, Mzilikazi makes a prophecy of his own: the Barolong, he predicts, will live to regret the alliance they have made with the Boers.

After so powerful and haunting a prophecy the remaining two chapters of the book come almost as an anti-climax, and are devoted mostly to tying up loose ends in the personal relationships developed by the main characters. Umnandi rejoins Mzilikazi, welcomed back as his rightful queen; De Villiers, Ra-Thaga's Boer friend, marries the girl he loves, Annetjie; whilst Mhudi and Ra-Thaga, after declining an invitation to stay on with their new-found friends, De Villiers and Annetjie, set off in an old waggon in the direction of Thaba Nchu: 'from henceforth', says Ra-Thaga to Mhudi, in the final lines of the book, 'I shall have no ears for the call of war or the chase; my ears shall be open to one call only – the call of your voice'.

◇

In many ways the actual sequence of events, the development of the individual characters and the interaction of their relationships, is not of primary importance. For Plaatje did not conceive of *Mhudi* as anything approaching a realistic novel in the western literary tradition. He himself gave his book the sub-title 'An epic of native life a hundred years ago', and it is as an epic that *Mhudi* is best defined. Just as in Shakespeare, clearly an important influence upon Plaatje in writing *Mhudi*, he expected his readers to suspend a sense of realism to allow for the delivery of long set-piece monologues and dialogues; to allow him to bring historical events backwards and forwards in time as it suited him in the construction of the narrative, and exploit for dramatic purposes an assumed historical knowledge on the part of his readers; and he composed his characters not so much to reflect the way they might realistically have behaved, as to provide a vehicle for the expression of a variety of human qualities and ideas which Plaatje wished to explore.[6]

Mhudi was the outcome of a quite conscious and deliberate attempt on Plaatje's part to marry together two different cultural traditions: African oral forms and traditions, particularly those of the Barolong, on the one hand; and the written traditions and forms of the English language and literature on the other. The full extent to which these African oral traditions have found their way into *Mhudi* may never be fully known, although if Plaatje's own collection of Tswana folk-tales had survived we would probably have been in a much better position to make some sort of assessment. But some of the ways at least in which Plaatje incorporated these traditions and cultural forms can be identified. The slaying of Bhoya, as Plaatje explained in his foreword, was one obvious example of the way in which he incorporated into his story what he had heard from old Barolong people he had talked to. His use of proverbs and African idiom was similarly a quite deliberate attempt to try and convey something of the richness of the cultural reservoir upon which he was drawing. Often the technique of literal translation was strikingly successful. 'I would rather be a Bushman and eat scorpions than that Matabele could be hunted and killed as freely as rockrabbits,' said Dambuza, one of Mzilikazi's warriors, at the Matabele court; and later he observes: 'Gubuza, my chief, your speech was the one fly in the milk. Your unworthy words stung like needles in my ears.'[7]

Plaatje was struck particularly by the way in which Tswana oral tradition and the written traditions of English literature – above all, Shakespeare, which he knew best – shared a common fund of literary and cultural symbols. In *Mhudi* he was concerned to explore the possibilities that this perception presented, above all in relation to omen and prophecy, and their association with planetary movements – characteristic both of Shakespeare and the oral traditions of his own people. It was something that had always fascinated him. 'In common with other Bantu tribes,' Plaatje had written in his newspaper at the time of the reappearance of Halley's Comet in 1910, 'the Bechuana attach many ominous traditions to stellar movements and cometary visitations in particular', and he had added: 'space will not permit of one going as far back as the 30s and 50s to record momentous events, in Sechuana history, which occurred synchronically with the movements of heavenly bodies'.[8] Ten years later Plaatje did find time to do exactly this in writing *Mhudi*, even if he had then to wait a further ten years before the results of this literary exploration were published.

Plaatje's awareness of the literary possibilities that lay in the manipulation of symbols that had meaning in both Tswana and English cultures also found expression in the humorous lion stories that appear in the early part of the book. These serve as a means of testing the courage of both Mhudi and Ra-Thaga, and are contrasted later on with the cowardly reaction of Lepane, a traveller, faced with a similar dilemma. That lion stories of this kind were a familiar motif in Tswana tradition emerges from the story that Plaatje himself reproduced in his *Sechuana Reader*: like the lion story that appears in Chapter 5 of *Mhudi*, its central point is the way in which the protagonist proves his bravery by holding on to the lion's tail. At the same time, lion stories of this kind, serving a similar function of demonstrating bravery and cowardice, are a familiar motif in English literature as well – in Bunyan's *Pilgrim's Progress*, and Shakespeare's *Love's Labour Lost*, *Julius Caesar*, and *A Midsummer Night's Dream*, all of which Plaatje knew well.[9]

In 1916, in his contribution to the *Book of Homage to Shakespeare*, Plaatje had expressed the view that he thought it likely that 'some of the stories on which his [Shakespeare's] dramas are based find equivalents in African folk-lore'. When he had looked into this question more closely he had found this prediction to be correct: the lion stories in *Mhudi* were one of the more humorous outcomes, and so too – in a more general sense – was Plaatje's exploration of the symbolism and meaning of planetary omens and prophecies. It was the kind of cultural borderland that Plaatje delighted in exploring. The tragedy was that so few people were in any kind of position to appreciate to the full just what it was that he was doing.

Plaatje had a number of other considerations in mind when he wrote *Mhudi*. Perhaps the most important of these he summed up in his foreword when he indicated that one of his main objectives in writing the book was 'to interpret to the reading public one phase of "the back of the Native mind" ': essentially, to write of a particular historical episode from an African, and more particularly, a Barolong viewpoint, rather than from the more familiar white perspective. It had long rankled in Plaatje's mind that the Boers, to whom he attributed so many of the later misfortunes of his people, owed their survival to the succour and help which one section of the Great Trek had received at the hands of the Barolong Chief Moroka at Thaba Nchu. It was a point to which he had often drawn attention in his political writings. 'In the eyes of most Natives the Prime Minister's campaign of calumny,' Plaatje wrote in the year before *Mhudi* was published, 'lumping us all as a barbarian menace to European civilisation was nothing but colossal ingratitude,' and he went on to outline – as he had done in *Native Life in South Africa* and on several other occasions since – the way in which Moroka's Barolong came to their assistance and helped them defeat the Matabele. Even more disturbing for Plaatje was the way in which the historical record was distorted for political purposes, something he came up against again and again.[10] It was not simply the politicians who exploited these distortions. 'It is a standing complaint among educated natives,' he wrote another time, 'that in South African history books (except where natives acted entirely under their own unaided initiative) tribal succour of Europeans is not even as much as mentioned, although tradition abounds with the stories of battle after battle carried by native legions in the cause of European colonisation in South Africa.'[11]

In *Mhudi* it was one of Plaatje's main intentions to counter these kind of distortions by writing of a familiar historical episode from a novel perspective. One theme that recurs throughout the book is an assertion of the fact that Barolong society prior to its contact with 'European civilisation' was not in the state of savagery so frequently used to justify its subsequent conquest by white colonists. At the very beginning of the book Plaatje implicitly contrasts the communal values of pre-colonial Barolong society with its later transformation under the impact of white settlement:

> Strange to relate, these simple folk were perfectly happy without money and without silver watches. Abject poverty was practically unknown; they had no orphanages because there were no nameless babies. When a man had a couple of karosses to make he invited the neighbours to spend the day with him, cutting, fitting in and sewing together the sixty grey jackal pelts into two rugs, and there would be intervals of feasting throughout the day. On such an occasion, some one would announce a field day at another place where there was a dwelling to thatch; here too the guests might receive an invitation from a peasant who had a stockade to erect at a third homestead on a subsequent day; and great would be the expectation of the fat bullock to be slaughtered by the good man, to say nothing of the good things to be prepared by the kind hostess. Thus a month's job would be accomplished in a day.
>
> But the anomaly of this community life was that, while the many seams in a rich man's kaross carried all kinds of knittings – good, bad, and indifferent – the wife of a poor man, who could not afford such a feast, was often gowned in flawless furs. It being the skilled handiwork of her own husband, the nicety of its seams seldom failed to evoke the admiration of experts.[12]

The absence of extremes of wealth, a tradition of communal hospitality – both are portrayed as attractive features of Barolong society before its contact with white civilisation. Elsewhere in *Mhudi* other characteristics of traditional Barolong society are also presented in a favourable light. At Thaba Nchu, for example, Chief Moroka is called upon to make a 'Solomonic' decision in a case involving two married couples who have exchanged partners; contrary to the precepts of Christian morality, his decision is that the new arrangement should continue since it was now obvious that this was the judgement that would give satisfaction to all parties concerned.[13] A kind of consensus justice, in other words, was preferable in certain circumstances to adherence to a rigid legal or moral code. In another decision made by Chief Moroka, the qualities emphasised were the seriousness with which physical assault was viewed in Barolong society, and the mercy bestowed in dealing with those guilty of this offence.[14]

So Plaatje was concerned to offer something of a corrective to the predominant view in the literature and the stereotypes of white South Africans (and others) that his people were murderous savages, saved only by the coming of the white man. He also has a fresh perspective to offer upon the Boers themselves. In *Mhudi* they are viewed not as the embodiment of the advance of civilisation, but as a strange and far from heroic group of travellers who are obliged to turn to Moroka for succour and assistance. When they first make their appearance, over a third of the way through the book, they are seen from a novel Barolong perspective, their credentials somewhat open to question:

They were mounted and each carried a rifle. It was a travel-stained party, and the faces of the older men bore traces of anxiety. Apart from that they were well-fed on the whole, as the open air of a sunny country had impressed health, vigour, and energy on their well-clothed bodies, especially the younger men of the party. The spokesman of the riders was their leader, a Boer named Sarel Cilliers, who headed a large band of Dutch emigrants from Cape Colony. They were travelling with their families in hooded waggons, and driving with their caravans their wealth of livestock into the hinterland in search of some unoccupied territory to colonise and to worship God in peace.

'But,' asked Chief Moroka, 'could you not worship God on the south of the Orange River?'

'We could,' replied Cilliers, 'but oppression is not conducive to piety. We are after freedom. The English of the Cape are not fair to us.'

'We Barolongs have always heard that, since David and Solomon, no king has ruled so justly as King George of England.'

'It may be so,' replied the Boer leader, 'but there are always two points of view. The point of view of the ruler is not always the viewpoint of the ruled. We Boers are tired of foreign kings and rulers. We only want one ruler and that is God, our Creator. No man or woman can rule another.'

'Yours must be a very strange people,' said several chiefs simultaneously. 'The Bible says when the children of Israel had only one God as their ruler, they gave Him no rest until He anointed a king for them. We are just like them. There are two persons that we Barolongs can never do without: a wife to mind the home and a king to call us to order, settle our disputes and lead us in battle.'[15]

It was a picture of the Boers far removed from the conventional image of the chroniclers of the Great Trek: it was no part of this, it need scarcely be said, that the Boers were met at Thaba Nchu by Barolong chiefs quoting the Bible at them, and disputing their arguments on the nature of freedom and justice on biblical grounds. Thereafter, Plaatje presents the Boers in a distinctly unfavourable light, and with several individual exceptions they are portrayed as greedy, cruel and deceitful. They mistreat their Hottentot servants, they fail to appreciate the hospitality accorded to them at Thaba Nchu, and they try to strike a very unfair bargain over the spoils of war during the negotiations with the Barolong over mounting a joint expedition against the Matabele. On other occasions they are almost figures of fun: '"How long must it last, O God?", they [a group of Boer women] demanded, as though expecting an answer by return post.'[16] The Boers in Plaatje's *Mhudi*, in short, were far removed from the heroic image so carefully cultivated by their twentieth-century successors.

◇

Mhudi also contains a more direct political message, or warning. Although the action of the novel does not extend beyond the 1830s or the 1840s it is perfectly clear that Plaatje expects his readers to draw a connection between the circumstances of the Barolong of the period covered in the book, and the position they found themselves in in the early part of the twentieth century when the book was written.[17] In *Mhudi*, oppression and tyranny bring forth retribution with an inevitability emphasised throughout the book by the use of prophecy. When Bhoya is killed, it is prophesied that Mzilikazi will seek his revenge – even if, when this duly took place, the devastation and destruction was on a scale that none had imagined. Then, amongst the Matabele, Gubuza is the first to warn that the Barolong would never rest until they had secured their revenge for punishment which he believed went far beyond reasonable retribution for the offence they had committed. Ultimately, that prophecy, too, is fulfilled: the Barolong ally themselves with the Boers, defeat the mighty Matabele in battle, and Mzilikazi is forced to flee northwards with his people. But before he does so he himself utters the greatest prophecy of them all, recovering his dignity and stature in a magnificent, haunting exhortation to his people, warning the Barolong of the inevitable outcome of their fateful alliance with the Boers:

> The Bechuana know not the story of Zungu of old. Remember him, my people; he caught a lion's whelp and thought that, if he fed it with the milk of his cows, he would in due course possess a useful mastiff to help him in hunting valuable specimens of wild beasts. The cub grew up, apparently tame and meek, just like an ordinary domestic puppy; but one day Zungu came home and found, what? It had eaten his children, chewed up two of his wives, and in destroying it, he himself narrowly escaped being mauled. So, if Tauana and his gang of brigands imagine that they shall have rain and plenty under the protection of these marauding wizards from the sea, they will gather some sense before long.
>
> Chaka served us just as treacherously. Where is Chaka's dynasty now? Extinguished, by the very Boers who poisoned my wives and are pursuing us today. The Bechuana are fools to think that these unnatural Kiwas (white men) will return their so-called friendship with honest friendship. Together they are laughing at my misery. Let them rejoice; they need all the laughter they can have today for when their deliverers begin to dose them with the same bitter medicine they prepared for me; when the Kiwas rob them of their cattle, their children and their lands, they will weep their eyes out of their sockets and get left with only their empty throats to squeal in vain for mercy.
>
> They will despoil them of the very lands they have rendered unsafe for us; they will entice the Bechuana youths to war and the chase, only to use them as pack oxen; yea, they will refuse to share with them the spoils of victory.

They will turn Bechuana women into beasts of burden to drag their loaded waggons to their granaries, while their own bullocks are fattening on the hillside and pining for exercise. They will use the whiplash on the bare skins of women to accelerate their paces and quicken their activities: they shall take Bechuana women to wife and, with them, breed a race of half man and half goblin, and they will deny them their legitimate lobolo. With their cries unheeded these Bechuana will waste away in helpless fury till the gnome offspring of such miscegenation rise up against their cruel sires; by that time their mucus will blend with their tears past their chins down to their heels, then shall come our turn to laugh.[18]

Thereupon, Mzilikazi exhorts his people to move northwards to find a new home, 'far, far beyond the reach of killing spirits, where the stars have no tails and the woods are free of mischievous Barolong'. In *Mhudi* there is an inevitability about the overthrow of oppression and tyranny: prophecies, once made, are always realised. Mzilikazi's prophecy was the only one not to have been fulfilled in the course of the book. But by the time Plaatje was writing his book it had been realised: in the South Africa of the early twentieth century the Barolong had become the oppressed, the Boers – as Plaatje saw it – the oppressors. In directing his readers to the lessons of history Plaatje's point was a straightforward one: unless tyranny and oppression were ended peaceably, it was inevitable that violence would then remain the only alternative. It was not an outcome that Plaatje either welcomed nor even wished to contemplate: his concern was simply to warn that this was what would happen. *Native Life in South Africa* had ended on exactly the same note.

Yet *Mhudi* also contains a message of hope as well as this fateful warning, and Plaatje made it perfectly clear how he felt so violent an outcome could be averted. One element of this message of hope is expressed in the bond of friendship that develops in the book between Ra-Thaga, the Morolong, and De Villiers, the Boer. In this friendship they discover a common humanity, and as a result De Villiers is able to escape from the otherwise characteristic Boer attitudes towards black people, Matabele or Barolong. 'But to tell you the truth,' De Villiers eventually says to Ra-Thaga, 'I get on much better with you than with many of my own people.' For Plaatje, human brotherhood and individual, moral change provide the key to the resolution of South Africa's racial problems: the friendship between Ra-Thaga and De Villiers represents not only the 'literary wish fulfilment of what South African society could be if only the facts of the power struggle could conveniently be ignored', as one critic writing about *Mhudi* has it;[19] in Plaatje's view, it is also the means of actually attaining such a society, the means of altering these facts of power by peaceful means, the means of avoiding the violent but inevitable alternative. No stable, just South Africa, Plaatje said on another occasion, could ever be built 'on the rickety foundation of a race discrimination, which takes everything from a subject race without giving anything for it'.[20]

This theme of brotherhood provides one important strand which runs throughout *Mhudi*, even as the ideal of brotherhood sustained Plaatje throughout his own life. But its literary expression gains added meaning when it is recalled that the book was written at a time when Plaatje was particularly hopeful of what might be achieved for his own Brotherhood movement: he enjoyed the support and hospitality of members of the movement in England, he had promises of financial aid and support from the Canadian branch of the movement, and much of *Mhudi* itself may well have been written in the home of William Cross, president of the Southall Men's Own Brotherhood, and one of Plaatje's closest English friends. Having at that time just exhausted all constitutional options for bringing about change in South Africa through appealing for imperial intervention, Plaatje's commitment to the theme of brotherhood remained one of the few sources of hope left to him: *Mhudi* can perhaps be regarded as the literary expression of this theme, affirmation of a creed that was to be severely tested in the years to come.

Yet in *Mhudi* there is another, even more fundamental source of hope and inspiration: the character of Mhudi herself. She is the central, life-giving figure of the book, a woman of great beauty, courage, wisdom and determination. Her qualities stand in sharp contrast to the far weaker and less formed character of her husband, Ra-Thaga. Often Plaatje sets her qualities in a humorous way against the stereotypes of submissive female behaviour which he is intent on both making fun of and undermining as the book unfolds. Thus his conclusion to the first lion-killing episode:

> Leaving the dead lion, Ra-Thaga fetched his herbs and his buck, secured the openings to his enclosure with fresh wag-'n-bietjie bush, and followed Mhudi into the hut where he skinned his buck while sunning himself in the adoration of his devoted wife. Her trust in him, which had never waned, was this evening greater than ever. She forgot that she herself was the only female native of Kunana who had thrice faced the king of beasts, and had finally killed one with her own hand. Needless to say, Ra-Thaga was a proud husband that night.[21]

Thereafter Mhudi completely dominates the relationship with Ra-Thaga. Immediately after the lion-killing incident Mhudi and Ra-Thaga discuss their attitudes towards Mzilikazi. Plaatje leaves no doubt whatever as to who emerges with the credit:

> At times Mhudi and Ra-Thaga found fruitful subjects for animated discussion. On one topic there was a sharp difference of opinion between man and wife. Ra-Thaga at times felt inclined to believe that the land on which they lived belonged to Mzilikazi, and that Mzilikazi was justified in sending his marauding expedition against Kunana. This roused the feminine ire of Mhudi. She could not be persuaded that the crime of one chief who murdered two indunas was sufficient justification for the massacre of a whole nation.
>
> 'But,' protested Ra-Thaga, 'all the tribes who quietly paid their dues in kind were left unmolested. Mzilikazi did not even insist that larger tribes should increase the value of their tax in proportion to their numbers. So long as each tribe sent something each spring in acknowledgement of its fealty, he was satisfied.'
>
> Mhudi, growing very irritated, cried: 'I begin to think that you are sorry that you met and married me, holding such extraordinary views. You would surely have been happier with a Matabele wife. Fancy my husband justifying

our exploitation by wild Khonkhobes, who fled from the poverty in their own land and came down to fatten on us!'[22]

Mhudi's judgement of people and character is also far superior to that of her husband. Ra-Thaga, Plaatje says, 'benefited much from the sober judgement of his clever wife', during their stay in the wilderness; but he nevertheless failed to heed her warnings about Ton-Qon, the Koranna leader, who in due course tries to kill him. As a result it is left to Mhudi to venture out and save his life, and then to nurse him back to recovery from his wounds. Later, when they encounter the Boers, Mhudi is sceptical of Ra-Thaga's somewhat uncritical enthusiasm for his new friends, and she is outraged by their cruelty; he, by contrast, came almost to turn a blind eye to instances of this cruelty, to pretend it did not exist.

Mhudi is also a woman of great courage. This is demonstrated at the beginning of the book in relation to the lion stories, and is expressed on numerous occasions thereafter – above all during the epic journey she undertakes from Thaba Nchu to the camp of the Barolong and Boer allies. Her qualities, in short, dominate the book. But they are paralleled and emphasised by the qualities and character of Umnandi, Mzilikazi's favourite wife who is forced to flee his court as a result of the jealousies of her rivals. She, too, was a woman of great beauty, excellent at every royal duty except providing royal heirs. And like Mhudi, she is the source of strength of her husband, and it is her disappearance that coincided with the change in his fortunes. 'That daughter of Mzinyato,' Mzilikazi exclaims to himself in his hour of defeat,

> was the mainstay of my throne. My greatness grew with the renown of her beauty, her wisdom, and her stately reception of my guests. She vanished, and with her the magic talisman of my court. She must have possessed the wand round which the pomp of Inzwinyani was twined, for the rise of my misfortune synchronised with her disappearance.[23]

When Umnandi is reunited with her husband at the end of the book, the symbolism is clear: the rebirth of a nation beyond the reach of Boer and Barolong.

In the qualities displayed by these two women Plaatje seems to be offering a source of hope and inspiration for a South Africa of the future. As far as the character of Mhudi herself is concerned, it seems reasonable to assume that she is a composite, created in Plaatje's imagination from a variety of people, ideas, and associations. One fundamental element was the historical figure of Mhudi. Although there is nothing in the book to indicate that Mhudi was a 'real' historical figure, in his account of his own ancestry Plaatje wrote the following: 'My mother is a direct descendant of a grandson of Tau from the house of his youngest and dearest wife, Mhudi.' Mhudi, in other words, must have been Plaatje's great-great-grandmother.

Family tradition therefore provided Plaatje with a knowledge of Mhudi's existence, and very probably he had heard from his mother and other relatives something of the character and the life of this woman from whom he was descended.

At the same time it is evident that Mhudi is invested, in Plaatje's book, with qualities and characteristics which flow very directly from his own experiences and perceptions of women during his own life. Perhaps first and foremost Mhudi stands as a tribute to his own wife, Elizabeth, 'without whose loyal cooperation' his previous book, *Native Life in South Africa*, so he acknowledged, would not have been written. But it would be surprising if Plaatje did not also conceive of Mhudi as a kind of literary testimony to those women who gave him so much support and encouragement when the book was being written in London in 1920 – Georgiana Solomon, the Colensos, Betty Molteno, Jane Cobden Unwin, Alice Werner. From these women in particular Plaatje had derived a keen insight into the parallels between the racial and sexual discrimination, and through their actions and beliefs they had done much to strengthen his conviction that women, more than men, possessed the qualities from which a more just and humane society could emerge. He had once said as much, indeed, in a letter written to Mrs Lennox Murray, another woman in this circle of friends, when congratulating her upon the birth of her baby: 'The mothers of a past generation', he had written, 'bequeathed to us a happy and beautiful sub-continent – the healthiest end of the Dark Continent: and it is the work of the mothers of tomorrow to save South Africa from degeneration if their dear ones are to live and enjoy the blessed privileges that once were ours.'[24] *Mhudi*, in large measure, was the literary expression of this belief.

Plaatje's somewhat more humorous playing around with male/female stereotypes in the book followed from this same awareness of male dominance in the society in which he lived. Much of this is very tongue in cheek, and on occasions Plaatje simply reverses the conventional roles. When the Boers first arrive in the Barolong camp, for example, it is the men who are the first to flee in flight, the women who are the more curious to venture forth and meet them. Elsewhere, the stereotypes are contrasted ironically with Mhudi's own actions – her statement, 'Of course young women are timid and not as bold as men', for example, coming immediately after the account of her own bravery which directly contradicts this cliché; or later, when Mhudi first meets her long-lost cousin, Baile:

Baile (between sobs):   'And you escaped wholly unscathed?'
Mhudi (also sobbing):   'Yes, thanks to my husband.'[25]

– the point being, rather, that it had been thanks to *her* that Ra-Thaga was still alive, not vice versa. Plaatje took great delight, in other words, in exploiting the humour implicit in contrasting reality and stereotype, as well as being concerned to make the more serious point about the potential role that women could play in South Africa's future. Just as he felt that individual, moral change was the key to the solution of South Africa's problems, so did he believe that women possessed particular qualities, transcending barriers of race, that gave them a special role in initiating these changes and bringing a more just society into existence. *Mhudi* stands as an eloquent, often amusing, testimony to this conviction.

So *Mhudi* – the book – was many things: the literary creation of a man of complex sensibilities, who found in writing it not only an escape from the day-to-day struggles that preoccupied him at the time he wrote in 1920, but also the opportunity to give expression to many of his underlying values and beliefs. Just as a knowledge of Plaatje's life makes possible a fuller appreciation of the book, so too does the book itself shed light upon the values and beliefs which sustained him throughout life. In this sense *Mhudi*'s particular value is that it brings all this together, and at a level of detachment from reality which provides a glimpse into an underlying character so often obscured by the many different guises Plaatje had to adopt in circumstances over which, as he often complained, he could exercise so little control.

In *Mhudi* it is different. Plaatje is in control of both his characters and their circumstances, released from the constraints imposed upon his own activities and ambitions. There is scope for a much freer expression of his personality and beliefs, his fascination with the traditions of his people, his humour, his enjoyment in exploring the literary and cultural possibilities of mixing Tswana tradition and Shakespeare, his admiration for the qualities he believed women to possess, his vision of the consequences of continued injustice in South Africa, his hope that the ideals of human brotherhood might yet provide a solution to South Africa's evils; above all, perhaps, an optimistic faith, a generosity of spirit, a commitment to the idea of a South African nation – all these things are conveyed in *Mhudi*, and in a totality and coherence not expressed elsewhere. The result is both a revealing personal testimony and a pioneering, eminently readable novel, which anticipates in many of its themes the preoccupations of later generations of writers from the African continent.

In terms of the more technical qualities of the book, several other characteristics stand out: a breadth of vision and scope which more than justifies Plaatje's description of *Mhudi* as 'an epic of native life', a sense of grandeur which is conveyed in some of the great set-piece speeches – above all those of the tragic figure of Mzilikazi. Many of the descriptive passages, too, are finely drawn – the battle scenes, for example, but perhaps even more notably, Plaatje's descriptions of landscapes and natural phenomena, quite clearly the product of a man who knew and loved the countryside, who felt a closeness to nature, who spiritually was far more at home here than in the towns and cities where he lived for the greater part of his life.

<>

By any standards *Mhudi* was a rich and complex novel. There was, though, little recognition of this fact in the reviews and comments that followed its publication in September 1930. These were generally favourable, although often rather patronising – as in the comment 'the style is wonderfully good for a native' from the review published in the East London *Daily Dispatch*. The same reviewer was somewhat critical of Plaatje's handling of the relationship between De Villiers and Ra-Thaga ('no one who knows Boer character will take in the story of an intimate relationship between a young Boer and a native which is enlarged upon in the latter part of the tale'), but felt that on the whole the book was 'a welcome contribution to South African literature, and is very pleasant reading'.[26]

Other people who commented upon *Mhudi* generally emphasised the significance of the fact that it was the first novel in English to have been written by a black South African. Sir David Harris, Plaatje's old Kimberley friend, considered *Mhudi* to be 'as fascinating as it is enthralling' and 'a book of exceptional merit', and that anybody capable of such an achievement 'is capable of occupying high office in the Union'.[27] Another of Plaatje's old friends, Vere Stent, still editing the *Pretoria News*, was likewise struck by the contrast between the achievement of having written such a novel and the status and disabilities faced by its author: 'If Mr Plaatje was a French subject', he wrote, 'they would fête him and make him a member of the *Academie*. In South Africa he is only a Native, and may not even ride a tram in the capital of the Union.'[28]

When the reviews and notices concerned themselves with *Mhudi* itself the opinions, like that of the East London *Daily Dispatch*, were mostly favourable, if not very penetrating. 'M.S.S.' in the *South African Outlook* advised that 'all who are in search of a thrilling and well-written book should make a point of reading this work'.[29] The *Diamond Fields Advertiser* was similarly enthusiastic. Its reviewer, 'L.C.', thought Plaatje had accomplished his stated objective of 'interpreting one phase of the back of the Native mind' to Europeans 'with outstanding success', and had written 'a really readable narrative into the bargain which informs us of the conditions of life natives lived a century ago'. *Mhudi* was, moreover, 'a good honest tale told straightforwardly and without due artifice'; if any criticism was to be made it was of the dialogue which 'occasionally reads a little stiltedly' – an opinion echoed by several other reviewers. All in all, thought the *Advertiser*, *Mhudi* 'is a South African book for South Africans and it may cordially be commended to young readers whose parents, however, will probably refuse to hand *Mhudi* over till they have finished it themselves'.[30]

Mhudi was not a great deal noted in more literary circles in South Africa, for it simply fell outside any recognised literary tradition. A characteristic exception to this general lack of interest, though, was Stephen Black, editor of the *Sjambok*. Shortly after *Mhudi* was published Plaatje was in Johannesburg and went along to see Stephen Black – probably the same occasion on which they discussed his Shakespeare translations. In the office that day was a young Zulu writer by the name of H. I. E. Dhlomo, whose brother, R. R. R. Dhlomo, was a regular and highly promising short-story writer for the *Sjambok*. 'I remember as if it were but yesterday,' H. I. E. was to recall, over fifteen years later,

> when that remarkable and talented man, Sol T. Plaatje (an admirer of Stephen Black), called at the *Sjambok* offices to get Plaatje's opinion on his (Plaatje's) novel, *Mhudi*. Black told Plaatje quite frankly that one of his faults was to make all his characters speak in high-sounding language and advised the grand old man to read some of the sketches of Dhlomo already published. Here, although the characters spoke in English, their language was natural.[31]

Black was another, in other words, who treated *Mhudi* as a realistic novel in the predominant western literary tradition and judged its characters and their dialogue accordingly. In a letter to another literary friend of his, W. C. Scully, author of *Daniel Venanda* (the book which Black advised Plaatje to translate into Setswana), Black acknowledged that he was reading *Mhudi* 'with great interest and a good deal of pleasure' and that he thought there was 'a charming authority in this book'; but he added, as an afterthought, as though such praise was too excessive, 'Of course it is crude.'[32] Stephen Black in fact had little liking for Plaatje's Shakespeare-like monologues and dialogues (nor indeed for Shakespeare himself) and little sympathy for the kind of cultural cross-fertilisation which is at the essence both of *Mhudi* and Plaatje's Shakespeare translations; his preference, rather, was for the realistic short stories of contemporary African life of the kind that R. R. R. Dhlomo was busy writing for him.

Stephen Black then voiced further criticism via the columns of 'The Telephone Conversations of Jeremiah', a regular feature that appeared in the *Sjambok*, which took *Mhudi* as its subject in its issue of October 1930. The point Stephen Black sought to make, in the convoluted style of the 'Conversations', was inspired by a similar feeling to that which underlay his views on the suitability of Shakespeare in African translation. Plaatje had 'forgotten Bechuanaland sometimes', Jeremiah says, 'and remembered only the kingdoms of Shakespeare, and those two people, Mhudi and Ra-Thaga, speak like, like . . . literature'. *Mhudi*, Jeremiah goes on to say, 'is composed of two parts . . . Sol Plaatje, the Bechuana writer, and all the white authors whom he has been reading'. In future, Jeremiah concluded, Plaatje should concentrate upon writing a novel that was about black life alone, and did not involve whites in it at all.[33]

Stephen Black was not alone in these views. When the *Times Literary Supplement* got around to reviewing *Mhudi* several years later the view it expressed was that while the book was 'definitely memorable – a torch for some other to carry on', Plaatje would have been better advised to steer away from 'Europeanism'. 'One wonders,' said the anonymous *TLS* reviewer,

> what secret fountain of African art might not have been unsealed if, in interpreting his people, a writer of Plaatje's insight had thought and written 'like a Native'. That might well have been the first authentic utterance out of the aeons of African silence.[34]

There was an element of this line of thinking in Clement Doke's reaction to the book as well. Whilst he acknowledged (in a review in *Bantu Studies*) that 'Mr Plaatje has done a good service in writing this', he added that it was 'a great pity that for Bantu publications the demand is at present so small among the Bantu themselves that books such as this have to be written in English. *Mhudi* written in Chwana would have been a still greater contribution, and Chwana sadly needs such additions to its present meagre literature.'[35] With this last comment about the state of Tswana literature Plaatje would have been in full agreement. Indeed, Doke need have read no further for confirmation of this than the Preface to *Mhudi*, wherein Plaatje says, amongst other things, that he hoped 'with the readers' money to collect and print (for Bantu schools) Sechuana folk-tales which, with the spread of European ideas, are fast being forgotten', and thereby 'to arrest this process by cultivating a love for art and literature in the vernacular'.

But with the earlier part of Doke's remarks – that *Mhudi* would have been 'a still greater contribution' had it been written in Setswana – Plaatje would have been rather uneasy, for it carried with it the implication, explicit in what both Stephen Black and the *Times Literary Supplement* said as well, that Africans should concentrate exclusively on interpreting their own people and culture. This was a view that Plaatje could never share: he contributed more to the development and preservation of Tswana literature than anybody else, but he could not accept that either he or his people should be denied the right to explore to the full the cultural possibilities of English (or any other language) if they so pleased. Quite apart from the unacceptable political connotations that were bound up in this, the whole basis to Plaatje's literary endeavours, in English or Setswana, was his insistence upon his right to interpret the one culture to the other as he wished. It was the inevitable consequence of such a position that he found himself being criticised on two fronts at the same time: and a sad paradox that it tended to be Africans who insisted upon the primacy of English, Europeans who sang the praises of concentrating upon Setswana.

◇

Whatever the reactions *Mhudi* elicited, Plaatje himself was well pleased to have finally seen his book published after such a long delay. In the three months after publication he himself ordered 250 copies from Lovedale, most of which he must have then sold himself. But he also sent copies to old friends and colleagues – an appropriate way, he felt, of repaying past debts of help or hospitality.[36] Ernst Westphal, the missionary at Pniel where Plaatje had grown up, had died in 1922, but his widow was still alive, and Plaatje sent her a copy for Christmas 1930, inscribed 'with the author's filial compliments and affectionate wishes for a blessed Christmas and a happy New Year'.[37] Sir Ernest Oppenheimer also received a copy, inscribed – somewhat mysteriously – 'with the author's compliments, in grateful recollection of courtesies during foggy nights in London';[38] so too did Mr Morris, Kimberley's City Electrical Engineer, who had earned Plaatje's appreciation for persuading the City Council to pay for the installation of street lighting in No. 2 Location.[39] To other people Plaatje sent copies of *Mhudi* in the hope of receiving books in exchange to add to his library. 'I should be glad to receive in exchange,' he wrote to Dr W. E. B. Du Bois, after sending him a copy of *Mhudi*, 'any Negro book – particularly *Darkwater* or *The Quest of the Silver Fleece*, as some sinners have relieved me of those two. I still treasure *The Soul, The Gift of Black Folk* etc.'[40]

Not that this ploy was always successful. Professor Victor Murray, a well-known educationist at Selly Oak College in Birmingham, England, and author of a recent study on education in Africa, received an unsolicited copy of *Mhudi* from Plaatje but he was somewhat reluctant to send his own book in return (since it was more expensive), and so sent him another one instead. 'Poor old Sol,' he wrote afterwards, 'was very peeved, but what could he do? He wrote back very bad tempered but as he was 6d up on the transaction I doubt if he could convince anybody that he has a case against me!'[41] It was not the most sympathetic of responses: Plaatje simply did not have the money to build up his library by purchasing the books he wanted, and sending copies of *Mhudi* to people who had written books themselves seemed, in the circumstances, one of the few means open to him of keeping up with subjects in which he had an interest. He may have had a further consideration in mind: while Plaatje would not have received royalties on copies of *Mhudi* which he obtained from Lovedale (at a 33 per cent discount), these would nevertheless have been taken into account in reaching the total of 700 copies which, according to his contract, had to be sold before royalties were payable. In less than a year after *Mhudi*'s publication Plaatje himself had purchased, so the Lovedale Press's records reveal, over 500 copies of his book.[42]

Plaatje also took a keen interest in seeking to arrange an edition of the book for potential readers in England and the United States, a possibility which he raised in July 1931 in letters to both Dr Du Bois and Dr Robert Moton. To Dr Moton he wrote as follows:

> Can we not get a publisher over there to issue a SECOND edition? Any good publisher should successfully exploit the English and North American market with an overseas edition – 2nd print. Lovedale not being commercial have no agencies abroad and the field here is so limited that I am afraid by the end of the year when this edition is exhausted, every South African reader will have a copy of *Mhudi*.[43]

The response does not seem to have been encouraging: from Dr Du Bois there is no record of a reply at all, and G. Lake Innes, Moton's assistant, who replied to the letter in Moton's absence, could offer little hope. While Innes himself had enjoyed reading *Mhudi* (he found it 'delightful and informing', and was 'impressed with the fidelity of the narrative and particularly the sympathetic reflection of the heart and mind of the native people'), he wrote:

> I am doubtful, however, if 'Mhudi' would find the circulation in America all that you would hope to achieve for it. It is true that Negro literature is in vogue at the present time, but not of the type which your book represents. I do not think any publisher would volunteer to issue it, but I am not sure that any of the Foundations would sponsor it. I think, however, that Dr Moton would be glad to feel them out and see what could be done.[44]

Plaatje did not succeed in arranging an American edition of *Mhudi* in his lifetime. Forty years, indeed, were to pass before an American edition was published. After his own experiences with the dubious J. S. Neale Publishing Company in the United States in 1922 he would perhaps not have been wholly surprised that when an American edition did finally appear, it should have been a pirated edition from which neither the Lovedale Press nor his heirs benefited at all.[45]

Mhudi was Plaatje's only English-language novel (if novel is the right word to describe it) to have been published. According to Isaiah Bud-M'belle, though, in an obituary notice written immediately after Plaatje's death, he had also written another novel in English with the intriguing title of 'Monkey Voodoo', which was, as Bud-M'belle said, 'as yet unpublished'.[46] Bud-M'belle gave no further indication here or elsewhere as to what the book was about, and it seemed to have been lost for ever. But in 1977 an incomplete 70-page manuscript, partly written in Plaatje's hand, partly typed on his typewriter, came to light. Overall, it has the appearance of a rough, early draft, and does not have a title. But from what has survived of the manuscript it is clear that Plaatje toyed with several possible alternative titles, and he set these out after writing some fifty pages in the notebook:

'A forty years romance in the life of the Ama-Baca, a South East African Tribe'

'With Other People's wives: a Romantic Epic of the Baca, a South East African Native Tribe'

| 'The Other Fellow's Wives' | An Epic covering two generations in the |
| 'Other People's Wives' | history of the Baca, a South East African Tribe.[47] |

There is no mention here of the term 'Monkey Voodoo', nor is it offered as a possible title anywhere else in the part of the manuscript that has survived. But it may well be that this was a thought which Plaatje had later on, and there is some evidence to suggest, as we shall see, that 'With Other People's Wives' and 'Monkey Voodoo' may well have been one and the same thing.

But the subject and source of inspiration of Plaatje's manuscript is clear: it is concerned with the dramatic history and migrations of the Ama-Baca tribe of the eastern Cape. Historically, the Baca originated in an area that was to become the colony of Natal. During the reign of the Zulu King Chaka in the early nineteenth century, so most accounts and traditions agree, they fled from that part of the country and then, under the leadership of their great Chief Madikane, travelled southwards, ultimately settling in the Mount Frere district of the eastern Cape.[48] Madikane himself seems to have been killed in battle with the Tembu some time between 1830 and 1834. He was succeeded by his elder son, Ncapayi, another great warrior, who fought a further series of battles and acquired for his army a reputation which – in the view of the British naval captain, A. F. Gardiner, who visited Ncapayi's court in 1835 – would rival that of Chaka himself, were their population more numerous. Thereafter the Baca entered into a short-lived alliance with the Mpondo against the Tembu, and clashed with a Boer commando sent down from Natal, before Ncapayi himself was finally killed in battle in the mid-1840s in an attack upon the Mpondo chief, Faku. Then, after a period of regency under Diko, Makhaula assumed the regency, and his people were peacefully incorporated into the Cape Colony, inhabiting the Mount Frere district where their descendants live to this day.

Their history was a dramatic and eventful one, and for Plaatje it held great fascination. He had some very interesting remarks to make about the reasons for this in a 'preface', although this does not actually appear at the beginning of the manuscript:

Why did I do it?
Outside the Baca tribe my limited reading has not disclosed another people whose history within living memory furnished miracles that approximate to Moses and the destruction of Sannacherib's army. The more I investigated their history the prouder I felt that this South Africa of ours can show a tribe

whose history includes epical topics paralleled only by some of those found in the annals of the ancient Israelites and I have often wondered why, apart from occasional sketches by Mr W. C. Scully, epical incidents like those of the Baca escaped the notice of all able writers.

So while many stories are written to provide readers with a thrill or a shock and incidents are recorded to fill a gap in some narrative, this book is the expression of pride – race pride – in the fact that South Africa . . . [*incomplete*][49]

Despite being incomplete, Plaatje's remarks are a revealing indication of what was in his mind when he set out to explore the history of the Baca. He was quick to recognise the quality of an epic in what he had found, and with his knowledge of the Bible could not fail to be struck by the parallels between the historical experience of the Baca and the biblical story of the exodus of Moses and the children of Israel from the land of Egypt. And he had a fascination in any case with the period of the *mfecane* in South African history – the forced migrations of the 1820s and 1830s which did so much to create the identities of the different African peoples of the sub-continent. For this was the heroic age of African history: a time that saw great leaders arise, brave exploits performed, a time when nations could be created or destroyed; and from the perspective of subsequent South African history a time of independence, the era before the white man began to assert his control over the lives of those who lived in the interior of southern Africa. Plaatje was not alone in looking back upon these years – for all their violence and turbulence – as a kind of golden age. In literary terms he viewed these times very much as Shakespeare viewed the adventures of the medieval kings of England from the perspective of the late Elizabethan era: both looked back to a heroic past for inspiration. For a man who knew Shakespeare so well it would be surprising if Plaatje himself was not struck by the comparison.

So Plaatje perceived in the history of the Baca material for the construction of an epic: his stated intention was not 'to provide readers with a thrill or a shock', or simply to fill in some gaps to an interesting historical episode, but to demonstrate that in South Africa's own neglected past there lay traditions that could provide a source of 'race-pride' for the African people; to emphasise that they need look no further than their own past, in other words, for that sense of identity and pride which South Africa's subsequent history had done so much to destroy.

Perhaps the single most important phrase that appears in this 'preface' was the term 'within living memory'. When Plaatje talked of investigating Baca history he must have been doing so at first hand, for at the time his manuscript was written – during the course of 1931, judging from the evidence of a letter and several newspaper clippings interleaved in the pages of the notebook in which it was written – there were no comprehensive written sources available upon which his account could have been based. W. C. Scully's writings on the Baca – published in *The State* in 1909, and his *Further Reminiscences of a South African Pioneer*, published in 1913 – may have provided Plaatje with the impetus to investigate the subject further, but what Scully has to say bears little resemblance to Plaatje's own account; and Bryant's *Olden Times in Natal and Zululand* and

J. H. Soga's *The South-Eastern Bantu*, both of which Plaatje would have been familiar with, do not throw very much light on the history of the Baca either.[50] And none of these accounts contain anything like the level of detail that Plaatje goes into.

Plaatje's manuscript must have been the product, rather, of his own first-hand investigations into Baca tradition, which he then re-worked in dramatic form: similar in this sense to *Mhudi*, but standing closer in both form and content to oral tradition. From what survives of 'With Other People's Wives' it seems Plaatje was much less concerned to work into it the degree of individual characterisation and the personal relationships that are developed in *Mhudi*. Individual characters there certainly are, but it is as though they are now subordinate in importance to the epic story of the Baca people as a whole; enough of 'With Other People's Wives' has survived to make it clear that history, or the Baca people generally, constitute the real hero. But there are similarities with *Mhudi* as well. As in *Mhudi*, prophecies play a vital part in carrying the tale along. At the beginning of 'With Other People's Wives' an old Baca woman, on her deathbed, prophesies the departure of the Baca from the land of Chaka, and exhorts them to be prepared for the tribulations that lie ahead: 'Great are the battles that you will fight with your son, Ncapayi,' she says to Madikane, the Baca chief, and she warns them to be ready to take in the women and children of other tribes whom they defeat in battle.

As in *Mhudi*, much of what follows sees the working out of these prophecies: Madikane and his people decide they can no longer endure the oppressive rule of Chaka; they plan secretly for their escape, and flee southwards. At the Tugela river they are saved from Chaka's pursuing army by a miracle. As the Zulu prepare to cross the river after them, a wall of water suddenly appears, blocking their route. They try to cross:

> The Bacas watched and the Zulus surged. Swarms of Zulus lined the water's edge with shields poised and spears aloft. In obedience to the orders of the commanders to swim across they plunged side by side in a straight line into the angry waters. This was the signal for a second line and third to follow suit in like formation – the fourth line came to the water's edge and halted. These did not plunge in, for in five minutes the billows, having completely disorganised the ranks of the surviving pursuers, heaved and tossed with them. Already some Zulus disappearing below the waves a myriad heads floated past . . . like balls, with the bodies drowning some fathoms below the surface of the water, while the surface was tossing with a myriad heads and bodies of dead and drowning Zulus and all rushing with the angry stream towards the Indian ocean with a thundering sound.[51]

So the Baca are saved by the miracle of the Tugela river, 'an episode', Plaatje says, 'that in every respect resembled the flight of the Israelites at the Red Sea'. Then they press on southwards, celebrating their bloodless victory, composing praise songs to commemorate the event. In Chaka's court, in contrast, the loss of so many of his bravest warriors to the upstart Baca causes great consternation, for the example of their escape is bound to have consequences for other tribes under Chaka's dominion: 'the Baca became an abiding menace long after their exodus',

Plaatje writes, 'for whoever mentioned them his tongue was forfeit because it mentioned a taboo, and whoever denied knowledge of their existence forfeited his tongue because it told untruths'.[52]

Yet for the Baca their difficulties are far from over. Apart from the ever-present danger of Chaka despatching a further expedition after them, as they travel southwards they encounter opposition from other people along their route. Amongst these are the Ama-Hola and Ama-Lala, but the Baca escape defeat at their hands because the Ama-Hola and Ama-Lala, intending to attack Madikane and his people, mistake one another for the intruders, and attack and destroy themselves. The Baca are left instead with their enemies' womenfolk, and in fulfilment of the prophecy, incorporate them into their tribe, taking the young women as wives for the Baca warriors; hence it is 'with other people's wives' that the Baca build up their strength as a nation. They move on to find a place of settlement at Amoshonemi, but soon have to fight off further attacks from the people on whose land they now find themselves. Their survival is due to the ingenuity of their chief, Madikane:

> The consistent luck of Madikane's armies had acquired for their King the fame of being a great witchdoctor. Madikane, who knew that he was no doctor, but profiting by this reputation which made his neighbours fear him, had no intention of disillusioning them. His fertile brain was constantly devising methods of keeping the illusion alive. One day the [?] army . . . mouths watering for the possession of the numerous Baca herds prepared to attack them and raid the cattle.
>
> Getting news of the impending attack, Madikane at once mobilised the Baca. They travelled across the mountains with outspread flanks and marching determinedly and arriving in due time they forced the enemy's hand before his plans had matured. The consternation can be imagined when a people had trained for a surprise attack on foreign . . . suddenly finding themselves compelled to give a defensive battle on their own home and within view of their women and children amidst their own cattle posts.[53]

In the battle that follows Madikane displays his resourcefulness yet again when he turns to his advantage the ominous appearance of a troop of monkeys, thereby defying the 'monkey voodoo':

> The evening before the delivery of the fatal blow a troop of monkeys made themselves very conspicuous on the mountain side below which position Madikane's army was encamped.
>
> Now among Bantu races these mischievous animals are regarded as walking voodoos and the proudest witchdoctor is he who can cleanse his path of any omen of evil and turn it to his enemy's detriment.
>
> The monkeys scampered and kept shouting at his men. So Madikane quickly thought of a plan. The Baca were really despairing as according to custom they knew that the die was cast against their enterprise and they were calmly awaiting the order to retreat and give up a hopeless battle. They had no faith that they could change the edicts of fate . . . [*unclear*]

But Madikane, like a resourceful wizard, quietly thought of a plan without the aid of his [witchdoctors].[54]

The page containing the details of Madikane's scheme is missing, but as the narrative continues it is evident that it achieved the desired outcome:

The running battle was swift and decisive, commencing with the race of the baboons by sunrise. The afternoon had led Madikane . . . collected a rich booty and the next day began the march back to the banks [of] the Kinra with hundreds of women and their children too.[55]

Once again Madikane is able to build up the strength of his nation 'with other people's wives'. Ultimately he meets his death in battle with the Tembu. And just as Madikane had himself defied the 'monkey voodoo' in their earlier battle, so now did his son, Ncapayi, the new chief of the Baca, turn to his advantage the awesome effects of the total eclipse of the sun which took place during the fighting between the two armies:

'They have killed Madikane!' yelled a leather-lunged Tembu, regardless of the orders of his army leader. 'They have killed Madikane and his spirit has stolen our sun. Madikane alive was always a dangerous being but Madikane dead – Hewu, he has blackened the sun.' This cry struck terror into the hearts of the bravest Tembu warriors. They could fight the Baca alive but an angry spirit that controlled the skies was surely too much.[56]

The tide of battle was turned. Ncapayi's warriors, though they were 'also wondering what was the matter with the sky', took full advantage of the fear struck into the Tembu army by the eclipse of the sun, and pressed home their advantage. But at this point, the moment that saw both the death of the great Chief Madikane and the decisive victory of his army over his foes, Plaatje's manuscript comes to an abrupt end, having covered only one generation of the two that he seems to have envisaged.

◇

It is impossible to reach any conclusive assessment of 'With Other People's Wives': at least half of it is missing, leaves are missing from the notebook in which it is written, parts are impossible to decipher or are very obscure, and virtually the whole of it is in a very early draft. Nor is there any way of knowing whether Plaatje had indeed completed the remaining part of the manuscript, or whether the death of Madikane was simply as far as he had got with it. While Plaatje's knowledge of the Bible, and Shakespeare, undoubtedly helped to give shape to his recognition of the epic character of the story of the Baca people, there is no indication of when and how he was able to collect the information upon which 'With Other People's Wives' is based: perhaps he had been to the Mount Frere district on one or more of his visits to the eastern Cape in the 1920s and had the opportunity of talking to old people there; possibly, too, his interest had been aroused by Isaiah Bud-M'belle, or Elizabeth, both of them descended from a Hlubi family and clan whose history was closely associated with that of the Baca.

But whatever the sources of Plaatje's interest and information on the Baca, even the incomplete, fragmentary manuscript that has survived provides an insight into the direction that Plaatje's future literary plans might have taken. It was significant, amongst other things, that these were not confined to exploring the traditions of the Tswana people alone: there was a wider body of historical tradition which Plaatje was already exploring. It was a great pity that H. I. E. Dhlomo never elaborated further upon the 'many literary plans' that Plaatje had told him about during the several hours' conversation they had on the last occasion they met.[57] Perhaps then he could have provided some clue as the nature of another manuscript with the title 'Chicago in the Bush' which (so Dr Molema at least had reason to believe) Plaatje had also written. Of this no trace whatever survives.

16

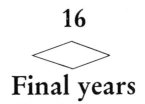

Final years

During the late 1920s and early 1930s Plaatje's most urgent preoccupation was with what could broadly be described as literary concerns: working upon his Shakespeare translations, his collection of Tswana folk-tales, the new edition of the *Sechuana Proverbs*, collecting data for his dictionary, writing – perhaps researching – his epic on the history of the Baca; arguing his case over Tswana orthography; and, probably most time-consuming of all, seeking the whole time to raise the funds to print and publish all this work, and then dealing with the various printers and publishers he approached.

At times it was a lonely, dispiriting struggle, and there was often little support or encouragement. One letter he wrote to Robert Moton, in July 1931, reveals something of the depth of frustration he was at that time feeling about the obstacles in his path:

> There is much data that wants writing in the line of old Native research, but valuable data lies unprinted, of immense historic and anthropological value; I have no financial aid to visit such localities and the old people are fast dying out and being buried with the information which is thus being lost to posterity.
>
> I frequently appealed to Dr Loram to use his influence in America for such financial aid. He would listen and question me so sympathetically – the net result was that after two years raising false hopes, I read in the [papers] how he secured £250, from the Government, and £900.0.0. from the Carnegie Trust for a White man to do in Zululand the kind of research that I have been explaining to him about my researches in Bechuanaland. I believe if a White man came along and stole my powder, he would have no difficulty in getting a £1,000 for half-cooked second-hand information (often distorted) about Natives. Yet a couple of hundred stirling could bring a Sechuana dictionary and a volume of Native fables and Traditional Poems in the vernacular to the printing press.[1]

Others were somewhat more appreciative of the wider value of Plaatje's literary endeavours. When reviewing *Mhudi* in May 1931, *Imvo* was moved to congratulate Plaatje on being amongst the few leaders who had found 'the time and inclination for striving to attain achievement in literature notwithstanding their political activity and anxiety to rescue their people from the state of oppression that must obsess them'; and it hazarded the opinion that 'the Bantu race of the future, long after his political efforts have been forgotten, will place him in a position of high esteem as a pioneer of literature'.[2] Earlier that year H. I. E. Dhlomo, an aspiring writer himself, reviewing the events of the previous year for *Umteteli wa Bantu*, drew attention to Plaatje's achievements: 'Mr Plaatje,' he said, 'is one of the new artists who deserve more support and sympathy for the priceless work they are doing for the nation.'[3] In these circles, at least, Plaatje was now beginning to acquire an honoured reputation as a writer of literature: no nation with any claim to self-esteem, it was widely felt, could do without this.

Not that literary concerns were a total preoccupation for Plaatje during these years. He had, after all, to earn a living, and so he continued to write – not as frequently as before, it is true – for the *Diamond Fields Advertiser* and *Umteteli wa Bantu* on the issues of the day. He was much involved, too, in the affairs of the Cape Native Voters' Association; he campaigned with growing impatience in the acrimonious orthographic debate; he travelled around with his bioscope apparatus, putting on shows in and around Kimberley; he continued to promote the cause of the International Order of True Templars, probably also one of his main sources of income at this time. And in December 1930 he attended the government's Native Conference in Pretoria, the first time it had been convened since 1926.

From the official minutes of the conference it is evident that Plaatje did not have as much to say as in previous Native Conferences. Perhaps it was that he now saw his main concern as lying in his work on Tswana literature; or perhaps he simply believed that it was time for younger spokesmen to come to the fore. Z. K. Matthews, at this time headmaster of Adams High School in Natal, recalled later that Plaatje had been particularly impressed by the emergence of R. H. Godlo, of East London, with whom he had worked closely in the Cape Native Voters' Association.[4] Now that Godlo was attending the Native Conference for the first time Plaatje seems to have been happy to let him take the initiative.

Certainly Richard Godlo made an impressive debut during the discussion which took place over the proposed Native Service Contract Bill, a measure designed to give white farmers an even greater degree of control over their black labour force than they enjoyed already, and to prevent them, and their families, from departing from the towns. He roundly condemned the bill as 'a measure aimed at the introduction of slave conditions', and it was he who moved conference's resolution on the subject.

Plaatje's only contribution to the debate was to ask why it was intended that the controversial 'whipping clause' (the method the government proposed to use to enforce the legislation) should apply only to Africans living in the Transvaal and Natal, and not to those in the other two provinces. 'Are not the Natives of the Cape and Orange Free State cheeky?' he enquired. For there were occasions now when Plaatje's wit took on a more biting, sarcastic tone, and people sensed, so Z. K. Matthews wrote, 'a note of despondency and a tone of harshness in his conversation about the trend of events in South Africa'. This particular Native Conference was clearly one of the occasions where these feelings were in evidence. Very likely it was also this same conference Vere Stent had in mind when he related the following anecdote:

At a certain conference he [Plaatje] was rebuked by one of the Government nominees for ingratitude. 'You should remember', said this maudlin person, 'all the blessings the white man has bestowed upon you.'
'I do,' said Plaatje, 'always I do, especially brandy and syphilis.'[5]

It was not the kind of exchange likely to find its way into the official conference record.

Richard Godlo's resolution on the Native Service Contract Bill was passed unanimously, despite a rather heavy-handed threat from Senator van Smit, one of the 'Native Senators' appointed to look after African interests (and possibly the 'government nominee' mentioned above). He warned the delegates not to reject the various measures that were being laid before them, 'as in that case a Conference might not be called again'; nor did he consider the 'whipping clause' to be – as the Reverend Z. Mahabane had claimed – 'contrary to the principles of Christianity'.

Plaatje did make his voice heard during the conference's debate on the proposed extension of the 'tot' system to the Transvaal; he asked the government what their intentions were on the orthographic question, and he wondered, too, whether the government would not consider raising the delegates' attendance allowance above the level of 12s 6d per day. On this last point, the Minister of Native Affairs, Mr Jansen, who had at least taken the trouble to attend the conference for most of its sittings, replied that 'he did not think it was possible to increase the allowance of members at present', and added that he took it that delegates 'were prepared to make some sacrifice for their people'. Plaatje, of all people, was hardly the person for him to have chosen to lecture on this subject.[6]

Although both the minister and the chairman of the conference, Mr J. F. Herbst, Secretary for Native Affairs, were duly thanked for their contributions to the proceedings at its close, few of the delegates present can have returned home with any illusions as to the effect their deliberations and resolutions, respectfully framed as they were, were likely to have. The government, for its part, was not pleased by the opposition expressed to the measures it had submitted for discussion, and the Native Conference was never again summoned.

The following month – January 1931 – Plaatje travelled to Johannesburg to attend another conference, a rather more fruitful one as it turned out, held under the auspices of the Independent Order of True Templars, for whom he had now been working, off and on, since 1927 in his capacity as 'Special Missioner'. Over the three days of the conference the triumphs and failures of the previous five years were debated and discussed, and Plaatje was given special credit for the progress of the movement amongst Africans in the Transvaal and Orange Free State. From Plaatje's point of view by far the most significant outcome of the conference was the decision to launch a monthly or quarterly newspaper for the movement, the objective being 'to keep us all in touch with each other but even more than that to spread our message through such a medium'.[7] The idea had been discussed on several previous occasions, but it had always been difficult to find the necessary financial backing, and no firm initiative had ever been taken.

Now, however, the need for such an organ seemed more urgent than ever before, firm promises of support from the different branches and jurisdictions of the Order were given, and the head of the Order, the Right Worthy Templar, J. W. Mushet, was very keen on the idea – and seems to have been willing to put up the capital required to launch it. The delegates to the conference accordingly resolved to 'start the paper as soon as arrangements could be made and to issue 3,000 copies to start with', the intention being – so Mushet explained – 'to publish the paper in English, but that Afrikaans items and any other items in Bantu languages would be published in these languages'. Mushet himself then offered to act as its first editor.[8]

The necessary arrangements took some months to complete, and they were probably one of the reasons for Plaatje's visit to Cape Town the following May. Although his name had not been mentioned in connection with editing the paper in the minutes of the January conference, it is clear that he was very much involved in the preparations. When the first number of *Our Heritage* (as the paper was called) appeared in June 1931 it gave two editorial addresses: Box 1432, Cape Town, the box number of the IOTT's head office; and Box 143, Kimberley, Plaatje's personal box number: Plaatje, it seems, was to be a joint editor. From the content of the first issue of *Our Heritage* it was evident that the new paper was not going to confine itself in a narrow way to the affairs and interests of the temperance movement alone, but would also be concerned with issues of much broader social and political interest. Thus the beginning of its first editorial:

> The starting of 'Our Heritage' on the anniversary month of the date of Union is a mere coincidence. But it is also a great and significant act. Today our Coloured and Native people, after twenty-one years of Union, find themselves being pushed back step by step. More and more they are being denied the inherent rights of all mankind, and more and more are they being denied civic and political rights in their own birthland. It is fitting that they should be able to tell the world – and South Africa – just how they fare twenty-one years after Union and how they feel about it.[9]

Over the next few months *Our Heritage* came to bear unmistakable signs of Plaatje's editorial imprint. Certainly there was news of the affairs of the IOTT, but there was much else of a more directly political nature as well – an article on 'Land Hunger', for example, in the issue of August–October 1931; articles on the orthographic debate along the same lines as Plaatje was writing elsewhere; and a great deal of material in Setswana, including a regular column entitled 'Mma-Mmaitisho' ('Conversations') printed, it should be added, in the orthography that Plaatje was so anxious to protect from the university professors and the Central Orthography Committee. Whether or not Plaatje was ever formally appointed sole editor of *Our Heritage*, in practice it seems that this was what his position amounted to. *Our Heritage* was certainly not *Tsala ea Batho* revived, but it was the first paper he had edited since departing on his first voyage overseas in May 1914. By July 1931 Plaatje was writing to Dr W. E. B. Du Bois in America to say that he hoped to turn it into a fortnightly 'very soon'.[10]

Plaatje's visit to Cape Town that winter was notable for one other development that could hardly have been predicted when he set out from Kimberley in April. After his arrival in Cape Town he happened to notice some advertisements for an international exhibition due to be held shortly in Elizabethville, capital of the Katanga province of the Belgian Congo. It provoked an immediate interest. 'It struck me at the time,' Plaatje wrote subsequently,

> that a visit up there and a study of race relationships on the spot might yield information of some value to Native Welfare Associations in the South. The General Manager of Railways obligingly concurred in the idea, and opened the way with a free press ticket to the Congo border, 2,165 miles away; so, without further ado, one wet and misty Wednesday, I bade goodbye to R.W.T. and Cape Town friends and boarded the mail train for the north.[11]

Five days later, after stopping for only a few hours in Kimberley, and passing through Bechuanaland and Northern Rhodesia, and across the Victoria Falls, Plaatje was in Elizabethville.

Plaatje reacted to what he saw in the Belgian Congo in much the same manner as when he was in the United States of America ten years earlier, being struck above all by the differences with South Africa's 'native policies' and treatment of its African population. Variations in employment policies were evident even before he reached Elizabethville from the Northern Rhodesian border:

> Train officials speak to us in French or Swahili, the two languages of the Congo. We speak foreign languages under a foreign flag, in a foreign express train, operated by a Native driver, and Native stoker, and a Native guard. At the stops in the dense jungle a Native pumper attends to the engine, and a Native stationmaster gives us the right away. Only the ticket collector in the van and Chief Steward in the dining-car are Belgians – a brand new experience.
>
> It was obvious that all passengers did not approve of this . . . in the skilled departments of the line, but our friends the Belgians are philosophers. Two of their most affable officials were chatting with a group of South Africans at Sakania station this morning, when a shunting engine purred past them. At sight of the black crew on the engine one South African very nearly fainted. Recovering from the shock, he protested vehemently against that method of keeping back the industries of the country. 'In the Union we don't allow them to do it', he exclaimed.
>
> 'You see,' said the affable Belgian in his accented English, 'in England, the home of the British Government they make no distinction; in Belgium, the home of our Government, they make no distinction; why should we make distinctions here in the Congo?' The South African was not satisfied. 'In this country,' he asked, 'are you going to entrust your safety to these people?'
>
> 'Quite so. They are very good. And they make good soldiers. In the war they fought very well; everybody was safe.'[12]

It was the kind of story Plaatje delighted in recounting, and – as he was taken in hand by the Belgian authorities, and treated very much, it would seem, as a

VIP – he found much else in the Belgian Congo to contrast with South African methods of dealing with its 'native' population. Another difference, which Plaatje was quick to perceive, was in the way in which labour was organised for the mines of Elizabethville and the Witwatersrand respectively. Whilst in South Africa the mining industry depended upon an institutionalised system of migrant labour, in which the industry's costs were in effect subsidised by the 'reserves', in Elizabethville the policy was one of labour stabilisation, designed to encourage the development of a skilled as well as unskilled labour force, for in the Belgian Congo there was to all intents and purposes no white working class to fulfil such a role.

The working of the Belgian Congo's judicial system, too, given Plaatje's longstanding interest in such matters, provided further food for thought. Introduced to the Chief Justice, Plaatje spent some time in the law courts (listening, he wrote, 'to some very interesting forensic duels'), was impressed by the system of utilising assessors from the different tribes involved in legal cases, and was assured that this system was 'giving the utmost satisfaction and inspiring a great respect for the laws of the country'. The contrast with what was being done within the South African judicial system could not have been clearer:

I hardly think that anyone in the Union could possibly object to a system of Native administration which inspires respect for law. Under such a system it would scarcely be possible to endure an unedifying spectacle like the Native Administration Act whereby the Union Parliament has legalised the sale of Native girls, like so many horses, and called the sale lobola! It is as if a Mohamedan power were to enact laws over Christians, and straightway dispensed with hymns and prayers, abolished sermons on Sundays, legalised only the collection, and called it divine service.[13]

On policies and practices in education and taxation, both subjects in which Plaatje was very much interested, his conclusions were broadly similar. On the latter topic, indeed, he later pointed to 'the senseless taxation methods of my country in contrast with the thoughtful administration of the poll tax laws inspired by the Belgian authorities'.[14] If Plaatje had any private reservations about what he saw in the Belgian Congo he did not give expression to them publicly. He went in search of new perspectives upon what went on in his own country, and this coloured all he wrote about his observations and experiences there. Just as with his visit to North America ten years previously, Plaatje's observations reveal as much about the perceptions he took with him as the situation in the Belgian Congo.

◇

After several weeks in the Belgian Congo Plaatje set out on the long journey southwards. Instead of travelling straight back home to Kimberley he had decided to break his journey in Bulawayo, having been invited by the Native Welfare Society of Matabeleland to address a meeting of Europeans. It proved to be a notable occasion. The hall was full to capacity; it was the first time that any white Rhodesian audience had given a hearing to a black South African; and the proceedings were given extended treatment in the local newspaper, the *Bulawayo*

Chronicle. From the report it carried it is quite evident that Plaatje had lost none of his customary eloquence on the public platform, nor his great talent for speaking to almost any audience imaginable in the most appropriate manner. Confining his remarks to South Africa, the gist of Plaatje's address – followed by a question and answer session – was a fierce attack upon the South African government's treatment of its African population, and a warning of the dangers of abrogating the rule of law in favour of policies that discriminated against any section of the population. 'I can tell you from experience,' he said, 'that if you allow the law to take sides with one group against another, it will not be many years before it takes sides with one section of the group.' At this point, so the *Bulawayo Chronicle*'s reporter considered, Plaatje 'seemed to feel he was touching upon difficult ground, and complained that he was limited by the presence of a Judge of the Supreme Court [Mr Justice Russell, President of the Native Welfare Society, who was presiding at the meeting]; whereupon he 'told a funny story to relieve the position', and suggested that proceedings should continue in the form of questions, to which he would then respond.

These were predictable enough: the answers – from the point of view of those present at the meeting – rather less so. Thus Plaatje's response to the question: 'What do you think of segregation?'

> It depends upon what you mean by the word . . . There was a time when the natives thought segregation would be a desirable thing – that was the segregation you read of in Johnson's dictionary. But poor Johnson did not know what segregation means. Segregation in practice does not mean that the white people should have their own area and sphere of control, and the natives theirs. No! It means that the native must live cheek by jowl with the white man, and the only segregation you have is between the native and his money. That is what we call segregation in action.

It was perhaps inevitable, given the composition of his audience, that there should have been a question raising the spectre of 'miscegenation'. In response, said the *Bulawayo Chronicle*, Plaatje was 'vigorously outspoken':

> This is a point upon which the Native is very much misrepresented. The task of the friends of the native is rendered very difficult by some people who, whenever you suggest anything in the interests of the native, turn round and ask you whether you would like to see your daughter marry a kafir. That shows that some people in this world are absolutely good for nobody except their sons-in-law (laughter). I wish these people would understand that we natives have no intention of doing anything of the sort. We, too, have a proverb like your 'birds of a feather'. It is 'the people know each other by their spots'.[15]

Plaatje's sense of humour had helped him to surmount many crises and difficulties in the past; it was not likely to desert him before Chief Justice Russell and the European audience which came to hear him talk that Monday evening in Bulawayo.

Plaatje returned home to the task of establishing *Our Heritage* as a viable concern. Early indications were not altogether encouraging. Despite his hope that it might soon be possible to turn *Our Heritage* into a fortnightly, the editorial in the second issue, July 1931, was already complaining that the response *Our Heritage* had evoked was 'a little disappointing', and that by now every 'Grand Secretary from every Grand Temple [should] have communicated with the Editor as was agreed at the Rt. Worthy Temple held in Johannesburg in January'; this, however, had not happened.[16] The blank space on the pages set aside for advertising was not an encouraging sign either, and nor was the non-appearance of *Our Heritage* in August or September – a matter alluded to, somewhat ambiguously, in the editorial in the combined August–October issue when this did finally appear:

> We cannot fully go into the difficulties that arose accounting for this break but we can assure readers that we were up against, what were for the time being, insuperable obstacles. We trust we have now successfully overcome these and that the future publication of 'Our Heritage' will be regular.
>
> Some of the difficulties we may indicate. A section of our readers wants *their* Native language. Another wants Afrikaans. (We are trying particularly to meet this.) Another wants one language only, English. Amongst all these conflicting demands it will be seen that a grave problem of policy is at stake. In the issue, we have only got thus far. For the future we will endeavour to arrange regular Afrikaans contributions. (This, however, will largely depend on Afrikaans contributors themselves.) We cannot agree to have more than one Native language used. And since most of our Native readers understand English as a reading medium we will endeavour to have more English used in future numbers.[17]

Such disagreements over exactly what form and function *Our Heritage* was to fulfil cannot have been wholly unexpected, given the different regions, languages and races represented in the IOTT itself. In particular, non-Tswana sections of the movement would have had good reason to complain about the way in which Setswana had taken over as the 'one African language' whose use the above editorial could agree to, and the very considerable amount of material in Setswana which then appeared in its columns. Even the English columns tended to be dominated by news of goings-on in Bechuanaland and other Tswana-speaking areas of the Union of South Africa. This might have suited Plaatje's purposes very well, but it was unlikely to commend itself to other parts of the IOTT, whose support was essential to the journal's survival; nor were they likely to countenance the use of IOTT funds to support such a journal for very long either.

Even without difficulties of this kind *Our Heritage* would have found it extremely difficult to have survived for very long. The goal it set itself of achieving an immediate circulation of 3,000 was very ambitious, and its prospects were further undermined by the severe economic depression prevailing at the time it was launched; as ever, the African population, its main prospective market, was worst affected by this. At some point in 1931 Plaatje is known to have approached the authorities in the Bechuanaland Protectorate for a subsidy – on the grounds, it seems, that they had an interest and obligation to support the only Tswana-language paper in existence; but they failed to respond.[18] The November issue of *Our Heritage* contained encouraging words ('There is little doubt that *Our Heritage* has captured the imagination of our Native people . . .'), and a further issue appeared in December with the promise of more from Plaatje about his Belgian Congo trip in the next issue, but this almost certainly never appeared.

Our Heritage was to be the last paper, or journal, over which Plaatje presided as editor. Ever since the demise of *Tsala ea Batho* he had cherished the hope of being able to edit his own newspaper, and over the years he had sought various kinds of backing and support. For a while he obtained this from the IOTT, but after just five issues *Our Heritage*, too, ceased publication.

In late 1931 or early 1932 Plaatje was offered the editorship of another newspaper, a new venture launched in Johannesburg as the weekly *Bantu World*. In many respects this paper represented an important new departure in the history of the African press in South Africa. The idea of a thirty-year-old failed farmer by the name of B. G. Paver, the *Bantu World* was conceived as the first in a range of publications which were to act as an advertising medium to enable white businessmen to reach the growing African market. Whereas *Umteteli wa Bantu* had been established ten years earlier for what were essentially political motives, the *Bantu World* heralded the arrival of European commercial interests into the African newspaper world. And unlike the under-capitalised African proprietors and syndicates who had struggled over the years to keep their newspapers going, the Bantu Press (Pty) Ltd – the organisation set up to run the *Bantu World* – succeeded in attracting the capital and in setting up the means of distribution denied to the dwindling band of independent African pressmen.[19] Within the next few years, indeed, the Bantu Press was to take over the few independent African newspapers which remained: there was no room in the South Africa of the 1930s for the kind of newspaper Plaatje had once run.

Although Plaatje was amongst those whose 'assistance and guidance' was acknowledged by the management and staff of the *Bantu World* when its first issue appeared in April 1932, he declined the editorship, which went instead to Richard Selope Thema.[20] Probably his reasons for doing so were not very different from those which had led him to turn down the opportunity to edit *Umteteli wa Bantu* ten years earlier. Now, as then, he valued his independence, and he preferred to live in Kimberley rather than Johannesburg. In his various literary ventures he had, besides, other priorities.

<>

So Plaatje remained in Kimberley. Personal considerations in any case probably made him reluctant to consider uprooting himself and his family by moving to Johannesburg, even if he had been tempted by the editorship of the *Bantu World*. For in Kimberley Plaatje enjoyed a position of influence and esteem in the local community, and he had many friends of all races. To them he now owed a special debt: the gift of his house, 32 Angel Street, purchased for him by a committee, headed by Mr William McLeod, a well-known Coloured leader, in

1929 – 'a tangible expression', so it was said, of Plaatje's '25 years of unsalaried service on behalf of non-Europeans'. He had been deeply moved by the gesture.[21]

Today, the dominant memory of Plaatje in his home town of Kimberley is of his unrivalled ability as a public speaker, a man whose wit and humour could hold the attention of any audience. He used to appear on a variety of local platforms, and at election time, particularly, his services were much in demand. As one who used to attend these meetings remembers:

> In those days we had the SAP, the South African Party, Sol Plaatje was always the speaker. They always left Sol Plaatje to speak last. And whenever the meeting got a little boring, you know, they would say, 'Sol Plaatje, Sol Plaatje', and in no time at all there would be roars of laughter . . . he was an eminent politician and speaker.[22]

One occasion at which Plaatje distinguished himself is remembered more than any other: his performance at a 'non-European function' in the City Hall, held in honour of Lord Clarendon, the Governor-General of South Africa, during his visit to Kimberley in November 1931. Representatives from Coloured, Indian and African communities had all been called upon to make appropriate speeches of welcome, and Plaatje – having been selected for the task – duly spoke on behalf of the African community in Kimberley. He made a typically humorous speech, the gist of which was to express his sympathy for the Governor-General in the difficult task he faced in fulfilling his duties 'in a land of two official languages, two white races, two capitals hundreds of miles apart, and two flags'; and he concluded with the observation that he was 'particularly pleased to hear the King's English spoken by a representative of His Majesty'. It was just the speech the occasion demanded, and it went down very well.

But what everybody present remembered about that function was Lord Clarendon's reply to Plaatje's words of welcome, which he singled out for special mention when he addressed the gathering. He was very glad to hear Plaatje's remarks about the King's English, he said, but he, Lord Clarendon (so it was reported by the *Diamond Fields Advertiser*) 'was not altogether sure that he could not have learned a lesson from Mr Plaatje in the speaking of the English language'.[23] Coming from the Governor-General of South Africa it was high praise indeed, and words which Simon Lekhela, a relative of Plaatje's, then training as a teacher, remembers to this day. 'You felt proud,' he recalls, 'that you were related to a man of that stature.'[24]

In the memories of those who knew Plaatje during these years some more personal impressions also survive. Michael van Reenen, who lived in 31 Angel Street, remembered the long discussions they used to have over Shakespeare, and about the proverbs Plaatje was collecting for the new edition of his book; and the late night conversations, over a cup of coffee in his kitchen, about newspaper articles Plaatje had just completed.[25] What stands out in Simon Lekhela's memory is the interest Plaatje took in his own educational progress, and the encouragement he was always ready to offer. At one time Simon Lekhela was amongst a small group of Africans studying at the predominantly Coloured Perseverance Teachers' Training School – there 'on sufferance', as they were constantly reminded by the staff whenever one of them stepped out of turn. They used to go to Plaatje whenever they thought they were being unfairly treated: a quiet word between him and Mr Meadows, the principal of Perseverance (who also lived in Angel Street) and things would suddenly improve.[26]

Even closer to Plaatje was Mary Plaatje (née Moikoatlhai), who had married Plaatje's second son, Richard, in 1927, and then lived for a while with the Plaatje family in Angel Street. She has some vivid memories of those years. It was often, she remembers, a crowded household. Apart from herself and her husband, and Plaatje and Elizabeth, there was also Halley, the youngest son; Violet (or 'Doodles', as she was known), now teaching at the Lyndhurst Road Native School; and, at various other times, Jane Ntingana, Elizabeth's sister, who worked as a cook at the Kimberley Boys' High School; St Leger and his wife, Mita, who sometimes stayed there; Gabriel Plaatje, one of Plaatje's nephews; and three girls from the Moyanaga family in Thaba Nchu, staying in Kimberley to attend the Lyndhurst Road Native School. Frequently there were other visitors, too, from both Kimberley and beyond. Mary Plaatje particularly remembers Dr Abdul Abdurahman, the Coloured leader from Cape Town, and a longstanding friend of Plaatje's, who visited Angel Street several times when she was there.[27]

When he was at home Plaatje spent a lot of his time working in his study, often – as Mary Plaatje remembers – tapping away on his typewriter until the early hours of the morning. Music was another sound often heard in the house. Violet, like her father, was an accomplished pianist, and like her mother had an extremely good singing voice; often she and her father used to play together on the piano. Fundamental to the daily routine of the household were family prayers, held each evening, after dinner. On Sundays there were sometimes family picnics, when Plaatje would drive the family in his car (for a while he owned a 14 hp Renault, the first motor vehicle to be run by an African in Kimberley) to Modder river, or to Pniel where Simon Plaatje – by this time in his late 70s – was still living.[28] Anybody wishing to accompany Plaatje on these family outings, though, had to be ready on time. If they were not, so Mary Plaatje recalls, Plaatje would simply depart without them, for punctuality was by now something he insisted upon. In his younger days, as his Mafeking diary showed, this had not always been so; now, with a busy life to lead, it had long been a necessity. Paul Mahabane, son of the Reverend Z. Mahabane, a close family friend, was sometimes fortunate enough to go along on these outings as well.[29]

Mostly the memories of those who knew Plaatje in Kimberley during the late 1920s and early 1930s were happy ones, inevitably coloured by the passage of time. Yet all are agreed that there was one thing which caused Plaatje much unhappiness during these last few years of his life: his sons' attitude towards liquor. All three sons, St Leger, Richard and Halley, were able and talented young men, and all had had a far better formal education than their father: St Leger and Richard at Lovedale, Halley at Lyndhurst Road and Perseverance in Kimberley. St Leger had had a variety of jobs since leaving Lovedale, but in 1927 Plaatje had managed to secure for him, with the assistance of Dr Abdurahman, the post of head clerk in the office of the location superintendent in Maitland,

Cape Town – the only African to be occupying such a position in the country; but it had not lasted, apparently because of his excessive drinking, and after a while St Leger returned to live in Kimberley.[30]

Halley, the youngest, was regarded as the playboy of the family; he was popular with his friends; he dressed in the latest fashion; he was a keen cricketer; and he had – like his father – a marvellous aptitude for languages. Unlike his father, though, he saw no great virtue in total abstinence, and he enjoyed a drink with his friends. Once this was in the company of several young teachers from Lyndhurst Road, amongst whom was his friend Simon Lekhela, both of them having just completed their training at Perseverance. Simon Lekhela remembers Plaatje's angry reaction when he heard about the state into which they had got themselves:

> From the old chap there was very strong talk about the evils of liquor. He likened alcohol to the blood of the lion, the blood of the fox, the blood of the pig: the lion in that it gives you a false sense of strength, the fox because it gives you a false sense of intelligence, but the only true representation is that of the pig. Because when you are drunk you grovel in the mire, like the ordinary pig. He couldn't understand how the young men could allow themselves to descend to that level. He was uncompromising on temperance, absolute temperance.[31]

It was not an isolated occasion: Mary Plaatje and Michael van Reenen both remember other times when Plaatje flew into a furious temper with St Leger and Halley when they had returned home after drinking sessions. Living as he did by the strict moral standards he set himself, it was obviously a bitter disappointment that his uncompromising attitude towards liquor was not shared by his own sons, particularly since he was at that time busy preaching the virtues of temperance in his work with the IOTT. On such matters there could be no question of an attitude of tolerant understanding.

Yet the situation in which Halley and St Leger found themselves was hardly an enviable one. Quite apart from having to grow up in the shadow of so eminent a father, whose achievements it would be virtually impossible to emulate, they now lived in a society which really had no place for them. Plaatje used to point out himself that his sons were now excluded by law from employment even as messengers in the Post Office in Kimberley where he had begun his career. There were few other opportunities for them. For their father none of this could of course excuse their lapses from the straight and narrow path of temperance. He himself had learnt to cope with what was happening to his country, to the disappearance of so many of the hopes and ideals to which he had grown up. It was much less easy to cope with the pressures that he saw getting the better of his children. Not everybody could have his sense of purpose and extraordinary strength of moral conviction.

◇

Conscious as ever of the need to set an example to those around him, Plaatje never eased up in his work. He would not be deterred by the advice he was now receiving from his doctors to limit his activities so as to avoid putting unnecessary strain upon his weak heart. How far he had been troubled by this after his return to South Africa in 1923 is unknown, but by the early 1930s (judging from several photographs which have survived) Plaatje was looking much older than a man in his mid-fifties. He took scant notice of his doctors' warnings: as Z. K. Matthews recalled, he regarded their advice 'as a counsel of perfection which he could not heed when there was so much to be done, and so little time in which to do it'.[32]

In late 1931 and early 1932 Plaatje was as involved as ever in his customary range of activities, the severe economic depression notwithstanding. In December 1931 he travelled to Aliwal North to give the presidential address (in the absence of Professor D. D. T. Jabavu, who was overseas) to the Cape Native Voters' Association – delivered, so *Imvo* thought, with 'his characteristic forceful eloquence', and widely noticed in the press.[33] It began with a gloomy review of the political events of the past year:

> We welcome you once again at the end of another year and I am sorry to say that we have absolutely no progress to report. On the contrary, at the close of this barren year, we are threatened with more repressive legislation such as the opening of facilities for our people to obtain more intoxicants, a Service Contract law which turns farm Natives into property in the lawful possession of farm owners, the extension and enforcement of the Natal Native Code which proclaims the Governor-General as the Supreme Chief of the Natives with power to legislate for them without the advice of a single Native induna, and new powers to imprison Natives for three months without any process of law – in short the complete demolition of the liberty of the subject which, under the Constitution of the old Colony of the Cape of Good Hope, became the heritage of natives in this country.

The prevailing economic depression had of course hit Africans far harder than anybody else, and many had been unable to pay the £1 poll tax that the law required, regardless of their income:

> The result of this thoughtless want of discrimination is that many Natives are gaoled for not being able to pay the tax – and the law makes of us a race of gaol birds. In these circumstances the effects of the present depression are accentuated by our double standard of justice which, as the proverb would say, places a Bantu between the horns of a buffalo. On the one hand he is gaoled for being poor, while on the other hand work – the only remedy to poverty – is denied him because it is now the prerogative of the white man.

Plaatje considered, too, the threats to the Cape franchise with which the Cape Native Voters' Association was particularly concerned: a campaign by the Nationalists to challenge the qualifications claimed by African voters, and the extension of the franchise to white (but not black) women. On this last subject Plaatje made an appeal to white women to behave in a more sensible political manner than their sons and husbands: 'What we expect from them when the time comes is for women to clean up the man-made political mess from which the world is suffering today.' He had made very much the same point in *Mhudi*, published six months previously, as some of the more perceptive readers of the book might have noticed.

Plaatje concluded his address as he had in so many other speeches and articles: with an appeal to the African people not to despair, not to blame all their troubles upon the apparently hopeless situation in which they found themselves. 'Finally,' he said,

> it is a mistake to suppose that all our troubles are due to the prejudice of the other race. Much of it is due to our own inertia, or to false starts in the wrong direction. Let us resolve to turn over a new leaf in 1932 and that there shall be closer cooperation and better understanding among the different groups of our community, so that by cooperation and better organisation we may command the ear of our rulers as the Indians have long since done. Let us subject ourselves to discipline, self-control and sacrifice and strengthen the hands of our friends and sympathisers among another race. If standing shoulder to shoulder, with a pull together, we can manage to keep South Africa solvent we surely could combine in our own interest, for that power lies in our hands, as Shakespeare very truly put it:
> Our remedies oft in themselves do lie
> Which we ascribe to heaven the fated sky
> Gives us free scope, only doth backward pull
> Our slow designs when we ourselves are dull.

There was no clearer exposition of both the strengths and weakness of Plaatje's philosophy, and it was altogether characteristic that he should have found in Shakespeare the words to conclude his address.[34]

Early in the New Year – 1932 – it was the affairs of the IOTT which had first claim on Plaatje's time, and he attended the annual sessions of both the Transvaal and Orange Free State jurisdictions of the movement.[35] Then he was very preoccupied with local educational affairs in Kimberley, which led to a visit to Cape Town in April to see the Minister of Education over the provision of secondary education facilities at the Lyndhurst Road school.[36] This struggle had a long history. Back in 1925 Plaatje, David Ramoshoana, and several others had managed to extract a promise from the Cape provincial authorities to provide Standards VII and VIII at the Lyndhurst Road school, but they had been unable to get the necessary funds from the Department of Native Education. As a result, African children completing their primary education there had to go to a boarding institution like Tigerkloof (which very few parents could afford), or secure one of the handful of places that the Coloured Perseverance School in Kimberley reserved unofficially for Africans. After persistent lobbying over the issue, a deputation consisting of Plaatje, the Reverend Z. Mahabane, and the Reverend C. B. Liphuko had seen the Minister of Education in Cape Town in May 1931 – just before Plaatje departed for the Belgian Congo – and finally extracted the promise they were after. Higher secondary education was begun, at long last, at the commencement of the new school year in January 1932, room for the classes being found in the Lyndhurst Road Native Institute, the building Plaatje had acquired from De Beers in 1918. But at the last minute there was an unexpected setback. Although it had been understood that 95 places would be available, it now transpired that there was provision only for 40: 55 unfortunate children had therefore to be turned away.[37]

During the same trip to Cape Town, Plaatje hoped also to persuade the government to take some measures to relieve the acute distress amongst Africans on the diamond fields caused by unemployment and the general economic depression. 'I have to leave for Cape Town tonight,' Plaatje informed the General Manager of De Beers, 'on the local unemployment among natives – their physical starvation by the policy of the Union Government and their mental starvation by the Provincial authorities'; it was, he added, 'an involved problem with intricacies between the Union government and the Cape Education Department and it may take weeks to clarify'.[38] Plaatje may no longer have represented any national organisation, or carried the political weight he once had, but he remained as determined as ever to bring local grievances to the attention of the highest authorities in the land.

Plaatje spent two months in Cape Town. During this time he managed to obtain an interview with the Minister of Native Affairs, Mr Jansen (through the good offices of Senator 'Matabele' Thompson, a large landowner in the Kimberley district), but got absolutely no satisfaction on either the education or the employment issue. On the question of unemployment, the minister indicated that 'their distress was not escaping his notice', but made it clear that he felt it was a matter for the provincial authorities to deal with, not the central government. 'It will be seen,' Plaatje concluded his subsequent account of the meeting, 'that natives unemployed would remain unemployed as long as the present Government remains in power.'[39]

In the circumstances Plaatje did well even to obtain an interview. He was rather less successful, however, in the lobbying in which he was engaged at the House of Assembly over the Native Service Contract Bill, the measure which had been submitted in preliminary form for the consideration of the Native Conference in Pretoria at the end of 1930. Even with the support of Sir James Rose Innes and Sir Clarkson Tredgold, ex-Chief Justice of Southern Rhodesia and now chairman of the Cape Town Joint Council, Plaatje was unable to see Mr Oswald Pirow, the Minister of Justice.[40] In parliament, Plaatje attended a number of sessions when the bill – fiercer still in its provisions than the earlier version which the Native Conference condemned – was debated; with only one small amendment it passed through both Houses and became the law of the land. The white farmers could scarcely have asked for tougher legal controls over their labourers; its effect, in Plaatje's view, was 'to turn rural natives into so much property, to be, with their families, virtually owned by the European landowner'.[41]

Plaatje was heartened, though, by one aspect of the debate – the strong speech made against the bill by J. H. Hofmeyr, the rising star of the liberal wing of the South African Party. Such, at any rate, was how Claire Goodblatte, secretary of the Cape Town Joint Council, who had Plaatje to lunch early in April, reported his reaction to it. Besides this, she wrote afterwards, in a letter to a friend, she got

a number of other 'pleasant anecdotes' and 'scraps of interest' from him; she did
not elaborate upon what they were. But beyond securing one small amendment,
Hofmeyr had been unable to do any more than Plaatje in preventing the passage
of the Native Service Contract Bill.[42]

Plaatje's visit to Cape Town that April was notable for one other incident,
recorded – like the debates on the Native Service Contract Bill – in the official
record of the proceedings of the House of Assembly. This reveals that the
following parliamentary question (under the heading 'Native Addressed White
Girls') was asked by Mr Harm Oost, Nationalist member of parliament for
Pretoria:

Question
    (1) Whether a Native was invited to address the pupils of the girls' high
school established in the old residence of Governor Adriaan van der Stel
('Rustenburg') at Rondebosch.
    (2) Whether the said native addressed about eighty girls during school hours
on the 20th April, the gist of his address being that the natives are being badly
treated by the white people and that the pupils should afterwards use their
franchise to remedy this state of affairs.
    (3) Whether the principal of the school thereafter had tea with the said native
in her sitting-room, and
    (4) Whether the Minister will take steps to prevent a recurrence of such
incidents?

Reply
    I have referred the question to the provincial authorities concerned under
whose jurisdiction the school referred to by the hon. gentleman falls. The
reply which I have received is as follows:
    (1) Yes.
    (2) The said native addressed about 80 girls, but not actually during school
hours. The principal reports that 'his address was a balanced statement of
conditions in South Africa and was divided into two parts:
        (a) the benefits conferred on natives by Europeans;
        (b) the economic and educational disabilities of natives.
He asked the pupils to give their consideration to these disabilities, and if they
thought well to use their influence in the future to remove them.'
    (3) Yes.
    (4) The reply to (4), which is more particularly directed to myself, is that as
the matter is one which falls under the provincial administration, I do not
contemplate taking any steps as suggested.[43]

The 'said native' was of course Plaatje. His own reaction to the incident is
unrecorded, but he must have wondered at the direction in which his country
was going if this sort of exchange could take place in the House of Assembly. In
the Cape Town press there was at least some hostile reaction from
correspondents deprecating the fact that such a question could have been asked.
One letter came from A. S. Williams, the former General Manager of De Beers,
whom Plaatje knew well, now living in Cape Town. He recalled Plaatje's success

on the occasion of his first visit to Cape Town in 1900 to take the civil service examinations, and wondered what harm Mr Oost could see in 'students listening to a native lecturer who outclassed their elders in the examination room 30 years ago'.[44] Another letter came from an 'ex-Professor UCT', who wrote to the *Cape Times* as follows:

> After reading your report in your issue of Saturday of a question in the House about the lecture given by a native out of school hours to those girls who wished to attend, I made enquiries about the identity of the lecturer and discovered him to be my old friend, and your occasional contributor, Mr Sol Plaatje, known throughout the world to those interested in African development as the author of many valuable books of use to the anthropologist, the historian and the student of the native peoples and of social science.
>
> As a parent of one of the scholars, it seems to me that their distinguished principal is to be thanked for her idea of giving those pupils who, like our modern University students, wished to hear the native view at first hand (reasonably and moderately put) so good an opportunity of doing so.[45]

Plaatje did take one very good piece of news back with him to Kimberley. Whilst in Cape Town he persuaded Countess Labia, daughter of the mining magnate Sir J. B. Robinson, now married to the Italian Minister Plenipotentiary in South Africa, to give him a cheque for the £92 needed to pay the printing costs of one of his unpublished Tswana manuscripts – described in a newspaper report as a book of 'Sechuana Nursery Rhymes', but almost certainly the 'Bantu Folk Tales – Traditional and Modern' mentioned in *Mhudi* as being ready for publication.[46] For Plaatje, this was a successful conclusion to a long struggle to raise funds to print the book, ranging from a public meeting in Kimberley one 'cheerless evening' in August 1931, to more personal approaches to a variety of other individuals; J. W. Jagger, Sir Abe Bailey and Mr J. Garlick were amongst the public figures from whom Plaatje had already successfully solicited contributions.[47]

One of the first issues of the *Bantu World*, the new weekly, reported the good news: 'Hard as it is to write a book,' it said, 'it is infinitely harder to get one's manuscript into print; and in thanking Her Excellency for her thoughtful gift, "The Bantu World" would like to congratulate the Sechuana author, Mr Sol T Plaatje, in connection with the Countess's gift which will get [an] important manuscript off his hands and [to] the Press.' Moreover, commented the same paper, the gift was of added significance in view of the 'series of unpleasant questions in Parliament' that had recently been asked in connection with Plaatje's address to the Rondebosch Girls' High School. 'In one sense,' concluded the report, 'Countess Labia's generous gift is a striking answer to Mr Harm Oost, showing that the best people in the land recognise only merit in men, and not the pigmentation of the skin, nor the texture of their hair.'[48]

Plaatje returned home in May, and on Empire Day, 24 May 1932, he addressed what was to be his last public meeting in Kimberley in the new Abantu–Batho Hall, in No. 2 Location, to communicate the results of his trip to Cape Town to those who were interested. He was received, so he noted in his own account of the meeting, 'with cheers', and was thanked for his efforts.[49] Then, in June, several weeks later, he set off for Johannesburg, intending to arrange for the publication of several of the books he now had ready – most notably the 'Bantu Folk Tales' for which he now had the funds.[50] He went to stay, on this occasion, as he had probably done on other visits in the past, with Mrs Moroa Smouse, one of his wife's relatives, who had a house in Pimville, an African residential area some ten miles from the centre of Johannesburg.[51]

But some time after arriving there, so Modiri Molema recalled, Plaatje caught influenza and had to retire to bed. Molema visited him on Thursday 16 June and considered him to be very ill. The next day, though, he felt rather better, and got up from his sickbed, anxious to keep appointments he had made in town with a bank and some printers in connection with the publication of the manuscripts he had in hand – which he had continued to work on whilst confined to bed. So he walked to the nearby Nancefield station to catch the train into town, kept both appointments, but on the way back to the station in Johannesburg was taken more seriously ill. Dr A. B. Xuma, the medical student whom Plaatje had first met in Chicago in 1922, by now a very well-known medical practitioner and public figure in Johannesburg's African community, was summoned, and he drove Plaatje back to Pimville in his car.

It was obvious that Plaatje was very ill, and that afternoon an urgent telegram was sent to Elizabeth in Kimberley to inform her of her husband's serious condition. It seems to have worsened quickly. What had begun as influenza then developed into double pneumonia.[52] Elizabeth arrived on the morning of Sunday 19 June. Plaatje died at 5 o'clock that afternoon.

<><

Over a thousand people attended Plaatje's funeral, held in Kimberley three days later.[53] It was an elaborate affair, and fitting tribute to his status as a public figure. The funeral cortège set out from Angel Street early in the afternoon, made its way to the Lutheran Church in No. 3 Location, Plaatje's regular place of worship, and then on to the graveside in the West End Cemetery. The memorial service in the Lutheran Church was conducted not by the Lutheran minister, but by the Reverend Z. Mahabane, the Methodist minister, an old friend of Plaatje's, until recently President-General of the African National Congress. Of such an arrangement Plaatje, a critic of denominational rivalries to the last, would have thoroughly approved.

Plaatje's death, so Mahabane told his packed congregation, had robbed the African people of one of its ablest sons. He was a great writer, a great orator, but above all, he said, a great leader of his people:

A great patriot, he devoted his great talents to the service of his people and country. In this service he did not spare himself, but worked day and night. He lived not for himself, but for others, and ultimately laid down his life on the altar of national interests.

Mahabane's words were echoed by many other speakers who proffered tributes at the graveside. In his funeral oration, the Reverend G. Kuhn, the Lutheran minister officiating at the burial service, chose as his text a few lines from the second book of Samuel, Chapter 3, verse 38: 'And the King said to his servants, Know ye not that there is a prince and a great man fallen to this day in Israel'. 'Our deceased friend, Solomon Plaatje,' he declared, 'may also be rightly called a prince and a great man, that is why we have gathered here in such numbers to pay him the last respect.'[54] Among the many speeches which followed was one from Mr G. A. Simpson, editor of the *Diamond Fields Advertiser*: 'Mr Plaatje', he said, had 'done a great service not only to the race from whom he sprang, but to the whole community, both black and white, for he was a link between them, and enabled each to understand something of the nature, feelings and interests of the other'; he 'was proud to have counted him among his most cherished friends'.[55]

In the weeks that followed many more tributes appeared in the African press. For *Ilanga lase Natal*, 'the sad news of his demise' came 'as a thunderbolt from a clear sky', and 'the whole Native race' was poorer by his death;[56] for *Imvo Zabantsundu* 'the ranks of recognised Bantu leaders' had 'suffered a severe depletion in the deplorable demise of a staunch patriot and indefatigable toiler in the service of his fellow men . . . His soul is departed but the memory of him and his works will live untarnished in the annals of Native history.'[57] Both *Umteteli wa Bantu* and the *Bantu World* carried special commemorative supplements, recalling the many achievements of Plaatje's career. His 'life motive', said *Umteteli*, 'had been the national weal', while his 'mature knowledge, quiet humour and innate kindliness had enriched his kind and built for himself a never-dying monument of public esteem. For Plaatje, Scholar and Patriot, the most fitting epitaph would be: "He loved his people" .'

In 1935, three years after Plaatje's death, a tombstone was erected on his grave in Kimberley. Again a large crowd gathered to do honour to his memory, and to witness the unveiling of the tombstone by one of his greatest admirers, Mr G. A. Simpson, invited to perform this task by Isaiah Bud-M'belle. On it were inscribed the following words:

I Khutse Morolong: Modiredi Wa Afrika
Rest in Peace Morolong, You Servant of Africa.[58]

◇

Posterity has been far less generous in its recognition of Plaatje's life and work. Much of what he strove for came to nought, his political career was gradually forgotten, his manuscripts were lost or destroyed, his published books largely unread. His novel *Mhudi* formed part of no literary tradition, and was long regarded as little more than a curiosity. Even to a later generation of black South African writers – like the talented *Drum* generation of the 1950s – it was a curiously old-fashioned, backward-looking book which could provide no inspiration for the élite of the new urban generation; they had no time for forging traditions with a past from which they sought, more than anything, to liberate themselves.

Nor has Plaatje's contribution to the preservation of the Tswana language found the recognition it deserves. The tragedy is not simply that so much of what he wrote was lost, but that the effect of subsequent political developments in

South Africa was to turn his natural successors away from anything which appeared to give sustenance to ethnic nationalism. In Plaatje's mind there was no conflict between his devotion to the Tswana language and the furtherance of its literature, and the wider political ideals for which he strove. But for those who came after him, who lived under a government intent on dividing the African people along ethnic lines, the contradiction became too great: untold damage was done not only to Setswana but to the literary development of all the other African languages of South Africa.

And what of those political ideals – that vision of a common society, free from discrimination on grounds of race or colour, which sustained Plaatje in a lifetime of struggle? They have yet to be realised. In 1935, General Hertzog achieved his longstanding ambition of abolishing the non-racial Cape franchise; it was perhaps as well for Plaatje that he did not live to experience this. Since then South Africa's rulers have taken the country further down the path of segregation; the official terminology may have changed, the underlying realities less so. Were Plaatje to return to South Africa today he would have little difficulty in recognising in the 'homelands' and 'independent black states' (the 'reserves' of his day) the logical outcome of the policies against which he had, in his own lifetime, fought so long and hard.

And yet those ideals for which he stood, which he did so much to keep alive, are far from dead and buried. The memory of his life of commitment to the African political struggle may yet contribute to their realisation.

Above all Plaatje should be remembered as a great South African. A man of deeply conservative instinct, he drew inspiration from both African and European traditions, and was sustained throughout a life of ceaseless endeavour by a vision of what South Africa could be, given only the freedom to draw upon what he saw as the best of those traditions, created from South Africa's unique historical experience. In his own life, in the exercise of his many talents, Plaatje demonstrated to the full the rich potential that lay therein.

NOTES

Abbreviations

AS/APS	Archive of Anti-Slavery and Aborigines' Protection Society, Rhodes House, Oxford, UK
BNA	Botswana National Archives, Gaborone, Botswana
CA	Cape Archives Depot, Cape Town, SA
CAD	Central Archives Depot, Pretoria, SA
DB	Archives of De Beers Consolidated Mines Ltd., Kimberley, SA
NAD	Natal Archives Depot, Pietermaritzburg, SA
PRO	Public Record Office, London, UK
SAL	South African Library, Cape Town, SA
SOAS	School of Oriental and African Studies (University of London), UK
TI	Tuskegee Institute, Tuskegee, Alabama, USA
UCT	University of Cape Town, SA
UNISA	Documentation Centre for African Studies, University of South Africa, Pretoria, SA
UW	University of the Witwatersrand (Historical and Literary Papers), Johannesburg, SA

1 Early Years

1 Anthony Trollope, *South Africa* (London, 1878), Vol. I, p. 7.
2 Ibid., Vol. II, p. 280.
3 S. M. Molema, *Montshiwa: Barolong Chief and Patriot* (Cape Town, 1966); J. Comaroff, 'Competition for office and political processes among the Barolong boo Ratshidi of the South Africa–Botswana borderland' (PhD thesis, University of London, 1973), esp. pp. 298–303.
4 The details, circumstances and location of Plaatje's birth are derived from a variety of sources, of which the following are the most important: S. M. Molema, 'Botshelo jwa ga Solomon Tshekisho Plaatje: Moratabo' (henceforth 'Biography') in UW, Molema/Plaatje Papers, Ad 6.4 (English translation), p. 18; Bethanie Mission Register, entry 795, 9 October 1876 (microfiche copy in SOAS library); UCT, Molteno Family Papers, BC 330 A81.2.4, Plaatje to Mrs Lennox Murray, 17 November 1922; SOAS Library, Plaatje Papers (English MS 375495), STP 3/4, passport entry; PRO/CO 537/1137, 3473 (secret), 'Minutes of deputation of South African Natives', 21 November 1919, statement by S. T. Plaatje, p. 11; Orange Free State Archives Depot (Bloemfontein), Land Registry files Akt. 2/1/36 and 2/1/31, 508, entries for Doornfontein; interview (November 1977) with Mr J. DuPlessis, current owner of the farm on which Plaatje was born. I should like particularly to express my gratitude to the late Rev. J. Dire, of Edenburg, OFS, for allowing me access to the Bethanie Mission Register; to Mrs Martha Bokako, of Thaba Nchu, OFS, for information leading to this; and to the Rev. Derek Jones, of the Botswana Book Centre, Gaborone, for giving me access to Molema's unpublished biography of Plaatje. See also B. P. Willan, 'Sol T. Plaatje's date and place of birth', *Africana Notes and News*, Vol. 23, No. 4, December 1978, pp. 172–4.
5 S. M. Molema, 'Biography', appendix; interview with Mrs Martha Bokako, Thaba Nchu, 26 March 1976.
6 Interview with Mrs Martha Bokako.
7 Bethanie Mission Register, entry 795.

8 Interview with Mrs Martha Bokako, 22 April 1976; 'Biography', p. 18.

9 SOAS, Plaatje Papers, STP 1/2, 'Ancestry'.

10 Molema/Plaatje Papers, Cc1, 'Historical account of the Barolong', pp. 1–2.

11 UCT, Lestrade Papers, BC 255 F7, 'Daniel Mokhatle and others *vs* Minister for Native Affairs', transcript of evidence of S. T. Plaatje, p. 221.

12 See especially Z. K. Matthews, 'A short history of the Tshidi Rolong', *Fort Hare Papers*, 1, 1945, p. 11; Molema/Plaatje Papers, S. M. Molema, 'History of the Barolong', Ad 6.1, pp. 31–2.

13 Interview with Mrs Martha Bokako, 22 April 1976.

14 Molema, 'History of the Barolong', pp. 31–2.

15 Ibid.

16 For the eighteenth-century history of the Barolong, see particularly Comaroff, 'Competition for office'; Matthews, 'A short history of the Tshidi Rolong', p. 12; Molema, 'History of the Barolong', p. 39 *et seq.*

17 Plaatje Papers, STP 1/2, 'Ancestry'.

18 J. Comaroff (ed.), *The Boer War Diary of Sol T. Plaatje* (London and Cape Town, 1973), Introduction, p.xiv; S. M. Molema, 'History of the Barolong', p. 32.

19 For the effects of the *mfecane* upon the Barolong, see J. D. Omer Cooper, *The Zulu Aftermath: A Nineteenth Century Revolution in Black Africa* (London, 1966); M. Legassick, 'The Griqua, the Sotho-Tswana, and the missionaries (1780–1840): the politics of a frontier zone' (PhD thesis, UCLA, 1969); R. L. Cope (ed.), *The Journals of the Rev. T. L. Hodgson, Missionary to the Seleka Rolong and the Griqua* (Johannesburg, 1977).

20 Plaatje Papers, STP 1/2, 'Ancestry'.

21 Plaatje family prayer book, p.iii. I am most grateful to Mr Johannes Plaatje, Kimberley, for allowing me access to this valuable document.

22 Prayer book, p.ii; interviews with Mrs Martha Bokako, Thaba Nchu, 26 March and 4 April 1976, and 16 August 1980; inscription on Simon Plaatje's gravestone, Pniel mission, near Barkly West; notebook recording births and deaths in Plaatje family (I am most grateful to Mr Johannes Plaatje for letting me see this document).

23 Interview with Mrs Bokako, 22 April 1976.

24 For the history of the Griqua, see especially Robert Ross, *Adam Kok's Griquas* (London, 1976).

25 Ruth First and Ann Scott, *Olive Schreiner* (London, 1980), pp. 37–9.

26 Interview with Mrs Bokako, 22 April 1976; Plaatje Papers, STP 1/2, 'Ancestry'.

27 Ross, *Adam Kok's Griquas*, pp. 66–74.

28 S. T. Plaatje, 'Descendants of the Koks', *Diamond Fields Advertiser (DFA)*, 7 December 1926.

29 Bethanie Mission Register, misc. entries 1867–76.

30 'The Berlin mission', *DFA* (weekly edition), 2 October 1909; J. Duplessis, *A History of Christian Missions in South Africa* (London, 1911), chapter 22, 'The beginnings of the Berlin mission'; W. J. de Kock (ed.), *Dictionary of South African Biography*, Vol. I, p. 891, entry for Carl Friedrich Wuras.

31 *Report of South African Native Affairs Commission* (1905), *Minutes of Evidence*, Vol. 4, p. 264, evidence of S. T. Plaatje; Michael van Reenen, letter to the editor, *The Star* (Johannesburg), 1 August 1932.

32 *Berliner Missionsberichte* (Journal of the Gesellschaft zur Beförderung der Evangelische Missionen zu Berlin) [Berlin Mission Society], 1880–1, p. 132, report on Pniel for 1879–80.

33 Physical description of Pniel derived from: E. Rosenthal, *Rivers of Diamonds* (Cape Town, n.d.), pp. 16–19, 26–7; Gardiner Williams, *The Diamond Mines of South Africa: Some Account of their Rise and Development* (London, 1902), pp. 137–9; miscellaneous reports from Pniel in *Missionsberichte* in the 1880s; S. T. Plaatje, *Native Life in South Africa* (London, 1916), pp. 61–2.

34 'The Pniel Jubilee', *DFA*, 22 July 1895; *Missionsberichte*, 1891, pp. 134–8, report on Pniel for 1890; Dr G. J. Fock, 'An early history of Pniel', *DFA*, 1 March and 5 April 1963; *Report on the Land Question in Griqualand West* (Colonial Office, London), June 1880, report no. 35, pp. 81–3.

35 For details of the dispute, see Cape Archives Depot (CA), SGGW 23 (Pniel lands), 'Historical statement'; Colonial Office, *Report on the Land Question in Griqualand West*, pp. 81–3.

36 *Missionsberichte*, 1884, pp. 156–8, report on Pniel for 1883.

37 *Missionsberichte*, 1882, pp. 107–9, report on Pniel for 1881; *Missionsberichte*, 1885, p. 154, report on Pniel for 1884.

38 *Missionsberichte*, 1882, pp. 107–9, report on Pniel for 1881.

39 Archives of Berlin Mission Society (East Berlin), Abteilung 3, Fach 3, nr.10, Stationsakten/ Tagebücher, Pniel, 1876–84 (Vol. 4), Tagebücher, July–October 1881; Inventor, January 1882. I am indebted to Dr Werner von der Merwe, University of South Africa, for copies and translations of this material.

40 Prayer book, p.ix.

41 Interview with Mr Johannes Plaatje, Kimberley, 29 March 1976.

42 See especially K. Shillington, 'The impact of the diamond discoveries on the Kimberley hinterland', in S. Marks and R. Rathbone (eds), *Industrialisation and Social Change in South Africa: African Class Formation, Culture and Consciousness 1870–1930* (London, 1982).

43 *Native Life in South Africa*, pp. 61–2.

44 South African Institute of Race Relations Archives (Johannesburg), Evidence of S. T. Plaatje to Native Economic Commission (typescript), p. 5326.

45 Plaatje Papers, STP 2/2, unpublished notebook (unpaginated).

46 S. T. Plaatje, *Sechuana Proverbs and their European Equivalents* (London, 1916), p. 17.

47 Plaatje Papers, STP 1/2, 'Ancestry'.

48 'Solomon T. Plaatje – as a very young man', unpublished account by Miss E. C. M. Westphal, August 1980, p. 2.

49 See especially *Missionsberichte*, 1890–1, p. 164, report on Pniel for 1889.

50 Stationsakten/Tagebüch, Pniel, July–October 1881; Inventor, January 1882.

51 Tagebüch, entries for 17 August and 27 October 1883.

52 Tagebüch, entries for 6 December 1882, 14 October, 27 April 1888.

53 'Solomon T. Plaatje – as a very young man', p. 3; also, interviews with Miss Westphal, Johannesburg, October and November 1977, and private communication dated 3 December 1980.

54 Tagebüch, July–September 1886; *Missionsberichte*, 1887, pp. 146–7.

55 Interview with Mrs Martha Bokako, 16 August 1980; S. M. Molema, 'Biography', p. 20; UNISA, Molema Papers (acc. 142), autobiographical fragment in Plaatje's hand; for Simon Plaatje, see obituary in *Umteteli wa Bantu* (Johannesburg), 2 September 1939. I am indebted to Bob Edgar for the last reference.

56 Tagebüch, January–March 1886; *Missionsberichte*, 1888, pp. 162–73.

57 Tagebüch, July–September 1887; *Missionsberichte*, 1888, pp. 162–73.

58 Interviews with Mrs Martha Bokako, 26 March 1976 and 16 August 1980; S. M. Molema, 'Biography'.

59 Obituary of Rev. G. E. Westphal in *DFA*, 17 January 1922; interviews with Miss E. C. M. Westphal, October and November 1977. For the background to Berlin Society missionaries at this time, see M. Wright, *German Missionaries in Tanganyika, 1891–1941* (Oxford, 1971), Chapter 1; *Missionsberichte*, 1885, pp. 151–3, Pniel report, January–June 1884.

60 Cape Colony, *Annual Report of Supt.-General of Education for 1882* (G3 1883), Supplement pp. xxxvi–xxxvii, report on Pniel mission school; see also CA, SGE 1/ 130, Misc. letters received 1892, B-CI, Westphal to SGE, Cape Town, 19 April 1892.

61 H. T. Wangemann, *Ein Zweites Reisejahr in Sud-Afrika* (Berlin, 1886), p. 63.

62 CA, SGE 2/6, Inspectors' Reports, 1894, Vol. 1, A-B, report on Pniel mission school; SGE 2/ 15, Inspectors' Reports, 1895, Vol. I (Aberdeen to Bedford), report on Pniel mission school, 23 August 1895.

63 Molema, 'Biography', p. 21; I am indebted to Miss Westphal for showing me her photographs of Pniel from this period.

64 Letter from D. M. Ramoshoana to *The Star*, 2 August 1932.

65 W. D. Crisp, *Some Account of the Diocese of Bloemfontein in the Province of South Africa* (Oxford, 1895), pp. 73–4; also *Griqualand West Church Magazine*, 9 (104), December 1892, p. 7; C. Lewis and G. Edwards, *Historical Records of the Church of the Province of South Africa* (London, 1934), pp. 483–4; obituary of Crossthwaite in *Quarterly Papers of the Bloemfontein Mission*, January 1901, pp. 29–33.

66 *Quarterly Papers of the Bloemfontein Mission*, 82, 15 October 1888, p. 147.

67 CA, SGE 1/92, Misc. letters rec'd, 1887, M. Baumbach to SGE, Cape Town, 26 April 1887; SGE 1/130, Misc. letters rec'd, 1892, B-CI, Westphal to SGE, Cape Town, 19 April 1892; *Missionsberichte*, 1888, report on Pniel for 1887, p. 32.

68 'Solomon T. Plaatje – as a very young man', pp. 6–7.

69 Obituary of G. E. Westphal, *DFA*, 17 January 1922; *Missionsberichte*, 1886, p. 81.
70 Interview with Miss Westphal, October 1977.
71 S. T. Plaatje, *Mhudi* (Lovedale, 1930), inscribed copy in possession of Professor E. O. J. Westphal (University of Cape Town). I am most grateful to Professor Westphal for informing me of this.
72 Plaatje Papers, STP 2/2, unpublished notebook (unpaginated).
73 Molema Papers, typescript fragment.
74 *Missionsberichte*, 1893, statistical tables for 1892, p. 287; CA, AG 630 120/98, Plaatje to RM, Mafeking, 5 August 1898, enclosure (Annexure F) in RM, Mafeking, to Secretary, Law Department, 15 September 1898.
75 S. T. Plaatje, letter to editor, *Christian Express*, May 1913.
76 Cape Colony, *Report of Supt.-Gen of Education for 1892*, (G29 1893), p. 17.
77 CA, SGE 3/23, Deputy Inspectors' Reports, 1892, Vol. I, A–M, report on Pniel mission school, 1892; Tagebüch, Pniel, January 1893.
78 CA, SGE 2/1, Inspectors' Reports, Vol. 1, A–C, 1893–4, Report no. 5 (Pniel), 11 August 1893.
79 S. T. Plaatje, *Boer War Diary*, p. 52.
80 *Nelson's Royal Reader* (London, 1872), 'The Wonderful Pudding', pp. 26–8, and 'The Boy Who Was Always Too Late', pp. 21–3.
81 Tagebüch, July–October 1982; interviews with Miss E. M. Westphal.
82 CA, SGE 5/116, District Education Inspectors' Reports, Pniel mission school, report of M. Solomon, 8 November 1892.
83 S. T. Plaatje, letter to editor, *Christian Express*, May 1913.
84 *Missionsberichte*, 1891, statistical tables for 1890, p. 237; interview with Mrs Martha Bokako, 16 August 1980.
85 Molema, 'Biography', pp. 20 and 25; interview with Mrs Bokako, 16 August 1980.
86 I. Schapera, 'The system of land tenure on the Barolong Farms' (unpublished report for Bechuanaland Protectorate Government), 1943, p. 1 (copy in Botswana National Archives, SMS).
87 S. T. Plaatje, 'Along the road to Cairo land', *Our Heritage* (Cape Town and Kimberley), August–October 1931.
88 Plaatje Papers, STP 2/2, unpublished notebook.
89 Tagebüch, September 1893.
90 Ibid.
91 CA, AG 739 28/99, Plaatje to RM, Mafeking, 1 March 1899, enclosure in RM, Mafeking, to Secretary, Law Department, Cape Town, 5 April 1899. I am indebted to Andrew Reed for providing me with copies of material relating to Plaatje in the AG series.
92 Molema Papers, autobiographical fragment in Plaatje's hand.
93 J. Stewart, *Lovedale Past and Present* (Lovedale, 1887), pp. 224 and 525.
94 Molema Papers, autobiographical fragment.
95 'Mr Sol T. Plaatje honoured: tributes to his work for non-Europeans', *DFA*, 12 November 1928.

2 Kimberley 1894–8

1 Quoted in C. W. De Kiewiet, *A History of South Africa: Social and Economic* (Oxford, 1966), p. 90.
2 James Bryce, *Impressions of South Africa* (London, 1899), p. 202; for Kimberley in this period, see also B. Roberts, *Kimberley: Turbulent City* (Cape Town, 1976).
3 Max O'Rell (pseud. for M. Blouet), *John Bull and Co.* (London, 1894), p. 266.
4 Civil Commissioner's Report for Kimberley, 1892, *Blue Book on Native Affairs*, Cape Government, G7, 1892.
5 *Report of General Manager of Telegraphs for the Year 1882*, Cape Government, G23/83; reproduced also in R. Young, *African Wastes Reclaimed* (London, 1902). I am most grateful to Mrs M. Macey, Africana Librarian, Kimberley Public Library, for drawing the latter to my attention.
6 Address by John Knox Bokwe to the Lovedale Training Society, *Imvo Zabantsundu*, 11 July 1894.
7 *Diamond Fields Advertiser* (*DFA*), 18 June 1892.

Notes

8 'Mr Alfred S. Moletsane', *Koranta ea Becoana*, 13 April 1904; E. H. Kilpin (ed.), *Cape of Good Hope Civil Service List* (Cape Town, 1892), Post Office establishment.
9 'A good example to his brothers', *DFA*, 4 March 1895.
10 'The capital revisited: interview continued', *Tsala ea Becoana*, 16 December 1911.
11 CA, Attorney-General's files, AG 739, 28/99, Annexure A, Plaatje to Resident Magistrate, Mafeking, 1 March 1899.
12 Names of Plaatje's colleagues taken from Cape Voters' Lists of 1895 and 1897, which list occupations (CA, CCP 11/1/33 and CCP 11/1/3).
13 'Worked day and night', *Pretoria News*, 1 April 1927.
14 CA, Kimberley Magistrate's Records, 1/KIM, 2/1/46 (Civil Records), record of case no. 1192, Aaron Nyusa *vs* E. Street, 29 November 1898.
15 CA, 1/KIM, 4/1/2/11, RM to T. Binase, 18 March 1897.
16 'Mr Sol T. Plaatje honoured', *DFA*, 12 November 1928.
17 UW, Molema/Plaatje Papers, Ad 6.4, 'Biography' (English translation), p. 22.
18 DB, General Secretary's Correspondence (microfilm), S. T. Plaatje to De Beers, 25 September 1929.
19 S. T. Plaatje, 'The Joint Council and the constitution', *Umteteli wa Bantu* (Johannesburg), 28 February 1925; interview with Mr Ben Tyamzashe, Zinyoka, Kingwilliamstown, 15 August 1976.
20 CA, AG 1984/1898, Record of Service of Messengers and Interpreters, entries for J. S. Moss and G. B. Polisa; AG 1970/1899, Record of Service, entry for J. S. Msikinya.
21 See especially 'Jubilee Commemoration Hall', *Imvo*, 18 November 1897; 'Native Wesleyan Church', *DFA*, 21 June 1897; and, more generally, B. P. Willan, 'An African in Kimberley: Sol T. Plaatje, 1894–1898' in S. Marks and R. Rathbone (eds), *Industrialisation and Social Change in South Africa: African Class Formation, Culture and Consciousness, 1870–1930* (London, 1982), pp. 242–3.
22 Interview with Mrs Martha Bokako, Thaba Nchu, 22 April 1976.
23 *Daily Independent* (Kimberley), 22 December 1882 and 12 July 1883. I am most grateful to Rob Turrell for these two references.
24 For Isaiah Bud-M'belle's career, see 'U Mr I. B. M'belle', *Imvo*, 5 January 1894; 'A government appointment', *Imvo*, 7 March 1894; T. D. Mweli Skota (ed.), *African Yearly Register* (Johannesburg, 1930), pp. 104–5; 'A scholarly native', *DFA*, 9 January 1893; 'Native interpreter retires' and 'Mr Bud-M'belle's retirement', *DFA*, 1 February 1916.
25 'Mr Bud-M'belle's retirement', *DFA*, 1 February 1916. I am most grateful to Mrs M. Macey for drawing this reference to my attention.
26 'The South Africans Improvement Society', *DFA*, 23 August 1895; S. T. Plaatje, 'An example to our youth', *Umteteli*, 17 October 1925.
27 'Native teachers – the want of literature' (editorial), *Imvo*, 29 August 1895.
28 'The South Africans Improvement Society', *DFA*, 23 August 1895.
29 Ibid.
30 Ibid.
31 'The Wesleyan Synod and ukulobola', letter from 'Biza' to *DFA*, 17 January 1896.
32 CA, CCP 11/1/33, Cape Voters' List (Kimberley), 1895, entry no. 1571 (P. Lenkoane).
33 J. Comaroff (ed.), *The Boer War Diary of Sol T. Plaatje* (London and Cape Town, 1973), entry for 27 December 1899, pp. 51–2.
34 Interview with Mrs Maud Zibi (née Sidzumo), Kayakulu, W. Transvaal, 2 December 1981. I am indebted to Andrew Reed for making this possible.
35 'The South Africans Improvement Society', *DFA*, 23 August 1895.
36 'Mr Sol T. Plaatje honoured', *DFA*, 12 November 1928.
37 CA, AG 630 120/98, Annexure A, Plaatje to RM, Mafeking, 5 August 1898; AG 630 120/98, RM, Mafeking, to Law Department, Cape Town, 15 December 1898.
38 S. T. Plaatje, 'A South African's homage', in I. Gollancz (ed.), *A Book of Homage to Shakespeare* (Oxford, 1916), pp. 336–9; reproduced in *English in Africa* (Grahamstown), Vol. 3, No. 2, September 1976, pp. 7–8.
39 'Interview with Mr William Haviland', *DFA*, 16 October 1896; 'The Merchant of Venice', *DFA*, 26 October 1896; advertisement for performance of 'The Merchant of Venice', *DFA*, 4 December 1897.
40 'A little function', *DFA*, 25 August 1896.
41 'Death of a native student', *DFA*, 18 April 1898; personal communication from the Registrar, Wilberforce University, 11 October 1978.

42 DB, General Secretary's Correspondence, YMCA appeal, 21 September 1896, enclosure in Plaatje to De Beers, 22 September 1896. I am most grateful to Dr M. Buys, De Beers Archivist, for providing me with copies of this correspondence.

43 *Koranta ea Becoana*, 11 October 1902.

44 'Concert', *DFA*, 23 July 1896.

45 'Hon. Marcus Garvey returns to Liberty Hall', *Negro World* (New York), 12 February 1921.

46 'The debut of the Philharmonic Society', *DFA*, 13 March 1897.

47 Ibid.

48 For further details and references, see 'An African in Kimberley' in Marks and Rathbone (eds), *Industrialisation and Social Change*, pp. 250–2.

49 'Beaconsfield – Eccentrics C.C.', *Imvo*, 22 September 1896.

50 See especially S. Trapido, 'White conflict and non-white participation in the politics of the Cape of Good Hope, 1853–1910' (PhD thesis, Univ. of London, 1970).

51 S. T. Plaatje, *Native Life in South Africa* (London, 1916), p. 165.

52 Quoted in L. D. Ngcongco, 'John Tengo Jabavu 1859–1921', in C. Saunders (ed.), *Black Leaders in South African History* (London, 1979), p. 146.

53 Trapido, 'White conflict and non-white participation', p. 312.

54 'Mr P. R. Frames', letter from P. Lenkoane to *Koranta ea Becoana*, 29 November 1902.

55 Reproduced in *DFA*, 21 August 1895, later published as O. Schreiner and S. C. Cronwright-Schreiner, *The Political Situation* (London, 1896); R. First and A. Scott, *Olive Schreiner* (London, 1980), pp. 218–21; S. C. Cronwright-Schreiner, *The Life of Olive Schreiner* (London, 1924), pp. 274–5; S. T. Plaatje, 'Friends of the natives', *DFA*, 15 June 1925.

56 'Mr Cronwright-Schreiner and the natives', *DFA*, 27 August 1895.

57 'The South Africans Improvement Society', *DFA*, 23 August 1895.

58 'The political situation', *DFA*, 26 August 1895.

59 J. C. Smuts, *Jan Christian Smuts* (London, 1954), p. 32; *DFA*, 30 October 1895, reproduced also in K. Hancock and J. van der Poel (eds), *Selections from the Smuts Papers*, Vol. I (Cambridge, 1966), pp. 80–100.

60 Comaroff (ed.), *Boer War Diary*, entry for 18 March 1900, p. 118.

61 *Imvo*, 15 June 1898.

62 *Koranta ea Becoana*, 7 September 1904.

63 Ibid.; see also *Imvo*, 22 February and 15 June 1898; S. T. Plaatje, 'Natives and law and order', *DFA*, 10 November 1930; S. T. Plaatje, 'Transvaal and natives', *DFA*, 25 January 1928; 'Native rights under pass laws', *Cape Times*, 14 June 1928; S. T. Plaatje, 'The pass law in Kimberley', *DFA*, 26 March 1925.

64 'Mr Sol T. Plaatje honoured', *DFA*, 12 November 1928.

65 Interview with Mrs Martha Bokako, Thaba Nchu, 22 April 1976.

66 'Practical brotherhood', *DFA*, 17 January 1919.

67 Plaatje family prayer book, p. ix, entry recording Johannes Plaatje's death in Mafeking district, 26 September 1896.

68 Molema, 'Biography', p. 27.

69 S. T. Plaatje, *Native Life in South Africa*, p. 92.

70 'Late Mrs E. Sol T. Plaatje', *Umteteli*, 30 January 1943; CA, 1/KIM, 8/1/15, Civil Marriage Affidavit, 25 January 1898. I am most grateful to Andrew Reed for providing me with a copy of this last document.

71 S. M. Molema, 'Biography', p. 27; interview with Mrs Martha Bokako, April 1976.

72 *Boer War Diary*, entry for 25 December 1899, p. 50.

73 'A South African's homage', p. 336.

74 Molema, 'Biography', p. 28.

75 Ibid.

76 *DFA*, 26 January 1898.

77 'A South African's homage', p. 338.

78 See particularly, S. Trapido, 'White conflict and non-white participation', p. 332.

79 *DFA* (weekly edition), 6 August 1898.

80 Rhodes House Library, Oxford, Rhodes Papers, no 233, T. D. Patrick Lenkoane to C. J. Rhodes, 20 June 1900.

81 *Boer War Diary*, entry for 18 March 1900, p. 118.

82 Trapido, 'White conflict and non-white participation', p. 165.

83 First and Scott, *Olive Schreiner*, p. 232.

84 Cape Colony, *Report of Postmaster-General for Year 1897*, G39 '98, p. 92.
85 UW, Rheinallt Jones Papers, Joint Councils file, proceedings of 1924 Joint Council Conference, address of S. T. Plaatje, 'Treatment of natives in the courts', p. 3.
86 CA, 1/MAF, 5/1/9/2, misc. letters received (January 1898–October 1899), Detective Dept, Kimberley, to RM, Mafeking, 17 January 1898, and J. A. Molkoe to RM, Mafeking, 28 February 1898.
87 CA, AG 630, 120/98, Plaatje to RM, Mafeking, 5 August 1898.
88 CA, AG 630, 120/98, Plaatje to RM, Mafeking, 13 September 1898.
89 CA, AG 630, 120/98, RM, Mafeking, to Law Department, Cape Town, 15 September 1898.
90 CA, AG 630, 120/98, Annexure D, testimonial dated 9 September 1898.
91 CA, AG 630, 128/98, Annexure A, form of application for employment.
92 CA, AG 630 138/98, Annexure C, application for leave dated 2 November 1898, and medical certificate dated 1 October 1898.
93 CA, AG 630 138/98, Annexure C, application for leave dated 2 November 1898.
94 CA, AG 630 120/98, Annexure F, handwritten memo to chief clerk.
95 CA, AG 630 128/98, Annexure A, form of application for employment.

3 'The Essential Interpreter': Mafeking 1898–9

1 Quoted in B. Gardner, *Mafeking: a Victorian Legend* (London, 1966), pp. 28–9.
2 Unpublished typescript of correspondence between Major Alexander and Mrs Godley (in author's possession), Mrs Godley to Major Godley, 5 September 1899.
3 'The story of Mafeking', *Diamond Fields Advertiser*, 13 July 1897.
4 SOAS, Methodist Missionary Society archives, Box 330/102, Rev. F. Briscoe to Rev. Marshall Hartley, 15 October 1898.
5 CA, Mafeking Magistrate's records, 1/MAF, Letterbook D, 1898, C. G. H. Bell to Colonial Secretary, Cape Town, 9 November 1898.
6 CA, NA 248, M. M. Rushton (Inspector of Native Reserves, Mafeking), 1 November 1898; quoted in K. Shillington, 'Land, labour and dependence: the impact of colonialism on the southern Tswana *c.* 1870–1900' (PhD thesis, Univ. of London, 1981), p. 340.
7 S. M. Molema, *Montshiwa: Barolong Chief and Patriot, 1815–96* (Cape Town, 1966); J. Comaroff, 'Competition for office and political processes among the Barolong boo Ratshidi of the South Africa–Botswana borderland' (PhD thesis, Univ. of London, 1973); S. T. Plaatje, 'Montsioa', in T. D. Mweli Skota (ed.), *African Yearly Register* (Johannesburg, 1930), pp. 53–7.
8 *Koranta ea Becoana*, 16 December 1903; reports in *Bechuanaland News* (Vryburg), 18 June and 6 July 1898; CA, 1/MAF, Letterbook M (May–December 1898), Bell to Wessels Montshiwa, 6 October 1898.
9 *South African Native Affairs Commission, Minutes of Evidence*, Vol. 4, evidence of S. T. Plaatje, p. 264.
10 S. T. Plaatje, 'The late Chief Silas Molema: passing of a progressive Barolong chief', *Cape Times*, 13 September 1927; see also entry for Silas Thelesho Molema in Mweli Skota (ed.), *African Yearly Register*, p. 51.
11 S. T. Plaatje, 'The late Chief Silas Molema'.
12 DB, Lyndhurst Road Estate file, Silas Molema to S. T. Plaatje, 25 May 1918.
13 Standard Bank archives (Johannesburg), Inspection Report, Mafeking branch, 26 December 1903.
14 CA, 1/MAF, Letterbook M (May–December 1898), marginal comment by Bell re Molema's application for a firearms licence, Supt. of Native Affairs to RM, Mafeking, 20 October 1898.
15 See chapter 2, p. 56; interview with Mr Rex Molema, Mafeking, August 1977.
16 J. Comaroff (ed.), *The Boer War Diary of Sol T. Plaatje* (London and Cape Town, 1973), Introduction, p. xvi; and see, e.g., Plaatje's diary entry for 16 February 1900, *Boer War Diary*, pp. 95–6.
17 UW, Ad 6.4, 'Biography', p. 1, pp. 4–6.
18 *Boer War Diary*, p. 49.
19 CA, AG 630 84/98, 'Application for a third clerk at Mafeking', Bell to Law Department, Cape Town, 29 May 1898.
20 CA, AG 630 84/98, recommendation for Grayson to be placed on fixed establishment, 7 July 1898.

21 Interview with Mrs Maud Zibi, Kayakulu, W. Transvaal, 2 December 1981.
22 Molema/Plaatje Papers, Db2, 'The Essential Interpreter', IV, p. 7.
23 E. F. Kilpin (ed.), *Cape of Good Hope Civil List* (Cape Town, 1902), p. 289; see also *Men of the Times: Old Colonists of the Cape Colony and Orange River Colony* (Johannesburg, 1906), p. 37.
24 Obituary in *Port Elizabeth Daily Telegraph*, 13 August 1908.
25 CA, AG 837 714/1900, 'Application for leave' from C. G. H. Bell, 20 June 1900.
26 'Departure of Mr Bell', *Mafeking Mail*, 31 October 1900.
27 Unpublished Godley correspondence, Godley to Mrs Godley, 19 February 1900.
28 *Boer War Diary*, p. 52.
29 CA, 1/MAF, Letterbook D, Bell to Supt. of Native Affairs, 15 September 1898.
30 CA, AG 739 28/99, Bell to Law Dept, Cape Town, 5 April 1899.
31 CA, 1/MAF, 1/2/1/1/2, Criminal Record book, 1898.
32 CA, 1/MAF, Letterbook D (January 1899–June 1900), schedule of types of cases heard in RM court, Mafeking, April 1881–99.
33 CA, 1/MAF, 1/2/1/1/2, Criminal Record book, entries for cases 290 and 291, October 1898.
34 CA, 1/MAF, Letterbook D (January 1899–June 1900), Bell to Law Dept., Cape Town, 29 March 1899; 'IDB at Mafeking', *Bechuanaland News*, 4 March 1899.
35 Molema/Plaatje Papers, Db2, 'The Essential Interpreter'.
36 'Essential Interpreter', IV, p. 11.
37 Ibid., IV, p. 11.
38 Ibid., IV, p. 8.
39 Ibid., IV, p. 10.
40 Ibid., IV, p. 17.
41 CA, AG 739 28/99, Plaatje to Bell, 1 March 1899, enclosure (annexure A) in Bell to Law Dept, Cape Town, 5 April 1899.
42 CA, AG 739 28/99, marginal comment by Acting Postmaster-General, Kimberley, 28 April 1899, on despatch cover, Bell to Law Dept, Cape Town, 5 April 1899.
43 'Essential Interpreter', IV, pp. 2–4.
44 Ibid., IV, p. 2
45 CA, 1/MAF, 2/1/1/16, Civil records, case no. 91, Solomon T. Plaatje *vs* Alfred Ngidi, 9 June 1899; 2/2/1/2, Civil record book 1898–1903, case no. 91, p. 121.
46 CA, 1/MAF, 2/1/1/16, Civil records, case no. 142, 29 August 1899, Joseph Whiffler *vs* Solomon Plaatje; 2/2/1/2, Civil record book, 1898–1903, case no. 142, p. 132.
47 S. T. Plaatje, 'The Native Congress Deputation', *Diamond Fields Advertiser*, 17 July 1914.
48 CA, Records of Civil Service Commission (unclassified), Letterbook (6 July 1899–31 December 1900), Secretary of Civil Service Commission to Plaatje, 10 August 1900; CA, AG 837 3/1900, Plaatje to Bell, 6 June 1900, enclosure in Bell to Law Department, 8 June 1900.
49 CA, Records of Civil Service Commission, Letterbook (28 March 1893–5 July 1899), Secretary, Civil Service Commission, to I. Bud-M'belle, 23 May 1899.
50 For the origins of the Anglo-Boer war, see particularly S. Marks and S. Trapido, 'Lord Milner and the South African state', *History Workshop*, 8, 1978; G. H. Blainey, 'Lost causes of the Jameson Raid', *Economic History Review*, 18, 1965; P. Warwick (ed.), *The South African War* (London, 1980), Part I.
51 For Mafeking on the eve of the siege, see Gardner, *Mafeking: A Victorian Legend*; B. Willan (ed.), *Edward Ross, Diary of the Siege of Mafeking, October 1899 to May 1900* (Van Riebeeck Society, Cape Town, 1981), Introduction; and issues of the *Mafeking Mail and Protectorate Guardian*, May–October 1899.
52 *Boer War Diary*, Prologue, xi.
53 S. T. Plaatje, *Native Life in South Africa* (London, 1916), p. 239.
54 Ibid.
55 Ibid.
56 CA, 1/MAF, 5/1/9/2, Misc. letters received (January 1898–October 1899), Wessels Montshiwa to Sec. for Native Affairs, 9 October 1899. I am most grateful to Andrew Reed for providing me with a copy of this and other material in the 1/MAF series.
57 S. T. Plaatje, 'Segregation: idea ridiculed', *Transvaal Chronicle* (n.d.), reproduced in *Tsala ea Becoana*, 28 January 1911.
58 *Imvo*, 21 August 1899; Natal Archives Depot (Pietermaritzburg), Colenso Papers, Box 55, Plaatje to Mrs S. Colenso, 26 February 1915.

59 CA, Records of Cape Civil Service Commission, Letterbook (6 July 1899–31 December 1900), Secretary of Civil Service Commission to Plaatje, 10 August 1899.
60 CA, AG 838 3/1900, Plaatje to Bell, 6 June 1900, enclosure in Bell to Law Dept, Cape Town, 8 June 1900.

4 The siege and after: Mafeking 1899–1902

1 For the siege of Mafeking, see particularly B. Gardner, *Mafeking: A Victorian Legend* (London, 1966); T. Pakenham, *The Boer War* (London, 1979), chapter 33; J. A. Hamilton, *The Siege of Mafeking* (London, 1900); B. Roberts, *Churchills in Africa* (London, 1970); B. Willan, 'The siege of Mafeking' in P. Warwick (ed.), *The South African War* (London, 1980).
2 B. Willan (ed.), *Edward Ross, Diary of the Siege of Mafeking, October 1899 to May 1900* (Cape Town, 1981) p. 98.
3 J. Comaroff (ed.), *The Boer War Diary of Sol T. Plaatje* (London and Cape Town, 1973).
4 Rhodes University Library, Cory Library, C. G. H. Bell Papers (MS 7348), 'Diary during the siege of Mafeking'.
5 *Boer War Diary*, p. 1.
6 Ibid., p. 2.
7 Ibid., p. 11.
8 Ibid., p. 85.
9 Ibid., p. 64.
10 Ibid., pp. 96–7.
11 Ibid., p. 49.
12 Ibid. p. 50.
13 Ibid., p. 16.
14 Bell Papers, Plaatje to Lord Edward Cecil, 26 January 1900.
15 *Boer War Diary*, p. 67.
16 Ibid., p. 43.
17 Ibid., p. 17.
18 Bell Papers, Plaatje to Cecil, 26 January 1900.
19 Bell Papers, Plaatje to Bell, 30 January 1900.
20 Bell Papers, 'Diary', p. 169.
21 Bell Papers, Report from Plaatje to Bell, 7 November 1899.
22 Bell Papers, 'Diary', p. 169.
23 *Boer War Diary*, p. 88.
24 S. T. Plaatje, *Native Life in South Africa* (London, 1916), p. 10.
25 First pointed out in Andrew Reed's unpublished article, 'An apprenticeship in the African press'.
26 On the food question and Baden-Powell's policy towards the African population, see particularly Pakenham, *The Boer War*, chapter 33.
27 *Boer War Diary*, p. 101.
28 Ibid., p. 121.
29 Ibid., pp. 77–8.
30 Ibid., p. 68.
31 *The Star* (Johannesburg), 5 July 1932, letter to the editor from Vere Stent; Vere Stent, 'South Africa's first native novelist', *Pretoria News*, 8 November 1930. I am most grateful to Andrew Reed for providing me with a copy of the last item.
32 *Boer War Diary*, p. 6.
33 Ibid., p. xxxi.
34 Ibid., p. 122.
35 For details of this incident, see especially Bell's 'Diary', pp. 145–6.
36 'Correspondence: the Barolongs and Eloff's Day', *Mafeking Mail*, 27 September 1904.
37 Bell, 'Diary', p. 167 and 170.
38 CA, 1/MAF, Letterbook D (January 1899–October 1900); C. G. H. Bell, 'Report on the Natives, state of', p. 2.
39 *Native Life in South Africa*, p. 251.
40 Ibid., p. 250.
41 Willan, 'The siege of Mafeking' in Warwick (ed.), *The South African War*, p. 160.
42 Editorial, *Koranta ea Becoana*, 18 November 1903.

43 For a general treatment of this, see P. Walshe, *The Rise of African Nationalism in South Africa: the African National Congress, 1912–1952* (London and Stanford, 1970), pp. 15–16; T. Karis and G. M. Carter (eds), *From Protest to Challenge*, Vol. I, *Protest and Hope, 1882–1934* (Stanford, 1972), pp. 8–9.

44 CA, AG 837 3/1900, 364, Bell to Law Dept, Cape Town, 29 June 1900.

45 CA, AG 837 3/1900, Bell to Law Dept, Cape Town, 19 May 1900, enclosing doctor's certificate.

46 CA, AG 837 3/1900, Plaatje to Bell, 6 June 1900.

47 CA, AG 837 3/1900, Bell to Law Dept, Cape Town, 15 June 1900.

48 Ibid.

49 CA, Records of Civil Service Commission (unclassified), Letterbook (6 July 1899–31 December 1900), M. Garrett (Secretary, Civil Service Commission) to Plaatje, 10 August 1900.

50 Civil Service Commission Records, Letterbook (6 July 1899–31 December 1900), Garrett to P. M. J. Sidzumo, Vryburg, 21 September 1900.

51 'Bloemfontein: from our correspondent', *Koranta ea Becoana*, 21 March 1903.

52 Civil Service Commission Records, Letterbook (6 July 1899–31 December 1900), Garrett to all candidates taking Special Examinations, 15 November 1900; CA, AG 837 63/1900, Plaatje to CC and RM, Mafeking, 22 November 1900, enclosing application for leave.

53 UW, I. Bud-M'belle Papers, typescript c.v., p. 1; Secretary of the Civil Service Commission to I. Bud-M'belle, 24 April 1899; CA, Civil Service Commission Records, Letterbook (6 July 1899–31 December 1900), M. Garrett to I. Bud-M'belle, 30 November 1900; Cape Colony, *Report of the Civil Service Commission* (G20, 1901).

54 CA, AG 923 65/1901, application for leave, dated 16 April 1901.

55 Cape Colony, *Report of the Civil Service Commission*, 1900 (G20, 1901); also, CA, AG 923 106/1901, Plaatje to CC and RM, Mafeking, 18 July 1901; *Native Life in South Africa*, p. 10; *Cape Times*, 16 May 1932, letter to editor from A. S. Williams.

56 *Report of the Civil Service Commission*, 1900, pp. 4 and 5.

57 Civil Service Commission Records, Letterbook (6 July 1899–31 December 1901), Garrett to Plaatje, 10 June 1901.

58 Ibid.

59 CA, AG 923 146/1901, E. Graham Green to Accounting Officer, Attorney-General's Office, Cape Town, 7 November 1901, enclosing claim in favour of S. T. Plaatje, 5 November 1901.

60 CA, AG 837 26/1901, J. B. Moffat to Law Dept, Cape Town, 19 December 1900; 1/ MAF, 6/1/
3/5, Letterbook M (October 1901–May 1902), Moffat to Commandant, 24 March 2901; 1/ MAF,
5/1/9/4 (Misc. letters received, January–August 1901), Plaatje to CC and RM, 20 May 1901.

61 CA, AG 837 97/1900, Moffat to Law Dept, Cape Town, 19 December 1900; AG 923 106/1901, Moffat to Law Dept, Cape Town, 23 July 1901.

62 CA, 1/MAF, 5/1/9/3 (Misc. Received, May–December 1900), memo from Bell to Commandant, 5 September 1900, and reply from Commandant, 6 September 1900.

63 CA, 1/MAF, 5/1/9/4 (Misc. letters received, January–August 1901), Plaatje to CC and RM, Mafeking, 8 January 1901.

64 CA, 1/MAF, 5/1/9/4 (Misc. letters received, January–August 1901), OC Ox Transport Dept to RM and CC, Mafeking, 9 January 1901.

65 CA, 1/MAF, 1/1/1/30, Criminal Records 101–154 (February–April 1901), case no. 152, R. *vs* S. T. Plaatje, 1 April 1901.

66 J. Comaroff, 'Competition for office and political processes among the Barolong boo Ratshidi of the South Africa–Botswana borderland' (PhD thesis, Univ. of London, 1973), pp. 237 and 304–5; S. M. Molema, *Montshiwa: Barolong Chief and Patriot, 1815–1896* (Cape Town, 1966), pp. 181–3.

67 UW, Molema/Plaatje Papers, Cc2, compensation claim for Kolobe for loss of left leg and right foot, in Plaatje's handwriting, 3 August 1900; Cc3, compensation claim from Chief of Bangwaketse, 7 August 1900; see also CA, 1/MAF, 6/1/2/6, Letterbook D (August–March 1901), E. Graham Green (CC and RM) to UCS, Health branch, Cape Town, re 'Wooden leg for native, Kolobe'.

68 British Library (MSS Dept.), Weil Papers (Add. Mss 468481), Plaatje to Ben Weil, 28 March 1900.

69 S. T. Plaatje, 'A friend of the natives: the late Sir William Solomon', *Pretoria News*, 21 June 1930.

70 Case fully reported in *Mafeking Mail*, 6–8 November 1901; see also CA, AG 2038/9, Treason cases, R. *vs* B. C. Lottering and J. S. Maritz, November 1901, transcript of trial proceedings.

71 Judge Solomon's summing-up, 'The murder trial', *Mafeking Mail*, 8 November 1901.

72 'A friend of the natives', *Pretoria News*, 21 June 1930.

73 Editorial, quoting English translation of letter from Joseph Gape to editor, *Koranta ea Becoana*, 6 December 1902.

74 'Sentencing of four rebels', *Mafeking Mail*, 16 November 1901.

75 'A friend of the natives', *Pretoria News*, 21 June 1930; UW, J. D. Rheinallt Jones Papers, Joint Councils file, 'Treatment of natives in the courts', address by S. T. Plaatje to 1924 Joint Council, p. 4.

76 *Mafeking Mail*, 4 September and 17 December 1901.

77 'Acts, rules and regulations of the Cape Civil Service', section III, clause 32, in E. F. Kilpin (ed.), *Cape of Good Hope Civil List* (Cape Town, 1892), p. 167.

78 *Koranta ea Becoana*, No. 1, 27 April 1901.

79 Molema/Plaatje Papers, A3.6.1, Memorandum of Agreement between G. N. H. Whales and S. T. Molema, 5 September 1901.

80 Molema/Plaatje Papers, A3.6.1, undated draft of letter from S. T. Molema to G. N. H. Whales, in Plaatje's hand.

81 'Our new departure', *Koranta ea Becoana*, 23 August 1903; see also CA, CO 2535, Index (administrative) of letters received (individuals), 1901, entry re letter from S. Molema, 19 December 1901, re 'enlargement of paper and charges'.

82 BNA, RC 117 3/10/01, Res. Commissioner, Mafeking, to Asst. Governor, Gaborone, 3 October 1901.

83 'The colour of the *Koranta*', *Koranta ea Becoana*, 6 September 1902; *Koranta ea Becoana*, 25 April 1903.

84 *Koranta ea Becoana*, 25 April 1903.

85 Standard Bank archives (Johannesburg), Inspection Report (Mafeking branch), 26 October 1903, estimate of Molema's assets and value of printing machinery.

86 SOAS, Plaatje Papers, STP 3/1, S. T. Molema to Commandant, Mafeking, 18 February 1902 (in Plaatje's hand).

87 *South African Native Affairs Commission, Minutes of Evidence*, Vol. 4, evidence of S. T. Plaatje, p. 264.

88 Molema/Plaatje Papers, Aa3.6.1, Memorandum of Agreement, March 1902 and 4 April 1902.

89 CA, AG 1002, 53/1902, Plaatje to Civil Commissioner, Mafeking, 19 May 1902, and RM and CC, Mafeking, to Law Dept, Cape Town, 11 June 1902.

90 CA, AG 1002 53/1902, Plaatje to Civil Commissioner, Mafeking, 19 May 1902.

91 CA, AG 1986, Annual Confidential Reports on Messengers and Interpreters for 1902, 14 April 1902.

92 CA, AG 1002 106/1902, E. Graham Green to Secretary, Law Dept, Cape Town, 6 October 1903.

93 CA, AG 1077 79/03, E. Graham Green to Secretary, Law Dept, Cape Town, 6 October 1903.

94 S. T. Plaatje, 'Friends of the natives', *Diamond Fields Advertiser*, 15 June 1925; 'The black man's burden: interview with Mr Solomon T. Plaatje', *Christian Commonwealth* (London), 3 January 1917.

95 Molema/Plaatje Papers, Db2, 'The Essential Interpreter', IV, pp. 19–20.

5 Editor of *Koranta ea Becoana* 1902–5

1 Quoted by W. R. Nasson in 'Black society in the Cape Colony and the South African war of 1899–1902: a social history' (PhD thesis, University of Cambridge, 1983), p. 223.

2 CA, 1/MAF, 6/1/2/7, Letterbook D, E. Graham Green (Acting RM, Mafeking) to Compensation Commission, Cape Town, 21 November 1902, enclosing late compensation claims; *Koranta ea Becoana*, 30 August 1902; UW, Molema/Plaatje Papers, A979 Cc3, 'Grievances of the Barolong'.

3 CA, 1/MAF, 6/1/2/6, Letterbook D (August 1901–March 1902), Green to the Secretary, Law Dept, Cape Town, 22 January 1902.

4 CA, 1/MAF, 6/1/2/6, Letterbook D (August 1901–March 1902), Green to the Secretary, Law Dept, Cape Town, 7 February 1902.

5 'Our apology', *Koranta*, 23 August 1902.

6 'Masonic Hall', *Mafeking Mail*, 21 May 1902; 'Philharmonic Society's concert', *Mafeking Mail*, 24 May 1902; 'The little peach dilates on the Philharmonic Concert', *Mafeking Mail*, 27 May 1902.

7 Molema/Plaatje Papers, Db2, 'The Essential Interpreter', IV, pp. 19–20.

8 'Our new departure', *Koranta*, 23 August 1902.

9 *Koranta*, 25 October 1902 and subsequent issues.

10 CA, CCP, 11/1/43, Cape Voters' Roll, electoral division of Mafeking (Native Reserves), 1903.

11 CA, Records of Supreme Court, Northern Circuit (September 1902–September 1903), R. *vs* Salatiele, 8 September 1902; *Mafeking Mail*, 8 and 27 September 1902.

12 *South African Native Affairs Commission, Minutes of Evidence*, Vol. 4, evidence of S. T. Plaatje, p. 267.

13 Union of South Africa, *Report of Natives' Land Commission*, Vol. II (evidence) (UG 22, '16), p. 93.

14 'Englishmen and *Koranta*', *Koranta*, 13 September 1902.

15 'Languages', *Koranta*, 30 March 1904.

16 'The negro question', *Koranta*, 7 September 1904.

17 'Bruce Grit's column', *Negro World* (New York), 16 July 1921. I am most grateful to Professor Robert Hill for providing me with a copy of this article.

18 'Bogwera', *Koranta*, 11 April 1903.

19 Editorial, *Koranta*, 13 December 1902.

20 'Haikonna annexation' (editorial), *Koranta*, 17 January 1903.

21 'Translation', letter from Badirile Montshiwa to editor, *Koranta*, 7 February 1903; *Mafeking Mail*, 12 February 1903.

22 Molema/Plaatje Papers, Bb3, account to Sol T. Plaatje from Mallett and Bowen (Solicitors), 29 January 1903.

23 Molema/Plaatje Papers, Bb3, Petition to Joseph Chamberlain, *Koranta*, 31 January 1903; also PRO, CO 529/1, 17754 and 17803, Petition and Supplementary Petition of Barolong to Joseph Chamberlain, January 1903.

24 University of Birmingham Library, Chamberlain Papers, JC 23/2/1–2, Mary Chamberlain's sketchbook, unpaginated.

25 'Mr Chamberlain's reply', *Koranta*, 31 January 1903.

26 Quoted in *Koranta*, 7 February 1903.

27 Testimonial from Joseph Chamberlain to S. T. Plaatje, 9 February 1903 (in Library of Congress, Washington DC, USA, Booker T. Washington Papers, Con. 13, enclosure in Plaatje to Emmett Scott, 27 August 1914).

28 Molema/Plaatje Papers, Bb3, Mallett and Bowen to Plaatje, February 1903.

29 'The compensation debate', *Koranta*, 1 August 1903.

30 'Personalia', *Koranta*, 1 August 1903; 'Koranta "Special" ', *Koranta*, 15 August 1903; CA, NA 7/B1907 (Barolong claims), misc. correspondence between F. Z. S. Peregrino and W. C. Cummings, 20–29 August 1903.

31 *Mafeking Mail*, 9 September 1903.

32 'The Argus plea', *Koranta*, 15 August 1903.

33 e.g. *Koranta*, 14 October 1903; editorial, *Koranta*, 6 June 1904, 'The Central S.A. Railways', *Koranta*, 30 March 1904.

34 'Whae's your pass?' *Koranta*, 13 July 1904.

35 'Occasional notes', *Koranta*, 13 April 1904.

36 'Segregation: idea ridiculed' (*Transvaal Chronicle*), reproduced in *Tsala ea Becoana*, 28 January 1911.

37 Editorial, *Koranta*, 9 November 1904.

38 'Maitisho', *Koranta*, 9 November 1904.

39 L. and D. Switzer, *The Black Press in South Africa and Lesotho* (Boston, 1979), pp. 38, 44, 54.

40 *Koranta*, 16 September 1903; 'Notice', *Koranta*, 7 October 1903; letter from F. Z. S. Peregrino, *Izwi la Bantu*, 24 March 1908 and editorial, *Izwi*, 14 April 1908; *Imvo*, 7 January 1913.

41 *South African Native Affairs Commission, Minutes of Evidence*, Vol. 4, evidence of S. T. Plaatje, pp. 267–9; CA, NA 428 (Misc. letters received), Plaatje to Secretary for Native Affairs, 16 February 1904.

42 'The educated nigger and his paper', *The Friend*, 9 March 1903. I am grateful to Andrew Reed for providing me with a copy of this article.
43 *Koranta*, 21 March 1903.
44 '*Imvo* and *Koranta*', *Imvo*, 8 September 1903; extract from *Times of Natal*, *Ipepa lo Hlanga*, 28 August 1903.
45 Extract from 'A Johannesburg paper', *Mafeking Mail*, 9 May 1905.
46 'Martyrdom of the saints', *Koranta*, 22 November 1902; 'A murder trial', *Koranta*, 29 November 1902; editorial, *Koranta*, 6 December 1902.
47 CA, 1/MAF, Letterbook D (September 1903–May 1904), Green to Secretary for Native Affairs, 22 January 1904; Green to Director of Census, Cape Town, 4 March 1904.
48 *South African Native Affairs Commission, Minutes of Evidence*, Vol. 4, evidence of S. T. Plaatje, p. 268.
49 CA, 1/MAF, Letterbook D (September 1903–May 1904), Green to Secretary, Law Dept, Cape Town, 24 October 1903, enclosing copy of an article on Inter-Colonial Commission on Native Affairs, 21 October 1903.
50 CA, 1/MAF, 6/1/3/8, Letterbook M (June 1903–March 1904), Green to editor, *Koranta ea Becoana*, 19 January 1904.
51 BNA, RC 10/7, Resident Commissioner, Bechuanaland Protectorate, to High Commissioner, 19 November 1903.
52 *South African Native Affairs Commission, Report*, p. 65, para. 322.
53 *Koranta ea Becoana*, 5 October 1904.

6 *Koranta* and after: 1905–10

1 *Koranta ea Becoana*, 27 June 1903.
2 UW, Molema/Plaatje Papers, Ac3.6.1, General bond passed by Silas Tau Molema and the firm of 'Silas Molema' in favour of Charles Wenham.
3 *Mafeking Mail*, 9 May 1905; CA, SNA, letters received (Secretary for Native Affairs), Dower to CC, Mafeking, 2 September 1905; 'Native education', *Ilanga lase Natal*, 29 December 1905.
4 Molema/Plaatje Papers, Aa3.6.2, G. N. H. Whales to S. Minchin (copy), 8 January 1906.
5 CA, 1/MAF, Letterbook M (July 1906–February 1907), RM (Mafeking) to The Commissioner, Robben Island, 27 August 1906.
6 Molema/Plaatje Papers, Aa3.6.2., Minchin to Silas Molema, 25 October 1906.
7 Molema/Plaatje Papers, Aa3.6.2., Minchin to Molema, 25 October 1906 and 26 November 1906; CA, 1/MAF, 2/2/1/3, Civil Record Book (12/6/03–5/1/09), case 134 (1906), Helen Moroney *vs* S. T. Molema and S. T. Plaatje.
8 Molema/Plaatje Papers, Aa3.6.2., Minchin to Molema, 7 January 1907.
9 *Mafeking Mail*, 30 January 1907.
10 'The Koranta trouble', *Ilanga lase Natal*, 1 March 1907.
11 Molema/Plaatje Papers, Aa3.6.2., Whales to Molema, 19 February 1907.
12 'The Bechuanaland Press Ltd', *Mafeking Mail*, 23 April 1907.
13 Selly Oak College Library, Birmingham, Willoughby Papers, file 743, cuttings from *Koranta ea Becoana* of 10 May and 16 August 1907; *Izwi la Bantu*, 30 April 1907.
14 Molema/Plaatje papers, Db2, 'Sekgoma: the Black Dreyfus', ff. 12–13.
15 British and Foreign Bible Society archives, London, Editorial sub-committee minutes, 1907–8, extracts from letters from Rev. A. J. Wookey, 3 December 1907 and 26 February 1908; Rev. A. H. W. Behrens, 26 October 1907; Rev. G. Lowe, 8 May 1908.
16 W. C. Willoughby, *Race Problems in the New Africa* (London, 1923), p. 238. I am indebted to the Rev. John Rutherford for drawing this reference to my attention.
17 Moeding College archives (Botswana), W. C. Willoughby to W. O. Barratt, 21 September 1904.
18 'Bechuanas and education: meeting at Mafeking', *Diamond Fields Advertiser* (weekly edition), 10 October 1908.
19 S. T. Plaatje, *Sechuana Proverbs with Literal Translations and their European Equivalents* (London, 1916), pp. 15–16.
20 *Koranta*, 23 November 1903; CA, NA 752/F.718, E. Graham Green to Secretary for Native Affairs, 29 November 1904.
21 CA, NA 752/F.718, Commissioner of Taxes to Secretary for Native Affairs, 6 August 1906.
22 Ibid.; *Mafeking Mail*, 15 May 1908.

23 CA, NA 752/F.718, Plaatje to Secretary for Native Affairs, Cape Town, 2 April 1911.

24 CA, NA 752/F.718, Peregrino to Secretary for Native Affairs, 31 January 1910.

25 Interview with Mrs Maud Zibi, Kayakulu, W. Transvaal, 2 December 1981.

26 'Concert at the Location in Wesleyan Church', *Mafeking Mail*, 3 July 1908.

27 'Correspondence: colour in the town hall', *Mafeking Mail*, 11 April 1906.

28 'Mafeking Town Council: proceedings', *Mafeking Mail*, 26 April 1906.

29 Plaatje Papers, STP 2/2, unpublished notebook (unpaginated), 'With the kids'; interview with Mrs Mary Plaatje, Natalspruit, Johannesburg, November 1980.

30 'With the kids'.

31 Ibid.

32 'Olive and I', *Koranta ea Becoana*, 15 November 1907 (clipping in Willoughby Papers, file 743).

33 Clippings in Willoughby Papers, file 743.

34 CA, 1/MAF, Letterbook D, XII (December 1906–September 1907), CC and RM to Controller of Printing and Stationery, 4 September 1907.

35 *Imvo*, 22 October 1907 (Xhosa section).

36 CA, 1/MAF, Letterbook D, XII (December 1906–September 1907), CC and RM to Controller of Printing and Stationery, 13 September 1907.

37 CA, 1/MAF, Letterbook D, XIII (September 1907–June 1908), CC and RM to Under-Colonial Secretary, Cape Town, 14 October 1907.

38 'Extracts from the native press' (reproducing passage from *Koranta*, 1 November 1907), *Christian Express*, December 1907.

39 'Pettyfogging black politicians', *Izwi*, 14 January 1908.

40 *Mafeking Mail*, 15 February 1908.

41 Molema/Plaatje Papers, Aa3.6.2. Minchin to Molema, 9 December 1907.

42 Molema/Plaatje Papers, Aa3.6.2. Minchin to Molema, 13 February 1908.

43 Ibid.

44 CA, 1/MAF, 2/2/1/3, Civil Record Book (12 June 1903–5 January 1909), misc. entries. I am most grateful to Margy Keegan for these references.

45 CA, 1/MAF, Letters received M (January–December 1907), Inspector of Native Reserves, Setlagoli, to Magistrate, Mafeking, 13 January 1907.

46 CA, 1/MAF, 2/2/1/3, Civil Record Book, case 1, 1907, Colonial government *vs* S. T. Plaatje.

47 CA, 1/MAF, Letters received M (January–December 1906), Plaatje to RM and CC, Mafeking, 3 January 1906).

48 CA, 1/MAF, Letterbook D (December 1906–September 1907), CC and RM, Mafeking, to Controller and Auditor-General, 4 September 1907.

49 Conveniently collected in CA, T. 1942/67 (Treasury).

50 CA, 1/MAF, Letterbook D (December 1906–September 1907), RM to Secretary for Public Works, Cape Town, 7 March 1907.

51 CA, 1/MAF, SNA Letters received (1896–1903), Secretary to Native Affairs Dept. to Civil Commissioner, Mafeking, 31 August 1903; CAD NA 556/950, Capt G. Goodyear to RM, 15 August 1906.

52 CA, 1/MAF, Letterbook M (December 1908–July 1909), RM to Plaatje, 21 January 1909 and subsequent correspondence.

53 CA, 1/MAF, Letterbook D (June 1908–April 1909), RM to Secretary, Native Affairs Dept, Cape Town, 1 February 1909.

54 CA, 1/MAF, Letters received M (1909), Plaatje to RM, 22 March 1909.

55 Ibid.; 1/MAF, Letters received M (1909), RM, Mafeking to RM Zeerust, 22 March 1909 (with reply of RM, Zeerust).

56 CA, 1/MAF, Letters received M (1908), telegram dated 8 April 1908.

57 CA, T.1942/07, Secretary for Public Works to Asst. Treasurer, Cape Town, 8 September 1909.

58 CA, CMT 3/573, Circular no. 34, Asst. Chief Magistrate (Transkeian Territories), 15 October 1909. I am most grateful to William Beinart for this reference.

59 CA, 1/MAF, Letters received M (1909), Minchin to CC and RM, Mafeking, 30 March 1909.

60 CA, 1/MAF, Letterbook D (April 1909–January 1910), RM to Controller of Printing and Stationery, Cape Town, 5 August 1909; RM to Under-Colonial Secretary, Cape Town, 9 August 1909.

61 Notice, *Mafeking Mail*, issues between 14 and 30 June 1909.

62 L. M. Thompson, *The Unification of South Africa* (London, 1960), pp. 325–7; P. Walshe, *The Rise of African Nationalism in South Africa: the African National Congress, 1912–1952* (London and Stanford, 1970), pp. 19–24; *The Friend*, 25–7 March 1909.

63 *The Friend*, 25–7 March 1909.

64 'Native convention: meeting in Waaihoek', *The Friend*, 25 March 1910.

65 'Native convention: meeting in Waaihoek'; 'Natives and Chinese', *Mafeking Mail*, 6 April 1910; *Ilanga lase Natal*, 15 April 1910.

66 'Prize essay competition on native segregation', *Christian Express*, July 1910; also, 'Prize essay competition', *Christian Express*, June 1910.

67 'Segregation: idea ridiculed' (*Transvaal Chronicle*), reproduced in *Tsala ea Becoana*, 28 January 1911.

68 CA, 1/MAF, 2/1/1/1/23, Civil Cases, case 57, 1910, Kemp and Co. *vs* S. T. Plaatje, 12 April 1910, warrant dated 28 April 1910.

7 *Tsala ea Becoana*, Congress and the Land Act of 1913: Kimberley 1910–14

1 S. T. Plaatje, *Native Life in South Africa* (London, 1916), p. 10; S. T. Plaatje, 'The late Chief J. M. Nyokong', *Umteteli wa Bantu*, 6 September 1930; S. T. Plaatje, 'Lesho loa morena mokitlane oa ga Motlala', *Umteteli*, 30 August 1930.

2 'The S.A. Native Convention, *Tsala ea Becoana*, 9 July 1910.

3 Orange Free State Archives Depot (Bloemfontein), Col. Sec., ORC, 1192/1908, T. M. Mapikela to Colonial Secretary, Bloemfontein, 1 August 1908; Bloemfontein municipality, MBL Box 44, Mapikela to Town Clerk, Bloemfontein, 20 August 1908. I am grateful to Andrew Reed for this last reference.

4 CA, Kimberley Magistrate's records, 1/KIM 9/4, Register of Newspapers (1884–1929), entry for *Tsala ea Becoana*, 13 June 1910. I am most grateful to Andrew Reed for providing me with a copy of this document.

5 B. Roberts, *Kimberley: Turbulent City* (Cape Town, 1976), pp. 356, 360.

6 S. T. Plaatje, 'Through native eyes: annexation and the protectorates', *Pretoria News*, 16 January 1911.

7 *Ilanga lase Natal*, 29 July 1910; CA, Kimberley Magistrate's records, 1/KIM 9/4, Register of Newspapers (1894–1929).

8 Editorial, *Tsala ea Becoana*, 8 October 1910.

9 Ibid.

10 SAL, W. P. Schreiner Papers, 1689, Plaatje to Schreiner, 17 December 1910.

11 UW, Molema/Plaatje Papers, Da22, Plaatje to Silas Molema, 12 December 1912.

12 Editorial and 'The capital revisited', *Tsala*, 2 December, 1911; 'The capital revisited: interview continued', *Tsala*, 16 December 1911.

13 UW, J. D. Rheinallt Jones Papers, Joint Councils file, 'Natives in the courts', address by S. T. Plaatje to 1924 Joint Councils Conference, pp. 5–6.

14 SOAS, Plaatje Papers, STP 1/1, typescript biography of Plaatje by I. Bud-M'belle, p. 14.

15 Molema/Plaatje Papers, Aa2, Goronyane to Molema, 8 June 1911.

16 Molema/Plaatje Papers, Da14, Plaatje to Silas Molema, n.d. [*c*.April 1911]; Da10, Plaatje to Silas Molema, 5 March 1911; Chief W. Z. Fenyang to S. T. Plaatje, 27 February 1911; Da16, Plaatje to Silas Molema, n.d. [*c*.1911].

17 Molema/Plaatje Papers, Da14, Plaatje to Molema, n.d. [*c*.April 1911]; Da17 and Da18, unaddressed letters from Plaatje, n.d. [*c*.1911].

18 S. T. Plaatje, 'Natives and Mr Merriman: an appreciation', *Diamond Fields Advertiser*, 10 August 1926.

19 'I Konyenslani Yabantsundu', *Imvo Zabantsundu*, 29 August 1911; 'Izindaba ze Komiti lokuhlela le South African Native Convention', *Ilanga lase Natal*, 1 September 1911.

20 S. T. Plaatje, 'Umfiko e Kaya', *Umteteli wa Bantu*, 15 December 1923; S. T. Plaatje, 'Kgakala ko Amerika', *Umteteli wa Bantu*, 22 December 1923.

21 Letter from Pixley Seme to editor, *Ilanga lase Natal*, 15 December 1911; *Imvo*, 21 November 1911; see also R. V. Selope Thema, 'How Congress began', in Mothobi Mutloatse (ed.), *Reconstruction* (Johannesburg, 1981), p. 108.

22 DB, General Secretary's correspondence, Plaatje to De Beers, 17 July 1913.
23 'Native Union', letter from Seme to editor, *Ilanga lase Natal*, 20 October 1911; 'Native Union', letter from Seme to editor, *Tsala ea Becoana*, 28 October 1911.
24 'Proposed Native Congress: caucus meeting', *Imvo*, 5 December 1911; 'Native Union', *Ilanga lase Natal*, 1 December 1911.
25 'Native Congress: doings at Bloemfontein', *Pretoria News*, 11 January 1912: 'Native Congress to emulate the whites', *Pretoria News*, 13 January 1912; also, 'SA Native National Congress', *Tsala ea Becoana*, 10 and 17 February 1912; 'The South African Native National Congress', *Ilanga lase Natal*, 26 January 1912.
26 On John Dube, see particularly S. Marks, 'The ambiguities of dependence: John L. Dube of Natal', *Journal of Southern African Studies*, Vol. 1, No. 2, 1976; P. Walshe, *The Rise of African Nationalism in South Africa: the African National Congress, 1912–1952* (London and Stanford, 1970), pp. 35–6.
27 Molema/Plaatje Papers, A979, Cc9, Dube to Chief Lekoko Montshiwa, 13 April 1912.
28 Editorial, *Tsala ea Becoana*, 10 February 1912; see also H. J. and R. E. Simons, *Class and Colour in South Africa* (Harmondsworth, 1969), pp. 134–5.
29 'The capital revisited', *Tsala ea Becoana*, 2 and 16 December 1911; 'Mr Sol Plaatje', *Ilanga lase Natal*, 5 January 1912.
30 Editorial, *Tsala ea Becoana*, 10 February 1912.
31 'S.A. Native Congress', *Tsala ea Becoana*, 17 February 1912.
32 Ibid.
33 'A memorable meeting: the first step to union of non-Europeans', *Tsala ea Becoana*, 6 April 1912; see also 'The Native Congress and the APO', *Ilanga lase Natal*, 29 March 1912.
34 'Deputation to Government', *Tsala ea Becoana*, 6 April 1912.
35 Ibid.; CAD, NA 3250/11/F1131, 'Notes of interview with the Minister of Native Affairs of representatives of the South African Native National Congress', Cape Town, 15 March 1912.
36 P. Rich, 'The agrarian counter-revolution in the Transvaal and the origins of segregation, 1902–1913', in P. L. Bonner (ed.), *Working Papers in Southern African Studies* (University of the Witwatersrand, Johannesburg, 1977).
37 'Notes of interview'.
38 CA, 1/KIM 9/4, Register of Newspapers.
39 Molema/Plaatje Papers, Da19, Plaatje to Molema, 8 August 1908.
40 S. T. Plaatje, *Native Life in South Africa* (London, 1916), pp. 123–4.
41 Molema/Plaatje Papers, Da22, Plaatje to Molema, 12 December 1912.
42 'Notes of interview'.
43 For the text of the Act, see Plaatje, *Native Life in South Africa*, pp. 46–51; for its passage through parliament, see C. M. Tatz, *Shadow and Substance in South Africa* (Pietermaritzburg, 1962), pp. 17–22.
44 See especially, T. Keegan, 'The sharecropping economy, African class formation and the Natives' Land Act of 1913 in the highveld belt', in S. Marks and R. Rathbone (eds), *Industrialisation and Social Change in South Africa: African Class Formation, Culture and Consciousness, 1870–1930* (London, 1982), pp. 195–211, and 'The restructuring of agrarian class relations in a colonial economy: the Orange River Colony, 1902–1910', *Journal of Southern African Studies*, Vol. 5, No. 2, April 1979.
45 S. T. Plaatje, 'Along the colour line', *Kimberley Evening Star*, 23 December 1913.
46 *Native Life in South Africa*, pp. 172–3.
47 *Native Life*, p. 68.
48 'Natives and Federation of Trades: the Congress and the strike', letter from Plaatje to the editor, *DFA*, 18 February 1914; 'Along the colour line', *Kimberley Evening Star*, 23 December 1913.
49 'Along the colour line', *Kimberley Evening Star*, 23 December 1913.
50 'Natives and the government: the new land act', *Tsala ea Batho*, 9 August 1913.
51 'The war of extermination: now in full swing', *Tsala ea Batho*, 23 August 1913.
52 *Native Life*, pp. 102–16.
53 *Native Life*, p. 116.
54 S. T. Plaatje, letter to the editor, *Christian Express*, December 1913, pp. 187–9.
55 *Umteteli wa Bantu*, 23 July 1921; *Native Life*, p. 168.
56 'Sub-Rosa', *Tsala ea Batho*, 30 August 1913.
57 *Native Life*, chapter 13, reproducing correspondence published previously in *Cape Mercury*

and *Tsala ea Batho*; 'Kingwilliamstown and the Land Act', letter from Plaatje to the editor, *APO*, 6 December 1913.

58 'Native Congress: delegates assemble in Kimberley', *DFA*, 28 February 1914, reporting remarks by J. L. Dube.

59 *Native Life*, pp. 181–93; CAD, NA 3248/13/F.814, E. Barrett (Under-Secretary of State for Native Affairs) to Plaatje, 19 February 1914; S. T. Plaatje, 'S.A. Native National Congress: special conference in Kimberley', *DFA*, 26 February 1914.

60 *Native Life*, pp. 185–7; 'Native Congress', *DFA*, 28 February 1914; 'Native Land Act', *DFA*, 2 March 1914; 'S.A. Native Congress', *DFA*, 3 March 1914.

61 *Native Life*, p. 188.

62 'A happy new year', *Tsala ea Batho*, 3 January 1914.

63 e.g. in *Tsala ea Batho*, 9 May 1914.

64 Union of South Africa, *Report of Natives' Land Commission*, Vol. 2 (Minutes of Evidence), evidence of S. T. Plaatje, pp. 93–4.

65 *Native Life*, p. 40, reproducing speech of T. L. Schreiner in the South African House of Assembly during debate on Natives' Land Bill.

66 *Native Life*, p. 10; 'Through native eyes', editorial in *Pretoria News*, 16 January 1911.

67 'Resignation', *Tsala ea Batho*, 23 May 1914; *Tsala*, 7 March 1914.

68 SOAS, Plaatje Papers, STP 2/2, unpublished notebook, passage headed 'With the children'.

69 'Along the colour line', *Tsala ea Batho*, 10 January 1914.

70 Plaatje Papers, unpublished notebook, 'With the children'.

71 *Native Life*, p. 126.

72 'In memoriam', *Tsala ea Batho*, 7 February 1914.

73 See R. W. Msimang, *Natives' Land Act 1913: specific cases of evictions and hardships (collected and compiled by R. W. Msimang by the authority of the records committee of the South African Native National Congress)*, n.d. [1913]; 'Land Act, 1913', *Abantu-Batho*, 22 May 1913, reporting meeting of Preparation Committee (English translation in CAD, NA 3248/13/F.814).

74 Plaatje Papers, STP 1/3, typed sheet of references, testimonial from Sir E. Oppenheimer, 25 April 1914.

75 CAD, NA 3248/13/F.817, Plaatje to Henry Burton, 7 May 1914.

76 SAL, J. X. Merriman Papers, 1914, 236, Dube to Merriman, 6 May 1914. I am most grateful to Miss M. F. Cartwright, Senior Librarian, SAL, for providing me with copies of this and the following items.

77 Merriman Papers, 1914, 241, Botha to Merriman, 8 May 1914.

78 Merriman Papers, 1914, 244, Memo of conversation with Dube, 9 May 1914.

79 Merriman Papers, 1914, 241, Botha to Merriman, 8 May 1914.

80 'Natives' Land Act: deputation to England', *Cape Times*, 16 May 1914.

81 *Native Life*, p. 192.

82 S. T. Plaatje, 'Native Delegation to England', *DFA*, 29 June 1914.

83 'Natives' Land Act', *Cape Times*, 16 May 1914.

84 'The cult of leadership', *Umteteli*, 25 April 1925; PRO, CO 551/64, H.Cr. 20147, Report of Apthorpe's meeting with CO, 2 June 1914.

85 'The Natives' Land Act', *Cape Times*, 16 May 1914; 'The Native Deputation', *Cape Argus*, 16 May 1914.

86 'Natives' Land Act', *Cape Times*, 16 May 1914.

87 Molema/Plaatje Papers, Da38, Paramount Chief of the Barolong Nation to Plaatje, 13 May 1914.

88 NAD, Colenso Papers, Box 55, Plaatje to Mrs Colenso, 26 February 1915.

8 England 1914–17

1 S. T. Plaatje, 'Native Congress Mission to England', *DFA*, 14 July 1914.

2 S. T. Plaatje, 'The Native Congress Deputation', *DFA*, 17 July 1914.

3 Ibid.

4 AS/APS, S19 D3/11, Harris to Dube, 18 May 1914.

5 AS/APS, S22 G203, deputation's memorandum to the Colonial Secretary, Lord Harcourt, 15 June 1914.

6 B. P. Willan, 'The Anti-Slavery and Aborigines' Protection Society and the South African Natives' Land Act of 1913', *Journal of African History*, Vol. 20, No. 1, 1979, pp. 83–102.

Notes

7 AS/APS, S22 G180, Congress delegates to Messrs Morgan Price and Co. (Solicitors), 6 July 1914.

8 AS/APS, S19 D3/8, Mrs S. Solomon to Travers Buxton, 29 March 1917; see also S19 D3/15, Harris to Mrs J. Cobden Unwin, 25 October 1916.

9 S. T. Plaatje, 'The Native Congress Deputation', *DFA*, 17 July 1914.

10 PRO, CO 551/64, H.Cr. 20301, comments on dispatch cover, 4 June 1914.

11 PRO, CO 551/67, H.Cr. 24531, comments on dispatch cover on letter from AS and APS to CO, 6 July 1914.

12 Ibid.; AS/APS, S22 D4/4, Harcourt to Harris, 11 July 1914; Central Archives Depot (Pretoria) Gov.-Gen. 50/452, report on meeting with Congress deputation, 26 June 1914.

13 S. T. Plaatje, 'An appeal to the British Brotherhoods', *Brotherhood Journal*, August 1914, pp. 226–7; S. T. Plaatje, 'No room to live: South African natives and the land law', *Daily Chronicle* (London), 14 July 1914; *Native Life in South Africa*, pp. 194–5.

14 CAD, Gov.-Gen. 50/448, telegram from Gov.-Gen., Cape Town, to Colonial Secretary, London, 4 July 1914, and minute from General Botha, 3 July 1914.

15 PRO, CO 551/67, 20301, Sir A. Ponsonby to CO, 13 June 1914.

16 PRO, CO 551/64, 23292, Harris and Buxton to CO, 26 June 1914; also, AS and APS, S19 D3/12, Harris to Cecil Beck, MP, 9 June 1914.

17 AS/APS, S19 D3/12, Harris to Dube, 14 July 1914 (private).

18 *Native Life*, pp. 194–5.

19 Ibid., p. 225.

20 *Ilanga lase Natal*, 28 August 1914, quoting *Westminster Gazette*, 20 July 1914.

21 *Native Life*, pp. 195–8.

22 NAD, Colenso Papers, Box 54, Plaatje to Mrs S. J. Colenso, 31 August 1914.

23 CAD, Gov.-Gen. 50/403, Louis Botha to H. J. Stanley, 4 March 1914; Colenso Papers, Box 57, Alice Werner to H. Colenso, 10 May 1916.

24 AS/APS, G203, Harris to Sir H. Johnston, 6 August 1914.

25 Colenso Papers, Box 54, Plaatje to Mrs S. J. Colenso, 31 August 1914; *Native Life*, p. 261.

26 Colenso Papers, Box 54, Plaatje to Mrs S. J. Colenso, 31 August 1914.

27 Ibid.

28 Ibid.

29 Ibid.

30 Ibid.

31 AS/APS, G203, APS to Dr H. Haigh, Wesleyan Missionary Society, 12 January 1917; S. T. Plaatje, 'Why I remained in England and what I am doing', *Abantu-Batho*, 30 September 1915, and letter from J. H. Harris and T. Buxton to *Abantu-Batho*, 5 November 1915, both enclosures in AS/APS, S22 D4/8, Mrs G. Solomon to J. Harris, 27 January 1916.

32 S. T. Plaatje, 'The cult of leadership', *Umteteli wa Bantu*, 25 April 1925.

33 PRO, CO 551/64, H.Cr. 20147, report of meeting between A. P. Apthorpe and CO officials; AS/APS, S22 G203, Harris to A. Wynne, 5 June 1914, re meeting with Apthorpe at AS and APS offices.

34 S. T. Plaatje, 'Why I remained in England and what I am doing', *Abantu-Batho*, 30 September 1915, enclosure in AS/APS, S22 D4/8, Mrs G. Solomon to Harris, 27 January 1916; Colenso Papers, Box 54, Plaatje to Mrs S. J. Colenso, 31 August 1914.

35 Colenso Papers, Box 54, Plaatje to Mrs S. J. Colenso, 24 October 1914.

36 Colenso Papers, Box 55, Plaatje to Mrs S. J. Colenso, 26 February 1915; interview with Mr Charles Newton (36 Carnarvon Rd), 3 March 1984.

37 UNISA, Molema Papers, Plaatje to Chief Lekoko Montsioa, 10 December 1914 (original in Setswana).

38 Molema Papers, Plaatje to Chief Lekoko Montsioa, 6 November and 10 December 1914; UW, Molema/Plaatje Papers, Da40, R. S. S. Baden-Powell to Plaatje, 20 November 1914.

39 S. T. Plaatje, 'The late Allan King', *African World Annual* (London, December 1915); 'The late Allan King', *African World*, 5 December 1914.

40 'The "Volkstem" and colour', *African World*, 20 March 1916; CAD, NA 3248/13/814, 'Translation of extract from *De Volkstem*, dated the 12 January 1915'.

41 W. E. G. Solomon, *Saul Solomon: the Member for Cape Town* (Cape Town, 1948), esp. pp. 348–50; interview with Miss D. D. Solomon, Cape Town, July 1976; obituaries in *The Times*, 3 July 1933 and *The Vote*, 7 July 1933 (in Solomon Family Papers, South African Library, Cape Town); S. T. Plaatje, 'A friend of the natives: the late Sir William Solomon', *Pretoria News*, 21 June 1930.

42 Molema/Plaatje Papers, Photograph Fca 7, 1916.

43 Colenso Papers, Box 54, Plaatje to Mrs S. J. Colenso, 31 August 1914; Plaatje to Mrs S. J. Colenso, 24 October 1914; Box 55, Mrs S. J. Colenso to Harriette Colenso, 26 November 1915.

44 Obituary of Percy Molteno in *The Times*, 21 September 1937, *African World*, 25 September 1937, *South Africa*, 2 October 1937, (from Molteno family scrapbook in possession of Mr and Mrs T. Ashfield, Fortingall, Perthshire).

45 Obituary of Alice Werner in *The Times*, 11 June 1935.

46 'Mr C. W. Cross: retirement of tax collector', *Middlesex County Times and Gazette*, 19 November 1925; obituary, *Middlesex County Times and Gazette*, 27 March 1954. I am indebted to Mr Graham Stapleton for further information about Mr Cross.

47 *The Papers of W. E. B. Du Bois, 1803 (1877–1963) 1965* (Microfilming Corp. of America, Sanford, NC, 1980–81), r8 f36–37, Plaatje to Du Bois, 19 May 1919.

48 Molema/Plaatje Papers, Ad1, Modiri Molema to Silas Molema, 7 August and 9 October 1914; interview with Dr James Moroka, Thaba Nchu, 19 April 1976.

49 Molema Papers, Plaatje to Chief Lekoko Montsioa, 6 November 1914.

50 Ibid.

51 Colenso Papers, Box 55, Plaatje to Mrs S. J. Colenso, 26 February 1916.

52 I am indebted to Andrew Roberts for information on P. S. King's list.

53 Molema/Plaatje Papers, Da42, Plaatje to Silas Molema, 15 June 1915.

54 AS/APS, S22 D4/6, Johnston to Harris, 16 August 1914; S22 D4/4, Johnston to Harris, 14 March 1915.

55 Colenso Papers, Box 63, Johnston to Plaatje, 4 June 1915, and Johnston to Alice Werner, 4 June 1915, enclosure in Alice Werner to H. Colenso, 18 June 1915.

56 Colenso Papers, Alice Werner to H. Colenso, 18 June 1915.

57 Molema/Plaatje Papers, Da41, Plaatje to Philemon Mosheshoe, 16 June 1915.

58 Molema/Plaatje Papers, Da42, Plaatje to Silas Molema, 15 July 1915.

59 AS/APS, S19 D2/16, Circular letter signed by Alice Werner, 18 September 1915.

60 AS/APS, S19 D3/13, D2/7, D2/16, D2/17, correspondence between Alice Werner, J. H. Harris and T. Buxton, October–November 1915.

61 AS/APS, D2/7, A. Werner to T. Buxton, 28 October 1915; Colenso Papers, Box 63, A. Werner to H. Colenso, 18 February 1916; AS and APS, S19 D2/7, Mrs G. Solomon to T. Buxton, 5 February 1916.

62 Colenso Papers, Box 63, Alice Werner to H. Colenso, 18 February 1916.

63 Colenso Papers, Box 56, Plaatje to Mrs Sophie Colenso, 28 January 1916.

64 S. T. Plaatje, *Sechuana Proverbs with Literal Translations and Their European Equivalents* (London, 1916).

65 Courtesy of Mr Graham Stapleton, who now owns this copy of the book.

66 D. Jones and S. T. Plaatje, *A Sechuana Reader in International Phonetic Orthography (with English Translations)* (London, 1916), p. viii.

67 Ibid., p. v; SOAS, Daniel Jones Papers (MS 349205), 'How to use phonetics with little known languages', lecture delivered by D. Jones at University College, London, 30 October 1916.

68 'The black man's burden: interview with Mr Solomon T. Plaatje', *Christian Commonwealth*, 3 January 1917.

69 A. Werner, review of *A Sechuana Reader* in *Man*, Vol. 18, 1917; see also Royal Commonwealth Society archives, Migeod Papers, A. Werner to Migeod, 19 July 1917.

70 I. Gollancz (ed.), *A Book of Homage to Shakespeare* (Oxford, 1916).

71 Review in *New Statesman*, 13 May 1916.

72 AS/APS, S19 D2/7, Mrs G. Solomon to T. Buxton, 5 and 6 October 1915; S. T. Plaatje, 'An inflammatory bioscope film', *Umteteli wa Bantu*, 18 July 1931.

73 Gollancz, *Book of Homage*, p. 339; Plaatje's contribution is also reproduced in *English in Africa* (Grahamstown), Vol. 3, No. 2, September 1976, pp. 7–8.

74 'Mr Sol Plaatje at the PSA Brotherhood', *Stratford-upon-Avon Herald*, 10 November 1916.

75 Colenso Papers, Box 55, Plaatje to Mrs Colenso, 26 February 1915.

76 *Du Bois Papers*, r8 f36–37, Plaatje to Du Bois, 19 May 1919.

77 Copies in Bud-M'belle Papers, UW (unsorted).

78 Colenso Papers, Box 55, Plaatje to Mrs Colenso, 3 April 1916.

78 *Freedom For My People: the Autobiography of Z. K. Matthews* (Cape Town, 1981), pp. 30–1.

80 Molema/Plaatje Papers, Da61, Plaatje to Modiri Molema, 11 July 1920.

81 *Native Life*, p. 15.

82 Review of *Native Life* in *Birmingham Post*, 2 July 1916.

83 Review of *Native Life* (n.d.), quoted in flyleaf in second edition of *Native Life in South Africa*.
84 Review of *Native Life* in *United Empire* (n.d.), quoted in flyleaf in second edition of *Native Life in South Africa*.
85 Review of *Native Life* by 'Delta', *African World*, 3 June 1916.
86 SAL, Solomon Family Papers, Olive Schreiner to Mrs G. Solomon, 5 October 1916.
87 UCT, Molteno Family Papers, BC330, undated letter [1916] from Mrs Solomon to Betty Molteno.
88 Solomon Family Papers, Box 4, General Botha to Mrs G. Solomon, 31 August 1915.
89 S. T. Plaatje, 'Through native eyes: the late General Louis Botha', *African World*, 6 September 1919.
90 PRO, CO 417/629, 34975, Plaatje to Sir D. Chaplin, 6 April 1919.
91 J. H. Harris, 'General Botha's Native Policy', *Journal of the Royal African Society*, Vol. 16, October 1916.
92 Ibid.; see also Harris's articles in *Manchester Guardian*, 27 December 1916, *Fortnightly Review*, CI, January–June 1917.
93 Union of South Africa, *Report of the Natives' Land Commission*, UG 25, 1916.
94 *Native Life* (second edition), pp. 379 and 382.
95 P. Walshe, *The Rise of African Nationalism in South Africa: the African National Congress, 1912–1952* (London and Stanford, 1970), pp. 59–60; AS/APS, S22 G203, R. V. S. Thema to Buxton, undated, enclosing SANNC resolutions of 2 October 1916.
96 AS/APS, S22 G203, Harris to Secretary, SANNC, 29 March 1918; University of Bristol Library, Archives DM 851, Cobden Unwin Papers, APS file, Plaatje to Mrs Cobden Unwin, 10 July 1917 (originally consulted in the National Liberal Club Library, London). I am indebted to Ruth Edgecombe for informing me of the existence of this collection.
97 AS/APS, S22 G204, memorial to General Botha, 13 November 1916, quoting resolution passed at executive committee of APS, 3 August 1916; *Anti-Slavery Reporter and Aborigines' Friend*, series v, Vol. 6, no. 4 (January 1917).
98 AS/APS, S22 G203, Edward Dower (Secretary for Native Affairs) to AS and APS, 15 December 1916.
99 *Native Life*, p. 223.
100 For information on the Brotherhood movement, see Basil Matthews (ed.), *World Brotherhood* (London, 1920); A. E. H. Gregory, *Romance and Revolution: the Story of the Brotherhood Movement* (Sevenoaks, 1975); J. W. Tuffley, *Grain from Galilee* (London, 1935).
101 *Leighton Buzzard Observer*, 3 August 1915; *Hastings and St Leonards Observer*, 11 December 1915; *Northampton Daily Echo*, 20 December 1915; see also 'A Native African editor', *African World*, 7 August 1915, reproducing report of Plaatje's address to New England PSA, from *Hunts County News*.
102 'Reception to Mr Sol Plaatje', *DFA*, 28 March 1917; AS/APS, S22 G203, circular letter from Alice Werner (secretary of the committee), 17 February 1917.
103 AS/APS, S22 G203, Harris to Dr Clifford, 20 February 1917.
104 'Reception to Mr Sol Plaatje', *DFA*, 28 March 1917.

9 South Africa 1917–19

1 'Shakespeare in Setswana', *The Star* (Johannesburg), 26 July 1930.
2 B. P. Willan, 'The South African Native Labour Contingent, 1916–1918', *Journal of African History*, Vol. 14, No. 1, 1978.
3 'Coloured men on the European front', letter from S. T. Plaatje to the editor, *Pretoria News*, 14 May 1917. I am most grateful to Andrew Reed for this reference.
4 SAL, J. X. Merriman Papers, Plaatje to J. X. Merriman, 28 February 1917; TI, R. R. Moton Papers, GC 109/810, Plaatje to Moton, 22 September 1924; National Archives of the USA, Washington DC, Dept of State, RG 59.848a, 55/20, 'Statement relative to Rev. H. A. Payne and his wife, missionaries, who are prohibited from remaining in the Union of South Africa'; RG 59.848a, 55/27, copy of letter from Rev. H. A. Payne to American Consul, Cape Town, 25 June 1917; S. T. Plaatje, letter to the editor, *Imvo Zabantsundu*, 24 April 1917; Lawrence H. Mamiya and Patricia A. Kaurouma (eds), *For their Courage and for their Struggles: the Black Oral History Project of Poughkeepsie, New York* (Urban Center for African Studies, Vassar College, 1978), transcript of interview with Mrs Bessie Harden Payne, p. 20. I am indebted to Randall Burkett for making this last item available to me.

5 'The call for native recruits', *DFA*, 28 June 1917.
6 University of Bristol Library, Archives DM 851, Cobden Unwin Papers, APS file, Plaatje to Mrs Cobden Unwin, 18 May 1917.
7 For details of the Native Administration Bill, see C. M. Tatz, *Shadow and Substance in South Africa* (Pietermaritzburg, 1962).
8 M. Lacey, *Working for Boroko* (Johannesburg, 1981), pp. 86–8.
9 CAD, Dept of Justice, F3/527/17, 108, CID report of meeting at Boomplatz, near Lydenburg, Transvaal, 19 April 1917.
10 Cobden Unwin Papers, APS file, Plaatje to Mrs Cobden Unwin, 18 May 1917.
11 'A worthy defender', *Ilanga lase Natal*, 6 April 1917; see also 'U Mr Sol T. Plaatje Uyabuya Pesheya', *Ilanga lase Natal*, 16 February 1917.
12 UW, Molema/Plaatje Papers, Dd1, 'Mr and Mrs Sol T. Plaatje in the Transvaal', reprinted from *Abantu-Batho*, 28 June 1917.
13 'Reception to Mr Sol T. Plaatje', *DFA*, 28 March 1917.
14 Cobden Unwin Papers, APS file, Plaatje to Mrs Cobden Unwin, 18 May 1917.
15 Report of proceedings of parliament, *Cape Times*, 5 April 1917; see also *DFA*, 29 June 1917.
16 CAD, NTS 619/17/1131, Inspector and Protector of Natives, Kimberley, to Director of Native Labour, Johannesburg, 12 May 1917.
17 'Native Life in South Africa', *The Star*, 4 June 1917.
18 CAD, NTS 619/17/1131, Acting Director of Native Labour to Secretary for Native Affairs, Pretoria, 15 May 1917, handwritten comments re opinion of General Botha.
19 S. T. Plaatje, *Native Life in South Africa* (London, 1916), pp. 260–64.
20 Willan, 'The South African Native Labour Contingent, 1916–18', pp. 64–5.
21 CAD, NTS 2337/14/F.1131, E. Barrett to the Secretary for Native Affairs, Cape Town, 20 February 1917.
22 'No chance to lay proper foundations: inner history of A. N. Congress being revealed', *Bantu World*, 13 January 1934; R. V. Selope Thema, 'The African National Congress: its achievements and failures', *Umteteli wa Bantu*, 14 and 21 September 1929.
23 Ibid.
24 'South African Native Congress', *DFA*, 5 June 1917.
25 'Come out or starve', *Rand Daily Mail*, 2 June 1917; see also 'The native question: Sol Plaatje's speech', *The Star*, 2 June 1917.
26 Report of proceedings of parliament, *Cape Times*, 29 June 1917.
27 'The Native Congress', *The Star*, 4 June 1917; 'Native Congress', *DFA*, 5 June 1917.
28 Cobden Unwin Papers, APS file, Plaatje to Mrs Cobden Unwin, 10 July 1917.
29 R. V. Selope Thema, 'The African National Congress: its achievements and failures, II', *Umteteli wa Bantu*, 21 September 1929; 'National Congress', *Ilanga lase Natal*, 15 June 1917.
30 'The Union segregation and separation policy', letter from Mrs G. M. Solomon to the editor, *The African Times and Orient Review*, January 1918, p. 138.
31 S. T. Plaatje, 'The "Good Times" and the "New Native" ', *Umteteli*, 9 November 1929; see also, S. T. Plaatje, 'Leadership', *Umteteli*, 18 February 1928.
32 S. T. Plaatje, 'Through native eyes', *DFA*, 5 September 1917.
33 Cobden Unwin Papers, APS file, Plaatje to Mrs Cobden Unwin, 10 July 1917.
34 Ibid.
35 S. T. Plaatje to the editor, *Imvo Zabantsundu*, 12 February 1918.
36 PRO, CO 537/1197, 3473 (secret), 'Minutes of Deputation of South African Natives', statement by S. T. Plaatje, p. 11.
37 PRO, CO 417/629, 34975, Plaatje to the Administrator of South Rhodesia (Sir Drummond Chaplin), 6 April 1919.
38 'The call for native recruits', *DFA*, 28 June 1917; see also 'Native grievances: a labour recruiting speech', *DFA*, 22 August 1917.
39 'Come out or starve', *Rand Daily Mail*, 2 June 1917.
40 DB, Estate Records, Lyndhurst Road Native Institute file, Plaatje to W. Pickering, 15 March 1918.
41 Native Institute file, De Beers General Secretary to Plaatje, 9 May 1918.
42 Native Institute file, Sir David Harris to Asst. Secretary, De Beers, 20 March 1918.
43 Native Institute file, Plaatje to A. S. Williams, 22 March 1918.
44 Native Institute file, Plaatje to General Manager, 22 March 1918.
45 'De Beers company and the natives', *DFA*, 25 June 1918.

46 Native Institute file, Plaatje to Estate Dept, 11 July 1918.
47 See especially, P. L. Bonner, 'The Transvaal Native Congress, 1917–1920: the radicalisation of the black bourgeoisie on the Rand', in S. Marks and R. Rathbone (eds), *Industrialisation and Social Change in South Africa: Afrcian Class Formation, Culture and Consciousness, 1870–1930* (London, 1982), pp. 270–313.
48 R. V. Selope Thema, 'The African National Congress: its achievements and failures, III', *Umteteli*, 2 November 1929; CAD, NTS 2337/14/F.1131, J. M. McKenzie to District Commandant, South African Police, Bethlehem, 6 April 1918, reporting proceedings ' of annual meeting of SANNC; Presidential address by S. M. Makgatho, esp. pp. 7–8.
49 UW, Rheinallt Jones Papers, Joint Councils file, 'Treatment of natives in the courts', address by S. T. Plaatje to 1924 Joint Councils Conference, p. 7.
50 CAD, NTS 2337/14/F.1131, 'Resolutions passed by the executive committee of the National Congress at Bloemfontein on August 1st, 2nd and 3rd 1918', pp. 1–3; DB, Native Institute file, Plaatje to the Secretary, De Beers, 3 August 1918.
51 Native Institute file, 'South African Native Congress', 2 August 1918; reproduced in 'Natives' Assembly Hall', *DFA*, 9 August 1918.
52 S. T. Plaatje, 'Through Native Eyes: the late General Louis Botha', *African World*, 6 September 1919.
53 'Assembly Hall for natives', *DFA*, 8 August 1918; 'Natives' Assembly Hall', *DFA*, 9 August 1918.
54 Native Institute file, Plaatje to the Secretary, De Beers, 3 August 1918.
55 S. T. Plaatje, 'Mr Saul Msane: death of a Rand native leader', *African World*, 25 October 1919.
56 Molema/Plaatje Papers, Da47, Plaatje to Silas Molema, 3 August 1918; Da49, Plaatje to Silas Molema, 11 August 1918.
57 Molema/Plaatje Papers, Da49, Plaatje to Silas Molema, 11 August 1918.
58 B. Roberts, *Kimberley: Turbulent City* (Cape Town, 1976), pp. 365–7.
59 Molema/Plaatje Papers, Da51, Plaatje to 'Morolong', 6 November 1918.
60 S. T. Plaatje, 'Native doctors at hospitals', *Cape Times*, 4 June 1927.
61 PRO, CO 537/1197, 3473 (secret), 'Minutes of Deputation of South African Natives', statement by S. T. Plaatje, p. 11.
62 'The Natives and the epidemic', S. T. Plaatje to the editor, *DFA*, 12 November 1918.
63 S. M. Makgatho, 'Presidential address' to SANNC annual conference, 6 May 1919, reproduced in T. Karis and G. M. Carter (eds), *From Protest to Challenge*, Vol. I (Stanford, 1972), pp. 107–10.
64 e.g. Plaatje's reported comments at 1918 annual SANNC conference in Bethlehem (CAD, NTS 2337/14/F.1131, J. M. Mckenzie to District Commandant, South African Police, Bethlehem, 6 April 1918); P. Walshe, *The Rise of African Nationalism in South Africa: the African National Congress, 1912–1952* (London and Stanford, 1970), pp. 61–2.
65 Speech by King George V to South African Native Labour Contingent at Abbeville, 10 July 1917, reproduced in SANNC petition to King George V, 16 December 1918, in Karis and Carter, *From Protest to Challenge*, pp. 139–40.
66 For details, see B. P. Willan, 'The Anti-Slavery and Aborigines' Protection Society and the South African Natives' Land Act of 1913', *Journal of African History*, Vol. 20, No. 1 (1979), pp. 99–100.
67 S. M. Makgatho, 'Presidential address', Karis and Carter, *From Protest to Challenge*, p. 109.
68 'The Native Congress', *Cape Argus*, 23 December 1918; 'The Native National Congress', *The Star*, 23 December 1918.
69 'Native Congress', *Cape Argus*, 17 December 1918; 'Native Congress', *The Star*, 21 December 1918.
70 'Petition to King George V from the South African Native National Congress, December 16, 1918', reproduced in Karis and Carter, *From Protest to Challenge*, pp. 137–42.
71 Molema/Plaatje Papers, Da52, Plaatje to Silas Molema, 20 December 1918.
72 'Presidential address', Karis and Carter, *From Protest to Challenge*, p. 139.
73 See especially I. Geiss, *The Pan African Movement* (London, 1974), chapter 12, pp. 229–62.
74 Molema/Plaatje Papers, Da55, Plaatje to Silas Molema, 14 March 1919; undated letter (no ref. number), Plaatje to Silas Molema [February 1919].
75 'Free State natives', *The Friend*, 19 February 1919 (reporting speech by S. T. Plaatje).
76 CAD, Dept. of Justice, F3/527/17, 108, CID report of meeting at Boomplatz, nr Lydenburg,

Transvaal, 19 April 1919; 'Natives in the Free State', *Cape Times*, 8 March 1919; PRO, CO 551/111, 15305, draft of minute from CO to SA High Commission, London, 14 April 1919.

77 Molema/Plaatje Papers, Da55, Plaatje to Silas Molema, 14 March 1919; see also Da58, Plaatje to Silas Molema, undated [June 1919].

78 'Native Brotherhood Institute', *DFA*, 3 April 1919; 'Native Brotherhood', *DFA*, 18 March 1919; 'Farewell meeting for Mr Arthur D. Tsengiwe', *DFA*, 8 April 1919.

79 Basil Matthews (ed.), *World Brotherhood* (London, 1920), p. 93.

80 Molema/Plaatje Papers, Da56, Plaatje to Silas Molema, 10 May 1919.

81 'A Native pamphlet', *Cape Times*, 21 May 1919; 'Presidential address', Karis and Carter, *From Protest to Challenge*, p. 110.

82 *Du Bois Papers*, r8 f36–37, Plaatje to Du Bois, 19 May 1919.

83 Native Institute file, Secretary, De Beers, to Secretary, Assembly Hall for Natives, 23 August 1920.

84 Molema/Plaatje Papers, Da58, Plaatje to Silas Molema, n.d. (June 1919).

10 England 1919–20

1 PRO, CO 551/111, 2203, W. P. Schreiner to Colonel Amery, 6 May 1919.

2 CO 551/111, 22003, minute of interview, 8 May 1919.

3 Colonel Amery's private diary, entry for 8 May 1919, quoted in A. Young, 'British policy and attitudes towards the treatment of Africans in South Africa, 1919–24', in University of York, Centre for South African Studies, *Collected Papers*, 1, p. 55.

4 CO 551/111, minutes dated 21 and 22 May 1919; CO 551/114, 58532, minute from H. Thornton to Sir H. Lambert, 30 October 1919 and 21 November 1919.

5 CO 551/114, 58532, minute from Thornton to Lambert, 21 November 1919; CO 537/1137, 3473 (secret), 'Minutes of Deputation of South African Natives to the Rt Hon. D. Lloyd George, MP (Prime Minister) on the colour bar and other questions', p. 12, statement by the Prime Minister.

6 S. T. Plaatje, 'Through native eyes: the late General Louis Botha', *African World*, 6 September 1919.

7 NAD, Colenso Papers, Box 56, Plaatje to Mrs Sophie Colenso, 17 July 1919.

8 Colenso Papers, Box 56, Mrs Sophie Colenso to Harriette and Agnes Colenso, 24 July 1919; UCT, Schreiner Papers, BC27, Olive Schreiner to Mrs Solomon, 26 July 1919; CO 551/123, 60993, Mrs G. Solomon to Lloyd George, 15 October 1919; CO 537/1137, 3473, 'Minutes of Deputation of South African Natives', p. 12, statement by Prime Minister; CO 551/123, 48382, Charles Garnett to the King, 12 August 1919; House of Lords Record Office (London), Lloyd George Papers, Series F/Box 227/Folder 1 [2/2(–1)], G. B. Clark to Lloyd George, 26 July 1919.

9 Colenso Papers, Box 56, Plaatje to Mrs Sophie Colenso, 25 July 1919.

10 Hansard, *House of Commons Debates*, 30 July 1919, p. 2198.

11 Ibid., p. 2237.

12 Molema/Plaatje Papers, Da59, Plaatje to Fenyang, 2 August 1919.

13 CO 551/122, 3780, minute of meeting between Colonel Amery, S. T. Plaatje, and J. Gumede, 20 August 1919.

14 'A London African gathering', *West Africa*, 16 August 1919; 'A "Many-millioned cry for justice" ', *African World*, 23 August 1919.

15 S. T. Plaatje, 'Our London letter', *The Clarion* (Cape Town), 17 January 1920.

16 See, for example, 'Rights of natives in South Africa', *Manchester Guardian*, 10 October 1919; 'Britain's soul in danger', *West Africa*, 25 October 1919; 'The peril of South Africa', *The Church Times*, 28 November 1919.

17 CO 551/122, MI 49541, W. Procktor, President, Abney Brotherhood, to Walter Long, Secretary of State for the Colonies, 21 August 1919.

18 S. T. Plaatje, 'Our London letter', *The Clarion*, November/December 1919.

19 Ibid.

20 Colenso Papers, Box 56, Plaatje to Mrs Sophie Colenso, 12 September 1919; Box 63, Alice Werner to Harriette and Agnes Colenso, 4 December 1919.

21 Colenso Papers, Box 56, Plaatje to Mrs Sophie Colenso, 12 September 1919; S. T. Plaatje, 'Our London letter', *The Clarion*, January 1920.

22 S. T. Plaatje, 'Mr Scully and native policy', letter to the editor, *Cape Argus*, 20 November 1919; CO 551/117, 5310, R. Blankenburg (Secretary, South African High Commission in London) to Minister of the Interior, Pretoria, 3 October 1919 (copy), and further correspondence in this series.

23 AS/APS, S19 D2/2, Plaatje to Travers Buxton, 5 and 7 November 1919, 22 January 1920.

24 For Plaatje's view of the matter, see particularly AS/APS, S19 D2/12, Plaatje to Travers Buxton, 29 October 1919.

25 See, e.g., CO 551/118, 69498, Plaatje to South African High Commission, 4 December 1919.

26 CO 551/118, 3824, 'Memorandum: South African Native Delegation', 17 November 1919.

27 Colenso Papers, Box 63, Alice Werner to Harriette and Agnes Colenso, 4 December 1919 and 16 June 1920; Box 56, Plaatje to Mrs Sophie Colenso, 29 December 1919.

28 CO 537/1137, 3473 (secret), 'Minutes of Deputation of South African Natives', statement by Prime Minister, p. 12.

29 CO 551/114, 58532, minute from Major H. C. Thornton to Sir Henry Lambert and copy of letter to Philip Kerr, 3 October 1919.

30 'The Prime Minister and South African Native Deputation', *African Sentinel* (London), 17 January 1920; Lloyd George Papers, Series F/Box 227/F.2, L. T. Mvabaza to Philip Kerr, 24 November 1919.

31 CO 537/1137, 3473 (secret), 'Minutes of Deputation of South African Natives', statement by Plaatje, pp. 7–12.

32 'Minutes of Deputation', statement by Lloyd George to members of deputation, p. 13.

33 'The Brotherhood: a record attendance', *Evening News* (Portsmouth), 19 January 1920; 'The Prime Minister and South African Native Deputation', *African Sentinel*, 17 January 1920; *African World* (Supplement), 30 September 1921, remarks of J. Eldred Taylor to Pan-African Congress, September 1921.

34 CO 537/1197, 1486 (secret), Lloyd George to Smuts, 3 March 1920.

35 CO 537/1197, 1486 (secret), Lloyd George to Smuts, 3 March 1920.

36 CO 537/1198, 27397 (secret), Smuts to Lloyd George, 12 May 1920.

37 See M. Chanock, *Unconsummated Union* (Manchester, 1977), pp. 132–4.

38 CO 551/118, 3824, Secretary, South African High Commission, to Secretary for Native Affairs, Pretoria, 10 December 1919, p. 3.

39 AS/APS, S19 H2/50, Gumede to Archbishop of Canterbury, 25 August 1919; Archbishop of Canterbury to J. H. Harris, 13 October 1919; Harris to Plaatje, 21 October 1919; 'Homeless! Landless! Outlawed! The plight of South African natives – interview with Solomon Plaatje', *The Labour Leader*, 11 December 1919; interview with Lord Fenner Brockway, House of Lords, London, August 1978; S. T. Plaatje, *Some of the Legal Disabilities Suffered by the Native Population of the Union of South Africa and Imperial Responsibility* (London, 1919).

40 AS/APS, S19 D2/12, Plaatje to AS and APS, 29 October 1919.

41 AS/APS S19 H2/50, Harris to Plaatje, 20 November and 20 December 1919.

42 Molema/Plaatje Papers, Ad 1, Modiri Molema to Silas Molema, n.d. [December 1919].

43 'Impartial interviews of the week: Mr Sol Plaatje on slavery in South Africa', *Forward* (Glasgow); 'In the Union of South Africa', *Falkirk Herald*, 13 December 1919; S. T. Plaatje, 'Our London letter', *The Clarion*, January 1920.

44 Colenso Papers, Box 56, Plaatje to Mrs Sophie Colenso, 29 December 1919; see also 'The colour bar: native leader describes his overseas tour', *The Star* (Johannesburg), 13 December 1923.

45 'The colour bar', *Workers' Dreadnought*, January 1920; see also 'British government refuses to protect Negro subjects', *The Emancipator*, 20 March 1920. I am grateful to Professor Robert Hill for this last reference.

46 Colenso Papers, Box 63, Alice Werner to Harriette and Agnes Colenso, 4 December 1919; Box 57, Mrs Sophie Colenso to Harriette and Agnes Colenso, 2 January 1920.

47 Colenso Papers, Box 57, Plaatje to Mrs Colenso, 6 January 1920.

48 Colenso Papers, Box 56, Mrs S. Colenso to Harriette and Agnes Colenso, 7 August 1919.

49 'The Brotherhood: a record attendance', *Evening News* (Portsmouth), 19 January 1920.

50 S. T. Plaatje, 'Our London letter', *The Clarion*, November/December 1919; Basil Matthews (ed.), *World Brotherhood* (London, 1920), 'The Brotherhood message', pp. v–ix.

51 DB, Estate Records, Lyndhurst Road Native Institute file, Griffiths Motsieloa to De Beers, 30 October 1920; National Adult School Union Minute Book (Drayton House, London), Minute 181, 27 October 1919; Minute 193, 19 November 1920.

52 S. T. Plaatje, 'Our London letter', *The Clarion*, November/December 1919.
53 AS/APS, S23 H2/50, AS and APS to S. T. Plaatje, 1 March 1920.
54 Papers in private possession of Professor Adelaide Cromwell Gulliver (Boston, USA), J. E. Bruce to John W. Cromwell, 19 October 1919; Archives of the United States of America (Washington, DC), Military Archives Division, File L0218–364/21, Report on Negro Subversion from Office of MID, New York, to Director of Military Intelligence, details of work of 'South African Delegation' and Plaatje's letter to J. E. Bruce, published in *Negro World*, n.d; Moorland-Spingarn Research Center (Howard University, Washington, DC), Cromwell Family Papers, John W. Cromwell Record Book, 1919–26, Box 24–3, Folder 52, record of letter from Plaatje (January 1920) and to Plaatje (February 1920). I am most grateful to Greta S. Wilson for drawing these items to my attention.
55 *Du Bois Papers*, r9 f248, W. E. Du Bois to Louis F. Post, Asst. Secretary Labour, 6 December 1920; Archives of the United States of America, General Services Division, Dept of State central decimal file (RG 59), request of Solomon T. Plaatje for US visa, 24 March 1920 (811.111); Diplomatic Section, Records of US Consulate, London, Register of Correspondence, p. 61, letter to Plaatje, 30 March 1920.
56 CAD, NTS 619/17/1131 (file on S. T. Plaatje), Secretary for Native Affairs to Consul General for the United States of America, Cape Town, 23 March 1920.
57 CAD, NTS 619/17/1131, telegram from South African High Commissioner (London) to Secretary for Native Affairs (Pretoria), 26 March 1920 and E. Barrett (Secretary for Native Affairs) to F. S. Malan (Minister for Native Affairs), 31 March 1920; PRO, CO 705/7, Register for Correspondence, 1920–21, entries for 31 March 1920 (H.Cr. 16567) and 7 April 1920·(H.Cr. 17458).
58 CAD, NTS 619/17/1131, Protector of Natives (Kimberley) to Director of Native Labour (Johannesburg), 12 March 1917; Molema/Plaatje Papers, Da48, Plaatje to Molema, 10 August 1918.
59 CAD, NTS 619/17/1131, Barrett to Malan, 31 March 1920 (see also Robert Hill, ' "Africa for the Africans": Marcus Garvey, the UNIA, and the struggle of African nationalism in South Africa' (unpublished paper), p. 27.
60 Ibid.; see also CA, 1/KIM/2/2/48, Civil Record Book, 1919, Hill and Hill *vs* A. D. Tsengiwe and S. T. Plaatje, 8 March 1919.
61 Archives of the United States of America, records of the Office of the Counselor, RG 59, 504.69–504.100, Box 30, report on address by Plaatje to Falkirk ILP meeting, 12 December 1919, enclosure in Wright to W. L. Hurley, 29 December 1919 (confidential).
62 Colenso Papers, Box 63, Alice Werner to Harriette and Agnes Colenso, 3 December 1920; SOAS, M. Benson Collection (MS 348942), transcript of interview with T. D. Mweli Skota (n.d.).
63 'The objects of this paper', *Umteteli wa Bantu*, Vol. 1, No. 1, May 1920; 'Class hatred', *Umteteli*, 30 August 1924.
64 Harold Mayer (Native Recruiting Corporation) to Secretary, Compound Manager's Association, 12 March 1920, quoted in *South African Review*, 1923. I am most grateful to Stephen Gray for this reference.
65 M. Benson Collection, Skota interview transcript.
66 Molema/Plaatje Papers, Da62, Plaatje to Molema, 25 August 1920.
67 Skota interview transcript.
68 Molema/Plaatje Papers, Da62, Plaatje to Molema, 25 August 1920.
69 S. T. Plaatje, 'Departed friends of the natives', *Umteteli*, 17 September 1927.
70 Molema/Plaatje Papers, Da61, Plaatje to Dr Modiri Molema, 11 July 1920.
71 Molema/Plaatje Papers, Da62, Plaatje to Molema, 25 August 1920.
72 PRO, CO 417/629, 34975, Plaatje to the Administrator of Southern Rhodesia (Sir Drummond Chaplin), 6 April 1919.
73 SOAS, Plaatje Papers, STP 2/2, Plaatje's notebook (unpaginated).
74 *Brotherhood Journal*, Vol. 1, No. 8, p. 157; 'A coaster's London log', *West Africa*, 4 and 11 September 1920.
75 J. A. Langley, *Pan-Africanism and West African Nationalism* (Oxford, 1973), chapter 5.
76 Cited in Langley, *Pan-Africanism and West African Nationalism*, p. 253 (but not in Macaulay Papers as stated).
77 University of Ibadan Library (Ibadan, Nigeria), Herbert Macaulay Papers, Box 18, File 3, National Congress of British West Africa, 1920, minutes of meeting held on 8 October 1920.

78 UCT, Molteno Family Papers, BC 330 A81.2.3, Plaatje to Mrs Lennox Murray, 17 November 1922.
79 CAD, J269 3/1064/18, A. E. Trigger (Divisional CI Officer, Witwatersrand Division) to Deputy Commissioner, South African Police, Witwatersrand Division, Johannesburg, 22 December 1923.
80 CAD, NTS 619/17/1131, Hubert S. Martin (Chief Passport Officer, UK) to Secretary, South African High Commission, 15 February 1921.
81 UCT, Molteno Family Papers, BC 330 A81.2.1, Plaatje to Miss Molteno, 16 December 1920. I am most grateful to Mrs P. E. Stevens for providing me with copies of this and other material in the Molteno Family Papers.
82 Ibid.

11 Canada and the USA 1920–22

1 UCT, Molteno Family Papers, BC 330 A81.2.1, Plaatje to Miss Molteno, 16 December 1920.
2 R. Allen, *The Social Passion: Religion and Social Reform in Canada, 1914–1928* (Toronto, 1971).
3 'Welcome to Plaatje, a distinguished African; an appreciation by Arthur C. Holder, Toronto, Can', *Negro World* (New York), 5 February 1921; also reproduced in *Pose ea Becoana*, No. 2. I am most grateful to Professor Robert Hill for this and other references from the *Negro World*.
4 Molteno Family Papers, BC 330 A8.1.2.1, Plaatje to Miss Molteno, 16 December 1920.
5 'Welcome to Plaatje'.
6 Molteno Family Papers, BC 330 A8.1.2.1, Plaatje to Miss Molteno, 16 December 1920.
7 'Hon. Marcus Garvey returns to Liberty Hall', *Negro World*, 12 February 1921.
8 S. T. Plaatje, 'Native doctors at hospitals', *Cape Times*, 4 June 1927.
9 *Du Bois Papers*, r9 f248, Du Bois to Louis F. Post, 6 December 1920.
10 *Du Bois Papers*, r9 f205, Plaatje to Du Bois, 19 December 1920.
11 *Du Bois Papers*, r9 f205, Plaatje to Du Bois, 29 December 1920.
12 'Welcome to Plaatje'; Du Bois Papers, *The Daylight*, 15 Jan 1921.
13 'Welcome to Plaatje'.
14 SOAS, Plaatje papers, STP 3/4, Canadian passport no. 79551, issued to S. T. Plaatje, 21 December 1920; UW, Molema/Plaatje Papers, Db1, 'Account of visit to Canada and United States of America', p. 6.
15 CAD, NTS 619/17/1131 (file on S. T. Plaatje), Secretary, South African High Commission, London, to Chief Passport Officer, 12 February 1921, and Chief Passport Officer to South African High Commission, 15 February 1921.
16 'Account of visit', p. 7; *Negro World*, 26 February 1921, report from UNIA branch, Buffalo, NY.
17 For the UNIA and Garveyism, see especially E. D. Cronon, *Black Moses: the Story of Marcus Garvey and the Universal Negro Improvement Association* (Madison, 1955).
18 'Bruce Grit's column', *Negro World*, 16 July 1921; see also 'Plaatje, famous African scholar and author, to visit New York', *Negro World*, 27 November 1920, enclosure in Molteno Family Papers, BC 330 A8 1.2.1, Plaatje to Miss Molteno, 16 December 1920.
19 S. T. Plaatje, 'Native doctors at hospitals', *Cape Times*, 4 June 1927.
20 'Hon. Marcus Garvey returns', *Negro World*, 12 February 1921.
21 NA, Colenso Papers, Box 11, Plaatje to 'Mrs Gebuza' (Colenso), 15 February 1921.
22 Plaatje Papers, STP 3/5, poster advertising Plaatje's meetings.
23 'Mr Sol Plaatje addresses the Brooklyn UNIA', *Negro World*, 19 March 1921; see also 'Interesting Harlem notes', *Negro World*, 19 February 1921; 'A digest of Brooklyn happenings', *Chicago Defender*, 19 March 1921; *New York Age*, 19 and 26 March 1921.
24 'Hon. Marcus Garvey returns'.
25 'Special Easter services held in Liberty Hall', *Negro World*, 2 April 1921.
26 Colenso Papers, Box 57, Plaatje to Mrs Colenso, 31 March 1922.
27 'Special Easter services', *Negro World*, 2 April 1921.
28 Library of Congress Manuscripts Division, NAACP collection, Box C8, General correspondence, Asst. Secretary NAACP, to Miss E. T. Wood, Treasurer, South African Bantu Brotherhood Mission, 5 and 15 July 1921; Ellen Wood to Secretary, NAACP, 12 August 1921; personal communication from Jeff Green, December 1981, re interview with Miss Amy Barbour James, London.

29 Schomburg Library, New York, J. E. Bruce Papers, John W. Cromwell to J. E. Bruce, 21 January 1921; Library of Congress, Manuscripts Division, Carter G. Woodson Papers, m/f reel 3, Mrs Booker T. Washington to Carter Woodson, 4 September 1922; Bruce to Mr J. Bronson, 7 January 1923.
30 Advertisements for *Native Life in South Africa*, July and August 1921.
31 S. T. Plaatje, *Mhudi: an Epic of Native life a Hundred Years Ago* (Lovedale, 1930), Preface.
32 'Special Easter services', *Negro World*, 2 April 1921.
33 'With the contributing editor', *Negro World*, 23 April 1921.
34 'Mr Sol T. Plaatje explains his mission', *Negro World*, 18 June 1921.
35 Report on Equal Rights League meeting, *The Guardian* (Boston), quoted in Frederick G. Detweiler, *The Negro Press in the United States* (Chicago, 1922), p. 95; S. T. Plaatje, 'Counteracting negrophilism in SA: race hatred and a film', *DFA*, 10 July 1931. I am indebted to Randall Burkett for the first of these references.
36 NAACP collection, Series B, Con. 4, 1921, Pan-African Conference file, Plaatje to Du Bois, 22 June 1921.
37 *Du Bois Papers*, r9 f249, Du Bois to S. M. Makgatho, 6 April 1921.
38 NAACP collection, Plaatje to White, 6 July 1921 and White to Plaatje, 12 July 1921. I am indebted to Robert Hill for these two references.
39 'Bruce Grit's column', *Negro World*, 16 July 1921; see also 'Negroes told to have unity', *Detroit News*, 1 July 1921; *The Crisis*, Vol. 22, No. 4, August 1921; NAACP collection, Box C8, General correspondence, Plaatje to J. W. Johnson, 12 September 1921.
40 'South Africa in grip of British Jim Crow rule: editor tells how British kill Natives', *Chicago Defender*, 22 October 1921; *Umteteli wa Bantu*, 23 July 1921.
41 UW, Molema/Plaatje Papers, Aa2.98, D. Goronyane to Chief William Letsapa, 18 July 1921.
42 'Pan-Africans in Congress', *Cape Times*, 21 September 1921.
43 *Du Bois Papers*, r10 f65–73, Plaatje's address to the Pan-African Congress, 1921, esp. pp. 3,8,11.
44 'Pan-Africans in Congress', *Christian Express*, 1 October 1921.
45 'South African entertained', 'Appotomattox Club reception', and 'Grace Lyceum', *Chicago Defender*, 1 October 1921; also 'Savagery kisses civilization on cheek in S. Africa', 'Grace Lyceum audience hears African lecturer', *Chicago Defender*, 8 October 1921; 'Capacity audience hears W. H. Barrett at Lyceum', *Chicago Defender*, 22 October 1921.
46 'South Africa in grip of British Jim Crow rule: editor tells how British kill Natives', *Chicago Defender*, 22 October 1921.
47 'Meeting of race leaders', *Washington Bee*, 19 November 1921; 'Conference on fundamentals in Washington', *Chicago Defender*, 3 December 1921; 'Conditions in South Africa described here', *Washington Tribune*, 3 December 1921.
48 Cromwell Papers, Plaatje to J. W. Cromwell, 28 November 1921. I am most grateful to Professor Adelaide Cromwell Gulliver for providing me with copies of letters from her grandfather's papers.
49 'The Natives' musical soul', *DFA*, 26 June 1926 and *Cape Argus* 31 May 1926; *Chicago Defender*, 19 November 1921.
50 'Account of visit', p. 20.
51 NAACP collection, Box C8, General correspondence (admin.), Plaatje to J. W. Johnson, 12 Sept 1921; *Du Bois Papers*, r11 f76–77, Plaatje to Du Bois, 1 February 1922.
52 S. T. Plaatje, 'The "New Native" and the new year', *Umteteli wa Bantu*, 12 January 1929; Colenso Papers, Box 57, Plaatje to Mrs S. Colenso, 31 March 1922; Hoover Institution Library, California, inscribed copy of *Native Life in South Africa* presented to J. A. Johnson. I am most grateful to Colin Bundy for bringing this last item to my attention.
53 Colenso Papers, Box 57, Plaatje to Mrs S. Colenso, 31 March 1922.
54 Ibid.
55 *Du Bois Papers*, r11 f76–77, Plaatje to Du Bois, 1 February 1922.
56 See especially A. Locke (ed.), *The New Negro* (New York, 1925).
57 *Du Bois Papers*, r11 f76–77, Plaatje to Du Bois, 1 February 1922.
58 *Du Bois Papers*, r11 f78, Du Bois to Plaatje, 20 February 1922.
59 Schomburg Center for Research in Black Culture, New York Public Library, William Pickens Papers, Box 1, File 8, James S. Stemons to William Pickens, 4 July 1916.
60 'Boston division celebrates Easter', *Negro World*, 29 April 1922.
61 'Account of visit', p. 22.

100

100

62 'Sol Plaatje to lecture at YMCA', *Washington Tribune*, 22 April 1922; 'YMCA', *Washington Tribune*, 6 May 1922; 'Race Congress closes seventh convention here', *Washington Tribune*, 6 May 1922; 'African editor exposes Jim Crow laws', *Chicago Defender*, 3 June 1922; Hampton Institute visitors' book, entry for 10 May 1922. I am most grateful to Mr Fritz Malval for providing me with a copy of this last item.
63 *Du Bois Papers*, r11 f79, Plaatje to Jessie Fausset, 16 May 1922.
64 'Account of visit', p. 19.
65 TI, Moton Papers, GC 83, Plaatje to Holsey, 20 May 1922.
66 Moton Papers, GC 83, Plaatje to Holsey, 26 May 1922; Molteno Family Papers, BC 330 A81.2.2, Plaatje to Miss Molteno, 8 November 1922; Moton Papers, GC 109/810, Plaatje to Moton, 22 September 1924.
67 'Mrs Ida B. Wells Barnet', *Washington Bee*, 28 May 1921; 'South African Visitor', *Chicago Defender*, 17 June 1922; Moton Papers, GC 83, Plaatje to Holsey, 26 May 1922.
68 'African to speak', *Chicago Defender*, 24 June 1922; 'To help Africans', *Chicago Defender*, 15 July 1922.
69 'To help Africans'; 'Africans on the program', *Chicago Defender*, 22 July 1922.
70 Richard D. Ralston, 'American episodes in the making of an African leader: a case study of Alfred B. Xuma (1893–1962)', *International Journal of African Historical Studies*, Vol. VI, No. 1 (1973), pp. 84–5.
71 Plaatje Papers, STP 3/4, passport; 'Shakespeare in Sechuana', *The Star* (Johannesburg), 26 July 1930.
72 Allen, *The Social Passion*, chapter 14.
73 UW, Xuma Papers, Plaatje to Xuma, 19 July 1923.
74 'Shakespeare in Setswana'; Moton Papers, GC 83, Plaatje to Holsey, 20 Sept 1922.

12 England 1922–23

1 UCT, Molteno Family Papers, BC 330 A81.2.2. Plaatje to Miss Molteno, 8 November 1922.
2 NA, Colenso Papers, Box 11, Plaatje to Mrs Colenso, 20 November 1922.
3 AS/APS, S19 D3/31, Harris to G. Gale, 25 October 1922; 'West Africa and the elections', *West Africa*, 18 November 1922.
4 Colenso Papers, Box 11, Plaatje to Mrs Colenso, 20 November 1922.
5 Ibid.
6 Colenso Papers, Box 63, Alice Werner to Harriette Colenso, 30 November 1922; S. T. Plaatje, *Dintshontsho tsa bo Juliuse Cesara* (Johannesburg, 1936), Preface by G. K. Lestrade; UNISA, Molema Papers, report on research by S. T. Plaatje, p. 5.
7 Hilda Kuper, *Sobhuza II: Ngwenyamu and King of Swaziland* (London, 1978), pp. 82–4; J. S. M. Matsebula, *A History of Swaziland* (Cape Town, 1976), pp. 140 and 168; 'Swazi chiefs in London', *South Africa*, 12 January 1923; 'Swazi chiefs and the king', *South Africa*, 2 February 1923; 'Swazi chiefs leave', *South Africa*, 9 February 1923; 'Swazi chiefs' visit', *African World*, 13 January 1923; 'Swazi ruler and chiefs say "au revoir" ', *African World*, 3 February 1923.
8 Colenso Papers, Box 57, Mrs Sophie Colenso to Harriette Colenso, 1 February 1923; 'The Swazi king and West African students', *West Africa*, 20 January 1923.
9 *Sobhuza II*, p. 84; personal communication from Mr J. S. M. Matsebula, 1 June 1981, reporting conversation with King Sobhuza II.
10 Molteno Family Papers, BC 330 A81.2.5, Plaatje to Miss Molteno, 12 December 1922.
11 Molteno Family Papers, BC 314 SP/1.2, Plaatje to Miss Molteno, 27 February 1923.
12 TI, Moton Papers, GC 93, Plaatje to Holsey, 13 March 1923.
13 National Adult School Union minute book (Drayton House, London), minute 210, p. 134, 2 December 1921.
14 Colenso Papers, Box 11, Plaatje to Mrs Colenso, 24 May 1923.
15 Molteno Family Papers, BC 314 SP/1.3, Plaatje to Miss Molteno, 29 June 1923.
16 Molteno Family Papers, BC 314 SP/1.4, Plaatje to Miss Molteno, 21 July 1923.
17 Molteno Family Papers, BC 330 A81.2.9, Plaatje to Mrs Solomon, 2 August 1923.
18 Molteno Family Papers, BC 330 A98.6, Mrs G. M. Solomon to Miss Colenso, 1 August 1923.
19 'Film of the week', *The Times*, 13 August 1923.

20 'The Cradle of the World', *South Africa*, 24 August 1923.
21 'A great African film', *African World*, 25 August 1923; see also 'A new film of African life', *West Africa*, 18 August 1923.
22 'Union of Students of African Descent', *West Africa*, 28 October 1922.
23 Molteno Family Papers, BC 314 SP/1.5, Plaatje to Miss Molteno, 21 September 1923, enclosing copy of letter to Miss Molteno (n.d.)
24 'The law, the land and the native', *South Africa*, 26 October 1923.
25 Personal communication from Mr D. J. M. Abdey (Record archivist, EMI), 17 March 1977.
26 'For a good cause', *West Africa*, 25 August 1923; 'Brotherhood Mission', *African World*, 25 August 1923.
27 Molteno Family Papers, BC 330 A81.2.11, Plaatje to Miss Solomon (copy), *c.* 8 October 1923; see also BC 314 SP/1.5, Plaatje to Miss Molteno, 21 September 1923.
28 'Mr Sol Plaatje', *South Africa*, 12 October 1923; Colenso Papers, Box 57, Mrs G. M. Solomon to Mrs Colenso, 11 October 1923; CAD, NTS 619/17/1131 (file on S. T. Plaatje), Programme of Farewell Concert, 9 October 1923.
29 Colenso Papers, Box 11, Mrs G. M. Solomon to Mrs S. Colenso, n.d. (*c.* December 1923).
30 CAD, J269 3/1064/18, telegram from South African High Commission, London, to Ministry of Justice, Pretoria.
31 'The law, the land, and the native', and 'Here and there', *South Africa*, 26 October 1923.

13 The 1920s: a leader without a people

1 DB, General Secretary's correspondence, W. T. McLeod to De Beers, 31 August 1929.
2 UCT, Molteno Family Papers, BC 314, SP/1.7, Plaatje to Mrs Solomon, 21 December 1923.
3 DB, General Secretary's correspondence, General Secretary to Hon. Treasurer, Kimberley Native Institute, 8 June 1923; Hon. Treasurer, Kimberley Native Institute, to Secretary, De Beers, 15 June 1923; James A. Swan to Secretary, De Beers, 16 March 1932.
4 DB, General Secretary's correspondence, Plaatje to General Manager, De Beers, 15 March 1932.
5 SOAS, Methodist Missionary Society archives, Transvaal corresp. 1921–4, 'Statement re Social Institute, Johannesburg', enclosure in J. W. Alcock to Amos Burnet, 8 January 1924. I am most grateful to Deborah Gaitskell for this reference.
6 S. T. Plaatje, 'Native affairs after four years', *DFA*, 19 January 1924.
7 S. T. Plaatje, 'Native affairs after four years', *DFA*, 22 January 1924.
8 Molteno Family Papers, BC 314 SP/1.9, Plaatje to Miss Molteno, 1 February 1924; also, 'U S.T. Plaatje e Qonce', *Imvo Zabantsundu*, 28 October 1924.
9 S. T. Plaatje, 'The case for the Barolongs', *Cape Argus*, 4 March 1924; 'Native taxation: a reply to Dr Visser', letter from Plaatje to the editor, *The Star* (Johannesburg), 11 March 1924; 'Natives and taxation', *Imvo*, 1 April 1924; S. T. Plaatje, 'Nationalists and natives: a scathing indictment', *Cape Argus*, 29 April 1924.
10 CAD, NTS 619/17/1131 (Plaatje file), Secretary for Native Affairs to S. T. Plaatje, 2 April 1924.
11 University of Cambridge, Smuts Papers (microfilm), Vol. 33, no. 43, Plaatje to Smuts, 19 January 1925.
12 S. T. Plaatje, 'Natives and the election: why they should vote SAP', *DFA*, 16 June 1924.
13 S. T. Plaatje, 'Congress and the Pact', *Umteteli wa Bantu*, 14 June 1924.
14 'The native vote: strong support for Sir E. Oppenheimer', *DFA*, 7 June 1924.
15 Smuts Papers, Vol. 33, no. 43, Plaatje to Smuts, 19 January 1925.
16 Ibid.
17 CA, East London municipal archive, Town Clerk's correspondence, leaflet advertising Plaatje's bioscope in Bloemfontein (26, 27, 29 September 1924), enclosure in Plaatje to Town Clerk, East London, 9 October 1924. I am most grateful to Colin Bundy for drawing this item to my attention; also, 'Sol T. Plaatje's Travelogue and Coloured American Bioscope' (advertisement), *Imvo*, 14 October 1924.
18 'Natives at the films: leper asylum entertainment', *Pretoria News*, n.d. (September–October 1924), enclosure in Plaatje to General J. B. M. Hertzog, 7 October 1924, in CAD, Hertzog Papers, A32 Box 35. I am most grateful to Paul Rich for this reference.
19 'Mr Sol T. Plaatje's bioscope', *Umteteli*, 31 May 1924.

20 DB, General Secretary's correspondence, Plaatje to De Beers, 31 May 1925; Kimberley municipal records, Town Clerk's files, Plaatje to Kimberley Town Council, 7 March 1930. I am most grateful to Mrs M. Macey for this last reference.

21 TI, Moton Papers, GC 109/810, Plaatje to Moton, 22 Sept 1924; interview with Mr Simon Lekhela (London, October 1978), Professor E. P. Lekhela (Mmabatho, July 1983, with Suzie Newton-King), and Mr G. Hermans (New Brighton, Port Elizabeth), 30 June 1976.

22 Moton Papers, GC 109/810, Plaatje to Moton, 22 Sept 1924.

23 Hertzog Papers, A32 Box 35, Plaatje to Hertzog, 7 Oct 1924.

24 Smuts Papers, Vol. 33, no. 42, Plaatje to Smuts, 19 January 1925.

25 UW, Rheinallt Jones Papers, Joint Councils file, address by S. T. Plaatje to the 1924 Joint Councils Conference on 'The treatment of natives in the courts'.

26 'Colour bill protest', *Cape Argus*, 7 May 1926.

27 Rheinallt Jones Papers, Joint Councils file, Plaatje to Rheinallt Jones, 23 April and 3 May 1926. I am grateful to Baruch Hirson for these references.

28 C. M. Tatz, *Shadow and Substance in South Africa* (Pietermaritzburg, 1962), pp. 49–52; 'Native policy of the Union', *DFA*, 4 December 1925; 'Native leaders' views', *Cape Times*, 4 December 1925; 'Division and removal of tribes', *Cape Times*, 5 December 1925.

29 'Native leaders' views', *Cape Times*, 4 December 1925.

30 See especially M. Lacey, *Working for Boroko* (Johannesburg, 1981), pp. 94–119.

31 e.g. 'Recent Native Conference', *DFA*, 15 December 1925; 'Why segregation will not work', *Cape Times*, 21 April 1926.

32 'Native Conference on premier's bills', *Cape Times*, 3 November 1926.

33 D. D. T. Jabavu, 'The Government Native Conference', *Cape Times*, 19 November 1926.

34 'Native Conference on Hertzog's proposals', *Cape Times*, 4 November 1926.

35 S. T. Plaatje, 'The natives and the premier's bills', *DFA*, 19 November 1926.

36 'The Plaatje bioscope', *Umteteli wa Bantu*, 5 December 1925; DB, General Secretary's correspondence, Plaatje to De Beers, 30 May 1925; Moton Papers, GC 109/810, Plaatje to Moton, 18 June 1925.

37 S. T. Plaatje, 'Colour questions', *DFA*, 23 April 1925.

38 'Native Conference on premier's bills', *Cape Times*, 3 November 1926.

39 Rheinallt Jones Papers, Joint Council file, address by S. T. Plaatje to 1924 Joint Councils Conference.

40 S. T. Plaatje, 'Light and shade on native questions', *Umteteli*, 11 October 1924.

41 For example: 'The colour bar bill', *DFA*, 11 April 1925; 'The native bills', *DFA*, 22 March 1927.

42 'Through native eyes', *Cape Argus*, 30 June 1926.

43 S. T. Plaatje, 'Natives and the mission', *DFA*, 20 June 1925.

44 *Cape Times*, 7 and 9 May 1927; *Cape Argus*, 10 May 1927; *Daily Dispatch* (East London), 7 and 10 May 1927; *DFA*, 11 May 1927.

45 S. T. Plaatje, 'Natives and Mr Merriman: an appreciation', *DFA*, 10 August 1926; S. T. Plaatje, 'Friends and helpers of natives: a tribute to Mr J. W. Jagger and Mr Weinthal', *Cape Times*, 3 July 1930; S. T. Plaatje, 'A friend of the natives: the late Sir William Solomon', *Pretoria News*, 11 June 1930. See also 'Lord Milner and the natives', *DFA*, 23 May 1925; 'Friends of the natives', *DFA*, 15 June 1925; 'The late Chief Silas Molema: passing of a progressive Barolong chief', *Cape Times*, 13 September 1927; 'Departed friends of the natives', *Cape Argus*, 30 August 1927.

46 South African Institute of Race Relations (Johannesburg), typescript of evidence to Native Economic Commission, p. 5292.

47 S. T. Plaatje, 'Self-help', *Umteteli wa Bantu*, 28 February 1928.

48 S. M. Molema, 'Biography', p. 123.

49 e.g. in S. T. Plaatje, ' "The good times" and the "new native" ', *Umteteli*, 9 November 1929.

50 S. T. Plaatje, 'Leadership', *Umteteli*, 18 February 1928.

51 'The native vote and other matters', letter from Plaatje to the editor, *Umteteli*, 27 October 1928.

52 e.g. S. T. Plaatje, 'The leadership cult from another angle', *Umteteli*, 14 March 1925; 'The race problem', letter to the editor from 'Enquirer', *Umteteli*, 4 May 1929; S. T. Plaatje, 'Statesmen and the natives', *Umteteli*, 11 May 1929; 'The vote', letter to the editor from 'Enquirer', *Umteteli*, 3 November 1928; letter to the editor from R. W. Msimang, *Umteteli*, 20 October 1928; 'The native franchise', letter to the editor from 'Enquirer', *Umteteli*, 20 October 1928; 'Resurgam', 'Bantu politics', *Umteteli*, 31 March 1928; letter to the editor from 'Enquirer', *Umteteli*, 27 October 1928.

53 Moton Papers, GC 128/965, Plaatje to Moton, 29 June 1927; *Synopsis of Proceedings of the Thirteenth Session of the Right Worthy True Temple of the Independent Order of True Templars, held at Vrededorp, Johannesburg, 6–8 January 1931*, pp. 10–12 and xii.
54 S. T. Plaatje, 'South Africans at the Ottowa conference', *Umteteli*, 23 April 1932.
55 Editorial, *Our Heritage*, Vol. 1, No. 1, June 1931.
56 Library of Parliament, Cape Town, Manuscript Annexures, Plaatje to Clerk of the House of Assembly, 6 May 1927. I am most grateful to the Librarian of the South African House of Parliament for providing me with a copy of this; see also *Report of the Select Committee on the Native Administration Bill*, May 1927, SC 11, '27, p. xxiv.
57 *Minutes of the First Non-European Conference held in the City Hall, Kimberley, 23rd, 24th and 25th June 1927*, p. 32.
58 *Minutes of the First Non-European Conference*, p. 52; Moton Papers, GC 128/965, Plaatje to Moton, 29 June 1927.
59 S. T. Plaatje, 'Natives and taxation', *DFA*, 3 March 1931; see also S. T. Plaatje, 'The native bills', *DFA*, 15 February 1929.
60 e.g. S. T. Plaatje, 'Native conditions through European spectacles', *Daily Dispatch* (East London), 9 July 1927.
61 e.g. S. T. Plaatje, 'The Cape franchise', *Umteteli*, 29 September 1928 and *South African Outlook*,
1 October 1928; 'The native vote', *Umteteli*, 13 October 1928; 'The native franchise', *Umteteli*, 8 December 1928; 'Native voters', *Umteteli*, 19 January 1929; 'Native Voters' Association', *DFA*, 15 February 1929.
62 'African National Congress: bill of rights', *Umteteli*, 6 April 1929; see also, 'Black man's place in the Union', *DFA*, 3 April 1929.
63 '17th Annual convention of the ANC', *South African Worker*, 30 April 1929.

14 Language and literature: preserving a culture

1 'Points of view: the late Mr Sol Plaatje', letter to editor from D. M. Ramoshoana, *Diamond Fields Advertiser*, 29 June 1932.
2 For the state of literature in Setswana at this time, see C. M. Doke, 'A preliminary investigation into the state of the native languages of South Africa with suggestions as to research and the development of literature', *Bantu Studies*, Vol. 7, 1933, pp. 21–2, 31, 77–85; C. M. Doke, 'The linguistic situation in South Africa', *Africa*, Vol. 1, 1928; C. M. Doke, 'Vernacular textbooks in South African native schools', *Africa*, Vol. 8, 1935.
3 Interviews with Mr Simon Lekhela, London, October 1978 and December 1981.
4 BNA, S.144/5, Peter M. Sebina to Resident Commissioner, Bechuanaland Protectorate, 26 February 1931.
5 'Experts and languages', letter from D. M. Ramoshoana to the editor, *Bantu World*, 16 June 1934.
6 S. T. Plaatje, 'Native affairs after four years', *DFA*, 22 January 1924.
7 DB, General Secretary's correspondence, Plaatje to De Beers, 19 November 1929.
8 Ibid.
9 DB, General Secretary's correspondence, General Secretary to Plaatje, 25 November 1929.
10 S. T. Plaatje (translator), *Diphosho-phosho/Comedy of Errors* (Morija Printing Works, Morija, 1930), Introduction, p. iv.
11 *Diphosho-phosho*, title page; 'Shakespeare in Sechuana', *The Star* (Johannesburg), 26 July 1930.
12 'Language in decay' (editorial), *DFA*, 4 October 1930.
13 'Shakespeare in Sechuana'.
14 *Diphosho-phosho*, p. 29; A. Sandilands, *Introduction to Tswana* (LMS, Tigerkloof, 1953), p. 277.
15 BNA, DCS 14/6, Plaatje to Serowe District Commissioner, 25 September 1930.
16 Doke, 'A preliminary investigation', p. 22.
17 G. P. Lestrade, 'European influences upon the development of Bantu languages and literature', in I. Schapera (ed.), *Western Civilisation and the Natives of South Africa* (London, 1934), p. 124.
18 D. M. Ramoshoana, 'Shakespeare in Sechuana', *Umteteli wa Bantu*, 4 October 1930.
19 Ibid.; see also D. M. Ramoshoana, letter to the editor, *DFA*, 4 October 1930.

20 S. T. Plaatje, 'A South African's homage', in I. Gollancz (ed.), *Book of Homage to Shakespeare* (Oxford, 1916), p. 339.
21 C. M. Doke, review of *Diphospho-phosho*, *Bantu Studies*, Vol. 5, 1931.
22 UW, W. C. Scully Papers, Stephen Black to W. C. Scully, 23 October 1930. I am indebted to Jean Marquard and Tim Couzens for drawing this item to my attention.
23 S. T. Plaatje, *Dintshontsho tsa bo-Juliuse Kesara* (University of the Witwatersrand Press, Bantu Treasury Series, Johannesburg, 1937); UCT, Lestrade Papers, BC 255 B2, 'Introduction'.
24 W. Eiselen, Review of *Dintshontsho tsa bo-Juliuse Kesara*, *Bantu Studies*, Vol. 12, 1938, p. 154.
25 UNISA, Molema Papers, fragment.
26 NAD, Colenso Papers, Box 59, Plaatje to Mrs G. Solomon (copy), 13 May 1930.
27 For information about publishers' interest in publishing Tswana school books, see correspondence in Lestrade Papers, BC 255 G2 (Longmans, Green and Co.) and BNA, S68/14, H. J. E. Dumbrell (Inspector of Education, Bechuanaland Protectorate) to Stakesby Lewis, 8 December 1930 (Blackie's).
28 'The late Mr Sol Plaatje', letter from D. M. Ramoshoana to the editor, *DFA*, 29 June 1932.
29 Interview with Mr Michael van Reenen, Mitcham, S. London, 6 September 1976; SOAS, Plaatje Papers, STP 2/4, typescript of new edition of *Sechuana Proverbs*, p. 4.
30 S. T. Plaatje, *Sechuana Proverbs* (London, 1916), pp. 32 and 41.
31 Plaatje Papers, typescript of new edition, p. 3.
32 *Sechuana Proverbs*, p. 76.
33 Ibid., p. 64.
34 Typescript of new edition, pp. 1 and 7.
35 *Sechuana Proverbs*, Introduction, p. 13.
36 D. Jones and S. T. Plaatje, *A Sechuana Reader in International Phonetic Orthography (with English Translations)* (London, 1916), pp. 4, 6, 10, 14.
37 S. T. Plaatje, *Mhudi* (Lovedale, 1930), reverse of title page; Moton Papers, GC 60/130, Plaatje to Moton, 16 July 1931; University of Zimbabwe, C. M. Doke Collection, letter inserted in Doke's copy of *Sechuana Proverbs*, Plaatje to Doke, 6 August 1931. I am most grateful to Andrew Reed for the last reference.
38 Doke Collection, Plaatje to Doke, 6 August 1931.
39 List of Tswana praise poems formerly in possession of Mrs Frieda Matthews, now in Z. K. Matthews Papers, University of Cape Town. I am most grateful to Mrs Matthews for making this available to me.
40 Ibid.
41 S. T. Plaatje, 'Montsioa', in T. D. Mweli Skota (ed.), *African Yearly Register* (Johannesburg, 1930), p. 53.
42 Ibid., p. 57.
43 C. M. Doke, 'A preliminary investigation', p. 79 (Tswana survey by Lestrade).
44 Molema Papers, undated and incomplete report by S. T. Plaatje, pp. 4–5.
45 'Shakespeare in Sechuana', *The Star*, 26 July 1930.
46 Doke Collection, Plaatje to Doke, 6 August 1931.
47 Plaatje's annotated copy of J. T. Brown's *Secwana Dictionary*, pp. i–iv. I am most grateful to Professor D. C. Cole, formerly of the University of the Witwatersrand, for making this available to me.
48 Ibid., p. vi.
49 *Diphosho-phosho*, Introduction, pp. i–ii.
50 Ibid.; S. T. Plaatje, 'Letter to the editor: suggested new Bantu orthography', *South African Outlook*, 1 August 1931.
51 'Sechuana orthography', letter from M. M. Kendle to the editor, *Umteteli wa Bantu*, 20 December 1930.
52 C. M. Doke, review of *Diphosho-phosho*, *Bantu Studies*, Vol. 5, 1931.
53 BNA, DCS 14/6, Plaatje to Serowe District Commissioner, 25 September 1930.
54 BNA, S. 150/5, 1886, minute from H. J. E. Dumbrell to High Commissioner, 19 February 1931.
55 BNA, S. 150/5, handwritten note from Dumbrell to the Government Secretary, 26 January 1931.
56 Archives of International Africa Institute (London), Minutes of Business Committee, International Institute of African Languages and Cultures, 2 December 1930, pp. 155–6.
57 See, e.g., F. D. Lugard, 'The International Institute of African Languages and Cultures', *Africa*, Vol. 1, No. 1, 1928, pp. 1–2; also, G. P. Lestrade, 'Some remarks on the practical orthography of the South African Bantu languages', *Bantu Studies*, Vol. 3, 1927–9, pp. 261–73.

58 See esp. Martin Legassick, 'The rise of modern South African liberalism: its assumptions and social base' (Unpublished seminar paper, Institute of Commonwealth Studies, University of London, March 1972).
59 International Institute of African Languages and Cultures, *A Practical Orthography of African Languages* (London, 1927); see also various articles in the first issue of *Africa* in 1928, esp. Lugard, 'The International Institute of African Languages and Cultures', pp. 1–2, and A. Lloyd James, 'The practical orthography of African languages', pp. 125–9.
60 Doke Collection, Plaatje to Doke, 6 August 1931; 'A preliminary investigation', p. 7; Doke to Plaatje, 20 December 1929 (copy of letter in possession of Professor D. C. Cole).
61 'A practical orthography for Tswana', *Bantu Studies*, Vol. 11, 1937, pp. 137–8.
62 Ibid.; S. T. Plaatje, 'Suggested new Bantu orthography', *South African Outlook*, 1 May 1931, pp. 88–90
63 Lestrade Papers, BC 255 A1.7, minutes of meeting of Tswana sub-committee, 14 and 15 February 1929.
64 'A practical orthography', p. 138; BNA S.68/12, 463/1, Union Advisory Board on Bantu Studies and Research, Central Orthography Committee, Cwana District Committee, minutes of meeting held on 27 February 1930.
65 Lestrade Papers, BC 255, A1.11, minutes of meeting of Tswana sub-committee, 1 and 2 October 1929; also BNA S.68/11, Cuzen (RM, Kanye) to Government Secretary, Mafeking, 26 November 1929, re October committee meeting.
66 'Suggested new Bantu orthography', p. 88.
67 Ibid., p. 89.
68 Ibid., p. 90.
69 UNISA, Plaatje/Molema Papers, 142/2, Minutes of Conference on Orthography, University of the Witwatersrand, Johannesburg, 28 August 1937, p. 3.
70 S. T. Plaatje, 'Uniform spelling', *Umteteli wa Bantu*, 15 November 1930; see also S. T. Plaatje, 'A white man's native language', *Umteteli*, 5 December 1931 and 2 April 1932; 'Some native criticism of Bantu languages', letter from Plaatje to the editor, *The Star*, 2 December 1931; 'The Bantu orthography', *Our Heritage*, Vol. 1 No. 3, August–October 1931, pp. 10–11; 'Bantu orthography', *Our Heritage*, Vol. I, No. 5, December 1931, p. 9.
71 'Spelling native languages', *The Star*, 19 November 1931; 'Spelling of native languages', *The Star*, 27 November 1931; 'Some native criticisms of Bantu languages', letter from Plaatje to *The Star*, 2 December 1931.
72 S. T. Plaatje, 'Spelling of African languages: criticism of suggested reforms', *DFA*, 15 October 1930.
73 Lestrade Papers, BC 255 F.125, 'Minutes of meeting of orthography committee appointed by his honour the Resident Commissioner, held at Mafeking on Thursday, 4 December 1930'; see also BNA, S.68/13, letter from Chief Montshiwa (drafted by Plaatje) to Government Secretary, Bechuanaland Protectorate, 15 November 1930; S.68/13, 463/3/30, Government Secretary (Bechuanaland Protectorate) to Mr G. Welch (SGE, Cape Province), 22 January 1931; S.68/13, 'Minutes of meeting held with certain representatives of the Barolong tribe on March 7th, 1931 with reference to Secwana orthography'; BNA, DCL 7/2, R. Haydon Lewis to Capt. R. Reilly, RM, Lobatsi, 23 July 1931.
74 BNA, S.68/15, G. Welch (SGE, Cape Province) to Secretary, Provincial Education Dept, 30 July 1931; Lestrade Papers, BC 255 A1.26, 'Second inter-provincial conference of introduction of new orthographies held at Bloemfontein on 18th November 1931'.

15 *Mhudi*

1 NAD, Colenso Papers, Box 59, Plaatje to Mrs Georgiana Solomon (copy), 13 May 1930.
2 For Shepherd's role at Lovedale, see Jeffrey Peires, 'Lovedale Press: literature for the Bantu revisited', *English in Africa*, Vol. 7 No. 2, March 1980, pp. 71–85; R. H. W. Shepherd, *Lovedale, South Africa*, 1924–55, p. 122.
3 R. H. W. Shepherd, *Bantu Literature and Life* (Lovedale, 1955), p. 98; also R. H. W. Shepherd and B. G. Paver, *African Contrasts: the Story of a South African People* (Cape Town, 1947), pp. 279–80.
4 Contract between Plaatje and the Lovedale Institution Press, 19 March 1930. I am most grateful to Mr R. B. Raven, General Manager of the Lovedale Press, for showing this to me.

5 S. T. Plaatje, *Mhudi* (Heinemann Educational Books, London, 1978), p. 21 (subsequent page references are for this edition of *Mhudi*).

6 For an exploration of the influence of Shakespeare in *Mhudi*, see S. Gray, 'Sources of the first black South African novel in English', in *Munger Africana Notes*, December 1976; and T. J. Couzens, 'Sol Plaatje's *Mhudi*', *Journal of Commonwealth Literature*, Vol. 8, No. 1, June 1973; S. Gray, 'Plaatje's Shakespeare', *English in Africa*, Vol. 4, No. 1, March 1977.

7 *Mhudi*, pp. 55 and 57.

8 Editorial, *Tsala ea Becoana*, 10 July 1910.

9 For an elucidation of the sources of the lion stories, see Gray, 'Sources', pp. 21–7.

10 S. T. Plaatje, 'Another five years', *Umteteli*, 24 August 1929; also, S. T. Plaatje, 'Should the Nyandjas be deported?', *Umteteli*, 5 March 1928.

11 S. T. Plaatje, 'Descendants of the Koks', *Diamond Fields Advertiser*, 7 December 1926.

12 *Mhudi*, pp. 27–8.

13 Ibid., p. 121.

14 Ibid., p. 106.

15 Ibid., pp. 83–4.

16 Ibid., p. 134.

17 For an elaboration of this argument, see Couzens, 'Sol Plaatje's *Mhudi*' and his valuable introduction to the Heinemann edition of *Mhudi*, pp. 17–19.

18 *Mhudi*, p. 174–5.

19 Nadine Gordimer, 'English-language literature and politics in South Africa' in Christopher Heywood (ed.). *Aspects of South African Literature* (London, 1976), pp. 107–8.

20 South African Institute of Race Relations archives (Johannesburg), Evidence of S. T. Plaatje to Native Economic Commission (typescript), p. 5291.

21 *Mhudi*, p. 66.

22 Ibid., p. 66.

23 Ibid., p. 172.

24 UCT, Molteno Family Papers, BC 330 A81.2.3, Plaatje to Mrs Lennox Murray, 17 November 1922.

25 *Mhudi*, p. 83.

26 'Overthrow of Mzilikizi', *Daily Dispatch* (East London), 17 December 1930.

27 'Tributes to Sir David Harris', *DFA*, 5 December 1930.

28 Vere Stent, 'South Africa's first native novelist', *Pretoria News*, 8 November 1930; 'First native novel', *Our Heritage*, Vol. 1, No. 2, June 1931, p. 5.

29 Review of *Mhudi*, *South African Outlook*, 1 December 1930.

30 'The bookshelf' (review of *Mhudi*), *DFA*, 1 November 1930.

31 H. I. E. Dhlomo, 'Three famous African authors I know: R. R. R. Dhlomo', *Inkundla ya Bantu*, August 1946 (reproduced in *English in Africa*, Vol. 2, No. 1, March 1975, p. 9).

32 UW, W. C. Scully Papers, Stephen Black to W. C. Scully, 23 October 1930.

33 Stephen Black, 'The Telephone Conversations of Jeremiah: the first full-length Black novel', *The Sjambok*, 31 October 1930, pp. 27–8. I am most grateful to Tim Couzens for this reference.

34 Review of *Mhudi*, *Times Literary Supplement*, 31 August 1933.

35 Review of *Mhudi* by C. M. Doke, *Bantu Studies*, Vol. 5, 1931, p. 86.

36 Rhodes University Library (Cory Library), Lovedale Collection, S. T. Plaatje file, 'Statement of account – estate Solomon T. Plaatje', 14 July 1932. I am grateful to Mike Berning and Sandy Fold for copies of this material.

37 Inscribed copy of *Mhudi* in possession of Professor E. O. J. Westphal, University of Cape Town.

38 Inscribed copy of *Mhudi* in possession of Mr H. Oppenheimer, Johannesburg.

39 Interview with Mr Morris, Kimberley, April 1976.

40 *Du Bois Papers*, r35 f651, Plaatje to Du Bois, 16 July 1931.

41 UW, Rheinallt Jones Papers, A394, Victor Murray to Rheinallt Jones, 20 May 1931. I am grateful to Deborah Gaitskell for this reference.

42 Lovedale Collection, Plaatje file, 'Statement of account', 14 July 1932.

43 TI, Moton Papers, GC 160/1304, Plaatje to Moton, 16 July 1931.

44 Moton Papers, GC 160/1304, G. Lake Innes (Special Asst. to the Principal) to Plaatje, 15 August 1931.

45 Published by the American Negro Universities Press in 1969, the first 'legitimate' American edition of *Mhudi* (the HAWS version) was published by Three Continents Press in 1978.

46 I. Bud-M'belle, 'Scholar and patriot', *Umteteli* (Supplement) 6 August 1932; also SOAS, Plaatje Papers, STP 1/1, 'Solomon Tshekisho Plaatje', by I. Bud-M'belle (unpublished biography/obituary), p. 14.
47 UNISA, Molema Papers, 'With other people's wives', unpublished manuscript of Plaatje's, p. 52 (page references are for retyped copy).
48 See particularly D. Hammond Tooke, *The Tribes of the Mount Frere District* (Ethnological Publications no. 33, Union of South Africa, Dept of Native Affairs, Government Printer, Pretoria, 1955), pp. 32–43.
49 'With other people's wives', p. 8.
50 W. C. Scully, 'Fragments of Native history: the AmaBaca', *The State*, June 1909; W. C. Scully, *By Veldt and Kopje* (London, 1907), pp. 285–301; W. C. Scully, *Further Reminiscences of a South African Pioneer* (London, 1913), pp. 259–70; J. H. Soga, *The South-Eastern Bantu* (Johannesburg, 1930), Chapters 21 and 22; A. T. Bryant, *Olden Times in Natal and Zululand* (London, 1929), pp. 154, 352, 378–86.
51 'With other people's wives', p. 16.
52 Ibid., p. 56.
53 Ibid., p. 67.
54 Ibid., p. 67.
55 Ibid., p. 68.
56 Ibid., p. 70.
57 H. I. E. Dhlomo, 'An appreciation', *Umteteli*, 25 June 1932.

16 Final years

1 TI, Moton Papers, GC 160/1305, Plaatje to Moton, 16 July 1931.
2 Editorial review of *Mhudi*, *Imvo Zabantsundu*, 26 May 1931.
3 H. I. E. Dhlomo, 'Through Umteteli's pages: a review of 1930', *Umteteli*, 3 January 1931.
4 Z. K. Matthews, 'Continuing the Plaatje story', *Imvo Zabantsundu*, 1 July 1961.
5 Vere Stent, 'The strange life of Sol Plaatje', *The Star*, 5 July 1932.
6 *Report of the Native Affairs Commission for the Years 1927–1931* (UG 26 1932, Government Printer, Pretoria), Appendix D, minutes of Native Conference held in Pretoria, 9–13 December 1930, pp. 22–3.
7 *Synopsis of Proceedings of the Thirteenth Session of the Right Worthy True Temple of the Independent Order of True Templars, held at Vrededorp, Johannesburg, 6–8 January 1931*, pp. 10–12, and Report of R. Worthy Secretary, p. xii.
8 *Synopsis of Proceedings*, p. 11.
9 'Editorial notes', *Our Heritage*, Vol. 1, No. 1, June 1931.
10 *Du Bois Papers*, r35 f651, Plaatje to Du Bois, 16 July 1931.
11 S. T. Plaatje, 'Along the road to Cairo land', *Our Heritage*, Vol. 1, No. 3, August–October 1931, p. 14.
12 S. T. Plaatje, 'Along the Road to Cairo land', *Our Heritage*, Vol. 1, No. 4, November 1931, p. 11.
13 S. T. Plaatje, 'Taxation in the Belgian Congo,' *Umteteli wa Bantu*, 23 January 1932.
14 Ibid.
15 'Native's definition of segregation', *Bulawayo Chronicle*, 20 June 1931; see also 'To succeed Sir Murray Bisset', *Our Heritage*, Vol. 1, No. 5, December 1931, p. 10.
16 'Editorial notes', *Our Heritage*, Vol. 1, No. 2, July 1931, p. 2.
17 'Editorial notes', *Our Heritage*, Vol. 1, No. 3, August–October 1931, p. 2.
18 BNA, Secretariat Register, 3890, 'Our Heritage: Sechuana newspaper', 1931. I am grateful to Neil Parsons for drawing my attention to this reference.
19 See especially, T. J. Couzens, 'A short history of *The World* (and other black South African newspapers)', African Studies Institute (University of the Witwatersrand) seminar paper, 1976; L. and D. Switzer, *The Black Press in South Africa and Lesotho* (Boston, 1979), p. 27.
20 H. I. E. Dhlomo, 'Three famous African authors I know', *Inkundla ya Bantu*, August 1946, reproduced (p. 10) in *English in Africa*, Vol. 2, No. 1, March 1975.
21 'Mr Sol T. Plaatje honoured: tributes to his work for non-Europeans', *DFA*, 12 November 1928; see also DB, General Secretary's correspondence, W. T. McLeod to De Beers, 31 August 1929; interview with Michael van Reenen, Mitcham, Surrey, 6 September 1976.

22 Interview with Mr J. van Riet, Kimberley, April 1976.
23 'Non-European function: address presented by the community', *DFA*, 3 November 1931.
24 Interview with Mr Simon Lekhela, London, 26 October 1978.
25 Interview with Michael van Reenen.
26 Interview with Mr Simon Lekhela, October 1978 and December 1981.
27 Interview with Mrs Mary Plaatje, May 1976.
28 Interview with Mr J. van der Riet; interviews with Mrs Mary Plaatje, May 1976 and November 1981.
29 Interview with Mr Paul Mahabane, Thaba Nchu, April 1976.
30 Moton Papers, GC 128/965, Plaatje to Moton, 29 June 1927; interview with Mrs Mary Plaatje, November 1981.
31 Interview with Mr Simon Lekhela, London, 26 October 1978.
32 Z. K. Matthews, 'Continuing the Plaatje story', *Imvo*, 1 July 1961.
33 'Cape Native Voters', *Imvo*, 5 January 1932; see also reports in *Ikwezi le Afrika*, 9 January 1932; *The Star*, 24 December 1931; *DFA*, 25 December 1931.
34 'Cape Native Voters' Convention', *Ikwezi le Afrika*, 9 January 1932.
35 'IOTT session', *Imvo*, 17 February 1931; *Synopsis of Proceedings of the Thirteenth Session of the Right Worthy True Temple of the Independent Order of True Templars*, p. 4; 'True Templars annual session', *DFA*, 8 January 1932.
36 'Secondary education for natives: limited openings in Kimberley schools', *DFA*, 21 March 1931.
37 DB, Estate records, Lyndhurst Road Native Institute file, Plaatje to Mr Grimmer (General Manager), 15 March 1932; 'Kimberley secondary school: inadequate accommodation', *Umteteli*, 5 March 1932; *Our Heritage*, Vol. 1, No. 1, June 1931. p. 9.
38 DB, Estate records, Lyndhurst Road Native Institute file, Plaatje to Mr Grimmer, 13 April 1932.
39 'Native grievances: mass meeting in location', *DFA*, 26 May 1932; see also 'Unemployment: minister interviewed', *Umteteli*, 28 May 1932.
40 Ibid.
41 S. T. Plaatje, 'The crime factory', *Umteteli*, 13 February 1932.
42 SAL, Claire Goodblatte Papers, Goodblatte to 'Jack', 13 April 1932; Alan Paton, *South African Tragedy* (New York, 1965), pp. 139–41. I am most grateful to Baruch Hirson for the first reference cited.
43 Union of South Africa, *Debates of the South African House of Assembly*, 13 May 1932, 4602–3.
44 'Mr Sol Plaatje', letter to editor from A. S. Williams, *Cape Times*, 16 May 1932.
45 'A Native lecturer', letter to editor from 'Ex-Professor, UCT', *Cape Times*, May 1932.
46 'Countess' gift to Bantu children', *Bantu World*, 4 June 1932; see also 'Countess Labia and the natives', *DFA*, 26 May 1932.
47 S. T. Plaatje, 'Friends and helpers of natives: a tribute to Mr J. W. Jagger and Mr Weinthal', *Cape Times*, 3 July 1930. I am most grateful to Andrew Reed for this reference.
48 'Countess' gift to Bantu children', *Bantu World*, 4 June 1932.
49 'Native grievances: mass meeting in location', *DFA*, 26 May 1932.
50 UW, S. M. Molema, 'Unpublished biography', p. 106.
51 *Umteteli*, 23 July 1932.
52 Mrs E. L. Plaatje to Mrs S. J. Colenso, 22 September 1932. I am most grateful to Professor George Shepperson, University of Edinburgh, who owns the original, for providing me with a copy of this letter.
53 'Funeral of Mr Sol T. Plaatje', *DFA*, 23 June 1932.
54 SOAS, Plaatje Papers, STP 4/1, Funeral oration by Rev. G. Kuhn (typescript).
55 'Funeral of Mr Sol T. Plaatje'.
56 'The late Mr Sol Plaatje', *Ilanga lase Natal*, 24 June 1932.
57 'Mr Sol Plaatje passes', *Imvo Zabantsundu*, 28 June 1932.
58 'An outstanding figure in life of people of South Africa', *DFA*, 14 December 1935.

INDEX

Index

Index

Index

434

Index